Introduction to **MARKETING**

Introduction to
MARKETING
THEORY AND PRACTICE
3rd Edition

ADRIAN PALMER

OXFORD
UNIVERSITY PRESS

Great Clarendon Street, Oxford OX2 6DP,
United Kingdom

Oxford University Press is a department of the University of Oxford.
It furthers the University's objective of excellence in research, scholarship,
and education by publishing worldwide. Oxford is a registered trade mark of
Oxford University Press in theUK and in certain other countries

British Library Cataloguing in Publication Data
Data available

Library of Congress Cataloging in Publication Data
Data available

ISBN 978-0-19-960213-1

Printed in Italy
by L.E.G.O.S.p.A—LavisTN

PREFACE

Marketing is an exciting subject to study. Markets are the basis for the wealth of western economies, and marketers help make markets become more efficient and effective. It is marketers who have been a driving force in making an ever wider range of goods and services available to buyers, seeking a better understanding of buyers' needs, and trying to deliver better products at lower prices than competitors.

This book provides an introduction to the principles of marketing, beginning from the underlying theoretical bases which are often borrowed from the disciplines of economics, sociology, and psychology. Practical application of theory is provided through case studies and vignettes, and it is often noted that the theories of marketing are not always easy to implement in practice. This book tries not to present prescriptive solutions to marketing problems, but encourages discussion about causes and effects. Underlying much of the discussion in this book is the interplay between marketing as a rigorous science and as a creative art.

The book is arranged in four thematic parts. The first part begins by identifying the fundamental building blocks of marketing. Chapter 1 explores definitions of marketing and its essential characteristics. Marketing takes place within a complex environment of social, economic, political, and technological forces and the following chapter examines the continual interplay between marketing managers and their business environment. Social responsibility has become an increasingly important part of firms' business environment in recent years and Chapter 3 of this edition has been expanded to take a critical look at marketing in the context of current ecological concerns and the perceptions by some people of unethical practices by marketers.

The second thematic part of the book focuses on consumers, and on understanding the complex factors that lead to buying decisions. An understanding of buying processes (explored in Chapter 4) calls for appropriate information gathering, analysis, and dissemination (Chapter 5). Knowledge of buyer behaviour, backed by good quality research, leads to the concept of segmentation and targeting (Chapter 6).

The third thematic part of the book focuses on how companies use knowledge about consumers and the broader marketing environment to develop a sustainable competitive advantage. Chapter 7 introduces basic principles of competitive positioning. Subsequent chapters analyse how the elements of the 'marketing mix'—product, price, place, and promotion—are used to create a competitive advantage (Chapters 8, 9, 10, and 11).

The final thematic part of the book seeks to integrate the previous chapters and provides an overview of the marketing management process in the context of an increasingly globalized marketing environment.

The book has been divided into a number of chapters in order to provide some form of structure. In the real world, marketing cannot be neatly compartmentalized in this way. With a holistic vision, it will be seen that any change in one aspect of marketing is likely to have consequences in other aspects. In an attempt to emphasize these linkages, each chapter closes with a summary of how that chapter relates to other chapters. Vignettes and case studies provide integrative perspectives.

Current developments in technology affecting marketing (e.g. mobile broadband and RFID) are reflected in vignettes and case studies throughout the book. The growing recognition of the social and ecological responsibilities of marketing is stressed throughout the book. Vignettes reflect the growing globalization of marketing. This book is published at a time of great debate about the nature of marketing knowledge and theory. New ideas and even claims of shifts in marketing paradigms appear regularly. This book seeks to develop a well-founded and balanced view of marketing and makes no apology for raising as many questions as it answers. Marketing is more about a way of thinking than a series of prescriptive rules.

This book is supported by an Online Resource Centre: http://www.oxfordtextbooks. co.uk/orc/palmer3e/. Here, you will find supplementary reading lists and web links relevant to each chapter, which can be clicked through. For each chapter, additional case studies and questions are provided. Your knowledge can be tested with a series of multiple-choice questions. For tutors, PowerPoint slides and lecture plans are linked to each chapter. An additional multiple-choice test bank of questions is provided.

Adrian Palmer
January 2012
mail@apalmer.com

ACKNOWLEDGEMENTS

Countless colleagues, reviewers, and organizations, too numerous to mention here, helped to bring this book to fruition and their assistance is greatly acknowledged. Many authors and organizations kindly granted permission to reproduce copyright material and this is specifically acknowledged throughout the book.

Every effort has been made to trace and contact copyright holders but this has not been possible in every case. If notified, the publisher will undertake to rectify any errors or omissions at the earliest opportunity.

Crown Copyright material reproduced with the permission of the Controller, HMSO (under the terms of the Click Use licence).

The author: Adrian Palmer is Professor of Marketing at Swansea University, UK and Affiliate Professor at ESC Rennes, France.

NOTES

New to this edition

- The final two chapters, 'Managing the marketing effort' and 'Global marketing' from the 2nd edition have been merged to provide an integrative summary of marketing and to highlight the problems of implementation in an increasingly globalized world.

- An increased number of examples of international marketing have been introduced throughout the text to reflect the global nature of modern marketing practice and to appeal to an increasingly international student audience.

- There is increased coverage of more contemporary issues throughout the text, such as mobile internet, social network media, and marketing in a recession.

- A suite of video links has been added to the Online Resource Centre for individual or group use.

BRIEF CONTENTS

DETAILED CONTENTS

PART 3 Developing the marketing mix

PART 4 Bringing it together

GUIDED TOUR OF TEXTBOOK FEATURES

Chapter objectives

Each chapter sets out learning objectives which provide a route map through the chapter material and summarize the goals of each section, so that you know what you can expect to learn as you move through the text.

Marketing in Action boxes

Put the theory you have read about into context with examples from around the world demonstrating the application of marketing techniques.

Chapter summary and key linkages

Chapter summaries and key links help to reiterate the key points that have been covered in the current chapter, as well as providing useful cross-references to related topics featured in other chapters of the book.

Key principles of marketing

A bulleted list of key principles is included to alert you to issues and principles that are particularly significant as well as reinforcing the topics that you have covered to date.

Case studies

Each chapter ends with an extended case study where you will see the theories you have encountered so far brought to life in a contemporary, real life case study, helping you to reflect on the themes and application of particular marketing techniques.

E-Marketing

E-Marketing boxes highlight examples of digital technology.

Case study review questions

> Case study review questions
>
> 1. Using an appropriate frame
>   change in the marketing en

Each of the case studies in the book is accompanied by a list of questions which will help you to test your knowledge and understanding of the topics you covered in the chapter, and prompt you to think further about current issues.

Chapter review questions

> ✎ CHAPTER REVIEW QUE
>
> 1. Explain briefly what you understan
> 2. 'Suppliers and intermediaries are in

End-of-chapter questions are a great way to help you measure your understanding of the material covered, and provide a useful basis for group discussions, or simply to evaluate your own learning and development.

Activities

> ✎ ACTIVITIES
>
> 1. Develop a checklist of points th
>   whether an organization is resp

A series of suggested activities is included at the end of every chapter and will enable you to discuss what you have gleaned from the chapter by testing your ability to apply the theories and concepts you have learnt, either independently or in groups.

References

> ✎ REFERENCES
>
> Atkinson, J. (1984), 'Manpower Stra
> Management, August, pp. 77–93.

References are provided at the end of each chapter, which will point you in the direction of other reliable sources and information on the subject so that you can expand your knowledge of specific topics and areas of interest.

Suggested further reading

> ✎ SUGGESTED FURTHER
>
> A wide-ranging review of organizati
> Palmer, A. and Hartley, B. (2008). The

If you are interested in a particular aspect of a chapter, the author has provided a list of further reading materials where you can find out more about a specific topic, or read further to extend your own development and understanding of that area of marketing.

Key terms

> ✎ KEY TERMS
>
> • Accelerator effect
> • Birth rate

Marketing has its own language: to help you build your vocabulary, key terms and ideas have been defined in these bullet-pointed lists, which have been designed to alert you to key areas of importance as well as summarizing critical themes and perspectives from the book.

GUIDE TO THE ONLINE RESOURCE CENTRE

www.oxfordtextbooks.co.uk/orc/palmer3e/

Free resources available to students include:

Additional case studies with case questions

The best way to reinforce your learning and understanding is through frequent revision. Here you will find additional questions to encourage critical thinking.

Additional chapter review questions

Here you will find a variety of new questions and assignments unique to the Online Resource Centre where you can further test your knowledge of the topic.

Multiple choice questions

A selection of multiple choice questions are available for each chapter, supported by instant feedback.

Additional suggested reading

This feature contains a set of additional references provided for each chapter of the book, so that you can further explore areas of interest.

Web exercises

Here you will find a variety of new online exercises that will help you to improve your knowledge of the topics within the text.

Web links

An Online Resource Centre accompanies the textbook, and here you will be directed to further resources that support and enhance your learning experience.

Video suite

A new video suite features links to footage and a guide to the latest marketing topics and issues.

Browsable online glossary

A new browsable online glossary enables you to search through marketing terms and familiarize yourself with the terminology you have encountered in the textbook.

Resources for registered adopters of the textbook include:

Suggested answers to case study and chapter review questions

The lecturer section of the Online Resource Centre provides suggestions for answers to the case study questions encountered throughout the textbook, case study questions found on the student section of the Online Resource Centre, and also the chapter review questions.

Additional discussion points

Here you will find a useful collection of ideas and pointers to prompt class discussion on a variety of marketing topics.

PowerPoints with teaching guide

A set of customizable PowerPoint slides which are available for each chapter for your use in lectures and seminars along with some helpful guidelines.

Test bank

Here you can find an electronic bank of questions to test your students on their knowledge of the subject.

MARKETING
the fundamentals

Part 1

1 WHAT IS MARKETING?

CHAPTER OBJECTIVES

There is much misunderstanding about what marketing is. Many people equate it with promotion, or 'trying to sell things that people don't really want'. With higher levels of business education, that misperception is changing. This chapter sets out the foundations of marketing and distinguishes between marketing as a fundamental philosophy and marketing as a set of techniques. While the techniques have now been widely adopted, many organizations still have a long way to go in developing a true customer focus, which is at the heart of the marketing philosophy. This chapter discusses the relationship of marketing to other organization functions and reviews current debate about the nature of marketing. It is essentially a foundation chapter, and many themes discussed will be returned to in more detail in later chapters.

Introduction

Next time you are in a grocery store, stop and think about why there is such a wide choice of goods competing for your custom. You might be quite a selective shopper, with a strong preference for one brand of cola over another. Or you may be very price sensitive, and choose the one that appears to give you the best value. You might be so accustomed to being able to purchase your favourite drink each time you go into a shop, and very surprised if one day it is not there waiting for you on the shelves. Then think about the shop itself. You might take it for granted that the shop is open late into the evening, at times which may be convenient for you. You might have noticed that the shop has innovated with new services over recent years, so you can now top up your phone, or buy freshly made coffee, for example. So much in our patterns of consumption that we take for granted can be attributed to marketing. When you called in to buy a can of your favourite drink, you probably didn't have on your mind questions such as 'why does the shop stock this brand but not another one?'; 'how did they decide which sizes of packaging to sell the drink in?'; 'how did they decide on the range of flavours?'; 'how were selling prices decided?' 'who decided on the current special promotion offer of "buy one get one free"'? 'who evaluated whether this offer was successful?'. Some of these involve key strategic decisions—others are day to day matters, but they are all central to what marketing is about. To get a simple bottle of cola on to the shelf in your local store will have involved hundreds, possibly thousands of strategic and operational decisions by marketing people. When these decisions are the right ones, you're happy with a product that you enjoy, and the manufacturer and retailer are happy because they earn profits from you. If it makes the wrong decisions, you will not like the product, so you will not buy it, at least not repeatedly, and the company selling it will not get your money. If it makes a series of wrong decisions, it may eventually go out of business.

Think also of higher value new products that you see in the shops—new versions of iPods, this season's new fashion clothing, or a new microwaveable ready-prepared meal, for example. The companies behind these new products would have most likely invested a lot of time and money researching these new products and their targeted buyers, so that when they are launched, they are snapped up by buyers, rather than having to be sold at a discounted 'clearance' price. Marketers have to be aware of your changing needs and expectations, because if another company offers a shiny new product, possibly at a lower price, you would probably be tempted by it, wouldn't you?

Contrast the situation described above, which we take for granted in western countries, with the situation in a centrally planned economy. There, the goods offered for sale are more likely to be the result of an internal production decision, without much regard to the needs of consumers. Without a competitive market-based economy to spur a company into action, there is less need for marketing managers. Companies may just carry on making the things that they like making, rather than what buyers actually want. At best, they may have a poor understanding of the complex needs that buyers seek to satisfy, and may have little idea about how these may change over time. Indeed, change may be seen as a threat rather than an opportunity, so companies would just carry on doing what they always did. This was clearly seen in the design of cars and household goods in Eastern Europe during the period of communism, when many people claimed that design and innovation lagged a long way behind what was happening in western, market-based economies. Today, as markets become increasingly competitive, so, too, does the need for marketing. Rather than trying to justify the existence of marketing, just think what your next visit to the shops would be like if marketing didn't exist.

There are many definitions of marketing, which generally revolve around the primacy of customers as part of an exchange process. Customers' needs are the starting point for marketing activity. Marketing managers try to identify these needs and develop products that will satisfy customers' needs through an exchange process. To begin defining marketing, we can look at the origins of the term. 'Market' is a noun which traditionally describes a place, real or virtual, comprising buyers and sellers. By adding 'ing', the passive noun is turned into an active verb. By this logic, marketing is about bringing buyers and sellers together so that the sellers offer for sale products that the buyers want to buy.

Definitions of marketing have subtly changed over time, and in 2008 the American Marketing Association updated its definition, stating that:

'Marketing is the activity, set of institutions, and processes for creating, communicating, delivering, and exchanging offerings that have value for customers, clients, partners, and society at large.'

In the UK, the Chartered Institute of Marketing (CIM) has proposed a new definition of marketing, describing it as:

'The strategic business function that creates value by stimulating, facilitating and fulfilling customer demand—it does this by building brands, nurturing innovation, developing relationships, creating good customer service and communicating benefits.'

While customers may drive the activities of a marketing-oriented organization, the organization will be able to continue serving its customers only if it meets its own objectives. Most private sector organizations operate with some kind of profit-related objectives, and if an adequate level of profits cannot be earned from a particular group of customers, a firm will not normally wish to meet the needs of that group. Where an organization is able to meet its customers' needs effectively and efficiently, its ability to gain an advantage over its competitors will be increased (e.g. by allowing it to sell a higher volume and/or at a higher price than its competitors). It is consequently also more likely to be able to meet its profit objectives.

Even in fully marketing-oriented organizations, it is not just customers who are crucial to the continuing success of the firm. The availability of finance and labour inputs may be quite critical, and in times of shortage of either one of these an organization must adapt its production processes if it is to continue meeting customers' needs. During the 'credit crunch' of 2008, many companies with satisfied customers and full order books nevertheless went out of business because they could not obtain finance to keep their activities going. In addition, a whole range of internal and external pressures (such as government legislation and the emergence of new technologies) can affect its ability to meet customers' needs profitably. Organizations must adapt to a changing marketing environment if they are to survive and prosper. In Chapter 2 we will look more closely at these pressures on businesses.

⦿ Marketing as a philosophy and as a set of techniques

Marketing can be seen at two levels—as a fundamental, underlying philosophy, and as a set of applied techniques. As a business philosophy, marketing puts customers at the centre of an organization's considerations. This is reflected in basic values, such as the requirement to understand and respond to customers' needs and the necessity to search constantly for new market opportunities. In a truly marketing-oriented organization, these values are instilled in all employees and should influence their behaviour without any need for prompting. For a fast-food restaurant, for example, the training of serving staff would emphasize those items—such as the speed of service and friendliness of staff—that research has found to be most valued by existing and potential customers. The personnel manager would have a selection policy that recruited staff who could fulfil the needs of customers rather than simply minimizing the wage bill. The accountant would investigate the effects on customers before deciding to save money by cutting stockholding levels. It is not sufficient for an organization simply to appoint a marketing manager or set up a marketing department— viewed as a philosophy, marketing is an attitude that applies to *everybody* who works for the organization.

To many people, marketing is simply associated with a set of techniques. For example, market research is seen as a technique for finding out about customers' needs, and advertising is thought to be a technique for communicating the benefits of a product offer to potential customers. However, these techniques can be of little value if they are undertaken by an organization that has not fully taken on board the *philosophy* of marketing. The techniques of marketing also include pricing, the design of channels of distribution, and new product development. Although many of the chapters of this book are arranged around specific techniques, it must never be forgotten that all of these techniques are interrelated and can be effective only if they are unified by a shared focus on customers.

Of course, the principles of marketing are not new. Some of the elements of marketing orientation can be traced as far back as ancient Greece, the Phoenicians, and the Venetian traders. The bartering that still takes place in many eastern Kasbahs is a form of marketing. In modern times, marketing orientation developed in the more affluent countries, especially for products where supply was outstripping demand and suppliers therefore faced

MARKETING in ACTION

Are they really marketing oriented?

Companies that have wholly embraced the marketing philosophy put customers at the centre of everything they do, so that being 'marketing oriented' becomes a state of mind for *all of their employees*. They should all be aware that if they don't put customers first somebody else probably will, and will win their profitable business. Here are some tell-tale signs of a company that may claim to be marketing oriented but where, in fact, not all of its employees have taken on board a genuine marketing orientation.

- In the car park, the prime parking spots are reserved for directors and senior staff rather than customers.

- Opening hours are geared towards meeting the social needs of staff rather than the purchasing preferences of customers.

- Management's attitudes towards lax staff is conditioned more by the need to keep internal peace than by the need to provide a high standard of service to customers.

- When confronted with a problem from a customer, an employee will refer the customer on to another employee without trying to resolve the matter themselves ('it's not my job').

- The company listens to customers' comments and complaints, but has poorly defined procedures for acting on them.

- Advertising is based on what senior staff want to say, rather than a sound analysis of what prospective customers want to hear.

- Goods and services are distributed through channels that are easy for the company to set up, rather than on the basis of what customers prefer.

Can you think of any more tell-tale signs? Can you identify companies that exhibit the characteristics described above? Why do you think the company can behave in such a way? Are there insufficient competitive pressures facing the company to warrant change? What, if anything, would you do to bring about change in the company?

high levels of competition for custom. Marketing first became an important discipline in the United States in the 1930s and has since become dominant around the world. In a competitive business environment, an organization will survive in the long term only if it focuses on the needs of clearly defined groups in society and produces goods and services that satisfy their requirements efficiently and effectively. The emphasis is on the customer wanting to buy, rather than on the producer needing to sell.

There have been many attempts to define just what is meant by marketing orientation. (A good review has been provided by Lafferty and Hult 2001.) Among empirical attempts to measure marketing orientation, a study by Narver and Slater (1990) identified three important components (Figure 1.1).

- Customer orientation: An organization must have a thorough understanding of its target buyers, so that it can create a product of superior value for them. Remember that value can be defined only by customers themselves, and can be created by increasing the benefits to the buyer in relation to the buyer's costs or by decreasing the buyer's costs in relation to the buyer's benefits. A customer orientation requires that a company understand not only the present value to the customer, but also how this is likely to evolve over time.

- Competitor orientation: As well as focusing on its customers, a firm should look at how well its competitors are able to satisfy buyers' needs. It should understand the short-term strengths and weaknesses and long-term capabilities and strategies of current and potential competitors.

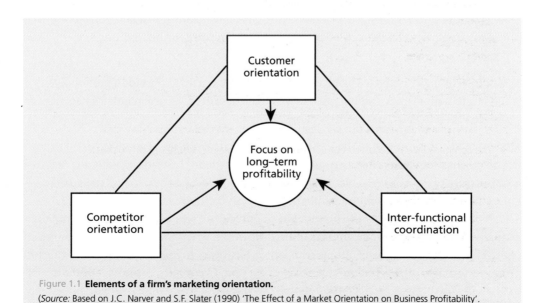

Figure 1.1 **Elements of a firm's marketing orientation.**
(*Source:* Based on J.C. Narver and S.F. Slater (1990) 'The Effect of a Market Orientation on Business Profitability'. *Journal of Marketing,* October, 20–35.)

- **Interfunctional coordination:** It is futile for marketing managers to develop marketing plans that are not acted upon by people who are capable of delivering promises made to customers. Many individuals within an organization have a responsibility for creating value—not just marketing staff—and a marketing orientation requires that the organization draws upon and integrates its human and physical resources effectively, and adapts them to meet customers' needs.

Foundations for success in business

So far, marketing has been presented as an indispensable approach to doing business. In fact, marketing is not appropriate to all firms at all times and in all places. Essentially, marketing is most important where the main factor constraining a firm's survival and growth is the shortage of customers for its products. If a firm can be assured of selling all that it produces, it may consider marketing to be the least of its worries. There are other factors that may be critical for success to some companies:

- Where the raw materials and components that a company requires are scarce but demand for its finished products is very strong, a company may consider that obtaining inputs to its production processes is its top priority. During the late 1990s, the shortage of organic vegetables, rather than a shortage of customers, posed the biggest challenge to companies seeking to develop the market for organic products (see 'Marketing in action' later in this chapter).

- For firms requiring high levels of skill among their employees, being able to recruit and retain the right personnel can be critical to business success. Firms in sectors as diverse as computer programming, direct marketing, specialist craft industries, and electrical engineering have had market-led growth held back by difficulties in filling key positions.

- Where a company is given a licence by government agencies to provide a monopoly service, its actions may be motivated more by the desire to keep the regulatory agency satisfied than to keep its customers happy.

Modern marketing emerged in the 1930s at a time when the volume of goods supplied to markets was increasing faster than consumers' demand for them. Instead of taking markets as a given element of their business plans, firms had to actively address the needs of their markets—if they didn't, the market would slip into their competitors' hands (see Figures 1.2 and 1.3).

It is common to talk about the production-oriented firm, where production and not marketing is the focal point for business planning. However, when markets become more competitive, the first reaction of many companies has been to take on board not the full philosophy of marketing, but only the selling function. Eventually, firms have come to realize that, instead of trying to sell products that buyers do not really want, it would be better to take on board the full philosophy of marketing, which puts customers' needs at the centre of all business planning.

Figure 1.2 **In 2010, tablet PCs became a hot new product which helped to reinvigorate the laptop computer market.** The market for laptops had become saturated and the basic laptop had become a commodity-type product. Tablet PCs allowed manufacturers to add features that consumers valued. Some innovators, such as Apple with its iPad created highly distinctive products which buyers were prepared to pay premium prices for. But how long would it be before *these* computers became standard and customers were no longer willing to pay a premium price for them? What would be the next features and benefits that customers will value as computing technology develops?
(*Source:* Reproduced with kind permission of Apple Inc.)
http://www.apple.com/pr/products/ipad.html

A production or a sales orientation may be appropriate to firms at certain stages in the evolution of markets. Where the dominant business environment is based on the need for good production planning above all else, the company that does this best will achieve the greatest overall business success. Likewise, in markets where customers face a lot of choice, the company that achieves the greatest business success is likely to be one that has the most effective marketing (see Figure 1.4).

Because they are business environments that still occur in some markets in some places, production and selling orientations are described below. There has, however, been an almost inevitable tendency for such business environments to progress to a full marketing orientation. Firms that have identified such trends and adapted have tended to survive, while those set in their traditional ways of doing business have fallen behind.

Production orientation

Marketing as a business discipline has much less significance where goods or services are scarce and considerable unsatisfied demand exists. If an organization is operating in a stable environment in which it can sell all that it can produce, why bother spending time and money trying to understand precisely what benefit a customer seeks from buying the product? If the market is stable, why take time trying to anticipate future requirements? Furthermore, if a company has significant monopoly power, it may have little interest in being more efficient in meeting customer requirements. The former state monopolies of Eastern Europe are frequently cited as examples of organizations that produced what they imagined consumers wanted, rather than what they actually wanted. Planning for full utilization of capital

Figure 1.3 **The fast-moving consumer goods (FMCG) sectors were the first to adopt modern marketing.**
The soap powder, toothpaste, and shampoo markets have become fiercely competitive and great efforts have been
made by the manufacturers to develop differentiated versions of a fairly standard product in order to meet the needs
of small groups of consumers more effectively than their competitors. Next time you are in a shop choosing
toothpaste, look at all of the different product formulations, packaging design, and price offers that companies have
deployed to try to get you to buy their product rather than the competitors'. It is often said that experience in the
tough world of an FMCG company's marketing department is the best apprenticeship that a new marketer can serve.
While FMCG sectors were early adopters of marketing, many more sectors have followed their example.

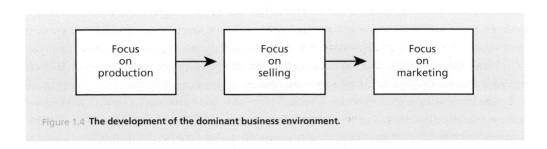

Figure 1.4 **The development of the dominant business environment.**

equipment was often seen as more important than ensuring that the equipment was used to provide goods and services that people actually wanted. Production-oriented firms generally aim for efficiency in production rather than effectiveness in meeting customers' needs.

In the developed countries of America and Europe, production orientation was quite pervasive until the 1930s; up to then, a general shortage of goods relative to the demand for them, and a lack of competition, resulted in a sellers' market. In many goods markets, however, the world depression of the 1920s and 1930s had the effect of tilting the balance of supply and demand more in favour of buyers, resulting in sellers having to address more seriously the needs of increasingly selective customers. In most countries markets for services have tended to retain a production orientation longer than most goods markets, reflecting the fact that many key services, such as postal services, telecommunications, electricity, gas, and water supply, have been dominated by state or private monopolies which gave consumers very little choice of supplier—if consumers did not like the service they received from their water supplier, they could not switch their business to another water company. Management in such circumstances had greater freedom to satisfy its own interests than those of the consumer, and could increase profits more effectively by keeping production costs down rather than applying effort and possibly taking greater risk through developing new services based on consumers' needs.

During periods of shortages, production orientation sometimes returns to an industry sector. The shortage might come about through supply limitations caused by strikes or bad weather, or it could be the result of a sudden increase in demand relative to supply. For example, during a bus or train drivers' strike, taxi operators may realize that there is a temporary massive excess of demand relative to supply and so may be tempted to lower their standards of service to casual customers (e.g. by responding to requests much more slowly and doing so in a less friendly manner than regular customers would have come to expect). During the boom in property prices that occurred in the UK during the mid-2000s, the services of builders were in short supply, especially in south-east England. Stories abounded of builders 'selecting' customers and delaying the completion of jobs because they knew that customers had very little choice.

Selling orientation

Faced with an increasingly competitive market, the natural reaction of many organizations has been to shout louder in order to attract customers to buy its products. Product policy was driven by the desire to make those products that the company thought it was good at producing, rather than seriously asking what benefits customers sought from buying its products. In order to increase sales, the focal point of the business moved away from the production manager to the sales manager, who set about increasing effective demand by the use of various sales techniques. Advertising, sales promotion, and personal selling were used to emphasize product differentiation and branding.

A sales orientation was a move away from a strict product orientation, but it still did not focus on satisfying customer needs. Little effort was made to research customers' needs or to devise new product offerings that were customer-led rather than production-led.

Demand boomed for organics, but where were the vegetables?

Supermarkets today sell a wide range of 'organic' fruit and vegetables, with rival supermarket chains competing against each other on the price and quality of their produce. Some have gone further, and added ethical sourcing as a point of differentiation, for example through compliance with Fairtrade standards. But in the early days of the boom in organic vegetables, competition was not so keen, and those early days illustrate the point that when a company faces acute problems of supply, it may simply not be realistic for it to be customer-led, at least in the short-term. In the UK during the late 1990s a combination of rising incomes, greater awareness of health issues, and a stream of food safety scares led to a rapid growth in demand for organic produce (see Chomka 2002). But how could farmers grow organically on land that had been saturated by decades of artificial fertilizers? The Soil Association, which operates an accreditation scheme for organic produce, required that farmland should be free of artificial fertilizer for at least five years before any crops grown on it could be described as organic. So, despite the rapid growth in demand and the price premiums that customers were prepared to pay, retailers found it difficult to satisfy demand. Furthermore, with a difficult and intermittent supply, could retailers risk their brand names by being seen as unreliable suppliers of second-rate produce? Marks & Spencer launched a range of organic vegetables in 1997, only to temporarily withdraw them soon afterwards, blaming the difficulty in obtaining regular and reliable supplies. In the short term, it was suppliers and not customers who guided the retailer's policy on organic produce. However, by 2002 previous initiatives to grow more organic food were finally coming on stream, resulting in a glut of produce which depressed the prices that farmers received. It was now a buyers' market.

A sales orientation has been characteristic of a number of business sectors. UK package holiday companies have often grown through heavy advertising of their competitive price advantage, supported by aggressive sales promotion techniques, such as free child places. There are signs that this sales-led approach is now being replaced by a greater analysis of the diverse needs that customers seek to satisfy when buying a package holiday, such as reliable aircraft departures, and assurance about the standards of the booked hotel.

If a company were accurately identifying consumer needs and offering a product that satisfied these needs, then consumers would want to buy the product, and the company would not have to rely on intensive sales techniques. In the words of Peter Drucker (1973):

'The aim of marketing is to make selling superfluous. The aim of marketing is to know and understand the customer so well that the product or service fits him and sells itself. Ideally, marketing should result in a customer who is ready to buy. All that should be needed is to make the product or service available . . .'

New marketing, or old ideas?

Among the favourite words of marketers are 'new', 'improved', and 'innovative'. Each year brings its crop of new ideas about the philosophy and practices of marketing, some of them being dressed up in pseudo-scientific terminology by consultants and academics, eager to use their knowledge base to sell a new idea to people who fear being left behind. In fact, basic principles of marketing have been quite enduring, and claims for completely new approaches to marketing should be treated cautiously. For the experienced marketer, most new ideas are based on age-old underlying theory, and there is usually some form of precedent for new ideas.

The Internet was hailed as a completely new approach to marketing, and at the height of 'dot. com' mania around 2000, some advocates had a vision of the Internet allowing almost infinite and cheap communication possibilities, breaking down monopolies, international trade and cultural barriers in the process. The world of marketing would never be the same again.

The Internet has certainly changed the way that many companies practise marketing, but underlying principles have often won out over the hype. 'Disintermediation' was held out as a great opportunity by which the Internet would cut out intermediaries, as people buy airline tickets, books, and financial services, directly from the producer, rather than using an agent, retailer, or broker as an intermediary. But basic theories of marketing suggest that people like to be presented with a manageable choice in one location. It should therefore have been no surprise that instead of 'disintermediation', many new information intermediaries such Expedia.com, Amazon.com, and moneysupermarket.com emerged to fulfil this role. Internet auction sites such as eBay have been proclaimed as a new way of marketing to customers on a one-to-one basis, but the basic principles underlying them can be traced back to marketing practices found in ancient Kasbahs. Many of the big Internet service providers realize that successful Internet marketing requires a sound understanding of basic human behaviour, and many have appointed teams of anthropologists to try to understand users' deep-seated motivations, and how these relate to modern technology. Among current burning questions are whether Web 2.0 and social networking sites, such as Facebook and Twitter, really represent a new marketing approach, as buyers seek out information from their peers rather than through conventional advertising. Again, theories based in social sciences may suggest that although the technology is new, the nature of people's need to belong and their methods of developing trust are longstanding.

Practitioners of marketing make excessive use of the word 'new', to describe anything from a 'new and improved' breakfast cereal to a new way of looking at the world. However, we should never forget that many of the underlying principles of marketing are quite timeless. We really need to distinguish between genuinely new marketing ideas—which are quite rare—and old ideas that have been applied to a new marketing environment.

Marketing and social responsibility

Marketing without markets?

Can you have marketing in a situation where there is no market? The link between marketing and markets has been extensively discussed, with some confusion about the role of marketing. Many public sector services have employed people with titles such as 'marketing officer', often with responsibilities which include services for which consumers may have little or no choice. Even many police forces have appointed marketing officers. Although there may be some instances where such a person would genuinely need to apply the principles of marketing (e.g. where police forces compete against each other to provide cover at regional football matches), most of their work is likely to be involved with promotion and possibly learning more about public opinion. For most services provided by police forces, there is no market, and indeed soliciting payment from some groups may sound like corruption. When one police force accepted sponsorship of its cars from the security company Chubb, it was widely accused of leaving itself open to accusations of favouritism if the sponsor was ever considered to be involved in an offence. Many of the tools of marketing, such as pricing and market segmentation, are clearly not available to the police service. It can also be difficult to identify who the customer is; it may be members of society more generally, who benefit from a safer community, but with whom there is no exchange relationship.

So can we have marketing without markets? Karl Marx once questioned whether you could have capitalism without capital. Perhaps marketing without a market is a similar oxymoron?

◉ Which organizations undertake marketing?

Marketing developed in competitive fast-moving consumer goods (FMCG) sectors, with private sector services following in their footsteps. More recently, marketing has been adopted by various public sector and not-for-profit organizations, reflecting the increasingly competitive environments in which these now operate. Operationalizing marketing within these organizations poses a number of challenges (see Sargeant 2009). If an organization has a market that it needs to win over, then marketing has a role. But without markets, can marketing ever be a reality? Many organizations claim to have introduced marketing when in fact their customers are captive, with no marketplace within which they can choose competing goods or services. What passes for marketing may be little more than a laudable attempt to bring best practice to their operations in selected areas, for example in providing customer care programmes for front-line staff. But if customers have to come to the company anyway (as they do in the case of many local authority services), is this really marketing?

Within the public/not-for-profit sectors, financial objectives are often qualified by non-financial social objectives. An organization's desire to meet individual customers' needs must be further constrained by its requirement to meet these wider social objectives. In this way, a leisure centre may set an objective of providing a range of keep-fit programmes for disadvantaged members of the local community, knowing that it could have earned more money by opening its facilities to the larger group of full fee paying visitors. Nevertheless, marketing can be employed to achieve a high take-up rate among this latter group, persuading them to spend their time and money at the leisure centre rather than on other leisure activities. It can also be used to appeal to disadvantaged groups by encouraging them to take part in keep fit activities rather than other forms of activity.

In recent years, the principles of marketing have been applied to organizations that essentially promote ideas, for example charities, political parties, and religious groups. Some of the principles of marketing may be evident in the way that the UK Labour Party 'rebranded' itself as New Labour after careful research of its audiences. This was backed up with a very effective advertising campaign, based on many of the principles of segmentation and targeting, which helped it to win the subsequent general elections. However, some purists would argue that, in its application to social and political causes, marketing is inappropriate because of the absence of markets and exchanges as conventionally understood by marketers.

◉ Key marketing concepts

In this section, the philosophy of marketing will be developed a little further by defining a number of key concepts which go to the heart of the philosophy. The concepts of customers, needs, value, exchange, and markets will be briefly introduced, but returned to in following chapters.

Customers

Customers provide payment to an organization in return for the delivery of goods and services and therefore form a focal point for an organization's marketing activity. Customers can be described by many terms, including client, passenger, subscriber, reader, guest, and student. The terminology can imply something about the relationship between a company and its customers, so the term 'patient' implies a caring relationship, 'passenger' implies an ongoing responsibility for the safety of the customer, and 'client' implies that the relationship is governed by a code of ethics (formal or informal).

The customer is generally understood to be the person who makes the decision to purchase a product, and/or who pays for it. In fact, products are often bought by one person for consumption by another, therefore the customer and consumer need not be the same person. For example, colleges must market themselves not only to prospective students, but also to their parents, careers counsellors, local employers, and government funding agencies. In these circumstances it can be difficult to identify who an organization's marketing effort should be focused upon. The role of influencers in the decision process is discussed further in Chapter 4.

For many public services, it is society as a whole, and not just the immediate customer, that benefits from an individual's consumption. In the case of health services, society can benefit from having a fit and healthy population in which the risk of contracting a contagious disease is minimized.

Different customers within a market have different needs which they seek to satisfy. To be fully marketing oriented, a company would have to adapt its offering to meet the needs of each individual. In fact, very few firms can justify aiming to meet the needs of each specific individual; instead, they target their product at a clearly defined group in society and position their product so that it meets the needs of that group. These sub-groups are often referred to as 'segments' and are explored in Chapter 3 (page 84).

> ## MARKETING in ACTION
>
> **When does a student become a customer?**
>
> As a hospital *patient*, would you cringe at being referred to as a 'customer'? Or what about the transformation of rail users from 'passengers' to 'customers'? Some universities now refer to their paying students as 'customers'. The use of the word 'customer' may sharpen minds within an organization, making everybody aware that they cannot take users for granted. 'Passenger', 'patient', and 'student' are relatively passive terms, but 'customer' provides a reminder that custom can be quite transient. Do terms used by professionals, such as 'patient' and 'student', imply a professional code of ethics which puts some groups of consumers in a very special, trusting relationship with their supplier? Is it realistic to describe as 'customers' the users of some public services (such as the police and fire services) when there is no alternative supplier they could customize? Does the use of the generic title of 'customer' undermine this special relationship? Could the use of the term 'customer' even be a double-edged sword, by raising consumers' expectations about standards of service to levels that may be undeliverable? Can being a patient in an NHS hospital ever be likened to being a customer of Sainsbury's supermarket?

Needs

Consumers are motivated by their desire to satisfy complex needs, and these should be the starting point for all marketing activity. We no longer live in a society in which the main motivation of individuals is to satisfy the basic needs for food and drink. Maslow (1943) recognized that, once individuals have satisfied basic physiological needs, they may be motivated by higher-order social and self-fulfillment needs. Needs as motivators are explored further in Chapter 4.

'Need' refers to something that is deep-rooted in an individual's personality. How individuals go about satisfying that need will be conditioned by the cultural values of the society which they belong to. So in some cultures the need for self-fulfilment may be satisfied by a religious penance, while other societies may seek it through a development of their creative talents.

It is useful to make a distinction between needs and wants. Wants are culturally conditioned by the society in which an individual lives. Wants subsequently become effective demand for a product where there is both a willingness and an ability to pay for the product. Marketers are continually seeking to learn more about underlying needs which may eventually manifest themselves as demand in the form of people actually being willing to pay money for its products (Figure 1.5).

It must not be forgotten that commercial buyers of goods and services also have complex needs which they seek to satisfy when buying on behalf of their organizations. Greater complexity occurs where the economic needs of the organization may not be entirely the same as the personal needs of individuals within the organization (Figure 1.6).

Value

For customers, value is represented by the ratio of perceived benefits to price paid. Customers will evaluate benefits according to the extent to which a product allows their needs to be

Nature of need	Likely sources of need satisfaction in primitive societies	Likely sources of need satisfaction in western Europe
Status	Ownership of animals Multiple wives	Make and model of car Type and location of house
Excitement	Hunting Inter-tribe rivalry	Fast car Adventure holiday
Identification with group	Body painting Adopting rituals of the group	Wearing branded clothing Patronizing 'cool' nightclubs and bars

Figure 1.5 **Some basic human needs and how people in different societies may go about satisfying them.**

satisfied (Figure 1.7). Customers also evaluate how well a product's benefits add to their own well-being as compared with the benefits provided by competitors' offerings:

$$\text{Customer perceived value} = \frac{\text{Benefits deriving from a product}}{\text{Cost of acquiring the product}}$$

Consumers often place a value on a product offer that is quite different from the value presumed by the supplier. Business organizations succeed by adding value at a faster rate than they add to their own production costs. Value can be added by better specifying a product offer in accordance with customers' expectations, for example by providing the reassurance of effective after-sales service.

Estimating customers' assessment of value is not easy for marketers. Essentially, marketers need to be able to estimate how much a buyer would be prepared to pay for its product—if the price is too high, it will not represent value to the buyer so they will not buy it. If the price is set too low, the buyer is getting a 'bargain' and the seller should try to get from the buyer the higher price that they would have been prepared to pay, just up to the point where the price no longer represents good value. Chapter 9 deals with theoretical and practical approaches to pricing which aim to set prices at a level that meets the needs of buyer and seller. Segmentation is crucial to this exercise, as some groups of buyers are likely to place significantly higher values on the firm's goods than others (Chapter 6). If the price of a good is set too high, no sale may take place, or at least only a one-off sale which may be regarded by the buyer as a 'rip-off'. If the price is set too low, the supplier may achieve high levels of sales, but fail to make any profit because the price is too low to cover its costs. Firms need to understand not just what constitutes value today, but how customers' perceptions of value will change over time.

Figure 1.6 **Traditional street markets and farmers markets have been experiencing a revival in the UK.** Although market traders may not use many of the terms used in books on marketing theory, they are nevertheless very adept marketers. Traders learn very quickly which product lines are selling quickly and the effects of price changes on sales levels, among other things. They must adapt quickly, or risk business going to another trader in the same market who is more in tune with customers' needs, or to another trader outside the market. Market traders do not have layers of bureaucratic control which may slow up a decision and individual traders cannot easily shelter in a bureaucratic structure where blame can be passed around without the fundamental issue of responding to customers' needs being addressed. It is not surprising that market traders who have survived and prospered in this environment have gone on to establish and run successful enterprises. Many marketers from large organizations could benefit by taking a walk through their local market and reconnecting with the fundamental principles of marketing. (Reproduced with kind permission of National Market Traders Federation.)

Exchange

Societies have different ways in which they arrange for goods and services to be acquired. In some less developed societies hunting for food, or begging, may be a norm. In centrally planned economies goods and services may be allocated to individuals and firms by central government planners. In modern market-based economies, goods and services are acquired

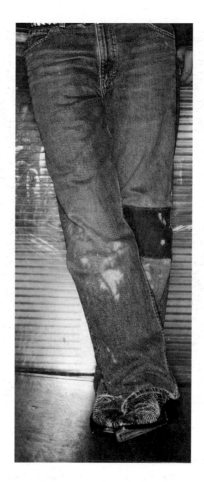

Figure 1.7 **Value can be a very personal issue, and one person's highly prized object may be regarded by somebody else as their rubbish.** Furniture and clothing has often been artificially aged to give it a used appearance. The denim jeans shown in this illustration have been cut and made to look worn at the knees before being sold to customers. Many buyers have been prepared to pay a premium price for a pair of jeans that looked as if they had been previously worn. To others, however, the idea of prematurely ageing clothes may sound like a sacrilege—for them, prematurely aged jeans should have a lower rather than a higher value. Value is essentially about personal judgements.

on the basis of exchange. Exchange implies that one party makes some sacrifice to another party in return for receiving something it values; the other party similarly makes a sacrifice and receives something that *it* values. Of course, the sacrifices and valuations of goods received and given up are essentially based on personal opinion and preferences, so there is no objective way of defining what is a 'fair' exchange, other than observing that both parties are happy with the outcomes. In market-based economies there is a presumption that each party can decide whether or not to enter into an exchange with the other. Each party is also free to choose between a number of alternative potential partners. Exchange usually takes

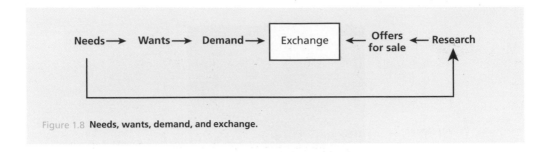

Figure 1.8 **Needs, wants, demand, and exchange.**

the form of a product being exchanged for money, although the bartering of goods and services is still common in some trading systems (Figure 1.8).

Can the concept of exchange be generalized to cover the provision of public services? Some have argued that the payment of taxes to the government in return for the provision of public services is a form of social marketing exchange. Within marketing frameworks, the problem with this approach to exchange is that it can be difficult to identify what sovereignty consumers of government services have in determining which exchanges they should engage in.

A single exchange should not be seen in isolation from the preceding and expected subsequent exchanges between parties. Marketers are increasingly focusing on analysing ongoing exchange relationships, rather than one-off and isolated exchanges. (We will come back to this in Chapter 4.)

Markets

The term 'market' has traditionally been used to describe a place where buyers and sellers gather to exchange goods and services (e.g. a fruit and vegetable market or a stock market). Economists define a market in terms of a more abstract concept of interaction between buyers and sellers, so that the 'UK cheese market' is defined in terms of all buyers and sellers of cheese in the UK. Markets are defined with reference to space and time, so marketers may talk about sales of a particular type of cheese in the north-west region for a specified period of time. Various measures of the market are commonly used, including sales volumes, sales values, growth rate, and level of competitiveness.

The marketing mix

Central to marketing management is the concept of the marketing mix (Figure 1.9). In this section the elements of the marketing mix are briefly introduced, but they are returned to in greater detail in following chapters. The marketing mix is not a theory of management that has been derived from scientific analysis, but a conceptual framework which highlights the principal decisions that marketing managers make in configuring their offerings to suit customers' needs. The tools can be used to develop both long-term strategies and short-term tactical programmes.

A marketing manager can be seen as somebody who mixes a set of ingredients to achieve a desired outcome in much the same way as a cook mixes ingredients for a cake. At the end

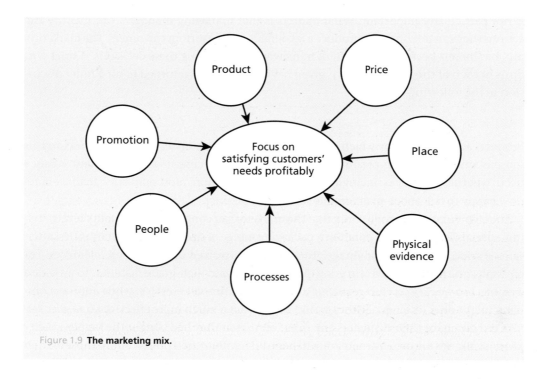

Figure 1.9 **The marketing mix.**

of the day, two cooks can meet a common objective of baking an edible cake, but using different blends of ingredients to achieve their objective. Marketing managers are essentially mixers of ingredients, and, as with the cooks, two marketers may each use broadly similar ingredients, but fashion them in different ways to end up with quite distinctive product offers. The nation's changing tastes result in bakers producing new types of cake, and so, too, the changing marketing environment results in marketing managers producing new goods and services to offer to their markets. The mixing of ingredients in both cases is a combination of a science—learning by a logical process from what has proved effective in the past—and an art form, in that both the cook and marketing manager frequently come across new situations where there is no direct experience to draw upon, and where a creative decision must therefore be made.

The concept of the marketing mix was first given prominence by Borden (1965), who described the marketing manager as

'A mixer of ingredients, one who is constantly engaged in fashioning creatively a mix of marketing procedures and policies in his efforts to produce a profitable enterprise.'

There has been debate about which tools should be included in the marketing mix. The traditional marketing mix has comprised the four elements of product, price, promotion, and place. A number of people have additionally suggested adding people, process, and physical evidence decisions, which can be important aspects of marketing planning in services industries. There is overlap between each of these headings, and their precise definition is not particularly important. What matters is that marketing managers can identify the actions they can take that will produce a favourable response from customers. The marketing mix has merely become a convenient framework for analysing these decisions. A brief synopsis of each of the mix elements is given below, and each is returned to for a fuller discussion in the following chapters.

Products

Products are the means by which organizations satisfy consumers' needs. A product in this sense is anything that an organization offers to potential customers which might satisfy a need, whether tangible or intangible. After initial hesitation, most marketing managers are now happy to talk about an intangible service as a product.

The elements of the product mix that the marketer can control include quality levels, styling, special design features, durability, packaging, range of sizes or options, warranties, after-sales service, and the brand image. Trade-offs are involved between these elements. For example, one firm may invest in good quality control and high-grade materials to provide a durable, top-quality product requiring a low level of after-sales service, while another company might offer lower quality but would ensure that a much more effective after-sales service did not make their customers any worse off than if they had bought the higher-quality product. Brands are used by companies to help differentiate their product from those of their competitors. A brand is a name, term, symbol, or combination of these intended to differentiate the goods of one seller from all other sellers (see Chapter 7).

The range of products offered by firms needs to adapt to changes in the marketing environment. As an example, cosmetics companies have responded to changes in male attitudes by launching new ranges of cosmetics targeted at men. (New product development is discussed in Chapter 8.)

Pricing

Pricing is a critical element of most companies' marketing mix, as it determines the revenue that will be generated. By contrast, the other mix elements are concerned essentially with items of expenditure. If the selling price of a product is set too high, a company may not achieve its sales volume targets. If it is set too low, volume targets may be achieved, but no profit earned. Setting prices is a difficult part of the marketing mix. In theory, prices are determined by the interaction of market forces, and the bases of such price determination is explored further in Chapter 9. In practice, marketers set prices for individual products on the basis of what they cost to produce, what the competition is charging, and what customers are prepared to pay. Marketing managers in many public utilities must additionally contend with interventions by government regulatory agencies.

Price decisions also involve deciding on the relationship between prices charged for different products within a firm's range (e.g. should the core product be sold at a low price in order to encourage sales of highly profitable optional extras?) and deciding a pricing strategy over time. (Should a new product be launched as a prestige product, and its price gradually lowered as it becomes more commonplace?)

Place

Decisions concerning place really comprise two related areas of decisions. Companies usually make their goods and services in places that are convenient for production, but customers prefer to buy them where the purchase process and/or consumption is easiest. So place decisions involve determining how easy a company wants to make it for customers to gain access to its goods and services. In the first place, this involves deciding which intermediaries to use in the process of transferring the product from the manufacturer to final consumer (usually referred to as designing a 'channel of distribution'). Intermediaries can either take a conventional form such as high street shops, or they can be Internet-based retailers and agents. Second, place decisions involve deciding how physically to move and handle the product as it is transported from manufacturer to final consumer (often referred to as 'logistics' or 'physical distribution management'). Place decisions are considered in more detail in Chapter 10.

Promotion

Promotion is used by companies to communicate the benefits of their products to their target markets. Promotional tools include advertising, personal selling, public relations, sales promotion, sponsorship, and—increasingly—direct marketing methods. Just as product ranges need to be kept up to date to reflect changing customer needs, so, too, promotional methods need to be responsive to changes in a firm's operating environment. Many companies are currently wondering how they can incorporate peer-to-peer communication derived from social network media into their promotional planning, for example by developing 'viral' advertising campaigns. Promotion decisions to be taken by companies typically include: what message to use; which media; what timing for an advertising campaign; how much to spend; how to evaluate this expenditure. Promotional decisions are considered in more detail in Chapter 11.

People

People decisions are particularly important to the marketing of services. In the services sector, in particular, people planning can be very important where staff have a high level of contact with customers. Marketing effectiveness is likely to be critically affected by the actions of front-line employees who interact with customers. While a car manufacturer's employees may be unseen by its customers, a restaurant's waiters can make or break the benefits that visitors to the restaurant perceive. People decisions call for close involvement between marketing and human resource management functions to answer such questions as: what are the pre-requisite skills for front-line employees? How should staff be rewarded and motivated?

Process

Process decisions are again of most importance to marketers in the services sector. The process of production may be of little concern to the consumer of manufactured goods, but it is often of critical concern to the consumer of 'high contact' services. A customer of a restaurant is deeply affected by the manner in which staff members serve them. For busy customers, the speed and friendliness with which a restaurant processes its customers may be just as important as the meal itself. Marketers must work closely with operations managers to design customer handling processes that are both cost efficient and effective in satisfying customers' needs.

Physical evidence

Physical evidence is important in guiding buyers of intangible services through the choices available to them. This evidence can take a number of forms. At its simplest, a brochure can describe and give pictures of important elements of the service product—a holiday brochure gives pictorial evidence of hotels and resorts for this purpose. The appearance of staff can give evidence about the nature of a service—a tidily dressed ticket clerk for an airline gives some evidence that the airline operation as a whole is run with care and attention. A clean, bright environment used in a service outlet can help reassure potential customers at the point where they make a service purchase decision.

Interdependency of the marketing mix

The definition of the elements of the marketing mix is largely intuitive and semantic. The list of mix elements has a lot of everyday practical value, because it provides headings around which management thoughts and actions can be focused. However, dividing management responses into apparently disconnected areas of activity may lead to the interaction between elements being overlooked. Promotion mix decisions, for example, cannot be considered in isolation from decisions about product characteristics or pricing. Within conventional definitions of the marketing mix, important customer-focused issues such as quality of service can become lost. A growing body of opinion is therefore suggesting that a more holistic approach should be taken by marketing managers in responding to their customers' needs. This view sees the marketing mix as a production-led approach to marketing in which the agenda for action is set by the seller and not by the customer. An alternative relationship marketing approach starts by asking what customers seek from a company and then proceeds to develop a response that integrates all the functions of a business in a manner that evolves in response to customers' changing needs. Although the chapters of this book roughly follow the elements of the marketing mix, the interlinkages between the mix elements must never be forgotten.

◉ Marketing management

Successful marketing does not generally come about by accident: it needs to be managed effectively. (Although there are nevertheless many cases of successful marketing that occurred more by good luck than by judgement!) Three fundamental aspects of marketing management can be identified: processes, structures, and outcomes.

The marketing management process

Some companies, as they emerge from a production orientation, may think that they need only 'do some marketing' when trading conditions get tough. In fact, for well-managed businesses, marketing is an ongoing process that has no beginning or end (Figure 1.10). It is usual to identify four principal stages of the marketing management process, which involves asking the following questions:

- Analysis: Where are we now? How does the company's market share compare with that of its competitors? What are the strengths and weaknesses of the company and its products? What opportunities and threats does it face in its marketing environment?

- Planning: Where do we want to be? What is the mission of the business? What objectives should be set for the next year? What strategy will be adopted in order to achieve those objectives (e.g. should the company go for a high price/low volume strategy, or a low price/high volume one)?

- Implementation: How are we going to put into effect the strategy that will lead us to our objectives?

- Evaluation and Control: Did we achieve our objectives? If not, why not? How can deficiencies be rectified? (In other words, go back to the beginning of the process and conduct further analysis.)

Marketing management structures

Internally, the structure and politics of an organization affect the manner in which it can respond to changing customer needs. An organization that gives all marketing responsibilities to just a narrow group of people may in fact create tensions within the organization that make it less effective at responding to change, compared with an organization where the philosophy and practice of marketing are shared more widely. Marketing plans cannot be developed and implemented without a sound understanding of marketing managers' relationships to other members of their organization. There has been extensive research into the internal barriers that prevent companies developing a marketing orientation (e.g. Harris 2002; Morgan 2002).

There are two aspects of management structures that particularly affect the role of marketers: the internal structure and processes of the marketing department itself (where one actually exists), and the relationship of the marketing functions to other business functions, which affects the marketing effectiveness of an organization. Issues of marketing management structures and processes are explored in Chapter 12.

Outcomes of the marketing management process

Ultimately, the aim of good marketing management is to allow a company to survive and produce an acceptable level of profits. Leading up to this, a tangible outcome of the management process is the marketing plan. A plan should be distinguished from the process of planning: a plan is a statement fixed at one point in time, while planning refers to an ongoing process, of which the plan is just one outcome.

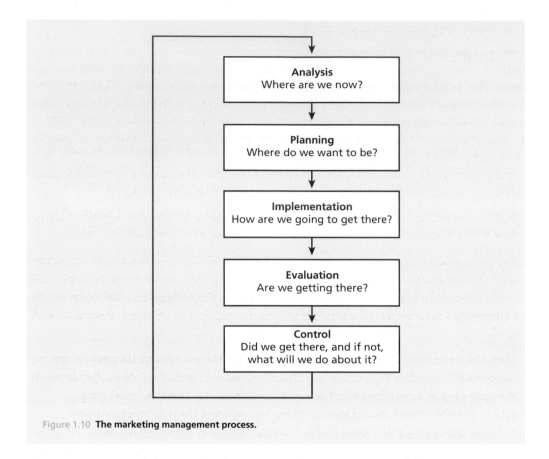

Figure 1.10 **The marketing management process.**

Companies typically produce a strategic marketing plan for a five-year period. Over this time period, projections can be subject to a lot of speculative estimation. Nevertheless, a five-year strategic plan can be vital to give a sense of direction to a company's marketing effort. Over the shorter term, companies usually produce an annual plan which gives more details of how the strategy will be implemented over the forthcoming 12-month period. Sometimes, where a marketing plan is based on a set of assumptions that are highly speculative, a company may choose to develop an additional contingency plan to use, should the assumptions on which the original plan was based turn out to be invalid.

There is continuing debate about the extent to which marketing plans should be flexible. If they are too flexible, they lose value in being able to act as a blueprint for all individuals in an organization to plan by. If the marketing department changes its sales targets halfway through the plan period, this might cause havoc in the production department, which had geared up to meet the original budgeted level of sales. On the other hand, fixed plans may become an irrelevance when the company's marketing environment has changed significantly.

⦿ Marketing and its relationship to other business functions

Companies have learned that their marketing departments cannot exist in isolation from the other functional departments of their organization. The importance attached to an organization's marketing activities is influenced by the nature of the environment in which the organization operates. In a production-oriented firm, a marketing department has little role to play, other than merely processing orders.

In a truly marketing-oriented company, marketing responsibilities cannot be confined to something called a marketing department. In the words of Drucker (1973):

> 'Marketing is so basic that it cannot be considered to be a separate function. It is the whole business seen from the point of view of its final result, that is, from the customer's point of view.'

In marketing-oriented organizations, the customer should be the concern not just of the marketing department, but also of all the production and administrative personnel whose actions may directly or indirectly create value in the mind of customers. In a typical company, the activities of a number of functional departments can affect customer value:

◉ The selection, training, motivation, and control of staff by personnel managers cannot be considered in isolation from marketing objectives and strategies. Possible conflict between the personnel and marketing functions may arise where, for example, marketing demands highly trained and motivated front-line staff, but the personnel function pursues a policy that places cost reduction and uniform pay rates above all else.

◉ A marketing manager may seek to respond as closely as possible to customers' needs, only to find opposition from production managers who argue that a product of the required standard cannot be achieved. Production managers tend to prefer long production runs of standardized products, but marketers increasingly try to satisfy market niches with specially adapted products.

◉ At a strategic and operational level, finance managers' actions in respect of the level of credit offered to customers, or towards stockholdings, can significantly affect the quality of service and the volume of customers with which the marketing department is able to do business.

Marketing orientation requires all of these departments to 'think customer' and to work together to satisfy customer needs and expectations. In practice, this can be very difficult to achieve, as witnessed by the many instances where it may appear that 'the left hand of the organization doesn't know what the right hand is doing'. A number of initiatives have sought to organize the activities of a company around processes that create value as perceived by customers (see Chapter 12). However, there is a danger that, as groups work more collectively, individual responsibilities and accountabilities can diminish.

Marketing and social responsibility

Traditional definitions of marketing have stressed the supremacy of customers, but this is increasingly being challenged by the requirement to satisfy the needs of a wider range of stakeholders in society. The depletion of the ozone layer, leading to potentially catastrophic climate change has led many consumers to question the values of the philosophy of marketing with its emphasis on personal need satisfaction rather than collective responsibility for the planet that we share. There have been many recent cases where companies have neglected these concerns, and we will look at some of these in Chapter 3. Scenes of protesters outside a company's premises and newspaper coverage of anti-social behaviour by firms can take away from the company something that its marketing department had spent years developing—its image. The opposite can be true where companies go out of their way to be good citizens.

There are segments within most markets that place high priority on ensuring that the companies they buy from are 'good citizens'. Examples can be found among consumers who prefer to pay a few pennies extra for products that have a low 'carbon footprint', or have been supplied by 'Fairtrade' companies.

Wider issues are raised about the effects of marketing practices on the values of a society. It has been argued by some that, by promoting greater consumption, marketing is responsible for creating a greater feeling of isolation among those members of society who cannot afford to join the consumer society where an individual's status is judged by what they own, rather than by their contribution to family and community life. Much advertising has been criticized as being socially harmful, for example for high-fat 'junk' food and alcohol, which may appeal against an individual's better judgement, bring bad health to millions, and raise the costs of health care for sufferers.

Determining the social responsibilities of organizations is a controversial subject and is discussed further in Chapter 3.

◉ Is marketing a science or an art?

Is marketing based on a scientific approach of inquiry, or is it essentially about an artistic process of creativity?

Studies of marketing using the scientific frameworks of the natural sciences have found favour with followers of the positivist approach. This holds that, from observations of the real world, it is possible to deduce models that are of general applicability. On this basis, models have been developed to predict consumer behaviour, the profitability of retail locations, and price–volume relationships, among many other phenomena.

The great merit of the scientific approach is its claim to great objectivity, in that patterns and trends can be identified with greater confidence than if they were based on casual observation. Many marketers have appreciated the value of this scientific approach. Most major retailers rely heavily on models of retail location before deciding where to locate their next

Marketing and social responsibility

Is marketing always good?

Marketing has come under increasing critical scrutiny in recent years, and it must not be assumed that a market-based approach is necessarily the best approach to making all goods and services available. Markets are motivated by the self-interest of individuals and companies. Without this self-interest, there will be little motivation for firms to provide better services, workers to work harder, and consumers to aspire for a higher level of consumption. But some moral philosophers have drawn a fine line between self-interest which helps markets work more effectively for the benefit of all, and a self-interest that becomes greed and a divisive force which undermines communities and is eventually self-destructive. Furthermore, there are many services that money used in market based transactions cannot—or should not—be able to buy.

The moral philosopher Michael Sandel has described a process by which markets triumphed during the three decades from the 1980s, but in doing so, undermined many vital public interests such as civic security, national defence, health, and welfare, which increasingly became outsourced, delivered, or created, through market-based mechanisms. Markets may lead individuals to commodify public services and undermine a sense of shared pride and moral righteousness in services provided for the community (Sandel 2009).

As an example of this, a creeping marketization of traditional community-based services has attracted strong criticism from those who see market forces 'crowding out' the efforts of the voluntary sector. One well-documented example of this is the case of blood donation services, which in many countries are operated as community-based voluntary activities, whereas in others blood donation is based on the market principles of paying money to individual donors in return for a valuable product. Richard Titmus showed how monetary compensation for donating blood could crowd out the supply of blood donors. Blood had been reduced to a commodity to be bought and sold, and this market-based calculation had crowded out individuals' evaluation based on moral rightness and benefit to the community (Titmus 1970). In short, there seemed to be evidence that introducing the principles of marketing might actually impede service provision.

In addition, some have argued that vital public services should not be left to decisions made by profit seeking companies whose individual objectives may be contrary to the greater public interest. In theory, markets would punish companies that did not serve the public interest, because they would lose customers and eventually go out of business. Unfortunately, the reality is that markets may not be efficient, or sufficiently rapid, in punishing companies that do not satisfy the wider public good. Critics of a market-led financial services sector blame its short-term, goal-driven culture for making a lot of high risk investments which began to unwind during the 'credit crunch' of 2008. Some would argue that as a result of short-term greed by market oriented banks, the banking system as a whole came close to collapse, with financial institutions reacting harshly by drastically reducing the amount of credit made available for investment by companies in the economy generally.

In short, did we all suffer because of our obsession with markets? Advocates of a centrally planned approach to the provision of essential public services pointed to countries such as France and Germany which had retained a much higher level of central control of essential public services, and their economies appeared to be less badly affected by the disruptive effects that occurred when bad, market-based decisions taken earlier by private sector companies harmed the rest of the economy.

In the UK, the government effectively nationalized Lloyds TSB bank and Royal Bank of Scotland, realizing that if these banks were to become bankrupt, there would be very serious implications for investment and financial transactions in all sectors of the economy. Was this humiliating evidence of the failure of markets?

outlet. Armed with trading statistics from their existing network of stores and background information about their locations (e.g. the number of people living within 20 minutes' driving time, passing vehicle traffic per day, proximity to competitors, etc.), a regression model can be developed which shows the significance of each specified factor in explaining sales success.

To many people, marketing has no credibility if it does not adopt a rigorous, scientific method of inquiry. This method of inquiry implies that research should be carried out in a systematic manner and results should be replicable. So a model of buyer behaviour should be able repeatedly to predict consumers' actions correctly, based on a sound collection of data and analysis. In the scientific approach, data are assessed using tests of significance and models are accepted or rejected accordingly. In the UK the Chartered Institute of Marketing has launched an initiative to improve the standards of 'marketing metrics'.

To counter this view, it has been argued that marketing cannot possibly copy the natural sciences in its methodologies. Positivist approaches have been accused of seeking meaning from quantitative data in a very subjective manner which is at variance with scientific principles (Brown 1995). Experimental research in the natural sciences generally involves closed systems in which the researcher can hold all extraneous variables constant, thereby isolating the effects of changes in a variable that is of interest. For social sciences, experimental frameworks generally consist of complex social systems over which the researcher has no control. So a researcher investigating the effects of a price change in a product on demand from customers cannot realistically hold constant all factors other than price. Indeed, it may be difficult to identify just what the 'other factors' are that should be controlled for in an experiment, but they may typically include the price of competitors' products, consumer confidence levels, the effects of media reports about that product category, and changes in consumer fashions and tastes, to name some of the more obvious. Contrast this with a physicist's laboratory experiment, where heat, light, humidity, pressure, and most other extraneous variables can be controlled, and the limitations of the scientific methodology in the social sciences become apparent. Marketers are essentially dealing with 'open' systems, in contrast to the 'closed' systems that are more typical of the natural sciences.

Post-positivists place greater emphasis on exploring in depth the meaning of individual case studies than on seeking objectivity and replicability through large sample sizes. Many would argue that such *inductive* approaches are much more customer-focused, in that they allow marketers to see the world from consumers' overall perspective, rather than through the mediating device of a series of isolated indicators. Post-positivist approaches to marketing hold that the 'real' truth will never emerge in a research framework that is constrained by the need to operationalize variables in a watertight manner. In real-life marketing, the world cannot be divided into clearly defined variables that are capable of objective measurement. Constructs such as consumers' attitudes and motivation may be very difficult to measure and model objectively. Furthermore, it is often the interaction between various phenomena that is of interest to researchers, and it can be very difficult to develop models that correspond to respondents' holistic perceptions of the world.

There is another argument against the scientific approach to marketing, which sees the process as essentially backward looking. The scientific approach is relatively good at making sense of historic trends, but less good at predicting what will happen following periods of turbulent change.

Creativity combined with a scientific approach can be essential for innovation. The scientific approach to marketing planning has a tendency to minimize risks, yet many major business successes have been based on entrepreneurs using their own judgement, in preference to that of their professional advisers. Consider the following cases.

- In the run-up to London's Millennium celebrations, the Millennium Dome was the outcome of a fairly bureaucratic process of planning. The forecasts turned out to be far too optimistic. By contrast, the London Eye was a great success, despite relying on largely intuitive estimates of likely demand.

- Demand for SMS text messaging services was greatly underestimated, partly reflecting a technological basis for forecasting, rather than a deeper understanding of individuals' lifestyles.

- A scientific analysis of the transatlantic airline market in the 1980s would have concluded that the market was saturated and there was no opportunity for a new British operator. This did not stop the entrepreneur Richard Branson from launching his own airline and, by using his own creative style, developing a distinctive and profitable service within the crowded market.

Marketing has to be seen as a combination of art and science. Treating it excessively as an art can lead to decisions that are not sufficiently rigorous. Emphasizing the scientific approach can lead a company to lose sight of the holistic perceptions of its customers. Successful firms seek to use scientific and creative approaches in a complementary manner.

◉ Marketing as an academic discipline

It is only since the 1970s that marketing has featured significantly on university syllabuses. To some of the more traditional academic institutions, marketing has been seen as essentially a topic of application rather than a discipline in its own right.

Marketing has borrowed heavily from other discipline areas. Its roots can be traced back to industrial economics, but in the process of growth it has drawn on the following discipline areas.

- Psychology has been central to many studies of buyer behaviour. Psychological theory in the fields of human motivation and perception has found ready application by marketers.

- Because of the importance of peer group pressures on many consumer and commercial purchases, a body of knowledge developed by sociologists has been used by marketers. As an example, social psychologists have contributed an understanding of the processes by which interpersonal trust develops, which has been applied to the study of long-term buyer–seller relationships (e.g. Dwyer et al. 1987).

- In its claim to be a science, marketers are constantly borrowing statistical techniques. Large-scale empirical research into buyer behaviour, product design preferences, and pricing effectiveness draws heavily upon previously developed statistical techniques which have conceptual and empirical validity.

- The law represents an embodiment of a society's values, and legal frameworks are becoming increasingly important to the study of marketing.

- Finally, economics remains an important discipline area on which marketing draws. As an example, marketers' pricing strategy has to be based on an understanding of the underlying theory of price determination in different market conditions.

As marketing has developed, the flow of theory has become more two-way. As well as borrowing from other discipline areas, marketers have developed theory and techniques that have been adopted by other discipline areas. (For example, marketers contributed significantly to the development of conjoint analysis in the study of consumer preferences, and this statistical methodology has now found widespread application elsewhere.) In universities the subject has benefited from multi-disciplinary teams being brought together to develop new techniques that are appropriate to marketing. Unfortunately, the structure of many universities still has a tendency to inhibit research between discipline areas that are based in different faculties.

◉ What makes a good marketer?

Finally, what characteristics make for a good marketer? Are good marketers born or bred? To answer this question, it is necessary to have a clear understanding of just what marketing is about. The ability to identify, anticipate, and respond to customer needs puts a lot of onus on skills of observation and analysis. Outdated ideas that marketing is all about selling harder by shouting more loudly were probably never appropriate to even the most aggressive sales personnel, for whom listening to customers' needs has always been crucial to developing a winning sales pitch. The great emphasis on listening skills is one explanation of the growing number of females who have made successful careers in marketing. Numerous studies have found that women have much stronger traits of empathy and listening ability than males.

Of course, marketing as a business function is very broad, and particular branches demand quite specific skills. Within the advertising sector, creativity is essential for successful copywriters, whereas a market analyst would be better equipped with patience and a rigorous methodical approach.

Can marketers be trained? There is a feeling among some employers that a little marketing knowledge by incoming employees may be quite dangerous. This idea holds that it may be better to take on staff who have an ability to think critically, communicate effectively, and show creativity. These abilities may have been developed in non-marketing environments, but the skills are easily transferable. Many engineers and biologists, to name but two science-based disciplines, have gone on to become very successful marketers, because of their ability to approach any new problem with clear, critical thinking combined with creativity.

This book seeks to cut through much of the jargon and mystique that has grown up around marketing and points out that many models are essentially based on straightforward critical analysis. By this argument, segmentation can be seen either as a specialist marketing technique or, more generally, as a logical process of breaking down a large problem (how to serve a market) into a series of smaller problems (how to serve different parts of that market). This book aims to develop a critical awareness of marketing theories and concepts, and to illustrate these with contemporary examples.

◉ Chapter summary and linkages to other chapters

This chapter has introduced the basic principles of marketing which act as building blocks for more detailed discussion in the following chapters. Having read this chapter, you should be aware of the wide definition of marketing as a philosophy and a set of practices. Although subsequent chapters analyse marketing practices under a number of headings, it should never be forgotten that all elements of the marketing mix should support each other. Customers take a holistic view of a company and its product. Product decisions (Chapter 8), price decisions (Chapter 9), place decisions (Chapter 10), and promotions decisions (Chapter 11) must focus on meeting targeted customer segments (Chapter 6) effectively and efficiently in the face of competitors' products (Chapter 7).

✎ KEY PRINCIPLES OF MARKETING

- Marketing is essentially about organizations meeting customers' needs as a means of achieving the organizations' own objectives.

- Marketing is both a philosophy and a set of techniques. Marketing techniques have less value if an organization has not embraced the philosophy of marketing.

- The principles of marketing are not new, but a continually changing marketing environment demands new ways of applying the basic principles.

- Marketing can be adopted by both profit-seeking and not-for-profit organizations.

- Marketing operates in an environment in which stakeholders have rising expectations for the ethical standards of marketers.

CASE STUDY

The Body Shop—good luck or good marketing?

The Body Shop may have grown rapidly during the 1970s and 1980s, but its founder, the late Dame Anita Roddick publicly dismissed the role of marketing. Roddick ridiculed marketers for putting the interests of shareholders before the needs of society. She had a similarly low opinion of the financial community, which she referred to as 'merchant wankers'. While things were going well, nobody seemed to mind. Maybe Roddick had found a new way of doing business, and if she had the results to prove it, who needed marketers? But how could even such an icon as Anita Roddick manage indefinitely without consulting the fundamental principles of marketing? By embracing ethical issues, was she way ahead of her rivals in understanding the public mood, long before the major retailers piled into Fairtrade and 'green' products? Or did the troubles that the Body Shop suffered in the late 1990s indicate that a company may publicly dismiss the value of marketing while the going is good, but sooner or later it will have to come back to earth with good old fashioned marketing plans?

Roddick had been the dynamo behind the Body Shop. From her first shop, which opened in Brighton in 1976, she inspired the growth of the chain of familiar green-fronted shops, which in 2006 comprised 2,100 stores in 55 countries around the world. She was the first to introduce socially and environmentally responsible business onto the high street and was talking about fair trade long before it became a popular corporate buzz word. Her pioneering products included naturally based skin and hair care preparations, such as Fuzzy Peach Bath and Shower Gel and Brazil Nut Conditioner. Her timing was impeccable, coming just at a time when increasingly affluent consumers were becoming concerned about animal testing and the use of chemicals in cosmetics. She had not gone down the classic marketing route of understanding consumer trends and then developing the appropriate products with the right positioning. She simply had a passion for humanely produced cosmetics and was just lucky with her timing—more consumers were coming round to her view just as she was launching her business. As for planning a promotion campaign, she didn't really need to do very much at all. With her boundless energy, outspoken views, and unorthodox dress sense she was continually being talked about in the media. Her flair for publicity won free editorial space for the Body Shop worth millions of pounds.

Much of the company's success has been tied up with its campaigning approach to the pursuit of social and environmental issues. But while Roddick campaigned for everything from battered wives and Siberian tigers to the poverty-stricken mining communities of southern Appalachia, the company was facing major problems in its key markets. Yet until the late 1990s she boasted that the Body Shop had never used, or needed, marketing.

By the late 1990s the Body Shop seemed to be running out if steam, with sales plateauing and the company's share price falling—from 370p in 1992 to just 65p in 2003. What was previously unique about Body Shop was now being copied by others, for example, the Boots company matched one of the Body Shop's earliest claims that it did not test its products on animals. Even the very feel of a Body Shop store—including its decor, staff, and product displays—had been copied by competitors. How could the company stay ahead in terms of maintaining its distinctive positioning? Its causes seemed to become increasingly remote from the real concerns of shoppers. While most UK shoppers may have been swayed by a company's unique claim to protect animals, how many would be moved by its support for Appalachian miners? If there was a Boots or a Superdrug store next door, why should a buyer pay a premium price to buy from the Body Shop? The Body Shop may have pioneered a very clever retailing formula over twenty years earlier, but, just as the product range had been successfully copied by others, other companies had made enormous strides in terms of their social and environmental awareness. Part of the problem of the

Body Shop was its failure fully to understand the dynamics of its marketplace. Positioning on the basis of good causes may have been enough to launch the company into the public's mind in the 1970s, but how could this position be sustained?

Many commentators blamed Body Shop's problems on the inability of Roddick to delegate. She is reported to have spent much of her time globetrotting in support of her good causes, but had a problem in delegating marketing strategy and implementation. Numerous strong managers who had been brought in to try to implement professional management practices apparently gave up in bewilderment at the lack of discretion that they had been given, and then left.

The Body Shop's experience in America had typified Roddick's pioneering style which frequently ignored sound marketing analysis. She sought a new way of doing business in America, but in doing so dismissed the experience of older and more sophisticated retailers—such as Marks & Spencer and the Sock Shop, which came unstuck in what is a very difficult market. The Body Shop decided to enter the US markets not through a safe option such as a joint venture or a franchising agreement, but instead by setting up its own operation from scratch—fine, according to Roddick's principles of changing the rulebook and cutting out the greedy American business community, but dangerously risky. Her store format was based on the British town centre model, despite the fact that Americans spend most of their money in out-of-town malls. In 1996 the US operations lost £3.4 million.

Roddick's critics claimed that she had a naive view of herself, her company, and business generally. She had consistently argued that profits and principles don't mix, despite the fact that many of her financially successfully competitors have been involved in major social initiatives.

Critics claimed that, had Roddick not dismissed the need for marketing for so long, the Body Shop could have avoided future problems. But by the early 2000s it was paying the price for not having devoted sufficient resources to new product development, to innovation, to refreshing its ranges, and to moving the business forward in a competitive market and fast changing business environment. It seemed that heroes can change the rulebook when the tide is flowing with them; but adopting the disciplines of marketing allows companies to anticipate and react when the tide begins to turn against them.

2006 turned out to be a turning point for Body Shop. In that year, the cosmetics giant L'Oréal acquired the company for £652 m. L'Oréal was part owned by Nestlé, and both companies had suffered long disputes with ethical campaigners. L'Oréal had been the subject of boycotts because of its involvement in animal testing, and Nestlé had been criticized for its treatment of third world producers. *Ethical Consumer* magazine, which rates companies' ethics on its 'Ethiscore' immediately down rated Body Shop from a rating of 11 to 2.5 out of 20 following the takeover by L'Oréal. A contributor to the magazine commented about Body Shop: 'I for one will certainly not be shopping there again and I urge other consumers concerned about ethical issues to follow my example. There are plenty of other higher scoring ethical companies out there.'

Not to be outdone, Roddick dismissed claims that she was 'selling out to the devil' by arguing that she would be able to use her influence to change L'Oréal from inside the company. Suppliers who had formerly worked with the Body Shop would in future have contracts with L'Oréal, and through an agreement to work with the company for 25 days a year Roddick would be able to have an input into its ethical sourcing decisions.

Roddick died soon after selling out to L'Oréal and her obituaries agreed that she had made a difference to the world. She certainly had put a lot of energy into her mission and had been lucky with her timing. But critics were more divided on whether she was a good marketer for the long haul, after all it is relatively easy to make money when the tide is going with you and your luck is in, but much more difficult to manage a changing and increasingly saturated marketing environment. Like many entrepreneurs who have been good at creating things, but not so good at maintaining them, was it simply time for Roddick to hand over to classically trained marketers who could rise to this challenge?

Case study review questions

1. Critically assess the extent to which you consider Body Shop to be a truly marketing oriented organization throughout its 30+ year history.

2. To what extent are the pursuits of profit and meeting the needs of wider groups of stakeholders incompatible? What companies, if any, have managed to sustainably reconcile these two aims?

3. What are the basic lessons in marketing that the Body Shop might have taken on board in its early years in order to improve its chances of long-term success?

CHAPTER REVIEW QUESTIONS

1. Discuss how a car wash business might operate if management embraced a production orientation? A sales orientation? A marketing orientation? A societal marketing orientation?

2. Analyse the nature of the needs which may be satisfied by a household mortgage.

3. What is the difference between selling and marketing?

ACTIVITIES

1. Go back to the 'Marketing in action' vignette on page 6 which describes some tell-tale signs about whether a company is truly marketing orientated. Now apply these tests, and any additional tests you can think of, to an organization with which you are familiar. If you are studying at a college or university, how marketing orientated is it?

2. Use the extended '7p' marketing mix to produce a checklist of the headings for a marketing plan for a fashion retailer. Are there any additional headings that you consider would be important to develop a sustainable competitive advantage?

3. Review literature produced by a selection of public or quasi-pubic sector service providers, such as a doctor's surgery, housing association, or state owned school. Assess the extent to which the organization balances its statutory duties with a marketing orientation.

REFERENCES

Borden, N.H. (1965) 'The Concept of the Marketing Mix'. In G. Schwartz (ed.), *Science in Marketing*. New York: John Wiley, pp. 386–97.

Brown, S. (1995) *Postmodern Marketing*. London: Routledge.

Chomka, S. (2002) 'Organic Market Figures Could Help Processors'. *Food Manufacture*, 77 (9), 7–9.

Drucker, P.F. (1973) *Management: Tasks, Responsibilities and Practices.* New York: Harper & Row.

Dwyer, F.R., Schurr, P.H., and Oh, S. (1987) 'Developing Buyer and Seller Relationships'. *Journal of Marketing*, 51, April, 11–27.

Harris, L.C. (2002) 'Developing Market Orientation: an Exploration of Differences in Management Approaches'. *Journal of Marketing Management*, 18, 603–32.

Lafferty, B.A. and Hult, G.T.M. (2001) 'A Synthesis of Contemporary Market Orientation Perspectives'. *European Journal of Marketing*, 35, 92–109.

Maslow, A. (1943) 'A Theory of Human Motivation'. *Psychological Review*, 50 (July), 370–96.

Morgan, N.A. (2002) 'Antecedents and Consequences of Market Orientation in Chartered Surveying Firms'. *Construction Management & Economics*, 20, 331–41.

Narver, J.C. and Slater, S.F. (1990) 'The Effect of a Market Orientation on Business Profitability'. *Journal of Marketing*, October, 20–35.

Sandel, M.J. (2009) *Justice: What's the Right Thing to Do?* New York: Allen Lane.

Sargeant, A. (2009) *Marketing Management for Non-Profit Organizations*, 3rd edition. Oxford: Oxford University Press.

Titmus, R. (1970) *The Gift Relationship: From Human Blood to Social Policy*. London: Allen and Unwin.

SUGGESTED FURTHER READING

This chapter has taken a very broad overview of marketing and sets the scene for the subsequent chapters. Further reading that relates to issues raised in this introductory chapter will be listed in chapters where introductory topics are returned to for a fuller discussion.

To review the debate about the nature of marketing, the following are significant contributors to the debate:

Gronroos, C. (1989) 'Defining Marketing: a Market-oriented Approach'. *European Journal of Marketing*, 23 (1), 52–60.

Gummesson, E. (2008) *Total Relationship Marketing: Marketing Management, Relationship Strategy and CRM Approaches for the Network Economy.* London: Butterworth-Heinemann.

Sargeant, A. (2009) *Marketing Management for Non-profit Organizations*, 3rd edition. Oxford: Oxford University Press.

Schultz, D. and Dev, C. (2005) 'In the Mix: A Customer-focused Approach Can Bring the Current Marketing Mix into the 21st Century'. *Marketing Management*, 14, (1).

Silk, Alvin J. (2007) *What is Marketing?* Boston, MA: Harvard Business School Press.

Vargo, S.L. and Lusch, R.F. (2004) 'Evolving to a New Dominant Logic for Marketing'. *Journal of Marketing*, 68 (1), 1–17.

 ONLINE RESOURCE CENTRE

Visit the Online Resource Centre for resources that are relevant to this chapter, including a flashcard glossary, web links, multiple choice questions, and additional case studies:

www.oxfordtextbooks.co.uk/orc/palmer3e/

KEY TERMS

- Competitor orientation
- Customer orientation
- Customers
- Demand
- Exchange
- Interfunctional coordination
- Marketing management
- Marketing mix
- Marketing orientation
- Markets
- Needs

- Not-for-profit organization
- Place
- Positivist approach
- Pricing
- Production orientation
- Products
- Promotion
- Scientific method
- Selling orientation
- Value
- Wants

THE MARKETING ENVIRONMENT

CHAPTER OBJECTIVES

In the previous chapter we established that marketing is essentially about firms identifying customers' needs and responding to those changing needs with appropriate product offers. In this chapter we will explore how customers' needs are derived from the nature of an organization's marketing environment. The marketing environment can be defined as everything that surrounds an organization's marketing function and can impinge on it. Macro-environmental factors, such as a change in the birth rate, may seem inconsequential now, but could quickly have a direct effect on a firm's micro-environment, expressed through demand for its products. This chapter explores the relationships between the different elements of a firm's environment and how the firm can respond effectively to environmental change.

◉ Introduction

In the previous chapter, marketing orientation was defined in terms of a firm's need to begin its business planning by looking outwardly at what its customers require, rather than inwardly at what it would prefer to produce. The firm must be aware of what is going on in its broader marketing environment and appreciate how change in this environment can lead to changing patterns of demand for its products.

An environment can be defined as everything that surrounds and impinges on a system. Systems of many kinds have environments they interact with. A central heating system operates in an environment where a key environmental factor will be the outside temperature. A good system will react to environmental change, for example by using a thermostat to increase the output of the system in response to a fall in the temperature of the external environment. The human body comprises numerous systems which constantly react to changes in the body's environment; for example the body perspires in response to an increase in external temperature.

Marketing can be seen as a system that must respond to environmental change. Just as the human body may die if it fails to adjust to environmental change (for example by not compensating for very low temperatures), businesses may fail if they do not adapt to external changes such as new sources of competition or changes in stakeholders' expectations of companies.

An organization's marketing environment is defined here as:

The individuals, organizations, and forces external to the marketing management function of an organization that impinge on the marketing management's ability to develop and maintain successful exchanges with its customers.

Naturally, some elements in a firm's marketing environment are more direct and immediate in their effects than others. Sometimes parts of the marketing environment may seem quite nebulous and difficult to assess in terms of their likely impact on a company. It is therefore usual to talk about a number of different levels of the marketing environment.

⊙ The micro-environment describes those elements that impinge directly on a company. The micro-environment of an organization includes customers, suppliers, and distributors. The company may deal directly with some of these, such as current customers. However, the micro-environment also includes companies and individuals with whom there is currently no direct contact, but their existence could nevertheless influence its policies (e.g. product policy could be affected by the changing attitudes of individuals a company may target in the future). Similarly, an organization's competitors could have a direct effect on its market position and form part of its micro-environment.

⊙ The macro-environment describes things that are beyond the immediate environment but can nevertheless affect an organization. A business may have no direct relationships with legislators as it does with suppliers, yet legislators' actions in passing new laws may have profound effects on the markets it seeks to serve, as well as affecting its production costs. The macro-environmental factors cover a wide range of nebulous phenomena— they represent general forces and pressures rather than institutions, to which the organization relates directly.

⊙ As well as looking to the outside world, marketing managers must also take account of factors within other functions of their own firm. This is often referred to as an organization's internal marketing environment.

The elements within each of these parts of an organization's environment are described in more detail below and illustrated schematically in Figure 2.1.

⊙ The micro-environment

The micro-environment comprises all those other organizations and individuals that, directly or indirectly, affect the activities of the organization. The following key groups can be identified.

Customers

These are a crucial part of an organization's micro-environment. For a commercial organization, no customers means no business. An organization should be concerned about the

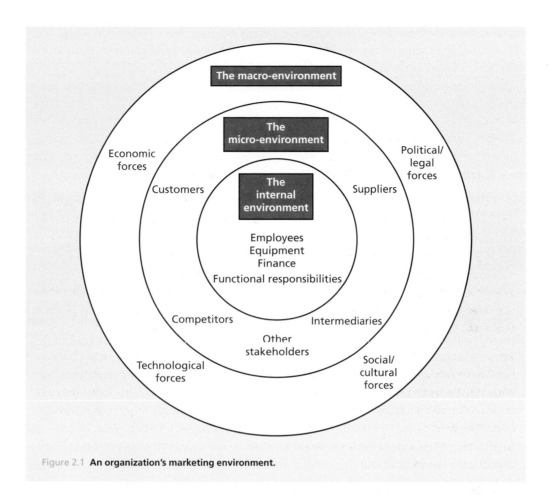

Figure 2.1 **An organization's marketing environment.**

changing requirements of its customers and should keep in touch with these changing needs by using an appropriate information gathering system.

Chapter 5 will return to the subject of collecting, analysing, and disseminating information. In an ideal world, an organization should know its customers so well that it is able to predict what they will require next, rather than wait until it is possibly too late and then follow. Most of this book is devoted to studying the interface between a company and its customers, for example in terms of customers' responses to promotional messages and prices.

Increasingly, companies are being expected to take into account not just what a customer says they want, but also what is good for them. The two can sometimes be quite different, as can be seen in the case of 'junk food' companies who may promote good tasting, but high fat food to people for whom it is harmful to their long-term health. Sometimes, firms' marketing efforts may wrongly suggest that their product would satisfy a customer's needs. As an example, in 2007 the website MoneySavingExpert.com launched a campaign against financial services companies which had sold payment protection insurance policies to individuals who could not possibly benefit from the insurance, because of terms and conditions which were not fully explained to them. Sales people may have been tempted by a high level of commission to sell a policy that the customer did not understand and was clearly not in their best interest (*Financial Times* 2008).

We will return to the issue of companies' broader responsibilities towards customers in the following chapter.

Competitors

You will recall from Chapter 1 that a competitor orientation is one of the defining characteristics of a marketing orientation. In highly competitive markets, keeping an eye on competitors and trying to understand their likely next moves can be crucial. Think of the manoeuvering and out-manoeuvering that appears to take place between competitors in such highly competitive sectors as soft drinks, budget airlines, and mobile phones. But who are a company's competitors? *Direct* competitors are generally similar in form and satisfy customers' needs in a similar way. So Coca Cola is a direct competitor for Pepsi Cola. *Indirect* competitors may appear different in form, but satisfy a fundamentally similar need. It is the indirect competitors that are most difficult to identify and to understand. What is a competitor for a cinema? Is it another cinema? A home rental movie? Or some completely different form of leisure activity which satisfies a similar underlying need for entertainment?

Because of the importance of competitors to a firm's marketing environment, in Chapter 7 we will have a more detailed analysis of competitors and how a company can position itself against these in order to gain a sustainable competitive advantage.

Intermediaries

Companies must not ignore the wholesalers, retailers, and agents who may be crucial interfaces between themselves and their final consumers. Large-scale manufacturing firms usually find it difficult to deal with each one of their final consumers individually, so they choose instead to sell their products through intermediaries. In some business sectors access to effective intermediaries can be crucial for marketing success. For example, food manufactures who do not get shelf space in the major supermarkets may find it difficult to achieve large-volume sales.

Channels of distribution comprise all those people and organizations involved in the process of transferring title to a product from the producer to the consumer. Sometimes products will be transferred directly from producer to final consumer—a factory selling specialized kitchen units directly to the public would fit into this category. Alternatively, the producer may sell its output through retailers; or, if these are considered too numerous for the manufacturer to handle, it could deal with a wholesaler who in turn would sell to the retailer. More than one wholesaler could be involved in the process.

Because of the importance of intermediaries in making a firm's goods and services accessible to its buyers, Chapter 10 of this book is devoted to understanding how they are selected, motivated, rewarded, and controlled. In addition, the chapter reviews physical distribution management and the decisions that firms make in physically moving goods from where they are produced to where customers wish to buy them.

Intermediaries may need reassurance about the company's capabilities as a supplier that is capable of working with them to supply goods and services in a reliable and ethical manner. Many companies have suffered because they have failed to take adequate account of the needs of their intermediaries. (For example, Body Shop and McDonald's have faced protests from their franchisees, which felt threatened by a marketing strategy that was perceived as being against their own interests.)

Suppliers

These provide an organization with goods and services that are transformed by the organization into value-added products for customers. For companies operating in highly competitive markets where differentiation between products is minimal, obtaining supplies at the best possible price may be vital in order to be able to pass on cost savings in the form of lower prices charged to customers. Where reliability of delivery to customers is crucial, unreliable suppliers may thwart a manufacturer's marketing efforts.

In business-to-business marketing, it is important to understand how suppliers, manufacturers, and intermediaries work together to create value. The idea of a value chain is introduced later in this chapter. Buyers and sellers are increasingly cooperating in their dealings with each other, rather than bargaining each transaction in a confrontational manner. (Buyer–seller relationships are discussed further in Chapter 4.)

There is an argument that companies should behave in a socially responsible way to their suppliers. Does a company favour local companies rather than possibly lower priced overseas producers? (For example, many supermarkets proudly promote locally produced ranges of food.) Does it divide its orders between a large number of small suppliers, or place the bulk of its custom with a small handful of preferred suppliers? Does it favour new businesses, or businesses representing minority interests, when it places its orders? We will return to the subject of responsible marketing in the next chapter.

Government

The demands of government agencies often take precedence over the needs of a company's customers. Government has a number of roles to play in a commercial organization's marketing environment:

- Government agencies, such as the Health and Safety Executive, regulate many activities that have a direct or indirect impact on what products a company can offer to its customers, for example UK legislation requiring employers to pay a minimum wage has added to the costs of companies, leading to price rises for many labour intensive service industries such as restaurants, and movement of capacity to low wage countries for many manufacturing companies.

- Governments—national, regional and local—levy taxes which will most likely have to be incorporated into a firm's selling prices, thereby affecting the size of demand for its products. Some retailers in central London reported a fall in their number of customers following the imposition of a congestion charge on motorists.

- Government is increasingly expecting business organizations to take over many responsibilities from the public sector, for example with regard to the payment of sickness and maternity benefits to employees.

- It is through business organizations that governments achieve many of their economic and social objectives, for example with respect to regional economic development and skills training.

As a regulator that impacts on many aspects of business activity, companies often go to great lengths in seeking favourable responses from such agencies. In the case of many private-sector utility providers, promotional effort is often aimed more at regulatory bodies than at final consumers. For UK water suppliers, promoting greater use of water to final consumers is unlikely to have a significant impact on a water utility company, but influencing the disposition of the Office of Water Regulation, which sets price limits and service standards, can have a major impact.

The financial community

This includes financial institutions that have supported, are currently supporting, or may support the organization in the future. Shareholders, both private and institutional, form an important element of this community and must be reassured that the organization is going to achieve its stated objectives. Many market expansion plans have failed because the company did not adequately consider the needs and expectations of potential investors.

Local communities

Market-led companies often try to be seen as a 'good neighbours' in their local communities. Such companies can enhance their image through charitable contributions, sponsorship of local events, and support of the local environment. This may be interpreted either as part of a firm's genuine concern for its local community, or as a more cynical and pragmatic attempt to buy favour where its own interests are at stake. If a fast-food restaurant installs improved filters on its extractor fans, is it doing this genuinely to improve the lives of local residents, or merely to forestall prohibitive action taken by the local authority? We will return to these issues in the following chapter.

Pressure groups

Members of pressure groups may have never been customers of a company and may never likely be. Yet a pressure group can detract seriously from the image of a company that its marketing department has worked hard to develop.

Pressure groups can be divided into those that are permanently fighting for a general cause, and those that are set up to achieve a specific objective and are dissolved when this objective is met. Pressure groups can also be classified according to their functions; for example sectional groups exist to promote the common interests of their members over a wide range of issues (e.g. trades unions and employers associations), while promotional groups fight for specific causes (e.g. the Countryside Alliance campaigns for a range of countryside issues).

Pressure groups can influence the activities of businesses in a number of ways:

◉ Propaganda is used to create awareness of the group and its cause (e.g. through press releases to the media). Many pressure groups have effectively used social networking media to rapidly mobilize opposition to companies that they see as operating in an anti-social way.

◉ The pressure group can seek to represent the views of the group directly to businesses on a one-to-one basis. (Many environmental pressure groups seek to advance their cause by 'educating' companies that may be ignorant of the pressure group's concerns.)

◉ Increasingly, pressure groups have resorted to direct action against companies, which can range from boycotts to physical attacks on a company's property. Organizations targeted in this way may initially put on a brave face when confronted with such activities by dismissing them as inconsequential, but often the result is to change the organization's behaviour, especially where the prospect of large profits is uncertain. Action by animal rights protestors contributed to the near collapse of Huntingdon Life Sciences (an animal testing laboratory), and many farmers have been discouraged from taking part in GM crops trials by the prospects of direct action against their farms.

It should not be forgotten that businesses themselves are often active members of pressure groups, which they may join as a means of influencing government legislation that will affect their industry sector. The British Road Federation and the Tobacco Advisory Council are two examples of high-profile, industry-led pressure groups.

Pressure groups themselves are increasingly crossing national boundaries to reflect the influence of international governmental institutions such as the EU and the increasing influence of multinational business organizations. Friends of the Earth and Greenpeace are examples of multinational pressure groups.

Value chains

The concept of a value chain will be explored more fully in Chapter 10 in the context of channels of distribution. Here it is introduced to help understand the complex marketing relationships that can exist between a company and its customers, suppliers, and intermediaries.

Most products bought by private consumers represent the culmination of a long process of value creation. The company selling the finished product probably bought many of its components from an outside supplier, which in turn bought raw materials from another outside supplier. This is the basis of a value chain in which basic raw materials progressively have value added to them by members of the value chain. Value adding can come in the form of adding further components, changing the form of a product, or adding ancillary services to the product offer.

Consider the example shown in Figure 2.2 of a value chain for instant coffee. The value of the raw beans contained in a jar of instant coffee may be no more than a few pence, but the final product may be sold for over £2. Customers are happy to pay this amount

Value chain member	Functions performed
Grower	produces a basic commodity product—coffee beans
Merchant	adds value to the coffee beans by checking, grading, and making beans available to coffee manufacturers
Coffee manufacturer	by processing the coffee beans, adding other ingredients and packaging, turns beans into jars of instant coffee; through promotion, creates a brand image
Wholesaler	buys bulk stocks of jars of coffee and stores in warehouses close to customers
Retailer	provides a facility for customers to buy coffee at a place and a time that is convenient to them, rather than from the manufacturer
Coffee shop	adds further value by providing a ready-made cup of coffee in pleasant surroundings

Figure 2.2 **A value chain for coffee.**

because a basic product that they place little value on has been transformed into something that they perceive as highly valuable. Some consumers would be happy to pay an even higher price to buy their coffee ready prepared for consumption in a coffee shop rather than make it themselves at home. In the case of some trendy coffee shops such as Starbucks, customers may be prepared to pay quite a hefty premium for the atmosphere in which the coffee is served—over £4 for a smartly presented cappuccino or a 'skinny latte' is not uncommon, even though the cost of the beans used in the coffee may be no more than a few pence. Value can be defined only in terms of customers' perceptions, so much of the transformation process described above may be considered by some people to have no value. Some coffee drinkers may consider that processing the coffee to make it into instant granules destroys value by spoiling the full taste that can be obtained from raw beans. For such people, the most important point in the value creating process probably derives from the growing and selection of the coffee beans. For others, paying £4 for a skinny latte in Starbucks may be considered good value, because they particularly like the atmosphere in which the coffee is served.

Who should be in the value chain? The coffee manufacturer might decide that it can add value at the preceding and subsequent stages better than other people are capable of doing. It may, for example, decide to operate its own farms to produce beans under its own control, or sell its coffee direct to customers. The crucial question to be asked is whether the company can add value better than other suppliers and intermediaries could. In a value chain, it is only value in the eyes of customers that matters. If high value is attached to having coffee easily available, then distributing it through a limited number of company-owned shops would not add much value to the product.

The Internet has led to the development of a modified form of 'virtual value chain' to try and explain how information-based industries operate a value chain that is distinct from traditional models based on raw materials, production, and distribution (Rayport and Sviokla 1995). Intermediaries such as Expedia.com (travel) and Confused.com (insurance) create value by making available to consumers in one website a range of travel and insurance products, saving the effort of buyers in having to shop around. These intermediaries are also likely to add value by providing after sales service.

Relationships between members of an organization's micro-environment

The discussion of value chains emphasizes the point that marketing effectiveness for a firm can be highly dependent upon its relationships with other members of its micro-environment. Very few organizations are able to produce and distribute everything they sell to customers entirely within their own resources. Instead, they will most likely outsource production, or use intermediaries to sell its products, for example. It follows that relationships between a company and these external organizations can be critical for delivering value to customers. The individuals and organizations that make up a firm's micro-environment are often described as its *environmental set*. An example of an environmental set for a computer manufacturer is shown in Figure 2.3.

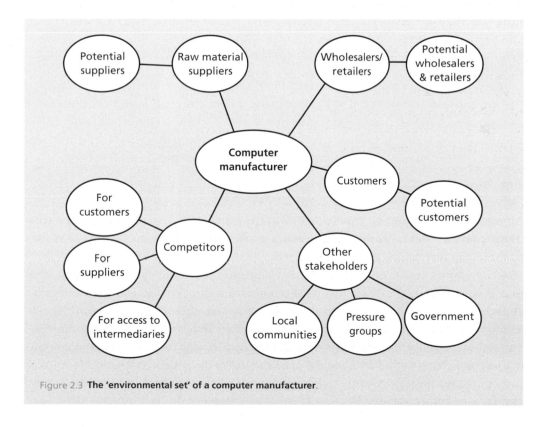

Figure 2.3 **The 'environmental set' of a computer manufacturer**.

An organization needs to be constantly alert to changes in the relationships between members of its environmental set. Consider the following recent changes in firms' environmental sets:

- There have been changes in the balance of power between set members (e.g. between retailers, wholesalers, and manufacturers).
- New groups of potential customers may emerge (e.g. elderly people have emerged as new groups of customers for fast-food restaurants), while other groups decline.
- New pressure groups are formed in response to emerging issues of widespread social concern.
- The role of government in many sectors has increased, with the introduction of new health and safety legislation (although in other sectors, deregulation and privatization have diminished the role of government).

In the UK in recent years there has been some significant redistribution in the power of manufacturers relative to retailers. The growing strength of retailers in many sectors has given them significantly increased bargaining power in their dealings with manufacturers whose goods they sell. By building up their own strong brands, large retailers are increasingly able to exert pressure on manufacturers in terms of product specification, price, and the level of promotional support to be given to the retailer. According to market research group TNS Worldpanel, the UK's big four grocery retailers—Tesco, Asda, Sainsbury's, and Morrisons— now account for more than three-quarters of the grocery market. However, while many manufacturers may be dependent on the big retailers for further sales, this dependency is not reciprocated, with very few retailers relying on one single supplier for more than one per cent of their supplies.

Increasingly, firms are changing the way they do business, away from one-off transactions that are individually negotiated, towards ongoing cooperative relationships. The process of turning casual, one-off transactions between buyers and sellers has often been described as relationship marketing. Chapter 4 provides further discussion of reasons for firms to seek closer relationships with their customers, and the methods adopted to achieve this.

Communication within the micro-environment

Communications bring together elements within a firm's environmental set. With no communication, there is no possibility for trading to take place. Although we talk today about a communications 'revolution', marketers of previous centuries have faced the challenge of rapid developments in communication, as evidenced by the great advances in trade that took place following the developments of canals, steamships, railways, and the telephone. Today, the Internet has become a versatile tool in an organization's relationship with its marketing environment, combining a communication function with a distribution function. The ability of companies to rapidly exchange information with their suppliers and intermediaries has allowed for the development of increasingly efficient supply chains. Without efficient communication systems, attempts to introduce 'just-in-time' production systems and rapid customer response (discussed further in Chapter 9) are likely to be impeded.

The Internet plays an increasingly significant role in allowing companies to communicate with their final consumers via email and SMS text messaging. Some companies have used the Internet to cut out intermediaries altogether through a process of disintermediation, although in reality the Internet has allowed a new generation of 'information intermediary' (e.g. Expedia.com and esure.com) to create value, as we saw above. Many companies are still trying to take on board the implications of Web 2.0 technologies such as Facebook and Twitter which have facilitated customer-to-customer communication, We will explore these implications further in Chapter 11.

The macro-environment

While the micro-environment comprises identifiable individuals and organizations with whom a company interacts (directly and indirectly), the macro-environment is more nebulous. It comprises general trends and forces which may not immediately affect the relationships that a company has with its customers, suppliers, and intermediaries, but sooner or later, as this environment changes, these trends and forces will alter the nature of such micro-level relationships. As an example, change in the population structure of a country does not immediately affect the way in which a company does business with its customers, but over time it may affect the numbers of young or elderly people with whom it is possible to do business.

Most analyses of the macro-environment divide the environment into a number of subject areas. The subject headings that are most commonly used are described below. It must, however, be remembered that the division of the macro-environment into subject areas does not result in watertight compartments. The macro-environment is complex and interdependent.

The macro-economic environment

An analysis of many companies' financial results will often indicate that business people attribute their current financial success or failure to the state of the economy. For example, in 2010, the low price retailer Poundland reported booming sales and profits as families cut their expenditure in response to falling levels of real wages and falling levels of consumer confidence. While Poundland's sales were booming, many mid-market retailers such as Debenhams suffered as consumers 'traded down'. Ten years earlier, a strong economy and high levels of discretionary income had led to booming sales and profits at Debenhams.

But what do we mean by the macro-economic environment? The following headings are useful analytic headings.

Economic growth and the distribution of income

Few business people can afford to ignore the state of the economy, because it affects the willingness and ability of customers to buy their products. Marketers therefore keep their eyes on numerous aggregate indicators of the economy, such as gross domestic product (GDP), inflation rates, and savings ratios. However, while aggregate changes in spending power may indicate a likely increase for goods and services in general, the actual distribution of spending power among the population will influence the pattern of demand for specific products.

In addition to measurable economic prosperity, the level of perceived wealth and confidence in the future can be an important determinant of demand for some high-value services. If consumers' confidence is low, a high proportion of income tends to be saved. If confidence is high, consumers are more likely to borrow, so that their expenditure is greater than their income (Figure 2.4).

The effects of government policy objectives on the distribution of income can have profound implications for marketers. During most of the post-war years, the tendency has been for income to be redistributed from richer to less well-off groups. In the UK, higher rate taxation and the payment of welfare benefits have been instrumental in achieving this. During the late 1980s, this trend was reversed by a number of measures introduced by the Conservative government. Even under the subsequent Labour government, there is some

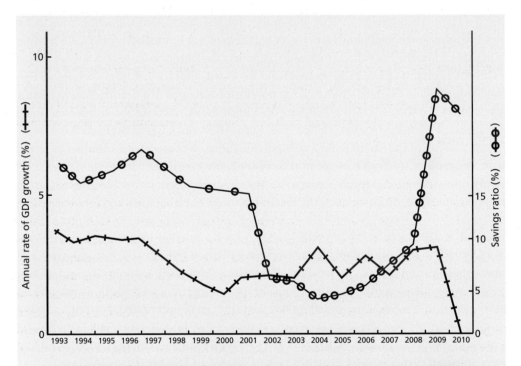

Figure 2.4 **Two key macro-economic indicators that marketers pay attention to are the annual rate of growth in GDP and the savings ratio. The first shows how rapidly the national economy is expanding, and therefore the capacity of the economy to purchase more products.** However, what is just as important to marketers is whether this economic wealth is saved or spent. If consumers' confidence is low, a high proportion of income tends to be saved. If confidence is high, consumers are more likely to borrow, so that their expenditure is greater than their income. The high levels of consumer confidence in the UK during 2002 saw record levels of mortgage borrowing, resulting in a house price boom and strong demand for many house-related items such as conservatories and furnishings By 2010, GDP was falling while the savings ratios rose, as consumers became more cautious in their spending, and banks became more cautious in their lending.
(*Source:* Based on Annual Abstract of Statistics.)

evidence that the richest groups in the UK got richer, while the poor have got poorer. Some evidence of this was found in ONS statistics showing that in 2008/09, average income, before taxes and benefits, of the top fifth of households in the UK was approximately 15 times greater than that for the bottom fifth (£73,800 per household per year compared with £5,000). Even after redistribution through taxes and benefits, the ratio between the top and bottom fifths is reduced to four-to-one (average final income of £53,900 compared to £13,600) (Office for National Statistics 2010).

Multiplier and accelerator effects

Through models of national economies, firms try to understand how increases in expenditure (whether by government, households, or firms) will affect their specific sector. The multiplier effect of increases in government spending (or cuts in taxation) can be compared to the effects of throwing a stone into a pond of water. The initial spending boost will first have an impact on households and businesses directly affected by the additional spending, but through a ripple effect will also be indirectly felt by households and firms throughout the economy.

A small increase in consumer demand can lead, through an accelerator effect, to a sudden large increase in demand for plant and machinery as manufacturers seek to increase their capacity with which to meet this demand. Demand for industrial capital goods therefore tends to be more cyclical than for consumer goods, so when consumer demand falls by a small amount, demand for plant and machinery falls by a correspondingly larger amount, and vice versa (Figure 2.5).

Business cycles

Companies are particularly interested in understanding business cycles and in predicting the cycle as it affects their sector. If the economy is at the bottom of an economic recession, this may be the ideal time for firms to begin investing in new production capacity, ahead of the eventual upturn in demand. Adding new production capacity during a period of recession is also likely to be much cheaper than waiting until an upturn in the economy puts upward pressure on its input prices. During periods of economic boom, firms should look ahead to the inevitable downturn that follows. A problem of excess capacity and stocks can result when a firm fails to spot the downturn at the top of the business cycle. Analysing turning points in the business cycle has therefore become crucial to marketers. To miss an upturn at the bottom of the recession can lead to missed opportunities when the recovery comes to fruition. On the other hand, reacting to a false signal can leave a firm with expensive excess stocks and capacity on its hands.

The business cycle also affects competition for resources, with peak prices for resources such as oil and metals being reached during periods of boom, and much lower prices during periods of economic recession.

It is extremely difficult to identify a turning point at the time when it is happening. In early 2006, the UK economy appeared to be going into recession, and many companies scaled back their investment in stocks and capacity. However, the economy soon bounced back after just a short blip, and the predicted recession did not set in until 2008. Understanding the business cycle can become particularly difficult during periods of great turbulence. During 2008 a

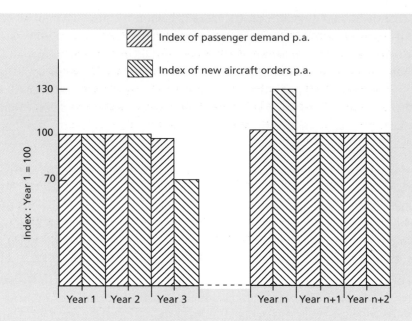

Figure 2.5 **The accelerator effect can lead to volatility in demand for companies supplying capital equipment, as customers will rapidly change their orders for equipment in response to just a small change in final consumer demand.** This can be illustrated by reference to the demand for new aircraft following a change in demand from passengers. In this simplified example, an airline operates a fleet of one hundred aircraft and during periods of stable passenger demand buys ten new aircraft each year and retires ten older aircraft, retaining a stable fleet size of one hundred aircraft. Then, some extraneous factor (e.g. a decline in the world economy) may cause the airline's passenger demand to fall by three per cent per year. The airline responds to this by reducing its capacity by three per cent to 97 aircraft (assuming that it can reschedule its aircraft so that it is able to accommodate all of its remaining passengers). The easiest way to achieve this is by reducing its annual order for aircraft from ten to seven. If it continued to retire its ten oldest aircraft, this would have the effect of reducing its fleet size to 97, in line with the new level of customer demand. What is of importance here is that, while consumer demand has gone down by just three per cent, the demand facing the aircraft manufacturer has gone down by 30 per cent (from ten aircraft a year to seven). If passenger demand settles down at its new level, the airline will have no need to cut its fleet any further, so will revert to buying ten new aircraft a year and selling ten old ones. If passenger demand picks up once more, the airline may seek to increase its capacity by ordering not ten aircraft but, say, 13.

'credit crunch' led to the collapse of several banks and many commentators predicted that established economic patterns would change forever. Just the existence of turbulence led to many individuals and organizations being much more cautious in the lending and borrowing decisions they made, which in turn had 'knock-on' effects elsewhere in the economy.

Marketers try to react to turning points as closely as possible. Many subscribe to the services of firms that use complex models of the economy to make predictions about the future performance of their sector. Companies can be guided by key lead indicators which have historically been a precursor of change in activity levels for their business sector. For a company manufacturing process plant equipment, the level of attendance at major trade exhibitions could indicate the number of buyers that are at the initial stages in the buying process for new equipment. An alternative to trying to predict the economic performance of their sector a long way ahead is to manage operations so that a firm can respond almost immediately to changes in its macro-economic environment. The use of short-term contracts of employment and outsourcing of component manufacture can help a company to downsize rapidly at minimum cost when it enters a recession, and to expand production when a recovery occurs. This approach is particularly important when an organization needs to respond to an unforeseen shock to the macro-economic environment, as occurred following the terrorist attacks of 11 September 2001.

Market competitiveness

An analysis of the macro-economic environment will also indicate the current and expected future level of competitor activity. An over-supply of products in a market sector (whether actual or predicted) results in a downward pressure on prices and profitability. Markets are dynamic, and what may appear an attractive market today may soon deteriorate as the market matures. Market dynamics are discussed further in Chapter 7.

The political environment

The political environment in its broadest sense comprises governments, politicians, and the pressure groups that bring pressure to bear on politicians and government. The political environment can be one of the less predictable elements in an organization's marketing environment. Marketers need to monitor the changing political environment because political change can profoundly affect a firm's marketing. Consider the following effects of change in the political environment on marketing.

- While the countries of western Europe are generally politically stable, the instability of many governments in less developed countries has led a number of companies to question the wisdom of marketing in those countries.

- In countries with well-developed political systems, firms should understand the consequences for their business of a change in government. For example, how would a manufacturer of luxury cars react if a Muslim fundamentalist government took over from a secular democracy, a prospect that looked realistic in the popular uprisings which affected many Arab countries during 2011? Firms should not just wait for the election results, but should try and predict the likely results.

- Governments are responsible for protecting the public interest at large, imposing further constraints on the activities of firms (for example controls on pollution, which may make a manufacturing firm uncompetitive in international markets on account of its increased costs).

- The macro-economic environment is very much influenced by the actions of politicians. Government is responsible for formulating policies that can influence the rate of growth in the economy and hence the total amount of spending power. It is also a political decision as to how this spending power should be distributed between different groups of consumers and between the public and private sectors.

- Government policies can influence the dominant social and cultural values of a country, although there can be argument about which is the cause and which is the effect. (For example, did the UK government's drive for economic expansion and individual responsibility during the late 1980s change public attitudes away from good citizenship and towards those of 'greed is good'?)

- Increasingly, the political environment affecting marketers includes supra-national organizations, which can directly or indirectly affect companies. These include trading blocs (e.g. the EU, ASEAN, and NAFTA) and the influence of worldwide intergovernmental organizations whose members seek to implement agreed policy (e.g. the World Trade Organization).

The social and cultural environment

It is crucial for marketers to fully appreciate the cultural values of a society, especially where an organization is seeking to do business in a country that is quite different to its own. Attitudes to specific products change through time and at any one time can differ between groups in society.

Even in home markets, business organizations should understand the processes of gradual cultural change and be prepared to satisfy the changing needs of consumers. Consider the following examples of contemporary cultural change in western Europe and the possible responses of marketers.

- Leisure is becoming a bigger part of many people's lives, and marketers have responded with a wide range of leisure related goods and services.

- Many western European countries are becoming ethnically and culturally much more diverse. In the UK, the large number of Polish people who entered the country from 2004 has led to the development of many retail and financial services aimed specifically at this group (*Financial Times* 2007).

- Attitudes to debt have changed and there is a tendency for increasing numbers of people to buy products for experiential values rather than to satisfy basic utilitarian needs.

- The role of women in society has changed, although worldwide, big differences in the role of women and men remain. For example, a report to the World Economic Forum in 2010 noted that in Nordic nations, women live longer, have high employment rates, high levels of participation in higher education and often enjoy generous maternity and paternity schemes. In the UK, a report by the Future Foundation predicted that women would be the major breadwinners in a quarter of families by 2030 (Doughty 2007). At the other end of the scale, Pakistan, Chad, and Yemen perform poorly. In the case of India, the World Economic Forum report noted that women suffered from persistent health, education, and economic participation gaps. In the western world, examples of business responses to the changing role of women include variants of cars designed to appeal to career women and ready-prepared meals which save time for busy working women who need to juggle work, family, and social roles.

⊙ Attitudes to healthy living have changed, for example in 1974, 26 per cent of men and 13 per cent of women in Great Britain who smoked regularly were classed as heavy smokers. But by 2008, these figures had fallen to seven per cent and five per cent respectively.

Marketing and social responsibility

Big mac, big business, big problem?

Business leaders have come under increasing levels of scrutiny from governments, the media, and the public in general. Some people have held grudges against particular companies, and others against the system of big business in general. In 2009, anti-globalization protesters damaged a Royal Bank of Scotland building during the G-20 summit of world leaders in London, and the object of the protestors was as much the world business environment in general, as RBS specifically. The advent of social network media had made it easier for groups of disenchanted individuals to connect with each other and to voice their concerns about the business environment.

Large, successful companies, it seems, just have to accept that they will never please some people, who hold large corporate organizations responsible for all of the world's problems. But just how hostile is the environment to business organizations?

A report by the Future Foundation appeared to challenge the idea that young people are becoming more hostile towards big business than their parents. According to a 2001 study by the organization, 16–24-year-olds have more positive feelings towards multinationals than older groups, particularly those who came of age in the 1960s, a period commonly associated with protest movements. Now in their sixties, this group seemed to be the most critical of big business. The research revealed that younger generations are less inclined towards direct action than their parents and grandparents. Nearly half of all 16–34-year-olds claimed they would not demonstrate if a multinational company had done something wrong. Further confounding the myth of young people wanting to change the world was the statistic that fewer than one in twenty strongly agreed that they 'would not buy the products of a large multinational company that had done something wrong'. A third of teens and twenty-somethings agreed to preserving the power of multinational companies and a further one in ten believed that multinationals are 'ultimately for the good of consumers' and should be encouraged to grow. By contrast, two-thirds of their grandparents—those aged 55 and above—claimed they would boycott goods to punish companies they considered guilty of corporate crimes. Even the issue of genetic engineering failed to provoke a strong response from young people, with only four in ten mistrusting the claims of the multinationals, compared to six in ten of their parents and grandparents.

Does this research indicate the ultimate supremacy for big business, where the golden arches of McDonald's and the Nike 'swoosh' are symbols of its global sovereignty? Should they feel safe in the knowledge of this study, or do they still need to be alert to possible trouble in the future? And even if a high proportion of young people support the idea of capitalism and big business, can such firms afford to ignore the vociferous and extreme minority whose direct action and boycotts can do costly and long-lasting harm to a firm's image?

Going global

EU legislators influence the UK, so UK marketers must try and influence the EU

The EU is playing an increasingly important role in firms' marketing environment. Protests at new legislation which would previously have been aimed at national legislators now often need to be aimed at the EU, because national legislators are simply implementing EU directives. The role of the EU in marketers' political environment was demonstrated when two EU directives came into force in 2005, placing all herbal medicines and vitamin and mineral supplements on the same regulatory basis as medicines. More than 300 widely used 'natural remedies' were banned altogether, and the cost of licensing each product—estimated at up £2,000 per product—would be beyond the means of many of the small producers who dominated the market for natural remedies. The big pharmaceutical companies had been lobbying the EU to get such a change, citing 'adverse reactions' from many herbal remedies and vitamin supplements such as vitamin B6. Of course, they knew that driving thousands of small herbal producers out of business would draw customers to the pharmaceutical companies' mass-produced products. The natural remedies producers were much more fragmented than the large pharmaceutical companies and were slow to get their lobbying together. In 2002, the sector presented to the UK government a petition protesting about the proposed changes. It contained over one million signatures, including those of Sir Paul McCartney and Sir Elton John, but it was too late, because the Directives had already been passed by the EU and hence there was little discretion left for the UK government. The lobbyists of the pharmaceutical industry seemed to have outsmarted the lobbyists of the natural remedies firms and understood where and when to apply pressure.

- Greater life expectancy is leading to an ageing of the population and a shift to an increasingly 'elderly' culture. This is reflected in product design which is increasingly emphasizing durability rather than fashionability.

- The growing concern among many groups in society with the ecological environment is reflected in a variety of 'green' consumer products.

These are just a few examples of changes which can have direct and indirect impact on the business environment. To take the example of the decline in the number of heavy smokers, this has encouraged many governments around the world to ban smoking in public spaces. Such legislation might have been difficult to agree and implement if smokers were still the dominant groups in society, but with declining numbers, legislation has been passed. Some business sectors have been affected by this, especially the hospitality and entertainment sector. As an example, in 2008 a UK-based bingo operator blamed a fall in profits on the smoking ban as many clients decided to smoke at home rather than visit the smoke free bingo hall.

Figure 2.6 **Busy lifestyles have opened new opportunities for marketers.** The increasing number of money rich, time poor households has been targeted by suppliers of services ranging from home shopping to domestic cleaning and personal coaching. Busy lifestyles have contributed to an increase in the number of parents seeking kindergartens for their young children. A desire for mothers to return to their career as soon as possible after the birth of their child and a decline in the geographically close extended family have led to an increase in private child care services. (Reproduced with permission of Bushbabies Kindergarten.)

Some indication of the minutiae of changing lifestyles and their implications for marketing was revealed in a report, *Complicated Lives II: The Price of Complexity* (The Future Foundation 2002). The report brought together quantitative and qualitative research, with extensive analysis of a range of trends affecting families and their finances (Figure 2.6). The findings show that, between 1961 and 2001:

- The average time women spent in a week doing cleaning and laundry fell from 12 hours and 40 minutes to 6 hours and 18 minutes.

- The average time that parents spent helping their children with homework had increased from 1 minute a day to 15 minutes a day.

- Time spent caring for children increased from 30 minutes a day to 75 minutes a day.

- The average amount of time spent entertaining went up from 25 minutes to 55 minutes.

- Time spent cooking has decreased for women, down from more than 1 hour and 40 minutes to just over an hour (73 minutes) per day. At the same time, men marginally increased their time in the kitchen, from 26 to 27 minutes per day.

There has been much discussion recently about the concept of cultural convergence, referring to an apparent decline in differences between cultures. It has been argued that basic human needs are universal in nature and, in principle, capable of satisfaction with universally similar solutions. Many companies have sought to develop one core product for a global market, and there is some evidence of firms achieving this (e.g. Coca Cola, McDonald's). The desire of a subculture in one country to imitate the values of those in another culture has also contributed to cultural convergence.

Critics of the trend towards cultural convergence point to a growing need for cultural identity which has been expressed, for example, in the rejection by some Muslim fundamentalist groups of the values of western society. This poses new challenges for western companies that seek overseas expansion. How can Coca Cola be sure that its brand name and product offer will be the object of aspiration for the dominant groups in a country, rather than a hated symbol of an alien system of capitalism?

The demographic environment

Demography is the study of populations in terms of their size and characteristics. Among the topics of interest to demographers are the age structure of a country, the geographic distribution of its population, the balance between males and females, and the likely future size of the population and its characteristics. Changes in the size and age structure of the population are critical to many firms' marketing. Although the total population of most western countries is stable, their composition is changing. Most countries are experiencing an increase in the proportion of elderly people, and companies who have monitored this trend have responded with the development of residential homes, cruise holidays, and financial portfolio management services aimed at meeting this group's needs. At the other end of the age spectrum, the birth rate of most countries is cyclical, resulting in a cyclical pattern of demand for age-related products such as baby products, fashion clothing, and family cars (Figure 2.7).

Consider the following changes in the structure of the UK population and their effects on marketers.

1. In 1970, life expectancy at birth for males in the UK was 68.7 years and for females 75.0 years. By 2009, life expectancy at birth for males had risen to 77.8 years and for females 81.9 years (Office for National Statistics 2010). Marketers are increasingly seeing elderly people as an opportunity, especially the active elderly 'baby boomers' who may retire with good pensions.

2. There has been a trend for women to have fewer children. (The average number of children for each woman born in 1930 was 2.35, it was 2.2 for those born in 1945 and it is projected to be 1.74 for those born in 1970.) There has also been a tendency for women to have children later in life. The mean age at which women in the UK have their first birth has increased from 25.2 years in 1986 to 27.4 in 2006 (Office for National Statistics 2008).

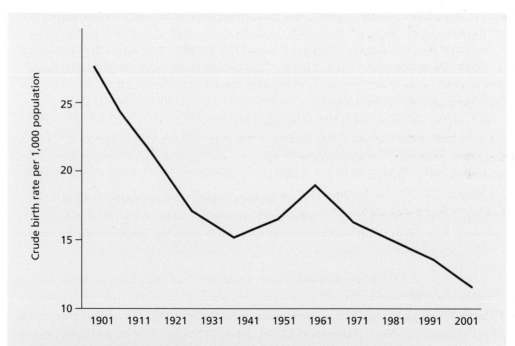

Figure 2.7 **The UK birth rate fluctuated greatly during the last century. As one 'baby boom' generation grew up, they had children which contributed to a further baby boom.** This figure shows how the number of births per 1,000 has fluctuated over time. For some companies, these changes can have a major effect on consumer demand. Inevitably, it is the specialist children's shops such as Mothercare that are first to feel the effects of a rise or fall in birth numbers, but eventually all companies who target specific age groups will experience a change in the number of buyers available to purchase their goods and services.

In addition, there has been an increase in the number of women having no children. (According to the Office for National Statistics, this has risen from 10 per cent of women born in 1950 to a projected 20 per cent of women born in the early 1960s.) Fewer children has resulted in parents spending more per child (more designer clothes for children rather than budget clothes) and has allowed women to stay at work longer (increasing household incomes and encouraging the purchase of labour-saving products).

3. Alongside a declining number of children has been a decline in the average household size. In 1971, the average household size in Great Britain was 2.9 people per household, with single person households accounting for 18 per cent of all households. By 2009, the average household size had fallen to 2.4, with the proportion of single person households rising to 29 per cent. There has been a particular fall in the number of large households with six or more people (down from six per cent of all households in 1971 to two per cent in 2009). (Office for National Statistics 2010). According to Euromonitor, only 32.7 per cent of all households in Western Europe were comprised of couples with children in 2006, compared to 51.0 per cent in Asia Pacific, and 54.3 per cent in Africa and the Middle East (Euromonitor 2007).

    The growth in small or one-person households has had numerous marketing implications, ranging from an increased demand for smaller units of housing to the types and size of groceries purchased. A single person buying for him or herself is likely to use different types of retail outlets compared with the household buying as a unit.

4. The ethnic composition of the UK population has become increasingly diverse. The Office for National Statistics has estimated that almost 60 per cent of the 4.3 million population increase expected to occur between 2000 and 2025 will be accounted for by inward migration (Office for National Statistics 2010). Ethnic diversity has created new opportunities to cater for ethnic preferences in fields as diverse as food, travel, and music.

5. Marketers also need to monitor the changing geographical distribution of the population (between different regions of the country and between urban and rural areas). The current drift towards rural and suburban areas has resulted in higher car ownership levels and a preference for using out-of-town shopping centres.

The technological environment

The pace of technological change is becoming increasingly rapid, and marketers need to understand how technological developments might affect them in four related business areas:

⊙ New technologies can allow new goods and services to be offered to consumers—mobile Internet, and new anti-cancer drugs for example.

⊙ New technology can allow existing products to be made more cheaply, thereby widening the market for such goods by enabling prices to be lowered. In this way, more efficient aircraft have allowed new markets for air travel to develop.

McDonald's recognizes new family values

Statistics have continued to chart the decline of the stereotypical nuclear family of two parents and 2.4 children. However, advertisers have often continued to portray this ideal type family in their advertising, despite the fact that fewer people can relate directly to it. The fast-food restaurant McDonald's recognized this trend with an advertising campaign that portrayed a boy arranging for a meeting between his separated parents in a branch of McDonald's. Behind the departure from the happy-families norm in fast-food marketing is the realization that the number of families in the UK with single parents has risen from eight per cent in 1971 to nearly one quarter in 2002. McDonald's claimed that it could not credibly position itself as a family restaurant and show only pictures of mum and dad and two kids without the risk of alienating parents and children from different households. But could McDonald's incur the wrath of critics who might accuse the company of actually contributing to family breakdown? With an eye on such worries, McDonald's advertisements left the impression that the couple were going to get together again.

◉ New opportunities for companies to communicate with their target customers have emerged, with many companies using computer databases to target potential customers and to maintain a dialogue with established customers. The development of mobile Internet services offers new possibilities for targeting buyers at times and places of high readiness to buy.

Technological developments have allowed new methods of distributing goods and services. (For example, amazon.com used the Internet to offer book buyers a new way of browsing and buying books.)

An example of the effects of a changing technological environment were seen in early 2011, when the music and books retailing group HMV reported falling sales and profits as consumers cut their discretionary expenditure following sharp increases in food, fuel, and housing costs. Furthermore, changes in technology, especially easier downloading of books and music, had left the group's high street stores looking vulnerable to new forms of distribution. Ten years earlier, a strong economy and high levels of discretionary income had led to booming sales and profits. Music and book downloading was seen as an opportunity which the company could embrace, but in fact subsequently failed to capitalize on.

E-Marketing

The Internet and the law of unintended consequences

The development of the Internet has had profound impacts on the marketing activities of some business sectors. As an example, the budget airline sector has capitalized on the ability of the Internet to cut out intermediaries and reduce the airlines' costs. The low-cost carrier easyJet now claims that over 95 per cent of its bookings are made online.

However, while many observers correctly predicted that travel and financial services would rapidly embrace the Internet, some other predictions have proved wide of the mark, suggesting that there is a very complex interaction between the technological, social, and economic environments. Consider the following predictions, which were made in 2000 when 'dotcom' mania was at its height.

- Predictions were made that commuting would lessen as more people would work from home, using the Internet to communicate with their work colleagues. Traffic congestion would disappear and commuter rail services would lose customers. In fact, 24/7 access to their work email has allowed many people to choose a pleasant residential environment and to live much further away from their work, because access to the Internet now allows them to work from home for two or three days a week. Overall, the travelling distances of many people in this situation have actually increased, resulting in more rather than less total commuting.

- Conferences were predicted to disappear in favour of video conferencing. Why bother travelling to a meeting or conference when you could meet 'virtually' from the comfort of your desk, and at lower cost? However, face-to-face conferences have continued to prosper. The technology that enables many people to work in isolation may have indirectly contributed to a desire to counter this with more face-to-face meetings with a greater social content.

- High street shops were being written off in 2000, when quite extraordinarily the pure Internet company lastminute.com had a market capitalization value far in excess of the 110-outlet Debenhams store. But the convenience of shopping in the high street or at out-of-town shopping centres and the problems of arranging home delivery of Internet suppliers were underestimated by advocates of Internet-based shopping.

We seem to have an inherent tendency to overstate the short-term effects of technological change, but to understate the long-term effects on our behaviour. With the development of new technologies enabling high-speed mobile Internet services, further predictions were being made in 2008. Would we really want to download full-length feature films to watch on our mobile phones? Would large numbers of people really want to surf the net on a small screen while travelling on a train? Would there be unforeseen 'killer applications' such as SMS text messaging which was almost left out of the specification of first-generation mobile phones, because no useful role for it was foreseen? Perhaps the long-term effects of the Internet may be more subtle, by contributing to individuals' sense of connectedness with narrowly selected commercial and social groups, no matter where they may be located, while reducing the sense of community which has traditionally been associated with diverse groups of people living together in close proximity.

The unforeseen consequences of the Internet emphasize how difficult it can be to understand the consequences for the marketer of a changing marketing environment. These examples demonstrate the importance of understanding the linkages between different elements of the marketing environment, so developments in the technological environment can be sensibly understood only in conjunction with changes in the social environment.

The ecological environment

Issues affecting our natural ecology have captured the public imagination in recent years. The destruction of tropical rain forests and the depletion of the ozone layer leading to global warming have serious implications for our quality of life—not necessarily today, but for future generations. Marketing is often seen as being in conflict with the need to protect the natural ecology. It is very easy for critics of marketing to point to cases where greed and mismanagement have created long-lasting or permanent ecological damage. Have rain forests been destroyed partly by our greed for more hardwood furniture? More locally, is our impatience for getting to our destination quickly the reason why many natural habitats have been lost to new road developments?

A market-led company cannot ignore threats to the natural ecology, for two principal reasons:

1. There has been growing pressure on natural resources, including those that, directly or indirectly, are used in firms' production processes. This is evidenced by the extinction of species of animals and the depletion of hardwood timber resources. As a result of overuse of natural resources, many industry sectors, such as North Sea fishing, have faced severe constraints on their production possibilities.

2. The general public has become increasingly aware of ecological issues, and, more importantly, some segments have shown a greater willingness and ability to spend money to alleviate the problems associated with ecologically harmful practices (see Leonidou and Leonidou 2011; Peattie and Peattie 2009).

Because of the growing importance of ecological considerations to the marketer, there is further discussion of the topic in Chapter 3.

◉ The internal environment

Marketers do not operate in a vacuum within their organizations. Internally, the structure and politics of an organization affect the manner in which it responds to environmental change. We are all familiar with lumbering giants of companies who, like a super-tanker, have ploughed ahead on a seemingly predetermined course, and found it difficult to change direction. During the late 1990s such well-respected companies as Sainsbury's and Marks & Spencer were accused of having internal structures and processes that were too rigid to cope with a changing external environment. Simply having a strong marketing department does not guarantee that a firm will be best able to adapt to change. The existence of a central marketing department may in fact create internal tensions, which make them less effective at responding to changing consumer needs than where marketing responsibilities in their widest sense are spread throughout the organization.

Two aspects to a marketing manager's internal environment are of importance here: the internal structure and processes of the marketing department itself (where one actually exists), and the relationship of the marketing function to other business functions.

Marketing departments allocate responsibilities to individual managers on a number of bases, the most common being functions performed, products managed, customer segments, and geographical areas; but in practice, most marketing departments show more than one approach to structure (Figure 2.8).

In a genuinely marketing-oriented organization, marketing activities cannot be confined to something called a marketing department. As Drucker (1973) noted, marketing is so basic that it cannot be considered a separate function: it has to be the whole business seen from the customer's point of view. In marketing-oriented organizations, customers should be the

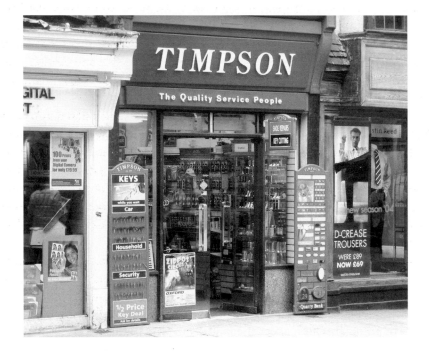

Figure 2.8 **Labour intensive service industries have long realized that recruiting, training, and motivating the right staff is an important basis for delivering value to customers.** In conditions of full employment, companies must sell themselves as a good employer so that they can recruit the people who will ultimately deliver marketers' promises to customers. The *Sunday Times* conducts an annual survey of Britain's best companies to work for, and the shoe repair and key cutting chain Timpson has scored highly for a number of years. Employee benefits include at least 16 weeks' maternity leave on full pay (compared to statutory minimum of six weeks at 90 per cent pay) and/or at least four weeks' leave above the statutory minimum of 40 weeks. One sign of the company's success is a low level of staff turnover—at least 40 per cent of its staff have worked at the company for more than five years. Managers are given considerable discretion in how they run their branch, for example the prices that they charge. Customers have come to trust the chain and rewarded it with sustainable long-term profits.

concern not simply of the marketing department, but also of all those operational and administrative personnel whose actions may directly or indirectly affect customers' perceptions of quality and value. Some of the most successful companies are those that have successfully integrated marketing into all functional areas of the organization.

An important element of an organization's internal environment is its dominant 'culture'. Culture in this sense refers to a set of values that are shared by all members of the organization. Some organizations, for example, have a culture that stresses that 'the customer is always right', while others have a bureaucratic culture that stresses the need to conduct business in an administratively 'correct' way. Numerous comparative studies into the performance of European, American, and Japanese-managed organizations have identified the concept of culture as a possible explanation for differences in competitive effectiveness.

It can be very difficult to change cultural attitudes within an organization, and the process of change can be painful for many. Some organizations appear to have successfully managed the transition from a production-oriented culture to one focused on customers (e.g. many former state-owned bus companies). In many cases, however, this change has been slow, leading to competitive disadvantage where culture does not keep up with changes in the external environment. As an example, some people have claimed that UK clearing banks have continued to be dominated by a culture based on prudence and caution whereas in some product areas such as home insurance a more aggressive approach to marketing management is called for.

For some firms, the availability of an adequate number of trained staff may by critical for satisfying customer needs. A marketing manager for a chain of fine dining restaurants may put together lots of promotional programmes to entice diners, but if the chain cannot find sufficient chefs to operate in its kitchens, it will not be able to meet its customers' needs and expectations. In order to encourage staff retention, in particular of women returning after having children, companies have offered attractive packages of benefits, such as working hours that fit around school holidays, and have sponsored various events in order to promote a caring image.

Can going beyond the legal requirement for employees ever be considered altruistic rather than just good business practice? Quaker companies such as Cadbury have a historic tradition of paternalism towards their staff. But might such altruism result in a payback in terms of better motivated staff?

The flexible organization

Organizations differ in the speed with which they are able to exploit new opportunities as they appear in their environment, partly reflecting the flexibility of their employment practices. Being the fastest company in a market to adapt can pay good dividends, so recent years have seen attempts by firms to increase their flexibility. This can be seen in the way that companies have moved personnel from areas in decline to those for which there is a prospect of future growth. For example, the major UK banks have moved staff away from basic banking activities—which face mature markets and challenges from new technology—towards broader financial services, which have been seen as more promising growth areas.

The management of change is becoming increasingly important to organizations, driven by the increasing speed with which the external environment is changing. Where the external environment is changing fast, employees of the organization may feel threatened, and it is important that management understands their fears and encourages them to take on board change. Sometimes, change needs to be considered at a strategic level, for example the role of post office employees is having to change in response to the threats posed by the Internet, and the declining volume of letter business. At other times, flexibility needs to be considered on a more short-term, operational basis, for example a restaurant may need the flexibility to take on or lay off staff a very short notice, depending upon the weather.

Flexibility within an organization's workforce can be achieved by segmenting it into *core* and *peripheral* components. Many organizations have given their core workers greater job security, with defined career opportunities. In return for this relative job security, core workers may have to accept what Atkinson (1984) termed 'functional flexibility' by becoming responsible for a variety of jobs, as and when required. During their career with a company, such employees may undertake a variety of roles. In contrast to this group, peripheral employees have less job security and relatively limited career opportunities. They are 'numerically flexible', and often are employed on short-term contracts or treated as self-employed subcontractors. It is not just operational staff whose jobs have been casualized in this way. Increasingly, many management jobs are being 'outsourced', and undertaken by consultants who are taken on as and when required. There is, however, debate about whether excessive use of short-term, flexible labour increases the effectiveness of an organization. Many have pointed to a possible downside in the form of reduced commitment of employees to the firm, which can ultimately damage the company's dealings with its customers.

◉ Monitoring and responding to environmental change

There are many examples of firms that have failed to read their marketing environment and have eventually withered and died. To avoid this fate, a firm must:

◉ Understand what is going on in its business environment, and

◉ Respond and adapt to environmental change.

As organizations become larger and national economies more complex, the task of understanding the marketing environment becomes more formidable. Information about a firm's environment becomes crucial to environmental analysis and response.

Information about the current state of the environment is used as a starting point for planning future marketing strategy, based on assumptions about how the environment will change. Information is also vital to monitor the implementation of an organization's marketing plans and to note the cause of any deviation from plan. Information therefore has both a planning function and a control function.

Information collection, processing, transmission, and storage technologies are continually improving, as witnessed by the development of electronic point of sale (EPOS) systems. These have enabled organizations to greatly enhance the quality of the information they have about their operating environment. However, information is becoming more accessible not just to one particular organization, but also to its competitors. Attention is therefore moving away from how information is collected, to who is best able to make use of the information.

Large organizations operating in complex and turbulent environments often use information to build models of their environment, or at least sub-components of it. Some of these can be quite general, as in the case of the models of the national economy which many large companies have developed. From a general model of the economy, a firm can predict how a specific item of government policy (e.g. increasing the rate of value added tax on luxury goods) will impact directly and indirectly on sales of its own products.

The crucial role of information in marketing analysis and planning will be returned to in Chapter 5.

SWOT analysis

SWOT is an acronym for strengths, weaknesses, opportunities, and threats. SWOT analysis is a useful framework for assessing an organization and its marketing environment, summarizing the main environmental issues in the form of opportunities and threats facing an organization. These external factors are listed alongside the organization's internal strengths and weaknesses. An opportunity in an organization's external environment can be exploited only if it has the internal strengths to do so. If, on the other hand, the organization is not capable of exploiting these because of internal weaknesses, then they should perhaps be left alone. For this reason, the terms 'opportunities' and 'threats' should not be viewed as 'absolutes', but assessed in the context of an organization's resources and the feasibility of exploiting them.

The principles of a SWOT analysis are illustrated in Figure 2.9 by examining how an established manufacturer of ready-prepared chicken products might view its strengths and weaknesses in terms of the opportunities and threats that it faces in its environment.

Marketing opportunities can come in many forms, and each should be assessed for its attractiveness and success probability. Attractiveness can be assessed in terms of potential market size, growth rates, profit margins, competitiveness, and distribution channels. Other factors may be technological requirements, the extent of government restrictions, availability of government grants, ecological concerns, and energy requirements. Measures of attractiveness must be qualified by the probability of success, which depends on the company's strengths and competitive advantage. Probability of success is likely to be influenced by, among other things, the firm's access to cash, lines of credit or capital to finance new developments, technological and production expertise, marketing skills, distribution channels, and managerial competence. A simple matrix can be constructed to show the relationship between attractiveness and success probability. We will return to this in Chapter 7.

Strengths	Weaknesses
Established and widely recognized brand name Good distribution network Strong financial base	Only has a narrow product range Shortage of production staff
Opportunities	**Threats**
Growing demand for chicken products Rising income will result in increased demand for ready prepared meals	Possibility of health scares Intense competition from supermarkets' own label products Tighter safety standards may increase costs

Figure 2.9 **SWOT analysis for a hypothetical established UK manufacturer of ready-prepared chicken meals.**

An environmental threat is a challenge posed by an unfavourable trend or development in a company's environment that would lead, in the absence of action by the company, to the erosion of the company's market position. In this case the threats should be assessed according to their seriousness and the probability of occurrence. A threat matrix can then be constructed.

In order for an environmental analysis to have a useful input to the marketing planning process, a wide range of information and opinions needs to be summarized in a meaningful way. The information collated from a detailed environmental analysis can be simplified in the form of an environmental threat and opportunity profile (ETOP). This provides a summary of the environmental factors that are most critical to the organization (Figure 2.10) and can be useful in stimulating debate among senior management about the future of the business. Some analysts suggest trying to weight these factors according to their importance, and then rating them for their impact on the organization.

Factor	Major opportunity	Minor opportunity	Neutral	Minor threat	Major threat	Probability of occurrence
Political						
New transport policy sees introduction of tax on use of cars in town centres					✓	0.1
Economic						
Tax on petrol increases by 5p				✓		0.4
Household spending falls for two quarters in succession					✓	0.2
VAT on new cars reduced	✓					0.1
Market						
Overseas competitors enter market more aggressively				✓		0.3

Figure 2.10 **An environmental threat and opportunity profile, applied to a car manufacturer.**

◉ Chapter summary and linkages to other chapters

The marketing environment comprises the individuals, organizations, and forces that impinge on the activities of marketers. Some of the effects are direct and relatively immediate (the micro-environment), while others are essentially forces for change in the future (the macro-environment). Marketers must also understand the internal structures and processes of their organization, as these can affect the development and implementation of marketing plans (the internal environment).

Marketers have developed methodologies for capturing information about the marketing environment and these will be developed in Chapter 5. Following analysis of their environment, marketers seek to develop a competitive position within that environment (Chapter 7). Increasingly, marketers are seeing the marketing environment in terms of not just the local market, but also the international environment (Chapter 12).

This chapter has stressed that marketers should understand the needs not just of their customers, but of a much broader range of stakeholders. Although social responsibility by firms can achieve long-term paybacks, there can still be doubt about what is the most responsible course of action. The issue of marketing's social responsibility is the focus for the next chapter.

✎ KEY PRINCIPLES OF MARKETING

- Marketing takes place within a broad system of economic, social, political, and technological relationships.

- Value is created through interaction with other individuals and organizations that make up the marketing environment.

- The marketing environment cannot be neatly divided into distinct areas. A good marketer seeks to understand the complex linkages between different parts of the marketing environment.

- Micro-environment influences may demand urgent attention, but macro-environment influences can have a more profound long-term effect on an organization's marketing.

CASE STUDY

Ready meal manufacturers ready to respond to a changing marketing environment

It is often said that 'we are what we eat', but it can also be said that what is on our dinner plates reflects the broader marketing environment. One big change in recent years has been growing demand for ready-prepared meals bought from a supermarket. Previously dismissed as unpalatable and a poor substitute for 'real' cooking, their sales have grown rapidly in recent years in many western developed countries. An analysis of the reasons for the growth in the ready-prepared meals markets indicates the effects of broader factors in the marketing environment on the size of a particular market.

The research company Mintel reported in 2007 that the market for ready meals in the five largest European countries increased by five per cent between 2006 and 2007 alone to reach 8.4 billion euro. Furthermore, it predicted a further 18 per cent growth to reach the 10 billion euro mark by 2011. In the UK, the market was worth a total of 2 billion euro, with a much higher level of sales per head of population than in France or Germany. Mintel predicted that between 2006 and 2011, UK ready meals sales would reach €3.7 billion, with about a quarter of all Brits likely to eat a ready meal at least once a week. It seemed that the appetite for ready meals would grow more slowly in other European countries, for example Mintel predicted that by 2011, only nine per cent of Germans would eat a ready meal each week.

What has driven the growth in the ready meals market in recent years, and why should there be differences in market potential between countries?

Technology has played a big role in the growing take up of ready meals. A report by the research body Leatherhead Food International described how new techniques have allowed companies to develop ready meals which preserve taste and texture, while still making them easy to use by the consumer. Furthermore, great advances in distribution management, in particular the use of information technology to control inventories, has allowed fresh, chilled ready meals to be effectively and efficiently distributed without the need for freezing or added preservatives.

The structure and values of society have contributed to the growth of the UK ready meal market, and may explain why grow here is greater than in France or Germany. Ready meals particularly appeal to single households, and those 'cellular' families in which individual family members tend to eat at different times. Mintel reported that the tradition of family meals together remains stronger in many continental European countries than in the UK, which may help to explain the greater popularity of individual ready meals in the UK. Some social commentators have reported that young people have lost the ability to cook creatively, as cookery has been reduced in importance in the school curriculum. Furthermore, many UK consumers no longer feel a social stigma attached to eating a ready meal, something which would be anathema to many French people, a country which takes great pride in its national cuisine. Any remaining stigma has been reduced by the number of 'celebrity chefs' who have endorsed ready meals with their own brand image.

The impact of the economic environment on sales of ready meals is slightly more ambiguous. As individuals get richer, they can afford to buy ready-prepared foods, rather than spend time and effort preparing it themselves. With a tempting range of ready meals now available, from duck à l'orange to beef bourguignon, the consumer with money in his or her pocket will be tempted to splash out on a ready meal, rather than persevere at home with a 'quick' jacket potato or pizza. Although rising incomes have been associated with rising consumption of ready meals, increased sales have also been attributed to a deteriorating economic environment. As recession bit the UK in 2008, the manufacturer Northern Foods—a major supplier of ready-prepared meals to Marks and Spencer—reported resilient sales. It seemed that consumers were trading down from expensive restaurant meals to the alternative of relatively cheap, gourmet, ready-prepared meals.

Of course, marketers should be more interested in predicting future effects of environmental change on consumption, rather than merely charting historical trends. So what do current trends hold for future sales of ready meals? The growing pressure on individuals' available time, matched with long-term rising disposable incomes, will doubtless continue to fuel the growth in UK ready meals sales.

In a market that is in its maturity stage, more attention will need to be paid to competitive differentiation, and understanding the way in which customers attribute value to a product. Many consumers have become increasingly concerned about the health implications of the food they eat, and ready meal manufacturers will need to continue responding to such concerns. For example, they have responded with a range of low calorie meals, and addressed specific, sometimes transient, health fads, with respect to trans-fatty acids and omega 3 supplements. Many consumers have also become concerned about the ecological environment, and some suppliers, such as Marks and Spencer have incorporated sustainability agendas into their ready meals, for example by reducing packaging and sourcing supplies from sustainable sources.

As other countries develop cellular household structures, with more professional, single people living alone, export opportunities may grow, and many companies in the sector have their eyes set on the Chinese and Indian markets, among others.

Sources: Based on: Mintel Oxygen Reports: Eating Habits: Improving the Appeal of Convenience Options, Aug 2007; *Financial Times*, Quality ready meals hit the spot, Jul 21, 2006; Leatherhead Food International, European Ready Meals Market, 2001.

Case study review questions

1. Using an appropriate framework of analysis, briefly summarize the effects of change in the marketing environment on sales of ready meals.

2. Critically discuss the link between the economic environment and sales of ready meals.

3. Discuss the factors that might affect sales of ready meals in your country over the next five years.

CHAPTER REVIEW QUESTIONS

1. Explain briefly what you understand by the 'marketing environment' of a business.

2. 'Suppliers and intermediaries are important stakeholders in the micro-environment of the business.' Explain the evolving role and functions of these stakeholders in today's marketing-orientated business.

3. Critically discuss the links between the internal environment of an organization and its external marketing environment.

ACTIVITIES

1. Develop a checklist of points that you consider to be important indicators of whether an organization is responsive to changes in its business environment. Why did you choose these indicators? Now apply your checklist to three selected organizations: one a traditional manufacturing industry, the second a service-based commercial organization, and the third a government organization that serves the public. What, if anything, should your chosen organizations do to become more responsive to changes in their business environment?

2. Using a company of your choice, produce and justify an environmental set.

3. Giving examples, explain what is meant by the term 'pressure groups'. Provide a résumé of the tactics you would advise a high profile company to use in managing relations with these groups.

REFERENCES

Atkinson, J. (1984) 'Manpower Strategies for Flexible Organizations'. *Personnel Management*, August, 77–93.

Doughty, S. (2007) 'Women to be the Major Breadwinners in a Quarter of Families by 2030'. *Daily Mail*, 3 August,17.

Drucker, P.F. (1973) *Management: Tasks, Responsibilities and Practices*. New York: Harper & Row.

Euromonitor (2007) *Countries and Consumers*. London: Euromonitor International.

Financial Times (2007) 'UK Immigration may be Close to Peak'. London: *Financial Times*, 24 July 2007.

Financial Times (2008) 'Insurance Threat to Loans'. London: *Financial Times*, 6 June, 5.

Future Foundation (2002) *Complicated Lives II: The Price of Complexity*. EU Office of Statistics, London: The Future Foundation.

Leonidou, C.N. & Leonidou, L.C. (2011) 'Research into Environmental Marketing/Management: a Bibliographic Analysis'. *European Journal of Marketing,* 45 (1/2), 68–103.

Office for National Statistics (2008a) Social Trends No. 38. London: Office for National Statistics (available online at http://www.statistics.gov.uk/downloads/theme_social/Social_Trends38/Social_Trends_38.pdf).

Office for National Statistics (2008b) *Population Trends*. Spring 2008, No. 131. London: Office for National Statistics (available online at http://www.statistics.gov.uk/downloads/theme_population/Population_Trends_131_web.pdf).

Office for National Statistics (2010) Social Trends No. 30. London: Office for National Statistics.

Peattie, K. and Peattie, S. (2009) 'Social Marketing: a Pathway to Consumption Reduction?' *Journal of Business Research,* 62 (2), 260–68.

Rayport, J.F. and Sviokla, J.J. (1995) 'Exploiting the Virtual Value Chain'. *Harvard Business Review*, November–December, 75–85.

SUGGESTED FURTHER READING

A wide-ranging review of organizations' environment is given in the following:

Palmer, A. and Hartley, B. (2011) *The Business Environment,* 7th edition. Maidenhead, Berks: McGraw-Hill.

The following provide further discussion of marketing relationships between a company and its suppliers and customers:

Donaldson, Bill and O'Toole, Tom (2007) *Strategic Market Relationships: From Strategy to Implementation*. London: John Wiley.

Egan, J. (2008) *Relationship Marketing—Exploring Relational Strategies in Marketing*, 3rd edition. Harlow: Pearson Education Ltd.

Mattsson, L.-G. and Johanson, J. (2006) 'Discovering Market Networks'. *European Journal of Marketing*, 40 (3/4), 259–74.

The difficulties of understanding and assessing the impacts of change in the economic environment on a firm's marketing activities are discussed in the following:

Blanchard, O., Giavazzi, F., and Amighin, A. (2010) *Macroeconomics, a European Perspective*. Harlow: Pearson Education.

Burda, M. and Wyplosz, C. (2009) *Macroeconomics: a European Text*, 5th edition. Oxford: Oxford University Press.

Griffiths, A. and Wall, S. (eds) (2009) *Economics for Business and Management*, 2nd edition. London: Prentice Hall.

Organizational culture has been referred to in this chapter as having a major impact on an organization's marketing effectiveness, and the following references explore internal and external dimensions of culture:

Hofstede, G. and Hofstede, G.J. (2004) *Cultures and Organizations: Software for the Mind*. Maidenhead: McGraw-Hill.

Zheng, W., Yang, B., and McClean, G.M. (2010) 'Linking Organizational Culture, Structure, Strategy, and Organizational Effectiveness'. *Journal of Business Research*, 63 (7), 763–71.

ONLINE RESOURCE CENTRE

Visit the Online Resource Centre for resources that are relevant to this chapter, including a flashcard glossary, web links, multiple choice questions, and additional case studies:

www.oxfordtextbooks.co.uk/orc/palmer3e/

KEY TERMS

- Accelerator effect
- Birth rate
- Business cycle
- Competitors
- Cultural convergence
- Demography
- Disintermediation
- Ecological environment
- Flexible organization
- Gross domestic product (GDP)
- Intermediaries
- Internal environment

- Internet
- Macro-environment
- Marketing environment
- Micro-environment
- Multiplier effect
- Pressure groups
- Relationship marketing
- Shareholders
- Stakeholders
- SWOT analysis
- System
- Value chain

3 SOCIALLY RESPONSIBLE MARKETING

CHAPTER OBJECTIVES

Marketing is coming under greater scrutiny by members of the public who have increasingly high expectations about the behaviour of commercial organizations. In the previous two chapters, we have presented marketing in simplistic terms whereby firms continually seek to maximize their profits by adapting what they sell to the needs of customers. Unfortunately, this simple approach may lead firms to adopt policies which society at large may consider to be irresponsible. This chapter explores the concept of marketing responsibility from a number of angles. It begins by reviewing the underlying philosophy of socially responsible business. It then explores the currently topical issue of sustainability in a world where many people have accused marketing of being responsible for unnecessarily depleting natural resources and harming the natural environment. Following this, the chapter will review issues of ethical standards by which marketers interact with their customers, suppliers, competitors, and government agencies. Finally, the chapter will make some observations on the duties of companies to communicate responsibly with their customers, in an era where customers and regulatory agencies are more prepared than ever before to criticize or sue firms for irresponsible communication.

Introduction

In Chapter 1, it was noted that satisfying customer requirements was a key defining element of marketing. The term 'customer is king' or 'the customer is always right' is often heard as the essential motivator which leads companies to try to satisfy customers' needs profitably. Of course, what the customer wants may be impossible for a company to provide at a profit, so the simplistic idea of 'customer is king' may not be followed through. It may also be highly irresponsible for a company to even attempt to satisfy customers' needs.

Issues of social responsibility frequently present themselves to buyers, and there is often no easy way to define what is right and what is wrong. Consider the case of two friends out shopping one Saturday afternoon in their local Primark, a chain of stores that has grown rapidly during the past 20 years by offering the latest fashions in clothing at very low prices.

It has achieved success through ruthless cost cutting, good trend spotting, and efficient sourcing and distribution. One of the friends spots an evening dress for £10—an irresistible bargain. Then the other remembered seeing a TV documentary which accused the company of buying clothes from subcontracted suppliers who used child labour and paid workers very little for working in bad conditions. She wanted to move her search for a dress to Marks and Spencer which had created a better impression on her for social responsibility. But the first friend was more cavalier in her approach—she didn't want to miss out on a bargain and rationalized that those underpaid workers in Vietnam should consider themselves lucky to have a job. This scenario which may be played out millions of times a day by individual consumers can directly influence company policy. To what extent should the company take on board issues of corporate responsibility towards disadvantaged groups and the ecological environment? Would buyers be prepared to forgo a bargain in order to buy from a company that is perceived as acting more responsibly? Are corporate responsibility and cost driven efficiency actually compatible? These issues are explored in this chapter.

We can generalize a number of situations in which it may be considered irresponsible for a company to provide customers with what they say they want:

1. A product may be harmful to customers, and although it may be seen by them as being beneficial in the short term, it may have long-term harmful effects, of which they are not aware at the time of purchase. Addictive drugs and high fat burgers may be sought by customers today, but they may regret their purchase in the future, when they are addicted to drugs, or obese from eating too much high fat food.

2. Some customers may not have the mental capacity to understand what they want. Children may choose to eat sweets and fizzy drinks all day, and may not be able to evaluate the consequences of their purchases.

3. Marketers have particular responsibility to vulnerable groups of customers. Young children may be vulnerable, because they have not developed the capacity to critically evaluate purchases. But vulnerability can have much wider effects, and a customer who is not vulnerable at one moment, may be vulnerable on another. A house owner who desperately needs repairs carrying out on his house following extensive storm damage in the area may be vulnerable to 'cowboy' builders who realize that customers suddenly have little choice of builders, and they can charge exploitative prices.

4. The company may present a false or misleading picture of a product, so the customer cannot realistically make an informed choice about whether or not it will satisfy their needs. In evaluating complex price details for mobile phones or gas tariffs, many customers may not understand exactly what they are buying, and what they are committing themselves to.

5. A customer may want to buy a product which is directly harmful to others, for example a shotgun. Should a company be allowed to supply it to them?

6. Similarly, a customer may wish to buy something which is harmful to society more generally, for example by undermining its core values. Should customers be able to buy

things from shops all day on Sunday, rather than treating Sunday as a day of rest and family togetherness?

7. Should companies promote products in a way that creates envy of those who have bought the product, and results in social divisions between a group of 'haves' and another group of 'have nots' which feels socially excluded? Should a teenager feel socially excluded because they do not have the latest fashion in trainers?

8. Could a customer's purchase harm future generations by depleting natural resources, or emitting harmful gases into the atmosphere? Customers may be happy to buy 'gas guzzling' cars, but should their choice be restricted in order to reduce the emission of 'greenhouse gases'?

9. Is the customer actually presented with all the choice that should be available to them? What if a cartel of producers got together to try to restrict choice of a particular category of products?

How should a profit orientated company act in each of these situations? Does it have a moral responsibility to treat its customers as an individual would treat their trusted friends? Is business essentially about letting the buyer beware, and if the customer says that they want something, why should the seller question this? Can forgoing sales and acting responsibly actually bring in more money to a company, because its brand comes to be seen more favourably by buyers?

In this chapter, we will explore issues of socially responsible marketing. Marketers have come under increasing levels of scrutiny by customers and the media, with newspapers and television programmes ever eager to pick up stories of bad practice by commercial organizations. Fast-food companies promoting high fat foods which lead to obesity; car manufacturers encouraging high emission four-wheel drive cars which are only going to be used around town; and insurance policies sold to customers who will never be able to make a claim on them, are typical of marketing irresponsibility that has been reported recently.

This chapter raises many more questions than it provides answers. Many of the issues discussed here involve value judgements, so one person's idea of responsibility may be viewed by another person as irresponsible. Even if the chapter provides no definitive answer on certain subjects, you should at least become aware of the issues involved, and frameworks for reconciling the sometimes conflicting aims of businesses and their broader group of stakeholders.

We will first explore the philosophical underpinnings of socially responsible marketing, before moving on to look at specific issues which may require us to modify the simple statement that marketing is primarily about satisfying customers' needs profitably.

◉ Philosophical principles underlying responsible marketing

It is difficult to define precisely what is meant by socially responsible marketing, because there are essentially two views about why companies should act in a socially responsible manner.

1. In models of 'good' societies, organizations have a duty to think about the interests of society, and not just their own narrow interests. Businesses should do their bit to contribute towards a just and fair society, alongside the contributions of other institutions such as the family and the church.

2. An alternative view is that firms take an instrumental approach to responsibility. If acting responsibly improves their chances of survival and prosperity, they will act responsibly—if not, they will act opportunistically and in their own self-interest.

For the purpose of this book, we will define socially responsible marketing as:

> Marketing activities which acknowledge corporate responsibilities to all stakeholders who may be affected by such activities. Socially responsible marketing need not be incompatible with a profit maximizing objective.

The philosophical approach of the firm as a 'good citizen' has been criticized by followers of Milton Friedman, who have argued that firms should concentrate on doing what they are best at—making profits for their owners. Expecting social responsibility by firms would allow business organizations to become too dominant in society. By this argument, any attempt by firms to contribute to social causes is a form of taxation on the customers of their businesses. Buyers should be aware of what they are buying, and make their own decisions about what is socially responsible.

The more pragmatic view is that where companies go out of their way to be 'good citizens', the cause of this can often be traced to a calculative, instrumental judgement by the company rather than philanthropy. There are a number of reasons for such instrumentality:

- In a market in which product offers are all broadly similar and with saturation advertising, support of socially valuable causes may allow a company to develop a unique identity for its products. Such support may be a cheap way of gaining attention and provide a unique selling proposition.

- Acting responsibly may actually reduce a company's costs, rather than increasing them, therefore being a good citizen comes with no additional cost implications for a company. As an example, a restaurant chain that sources a high proportion of its food locally may appear to be acting responsibly by reducing 'food miles', but may also actually reduce its total costs. Sometimes, the biggest barrier to a company acting responsibly is the mindset of staff which can be difficult to change.

- Some of the company's customers may prefer to buy from a responsible company rather than an irresponsible one. Where there is a lot of broadly similar choice available in a market, the cost to a customer of buying the 'responsible' product rather than an irresponsible one may be quite low. By appearing to be responsible, a company may have added to its brand reputation in much the same way as it would be investing in advertising and quality control.

⊙ Sometimes companies change their behaviour ahead of new legislation. By changing early, they can gain positive publicity, which would be lost if they were seen to be pushed into change by legislation. The company may also gain cost saving and learning advantages ahead of its competitors, before they, too, are forced to change when new legislation is introduced.

This chapter is about responsible *marketing*. However, it can often be difficult to separate marketing responsibility from other aspects of corporate responsibility. This reflects the recognition in Chapter 1 that marketing in its broadest sense is not just the responsibility of the marketing department, but of all functions within an organization. Consider some of the following cross functional issues that impinge on responsible marketing:

1. The marketing department of a food retailer is desperately trying to get its supply costs down, so that it can sell a range of ready-prepared foods below a critical price point. It has cut its overheads as far as it can, so the only realistic method of selling its food at the specified price point, while at the same time still retaining its profit margin, is to cut its production and wastage costs. Should it use chlorine in its washing processes which will reduce washing costs, and keep the finished product looking fresh for longer, even though there is a suggestion that chlorine may increase cancer risks and lead to the pollution of watercourses? The production manager may be happy to extend the shelf life, but what view should the marketing manager take?

2. Many service industries require a high level of flexibility by staff, with some staff being held on standby, and only called in for work if there is expected to be a high level of customer demand. Is it responsible that marketing's need to flexibly accommodate as many customers as possible, should lead to uncertainty among workers, who may come from disadvantaged groups in society anyway?

3. The marketing department of a retailer may desperately want to expand its store network, but the finance director needs to obtain new sources of funds. Should the finance director overstate recent profits in order to make raising new finance—and hence opening more stores—easier?

In all of these cases, it should be apparent that making decisions about what is responsible may not be easy. It is too naive and simplistic to say that commercial organizations should always act in a completely responsible manner. Just as there are few human beings who know no sin, so, too, there are very few companies that are beyond reproach. Acting responsibly may be crucial for a large organization with a differentiation strategy based on trust in its brand. In these cases, the brand is probably based on being perceived as a reliable, responsible one which customers can do business with. So companies such as Boots, Marks and Spencer, and Virgin have gone to great lengths to appear as a responsible member of the community. The Virgin group has used its reputation for responsibility to move into completely new markets, from music to airlines, trains, and telephones. For such companies, share values have sometimes suddenly fallen when stories or rumours have circulated about them acting in an irresponsible way. However, many smaller challenging companies may have less concern with being seen as a responsible organization. A clothing retailer which is seeking to expand fast and appeal to a price sensitive market through discount outlets may be prepared to take more risks when it comes to acting irresponsibly. If their main point of difference with competitors is price, rather than brand reputation, it may be more willing to turn a blind eye to dubious suppliers, or suppliers to those suppliers, who may have used toxic chemicals in their production process, or used child labour. They may reason that their brand is not particularly powerful, so therefore they have less to lose than a trusted brand. On the other hand, they would have everything to gain by undercutting the competition with cheaply sourced products. Refer back to the opening paragraph of this chapter and the dilemma faced by two shoppers looking for a new dress. Some segments may be quite happy to turn a 'blind eye' to socially poor practice, if it means they can buy a product that they want at a lower price.

Responsible marketing, then, is not a simple question of being good to all people at all times. In real life, marketing managers have to make hard decisions if they are to survive and stay in business. A business which was run purely on philanthropic lines probably wouldn't last very long. However, a business that has a shrewd understanding of its business environment, and understands the broader expectations of buyers and legislators, may consider that acting responsibly yields good long-term dividends. It may even find that acting responsibly is less costly than acting irresponsibly. Read the 'marketing in action' vignette (below) about the retailer B&Q's decision to stop selling patio heaters, and judge for yourself whether you think the company was being philanthropic or simply shrewd in its decision.

◉ Ecologically responsible marketing

There is no doubt that issues of ecological responsibility have been rising rapidly up the agenda of marketing. Global warming, tsunamis, violent storms, and the depletion of natural resources have led even the most doubting member of the public to the view that 'something must be done'. As individual consumers, we can decide to do our bit for the ecological environment, for example by walking rather than using the car, or buying locally produced food which has incurred fewer 'food miles'. But what should we expect businesses to do? Marketing is often seen as being irresponsible in its attitude to the natural ecology. Many of the products that we see in the shops probably have a substitute which is less harmful to the environment. Why should bottled water companies such as Volvic and Evian spend a lot of money promoting their product, and using environmentally harmful transport to move it over long distances, when there is plenty of evidence that locally available tap water is just as good? Indeed, marketing could be accused of encouraging a throwaway society, which is good for increasing sales, but less sustainable for the environment. Taken to its logical extreme, consumption of the vast majority of goods and services can result in some form of ecological harm. For example, the most ecologically responsible means of transport is to

Marketing and social responsibility

No more patio heaters at B&Q—who wins?

Global warming has become the big ecological issue of the early 21st century with a combination of financial incentives, new product development, and feelings of guilt leading to many consumers' desire to cut the greenhouse gas emissions that their consumption contributes to. Firms have been keen to associate with the cause of reducing greenhouse gas emissions, but how far would they go in helping the environment, or are they invariably guided by traditional corporate profit objectives? The DIY chain B&Q's decision in 2008 to end the sale of patio heaters at its stores illustrates the sometimes complex interplay between responsibility and profitability.

Patio heaters became a 'must have' accessory for many people during the prosperous years of the 1990s. For homeowners obsessed with style and obtaining the maximum utilization of their house space, a patio heater allowed use of their garden on chilly evenings. British people who had enjoyed alfresco eating in Benidorm could now enjoy the same on chilly evenings in Birmingham. Patio heaters were also a big hit with pubs, especially following bans on smoking in many countries. Pubs could still keep the trade of smokers, who could sit and smoke outside under a warm patio heater. According to the UK's Energy Saving Trust, there were 1.2 million patio heaters in the UK in 2007, and it predicted that within three years, this figure would almost double to 2.3 million.

Against this background of growing popularity among consumers, it may seem surprising that B&Q announced in January 2008 that it would stop selling patio heaters. Was it simply seeking favourable publicity, especially at a time when gas-powered patio heaters were drawing the wrath of environmentalists, who pointed out that each patio heater could emit as much carbon dioxide in a year as 1½ cars? Was it being altruistic in its concern for the environment? Or could there have been pragmatic business benefit of discontinuing patio heaters?

First, B&Q could have expected the profits of selling patio heaters to be gradually falling. They were no longer the new product which they were a decade earlier, and the company now faced competition for sales—and pressure on margins—from a wider range of retailers. Also, after a decade of falling energy prices, gas prices started to increase sharply from 2007; would patio heaters fall out of favour as they became more costly to operate?

More importantly, pressure was mounting in the EU for a ban on sales of patio heaters, which were seen as socially irresponsible. Was B&Q simply getting out while the going was still good? Did it foresee further government restrictions on the sale and use of such heaters, so if it got out now, it could gain the kudos for leading, rather than being pushed if it waited until later? Some cynics argued that B&Q had built up large stocks of patio heaters, and only committed itself to stop selling them when stocks ran out. Could the publicity have actually helped B&Q sell even more patio heaters than it would otherwise have done?

avoid the need for transport in the first place. The most ecologically responsible holiday is for an individual to stay at home. Individuals with a true concern for preserving their ecological environment would choose to reduce their consumption of goods and services in total. At the moment, such attitudes are held by only a small minority in western societies, but the development of a widespread anti-consumption mentality would have major implications for marketers.

There are two principal reasons why marketers should be concerned about ecological responsibility:

1. The general public has become increasingly aware of ecological issues and, more importantly, some segments have shown a greater willingness and ability to spend their money in a way which minimizes ecological harm (see Peattie and Peattie 2009). It has been suggested that concern for the ecological environment is a luxury which can be afforded by developed societies who have achieved their wealth. Some have questioned the morality of western developed nations seeking to restrict growth in the less developed countries by a imposing on them western standards of ecological protection.

2. There has been growing pressure on natural resources, including those that directly or indirectly are used in firms' production processes. This is evidenced by the extinction of species of animals and depletion of hardwood timber resources. As a result of overuse of natural resources, many industry sectors, such as North Sea fishing, have faced severe constraints on their production possibilities. The move towards sustainable resources implies that as resources are used in the consumption, they are replaced by freshly generated resources. In this way, timber grown in properly managed forests may be said to be sustainable, because a new tree will grow where an old one was felled. The use of other resources, such as oil, may be said to be unsustainable—when it is gone, it's gone, and it will take millions of years to create new oil. Many would argue that it is irresponsible of marketers to use unsustainable resources, when there are sustainable alternatives.

Marketers can face problems in coming to a view about what is ecologically responsible. Consumers (and marketers) may be confounded by alternative arguments about the consequences of their purchase decisions, with goods which were once considered to be environmentally 'friendly' suddenly becoming seen as enemies of the environment as knowledge and prejudice change (see marketing in action vignette on biodiesel fuels). Read the case study at the end of this chapter, and you might be surprised to hear that the chief executive of the airline Ryanair claimed to be a saviour for the ecological environment by using more efficient aircraft than its competitors.

Most consumers are not experts on ecological issues, and may therefore be easily persuaded by the most compellingly promoted argument, regardless of the technical merit of the case. Very often, a firm may have a technically sound case, but fail to win the hearts and minds of consumers who seem intent on believing the opposite argument that is in accordance with their own prejudices. For example, the nuclear power industry may claim to have won technical arguments about the much lower level of carbon dioxide emissions compared to fossil fuel energy sources, but many people remain implacably opposed to the concept of nuclear power.

Another confusing issue is the presumed benefits for the ecological environment of marketing new, efficient, low energy products. If we save ecological resources in one form of activity, will that simply leave us with spare money to use more resources in other forms of activity? Consider the example of cars. It is certainly true that for any class of car, the typical fuel consumption has dropped over the past decade or so. A family-sized car such as the Volkswagen Golf, which 20 years ago might have achieved 34 miles per gallon, today may achieve over 40. Unfortunately, the associated reduction in running costs of a car have meant that customers can now afford a bigger and better car, which will doubtless use more fuel. So over the past decade or so, the fastest growth in car sales to private consumers has been in larger sports utility vehicles and multi-people vehicles. It is as if individuals have a set proportion of their income that they allocate to transport. If the cost per mile of running their vehicle comes down, they may trade up to the larger 'luxury' vehicle. So although car manufacturers might have been acting responsibly by improving the efficiency of cars, this has sent an ambiguous signal to consumers, and the overall contribution to the ecological environment may be neutralized by consumers' changed patterns of expenditure. This apparently perverse effect has been seen in a number of other sectors. The ecological benefits of increasingly fuel-efficient aircraft have been partly offset by the resulting lower prices of air transport, leading to more people taking short-break holidays. The Boeing 737-800 series aircraft not only uses much less fuel than the original Boeing-737 of 20 years ago, but this has also allowed budget airlines to develop a whole new market of low-cost air travel. Friends of the Earth has estimated that half a billion tonnes of carbon dioxide was emitted by aircraft into the atmosphere in 2006, up on previous years, despite the development of more efficient aircraft engines. The advent of budget airlines may also have brought tourists flocking to previously underdeveloped areas, causing ecological damage in the process.

'Green marketing'

The term 'green marketing' has been used generically to describe marketing strategy and tactics which address green consumers' concerns for environmental issues (Charter and Polonsky 1999). From a product perspective, Schlegelmilch et al. (1996) identified a number of overlapping categories of green marketing: recycled products, products not tested on animals, organically-grown products, ozone-friendly products, and energy-efficient products. In addition to the ecological credentials of the focal product, the concept of green marketing has been applied to its promotional and protective packaging (Rooka and Uusitalo 2008) and transport and distribution (Carter and Rogers 2008).

'Green marketing' began to receive attention from marketing academics from the 1970s (Kassarjian 1971; Kotler and Levy 1969). The crystallization of latent concerns about ecological sustainability became prominent in many western countries from the 1980s, but initial expectations about rapid growth of the 'green' sector initially failed to materialize (Kalafatis et al. 1999; Peattie and Crane 2005). Even though increasing concern for the ecological environment by government, public, and commercial organizations has stimulated a growth of academic papers during the last two decades, it has been suggested that the topic is still in an evolving phase (Leonidou and Leonidou 2011).

From a consumer's perspective, green marketing implies a widening of pre- and post-consumption evaluation of a product to include not only costs and benefits that are directly attributable to them as a consumer, but also the external costs and benefits that occur in the broader ecological environment (Hepburn 2010).

The propensity for principles of green marketing to become pervasive has been related to a number of phenomena, including:

⊙ The wealth of a society, with some evidence that ecological concern may be regarded as a 'luxury' to be afforded when a society reaches a mature stage of economic development (Gurau and Ranchhod 2005).

⊙ Embedded cultures of a society, with an observation that respect for the ecological environment may be inherently stronger in societies with a collective, rather than an individualistic, market-based culture (Schumacher 2009).

⊙ Current manifestation of ecological concerns through the popular media, for example it has been noted that consumers' concern for the ecological environment has risen following events such as the discovery of a hole in the ozone layer.

⊙ Government policy has been instrumental in developing markets for ecologically sustainable products, for example through regulations requiring the use of recycled materials and through government procurement policies (Sarkar 2008).

⊙ Partly as a result of these phenomena, social norm has been observed to play an important role in the uptake of green products and to facilitate the transition of green products from market niche to mainstream (Peattie and Peattie 2009).

It has been observed that uptake of green products is balanced by the forces of green enthusiasts and those who are cynical of green claims (Mendelson and Polonsky 1995; Peattie and Crane 2005). The literature seeking to explain consumers' adoption of ecologically friendly products has predominantly taken the perspective of a logical and rational evaluation process, often based on the theory of reasoned action and the theory of planned behaviour (Chamorro et al. 2009). However, a number of studies have highlighted a gap between environmental concern and subsequent purchasing behaviour (Fraj and Martinez 2006; Lee and Holden 1999). There is evidence that a focus on logical and rational evaluations of green credentials of products is poor at explaining actual behaviour. For example, a study by Schlegelmilch et al. (1996) found that environmental conscience only explained 20 per cent of purchasing intentions of environmentally friendly products.

Opportunities for business arising from ecological concerns

The ecological environment can present opportunities as well as challenges for businesses. Proactive companies have capitalized on ecological issues by reducing their costs and/or improving their organizational image:

⊙ Many markets are characterized by segments that are prepared to pay a premium price for a product that has been produced in an ecologically sound manner. Some retailers, such as the Body Shop, have developed valuable niches on this basis. What starts off as a 'deep green' niche soon expands into a larger 'pale green' segment of customers who prefer ecologically sound products but are unwilling to pay such a high price premium. However, many companies may make token concessions to ecological responsibility without making any significant contribution to the ecological environment. Such 'greenwash' (or 'green tosh') is likely to be found out sooner or later, and the dishonesty of a company's claims may ultimately harm its reputation. On the other hand, many consumers are quite happy to go along with the crowd and to be seen 'doing something green' even if their actions have a negligible, or even harmful, effect. Somebody driving to a recycling centre to drop off an unwanted television may feel good about doing their bit for the environment, but they may actually cause more harmful consequences by driving their car. They may also fail to ask themselves why they didn't repair the television, thereby saving even more resources.

⦿ Being 'green' may actually save a company money. Often, changing existing environmentally harmful practices primarily involves overcoming traditional mindsets about how things should be done (e.g. fast-food chains using recycled packaging materials and overcoming a one-way logistics mindset by returning their waste materials for recycling) (see Unruh 2008).

⦿ In western developed economies, legislation to enforce environmentally sensitive methods of production is increasing. A company that adopts environmentally sensitive service processes ahead of compulsion can gain a competitive advantage.

⦿ The challenges of using resources in a more efficient and less polluting way has spurred research and development, and some companies have developed valuable niches. Wind turbines, solar panels, heat pumps, and carbon capture technology have presented tremendous opportunities for companies to improve the efficiency of a product and their marketing to business and consumers. For the future, there are many more new products awaiting further development, for example lightweight, long-life batteries for electric cars.

⦿ Ecological concerns may spur the development of completely new technologies, often with the support of government. Wind turbines presented a new opportunity in the early 21st century, which was exploited by aircraft manufacturing companies, among others. UK companies were relatively late to the scene, by which time competitive advantage had been gained by overseas manufacturers, and the one remaining large-scale wind turbine manufacturer based in the UK faced closure in 2009. However, the UK government saw advantages in being first to market with innovative 'carbon capture' technologies and in 2010 increased funding for research and development in this area.

Ethical responsibility

We now turn our attention to the broader subject of ethics, and the responsibilities of marketers to act according to a set of shared values, rather than simply pursuing short-term profits. Ethics has its roots in the study of philosophy, and for our purposes will be defined here as:

A philosophical framework within which decisions are made as to what constitutes right and wrong behaviour.

Marketing and social responsibility

Biodiesel—from clean and green to mean?

In 2006, 'biodiesel', derived from renewable agricultural crops, was hailed as a great way forward to reduce carbon emissions and avoid depletion of our finite resources of fossil fuels. In a world which would eventually run out of oil, the prospect of a renewable energy source which could be grown in clean and pleasant fields seemed like an answer from heaven. Moreover, biodiesel would have lower carbon dioxide emissions compared with alternative fossil fuels. The Virgin group, ever eager to gain a publicity advantage, announced that it would be converting part of its fleet of trains to run on biodiesel. The public were doubtless impressed by the ecological credentials of the boss of Virgin, Sir Richard Branson. They might just have seen through the hypocrisy of his attempts to save the planet by turning to bio fuels, while at the same time causing what many would regard as unnecessary and reckless ecological damage through his planned Virgin Galactica space travel project.

However, just a couple of years after Virgin's announcement, biodiesel had fallen out of favour with many groups. To many people, the analysis of carbon emission reductions was oversimplified and understated, for example destroying rainforest to make land available for bio fuels could actually increase greenhouse gas emissions. More seriously, there was a growing feeling that using agricultural crops to provide fuel for vehicles in the rich western countries would push up the price of basic food materials for people in developing countries. Was this ethical? Within a few months of Virgin seeking favourable reactions for its move to bio fuels, its rival, National Express, announced that it would be scaling back its project to use bio fuels. Did it have a better understanding of the reality of bio fuels and their likely future cost and availability? Had it responded to the publics' flip flop attitude on ecological issues, and sensed that a public now saw bio fuels as a problem rather than a solution?

However, it can be difficult to agree just what is right and wrong, because no two people have exactly the same opinions. It can also be difficult to distinguish between ethics and legality; for example it may not be strictly illegal to exploit the gullibility of children in advertisements, but it may nevertheless be unethical. Furthermore, culture has a strong influence on what is considered to be ethical, and culture's attitudes have a tendency to change over time, so that what is considered ethical today, may be considered unethical a few years later.

In western societies, ethical considerations confront business organizations on many occasions, as the following examples show:

- A food company may advertise a product and provide information which is technically correct, but omit to provide vital information about side effects associated with consuming the food. Should the company be required to spell out the possible problems of using its products, as well as the benefits?

- A dentist is short of money and diagnoses spurious problems which call for unnecessary medical treatment. How does he reconcile his need to maximize his earning potential with the need to provide what is best for his patient?

- In order to secure a major new construction contract, a salesperson must entertain the client's buying manager with a weekend all-expenses paid holiday. Should this be considered ethical business practice in Britain? Or in South America?

With expanding media availability and an increasingly media-literate audience, it is getting easier to expose examples of unethical business practice. Moreover, our expectations of business organizations are continually increasing. Many television audiences appear to enjoy watching programmes which reveal alleged unethical practices of household-name companies.

Firms are responding to increasing levels of ethical awareness by trying to put their own house in order. The following are some examples of how firms have gone about the task:

⊙ Many companies have identified segments of their market that are prepared to pay a premium price in order to buy a product that has been produced in an ethical manner, or from a company that has adopted ethical practices. In the food sector, many consumers would consider the treatment of cattle grown for meat to be inhuman and unethical and would be happy to buy from a supplier who they knew acted ethically in the manner in which the cattle were raised and slaughtered.

⊙ Greater attention to training can make clear to staff just what is expected of them, for example that it is unethical (and in the long term commercially damaging) for an insurance company's sales personnel to try and sell to a person a policy that doesn't really suit their needs. Training may emphasize the need to spend a lot of time finding out just what the true needs of the customer are.

⊙ More effective control and reward systems can help to reduce unethical practices within an organization. For example, sales personnel employed by a financial services company on a commission-only basis are more likely to try to sell a policy to a customer regardless of the customer's needs than a salaried employee who can take a longer-term view of the relationship between the company and its clients.

There are many documented cases to show that acting ethically need not conflict with a company's profit objectives, and indeed can add to profitability (e.g. Porter and Kramer 2006).

Some societies can effectively use social pressure to bring about compliance with ethical codes of conduct. For example, it has been noted that in many traditional Far Eastern cultures, the distinction between an individual's social role and their business role is less clearly defined than it would be in most western countries. Therefore, acting unethically in business may bring shame on an individual, which may be a powerful incentive to act ethically. In modern western societies, there tends to be a clearer distinction between an individual's work and social environments, therefore social pressures alone may be insufficient to bring about compliance.

Over time, the ethics of a society tend to be incorporated into its laws. Initially, a group of companies acting through a trade association may develop an industry sector code of conduct (Figure 3.1). Codes of conduct do not in themselves have the force of law, but they can be very important to businesses. In the first place, they can help to raise the standards of an industry by imposing a discipline on signatories to a code not to indulge in unethical marketing practices, which—although legal—act against the long-term interests of the industry and its customers. Second, business organizations are often happy to accept restrictions imposed by voluntary codes of practice as these are seen as preferable to restrictions imposed by laws. The tobacco industry in the UK for a long time avoided statutory controls on cigarette advertising because of the existence of its voluntary code which imposed restrictions on tobacco advertising. Third, voluntary codes of conduct can offer a cheaper and quicker means of resolving disputes between a company and its customers, compared with more formal legal channels.

One industry sector that has frequently been accused of unethical practice is the car repair business. As cars become increasingly sophisticated, the typical customer may have little knowledge about the precise nature of a problem with their car, and may have to trust the car repairer's diagnosis and their subsequent solution. It is not surprising, therefore, that there is often a knowledge imbalance, and some car repairers have been accused of acting unethically by talking customers into having repairs undertaken which are not really needed, and which the customer cannot realistically evaluate afterwards. Car repairers in the UK who subscribe to the voluntary code of the Vehicle Builders and Repairers Association agree, among other things, to: give clear estimates of prices; inform customers as soon as possible if additional costs are likely to be incurred; and complete work in a timely manner. In the event of a dispute between a customer and a member of the Association, a conciliation service is available which reduces the need to resort to legal remedies. However, in April 2005, the UK National Consumer Council accused the motor industry of failing to adequately regulate itself, by providing 'shoddy services and rip-off charges'. The council pledged to submit a 'super complaint' to the Office of Fair Trading (OFT), which would force the OFT to investigate its allegations, unless the industry took prompt remedial action. This raised the possibility of a licensing system for car repairers, something which the industry had resisted so far and realized would be more onerous than a voluntary code of conduct.

Marketing's responsibility for customers' privacy and security

In a technological environment in which information about customers can be very quickly collected and disseminated, concerns have been expressed about the privacy of consumers and the security of data that is held about them. Firms have a responsibility to respect customers' privacy and their personal data, and this moral responsibility is increasingly being enshrined in codes of conduct and legislation.

There is nothing new in consumers' expectations that companies will treat their personal data as confidential and ensure its safe storage. Stories of banks' unshredded confidential waste being left out in the street where criminals as well as refuse collectors can obtain it have raised alarm among consumers. Today, personal information is likely to be held on servers which are accessible remotely by a range of authorized employees and unauthorized hackers. Instead of having to laboriously break into several bank branches to obtain large volumes of customer data, there have been many reported cases (and probably many more unreported cases) of skilled hackers being able to get into a bank's database and view the records of thousands or even millions of customers (*Financial Times* 2007). Where customer information is held on transportable discs, huge amounts of data can accidentally or deliberately end up in the wrong hands. In November 2007, many people in the UK were concerned to hear that the Government had 'lost' two CDs containing personal information of 25 million recipients of government benefits. There was concern that this information could be used by criminals wrongly to impersonate another person and obtain credit or benefits to which they were not entitled.

There is also concern by some consumers that their personal data may be used irresponsibly, if not in a criminal way, certainly in a way that they would consider unethical. Junk mail,

Figure 3.1 **In market sectors which are dominated by basically similar product offers, an ethical positioning may give a business a competitive advantage in the eyes of some customer segments.** Many people would regard the major coffee shop chains as being essentially similar in what they offer, and many customers may question the disparity between the seemingly high price charged to consumers for a cup of coffee and the low price that third world producers receive for raw coffee beans. Starbucks has developed a loyal following of customers for whom the atmosphere of its stores warrants a premium price. However, the company is conscious of critics who point to low prices paid to producers, and addresses this by offering 'Fairtrade' certified coffee. Not only does Fairtrade ensure farmers receive a fair price for their harvest it also guarantees an additional social premium. The Fairtrade premium is a sum of money paid on top of the agreed Fairtrade price for investment in social, environmental, or economic development projects, decided upon democratically by producers within the farmers' organization or by workers on a plantation. Starbucks' goal is one hundred per cent ethically sourced coffee by 2015. For many western consumers, this ethical positioning is a basis for differentiating Starbucks from other coffee shops.
(Reproduced with kind permission of Starbucks Coffee Company.)

spam email, and uninvited telephone sales calls may be considered intrusive by many, and can result from a company using personal data for a purpose for which it was never originally intended or authorized. Of course much 'junk mail' is welcomed, and a survey by the Direct Marketing Association even claimed that a majority of UK consumers actually liked receiving it (DMA 2007). However, most consumers would expect that if they gave their personal information and contact details to a bank when they took out a new credit card, the bank would act responsibly and not then pass on this information to a double glazing company who would use the details to make sales calls to them.

Intrusive advertising messages may be linked to 'guerrilla marketing'. This has been defined as a way of getting a message through to the target audience when the audience would least be expecting a selling message (Levinson 2007). Instead of perceptually filtering out what might be seen as a sales message, the target may be more amenable to persuasion. When guerrilla tactics are linked to the Internet, the results can be even more ethically questionable, as illustrated by the case of FriendGreetings.com. The company had built up a list of email addresses and thousands of people followed its link to a greeting card which the company claimed was waiting for the recipient. Users were then invited to install an ActiveX control in order to view their e-card. Two lengthy end user licence agreements were displayed stating that by running the application the user is giving permission for a similar email to be sent to all addresses found in the user's Outlook address book. Of course, most users would not bother to read the licence agreement and therefore allowed numerous unwanted emails to be sent from their email address. Such a 'worm', which creates a flood of unwanted emails can be just as much a nuisance as a virus. Guerrilla tactics had achieved their aim of attracting attention. As the message took the form of an e-card sent by somebody that the user knew, they did not suspect that clicking onto the link would result in anything untoward occurring.

Would you consider the practices of companies such as FriendGreetings.com to be responsible marketing? Would such practices be self-defeating because the company would simply acquire a bad reputation for itself? Is it right that 999 people could be inconvenienced so that the company can get profitable business from just 1 person out of each 1,000 that it targets? Is it possible to stop practices of this type, after all users had technically given permission for a worm to get into their computer, even if the request was deviously hidden in a lengthy licence agreement?

The issue of privacy has also been raised by firms' attempts to collect information about them in a covert way. Marketers have used technology to covertly probe individuals' behaviour, but critics have argued that 'Big Brother' techniques may be exploiting consumers without their agreement. Many users of the Internet may be unaware that cookies lodged in their computer are 'spying' on them, trying to understand their buying behaviour. So when an Internet service provider flashes a banner advert for car rental on a user's screen, it may not have appeared by chance, but an analysis of their previous search behaviour that led the system to deduce that the user was in the process of looking for a rental car. Similarly, close circuit television (CCTV) has been used by researchers to study how people move around a supermarket and the processes used in searching for products. Would you be happy in the knowledge that all of your indecisions, strained facial expressions, and bad tempers were being recorded, possibly to be replayed over and over again by researchers? In a nation which has been gripped by voyeuristic 'reality' television programmes such as 'Big Brother', it is not surprising that businesses should also try and gain a better insight into behaviour that might previously have been considered private. But how far is it responsible for marketers to go in their pursuit of these better insights? And at what point does it become intrusive and irresponsible?

The response of marketers' to issues of privacy and security has followed the familiar pattern of some firms developing best practice which has then been used as a basis for industry association codes of conduct, and where these have not worked, legislation has followed.

The first stage of this process, developing best practice, may be achieved by companies in a sector which has the profit margins (and the client base) to support their efforts at doing more than the minimum required by legislation. Within the banking sector, a bank such as Coutts which has targeted high wealth individuals with high expectations about privacy could afford to implement more rigorous security and privacy procedures than a bank targeting mass market customers with more basic banking services. Over time, the standards of the upmarket banks would be expected to filter down to other banks, as customers' expectations rise. Widespread evidence of bad practice within a sector may lead the key players in the sector to cooperate in the development of a shared code of conduct which will avoid the whole sector being tarnished by the bad practice of a few firms. In the case of the banking sector, this has been achieved through the Banking Code, developed and monitored by the British Banking Association (www.bba.org.uk). This includes, among other things, a responsibility of member banks who subscribe to the code to treat customers' personal information as private and confidential, and operate secure and reliable banking and payment systems.

Voluntary codes of conduct have not managed to protect individuals' privacy in all sectors at all times, and one consequence of this failure has been legislation which all designated companies must comply with. Within the EU, the *European Convention for Individuals with regard to Automatic Processing of Personal Data*, implemented through Directive 95/46/EC provides a framework for data privacy and security. This has been implemented in the UK in the 1988 Data Protection Act, and policed by the Data Protection Commissioner. The Act covers electronically stored data which can be used to identify a living person, including names, birthday and anniversary dates, addresses, telephone numbers, fax numbers, email addresses, etc. A number of principles guide companies' use of data, and require, among other things, that personal data shall be processed fairly and lawfully, and shall not be used for any purpose which is not compatible with the original purpose. There is a requirement for companies to keep accurate records which are not unnecessarily excessive in detail, and should not be kept for longer than is necessary for the purpose of collecting it. Appropriate technical and organizational measures must be taken against unauthorized or unlawful processing of personal data and against its accidental loss or destruction.

Legislation and voluntary codes of conduct can provide a dilemma for marketing managers who must reconcile the need to protect individuals' privacy and security with the need to make goods and services easily available. The only really secure way of holding data is to create a barrier to the outside world which nobody can penetrate. The only really secure form of Internet banking is a system which is not accessible from outside a bank's offices. Of course, this would defeat the whole purpose of Internet banking, and firms will find themselves reducing the barriers to access from the outside world, which improves accessibility for legitimate customers, but also facilitates unauthorized access. Some customers may be reassured by lengthy security procedures to gain access to their account. Others may simply give up and either not buy, or go elsewhere.

Marketing's responsibilities to vulnerable people

We have seen that the basic principles of marketing are based on an assumption that customers know what they want and are able to evaluate the extent to which a product will meet their needs. Unfortunately, many people may not be able or willing to make a proper evaluation of a product and its likely impact on their physical and mental well-being. Some people may find themselves excluded from being able to buy in a market, leading to undesirable social consequences. Marketing managers are frequently faced with issues about what responsibilities, if any, they should have towards people who may not be able to make a free and fully informed choice by themselves.

The term *vulnerable customer* can be loosely used to describe any individual over whom a company has a high level of power which leaves the individual unable to apply their own judgement effectively. When anybody is taken out of their comfort zone or their area of expertise or knowledge base, they can potentially become vulnerable. In the UK, a 2007 report of an All Party Parliamentary Enquiry on Corporate Responsibility identified a number of generic bases for defining categories of vulnerable customers:

Vulnerabilities of personality: An inherent factor within someone that makes them vulnerable to falling into consumption patterns that do them harm, for example gamblers, alcoholics, people with eating disorders.

Vulnerabilities of experience/understanding: Where either lack of worldly experience or barriers to understanding leave people vulnerable to people or processes that may harm them, for example children, people without financial education or maturity, people without good language or literacy skills.

Vulnerabilities of physical disorders: Where physical reactions to normal circumstances may lead to harm, for example people with allergies, immunity deficiency, certain disabilities.

Vulnerabilities of access: Where lack of financial resources or other barriers to accessing key basic services exist, leading to harm that goes beyond mere inconvenience.

The parliamentary committee report suggested that commercial organizations owed responsibilities towards these vulnerable groups. It pointed to a number of examples of good business practice, including Barclays Bank which had introduced a basic bank account for groups who would not normally be accepted for full banking services. The bank had consulted extensively to ensure that this basic bank account met the target users' needs. It also pointed favourably to the mobile phone company O_2's policies towards children. Children were considered vulnerable, on account of the potential health risks, and their uncritical acceptance of advertising claims. The company worked with the Home Office and children's charities to draw up a Code of Practice to regulate the provision of content on mobile phones, for example any commercial content rated '18' has to be behind content controls, which can only be accessed by someone verified to be over 18. O_2 agreed to a policy of only advertising in magazines or between television programmes where more than 50% of the audience is over 16.

Companies may attempt to develop voluntary codes of practice towards vulnerable groups, but in fiercely competitive markets this may be difficult to achieve, in which case

....

E-Marketing

Taking a punt online

The gambling industry in the UK is substantial, with a turnover of over £84 billion in 2006/07 (Gambling Commission 2009). The most popular gambling activities in 2007 were the National Lottery Draw (57 per cent had participated in the past year), scratchcards (20 per cent), betting on horse races (17 per cent), and playing slot machines (14 per cent).

The use of traditional gambling methods in Britain, such as horse racing and slot machines has been in long-term decline. But, this masks a significant increase in online gambling, which according to research undertaken by Nielsen//NetRatings, increased by 45 per cent in just one year, from 2004 to 2005, when 3.2 million people were estimated to have visited an online gambling site. In 2007, Gambling Commission statistics estimated that 6 per cent of the population had used an Internet site for gambling, The National Lottery was the most popular online gambling site for punters, making it one of the top 40 most visited sites in the UK. William Hill came in second, followed by Partypoker.com.

The appeal of online service to gambling companies is overwhelming. Nielsen//NetRatings said UK growth has been driven by a range of gambling, betting, and online casino sites, and not just by the National Lottery. The firm's research showed that UK gamblers were attracted by the speed and convenience of betting online, and the availability of broadband Internet access greatly increased take-up of online gambling. The average gambler spent 20 minutes on a website.

Many of the traditional high street betting shops have developed a web presence, where they have much lower transaction costs compared to their town-centre and racecourse shops, for which they have to pay high overheads. By moving their customers online, the overhead costs of running a branch network can be greatly reduced. Companies can also use the Internet to overcome problems of inseparability by locating their operations in obscure offshore countries where taxation is lower. By going online, betting companies can get access to customers who might not traditionally have considered visiting a betting shop. The Internet also allows access to groups of people who may otherwise be prevented by law from being served. The Internet recognizes no international boundaries, and it has proved difficult to prevent citizens of a country where gambling is illegal from using a gambling website based in another country. It can also in practice be much more difficult to prevent access to under-age players, whose identity cannot be as readily established online as face to face.

Above all else, gambling companies like to go online because of the addictive nature of the Internet. Once an individual achieves a state of 'flow', they have a tendency to distort time and lose self-consciousness. Gambling meets many of the criteria for establishing flow, especially the interactivity of challenges and the rapid feedback.

Of course, online gambling has raised many ethical and legal issues. Many countries restrict access to gambling services, in the belief that they may be associated with a range of social disorders. However, the nature of the Internet makes the medium both particularly attractive to gambling operators and, at the same time, particularly difficult to control. The US government, frustrated by the inability of its anti-gambling laws to control offshore online operations, has resorted to a number of more indirect approaches to control these companies, including making it illegal for American banks to carry out transactions with such companies, and effectively preventing executives of the gambling companies from visiting the USA for fear of being arrested.

Is online gambling the perfect business model for online service delivery? Is the market so attractive that competition between companies would inevitably intensify, forcing down profitability? Or would intense competition result in even more devious practices being used to make customers addicted to gambling online? Given the international environment in which online companies cross national borders, how could governments hope to regulate this sector? Indeed, should it be regulated?

legislation may be imposed. As an example, gas, water, and electricity suppliers in the UK must comply with the government regulator Ofgem's guidelines before they can withhold supplies from certain designated vulnerable groups.

Marketing's responsibility to employees

We saw in Chapter 1 that for many firms, especially service-based firms, marketing cannot easily be separated from human resource management. Where customers mainly judge a company on the basis of its front-line personnel, the recruitment, training monitoring, and rewarding of employees should be something that the marketing department has a strong influence over, even if the marketing manager does not have final authority. It should also follow that the marketing manager owes some responsibility for the welfare of employees. Again, a fine balance often has to be made between what customers want, and what a responsible employer should provide for its employees. There is a widely held view that if employees are not happy with their jobs, customers will never be uppermost in their minds. Nevertheless, many have recognized the three-way fight between the firm, the employees, and the customer. Delivering goods and services is thus a 'compromise between partially conflicting parties' (Bateson 1989).

In less developed countries with abundant supplies of low cost and replaceable labour, employees have been expected to carry out tasks for customers which would be considered irresponsible in western developed countries. Circus acts in India, for example, have involved employees being shot from canons and performing dare devil stunts on motorbikes without safety equipment. Customers may have loved the acts, the employee may have welcomed the money they earned, but is it responsible for marketing to promote something which involves high levels of risk to employees?

Two recent issues illustrate the influences of responsibilities towards employees on the marketing function. First, many service-based companies have been keen to allow smoking in their establishments, on the basis that this is what a significant number of their customers want. For those customers who prefer to be in a smoke free environment, separate non-smoking areas can be offered. But what about the effects of smoke on the health of employees who serve customers in a smoky environment? There is growing evidence of the effects of passive smoking on individuals who are in the vicinity of smokers, so is it responsible for a firm to expose employees to such risk? In 2007, a ban on smoking was introduced in public places in England, Scotland, and Wales. Some companies had already voluntarily introduced bans, but following the ban some companies, such as Gala Bingo reported sharp falls in revenue, as smokers stayed at home where they were free to smoke. Without a change in the law, would marketers have been happy to go on satisfying their smoking customers' needs, while putting the health of their employees at risk? A second example which is currently exercising the minds of many marketing managers is the issue of 24/7 access to goods and services. What happens when a company's customers want access to its goods and services 24 hours a day, and they want immediate access, not a promise of delivery tomorrow or some time in the future? One consequence is often stress at work for those who are charged with responding to a company's promises which it must make if it is to stay alive in a competitive business environment. The 24/7 culture has had a big impact on employees' lifestyles, with many individuals having to adjust to varying and often unsocial shift patterns. Research undertaken by the Future Foundation (2004) predicted that by 2020, over 13 million people in the UK will be operating in an out-of-hours economy (outside the traditional Monday–Friday hours of 9 am–6 pm), compared to the seven million who did so in 2003 (Figure 3.2).

Another study, by the British Industrial Society, showed that juggling home and work demands was a major source of stress for 70 per cent of respondents, while half cited unrealistic deadlines and constant time pressures as an additional factor (British Industrial Society 2001). The Future Foundation research found that while relatively wealthy customers benefit from 24/7 service availability, the down side of a vibrant 24/7 economy is an army of low-paid staff, many working for little above minimum wage, often trying to juggle multiple part-time jobs with study or looking after children. Responsible employers have sought to alleviate stress, setting standards for others to follow. This has not been entirely altruistic, as companies have recognized hidden costs to their operations which can result from high levels of stress at work. However, in some fiercely competitive business sectors, a voluntary approach to stress management has been insufficient, so the law (in the UK the Health and Safety at Work Regulations 1999, specifically Regulations 3, 4, 13, and 19) is now requiring them to take some responsibility for employees' stress at work.

Marketing's responsibility for preserving the competitiveness of markets

Marketing is all about markets—the space where buyers and sellers come together and where market forces ensure that buyers have available to them a wide choice of products, and they choose the products of the seller who offers them the best value. Unfortunately, fiercely competitive markets can be bad news for sellers, who may have their work cut out raising their efficiency and lowering their costs so that they can offer better value to discerning buyers than is offered by their competitors. Most business people would publicly acknowledge that competitive markets are a good thing, but quietly, many would be only too happy to come to an agreement with their competitors to limit the amount of competition between them. For sellers, a cosy 'cartel' between them will put less pressure on them to reduce their costs. For buyers, the consequence would most likely be less choice

Figure 3.2 **Visitors to the Oktoberfest beer festival in Munich come away with memories of the beer and the barmaids.** The festival is made memorable by the distinctive dress worn by barmaids which combines tradition with visual appeal (especially to men, who make up a large part of the festival's market). The barmaids' dress, known as a 'dirndl', comprises a figure-hugging dress and apron with a tight, low-cut top. The sight of a barmaid dressed in a dirndl and carrying several glasses of beer helps to create a distinctive atmosphere for the festival, leading to visitors coming back year after year. Customers love the dress, festival managers love it, and apparently the barmaids do too. But some health professionals have expressed concern that the barmaid's low cut dress and short sleeves unnecessarily exposes them to the strong Bavarian sunshine, leading to increased risk of skin cancer. In the UK alone about 70,000 new cases of skin cancer are diagnosed each year. If an employer leaves scantily dressed employees exposed to the sun, they could face possible legal action by employees who subsequently develop skin cancer. Is it responsible of marketers to cater to customers' needs by insisting that staff wear skimpy clothes? How does a company strike a balance between the two apparently conflicting sets of needs? In the absence of voluntary action by employers to minimize the risks involved, the law may intervene. In 2006 the EU proposed an Optical Radiation Directive, by which employers of staff who work outdoors, such as those in Munich's beer gardens, must ensure that staff are protected against the risk of sunburn. Contrary to many newspaper reports, the EU directive does not specifically require Bavarian barmaids (or outdoor workers elsewhere) to cover up their low cut dresses. But an employer must undertake a risk assessment and take appropriate action.

(*Source:* © sehenswerk www.yaymicro.comww.yaymicro.com)

and/or higher prices. Is it responsible for marketers to seek to undermine the power of market forces?

Consider the case of fruit and vegetable markets, which in many towns would comprise several stallholders competing against each other on price and quality. Now just imagine that the market was the only source of food for miles around, and all the traders in it got together to agree prices that they would charge. They may agree, for example, that instead of them all selling a wide range of fruit and vegetables, each trader would sell only two or three ranges, thereby reducing their operating costs and reducing the amount of competition for each product. When customers visit the market, they will initially find less choice, and also prices would most likely have risen, because of the reduced level of competition for each product. This simple example may sound like an unrealistic scenario, but such collusion between suppliers is the basis for many attempts by businesses to undermine the power of markets, and to leave consumers worse off than they otherwise might have been.

A fine balance often exists between cooperation among firms which leads to lower prices/ better products for consumers, and irresponsible cooperation which leads to collusion and a reduction in consumers' choice. Cooperation between companies may result in greater benefits for consumers, for example life is made easier for bank customers who can use their ATM card at the ATMs of competing banks, and not just the bank which issued the card. However, government regulators at national (and EU) levels are increasingly taking action against irresponsible actions by businesses which have the effect of restricting competition in a market. Recent cases investigated have highlighted irresponsible and illegal behaviour by many well-known companies.

- In 2009, a UK Competition Commission enquiry concluded that the airports operator BAA had significant monopoly power, especially in the London area, and was ordered to sell both Gatwick and Stansted airports, and also either Glasgow or Edinburgh. However, BAA issued an initially successful challenge through the Competition Appeal Tribunal, accusing the competition commission decision of 'apparent bias'.

- In 2007, The Office of Fair Trading (OFT) fined British Airways £121.5 million for colluding with Virgin Atlantic over the imposition of fuel surcharges. British Airways and Virgin appeared to increase their charges in step from when they were first introduced in May 2004. British Airways introduced a £2.50 surcharge on 13 May and Virgin did the same thing six days later. By April 2006, both airlines were charging £35 extra on a long-haul flight. In addition to the fine, British Airways was faced with a potential compensation bill of £80 million from customers who had been overcharged. Virgin escaped a fine from the regulator, because it had 'blown the whistle' on the price fixing arrangement and provided evidence for the OFT. The investigation revealed a number of bad practices within British Airways, and shortly after publication of the report, the commercial director and communications director of BA resigned.

- Abuse of monopoly power can also occur at a local level. The Competition Commission has investigated several alleged abuses of monopoly power by local bus companies. In the

Lancashire town of Preston, for example, the bus operator Stagecoach acquired Preston Bus in 2009, prompting an investigation by the Competition Commission which found evidence of a monopoly situation which was against the public interest, and therefore ordered the Scottish-based Stagecoach to sell its recent acquisition.

These cases illustrate the growing expectations of regulators that marketers should act responsibly by putting consumers' interest above what may be a natural desire to control a market. Actually detecting irresponsible behaviour by marketers in the first place can be quite difficult. If all airlines change their fuel surcharge at the same time, is this evidence of collusion, or are they all simply responding simultaneously to the same external price pressures? Often, collusion is only revealed when one party decides to inform the regulatory authorities about what is going on. In return for being a 'whistleblower', an organization may escape punishment, in the way that Virgin Atlantic did not face the fines imposed on British Airways. Virgin could also claim to be acting in the public interest by exposing irresponsible practices, even though it had initially been part of that practice.

Responsible communication

The final aspect of responsible marketing that we will consider is in respect of firms' communication. In an ideal world, a company would act responsibly, and communicate honestly with its customers and key stakeholders. Unfortunately, there are too many cases where a company acts in an irresponsible manner, and then uses communication dishonestly to try and portray itself as acting responsibly. Responsibility in communication can be analysed at two levels: at a strategic level, whereby the company communicates an overall image of responsibility; and at a more tactical level, which involves the company acting responsibly in the way it communicates specific product features to its customers. We will look at these in turn.

Companies often go to great lengths in their communication to associate their brand with responsibility. Some organizations, such as the Body Shop, Innocent Smoothies, and Starbucks have associated themselves with good causes, and appeal to segments of customers who are happy paying a few pennies more for the peace of mind, or social recognition which may come from association with a socially responsible brand. Starbucks, for example, has gone out of its way by stressing its social responsibility through the use of 'Fairtrade' coffee. It has been suggested that organizations may be quite keen to support good causes which are popular with the public in general, or the particular groups of customers that they target. Many consumer goods companies, for example, have supported child and animal welfare charities, knowing that this will be popular with their target audiences. However, there may be other groups, such as refugees or the mentally ill, that represent even more deserving cases for a company to be associated with, but in general these groups have been shunned by the corporate sector.

Of course, where a company communicates a message to support a good cause, but does not in fact deliver its promise, this can add to criticism of the company by pressure groups who can now accuse it not only of the original bad practice, but also hypocrisy and dishonesty. In the case of companies making unjustified claims about their ecological responsibility, these claims may be dismissed as 'green wash' or 'green tosh'.

Communicating a position of responsibility can be a very long-term process, and a company cannot expect instant results from attempts to promote an image of responsibility. The true level of perceived responsibility can be tested during a crisis, when investigative journalists may dig deep into a company's past in the hope of digging up bad practice, which may help create a further news story to add to the crisis which a company finds itself in. A company which had a consistent policy of acting responsibly would have little to worry about, but a company with a record of bad practice cannot expect a short burst of public relations to overcome its problems. For example, the train crash that occurred in the UK at Hatfield, involving a London–Edinburgh train in 2000 came following a series of widely reported failures by the privatized Railtrack company, which was perceived as putting profits before safety. The crash, in which four people were killed, appeared to be an indication of everything that was wrong with Railtrack. Partly because of the public's general distrust of Britain's railway operators, the industry, through its regulatory agencies, was forced to respond with drastic and costly measures, including system wide speed restrictions. The industry was under intense scrutiny by a media which sensed that more bad practice would be found if it looked hard enough. It took several years for the sector to recover its trust in the eyes of its users. Railtrack, which was seen as incompetent, while rewarding its directors and shareholders, was subsequently taken into state ownership. By contrast, the coach operator National Express had a long history of safe operation, with very few major causes for complaints by its customers. It had been a long while since the public had read stories of overcrowded coaches travelling at excessive speed, driven by poorly trained, overworked, and tired drivers. When one of the company's coaches crashed in January 2007, killing two passengers and injuring several others, the media was generally sympathetic to the company. Senior executives were made available to answer media questions, the company provided an efficient and effective helpline for customers and the relatives of those affected. Above all else, the company had invested in a good reputation and even the most adversarial investigative reporters could not find a history of irresponsible management to prolong the crisis and open a 'can of worms' which would come back to haunt the company.

On some occasions, industry groups have got together to communicate a message of responsibility for the sector as a whole. As an example, many pub operators and alcoholic drinks manufacturers in the UK are members of the Portman Group, which has used a levy on members to pay for an advertising campaign to promote responsible drinking. One reason why members of the group are keen to promote social responsibility in drinking is to deter potentially harmful new legislation, such as restricted opening hours of pubs, or higher taxes on beer, which could harm members' interests (Figure 3.3). Industry wide communication of responsible behaviour may work where there is a consensus within the sector, but may be difficult to achieve where this consensus is lacking. For example, the British Retail Federation had difficulty in communicating its members' views on proposed food labelling regulations, because its members were divided over what would be the best policy to pursue. If a sector cooperates too closely to communicate its views, it may be accused of illegally operating a cartel which has the effect of restricting consumers' choice (see above).

Figure 3.3 **Like many bars, this one loudly promotes a 'happy hour' period during which alcohol is sold at a reduced price.** For pub operators, such promotions may be vital to boost turnover, especially if all bars in the area are offering equally low prices. Unfortunately, one consequence of cheap alcohol and 'buy one, get one free' offers is an increase in 'binge drinking', with many town centres becoming noisy and violent areas at night-time, fuelled by excessive drinking. For any individual pub, how does it balance the need for aggressive price promotion to customers with the need to appear socially responsible, for fear of further government regulation of the sector? Adverts for alcohol now routinely include warnings about the consequences for the customer of excessive drinking, but often in much smaller print than the main price information. Should a pub simply stop '2 for 1' offers and earn a higher margin on a smaller volume of sales? Although this may seem to be a responsible and profitable approach, it is unlikely to work if other pubs continue with their cheap beer promotions—determined drinkers will simply make their way to the cheapest pub, or pick up their beer at a nearby supermarket. To illustrate the complexity of the task facing the sector, bar owners in some towns have voluntarily got together to try and agree collectively to stop price promotions that many believe lead to binge drinking. Agreement of all bar owners would be crucial, because otherwise drinkers would simply find the cheapest outlet, and other bars would be forced to cut their prices defensively to retain business. But did government see this as an example of good, socially motivated cooperation? Not the Office of Fair Trading, which gave a veiled threat to a group of Essex bar owners that they could be prosecuted for operating a cartel by agreeing to keep prices artificially high.

Issues about responsibility in communications also affect organizations at a much more operational level. Indeed, it could be argued that the long-term image communicated by a company is largely determined by a series of possibly isolated tactical communications. The issue of responsibility in everyday advertising is of regular concern to companies and the general public at large. Three or four decades ago, UK companies might have been able to get away with advertising claims which, while not factually incorrect, were misleading because they may have missed out vital information. They may also have been able to get away with statements that are today considered socially unacceptable (for example adverts which are demeaning to women or ethnic minorities may have been considered acceptable then, but are not now).

In the UK, there are a number of voluntary codes which set standards for responsible advertising. The two most important codes affecting advertisers are administered by the Advertising Standards Authority (ASA) through two Committees of Advertising Practice: CAP-Broadcast (responsible for the TV and radio advertising) and CAP-Non-broadcast (responsible for non-broadcast advertisements, sales promotions, and direct marketing). The ASA codes are subscribed to by most organizations involved in advertising, including the Advertising Association, the Institute of Practitioners in Advertising, and the associations representing publishers of newspapers and magazines, the outdoor advertising industry, and direct marketing.

The Code of Advertising Practice (Non-broadcast) requires that all advertisements appearing in members' publications should be legal, honest, decent, and truthful. A case considered by the ASA in 2008 illustrates how the ASA interprets this. An advert in the *Daily Mail* for Ryanair under the headline 'Hottest back to school fares . . . one way fares £10' featured a picture of a teenage girl or woman standing in a classroom and wearing a version of a school uniform consisting of a short tartan skirt, a cropped short sleeved shirt and tie and long white socks. The ASA considered the model's clothing, together with the setting of the ad in a classroom strongly suggested she was a schoolgirl and considered that her appearance and pose, in conjunction with the heading 'Hottest', appeared to link teenage girls with sexually provocative behaviour. It considered the advert was likely to cause serious or widespread offence, and in breach of the Code's sections governing social responsibility and decency.

Numerous other forms of voluntary controls on advertising exist. Some professional trade associations have codes which impose restrictions on how they can advertise. Solicitors, for example, were previously not allowed to advertise at all, but now can do so within limits defined by the Law Society.

In general, the system of voluntary regulation of advertising has worked well in the UK. For advertisers, voluntary codes can allow more flexibility and opportunities to have an input to the code. However, the Control of Misleading Advertisements Regulations 1988 (as amended) provides the legislative back-up to the self-regulatory system in respect of advertisements which mislead. The Regulations require the Office of Fair Trading (OFT) to investigate complaints, and empower the OFT to seek, if necessary, an injunction from the courts against publication of an advertisement. In the case of television advertising, the Office of Communications (Ofcom) is the statutory regulator for broadcast advertising in the UK and has delegated its powers to the ASA. In addition, there are a number of laws that influence the content of advertisements in Britain. For example, the Trade Descriptions Act makes false statements in an advertisement an offence, while the Consumer Credit Act lays down quite precise rules about the way in which credit can be advertised.

Irresponsible communication by companies is about more than just misleading advertising. Many companies have been criticized for using dubious, high pressure sales techniques (see marketing in action case below). Again, such practices may not be strictly illegal, but society has increasingly high expectations about the behaviour of sales people. In previous times, a buyer who had made a bad purchase may have blamed themselves, but today, they may argue that the salesperson was irresponsible in selling them something which the salesperson knew was not suitable for the customer. Irresponsible selling may eventually cost the company money in terms of the poor reputation it gains, and possible fines from regulatory bodies.

Marketing and social responsibility

Irresponsible selling of payment protection insurance

Companies can sometimes be too eager to promote products that are not at all suitable for customers. Many sales people have responded to bonus incentives offered by their employers to vigorously achieve sales which looked good at the time, but later came back to haunt the company. One of the key characteristics of a good salesperson is their ability to listen and to gain a good understanding of a buyer's needs. But what happens when the product on sale is complex and the buyer doesn't have the willingness or ability to understand exactly what they are buying? Furthermore, what happens when you couple this with a sales person who would rather earn his sales commission as easily as possible than probe the true needs of the customer? The result has been a series of mis-selling scandals that have tarnished the reputation of a number of business sectors, especially financial services.

In the early 2000s, Payment Protection Insurance (PPI) became the latest financial product to be associated with irresponsible selling. The purpose of PPI is to cover loan or credit card repayments in the event of a borrower suffering an accident, sickness, or unemployment. It was estimated in 2008 that there were around 20 million PPI policies in the UK, generating over £5 billion a year for the companies involved (www.moneysavingexpert.com 2008). There is nothing wrong with the principle of PPI, which can give valuable peace of mind to individuals who suddenly find that they cannot afford to repay their loan when they become unemployed. Unfortunately, many PPI policies were sold by sales staff who did not undertake a rigorous analysis of whether the policy was right for a customer. In many cases, a buyer would pay for a policy, but hidden in the small print would be clauses that would effectively prevent them from ever being able to make a claim on the policy. For example, self-employed people would most likely not be covered against unemployment, and many sales people might have not mentioned that the policy would not pay out for existing medical conditions. A seller should have enquired about a customer's medical history, but many skipped over this, eager to earn their commission.

The term caveat emptor ('let the buyer be aware') has been used to excuse the situation where a sales person sold an individual an item that was not at all suited to their needs. It was assumed to be the buyer's fault for buying wrongly, rather the seller's fault for selling wrongly. The balance is now tilting in the consumer's favour as society's expectations of sellers rise. The Financial Services Authority (FSA) has a strict code of conduct which regulated sellers of financial services must follow. The Financial Services Authority guidelines require that a seller must establish the needs of a seller before completing a sale. Clearly, in the case of many PPI policies, these guidelines had not been complied with. The over-enthusiastic selling of PPI policies resulted in big fines being imposed by the FSA, and thousands of compensation claims from customers who claimed that they had been mis-sold a policy that was worthless to them. Companies were forced to rethink the way they managed their sales personnel, but this really just involved going back to traditional best practice for the sales force—listening to the customer and understanding what they really need; training the sales force with greater product knowledge; and structuring their rewards to recognize a balance between the need for short-term incentives and long-term relationships.

◉ Chapter summary and linkages to other chapters

The aim of this chapter has been to provide a counterbalance to the first two chapters of this book which have portrayed marketing managers as single mindedly seeking to satisfy customers' needs as a means of meeting their organizations' objectives. This chapter has shown how listening to customers and supplying them with what they say they want might actually be considered irresponsible and this chapter has reviewed reasons why this might be so. Marketers are increasingly being expected to act responsibly with a high standard of ethics. It usually makes sound business sense for a marketer to act responsibly rather than irresponsibly. Where there is a tendency for marketers to act irresponsibly, voluntary industry sector codes of conduct may help to raise standards throughout the sector. If this is insufficient incentive to change firms' behaviour, the law may subsequently force companies to change.

Just as Chapters 1 and 2 were integrative chapters in defining the tasks and processes of marketing, this chapter is also integrative. Responsibility permeates all aspects of marketing, so we will return to the subject when we look at responsibility in promotion (Chapter 11); responsible pricing (Chapter 9); problems of abuse of power within a distribution channel (Chapter 10); and product design (Chapter 8). As we saw in this chapter, undertaking market research can raise ethical issues and these will be further explored in Chapter 5).

✎ KEY PRINCIPLES OF MARKETING

- Marketing responsibility does not necessarily imply any conflict between a company's profit objectives and its social responsibilities.

- Ethics is a moral code which defines what is right and what is wrong.

- Voluntary codes of conduct are generally preferred to legislation as means of bringing about social responsibility by firms.

- The customer is not always 'king'—they may not know what is really good for them, or what patterns of consumption are acceptable to society.

- Marketers have a responsibility to preserve freedom and choice in a marketplace.

CASE STUDY

Problems in the air for low-cost flights?

Global warming has emerged as a major concern to consumers throughout the world. Initially, awareness of the causes and consequences of global warming was confined to a small part of the population, but linkages with the destructive tsunami of December 2004, and Hurricane Katrina of 2005 brought home to many people the possible long-term harmful consequences of excessive emissions off CO_2 to the atmosphere. Global warming was no longer a humorous subject where people in the developed countries of northern Europe and the United States focused on the benign consequences of mild winters and exotic new plants that they would be able to grow. Destructive winds, rising sea levels, and devastation of low-lying areas were increasingly coming to be seen as a consequence of our prodigious use of fossil fuels.

The reduction of carbon dioxide emissions had already been taken on board by many manufacturing companies, the largest of whom had seen reductions through a system of carbon trading initiated by the Kyoto treaty. But one business sector—Civil Aviation—had been quite notable for its apparent irresponsibility in not embracing the principles of reducing carbon emissions. Critics of the sector pointed out that as a result of worldwide agreements, aviation fuel was not taxed, in contrast to the steep taxation on most other forms of fuel. Although aircraft had become more efficient in their use of fuel during the 1990s, this was more than offset by booming demand for flights with no frills airlines such as easyJet and Ryanair. It seemed that the budget airline companies were very effective in communicating their low price message to customers who filled their planes, often with more thought about a cheap weekend break by the Mediterranean, than the unknown and remote possibilities of global warming. Indeed, the general public seemed to be somewhat hypocritical about the effects of global warming. Some still thought that the problem would go away, and may have recalled previous 'scares' such as the imminent depletion of fossil fuels and the effects of 'acid rain', neither of which had really affected most peoples' lives, and had subsequently slipped down the news agenda. Even in respect of 'greenhouse gas' emissions, people may profess to being sympathetic to green causes, but then buy something which is anything but green. As an example, one survey of holidaymakers conducted in 2007 suggested that consideration of greenhouse gas emissions came way behind other evaluation criteria when choosing a holiday, including the ease of getting a sun lounger, proximity to the beach, and the range of nightlife available.

How were airlines to respond to the apparent threat to their business model that had been thrown up by the issue of global warming? Should they put their head in the sand and hope that the problem would go away? Should they concentrate on giving customers what they have repeatedly said they wanted—cheap flights—and hope that human hedonism would win out over feelings of social responsibility? Or should airlines be on their guard against possible government intervention which could undermine their business model. How could they prevent new legislation? And if it was introduced, how could they respond to it?

Politicians were becoming increasingly frustrated by the airlines' seeming lack of willingness to address issues of climate change. Already, the Bishop of London had described air travel as 'immoral', for the way that wealthy western travellers could inflict harm on people in the developed world through climate change. Could a significant number of airline passengers really begin to feel guilty about flying away for a cheap weekend break, and cut back their travelling by air?

In January 2007, the communications battle was stepped up when a UK government minister described Ryanair as 'the irresponsible face of capitalism'. He had argued that while other industries and consumers were cutting down their emissions, Ryanair had expanded at a phenomenal rate, churning out more carbon dioxide into the atmosphere. Friends of the Earth, in a report 'Aviation and global climate change' noted that commercial jets were adding 600 million tonnes of carbon dioxide a year to global warming, almost as much as for the whole of Africa. With such negative communication, would Ryanair suffer as people felt guilty about flying, and governments increasingly moved to regulate civil aviation and make it more expensive, especially for the price sensitive segments that the no frills airlines had been targeting?

Rarely known to be quiet, the chief executive of Ryanair, Michael O'Leary went on a communications offensive. Dismissing the minister as 'knowing nothing', he presented Ryanair as a friend rather than an enemy of global warming. He argued that travellers should feel reassured that Ryanair used one of the world's most modern and fuel efficient fleets of aircraft. Moreover, Ryanair's business model of filling seats at the lowest price really meant that the carbon emissions per passenger were much lower than traditional full service airlines, who often flew half empty planes. And the fact that budget airlines operated an extensive point-to-point network avoided the costly and environmentally harmful effects of taking two indirect flights via a central hub airport.

The war of words that has ensued over airlines' contribution to global warming demonstrates the difficulty that many ordinary consumers have in evaluating rival environmental claims. Many may have taken to heart governments' and church leaders' claims that made them feel guilty about flying. But even if hypocritical consumers were happy to carry on flying and not backing their expressed concerns for climate change with changes in their behaviour, there was certainly a possibility that governments would intervene. Both the UK government and EU Commission had floated the idea of taxing aviation fuel, and bringing aircraft emissions within the scope of the EU Emissions Trading Scheme. Some airlines, such as Ryanair, continued to sound off against the government, positioning them as the consumer's champion. But others, including easyJet sensed the change in mood of the public and government bodies, and openly supported the idea of bringing aircraft emissions into the carbon trading regime. Was easyJet being philanthropic?

Was it simply putting out a message that it thought its customers would want to hear, helping them salve their conscience and avoid feelings of guilt? Or was there a shrewd underlying commercial advantage, in which the modern, efficient easyJet fleet may use less than its allotted share of carbon emission, which it could then sell on to less efficient 'legacy' carriers? Should the company begin planning for higher taxes on flying, and be prepared for reducing its growth plans if some marginal customers decided that a weekend break by the Mediterranean was no longer a luxury that they could afford?

Source: Based on: The Intergovernmental Panel on Climate Change's (IPCC's) '*Special Report on Aviation and the Global Atmosphere*', published 1999. available at www.unep.ch/ipcc/press/pr6-99.html; *Financial Times*, 'UK minister slapped down for attack on airlines', 5 January 2007; Ryanair corporate website (www.ryanair.com).

Case study review questions

1. If you were the marketing manager of an airline such as Ryanair, how would you address the ecological concerns raised in this article?

2. The case study refers to apparent hypocrisy of consumers who may claim to be concerned about the environment, but nevertheless continue to fly. What might bring about a narrowing of this gap between what consumers think and what they actually do? How could a company such as easyJet measure and monitor consumers' attitudes?

3. What might be the consequences for the marketing of a budget airline of government policy measures which have the effect of doubling air fares in real terms? Critically discuss how the marketing manager of a budget airline might respond.

CHAPTER REVIEW QUESTIONS

1. Critically discuss the view that there is no such thing as altruism in marketing, but apparently altruistic acts by marketers are in fact always calculated attempts to directly or indirectly improve profitability.

2. What do you understand by the term ethics? Discuss the benefits to a marketing manager of having a thorough understanding of ethics.

3. What should be the response of businesses to pressure groups' claims that their activities are causing ecological damage?

ACTIVITIES

1. You are employed by a phone company as a commission-based sales assistant. The more people you get to sign up and switch from other phone companies, the more commission you will be paid. However, you know in your heart that most of the people you are selling to could get a much better deal with another company. Moreover, you realize that hidden in the small print of the contract are clauses which will result in additional charges to the customer which are not mentioned in the glossy, colourful brochure that you send out.

    As a salesperson, would you consider yourself to be acting ethically by selling something when you know that buyers could get better elsewhere? Is it ethical not to alert buyers to the potentially disadvantageous terms contained in the small print, and just lure them to sign on the dotted line with the bait of free gifts and a glossy brochure? What would you do?

2. Select two or three campaigns by environmental pressure groups with which you are familiar, for example Greenpeace, Friends of the Earth, or the Countryside Alliance. Review their websites and recent press releases to assess the effects that their campaigning is likely to have on a manufacturer of consumer goods. How widely do you consider the opinions expressed by these groups represent the population as a whole? If you were a manufacturer, how would you address the issues raised?

3. Select a company with which you are familiar as a customer. Using some of the headings in this chapter, undertake an audit to assess how responsible you consider the organization to be in its marketing.

REFERENCES

Bateson, J.E.G. (1989) *Managing Services Marketing: Text and Readings*, 2nd edn. Fort Worth, USA: Dryden Press.

British Industrial Society (2001) Managing Best Practice, No.83, *Occupational Stress*, London: British Industrial Society. pp. 4–23.

Carter, C.R. and Rogers, D.S. (2008) 'A Framework of Sustainable Supply Chain Management: Moving Toward New Theory'. *International Journal of Physical Distribution & Logistics Management*, 38 (5), 360–87.

Chamorro, A., Rubio, S., and Miranda, F.J. (2009) 'Characteristics of Research on Green Marketing'. *Business Strategy and the Environment*, 18 (4), 223–39.

Charter, M. and Polonsky M.J. (eds), *Greener Marketing: A Global Perspective on Greening Marketing Practice*. Sheffield, UK: Greenleaf Publishing Ltd. pp. 233–54.

Direct Marketing Association (2007) *Census of the UK Direct Marketing Industry*. London: Direct Marketing Association.

Financial Times (2007) 'MI5 warns Banks of Chinese Hackers', *Financial Times*, London, 1 December.

Fraj, E. and Martinez, E. (2006) 'Ecological Consumer Behavior: An Empirical Analysis'. *International Journal of Consumer Studies*, 31, 26–33.

Future Foundation (2004) *Life in the 24/7? The Shape of Things to Come*. London: Future Foundation.

Gambling Commission (2009) *Industry Statistics 2008/09*. London: Gambling Commission.

Gurau, C. and Ranchhod, A. (2005) 'International Green Marketing: a Comparative Study of British and Romanian Firms'. *International Marketing Review*, 22 (5), 547–62.

Hepburn, C. (2010) 'Environmental Policy, Government, and the Market'. *Oxford Review of Econ Policy*, 26 (2), 117–136.

Kalafatis, S.P., Pollard, M., East, R., and Tsogas, M.H. (1999) 'Green Marketing and Ajzen's Theory of Planned Behaviour: A Cross-Market Examination'. *Journal of Consumer Marketing*, 16 (5), 441–60.

Kassarjian, H.H. (1971) 'Incorporating Ecology into Marketing Strategy: The Case of Air Pollution'. *Journal of Marketing*, 35 (3), 61–5.

Kotler, P. and Levy, S.L. (1969) 'Broadening the Concept of Marketing'. *Journal of Marketing*, 33 (1), 10–15.

Laroche, M., Bergeron, J., and Barbaro-Forleo, G. (2001) 'Targeting Consumers Who are Willing to Pay More for Environmentally Friendly Products'. *Journal of Consumer Marketing*, 18 (6), 503–20.

Lee, J. A. and Holden, S.J.S. (1999) 'Understanding the Determinants of Environmentally Conscious Behavior'. *Psychology & Marketing*, 16 (5), 373–92.

Leonidou, C.N. and Leonidou, L.C. (2011) 'Research into Environmental Marketing/Management: A Bibliographic Analysis'. *European Journal of Marketing*, 45 (1/2), 68–103.

Levinson, J.C. (2007) *Guerrilla Marketing*, 4th rev edition. London: Piatkus Books.

Mendelson, N. and Polonsky, M.J. (1995) 'Using Strategic Alliances to Develop Credible Green Marketing'. *Journal of Consumer Marketing*, 12 (2), 4–18.

Peattie, K. and Crane, A. (2005) 'Green Marketing: Legend, Myth, Farce or Prophesy?' *Qualititve Market Research: An International Journal*, 8 (4), 357–70.

Peattie, K. and Peattie, S. (2009) 'Social Marketing: a Pathway to Consumption Reduction?' *Journal of Business Research*, 62 (2), 260–68.

Porter, M.E. and Kramer, M.R. (2006), 'Strategy and Society: The Link Between Competitive Advantage and Corporate Social Responsibility', *Harvard Business Review*, 84 (12), December 2006, 78–92.

Rooka, J. and Uusitalo, L. (2008) 'Preference for Green Packaging in Consumer Product Choices—Do Consumers Care?' *International Journal of Consumer Studies*, 32 (5), 516–25.

Sarkar, R. (2008) 'Public Policy and Corporate Environmental Behaviour: A Broader View'. *Corporate Social Responsibility and Environmental Management*, 15 (5), 281–97.

Schlegelmilch, B.B., Bohlen, G.M., and Diamantopoulos, A. (1996) 'The Link Between Green Purchasing Decisions and Measures of Environmental Consciousness'. *European Journal of Marketing*, 30 (5), 35–55.

Schumacher, I. (2009) 'The Dynamics of Environmentalism and the Environment'. *Ecological Economics*, 68 (11), 2842–9.

Unruh, G.C. (2008) 'The Biosphere Rules', *Harvard Business Review*, 86 (2), February 2008, 111–17, 138.

SUGGESTED FURTHER READING

The following provides an overview of general issues of corporate social responsibility:

Blowfield, M.E. and Murray, A. (2008) *Corporate Responsibility: a Critical Introduction*. Oxford: Oxford University Press.

Issues of socially responsible and ecologically sound marketing are explored in the following:

Hitchcock, D. and Willard, M. (2006) *The Business Guide to Sustainability: Practical Strategies and Tools for Organizations*. Abingdon: Earthscan.

For a discussion of business ethics the following texts are useful.

Crane, A. and Matten, D. (2010) *Business Ethics: Managing Corporate Citizenship and Sustainability in the Age of Globalization*, 3rd edn. Oxford: Oxford University Press.

Bibb, S. (2010) *The Right Thing: An Everyday Guide to Ethics in Business*. Chichester: John Wiley.

Stanwick, P. and Stanwick, S. (2008) *Understanding Business Ethics*. Harlow: Prentice Hall.

Carrington, M.J., Neville, B.A., and Whitwell, G.J. (2010) 'Why Ethical Consumers Don't Walk Their Talk: Towards a Framework for Understanding the Gap Between the Ethical Purchase Intentions and Actual Buying Behaviour of Ethically Minded Consumers'. *Journal of Business Ethics,* 97 (1), 139–58.

Webb, D.J., Mohr, L.A., and Harris, K.E. (2008) 'A re-examination of socially responsible consumption and its measurement'. *Journal of Business Research,* 61 (2), 91–8.

 ## ONLINE RESOURCE CENTRE

Visit the Online Resource Centre for resources that are relevant to this chapter, including a flashcard glossary, web links, multiple choice questions, and additional case studies:

www.oxfordtextbooks.co.uk/orc/palmer3e/

KEY TERMS

- Cartel
- Codes of conduct
- Data protection
- Ecological responsibility
- Ethics

- Green consumers
- Privacy
- Sustainability
- Vulnerable customers

UNDERSTANDING CUSTOMERS

Part 2

BUYER BEHAVIOUR AND RELATIONSHIP DEVELOPMENT

4

CHAPTER OBJECTIVES

Faced with competing products, it is important for companies to understand how buyers go about choosing between the alternatives. A thorough understanding of buyer behaviour should be reflected in product design, pricing, promotion, and distribution, all of which should satisfy the needs of individuals' buying processes. This chapter explores basic theories of buyer behaviour. Distinctions between personal and organizational buyer behaviour are noted, especially in the composition of the decision-making unit. Companies generally seek to influence buyer behaviour so that the company becomes customers' first choice of supplier. This chapter reviews methods by which companies seek to turn one-off casual buying behaviour into ongoing buyer–seller relationships.

◉ Introduction

A company may think that it has developed the perfect product, one that customers will be queuing up to buy. But despite putting possibly years into new product development, it could find its efforts wasted as buyers reject its product in the few minutes, or sometimes even seconds, that it might take them to choose between competing products. The company may have failed to understand the complex processes by which buyers make purchasing decisions. It may, for example, have underestimated the role played by key influencers in the decision process and aimed its marketing effort at those individuals who really don't count for a lot in the final decision. It may have spent the bulk of its promotional effort at a time when buyers were not at a receptive stage in the buying process.

Companies undertake marketing activities in order to elicit some kind of response from buyers. The ultimate aim of that activity is to get customers to buy their products, and to come back again. Most of this book breaks marketing activities down into distinct areas of decisions that have to be made by marketing managers, for example pricing decisions and promotion decisions.

However, while companies may break their planning down into small manageable chunks, customers make an assessment based on a holistic view of the total product offer. How customers perceive the whole offer and react to it may be quite different from what the company had expected when it was developing its marketing plan. In the case of sales to commercial buyers, the task of understanding who is involved in the buying process and what procedures are adopted becomes even more complex. Faced with a sometimes bewildering array of choices, buyers seek to simplify the choice process, for example by sticking with brand names they are familiar with.

In short, buying processes can be complex, involving many people over a sometimes lengthy period of time. Making false assumptions about these processes can result in an otherwise good product not being bought.

This chapter will explore a number of dimensions in the complexity of buying behaviour:

- What factors motivate an individual to seek out a purchase in the first place?

- What sources of information are used in evaluating competing products?

- What is the relative importance attached by decision makers to each of the elements of the product offer?

- What is the set of competing products from which consumers make their final choice?

- Who is involved in making the purchase decision?

- How long the does the process of making a decision take?

- How can a seller affect buyers' subsequent behaviour so that it becomes the preferred supplier, tied by a formal or informal relationship?

Buying situations

Of course, buying processes vary between products and between individuals. For the purpose of studying buying behaviour, a number of categories of buying situations can be identified.

- Routine rebuy: The buyer makes a purchase decision in these situations almost instinctively, without giving the process any thought. It is like routinely buying the same daily newspaper.

- Modified rebuy: The buyer may be familiar with a class of product, but this time wants something a little different. For example, she may often buy a tin of paint, but on this occasion she needs paint specifically for a job in hand which may be novel to her (such as covering external masonry), so she is likely to engage in limited search processes to identify and evaluate alternatives.

- Completely novel: The buyer has no previous experience of buying this type of product, so the search process is likely to be longer, with a greater range of information sources being consulted.

In addition, the sophistication of the buying process is influenced by the level of involvement that a buyer has in the product being purchased.

⦿ With high-involvement products, buyers have a close relationship with the product. The manner in which the product is used has the capacity to deeply affect their happiness and they cannot easily ignore the product. Items of clothing and many personal medical services fall into this category.

⦿ Low-involvement products have less consequence for individuals' psychological well-being. If a mistake is made in choosing an unsuitable product, they will not worry about it unduly. They can normally live with the consequences of making a mistake in their washing powder purchase, but a mistake in their choice of outer clothing may affect their self-image.

Involvement is closely associated with risk. High-involvement purchase decisions are seen as being more risky in terms of their outcomes, so buyers are likely to spend more time and effort in trying to avoid a bad purchase for such products.

Further variety in the buying process is evident from the major differences that can occur between private individuals and organizations in the way they make purchase decisions. These differences are considered later in this chapter.

⦿ The buying process

The basic processes involved in purchase decisions are illustrated in Figure 4.1. Simple models of buyer behaviour usually see an underlying need triggering a search for need-satisfying solutions. When possible solutions have been identified, these are evaluated according to some criteria. The final purchase decision is often a result of the interaction

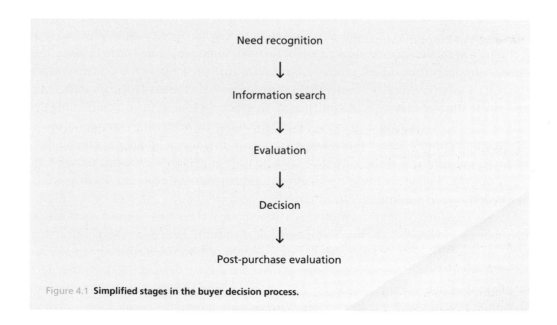

Figure 4.1 **Simplified stages in the buyer decision process.**

between the final decision maker and a range of influencers. Eventually, after purchase and consumption, the consumer will develop feelings about the purchase that will influence future purchase decisions. In reality, however, purchase decision processes can be complex iterative processes involving large numbers of influencers and a variety of decision criteria. It is often unrealistic to see the stages of the buying process as being completely separate; for example, evaluation often takes place while the search for information is still ongoing.

Needs as buying process initiators

A need for something triggers the buying process. Needs provide a motive for an individual's action and can be very complex. Because they are a deep-seated initiator of buying behaviour, marketers are very keen to understand how needs are formed and manifested.

A *need* can be defined as a perceived state of deprivation, which motivates an individual to take actions to eliminate that sense of deprivation. A need is deep-rooted in an individual's personality. How the individual seeks to satisfy a need will be conditioned by the society of which he is a member. As an example, the need for status may be fairly universal, but its expression differs between cultures. In many less developed economies the need for status may be acquired by owning large numbers of cattle. In western countries the need is more likely to be satisfied by ownership of a particular brand of car. These manifestations of needs are sometimes referred to as *wants*. Wants are the culturally influenced manifestation of a deep-seated need. Of course, we can all want many products, but not buy or be able to buy them. Marketers are ultimately interested in *demand*, which can be defined as a willingness and ability to buy a product that satisfies a need.

An individual's needs are influenced by a wide range of psychological and sociological factors. We can begin our understanding of needs by focusing on those psychological factors that are inherent to an individual.

Physiological and psychological bases of needs

Genetic make-up clearly has some effect on buying behaviour. For example, physiological factors can influence an individual's appetite for food. Some people are said to be more 'impulsive' shoppers than others, and researchers have attributed part of the explanation for this behaviour to genetics. Differences have also been noted in the needs of male and female buyers and the way they approach purchasing decisions. Of course, there is continuing debate about whether, and to what extent, such behaviours are inherent in our nature, or are the result of nurture through a socialization process. Either way, it is important for marketers to recognize differences between individuals in what motivates them to buy (Figure 4.2).

It is wrong to equate needs solely with physiological drivers. We no longer live in a society in which the main motivation of individuals is to satisfy the basic needs for food and drink.

Maslow recognized that, once individuals have satisfied these basic physiological needs, they may seek to satisfy social needs—for example, the need to have meaningful interaction with peers (see Figure 4.3). More complex still, western cultures see increasing numbers of people seeking to satisfy essentially internal needs for self-satisfaction. Products therefore satisfy increasingly complex needs. Food is no longer seen as a basic necessity to be purchased and cooked for self-consumption. With growing prosperity, people have sought to satisfy social needs by eating out with friends or family. Satisfaction of such social needs may

Figure 4.2 **The market for sun protection products has become increasingly complex, as consumers' needs have changed.** Marketers have recognized that the cheap bottle of sun oil from a pharmacy or supermarket is not going to satisfy the needs of increasingly discerning buyers who seek a sun oil that is suitable for their particular skin type. In addition, the desire for a natural tan has been supplemented with a growing awareness of the need to avoid the dangers of skin cancer. The Calypso brand has been progressively extended and developed to cater for these increasingly complex needs.
(Reproduced with kind permission of Linco CARE Limited.)

be supplemented with a higher-order need to experience different types of meals. The great growth in eating out that occurred during the 1970s and 1980s has been followed by a growing diversity of restaurants that cater for people's need for variety and curiosity—hence the emergence in most large European towns of Balti, Creole, and Far Eastern restaurants.

Maslow's **hierarchy of needs** is no more than a conceptual model, and it is difficult actually to measure where an individual is positioned on the hierarchy of needs. Furthermore, it is essentially based on western values of motivation, and there is a lot of evidence of cultural

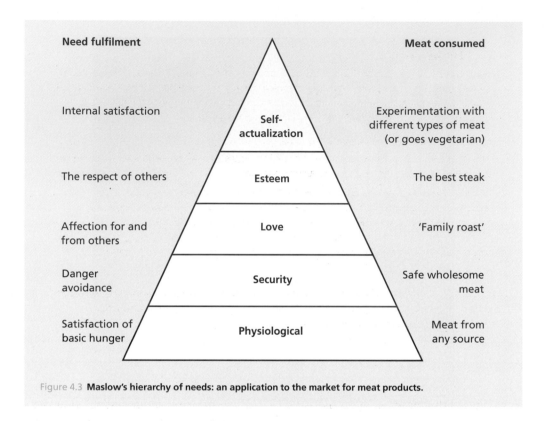

Figure 4.3 **Maslow's hierarchy of needs: an application to the market for meat products.**

influences on needs (e.g. Jai-Ok *et al.* 2002). How, for example, would you explain religious sacrifice and penance, which are important motivators for many non-western consumers?

Maslow has presented one model of motivation which marketers have adopted widely as a conceptual framework. There are other frameworks for understanding the psychological bases for understanding how people are motivated to satisfy their needs.

- **Freudian analysis** sees human behaviour as directed by a repression of feelings from early childhood. What comes naturally to a young child is often considered socially unacceptable, so such behaviour is socialized out before the child reaches adulthood. Behaviour is the outcome of the interaction between the id (the primitive unconscious basis of the psyche dominated by primary urges) and the ego (conscious perceptions that act as an inhibiting agency).

- **Stimulus–response models of motivation** have been widely used by marketers to understand needs. Analogies have been drawn between Pavlov's dog (who came to associate the sound of a bell with food) and everyday marketing situations. The existence of cues in the environment, such as advertising, can help trigger the buying process, even though the initial cue has no direct connection with the need an individual is seeking to satisfy. In this way, the sight of a well-known celebrity endorser can trigger the process of seeking out a brand of food that she endorses.

MARKETING in ACTION

Is Freud fit for marketing?

Freudian analyses of human motivation based on repression have sometimes achieved notoriety for their explanations of human behaviour. Is smoking really a substitute for the repressed desire of a child to suck its thumb? Think about the two following cases of supposedly repressed feelings, their explanation, and possible opportunities for marketers:

1. Children inherently dislike order and prefer creative chaos: it is only adults that teach children to be tidy and to structure their lives. Possible marketing opportunity—toys and novelties for adults that recreate a sense of chaos, such as 'silly string', party poppers, and some modern art.

2. Children like to be cared for by a mother figure. As adults we take on board such responsibilities, but we would sometimes be happy to go back to a simple dependent child–mother relationship. Possible marketing opportunity—a wide range of personal services aimed to pamper adults as if they were children again, including hairdressing, beauty salons, and health farms. Who else can exploit this desire to be a pampered, dependent child? Restaurants? Airlines?

Is an analysis of repression of any use to marketers in trying to understand human motivation? Or is it a highly speculative approach that may be intuitively appealing, but is only one of a number of possible explanations of the observed behaviour?

Sociological influences on needs

You will recall that needs were defined earlier as being inherent in an individual. However, the manifestation of these needs is influenced by the society in which an individual lives, and there is a lot of research evidence of how these social influences work (see e.g. Butcher et al. 2002). A number of levels of influence can be identified:

- The family influences a child's perception of the world, and this influence lasts into adulthood. Examples of this effect on buying processes can be found in adults' selection of a particular brand of breakfast cereal because it is the one that they were brought up with.

- Individuals are surrounded by peer groups (or reference groups) which act as a guide for behaviour. Peer groups can be primary and direct in their influence (e.g. colleagues at work and school), or they can be secondary and indirect (e.g. the guidance to behaviour provided by pop stars or media figures).

- Individuals can identify with a social class, and the values of this class can influence behaviour. As an example, individuals who identify with the 'working class' may feel alienated by an up-market retail outlet such as the Gap compared with the values epitomized in Primark.

- Culture in its widest sense influences our buying behaviour. Concepts such as self-centredness, the desire for immediate results, and deference to suppliers can differ significantly between cultures (see Hofstede 2004).

MARKETING in ACTION

The consumer culture is dead—long live the consumer?

In September 2008 it seemed that consumer behaviour had changed forever. As cherished institutions collapsed, it seemed that buyers would never be the same again. In the space of a few months, banks around the world had gone bankrupt, from the mighty Lehman Brothers down to the small savings and loans institutions which ran out of cash. Mighty retailers such as Woolworths—just one year short of its 100th birthday in the UK—were laid to ruin.

A generation had been brought up on the idea that 'greed is good' and that big end of year bonuses were to be celebrated, not condemned. But now greedy bonus seekers were seen as the cause of so many problems. In many circles, 'ostentatious consumption' was eclipsed by a new age of 'ostentatious utilitarianism'. At dinner parties, people who once would have boasted about how much they had paid for their Prada handbag or Jimmy Choo shoes now revelled in telling their friends how they had been so clever in 'discovering' good value bargains in Poundland and Lidl. This also coincided with a period of growing concern for the ecological environment, so any self-respecting socialite could now save their dwindling pennies and acquire street cred by convincing their friends that by shopping at Poundland they were helping to help save the environment. Where would all this lead? Some pundits saw an inexorable trend to an anti-materialistic world in which people felt guilty about earning bonuses (at least those who still had a job), and those who had the money felt bad about spending it. Surely marketing would never be the same again as consumers' new found values resulted in them spending less.

Reports of the death of the capitalist, consumer-led culture turned out to be premature. Some wealthy groups never stopped spending, for example the profits of the upmarket auction house Sotheby's remained strong following the financial crisis. Others appeared to have been lying low and soon came out spending again. By 2010 the profits of many luxury goods makers had begun to rise as shoppers rediscovered luxury.

Even the 'bonus culture' which had been so much maligned during the financial crisis seemed to be making a strong comeback. In February 2010, Royal Bank of Scotland, which had been brought close to bankruptcy partly as a result of its bonus culture, announced that it would be paying £1.3 billion in bonuses to its staff.

Trying to predict future attitudes of consumers can be fraught with difficulty. In the eye of a crisis, many thought that consumer culture had changed forever, but as this example illustrates, deep-seated social attitudes can be resilient. A difficult challenge for business leaders is to distinguish transient, self-correcting changes from these which bring about fundamental change. Maybe some things are quite constant, for example consumers' need to adapt to the norms of their peer group; this was just manifested in different ways at the depths of the recession. When the economy came out of recession, would the peer groups' values change again back to 'shopping as usual'?

Situational factors influencing needs

Our needs are also influenced by the situation in which we currently find ourselves. The subjects of age and socio-economic status can have profound effects on buying behaviour, as we will see in Chapter 5 when we look at market segmentation. In addition, the stage that an individual has reached in the **family life-cycle** has a significant influence on needs (see Tinson et al. 2008). There have been numerous descriptions of the typical family life-cycle.

One of the earliest—and still widely cited—classifications was developed by Wells and Gubar (1966), who identified a number of stages, each associated with distinctive sets of needs:

1. Bachelor stage: young, single people not living at home

2. Newly married couples: young, no children

3. Full nest 1: youngest child under six

4. Full nest 2: youngest child over six

5. Full nest 3: older married couples with dependent children

6. Empty nest 1: older married couples, no children living at home

7. Empty nest 2: older married couples, retired, no children living at home

8. Solitary survivor 1: still working

9. Solitary survivor 2: retired

More recent refinements of family life-cycle stages have sought to take account of their increasing complexity, brought about by the breakdown of the traditional nuclear family and the emergence of deviations from the norm such as single-parent families, extended cohabitation before marriage, and groups of young people sharing a house before they can afford their own. However, all family life-cycle models make the same important point: an individual's needs are likely to change as he or she goes through life. An individual moving from a bachelor stage to one with dependent children will face a re-ordering of priorities, reflecting a different set of needs. This will also most likely be matched by a reduction in discretionary expenditure.

Information search

Once a need has triggered a search for need-satisfying solutions, the search for information will begin. But where do buyers look for information when making purchases? In the case of the routine repurchase of a familiar product, probably very little information is sought about the product. But where there is a greater element of uncertainty, buyers will seek out information about the alternative ways in which they can satisfy their needs, especially where a high level of risk is involved. The following information sources are likely to be used (Figure 4.4).

   Personal experience will be a starting point, so, if a buyer has already used a company's products, the suitability of the proposed purchase may be assessed in the light of the previous purchases.

⊙ **Word-of-mouth** recommendation from friends is important for many categories of goods and services where an individual may have had no previous need to make a purchase (Sweeney et al. 2008). When looking for a plumber or a solicitor, for example, many people will seek the advice of friends. Increasingly, buyers are looking to the Internet to gather recommendations, through social networking sites, blogs, and discussion forums.

Figure 4.4 **In the UK domestic gas and electricity supply market, consumers are faced with a sometimes bewildering and confusing choice of suppliers, all offering a basic commodity product, which by law cannot be differentiated.** Evaluation is made more difficult because the different companies choose different bases for pricing, with many companies offering several different price plans. Some give introductory discounts, some give low user discounts and most give discounts for payment by direct debit. The website www.uswitch.co.uk has become a popular choice for many consumers seeking comparative information on a novel purchase. This calculator for gas and electricity guides consumers through all the choices available and identifies which supplier and price plan is best for them. It is claimed that an average family who switches suppliers on buy.co.uk or uSwitch.com saves £140 on their annual energy bills.
(*Source*: Reproduced with kind permission of uswitch.co.uk.)

- Rather than referring to people we know, we may use various other reference groups to guide us. What type of sports shoes are our sports heroes wearing at the moment? What kind of drink is considered to be fashionable with our age group?

- Newspaper editorial content and trusted consumer review sources such as 'Which?' magazine and www.moneysavingexpert.com may be consulted as a relatively objective source of information. Advertising and promotion in all of its forms is taken on board, sometimes being specifically sought and at other times just being casually noticed.

The greater the perceived risk of a purchase, the longer and more widespread is the search for information. Of course, individuals differ in the extent to which they are prepared to collect information methodically—some may make a purchase more impulsively than other, more calculating, individuals.

Perception

We may consciously seek out information, but may nevertheless fail to process the information that is presented to us. There are three key perceptual processes that can get in the way between the presentation of information and the using of that information for evaluation:

1. We may fail to perceive the information because it fails to attract our attention (*selective attention*).

2. We may perceive the information, but then distort its content (*selective distortion*).

3. We may perceive the information, but then forget it very quickly (*selective retention*).

There is evidence that each sense receptor requircs some minimum level of energy (or 'absolute threshold') to excite it before perception is organized. As well as the absolute threshold, there is a 'differential threshold', which is the smallest amount by which two stimuli must be different in order to be perceived as different. These thresholds are known to fluctuate, and differences between individuals' perceptions are influenced by their education, upbringing, experience, and many other factors.

We will return to the subject of perception in Chapter 10 when we look at communication processes within the context of the promotional mix.

....

E-Marketing

Can online gossip be more important than what you read in the newspapers?

Word-of-mouth recommendation can be an important way of influencing buyers' choices, but it has traditionally been a fairly slow means of spreading recommendation about a product. Now, the Internet allows the whole process to be speeded up and has widened its impact. From word of mouth, companies now talk about word of mouse, leading to 'viral marketing' in which a purchase recommendation can spread very quickly as one person passes on a message to half a dozen friends, each of whom in turn passes on the message to another half dozen friends. Viral marketing is becoming increasingly important to companies, with evidence that influencing customer behaviour by means of traditional marketing media is becoming less effective, with the proliferation of social media and falling readership levels of conventional media (Leskovec et al. 2008; Subramani and Rajagopalan 2003).

The power of referral through social network sites is becoming increasingly apparent, with reports that 64 per cent of social networkers in Europe will visit a website related to what they have seen on a friend's site, while more than 10 per cent of visits in 2007 to entertainment and music sites came by direct referral from social network sites (Hitwise 2008). It also seems that messages received through online communities are more believable and trusted than messages received through conventional media (Gillin 2007). Ipsos MORI (2006) reported that over half of European Internet users are more likely to buy a product if they have read positive comments on the Internet from other customers, while 34 per cent had not bought a product in the past on the basis of bad online reviews. In the UK, trust in online reviews is reported to be higher than trust in conventional marketing communications. In one study, 25 per cent of Internet users trusted reviews on a recognized review website and 15 per cent trusted reviews written by customers or private individuals on a blog. In contrast, only 14 per cent of Internet users trusted a newspaper article, 9 per cent a TV advertisement, 8 per cent trusted reviews of a company's products on its own website, 4 per cent trusted an email sent by a company and only 2 per cent trusted information written about a company by its CEO (Ipsos MORI 2006).

Increasingly, companies have been mingling in social networks sites, and have sometimes created their own sites as community forums. Dell, for example, established the Dell2Dell blog, in an attempt to gain some control over communication about it. But on other occasions, companies have sponsored blogs without declaring their hand. The retailer Walmart covertly sponsored a blog which was supposedly operated by a couple camping in the store's car-parks. It had hoped to manipulate content to put the company in a good light, but eventually the exercise turned into a PR disaster when news broke that the company had in fact been controlling the blog. In this case, even though technology may have advanced, old questions remain, especially: why did a company allow itself to get into the position of exposing itself to criticism? Could this not have been foreseen? If there is little material for people to spread bad stories about, the dissident websites would probably lose much of their support.

Evaluation

In the process of gathering information, the total range of products available in the marketplace is gradually filtered down to a manageable number for evaluation (Figure 4.5). Choice is made from a select set of possibilities, and these choice sets can be classified according to their selectivity:

⊙ The *total set* comprises all products that are capable of satisfying a given need.

⊙ The *awareness set* comprises all of those products that the consumer is aware of. (The *unaware set* is the opposite of the awareness set.)

⊙ The *consideration set* includes those items within the awareness set that the consumer considers buying.

⊙ The *choice set* is the group of products from which a final decision is ultimately made.

⊙ Along the way to defining the choice set, some products will have been rejected, as they are perceived to be unavailable, unaffordable, unsuitable, etc. These comprise the *infeasible set*.

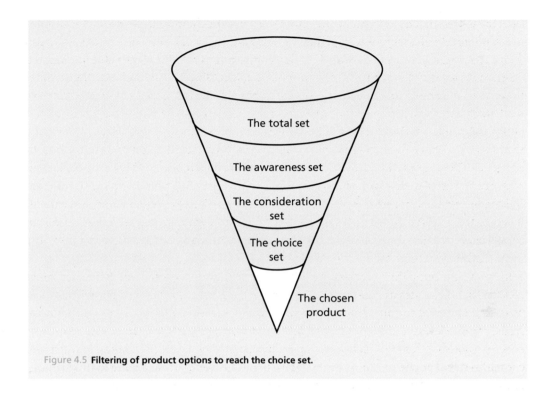

Figure 4.5 **Filtering of product options to reach the choice set.**

Research should seek to establish the choice set against which a company's product is being compared, and on this basis the marketing programme can be adapted in order to achieve competitive advantage against other members of the choice set.

A private buyer seeking to buy a low-value, low-involvement product such as an electric kettle may have narrowed down the choice set to four kettles. Analysts of buyer behaviour have developed a number of frameworks for trying to understand how a consumer chooses between these competing alternatives. In one such framework the consumer uses a sense of intuition as to which seems best. Such non-systematic methods of evaluation may be quite appropriate where the product in question involves low levels of cost, risk, and involvement.

Even apparently intuitive bases of evaluation can be reduced to a series of rules, implying some systematic foundation. One framework is a multiple-attribute choice matrix which holds that consumers refer to a number of component attributes of a product to evaluate its overall suitability. Figure 4.6 shows a typical matrix in which four competing MP3 players are compared in terms of five important attributes. In this matrix, the four short-listed MP3 players in the choice set are shown by the column headings A, B, C, and D. The left-hand column lists five attributes which research has suggested buyers use to make their purchase decision (price, reputation of the brand name, colour, styling, capacity). The second column shows the importance the consumer attaches to each attribute of the service (with maximum importance being given a score of ten and a completely unimportant attribute a score of zero). The following four columns show how each MP3 player scores against each of the five evaluation attributes.

	Importance weights (out of 10)	Scores for each attribute for each MP3 player (0 = poor, 10 = excellent)			
		A	B	C	D
Brand reputation	10	10	7	8	10
User-friendliness	9	10	9	8	8
Memory size	8	10	10	9	9
Price	7	10	10	10	5
Battery life	6	4	10	10	4
Overall rating		44	46	45	36
Weighted rating		7.3	7.2	7.0	6.1

Overall rating = the sum total of scores for all attributes.
Weighted rating = the sum total of scores for all attributes, in which each attribute has been multiplied by its importance weight. (The importance weight is expressed as a percentage of the maximum score of 10 points.)

Figure 4.6 **A hypothetical choice set for MP3 players: a multiple attribute matrix.**

If it is assumed that a consumer evaluates each product without weighting each attribute, MP3 B will be preferred, as it has the highest overall rating. However, it is more realistic to expect that some attributes will be weighted as being more important than others; therefore the alternative *linear compensatory* approach is based on consumers creating weighted scores for each product. The importance of each attribute is multiplied by the score for each attribute, so in this case player A is preferred, as the attributes of A that consumers rank most highly are also those that are considered to be the most important.

A third approach to evaluation is sometimes described as a *lexicographic approach*. This involves the buyer in starting his evaluation by looking at the most important attribute and ruling out those products that do not meet a minimum standard; evaluation is then based on the second most important attribute, with products being eliminated that do not meet this standard. The process continues until only one option is left. In Figure 4.6 price is given as the most important attribute, so the initial evaluation may have reduced the choice set to A, C, and D (which score highest on price). In the second round, brand name becomes the most important decision criterion; only A and D remain in the choice set, and as A has the highest score for brand name, it will be chosen in preference to D.

Decision

It is important to understand who is actually responsible for making a purchase decision. Both private and organizational purchases usually involve large numbers of people; for example household purchases may involve joint decision making between a husband and wife, with other family members acting as influencers. The subject of 'the decision-making unit' is considered later in this chapter.

The outcome of the evaluation process may be a decision to do any of the following:

1. Buy now

2. Do not buy at all

3. Defer the process

4. Start the process again

Even when a positive decision to buy a product (e.g. the MP3 player used in the example above) is made, further decisions have to be taken to put the main decision into effect, for example:

⦿ When will the product be bought?

⦿ From which retailer?

⦿ How many will be bought?

⦿ Will any optional accessories be bought?

⦿ How will the purchase be paid for (e.g. cash or credit card)?

⦿ Post-purchase evaluation

Wise marketers realize that purchasing activity doesn't end when a sale has been made. The buyer takes the product away and continues to develop feelings about it that will influence his decision next time he needs to make a purchase in that product category. The buyer will also be likely to tell his friends about the purchase, making either favourable or unfavourable comments. Many companies regard satisfied customers as their best form of promotion.

Cognitive dissonance

Buyers approach a purchase with a set of expectations about the performance of the product they are purchasing. A company's advertising and sales messages often serve to heighten expectations about the product's performance. Of course, these expectations are often not met. Maybe the product didn't perform adequately, or the buyer's expectations were simply unrealistically high. In either case, the result is to create what is often referred to as cognitive dissonance, in which our expectations are out of line with the reality around us. We can handle dissonance in a number of ways (Figure 4.7).

⦿ We can often simply return the goods and make a fresh purchase decision. The failed decision becomes part of a learning experience.

⦿ Sometimes it is not possible to return the product. In the case of services that have already been consumed, this option is generally impossible. We may, alternatively, go about complaining and telling our friends about the bad product. Estimates vary, but it is reckoned that on average a dissatisfied customer tells between five and ten people about his or her bad purchase.

Figure 4.7 **Many people faced with buying a product which they are not familiar with, or which is particularly important to them will seek the advice of friends to guide the decision-making process.** Increasingly, the network of friends that individuals refer to during this process is being widened with the development of social network media.

⦿ We can try and reduce dissonance by internal psychological processes. We may convince ourselves that we didn't really make a bad decision, but our expectations were simply too high. We may clutch at minor features of the product that we like, to offset the major features that we dislike. We do not like to think that we made a mistake, so we may try to convince ourselves that we were right in our choice.

Companies often devote part of their promotional budget to reminding customers that they made the right choice in their purchase. Many companies write a short letter to recent customers, providing further reassurance to waverers that they have made the best choice. A convinced happy customer will be more likely to recommend a product to friends and to return to the same supplier next time.

Consumer ethnocentricity and the buying decision

We are living in an increasingly multi-ethnic world in which distinct groups within a society may have quite different purchasing processes to other groups. Ethnocentrism is about belonging to groups, and identifying with an 'in crowd' which is presumed to be superior to an 'out-crowd' of people an individual would prefer not to identify with. This identification can be based on a wide range of values, attitudes, beliefs, and often physical characteristics which are shared by a group of people and passed down through generations.

Sociologists and political scientists have essentially sought to understand how individuals manifest their ethnic identity, with extensive discussion about the links between ethnicity and identification with a nation state.

An individual's ethnocentrism generally starts with the culture into which they are born. Over time, the values and behaviours of this culture will become accepted as a norm. When the individual subsequently becomes aware of other cultures with different values and behaviours, their need to belong may be manifested in identification with their own culture rather than that of others. A new culture may be encountered through migration and may serve to reinforce an individual's sense of identity.

Consumer ethnocentrism has been used to study the notion that domestically produced goods are perceived as superior to foreign ones. One interpretation is that domestically produced goods are produced by the 'tribe' to which a person belongs, whereas imported goods are produced by an alien tribe. A definition of consumer ethnocentrism in the context of an American consumption culture is 'the beliefs held by American consumers about the appropriateness, indeed morality, of purchasing foreign-made products' (Shimp and Sharma 1987, 280). Central to the concept of consumer ethnocentrism is the idea that consumers express identification with their ethnic or national group through the products that they purchase.

Although the concept of consumer ethnocentricity has generally been assumed to imply favouring domestically produced goods, it has been suggested that this reflects a western, developed nation perspective (Agbonifoh and Elimimian 1999). The situation may be different in developing countries where foreign goods may be presumed to be superior to poor quality locally produced goods. This observation is not inconsistent with the concept of consumer ethnocentrism. It merely reflects that some segments of consumers in developing countries may identify aspirationally with their peers in western, developed countries, and the purchase of foreign goods provides visible expression for this sought identity (Dasgupta 2004). It is not uncommon, for example, in some less developed countries in Asia and Africa to see young, relatively affluent people in an otherwise poor society patronizing western retailers such as McDonald's to identify with an aspirational lifestyle. By implication, they dissociate themselves from the culture of poverty from which they wish to escape.

Going global

Do national stereotypes help or hinder exporters?

There is an old joke that in a perfect world, the engineers would be German, the cooks would be Italian, the comedians would be Irish, and the road safety designers would be British. On the other hand, purgatory would be a world where the comedians were German, the engineers Irish, the cooks British, and the road safety experts Italian. Old stereotypes take a long time to die, but there is a lot of evidence that the country of origin of a product can influence buyers' perceptions of a product and their subsequent satisfaction. This is particularly true when very little other information is known about a product or category of products. Faced with choice between two otherwise similar coffee making machines, a consumer may, for example, presume that an Italian machine is better than one made in Korea (Lim and O' Cass 2001; Moon and Jain 2002).

For some products, country of origin effects are likely to be great when other bases for differentiation are low and there is a high level of buyer involvement in the purchase (Kotler and Gertner 2002). Cars and fashion clothing typically fit into this category of products. On the other hand, country of origin effects may be substantially less for low value, low involvement products such as laundry soap and tissue paper. Where there is an element of ostentatious consumption, the country of origin may itself be a means of gaining peer group approval for a purchase. For example, a German sports car may have a higher social approval rating than one that is made in Korea.

So far, the discussion has focused on manufactured goods, but can country of origin effects also have relevance to services? One of the distinguishing features of services is their inseparability, meaning that the production and consumption of a service cannot generally be separated. French restaurants and Italian pizza houses clearly exploit these effects by taking their service processes around the world. Sometimes the opposite may be true, and consumers might travel to a country with a positive country of origin effect in order to receive a service. For example, many people would travel to the United Kingdom or United States for specialist medical treatment.

Are consumers being naive in their evaluation of country of origin effects in a globalized world in which many commentators have talked about 'cultural convergence'? Is it even realistic to identify the country of origin of a complex product, for example a 'German' Mercedes Benz car might actually have been assembled in South Africa from components many of which were made in Turkey or Hungary. What is the 'Germanness' of the car? In the world of globalized business and cultural convergence, will country of origin effects diminish in importance, or will buyers still seek emotional identification through consumption of products associated with a particular area?

◉ Search, experience, and credence bases for buying

In an attempt to distinguish between different kinds of buying situations, products have often been divided into three groups according to the type of buying behaviour associated with them: search, experience, and credence services.

Search products are those for which it is generally easy to define the product in terms of known and measurable characteristics, and a buyer could be reasonably confident that the product they select will provide benefits as defined in the description. Such products are essentially commodities in which points of commonality between product offers are relatively high and points of difference relatively low. As an example, airline tickets between two points may be evaluated on their search characteristics, typically the price of the ticket, the number of changes involved, and the journey time. For short journeys, in particular, intrinsic qualities such as the comfort of the airline and the quality of its customer services may be relatively unimportant. Most airlines would be quite generic in the service they provide—safe transport between the two points. Many online search facilities, such as those of expedia. com and opodo.com allow customers to search for flights and for these to be ranked according to the customers' criteria, typically price and convenience of the timing.

Experience products can only be evaluated through consumption, because they are likely to be quite individual and incapable of being reduced to standardized, generic searchable characteristics. This type of product is likely to emphasize hedonistic rather than utilitarian benefits, typical of theatre performances and many health and caring services. Risk is likely to be perceived as quite high for experience based products, and buyers will seek to reduce this risk by seeking the opinions of friends and contributors to customer review sites.

Credence products are those for which it is very difficult or impossible to assess prior to purchase. Evaluation is therefore likely to be based upon the credibility of the supplier and its reputation for delivering its promises. If we are planning to buy a product for which we have no previous purchasing experience, we may base our evaluation on the credibility of a seller, which may be gained through personal experience of buying other types of products from the company, media reports about the company, or word of mouth recommendation from our friends. Many financial services companies promote themselves on credence values by stressing their long history and good past performance.

In general, goods are more likely to be evaluated on the basis of search qualities, whereas services are more likely to be evaluated on credence qualities., with most hybrid products being based on a combination of search, credence, and experience qualities. Figure 4.8 illustrates schematically a model showing the dominance of each characteristic.

⊙ The decision-making unit (DMU)

In practice, few purchase decisions are made by an individual without reference to others. Usually other people are involved in some sort of role and have a bearing on the final purchase decision. It is important to recognize who the key players in this process are, in order that a product can be configured to meet these people's needs, and that promotional messages can be adapted and directed to the key individuals involved in the purchase decision. A number of roles can be identified among people involved in the decision process (Figure 4.9).

Influencers

These are people or groups of people whom the decision maker refers to in the process of making a decision. You will recall that reference groups can be primary in the form of friends, acquaintances, and work colleagues, or secondary in the form of remote personalities with whom there is no two-way interaction. Where research indicates that the primary reference group exerts a major influence on purchase decisions, this could indicate the need to take measures that will facilitate word-of-mouth communication—for example giving established customers rewards in return for the introduction of new customers. An analysis of secondary reference groups used by consumers in the decision process can help in a number of ways. It will indicate possible personalities to be approached who may be used to endorse

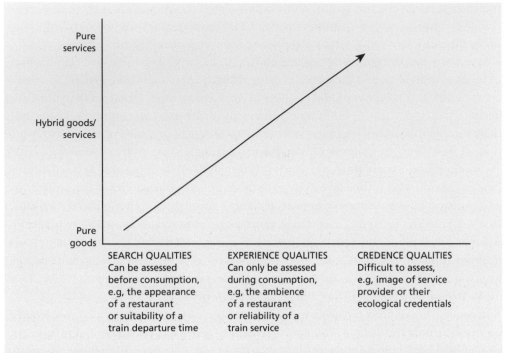

Figure 4.8 A classification of product evaluation characteristics, showing characteristics dominant in typical goods and services purchases.

(*Source*: Based on Mitra et al. 1999).

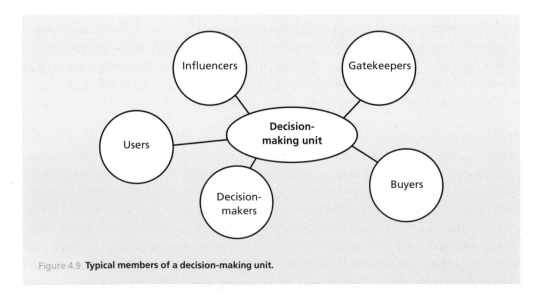

Figure 4.9 **Typical members of a decision-making unit.**

a product in the company's advertising. It will also indicate which opinion leaders an organization should target as part of its communication programme in order to achieve the maximum 'trickle-down' effect. The media can be included within this secondary reference group—what a newspaper writes in its columns can have an important influence on purchase decisions.

Gatekeepers

These are most commonly found among commercial buyers. Their main effect is to act as a filter on the range of products that enter the decision choice set. Gatekeepers can take a number of forms—for example a buying manager's personal assistant barring calls from sales representatives has the effect of screening out a number of possible choices. In many organizations it can be difficult to establish just who is acting as a gatekeeper; identifying a marketing strategy that gains acceptance by the gatekeeper, or bypasses him completely, is therefore made difficult. In larger organizations, and the public sector in particular, a select list of suppliers who are invited to submit tenders for work may exist—and if it is not on this list a supplier will be unable to enter the decision set.

Although gatekeepers are most commonly associated with purchases made by organizations, they can also be found in consumer purchase processes. In the case of many household goods and services, such as buying wallpaper or booking an overseas holiday, an early part of the decision process may be the collection of samples or brochures. While the final decision may be the subject of joint discussion and action, the initial stage of collecting the items for the decision set is more likely to be left to one person. In this way, one member of a family may pick up holiday brochures or samples of wallpaper, thereby acting as a gatekeeper and restricting the subsequent choice to the products of those companies whose brochures or samples were originally collected.

Buyers

The buyer actually undertakes the task of buying a product, for example by going into the shop, or ordering online. In the case of industrial goods and services, low-budget items that are not novel may be left to the discretion of a buyer. In this way, office stationery may be contracted by a buying clerk within the organization without immediate reference to anybody else. In the case of modified rebuys, or novel purchases, the decision-making unit is likely to be larger.

Users

The user of a product may not be the person responsible for making the actual purchase decision. This is typical of many items of clothing bought within household units. For example, it has been estimated that in the UK over half of all men's socks are bought by women. Parents buy products for their children, with varying levels of influence (or, pester power) from the children who will be the actual users of the product. In the case of organizational purchases, there is often a separation between users and buyers and research should be undertaken to reveal the extent to which users are important contributors to the decision process.

In the case of the business air travel market, it is important to understand the degree of pressure that individual travellers can exert on their choice of airline, as opposed to the influence of a company buyer (who might have arranged a long-term contract with one particular airline), a gatekeeper (who may discard promotional material relating to new airline services), or other influencers within the organization (e.g. cost centre managers might be more concerned with the cost of using a product, in contrast to the user's overriding concern with its quality.)

Decision maker

This is the person (or group of individuals) who makes the final decision to purchase, whether he executes the purchase himself or instructs others to do so. With many family-based consumer products, it can be difficult to identify just who within the family carries most weight in making the final decision. Research into family purchases has suggested that, in the case of package holidays and furniture, women dominate in making the final decision, whereas in the case of financial services it is men who dominate. An analysis of how a decision is made can realistically be achieved only by means of qualitative in-depth research. In the case of decisions made by organizational buyers, the task of identifying the individuals responsible for making a final decision—and their level within the organizational hierarchy—becomes even more difficult.

◉ Models of buyer decision making

The buying process has now been portrayed as a highly complex one, in which a variety of personal and environmental factors influence the decisions we make. We can process a lot of information with outcomes that can sometimes be seen as quite irrational. So how can we attempt to model the buying process in order to establish some general rules that explain why a buyer decides to purchase one product rather than another?

A simple starting point is a black box model of consumer response (Figure 4.10). The inputs to the decision process are the range of psychological, sociological, economic, and situational factors. The outcome is the decision (e.g. whether or not to purchase, whether to purchase now or to defer, where to buy from, how many, etc.). In between is the 'black box', comprising our decision-making processes. The black box determines how we translate complex information into decisions. As individuals, we differ in the way that our processing occurs.

Of course, a black box is a simple representation of the input–decision–outcome process. In itself, it does not explain how a decision is actually made. For this, a number of models of buyer behaviour have been developed. If a model is to have value to marketing managers, it should be capable of use as a predictive tool, given a set of conditions on which the model is based. Modelling buyer decision processes poses many problems. At one extreme, simple models may help in very general terms in developing marketing strategies, but are too general to be of use in any specific situation. At the other extreme, models of buyer behaviour

Pester power pays

What role do children play in the purchase of the goods that they ultimately consume? There has been considerable debate about the extent of pester power, whereby parents give in to the demands of children. Increasingly, advertisers are aiming their promotional messages over the heads of adults and straight at children. The ethics of doing this have been questioned by many, and some countries, such as Sweden and Greece, have imposed restrictions on television advertising of children's products. A report published by the UK children's research company Childwise (2010) showed how children had become increasingly sophisticated shoppers. In a survey of 2,245 children aged 5–16, 78 per cent of 10–12-year-olds said they enjoyed shopping. More than two-thirds liked collecting the latest things that their peers were collecting, and nearly half of 10–12-year-olds thought that brands are important when they buy. The average ten-year-old had internalized 300 to 400 brands, with a majority of even 5–6-year-olds able to name a brand of crisps or confectionery. In 2010, the average child received £9.70 per week from pocket money and jobs, but as a sign of the recessionary times, this had fallen from £9.90 the previous year.

There was speculation about how children came to learn about these brands, with some pointing the finger at television advertising, especially during the breaks in children's programmes, while others who have studied children's behaviour claimed that children pick up 'cool' brands from their peer group. Despite a denial of its effects on children, many marketers of products consumed by children are quietly concerned by any moves towards EU integration of legislation on advertising to children. As a sign of regulators' increasing concern about the vulnerability of children to advertising, Ofcom, the UK broadcast regulator issued new rules in 2007 banning television adverts for high fat, salt, and sugar foods from programming likely to be popular with under 16s. While this may have seemed like good news to harassed parents, many felt that the restrictions did not go far enough, and called for a total ban on advertising such foods.

Even with advertising restrictions, companies have managed to get through to children in more subtle ways, for example by sponsoring educational materials used in schools and paying celebrities to endorse their products. When it comes to such items as confectionery and toys, just what influence do children exert on the purchase decision? And when football clubs deliberately change their strip every season, is it unethical for the clubs to expect fanatical children to pester their parents to buy a new one so that they can keep up with their peer group?

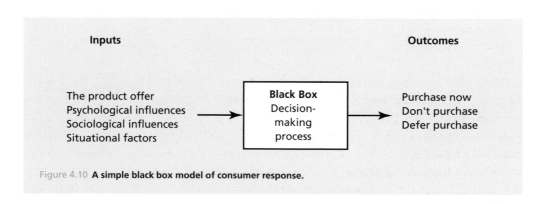

Figure 4.10 **A simple black box model of consumer response.**

based on narrowly defined sectors may lose much of their explanatory and predictive power if applied to another sector where assumptions on which the original model was based no longer apply. In any event, most models of buyer behaviour provide normative rather than strictly quantitative explanations of buyer behaviour, and there can be no guarantee that the assumptions on which the model was originally based continue to be valid.

One widely used model that has been widely applied and subsequently developed is that developed by Howard and Sheth (1969). The principles of their model are shown in Figure 4.11.

The framework incorporates a number of elements:

- **Inputs:** This comprises information about the range of competing products that may satisfy a consumer's need. Information may be obtained from personal or published sources.

- **Behavioural determinants:** Individuals bring to the purchase decision a predisposition to act in a particular way. This predisposition is influenced by the culture that they live in and family and personality factors, among others.

- **Perceptual reaction:** Inputs are likely to be interpreted in different ways by different individuals, based on their unique personality make-up, and conditioning which is a result of previous purchase experiences. While one person might readily accept the advertising messages of a bank, another might have been disappointed by that bank in the past, or by banks' advertising in general; she is therefore less likely to perceive such inputs as credible.

- **Processing determinants:** This part of the model focuses attention on the way in which a decision is made. Important determinants include the motivation of the individual to satisfy a particular need, the individual's attitude to a particular product or organization,

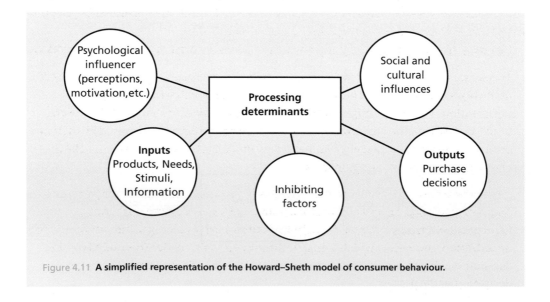

Figure 4.11 **A simplified representation of the Howard–Sheth model of consumer behaviour.**

and the weight attached to each of the factors used in the evaluation. For some consumers for some products, critical product requirements may exist which must be present if a product is to be included in the decision set. At other times, consumers attach weights to each of its attributes and select the product with the highest weighted 'score' (see Figure 4.6).

⊙ Inhibitors: A number of factors might prevent an individual from making a decision to purchase a particular product, such as the ease of access to the product, its price, and the terms and conditions for delivery.

⊙ Outputs: The outcome of the decision process may either be to go ahead and purchase, or alternatively, not to buy or to defer a decision to a later date.

More specific models of buyer behaviour have been developed as a result of research into specific sectors. Many of these have sought to rank in order of importance the factors that contribute towards the purchase decision, and to identify critical factors, the absence of which will exclude a possibility from a decision set. As an example, research into restaurant choice decisions by Auty (1992) identified five key factors, ranking food quality as the most important, then image and atmosphere. However, it was also noted that the importance attached to each of these factors differed according to the purpose of the visit to the restaurant; the factors influencing a choice of restaurant for a celebration were quite different from those used for a general social occasion.

⊙ Personal and organizational buyer behaviour compared

At the beginning of this chapter it was noted that buying processes are likely to differ for situations where it is an organization rather than an individual making a purchase. Instead of being seen as completely different processes, all personal and organizational buying processes can be placed along a continuum (Cova and Salle 2008).

However, there are a number of features which characterize organizational buying processes.

⊙ Two sets of needs are being met when an organization buys a product: the formal needs of the organization, and the personal needs of the individuals who make up the organization. The former might be thought of as being the more 'rational'. However, individuals within the organization seek to satisfy needs that are influenced by their own perceptual and behavioural environment, very much in the same way as would be the case with private consumer purchases.

⊙ More people are typically involved in organizational purchases. High-value purchases may require evaluation and approval at a number of levels of an organization's management hierarchy. Research might indicate, for particular organizations or types of organization, the level at which a final decision is normally made. The analysis of the decision-making unit might also reveal a wider range of influencers present in the decision-making process.

MARKETING in ACTION

Smells sell

Smell has been used for a long time by organizations to try and encourage buyers to buy. Coffee shops have often circulated the smell of freshly roasted beans by the entrance door in the hope that such smells would be an irresistible invitation to passers-by to enter. Supermarkets have managed smells carefully, for example by extracting unpleasant smells of fish and detergents, and instead circulating fresh bread smells.

The effect of smell on consumers' purchase/repurchase/recommendation, has been well researched (see, for example, Bosmans 2006). Among a number of reported findings, the smell of mulled wine has been seen to increase sales of Christmas food, and the smell of toast has been associated with sales of electric toasters. Improvements in technology no longer constrain a service provider to those smells that are an inherent part of their production processes—such as bread smells for a bakery and coffee smells for a coffee shop. Manufactured smells can be imported that are completely unrelated to production processes. The electrical shop selling toasters, for example, would almost certainly have to import an artificial smell, rather than producing it naturally by toasting bread.

Why are companies so keen to spend money creating artificial smells? Most simply, if a smell is seen to work, its use will be further developed. A large multi-outlet chain can experiment with smells by measuring the effects of specific smells on sales in experimental outlets, compared with sales in matched control outlets. More fundamentally, smell can act as part of a service organization's distinctive identity, in much the same way as its distinctive visual identity. Even with a blindfold, many book-buyers may be able to recognize the distinctive smell of a Waterstone's bookshop, or of a Starbucks coffee shop. Why do smells have such effects on buyers? Stimulus–response models can provide some explanation. Some responses may be part of our basic psychological make-up; for example the smell of fresh food to a hungry person is likely to create a desire for food. However, other stimuli may have a more indirect effect through association with evoked memories. There is no physiological reason why the smell of popcorn should help a DVD rental business to hire out more videos, but an effect arises from association of popcorn with previous visits to the cinema, maybe associated with happy childhood memories. Of course, a smell that evokes such a response in one person may have no effect in another, and companies expanding overseas need to understand cultural definitions of smell, as well as basic physiological responses.

Is the use of smells to sell ethical? Can the use of artificial smells be justified where there is no link to actual production methods, and some would argue the company is cynically exploiting consumers' subconscious memories? Are some groups of customers particularly vulnerable to such an approach, for example children, who may be attracted to a store by the smell of confectionery? Or is the use of smell evidence of organizations' strong customer focus and their determination to create a pleasant experience, whose success can be measured by customers returning and recommending the business to others?

⊙ Organizational purchases are more likely to be made according to formalized routines. At its simplest, this may involve delegating to a junior buyer the task of making repeat orders for goods and services that have previously been evaluated. At the other extreme, many high-value purchases may be made only after a formal process of bidding and evaluation has been undertaken.

Figure 4.12 **If a domestic telephone breaks down, it may cause no more than annoyance and inconvenience to the owner.** However, for business users, the consequences of a failure can be much more serious, possibly leading to lost sales, delayed orders, and missed production. Few members of the organizational decision-making unit would want to carry the blame for selecting a phone provider which subsequently lets the company down. For business customers, telephone providers must appeal to all members of the decision-making unit by stressing that its services are reliable and have benefits in use which will be good value to the company. BT, the largest provider in the UK telecoms market, offers numerous packages for its domestic market. However, this advertisement aimed at the business sector stresses a particular concern of business user—the need to get a faulty phone repaired quickly so that business is not interrupted.
(*Source*: Reproduced with kind permission of British Telecom PLC.)

- The elements of the product offer that are considered critical in the evaluation process are likely to differ. For many products, the emphasis placed on price by many personal buyers is replaced by reliability and performance characteristics by the organizational buyer. In many cases, poor performance of a product can have direct financial consequences for an organization—a low-price but unreliable computer might merely cause annoyance and frustration to a private buyer, but might lead to lost production output or lost sales for an organizational buyer (Figure 4.12).

- The greater number of people involved in organizational buying also often results in the whole process taking longer. A desire to minimize risk is inherent in many formal organizational motives and informally present in the motives of individuals within organizations. This often results in lengthy feasibility studies being undertaken. In some new markets, especially overseas markets, trust in suppliers might be an important factor for purchasers when evaluating competing suppliers, and it may take time to build up a trusting relationship before any purchase commitment is secured.

Developing ongoing relationships with buyers

It was noted earlier that the buying process generally does not end when a purchase is completed. For many products, the purchase and subsequent use of the product provides input to the next purchase decision. Companies have recognized that it can be profitable to cultivate long-term customers; hence the emergence of 'relationship marketing' as an alternative to a one-off, transaction-based approach to marketing. Marketing managers have seen the

MARKETING in ACTION

A £20 meal or a lifelong relationship?

What is the lifetime value of a restaurant customer? First-time customers may be spending only £20 on this occasion, but if they like what they get, how much are they likely to spend in the future? A typical diner eating out just once a month could be worth £2,000 in five years. If customers are happy, they are likely to tell their friends—if they're not, they are likely to tell even more of their friends. It follows that customers should be seen as investments, to be carefully nurtured over time. When things go wrong (e.g. through overbooking) it would probably be to the restaurant's advantage to spend heavily on putting things right for the customer (e.g. by offering money off a future meal). Judged on the basis of the current transaction, the restaurant may make a loss, but it will have protected its investment in a future income stream.

Like all investments, some are worth more than others. How should a company decide which customers are worth investing in? And what level of investment can be justified in terms of the speculative future income that could result from the relationship?

potential advantages of reducing levels of customer 'churn' by improving the retention rates of profitable customers (see Reichheld and Sasser 1990).

Reasons for the development of ongoing customer relationships

Relational exchange is not a new concept; it has been observed, for example, in the pattern of exchanges between textile manufacturers and intermediaries in Victorian England. Also, while relationships may have been rediscovered in the west, they have remained a fundamental part of exchange in many eastern cultures (Lee et al. 2001).

In recent times, organizations' growing interest in developing closer relationships with their private and corporate customers has come about for two principal reasons.

1. In increasingly competitive markets, good product quality alone may be insufficient for a company to gain competitive advantage. Superior ongoing relationships with customers supplement a firm's competitive advantage. This is evident in the car market, where the focal point of marketing has shifted from a preoccupation with better design, to better service and now to better relationships. Today, many private buyers of cars choose a car that comes with the best support package, keeping the car financed, maintained, insured, and replaced at the end of a specified period (Figure 4.13). For many, the three-yearly purchase of a car has been turned into an ongoing relationship with a car company to supply all the services that make a car available to the consumer.

2. The emergence of powerful, user-friendly databases has enabled large companies to know much more about their customers as individuals, recreating in a computer what the small business owner knew in his or her head. Many of the current developments in relationship marketing would have been unthinkable without modern information technology capabilities.

Figure 4.13 **One of the great marketing successes of the car industry in recent years has been to transform the sale of a car into what is effectively an ongoing relationship with the car manufacturer.** For many private buyers, the traditional way of buying a car has been to pay a sum of money for the car (either by cash or through a loan), keep the car for probably three or four years, then trade it in for a new one and make a fresh payment for the new car. Today, a wide variety of relationship-based service arrangements are available to private buyers which give them the use of a car for a defined period of time, and just as importantly, service benefits which allow them to make the greatest use of their car. A relationship-based approach to car sales typically includes a loan which is repaid over two or three years; an extended warranty; and a breakdown support service, some of which have been increasingly sophisticated in the benefits they offer car buyers to keep them mobile (e.g. many support packages include the provision of a temporary replacement car, and overnight accommodation if necessary). Many agreements give the car buyer the option of returning their car at the end of a specified period and exchanging it for a newer model. Instead of spending £15,000 every three years for a tangible object, the car buyer now typically pays two or three hundred pounds a month for a service-based relationship with a car company and its dealers.

The main differences between traditional one-off transaction-based exchanges and relationship-based exchanges are summarized in Figure 4.14.

The extent to which the development of ongoing relationships with customers represents a desirable marketing strategy is dependent upon three main factors:

1. **The characteristics of the product:** Where products are complex and involve a high degree of uncertainty on the part of buyers, the likelihood of customers seeking a relationship is increased. Relationships are often a necessity where the stream of product benefits is produced and consumed over a period of time—a programme of

Traditional transaction-oriented marketing	Relationship marketing
Focus on a single sale	Focus on customer retention
Short-term orientation	Long-term orientation
Sales to anonymous buyers	Tracking of named buyers
Salesperson is the main interface between buyer and seller	Multiple levels of relationships between buyer and seller
Limited customer commitment	High customer commitment
Quality is the responsibility of production department	Quality is the responsibility of all

Figure 4.14 **The components of transactional and relational exchange compared.**

medical treatment, for example. For some products, a relationship may allow preferential treatment or semi-automatic responses to requests for service, thereby reducing transaction costs associated with multiple service ordering. It has also been suggested that both suppliers and customers seek the security of relationships where the market environment is turbulent.

2. The characteristics of customers: Some customers may be happy to shop around each time they approach a purchase, while others may value the perceived security of an ongoing relationship with a supplier they have come to trust. Some buyers may value social aspects of an ongoing relationship and judge a transaction not just by its economic outcomes. Research has also suggested that the importance attributed to components of a relationship differ between groups, for example in the way that women place more emphasis on trust and commitment in their relationships than men (Shemwell et al. 1994).

3. The characteristics of suppliers: By developing relationships with their customers, suppliers add to the differentiation of their products and give customers a reason to remain loyal. The extent to which organizations are relationship-rather than product-oriented can be related to their structure, processes, and core values. Organizations differ in the extent to which they are able, or willing, to calculate the lifetime value of a customer (Figure 4.15).

Figure 4.15 **Many retailers offer benefits to customers who sign up for their loyalty programmes.**
A retailer's challenge is often to encourage the large number of people who visit its stores each day to spend more during their visit. A loyalty card offers an inducement to customers to place a larger part of their total expenditure with the store, especially where the rewards are seen as significant. However, the biggest benefit of a loyalty programme to most retailers is to get a much deeper insight into the shopping behaviour of their customers. No longer does it have to base its marketing planning simply on till receipt analysis, it can now understand each individual's pattern of buying over a period of time. It can also link data collected at the point of sale with other demographic data provided by card holders. Ideally, a company should have sufficient insight that it can make sales offers which are particularly suited to an individual's future needs. Although some retailers have dismissed loyalty programmes as an expensive gimmick which adds to a company's operating costs, many others have taken the view that the additional costs are a low price to pay for the rich data that is provided.

Methods used to develop ongoing relationships with customers

Companies seek to move buyers up what has often been described as a ladder of loyalty to the point where they become enthusiastic advocates for a firm's products (Figure 4.16). As customers move up this ladder, the relationship they have with a company changes from one based on convenience or necessity to one that is emotionally valued by the buyer.

However, considerable double-speak is often present in attempts by firms to develop customer relationships. In the service sector, many organizations are simplifying and 'industrializing' their processes, usually in an attempt to improve their operational efficiency and consistency of performance. Such companies may talk about relationship development with customers, based on dialogue that is driven by information technology. But such

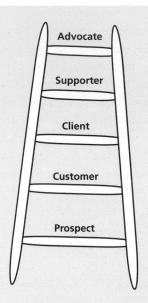

Figure 4.16 **Companies seek to turn a mere prospective customer into a strong advocate for the company.** Loyalty is generally a multi-stage process, which involves taking customers up to progressively higher rungs on a ladder of loyalty.

relationships can be qualitatively quite different from those based on social bonds founded on emotional commitment and trust. While UK clearing banks have become vigorous in their development of customer databases and named personal banking advisers, many customers may feel that the relationship with their bank today is qualitatively worse than when a branch manager was able to enter into a more holistic dialogue with them. Many unhappy customers do not switch banks, however, because the perceived financial and psychological costs are too great.

Managers of firms seeking to develop relationships with their customers should avoid the arrogant belief that customers seek such relationships. Surveys have indicated that many categories of buyers are becoming increasingly confident in venturing outside a business relationship and increasingly reluctant to enter into an ongoing relationship. Relationship marketing strategies may fail where buyers' perceptions are of reduced choice and freedom to act opportunistically rather than the added value to be derived from a relationship. Added value must be defined by sellers in terms of buyers' needs, rather than focusing on customers as captives who can be cross-sold other products from a firm's portfolio.

So, why should buyers wish to go back repeatedly to the same supplier? Below we consider some of the methods used by companies to create ongoing relationships with customers.

Customer satisfaction

In a competitive marketplace, customer satisfaction can be the most important reason for customers deciding to make a repeat purchase, and telling their friends about their satisfaction.

To achieve high levels of satisfaction requires the effort of all functions within an organization. Relationship development cannot simply be left to a relationship manager. There are many notable cases of companies that have not developed any explicit relationship marketing programme, but nevertheless achieve very high levels of recommendation by their customers. Consider, for example, the chocolate retailer Thorntons, which has developed strong loyalty from customers who return to its shops for indulgence and gift purchases of chocolate, despite having no formally stated relationship marketing programme.

Of course, many companies enjoy high levels of repeat business without providing high levels of customer satisfaction. Many train passengers may complain about the price and reliability of their train service, but they return because they have no realistic alternative.

Even companies that have an apparently poor standard of service can achieve high levels of repeat business in a competitive market by charging low prices. Retail chains such as Aldi and Lidl have developed strong loyalty from price-sensitive customers who consider that the total service offer (access to the store, range of products, cleanliness, friendliness, etc.) are acceptable in return for the price they have paid. The danger here is that competitors may enter the market with similarly low prices, but offering higher levels of service. Would customers still remain loyal?

Trust

The top of the loyalty ladder is more likely to be reached by a customer who trusts a company. Trust is a complex multi-faceted concept which has been extensively researched by marketers (e.g. Morgan and Hunt 1994). Some retailers, such as Boots and John Lewis, consistently score highly in surveys of customers' trust in firms, and these companies generally tend to have high levels of customer loyalty. However, merely being trusted doesn't guarantee profitability for a firm—the rest of its operational and financial strategies must also be right.

Adding value to a relationship

A relationship, to be sustainable, must add value in the eyes of customers. This value can come about in a number of ways, including:

- Making the reordering of goods and services easier (e.g. many hotels record guests' details and preferences so that they do not have to be re-entered each time the guest checks in).

- Offering privileges to customers who wish to enter into some type of formal relationship. As an example, many retailers hold special preview events for loyalty card holders, and send a free copy of the store's magazine. Loyalty cards allow companies to gather a lot of valuable data about their customers' buying behaviour (see Meyer-Waarden 2008). Customers will generally participate in a loyalty card programme only if they believe that they will gain something of value out of it. Many companies have been imaginative in creating value in the buyer's mind, beyond basic cash rebate schemes.

- Developing an ability to jointly solve problems. For example, a car repair garage may endeavour to identify exactly what the problem is that a customer wants put right, rather than leaving it to the customer to specify the work that she wants carried out. Such joint problem solving requires a considerable level of trust to have been developed between the parties. In some cases, professional codes of conduct govern the delegation of problem-solving responsibilities.

Creating barriers to exit

Companies can bring about repeat buying by trying to make it difficult for customers to defect to a competitor. Customers can unwittingly walk into traps where they become dependent upon a supplier for continuing support. Suppliers of industrial machinery create ongoing relationships whereby they are the sole supplier of the spare parts or consumable items that the purchaser must buy in order to continue using their equipment. Many companies negotiate exclusive supply agreements with a supplier in return for a promise of preferential treatment. In both cases, the customer becomes dependent in the short term. However, such ties can usually be broken eventually (e.g. when the machinery is replaced, or when an exclusive supply contract comes up for renewal), and it is at that point that the true loyalty of a customer is put to the test. It has been pointed out that such ties may lead to customer *detention* rather than *retention* (Dick and Basu 1994) and that a company that has not achieved a more deep-seated emotional relationship with its customers may be unable to sustain those relationships if the legal or technological environment changes.

Problems of creating ongoing relationships with buyers

There are many situations in which buyers are not responsive to firms' efforts to create ongoing relationships. Many companies serve market segments where customers have no underlying need to make further purchases of a category of product that the company is able to supply. In the extreme case, a small-scale company may appeal to the curiosity of buyers, for whom a second-time purchase will have little of its original value—curiosity. This phenomenon is present in many tourism-related businesses in destinations of symbolic rather than aesthetic quality. (For example, many people make a religious pilgrimage once in their lifetime with little incentive to return again.) In the case of supplies to governmental organizations (and often to larger private-sector organizations), rules for tendering of new purchases may nullify sellers' attempts to develop continuing and uninterrupted relationships. Where relationships between commercial buyers and sellers are deemed to be against the public interest (e.g. where they make it difficult for new entrants to enter a market), regulatory agencies may order them to be reduced in scope. (For example, soft drinks companies' exclusive supply agreements with retail customers have in some circumstances been held to be against the public interest.) Finally, attempts to create ongoing relationships by firms can be costly and may put a firm at a competitive disadvantage in markets where price is the most important decision factor.

Relationships between connected customers

Finally, we must not overlook the networks of relationships that can exist between the customers of a company and which, as we have seen above, can have a big impact on the buying decisions made by consumers. *Anthropological and sociological approaches* have contributed an understanding of individuals' desire to identify with groups and the goods and services that they consume (e.g. Sierra and McQuitty 2005). Relationships satisfy individuals' affiliation and attachment needs, and there is some evidence that commercial relationships have replaced church, family, and work-based relationships as a means of satisfying these needs (Palmer and Gallagher 2007). The term tribal marketing has been used to explain how marketers can take advantage of individuals' desire to belong to a group (Cova and Cova 2002).

The ability of customers to be connected with one another is not new, but today, the development of various Web 2.0 social network technologies has extended the possibilities for such connectedness. A distinguishing feature of social network sites is the apparent willingness and ability of individuals to communicate their thoughts to others, including people they do not know. Many strong service brands such as Skype have been built with very little paid for advertising and instead relied on referral through online communities.

Online communities can pose a threat as well as an opportunity to companies as they can rapidly spread the views of dissatisfied, angry customers. As an example, the bank HSBC announced in 2007 that it intended to end interest-free overdrafts for students after they had graduated, but was subsequently forced to do a U-turn and restore the facility. Many commentators attributed this change of heart to the strength of feeling expressed through Facebook circles of friends. Another example is provided by two employees from Domino's pizza in North Carolina who posted a video of disgusting food preparation on YouTube (Vogt 2009).

MARKETING in ACTION

Spurious loyalty?

Just because customers repeatedly come back to a company it does not necessarily mean that they have a loyal relationship to the company. This point was made, tongue-in-cheek, during a war of words between British Airways and Virgin Atlantic Airways. The latter had objected to BA's use of the advertising slogan 'The World's Favourite Airline'. Statistically, it was true at the time that more passengers travelled internationally with British Airways than with any other airline, but surveys of airline users had consistently put Virgin ahead of BA in terms of perceived quality of service. Virgin's Richard Branson claimed that on BA's logic the M25, London's notorious orbital motorway, could be described as the world's favourite motorway. Despite coming back to the motorway day after day, few motorists could claim to be loyal to it—they simply had no other choice.

The spat between BA and Virgin serves to underline the point that customer loyalty is about more than mere repetitious buying. True loyalty involves customers becoming enthusiastic advocates of a company.

⊙ Chapter summary and linkages to other chapters

A sound understanding of buying processes is essential for the development of an appropriate marketing mix. A purchase decision is influenced by a wide range of personal, social, economic, and situational factors, and varies between different types of product and different individuals. The outcome of the decision-making process may be to buy now, to not buy, or to defer a decision. Few buying decisions are made without reference to others, so it is important to identify the members of the decision-making unit. This is particularly true in the case of organizational purchases, where it is important to know what product features and promotional messages motivate different individuals.

Study of buyer behaviour is increasingly extending beyond the initial purchase by attempting to understand how buyers can be turned into loyal repeat customers. Relationship marketing is becoming an important part of many companies' marketing plans as they realize that it can be more profitable to take care to retain the customers they currently have, than to search expensively for new customers to replace lapsed ones.

In the first two chapters we noted in general terms that marketing is essentially about satisfying customers' needs profitably. This chapter has focused more specifically on buyers' evaluation of sellers' attempts to satisfy their needs. In subsequent chapters we will explore how companies undertake research into needs and buying processes (Chapter 5) and subsequently will group together buyers that have essentially similar needs (Chapter 6). Companies then develop a distinctive marketing mix which will give them a competitive advantage in satisfying the needs of the customers they are targeting (Chapters 7–11).

KEY PRINCIPLES OF MARKETING

- Buying is a process with a number of overlapping stages and a feedback loop from post-consumption to the start of the next buying cycle.

- The effort that buyers put into the buying process is influenced by their level of involvement with the product.

- We rarely make decisions entirely on our own. Marketers need to be aware of the broader decision-making unit of people who may knowingly or unknowingly influence a purchase decision.

- Models of buyer behaviour attempt to portray the buying process. Because of the situational nature of buying decisions, general models cannot hope to give anything more than a general indication of these processes.

- It is generally more profitable for companies to retain existing customers than to replace lapsed customers with new ones.

CASE STUDY

How do you really understand young people's buying behaviour?

How can any marketer get inside *your* mind to understand how *you* actually make purchase decisions? Structured questionnaire surveys may have a role for collecting large-scale factual data, but they have major weaknesses when it comes to understanding individuals' attitudes. Complex sets of factors that influence our buying decisions can only rarely be captured by a questionnaire. Qualitative approaches such as those using focus groups can get closer to the truth, but participants often still find themselves inhibited from telling the full story. Many marketing managers, especially those without large research budgets, inevitably end up relying on their own personal experiences to understand how consumers behave. This may be easy for target markets that are in the 20–40 age range (the age of typical marketers), but how do you get inside the mind of teenagers, or elderly people?

Ethnographic approaches are becoming increasingly popular among marketers as a means of getting closer to the truth about consumer behaviour. Ethnographic research is nothing new, having been used by anthropologists in their study of the rituals of tribal people. Marketers have been relatively recent converts to the techniques of ethnography.

One company that has applied ethnography to marketing is called EverydayLives. Its clients have included Unilever, Proctor & Gamble, Pedigree, and GlaxoSmithKline. On behalf of its clients, it seeks to uncover hidden truths about the way people lead their lives, by paying volunteers to be followed for days on end, being filmed, and having their every move recorded. According to the company, an observational survey would cost about £4,000–£6,000 per household, and a typical project for a client would involve a minimum of six households. For major international brands, many more than this number would be involved.

One essential feature of ethnographic research is that it must not have any predetermined agenda. There is little value in undertaking this type of research if the mindset of the researcher is expecting to see preconceived phenomena—it is the unexpected that is often of most interest, and which is so difficult to pick up through more structured forms of survey. Inevitably, participants in a survey may feel very self-conscious while they are being filmed, and the more interesting insights are likely to be observed when participants are feeling relaxed and off their guard. It is not just what people actually do that can be interesting, but what they almost do, and the body language used when members of the household are discussing an issue. It can take several hours of filming to yield just a few moments of true insights into participants' true attitudes and behaviour.

One example of the company's ethnographic research in action was provided by a project commissioned by the footwear brand Dr Martens. The company wanted to understand how young people used fashion brands in their everyday lives. Why, for example, did some brands, such as Nike trainers or baseball caps become so iconic in youth culture? The researchers identified groups of young people around the world who corresponded to Dr Martens' target market. In return for a payment, volunteers were followed for several days and their daily routines filmed with a handheld digital camera. In total, 180 hours of captured film was edited to just one hour of highlights showing the key drivers of youth culture which are relevant to the Dr Martens brand.

It seemed that young people preferred fashions that allowed them to customize an item of clothing and in some way take 'ownership' of it. This was seen in the way that many young people wore a baseball cap the wrong way round, or pulled the tongue of a pair of trainers from behind the laces. The research drew the conclusion that iconic fashion items for young people had to have a distinctive label or style that made their wearers stand out as part of a tribe. The company's research brief did not go as far as designing shoes that might appeal to the target market—this is where the research had to be picked up by the brand owner and operationalized. Given the research evidence of young people's need to belong to a tribe, yet still be individual, how could Dr Martens develop its product? Could coloured shoelaces be one means of allowing young people to associate with a respected brand, yet at the same time show their individuality through different coloured laces?

What makes for good ethnographic research? EverydayLives has a number of tips for making the most of the technique. It suggests avoiding telling households what the research project is about, until it is over. That way, the chances of participants deliberately playing to the camera can be reduced. But apart from that, involvement and total immersion of the researchers in the lives of the participants is key to understanding their attitudes, beliefs, and lifestyles.

Ethnographic research has not been without its critics. Some have described it as 'psycho-babble', arguing that it does not lead to original insights and explanation, but microscopic reflections of everyday events. At its worst, ethnographic research could be entertaining, easy, and quick, but superficial and the 'insights' of a poorly undertaken piece of research could be unduly influenced by the background and prejudices of the researchers. In short, hours of filming and 'analysis' could actually be a pointless cover for reinforcing established beliefs and prejudices. Some have questioned the ethics of ethnographic approaches, especially where participants are not fully informed about the purpose of the research. The participants themselves may not be representative of a product's target market, and insights may be biased towards outgoing, camera seeking types, rather than quieter, more private types of people whose views will remain difficult to assess.

Sources:

Daily Telegraph, 'Big brands turning to Big Brother', 29 March 2007, p. 17.

Miles, Louella, 'Market Research: Living their lives', *Marketing* 11 December 2003, p. 1.5

EverydayLives website: **www.everydaylives.com**

....

Case study review questions

1. Critically assess the role of ethnographic research as a means of learning more about buyer behaviour.

2. Discuss the ethical issues that are raised by ethnographic research.

3. Discuss possible alternative approaches by which marketers may learn more about 'youth culture'.

CHAPTER REVIEW QUESTIONS

1. Is it realistic to represent the buying process as a simple linear process? What factors might complicate such apparently smooth progress?

2. Discuss the main ways in which buying processes for airline travel typically differ between private buyers and business buyers. How might airlines adapt their product offer to take account of these differences?

3. Critically assess methods used by banks to develop ongoing relationships with their personal customers.

ACTIVITIES

1. Reflect on the last time that you went for a night out with a group of friends to a bar/restaurant or nightclub. Analyse the decision processes, information sources, and evaluation criteria that you used in arriving at a decision as to where to go and what to order.

2. Refer to the buyer evaluation matrix shown in Figure 4.6. Now apply this to the decision making process that you and your friends may go through if you were evaluating competing service offers from mobile phone service providers.

3. Review consumer magazines containing adverts for telecommunication services. Now review professional/trade magazines which also contain adverts for telecommunication service. Critically evaluate the ways in which the messages differ between the two types of magazine. What do the differences, if any, say about differences in buying process between private buyers and business buyers?

REFERENCES

Agbonifoh, B.A. and Elimimian, J.U. (1999) 'Attitudes of Developing Countries Towards Country-of-Origin Products in an Era of Multiple Brands'. *Journal of International Consumer Marketing*, 11 (4), 97–116.

Auty, S. (1992) 'Consumer Choice and Segmentation in the Restaurant Industry'. *Services Industries Journal*, 12, 324–39.

Berry, L.L. (1995) 'Relationship Marketing of Services: Growing Interest, Emerging Perspectives'. *Journal of the Academy of Marketing Science*, 23, 236–45.

Bosmans, A. (2006) 'Scents and Sensibility: When Do (In)Congruent Ambient Scents Influence Product Evaluations?' *Journal of Marketing*, 70 (3), 32–43.

Butcher, K., Sparks, B., and O'Callaghan, F. (2002) 'Effect of Social Influence on Repurchase Intentions'. *Journal of Services Marketing*, 16, 503–12.

Childwise (2010) *ChildWise Monitor Trends Report 2010*. Norwich: Childwise.

Clegg, P. (1956) *A Social and Economic History of Britain 1760–1955*. London: Harrap.

Cova, B. and Cova, V. (2002) 'Tribal Marketing: the Tribalisation of Society and its Impact on the Conduct of Marketing'. *European Journal of Marketing*, 36 (5/6), 595–620.

Cova, B. and Salle, R. (2008) 'The Industrial/Consumer Marketing Dichotomy Revisited: a Case of Outdated Justification?' *Journal of Business & Industrial Marketing*, 23 (1), 3–11.

Dasgupta, N. (2004) 'Implicit Ingroup Favoritism, Outgroup Favoritism, and their Behavioral Manifestations'. *Social Justice Research*, 17 (2), 143–169.

Dick, A.S. and Basu, K. (1994) 'Customer Loyalty: Toward an Integrated Conceptual Framework', *JAMS*, 22 (2), 99–113.

Gillin, P. (2007) *The New Influencers: a Marketer's Guide to the New Social Media*. Sanger: Quil Driver.

Gronroos, C. (1994) 'From Marketing Mix to Relationship Marketing'. *Management Decision*, 32 (1), 4–20.

Hitwise (2008) 'The Impact of Social Networking in the UK'. Available at: www.bergenmediaby.no/admin/ressurser/QCetFnO$_11_Social_Networking_Report_2008.pdf (accessed 2 April 2009).

Hofstede, G. and Hofstede, G.J. (2004) *Cultures and Organizations: Software for the Mind*. Maidenhead: McGraw-Hill.

Howard, J.A. and Sheth, J.N. (1969) *The Theory of Buyer Behaviour*. New York: John Wiley.

Ipsos MORI (2006) White Paper: European Blog Influencer Barometer with Ipsos MORI. Retrieved 2 April 2009, from http://www.hotwirepr.com/pdf/BlogWhitePaperUK.pdf

Jai-Ok, K., Forsythe, S., Qingliang, G., and Sook, J.M. (2002) 'Cross-cultural Values, Needs and Purchase Behavior'. *Journal of Consumer Marketing*, 19, 481–502.

Kotler, P. and Gertner, D. (2002) 'Country as Brand, Product, and Beyond: A Place Marketing and Brand Management Perspective'. *Brand Management*, 9 (4–5), 249–61.

Lee, D.-J., Pae, J.H., and Wong, Y.H. (2001) 'A Model of Close Business Relationships in China (Guanxi)'. *European Journal of Marketing*, 35 (1/2).

Leskovec, J., Adamic, L.A., and Huberman, B.A. (2007) 'The Dynamics of Viral Marketing'. *ACM Trans. Web,* 1 (1), 5.

Lim, K. and O'Cass, A. (2001) 'Consumer Brand Classifications: An Assessment of Culture-of-origin Versus Country-of-origin'. *The Journal of Product & Brand Management*, 10 (2), 120–36.

Maslow, A. (1943) 'A Theory of Human Motivation'. *Psychological Review*, 50, 370–96.

Meyer-Waarden, L. (2008) 'The Influence of Loyalty Programme Membership on Customer Purchase Behaviour'. *European Journal of Marketing* 42 (1/2), 87–114.

Mitra, K., Reiss, M.C., and Capella, M.C. (1999) 'An Examination of Perceived Risk, Information Search and Behavioral Intentions in Search, Experience and Credence Services'. *Journal of Services Marketing*, 13 (3), 208–28.

Moon, B.J. and Jain, S.C. (2002) 'Consumer Processing of Foreign Advertisements: Roles of Country-of-origin Perceptions, Consumer Ethnocentrism, and Country Attitude'. *International Business Review*, 11 (2), 117–38.

Morgan, R.M. and Hunt, S.D. (1994) 'The Commitment–Trust Theory of Relationship Marketing'. *Journal of Marketing*, 58 (July), 20–38.

Narver, J. and Slater, S. (1994) 'Marketing Orientation, Customer Value and Superior Performance'. *Business Horizons*, 37 (2), 22–9.

Ohame, K. (1989) 'The Global Logic of Strategic Alliances'. *Harvard Business Review*, 67, 143–54.

Palmer, A. and Gallagher, D. (2007) 'Religiosity, Relationships and Consumption: a Study of Church Going in Ireland'. *Consumption Markets & Culture*, 10 (1), 31–49.

Reichheld, F.F. and Sasser, W.E. (1990) 'Zero Defections'. *Harvard Business Review*, 68 (5), 105–11.

Shemwell, D., Cronin, J., and Bullard, W. (1994) 'Relationship Exchanges in Services: an Empirical Investigation of Ongoing Customer–Service Provider Relationships'. *International Journal of Service Industry Management*, 5 (3), 57–68.

Shimp, T.A. and Sharma, S. (1987) 'Consumer Ethnocentrism: Construction and Validation of the CETSCALE'. *Journal of Marketing Research*, 24 (3), 280–9.

Sierra, J.J. and McQuitty, S. (2005) Service Providers and Customers: Social Exchange Theory and Service Loyalty'. *Journal of Services Marketing*, 19 (6), 392–400.

Subramani, M.R., and Rajagopalan, B. (2003) 'Knowledge-sharing and Influence in Online Social Networks Via Viral Marketing'. *Commun. ACM*, 46 (12), 300–7.

Sweeney, J.C., Soutar, G.N., and Mazzarol, T. (2008) 'Factors Influencing Word of Mouth Effectiveness: Receiver Perspectives'. *European Journal of Marketing*, 42 (3/4), 344–64.

Tinson, J., Nancarrow, C., and Bruce, I. (2008) 'Purchase Decision Making and the Increasing Significance of Family Types'. *Journal of Consumer Marketing*, 25 (1), 45–56.

Vogt, P. (2009) 'Brands Under Attack: Marketers Can Learn from Domino's Video Disaster'. *Forbes*, available at: www.forbes.com/2009/04/24/dominos-youtube-twitter-leadership-cmo-network-marketing.html (accessed 20 May 2009).

Wells, W.D. and Gubar, G. (1966) 'Life Cycle Concepts in Marketing Research'. *Journal of Marketing Research*, 3, 355–63.

SUGGESTED FURTHER READING

There are numerous textbooks that provide a good overview of buyer behaviour, including the following:

Evans, M., Jamal, A., and Foxal, G. (2009) *Consumer Behaviour*, 2nd edition. Chichester: John Wiley.

Solomon, M., Bamossy, G., Askegaard, S., and Hogg, M. (2009) *Consumer Behaviour: A European Perspective,* 4th edition. Harlow: FT Prentice Hall.

For an update of buying behaviour in the context of the Internet, consult the following:

Barnes, S.J., Bauer, H.H., Neumann, M.M., and Huber, F. (2007) 'Segmenting Cyberspace: a Customer Typology for the Internet'. *European Journal of Marketing,* 41 (1/2), 71–93.

Dennis, C., Merrilees, B., Jayawardhena, C., and Wright, L.T. (2009) 'E-consumer behaviour'. *European Journal of Marketing*, 43 (9/10), 1121–39.

Eccleston, D. and Griseri, L. (2008) 'How does Web 2.0 Stretch Traditional Influencing Patterns?' *International Journal of Market Research*, 50 (5), Web 2.0 Special Issue.

For an introduction to the general principles of relationship marketing and its role in turning buyers into regular customers, the following are useful:

Buttle, F.D. (2008) *Relationship Marketing*, 2nd edition. London: Butterworth-Heinemann.

Das, K. (2009) 'Relationship Marketing Research (1994–2006): an Academic Literature Review and Classification'. *Marketing Intelligence & Planning*, 27 (3), 326–63.

Egan, J. (2008), *Relationship Marketing—Exploring Relational Strategies in Marketing*, 3rd edition. Harlow: Pearson Education Ltd.

@ ONLINE RESOURCE CENTRE

Visit the Online Resource Centre for resources that are relevant to this chapter, including a flashcard glossary, web links, multiple choice questions, and additional case studies:

www.oxfordtextbooks.co.uk/orc/palmer3e/

🔍 KEY TERMS

- Black box model
- Buying process
- Cognitive dissonance
- Decision-making unit (DMU)
- Family life-cycle
- Gatekeepers
- Hierarchy of needs
- Influencers
- Involvement

- Ladder of loyalty
- Models of buyer behaviour
- Need
- Peer groups
- Perception
- Pester power
- Reference groups
- Stimulus–response models
- Word-of-mouth

MARKETING RESEARCH

CHAPTER OBJECTIVES

So far in this book, we have spoken in general terms of marketing being essentially about providing what the customer wants. But how do we know what the customer *actually* wants? How can we find out how buyers *actually* go about the buying process? How can we tell whether a company has succeeded in providing the goods and service that a buyer seeks? And how does a company gather, analyse, and disseminate information about its marketing environment, which we looked at in general terms in Chapter 2?

This chapter explores information as a valuable resource which can help marketers improve their knowledge of customers and their ability to meet customers' needs profitably. Marketing research is essentially about keeping in touch with a company's customers and its broader marketing environment, and this chapter reviews the main methodological approaches. Sources of data are discussed in terms of their timeliness and relevance. It is important that a company knows about its markets not just as they are now, but as they are likely to be in the future; therefore, demand forecasting and knowledge management become crucial.

◉ Introduction

Most definitions of marketing focus on a firm satisfying its customers' needs. But how does a firm know just what those needs are? And how can it try and predict what those needs will be in a year's time, or five years' time? A small business owner in a stable business environment may be able to manage by just listening to her customers and forming an intuitive opinion about customers' needs and how they are likely to change slowly in the future. But how can such an informal approach work in today's turbulent business environments, where the senior managers of very large businesses probably have very little contact with their customers?

Marketing research is essentially about the managers of a business *keeping in touch* with their markets. The small business owner may have been able to do marketing research quite intuitively and adapt her product offer accordingly. Larger organizations operating in competitive and changing environments need more formal methods of collecting, analysing, and disseminating information about their markets. It is frequently said that information is a source of a firm's competitive advantage, and there are many examples of firms that have used a detailed knowledge of their customers' needs to develop better product offers which have given the firm a competitive advantage. Interestingly, a recent trend has been for market researchers to rename themselves as 'customer insight departments'. This is a recognition that marketers value insights above *everything* else—above being objective, above classic methodology, even above validity and reliability.

The range of techniques used by companies to collect information and turn it into actionable knowledge is increasing constantly. Indeed, companies often find themselves with more information than they can sensibly use. The great advances in electronic point of sale (EPOS) technology, for example, have given retailers a wealth of new data which not all companies have managed to make full use of. As new techniques for data collection appear, it is important to maintain a balance between techniques so that a good overall picture is obtained. Reliance on just one technique may save costs in the short term, but only at the long-term cost of not having a good holistic view of market characteristics.

◉ Market research *v.* marketing research

The terms market research and marketing research' are often used interchangeably. This is incorrect, and the distinctive characteristics of each should be noted.

◉ Market research is about determining the characteristics of a *market*, for example in terms of its size, requirements, growth rate, market segments, and competitor positioning.

◉ Marketing research is broader and is about researching the whole of a company's marketing activities. In most organizations, such research would probably include monitoring the effectiveness of its advertising, intermediaries, and pricing position.

This chapter focuses on how a company goes about assessing its customers' needs. Of course, research into areas such as customers' perceptions of advertising messages is closely related to an understanding of their needs and expectations, so it is unwise to see the two aspects of research as completely separate.

Market research should be seen as just one component of a firm's information gathering procedures. It is usual to talk about integrating market research within a company-wide marketing information system, which itself is part of a wider corporate management information system. From this, knowledge is created, and there is a lot of interest in how this knowledge can be shared to create a 'learning organization'.

In Figure 5.1, an attempt has been made to put market research into the context of a broader marketing information system.

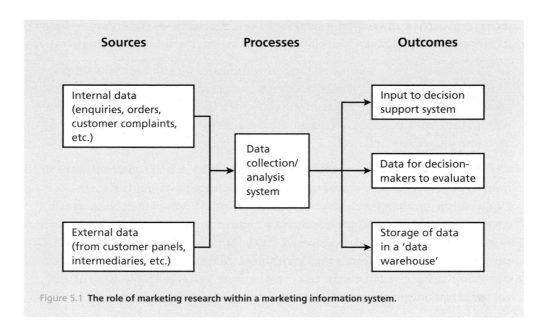

Figure 5.1 **The role of marketing research within a marketing information system.**

⊙ Major uses of marketing research

As markets become more competitive, marketing research is being called upon to perform an ever-increasing range of tasks. Some of the more important specific marketing research activities are listed below.

⊙ **Research into customer needs and expectations:** Research is undertaken to learn what underlying needs individuals seek to satisfy when they buy goods and services. Identifying needs that are currently unmet by existing products spurs new product development. Needs should be distinguished from expectations, and a variety of qualitative techniques are used to study the often complex sets of expectations that customers have with respect to a purchase. For example, when buying a personal computer, what are customers' expectations with respect to reliability, after-sales support, design, etc.?

⊙ **Customer satisfaction surveys:** Companies regularly try to find out from their customers how satisfied they are with the goods or services that they have bought. By identifying areas of dissatisfaction, a company can seek to improve its product offer in order to increase its sales. Customer surveys can have the dual function of providing a company with valuable information and providing a public relations tool, allowing customers to feel that they have made their feelings known to the company.

⊙ **Communication effectiveness:** Companies may spend a lot of money on various forms of communication, such as advertising, sales promotion, and public relations, but may have little idea about how effectively the money was spent. Regular surveys may help a company identify the communication channels which are most cost effective for producing sales leads.

⊙ **Similar industry studies:** By researching other companies, including competitors and companies in completely unrelated business sectors, marketing managers can learn a lot about how to improve their own marketing effectiveness. Through a process sometimes referred to as 'benchmarking', an organization can set itself targets based on best practice in its own, or a related, industry.

⊙ **Key client studies:** Where a company derives the majority of its income from just a small number of customers, it may make special efforts to ensure that these customers are totally satisfied with its standards of service and prices. The loss of their business as a result of shortcomings of which it is unaware could otherwise be catastrophic. In some cases, the relationship with key customers may be of such mutual importance that each partner may spend considerable time jointly researching shared problems (e.g. airport operators sharing with airlines the task of researching customers' perceptions of the airport's handling procedures).

⊙ **Research into intermediaries:** Agents, dealers, and other intermediaries are close to consumers and therefore form a valuable means for gathering information about consumers' needs and expectations. In addition, intermediaries are themselves customers of manufacturers and service principals. It follows that the latter should be very interested in how they are perceived by their intermediaries, for example in relation to reliability, delivery times, and after-sales service.

⊙ **Employee research:** For many services organizations, front-line employees are close to customers and are valuable sources of information about customers' needs. Research can also focus on employees as 'customers' of an organization, for example by measuring their attitudes towards the company. Employee suggestion schemes can form an important aspect of employee research.

⊙ **Environmental scanning:** We saw in Chapter 2 that a company's marketing environment can be highly complex and that it is crucial to understand how even quite nebulous changes today may affect the marketing activities of a company in the future. Environmental scanning is about gathering information on trends in the environment and disseminating this information to individuals who may be able to act on it.

⊙ The marketing research process

The small business owner may have been able to get by with a fairly intuitive system of market research. Larger organizations operating in complex environments need to adopt a more structured approach to their market research activities. To be useful, keeping in touch with customers' needs should be carried out objectively, accurately, and should use a variety of

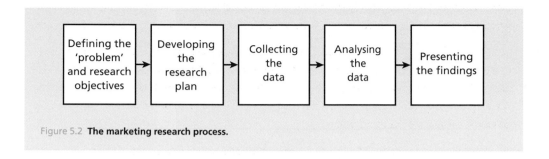

Figure 5.2 **The marketing research process.**

methods. Casual, unstructured research may at best be wasteful, and at worst misleading. Data collected should be as up to date and relevant to a problem as time and cost constraints allow.

The stages of the marketing research process can be described in a simple, linear format. A model of this process, which begins with the definition of the research problem and ends with the presentation of the findings, is shown in Figure 5.2. The process follows the basic pattern of scientific inquiry that is adopted for other forms research.

The trigger for research can usually be related to a gap in the information that is currently available to a firm. For example, a company may have comprehensive information on the current market for its products, but lack information on new market opportunities for which its product range could be adapted.

Very often, marketing research activity fails because the 'problem' to be researched has been inadequately thought through and expressed as a research brief. For example, a company may be facing declining sales of a product and may then commission research to investigate customers' liking of the product's features relative to competitors' products. However, the real problem may be to understand the macro-economic environment, which may explain why sales of that category of product are declining.

The marketing research process operates at a number of levels.

- At the simplest level, a researcher may simply be required to provide a normative *description* of market characteristics (e.g. defining the attributes that buyers evaluate when choosing between competing personal computer brands, or describing the buying behaviour of families buying a personal computer for the first time).

- The research task may additionally call for the *measurement* of market characteristics, for example by measuring the annual sales value of the UK personal computer market and the market shares of the main suppliers.

- A more thorough investigation would require an *analysis* of data, both quantitative and qualitative (e.g. an analysis of personal computer buying behaviour according to the age, income, or lifestyle of different segments of the population).

- With further analysis, a predictive model for targeting may be sought (e.g. a model to predict the level of computer sales based on individuals' occupation, family structure, and postcode).

159

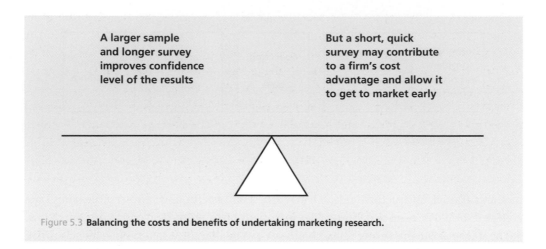

A larger sample and longer survey improves confidence level of the results

But a short, quick survey may contribute to a firm's cost advantage and allow it to get to market early

Figure 5.3 **Balancing the costs and benefits of undertaking marketing research.**

Once the objectives of a research exercise have been defined, plans can be developed to collect relevant data. Data collection methods are considered below. A time plan is essential to ensure that decision makers can have the most up-to-date information on market characteristics as they are at present, rather than as they were some time ago. In rapidly changing markets, timeliness can be crucial. The outcome of market research should be actionable by those who receive it.

How extensive should a firm's marketing research processes be? The amount of time and expense incurred in undertaking research must be compared with the benefits that will result from it in terms of making a better informed decision. Very often, the issue is how harmful a badly informed decision could be to a firm. Where the capital costs involved in developing a new product are low, and the market is changing rapidly, it may make sense to do very little research and go straight to the market with a new product. This is true of many fashion designers, who can run up sample items and see how well they sell. If they sell well, follow-up production can be put in hand rapidly; if they fail to sell, they can be consigned to a bargain clearance store. Little will have been lost, whereas had the designer taken time to carry out lengthy market research, he could have got his designs to the market just as the current fashion was changing again, rendering his research historic and obsolete. Contrast this with the marketing research needed for a much more risky major infrastructure investment such as an airport, which will have a high capital cost and a long lifespan. The research process here will typically last several years and take many forms (Figure 5.3).

◉ Primary *v.* secondary research

A further question is whether to use primary data collection techniques, secondary research, or a combination of the two. Data sources are traditionally divided into two categories according to the methods by which they were collected. Secondary research is often referred to as desk research, while primary research is often called field research.

Most organizations approach a research exercise by examining the available sources of secondary data. Secondary data refers to information which in some sense is second-hand to the current research project. Data can be second-hand because they have already been collected internally by the organization, although for a different primary purpose. Alternatively, the information may be acquired second-hand from external sources.

Secondary, or *desk research* can be a useful starting point for a research exercise. If somebody else has collected data or published a report in a closely related area, it is often much cheaper to buy that report than start to collect data afresh. Reports by organizations such as nVision and the Economist Intelligence Unit (EIU) may at first sight seem to be very expensive, but when set against the cost of undertaking the research from scratch the cost begins to look relatively good value.

Primary, or *field research* is concerned with generating new information direct from the target population. The phrase 'keeping in touch' was highlighted earlier, and marketing researchers spend most of their time designing and implementing such studies, either on a one-off or a continuous monitoring basis. Primary research tends to be much more expensive to conduct than secondary research, but the results are invariably more up to date and specific to a company's research objectives.

The range of primary research techniques is constantly increasing, and some of the important ones are discussed later in this chapter.

E-Marketing

How valuable is the Internet for market researchers?

The Internet has spawned a new generation of researchers who seem to have boundless amounts of web-generated data. But how valuable are these data?

One of the big advantages of doing business through the Internet is that all transactions are recorded in a form that is immediately available for analysis. No more transcribing the newspaper enquiry coupon into a database, or recording the essence of a customer's telephone call in a series of codes to be saved in notes. In both cases, creating a database can be time-consuming, costly, and subject to human transcription error—better to let the customer himself enter the data. Where a prospective customer approaches a company's website with an enquiry, the fact can automatically be recorded. Fairly simple software will allow a company to record how the visitor got to its site, how long was spent at each page and the results of the visit (e.g. a request for further information; quotation request; purchase order). More sophisticated data are provided by companies, such as doubleclick.com, which inserts 'cookies'—often unknowingly—into users' PCs which are then used to send back to the company information about all of the sites that the user has visited. This can be very valuable information that third-party companies buy to improve their targeting. Of course, collecting information through use of such 'spyware' raises ethical questions.

Faced with such a huge amount of research data, just how valuable is it to marketers? Inevitably, there are some gems amidst a mass of debris. The ability to measure response rates to different page designs and/or different links to a company's site can sharpen marketers' analytic skills and improve accountability for their actions. It is no longer good enough just to have a hunch that a website is effective when there is copious information to measure its performance.

Online communities present a number of opportunities for companies to get close to their markets, including observing and collecting information; hosting or sponsoring communities; providing content to communities (such as music, information, or entertainment); and participating as members of online communities (Miller et al. 2009). Companies would generally love their product to be at the heart of a community, and there have been many examples of companies who have developed social network media to put them at the centre of a community. Starbucks, for example, has a Facebook site which claimed to have 1,727,314 'fans' in 2009; it is present on Twitter; has its own YouTube channel and its own online community web pages (MyStarbucksIdeas, Starbucks V2V, and StarbucksRed). A company's involvement in social network sites can result in a wide range of strategic and operational benefits. By inviting feedback, or simply observing conversations, a company can learn about customers' needs and inform its new product development policy (Constantinides and Fountain 2008).

How useful are the statistics that marketers routinely collect from the web? Simple records of visitors to a website are prone to many errors, including the problem of identifying 'unique' visitors from those who might repeatedly enter and leave a site in quick succession. Many apparent visits are actually hits recorded by 'spiders'—search engines that routinely seek out websites for indexing. A bigger problem of Internet data is the difficulty that often prevents Internet-based databases being integrated with existing records of consumers' behaviour, lifestyles, and attitudes. With concerns over Internet security remaining high, individuals may be reluctant to divulge personal information through the Internet which would allow a company to build up a full picture. Unfortunately, the people with the greatest concerns about privacy are often the people that companies are most interested in learning more about (Ashworth and Free 2006).

The development of the Internet as a marketing research tool has not always been helped by the sometimes confused communications between marketing and IT departments within a company. IT systems often fail to meet marketers' expectations, because needs have not been defined accurately. Another complicating factor in many organizations occurs where management bans employees from using social network sites, for fear that they may be wasting paid time on social activities, overlooking the fact that they may be losing the opportunity of learning what customers are saying. As in other aspects of marketing, getting the inter-functional dynamics of a company right can be crucial in the quest for competitive advantage, and may explain the success of, among others, Direct Line Insurance and First Direct.

● Secondary research information sources

A good starting point for secondary research is to examine what a company already has available in-house. Typically, a lot of information is generated internally within organizations;

- Government departments and official publications—e.g. *General Household Survey, Social Trends, Transport Statistics*
- National media—e.g. *Financial Times* country surveys
- Professional and trade associations—e.g. Association of British Travel Agents, British Roads Federation
- Trade, technical, and professional media—e.g. *Travel Trade Gazette, Marketing Week*
- Local chambers of trade and commerce
- Yearbooks and directories, e.g. Dataquest
- Companies' Annual Reports and Accounts
- Subscription services, providing periodic sector reports on market intelligence and financial analyses, such as Keynote, Mintel, etc.
- Subscription electronic databases, e.g. Forrester Research, Gartner, Mintel Online

Figure 5.4 **Examples of secondary data used in marketing research.**

for example, sales invoices may form the basis of a market segmentation exercise. To make the task of desk research as easy as possible, routinely collected information should be analysed and stored in a way that facilitates future use. Of course, a balance needs to be struck between having data readily available, and spending money on the collection and storage of data that may subsequently (but not necessarily) be used.

The range of external sources of secondary data is constantly increasing, both in document and in electronic format. These sources include government statistics, trade associations, and specialist research reports. A good starting point for a review of these is still the business section of a good library. Some examples of secondary data sources are shown in Figure 5.4.

In many cases, other organizations, possibly even competitors, will have conducted similar studies to the one that is proposed. These may be available to purchase (or may be publicly available, as in the case of companies' annual reports, which often contain useful market information). There is also a dark world of espionage, where companies seek to gather information from competitors.

Primary research methods

Primary, or field, research is becoming increasingly sophisticated, and this chapter can give only a brief overview of the range of techniques available. There are now many texts that go into market research methods in great detail (see the suggestions for further reading). We will begin by looking at methodological issues concerning primary research. Later, we will look at how data collected using these methods can be analysed to give a company new insights.

Sampling procedures

Primary research involves looking directly at the phenomena or individuals that are of interest, and recording the characteristics about them that are of particular interest. In most circumstances, it would be impractical to measure details of everybody who makes up the 'population'. (For example, if we were interested in the preferences of intensive mobile phone users in the UK, it would not be practical to talk to every single intensive user in the country.) As an alternative, primary research usually uses just a *sample* of the population that we are interested in. From this small sample, we can extrapolate to infer characteristics of the population as a whole. Any inference made about the population is limited by the extent to which the sample is truly representative of the population as a whole.

Sampling is essentially concerned with quantitative techniques, and there are a number of widely used techniques for sampling:

- A random sample implies that everyone within the target population has an equal chance of being selected for inclusion in the sample. For a completely random sample of all adult members of the population, the electoral register is frequently used and a proportion of names selected at random. (However, from 2002, UK residents have been able to 'opt out' of the part of the electoral register that is made available to commercial organizations.) A variant on this approach is stratified random sampling, in which the population is divided into a number of sub-groups and a random sample obtained from each sub-group. The proportion sampled from each sub-group can be varied according to the researcher's interest.

- Rather than picking specific individuals to be included in the sample, the researcher can specify the characteristics of each sub-group and the number required from each such group. The interviewer is then free to include in her *quota* sample individuals who meet the specification. This method of sampling is only as good as the specification of the quota's characteristics. If data collectors are given too much freedom to choose their sample, it can best be described as a *convenience* sample and is likely to be biased in terms of respondents' characteristics. (The researcher may consciously or unconsciously recruit respondents who are easiest to find, rather than those whom it is most valuable to learn about.) A biased sample may limit the generalizability of the research results to the population as a whole.

- Many survey techniques are effectively *self-selecting* in their sampling procedure. Where questionnaires are made widely available to the public, the researcher has little control over who will actually return a questionnaire. There is evidence that responses can be dominated by vociferous minorities of individuals who hold extreme views, which may not be typical of the views of the large group of 'average' customers. There is also evidence that retired people and housewives with more time to spare are more likely to volunteer to complete a survey, even though a research exercise may be more interested in the views of busy working people.

Data collection methods

The range of field research techniques is constantly increasing. Two main approaches to collecting primary data can be identified: by observation of the individuals who the researcher is interested in, or by interaction with them through a survey.

Observation techniques

Observational techniques are limited to descriptions of behaviour, and cannot explore the reasons that might explain such behaviour. However, they do claim to be highly objective and free of bias from respondents.

The following are some examples of observation techniques.

- When a retailer is assessing the attractiveness of a proposed new store location, it may undertake observational research into pedestrian or vehicle flows past a proposed site.

- Many firms routinely monitor their competitors' marketing programmes, for example by collecting their brochures or by observing prices and products on offer in retail outlets and Internet sites.

- The use of mystery shoppers is becoming increasingly common among services companies who use them to check on standards of service delivery. Typical uses have been to assess the efficiency and friendliness of restaurant waiting staff, the attention received from staff in a car showroom, and whether a travel agent is recommending a sponsoring tour operator's products.

- Experimental laboratory research may observe how consumers interact with a product, for example by observing how, and in what order, an individual reads an advertisement.

- The Internet has created new opportunities for observing how individuals move around a company's website. Which hyperlinks were most productive in bringing visitors to the company's site? Which combination of pages did they visit? In what order were they visited? How long did they spend on each page? Companies often use alternative page designs which are randomly allocated to visitors, then the results (an order, further enquiry, etc.) are compared.

- Developments in radio frequency identity (RFID) technology is allowing tags to be attached to products, transmitting information to nearby receivers. This can potentially allow information about product usage to be transmitted back to a base station. However, RFID tags are still too expensive for widespread application to low value, high-volume products. Their use has also raised many ethical questions.

Observational techniques may be good at describing phenomena, but they do not in themselves provide explanations. For this, other techniques need to be used. Observational techniques can raise ethical questions, where those being observed are not aware that they are being studied. Many people may be unhappy at the thought that CCTV footage of them walking round a store is being used in a study of flow around the store. The use of unseen 'cookies' to observe Internet usage has been challenged by many on ethical and legal grounds.

A tiny spy in your shopping or a valuable new source of data?

Many inventions come along which have the potential to change the business environment, but the excitement of a launch may be matched with scepticism. Radio frequency identification is one new development that has taken some time in achieving widespread acceptance, while simultaneously raising concerns among many groups about its privacy implications.

Radio frequency identification involves placing a small radio transmitter on a product so that its movement can be tracked remotely. So far, RFID has mainly been applied to pallets and case loads of goods, rather than individual consumer goods. The cost of tags, as well as the equipment needed to read them and process the data, means that item-level tagging may be still some way off. But the prospect of rapidly falling costs and greater miniaturization has alerted companies to the opportunities, and some consumer groups to the potential threats. However, a report for the EU in 2008 talked about the 'hype cycle' which has affected RFID, like many new products (Schmitt and Michahelles 2008). The initial excitement is eventually seen as unrealistic and eventually adoption of the new technology settles down at a much more modest level than the previous hype might have led us to believe.

In addition to the technical issues of reducing the costs of producing RFID tags is the issue of privacy. RFID would seem like a blessing to companies keen to find out more about their products after they have left their shelves. But is their use ethical? In 2007, the EU's information society commissioner, called for a debate about the security and privacy issues surrounding RFID. Consumer groups and privacy campaigners have expressed concern that RFID tags could be used to build up massive databases of individuals' shopping, leisure, and travel habits. These databases could be exploited by unscrupulous businesses and also become a target for cybercriminals. The fact that RFID tags track the actual items that people buy has led to fears that RFID data could be much more intrusive than the information retailers typically collect through bar code data and loyalty card programmes. As the cost of RFID tags falls and their versatility increases, they have the potential to be read at a distance without a consumer's knowledge. Would you want a bookshop 'spying' on how and where you read a book that you recently bought from the shop?

Not to be outdone, proponents of RFID have gone on the offensive to present the positive elements of the technology, such as its use in preventing counterfeit drugs reaching consumers, or in aviation, where tags have been fixed to aircraft spares and safety equipment. Retailers have attached RFID tags to goods to monitor thefts and have argued that honest customers would have nothing to fear, and would benefit from lower prices resulting from less shoplifting.

If you were a commercial organization contemplating the use of RFID, which way do you think the privacy debate will go? Are pressure groups being paranoid about the data that companies can keep on an individual, when in reality, government agencies routinely collect much more information about us, for example through vehicle number plate recognition? Will consumers be won over by the safety and security aspects of RFID, in much the same way as many people would readily accept the necessity for 'sinister' monitoring of their movements by CCTV? Would the most likely outcome of the EU review of RFID be a compromise, perhaps limiting how long RFID data could be kept and who would be allowed access to it?

Survey-based research methods

A survey questionnaire involves some form of interaction with the subject being studied and would normally seek some attitudinal, personal, or historical information about the respondent. Questions in a survey can be asked face to face, by telephone, or distributed for self-completion.

- *Face-to-face interviewing* is a traditional method of carrying out surveys. It can achieve high rates of response and can be free of the self-selection bias commonly associated with self-completion surveys. Bias can, however, occur where respondents give an answer that they believe the interviewer expects them to give, rather than one they truly believe. Face-to face interviewing, whether carried out house to house (which is the best approach for sampling purposes), in the street, or in hired locations, is labour intensive. The cost and difficulty of obtaining good quality, trained staff to undertake survey research, often at unsociable times of the day, has led researchers to search for lower cost alternatives.

- An alternative to face-to-face interviewing is the *telephone survey*. While considerably cheaper than face-to-face interviews, the refusal rate for telephone surveys can be up to three times higher than for personal interviews, and response rates appear to be falling rapidly (Tuckel and O'Neill 2002). The increased use of computer-assisted information collection for telephone (CATI) and personal interviews (CAPI) has speeded up the whole survey process dramatically, with responses being processed as they are received. Immediately prior to the 2005 UK general election, these systems were used in the next day publication of survey results from total sample sizes extending into thousands.

- Online surveys have become increasingly popular, particularly among companies who target goods and services at young people who are likely to be heavy Internet users. There have been many reports of high response rates using this data collection method, although concerns have been expressed about the representativeness of samples obtained.

- In the case of *self-completion surveys*, respondents obviously self-select, so no matter how carefully the original sample to be contacted is chosen, the possibility of bias is highest. Furthermore, the response rate may be lower than 2 per cent, particularly where a postal survey is used (Figure 5.5).

- In qualitative research (see below), the open-ended nature of the questions and the need to establish the confidence of respondents preclude the use of telephone and self-completion interviews. Face-to-face in-depth interviews are used, particularly in business-to-business research, where confidentiality is especially important and the

Figure 5.5 **The UK supermarket operator ASDA (part of Walmart), appreciates the value of feedback from customers.** Like many well-run companies, ASDA provides comment cards and a freephone telephone number that customers can use to pass on their suggestions, complaints, and praise about the company's operations. ASDA recognizes the value of this customer insight and goes one step further by making a donation to charity for each call that it receives on its freephone number. It also completes the process of information exchange by displaying in its stores a list of suggestions that customers have made, and actions that the company has taken in response to them. (Reproduced with kind permission of Asda.)

scheduling difficulties and cost of getting a group of busy buyers together in one place can be a major problem; for this reason, it is usually most convenient for respondents to be interviewed at their place of work.

◉ In consumer markets, focus group discussions are frequently used. Groups normally consist of about eight people, plus a trained moderator who leads the discussion. Respondents are recruited by interviewers, who use recruitment questionnaires to ensure that those invited to attend reflect the demography of the target market, and to filter out unsuitable respondents. Focus groups do not claim to be statistically representative of the population that they come from, but nevertheless there would be little value in recruiting a group that was not typical of the target population as a whole. In national markets, groups are arranged at central points throughout the country, the number of groups in each region reflecting the regional breakdown of the target population.

◉ There has been recent excitement among marketers that developments in medical technology will allow market researchers to study brain functions directly, so that instead of getting a conditioned, verbalized response to a question, the researcher can get something closer to the 'real' truth by studying brain pattern responses. However, such 'neuro marketing' research raises major issues about ethics and practicality (see Fugate 2008).

◉ Quantitative v. qualitative research

It was noted earlier that research techniques need to be varied and appropriate to the problem being studied. One important decision that needs to be made when developing a survey-based research plan is whether to conduct a qualitative or quantitative survey, or a combination of the two. Although quantitative and qualitative research are often seen as opposite ends of a research techniques spectrum, their methods overlap. Market researchers need to feel comfortable 'operating in all slices of the information map' (Smith and Dexter 2001), incorporating harder, more scientific, objective data with softer, anecdotal, qualitative data.

Quantitative research

This is used to measure consumers' attitudes and behaviour where the nature of the research has been defined. Quantitative research is designed to gather information from statistically representative samples of the target population. The sample size is related to the size of the total population being studied, the variability within it, and the degree of statistical reliability required, balanced against time and cost constraints. In order to achieve margins of error small enough to make the final measurements useful, however, quantitative research, as its name implies, is usually conducted among several hundred, sometimes thousands, of respondents. For this reason, information is generally obtained using standardized structured questionnaires.

Unfortunately, many phenomena that marketers are interested in cannot be easily measured using single, simple indicators. In these cases, composite sets of scales are used and factor analysis is carried out to try and identify distinctive dimensions of a phenomenon. For example, marketers are often interested in whether customers trust a brand, but a lot of research evidence has suggested that trust is a complex phenomenon; hence it is not uncommon in quantitative studies to use 30 or more questions in a survey of trust. Perhaps the best known multiple item measure used by marketers is the SERVQUAL methodology for measuring service quality. A company may wish to learn more about customers' perceptions of its service and to compare these with what they had expected. The methodology uses 22 questions to probe a respondent's attitudes about service quality. Previous research has shown that these 22 questions are reliable indicators of five distinct dimensions of service quality: reliability, attentiveness, tangibles, empathy, and responsiveness. The survey instrument has been widely used in the services sector to compare customers' perceptions of service quality between different branches, and to plot changes in performance over time.

The marketer has available a wide range of quantitative techniques with which to collect and analyse data. The following is a brief summary of the techniques most commonly used by marketers. Further details can be found in any good research methods book (see suggested further reading at the end of this chapter).

Correlation analysis

Marketers are often interested in the extent to which two phenomena are associated with each other, for example whether change in household income is associated with the amount that a household spends on eating out. A correlation coefficient of 1 would indicate perfect association between the two variables and 0 would indicate no association at all. A correlation does not imply causation, and, as with all quantitative techniques, care needs to be taken in interpreting a correlation coefficient. Researchers have, for example, found significant correlations between firms' advertising expenditure on a product and sales revenue for it. However, this correlation could imply either that advertising expenditure leads to increased sales, or that firms increase their advertising expenditure in response to increasing sales revenue, because advertising is now more affordable. Each of these hypotheses is plausible, and the observed correlation must be interpreted in the context of theoretical foundations and previous evidence. In the light of theory, it may be concluded that the most relevant correlation is between sales in one period and advertising revenue in the preceding period.

Regression analysis

Regression models are used to build a model of causes (independent variables), which lead to an effect (the dependent variable). Companies would use a historical database to test models that are assessed for the amount of variance in the dataset that they explain. A regression analysis would comprise one dependent variable, a constant, and any number of independent variables. The significance of each of these independent variables is calculated, allowing a company to understand which of them are having a significant effect on the dependent variable.

A typical application of regression modelling is retailers' use of it to predict sales at possible new sales locations. A regression model will be able to discover, on the basis of performance of the company's other sites, the relative contribution to sales that will be made by such factors as passing pedestrian traffic, passing vehicle traffic, proximity to a major attractor, and the number/proximity of competitors. Regression analysis is only as good as the data and context on which the initial model was calibrated. The model may not be relevant if it is applied outside the context of the original dataset (e.g. a UK-based model applied to US retailing), and environmental factors may change the validity of the model over time.

Analysis of variance

Analysis of variance, or 'ANOVA', is used to test hypotheses about differences between two or more means. It is widely used in experimental frameworks where the researcher wishes to examine the effects of two or more 'treatments' on customers. A store interested in the effects of background music on the daily value of sales may develop an experiment in which shoppers are treated to one of three types of background music: (1) slow, soft music; (2) strident, loud music; or (3) no music. Analysis of variance can be used to test whether there is any significant difference between sales values associated with different types of music.

ANOVA designs can be used to test for differences within subject variables and between subject variables.

Conjoint analysis

This is a versatile marketing research tool that can provide valuable information for market segmentation, new product development, forecasting, and pricing decisions. Conjoint analysis can analyse the real-life trade-offs that shoppers make when evaluating a range of features or attributes that are present in a range of products. Once data are collected about consumers' preferences for particular attributes and features, the researcher can conduct a number of 'choice simulations' to estimate market share for products with different attributes/features. This can improve the researcher's ability to predict which formulation of a product will be successful before a product is launched on the market. A limitation of this technique is that consumers' evaluation of individual attributes of a product may be quite meaningless on their own, and it is the creative combining of attributes that determines their final choice.

Cluster analysis

Segmentation exercises involve trying to allocate individuals within a sample/population into distinctive groups, so that differences *within* the groups are minimized relative to the differences *between* the groups. Cluster analysis is frequently used in segmentation studies, but does not provide the marketer with a unique solution, as the process of clustering involves subjective decisions about the grouping of data.

Neural network analysis

This technique splits a dataset into a training set and a testing set. It essentially combines the features of regression modelling with an analysis of variance to give a 'best fit' model of dependent and independent variables.

Limitations to quantitative techniques

Quantitative surveys may give the appearance of a rigorous, scientific approach, and many marketers may delude themselves (and others) into thinking that you 'can't argue with the figures'. However, quantitative analysis techniques can suffer from a number of weaknesses.

Sampling error

Many quantitative studies fail because the sample is not truly representative of the population about which inferences are being made. A growing problem is non-response bias, which occurs when people who don't respond to a survey hold significantly different views from those who do respond, resulting in a biased estimate of population characteristics. A company will never know for sure what the views of non-respondents are, and how these differ from respondents, but there is some research evidence that, in the case of service quality surveys, responses are likely to be biased in favour of those who are either very happy or very unhappy with service levels, leaving the bulk of average customers under-represented. There are some methods to try and overcome this bias (e.g. comparing early respondents with late respondents), but the problem of non-response bias is a big one. (Typically, less than 5 per cent of targeted individuals reply to a mail survey.) Concerns over data privacy, among other things, are exacerbating the problem.

Measurement error

This occurs where there is a difference between the true value of the information being sought and the information that is actually obtained by the measurement process. There are many sources of measurement error, the most common being using measurement variables that are inappropriate to the research problem; interviewer bias (which often occurs in face-to-face surveys where the respondent may give a 'polite' or 'expected' response, rather than the truth); problems with the research instrument (e.g. loaded questions used in a questionnaire); and processing errors (e.g. incorrect coding and data entry).

Significance level

Sample surveys can give only an estimate of population characteristics, and this estimate is subject to a margin of error. In general, as the size of the sample relative to the population increases, the confidence with which population parameters can be predicted increases. Also, greater confidence in predicting population parameters occurs where the amount of variability within the population is low. Before accepting an estimate of population characteristics, it is important to note the confidence interval of these predictions.

Inappropriate tests

Estimates of population may be invalidated because of the use of inappropriate statistical tests. Many of the tests described above are based on an assumption that data are normally distributed. If they are not, the test is invalidated.

Inappropriate interpretation

The interpretation of results can be highly subjective. This can derive from the validity of the measures being used—do they really measure the phenomena that they purport to (e.g. does SERVQUAL truly measure service quality as it applies in a specific industry sector)? Often a variety of significance tests are available to the researcher and a test may be chosen that is the most significant, but not the most valid. Finally, all inferences are subject to interpretation of meaning; for example at what point does an observed fall in sales become a long-term trend rather than a temporary blip?

It should always be remembered that there are many 'noise' factors getting in the way of what is reported and the true state of the phenomenon that is being researched. Survey knowledge is a representation (researcher's interpretation) of a representation (data analysis) of a representation (survey instrument) of a representation (sample) of a representation (respondents' views of what really is going on) (Brown 1998).

Qualitative research

Qualitative techniques essentially seek to recreate the listening ear and interpretative mind that so many entrepreneurs use so well. In today's large corporation, key decision makers are likely to be some way removed from everyday transactions with customers, so they employ qualitative researchers to be their listening ears for them.

Qualitative marketing research involves the exploration and interpretation of the perceptions and behaviour of small samples of individuals, and the study of the motivators behind observed actions. It can be highly focused, exploring in depth, for example, the attitudes that buyers have towards particular brand names. The techniques used to encourage respondents to speak and behave honestly and un-selfconsciously are derived from the social sciences.

During the early stages of the research process, definitions and descriptions may be needed, and it is here that qualitative research is at its most useful. It can define the parameters for future studies, and identify key criteria among consumers that can subsequently be measured using quantitative research. For example, if a supermarket observed that its older customers were unwilling to register for its loyalty card programme, it might conduct some qualitative research among its older customers in order to develop greater understanding about why this particular group was reluctant to subscribe. (Perhaps it might uncover an underlying scepticism towards the idea of deferring rewards to the future; or there may be greater concerns over privacy; or perhaps a loyalty card may even subliminally bring back memories of wartime ration cards.)

Probably the most widely used qualitative approach in marketing research is the focus group. This entails inviting a group of individuals to discuss an issue that a company is interested in learning more about. Participants are invited to contribute to an understanding of an issue on the basis of their ability, rather than on the basis of being a statistically significant representation of the population being studied. A trained moderator will guide the discussion, but she needs to be careful not to put too many ideas into the minds of participants, which might stifle their originality of thought. There are numerous approaches to managing a focus group which have the aim of reducing the bias caused by the intervention of the moderator and stimulating contribution from the invited members. Some researchers have had success by recording conversations between friends which tend to be relatively uninhibited. Although focus groups do not aim to be statistically representative of the population, some concerns have been expressed that they may become dominated by semi-professional participants, who make a living out of payments made to participants. Their views may be quite different from those of 'ordinary' consumers.

An alternative to the focus group is to use a one-to-one discussion format, which is especially useful for studying the behaviour and attitudes of employees of organizations, and also where confidentiality is an important concern of participants. Although one-to-one discussions may reduce problems of confidentiality, this approach does not allow the researcher to study peer group interaction, which may be important when studying attitudes to items of ostentatious consumption.

Researchers have often turned to ethnographic methods to get a deeper insight to the behaviours, motivations, and expectations of consumers. This may involve observing minute detail about individuals, for example their body language and interaction with friends. The researcher can either be an observer, or participate in the lives of their research subjects in order to get a deeper interactive account of their behaviours and the underlying reasons for them.

In seeking to discover hidden meanings of phenomena, qualitative researchers use a number of techniques that are not available to the quantitative researcher. Projective techniques, including word association (often used in connection with research into proposed brand names), sentence completion, and interpreting a story board, are commonly used, but can demand skill in their interpretation.

Many additional sources of qualitative research data have been made possible using the Internet. Observation of blogs and social websites with a view to obtaining meaning has led to the development of a range of techniques, such as transaction log analysis (Jansen et al. 2000); verbal protocol analysis (Ericsson and Simon 1993; Nahl and Tenopir 1996), and 'webnography' or 'virtual ethnography' (Morton 2001). Morton (2001, 6) noted two principal methods for conducting ethnographic research on the Internet—distanced or involved. Many market researchers learn a lot about consumers by simply observing, or 'lurking' in social media sites—a form of distanced research. Others have been more practised and participated online, posing issues and recording the results. However, questions about the ethics of such behaviour have been raised where the true intent of the researcher has not been revealed and participants may be led to believe that the researcher is in fact just another member of the community.

It is very difficult to assess the validity of qualitative research techniques, and the tests for significance that are available for most quantitative techniques are largely lacking for qualitative techniques. So how can a client company that has commissioned qualitative research assess whether the findings are credible? Consider the following possibilities:

◉ Market research demands cooperation and trust between the client commissioning a study and the company carrying it out. The reputation that a market research agency has built for itself is particularly important where qualitative research is involved.

◉ Increasingly, qualitative research techniques are utilizing quasi-quantitative techniques in order to enhance their credibility (or at least the appearance of credibility). There are now a number of computer programs (e.g. NVivo) which essentially analyse the content of discussions and count key words, phrases, and contexts.

Qualitative research has been a major growth activity in marketing over the past couple of decades.

Who carries out marketing research?

Marketing researchers fall into two groups.

1. There are those employed by manufacturers and services companies (often referred to as 'client' companies) who collect internal data and commission research from outside organizations when needed.

2. A large industry of market research firms is available to carry out the research that client companies are unable or unwilling to carry out themselves. (Among the larger companies in this category are BMRB, Ispos MORI, and Taylor Nelson Sofres.) Staff employed by these companies can achieve a high level of expertise in particular research techniques or particular product areas. (For example, Verdict Research has achieved particular skills in the field of retailing.) Some of these companies undertake 'omnibus' surveys on behalf of a number of clients simultaneously, thereby reducing the costs to each client.

The research process shown in Figure 5.2 allows for the expertise of both groups to be used at different stages. Client company researchers initially define a research problem, after internal discussion with marketing and other management. This is usually communicated to potential suppliers in the form of a research brief. The objectives of the study are determined by matching management information needs with what can realistically be obtained from the marketplace, particularly in the light of time and budgetary constraints, and these may well be defined after initial discussions with possible suppliers.

Specialist market research suppliers tend to dominate at the stage of data collection, for two main reasons. First, very few client companies, however large or diverse their product range, can generate sufficient research to warrant employing full-time specialist interviewers throughout the country. Much research is seasonal or one-off, and it would be more expensive for a company to retain research capacity that is required only intermittently, than to buy it in as and when required. The second reason is that respondents may be more likely to give honest answers to third parties than when replying directly to representatives of the organization being discussed. Data collectors are also less likely to be biased when they are working for a company that is independent of their own employer. However, commercial market research companies have sometimes been accused of focusing more on techniques than on identifying really useful information to a company (Savage 2001).

Relationships between client companies and their suppliers can involve high levels of trust and cooperation, and many relationships between the two are very long-standing. Before deciding on the final plan, however, it is usual for client companies to approach several possible suppliers and ask for their suggestions in the form of a research proposal. The extent of involvement of the client company in the research process is largely dependent upon the size and expertise of its research department.

⦿ Marketing intelligence

Market research has so far been described in terms of establishing customers' characteristics and preferences in a structured manner. Another approach is to gather relatively unstructured information about the environment in a format that is often referred to as marketing intelligence. Business owners have developed over a long time the art of 'keeping their ear close to the ground' through informal networks of contacts. With the growing sophistication of the business environment, these informal methods of gathering intelligence often need to be supplemented. In contrast to market research, intelligence gathering concentrates on picking up relatively intangible ideas and trends, especially about competitors' developments.

Carson et al. (2001) described how marketing managers use networks, often haphazardly and informally, to gather information. They noted that for many small business owners, 'research' is inseparable from daily business. According to their study, research by networking is 'informal, often discreet, interactive, interchangeable, integrated, habitual, reactive, individualistic, and highly focused on the enterprise' (Carson et al. 2001, 56).

Marketing managers can gather this intelligence from a number of sources, including the following:

- By regularly scanning newspapers, especially trade newspapers, a company can learn about competitors' planned new product launches.

- There are now many specialized media cutting services which will regularly review published material and alert a company to items that fall within pre-determined criteria.

- Employees are a valuable source of marketing intelligence, especially in services organizations where they are in regular contact with customers. Sales personnel can act as the ears as well as the mouth for an organization. Staff suggestion schemes and quality circles are often used to gain market intelligence, in addition to informal methods of listening to front-line employees.

- Similarly, intermediaries are close to customers, and their observations are often encouraged through seminars, consultation meetings, and informal communication methods.

- When a firm feels that it doesn't have the resources to undertake any of the above, it may retain consultants to provide regular briefings.

Market intelligence is a valuable contributor to the development of corporate knowledge, which is considered next.

⦿ Knowledge management

Knowledge is one of the greatest assets of most commercial organizations, and its contribution to sustainable competitive advantage has been widely recognized (e.g. Pugh and

Dixon 2008). Information represents a bridge between the organization and its environment and is the means by which a picture of the changing environment is built up within the organization. Marketing management is responsible for turning information-based knowledge into specific marketing plans.

In 1991, Ikujiro Nonaka began an article in the *Harvard Business Review* with a simple statement: 'In an economy where the only certainty is uncertainty, the one sure source of lasting competitive advantage is knowledge' (Nonaka 1991). A firm's knowledge base is likely to include, among other things, an understanding of the precise needs of customers; how those needs are likely to change over time; how those needs are satisfied in terms of efficient and effective production systems, and an understanding of competitors' activities. We are probably all familiar with companies in which knowledge seems to be very poor—the hotel reservation that is mixed up, the delivery that does not happen as specified, or junk mail which is of no interest at all. On the other hand, customers may revel in a company that delivers the right service at the right time and clearly demonstrates that it is knowledgeable about all aspects of the transaction. The small business owner may have been able to achieve all of this by himself, but in large organizations the task of managing knowledge becomes much more complex. Where it is done well, it can be a significant contributor to a firm's sustainable competitive advantage.

We need to distinguish between the terms 'knowledge' and 'information'. Even though in some senses they may be used interchangeably, many writers have suggested that the two concepts are quite distinct. Knowledge is a much more all-encompassing term, incorporating the concept of beliefs that are based on information. Knowledge also depends on the commitment and understanding of the individual holding these beliefs, which are affected by interaction and the development of judgement, behaviour, and attitude. Knowledge has meaning only in the context of a process or capacity to act. Drucker noted that 'There is no such thing as knowledge management, there are only knowledgeable people. Information only becomes knowledge in the hands of someone who knows what to do with it' (Drucker 1999). Knowledge, then, is evidenced by its association with actions, and its source can be found in a combination of information, social interaction, and contextual situations which affect the knowledge accumulation process at an individual level. One outcome of a knowledge-based organization has often been referred to as the 'learning organization', in which the challenge is to learn at the corporate level from what is known by individuals who make up the organization.

Two different types of knowledge can be identified:

1. Knowledge that is easily definable and is accessible is often referred to as explicit knowledge. This type of knowledge can be readily quantified and passed between individuals in the form of words and numbers. Because it is easily communicated, it is relatively easy to manage. Knowledge management is concerned with ensuring that the explicit knowledge of individuals becomes a part of the organizational knowledge base and that it is used efficiently and contributes where necessary to changes in work practices, processes, and products.

2. The second type of knowledge comprises the accumulated knowledge of individuals, which is not explicit, but can still be important to the successful operation of an organization. This type of knowledge, often referred to as tacit knowledge, is not easy to see or express; it is highly personal and is rooted in an individual's experiences, attitudes, values, and behaviour patterns. Tacit knowledge can be much more difficult to formalize and disseminate within an organization. If tacit knowledge can be captured, mobilized, and turned into explicit knowledge, it will then be accessible to others in the organization and will enable the organization to progress, rather than require individuals within it continually to have to relearn from the same point. The owner of a small business could have all of this information readily available to him in his head. The challenge taken on by many large corporations is to emulate the knowledge management of the small business owner.

The transition from individuals' information to corporate knowledge requires a sharing of knowledge by all concerned. This raises problems in which employees perceive that knowledge is a powerful asset which they can use in their negotiations with senior management or

MARKETING in ACTION

Management by walking about

Information is often described as management's window on the world. But what happens if management works in a large corporate head office, far removed from customers and day-to-day operations? It is sadly all too familiar for senior management to become cut off from the operations that they manage. In a BBC television series, 'Back to the Floor', chief executives were invited to spend a few days changing their role to that of a front-line employee. For some of the participants this was unfamiliar territory, which hadn't been witnessed at first hand for some time (if ever). The gulf between what these key decision makers thought was happening and what was actually happening was sometimes quite marked. In one case, the then chief executive of the grocery retailer Sainsbury's seemed to be oblivious of customers' annoyance with shopping trolley design and availability, and in another the chief executive of Pickford's Removals couldn't understand why the company was so inflexible when minor changes in customers' requirements occurred. The managers of small businesses do not generally have such problems, as they are in regular contact with their customers and do not need structured information management systems to give them a window on the world. Their success in keeping in touch with customers has led many larger businesses to emulate some of their practices. Management by walking about has become a popular way in which senior executives try to gain knowledge about their marketing environment which is not immediately apparent from structured reporting systems. Archie Norman, when head of the retailer Asda, is reported to have introduced a number of innovations learnt during his regular visits to the company's shop-floors. Some companies have adopted a formal system of role exchanges where senior executives spend a period at the sharp end of their business.

If you are studying at a university, do you believe that the vice-chancellor really has a good understanding of the day-to-day issues that are of greatest concern to students? Some vice-chancellors have taken the bold step of trying to live student life for a day or a week. What benefits can you see in this approach? Are there any possible problems in this approach?

other functional departments. A knowledge management programme is needed to break down a *laissez-faire* attitude, and typically would include the following elements:

◉ a strong knowledge-sharing culture, which can emerge only over time with the development of trust;

◉ measures to monitor that sharing, which may be reflected in individuals' performance reviews;

◉ technology to facilitate knowledge transfer, which should be as user-friendly as possible;

◉ established practices for the capture and sharing of knowledge—without clearly defined procedures, the technology is of only limited value;

◉ leadership and senior management commitment to sharing information—if senior management doesn't share information, why should anybody else bother?

It must be remembered that marketing information cannot in itself produce decisions: it merely provides data which must be interpreted by marketing managers. Also, as information collection, processing, transmission, and storage technologies improve, information is becoming more accessible not just to one particular organization, but also to its competitors. Competitive advantage is more likely to go to those companies that are best able to make use of the available information.

◉ Demand forecasting

It should never be forgotten that a key task of marketing management in general, and of marketing research in particular, is to gather a better picture of the future so that a company can be prepared for it more efficiently and effectively than its competitors. Demand forecasting can involve predicting general changes in the marketing environment, which were discussed in Chapter 2. This in itself can be very difficult; for example economists frequently disagree in their forecasts of economic growth during the year ahead. When it comes to predicting macro-environmental change, larger companies often retain expert consultants, such as the Future Foundation (www.futurefoundation.net), who employ economists, sociologists, and psychologists, among others, to try to build a picture of the world as it will evolve. Such macro-level forecasts can inform more detailed forecasts about market size, growth rates, market share, etc.

There have been many cases of spectacular failures to forecast demand accurately, of which the following are a few examples (Figure 5.6):

◉ When Carphone Warehouse launched its new 'free' Broadband service in 2006, it experienced an unexpectedly high level of take-up, resulting in delays and frustration for potential customers.

- Many people in the industry expected the launch of 'Freeview' digital television services in 2002 to be a flop, following the previous low levels of takeup of ITV digital services. In fact, Freeview quickly became very popular, with reports of shortages of set-top adapter boxes.

- Each Christmas seems to witness another new toy which has become an unexpected success with children, leading to shortages, while other new toys fail to sell and end up being discounted in the January sales.

A forecast of likely demand is a crucial input to a firm's strategic and operational planning processes. In the case of Carphone Warehouse's broadband offer, the forecast of new customer applications was used as an input to the firm's human resource plan, so when the marketing demand forecast proved to be wrong, the human resource plan—which had recruited to cater for a lower level of forecast demand—also proved wrong.

Figure 5.6 **London's Millennium Dome (now known as the O$_2$ Arena), was open to the public for just one year in 2000, and proved to be a disappointment in terms of visitor numbers.** Against forecasts of 12 million paying visitors, only about half this figure actually visited. Forecasts were made difficult because of the absence of comparable previous projects which might have given some idea of the likely take-up. Many uncertainties remained during the forecasting process, including the effects of competing millennium attractions, the impact of press reviews, the state of the national economy, and the capacity of the local transport infrastructure. Also, low initial numbers appeared to develop a momentum of its own, as the media talked down the success of the project, leading to many more people deciding to give the event a miss.

The amount of effort that a firm puts into refining its demand forecasting techniques calls for a balancing of the cost of undertaking a detailed study against the cost of making an inaccurate forecast. Where capital costs are low, it may make sense to go straight to the market with a product to see what happens. It was noted earlier that this is common in the fashion clothing industry. At other times, a more analytic approach to demand forecasting is required (refer back to Figure 5.2).

Demand forecasting uses many of the analytic techniques—quantitative and qualitative—described earlier in this chapter. A starting point for demand forecasting is an examination of historical trends. At its simplest, a firm identifies a historic and consistent long-term change in demand for a product over time and seeks to explain this in terms of change in some underlying variables, such as household income levels or price levels. Correlation and regression techniques can be used to assess the significance of historical relationships between variables. However, a simple extrapolation of past trends has a number of weaknesses. One variable, or even a small number of variables, is seldom adequate to predict future demand for a product, yet it can be difficult to identify the full set of variables that have an influence. New variables may emerge over time. There can be no certainty that the trends identified from historic data are likely to continue in the future, and the data are of diminishing value as the length of time that they are used to forecast increases.

Models have become increasingly sophisticated in their ability to forecast consumer demand. This can be explained partly by a growing amount of readily available data (and staff who can use it), which can be used to build and validate a model. Reliability is improved by increasing the volume of data on which a model is based and the number of variables that are used for prediction.

Inevitably, models, no matter how sophisticated, need interpretation. This is where the creative side of marketing management is called for, especially in combining market intelligence with harder economic approaches. In interpreting quantitative demand forecasts, management must use its judgement, based on a holistic overview of the market situation.

◉ Chapter summary and key linkages to other chapters

Understanding customers is critical to business success, and this chapter has discussed some of the approaches to market research. Marketing management is a combination of a science and an art, and this is reflected in approaches to gathering and analysing marketing information. The chapter has built on our review of the marketing environment (Chapter 2) and buyer behaviour (Chapter 4), which marketers must try to understand and predict into the future. Appropriate research methods are necessary for conducting segmentation exercises, to be discussed in Chapter 6. In the following chapters we will look at how research is used to inform decisions about a company's product development, pricing, distribution, and promotion activities.

KEY PRINCIPLES OF MARKETING

- The ultimate aim of a company's research activity is essentially to gain a better understanding of its likely future marketing environment.

- Information is a source of a company's competitive advantage.

- Information on its own does not make decisions—management must use its judgement to interpret information.

- Learning organizations develop knowledge at a corporate level in order to provide a more efficient and effective response to environmental change.

- Research techniques need to be appropriate to the task in hand.

- Qualitative techniques provide for depth of understanding, while quantitative techniques provide for broad representation. The two techniques overlap.

CASE STUDY

Drowning in data, searching for insight?

Companies are able to capture ever-increasing amounts of information through electronically stored till receipts, order forms, registration cards, etc., from which almost endless correlation coefficients may be calculated. In recent times, researchers' analyses have shown correlations between an individual's height and his annual expenditure on clothing; shoe size and usage of gyms; and purchases of milk and purchases of paint. Some of these might at first sound quite spurious, and the researcher's task is to probe more deeply to establish whether there really is any direct causative relationship between the two variables, or whether there is some other intervening factor that may explain the observed correlation. Of course, sometimes the correlation is of little more than amusement value, and often it is used by research sponsors for its PR value. Would gym operators ever really want to target customers with large or small feet?

The retailer Tesco is one of many companies that routinely gathers large volumes of data about its customers. Each year, it accumulates literally billions of pieces of information from its retail operations—sales of individual product lines, how these products are combined in customers' shopping baskets, data relating to the time of purchase and place of purchase, etc. For customers who registered with the company's 'Clubcard' loyalty programme, the quantity and quality of information is even greater. The card allows the company to track an individual's purchases over time, allowing it an opportunity to try to understand long-term trends at both the individual customer level, and possibly trends which are general between customers. The company also buys in information about customers, for example Clubcard holders give their address, and the postcode is used to match their expenditure with a particular 'ACORN' customer profile. From this information, the company can begin to build up a picture of spending habits related to postcode types.

Tesco's clubcard has both operational and planning functions. As an operational tool, it has been invaluable for targeting individual customers with offers that are of particular value to them as an individual. As an example, the company operates a mother and baby club which targets new mothers, and mothers-to-be with product offers which they are likely to be particularly receptive to. As a planning tool, the Clubcard allows the company to look for patterns in consumer spending. This can be useful, for example, for planning the location of new stores, allowing the company to have a better idea of likely sales and the best product mix, depending upon the previous spending pattern of local postcode types.

Using research data, the company frequently conducts experiments and monitors the results. A promotional offer can be mailed to a sample of people on its database and the results studied before the promotional offer is refined and targeted at a larger segment of its database. Experiments can be conducted with store layouts, opening hours, and product ranges and the results assessed before being rolled out nationally.

Although Tesco is sitting on a mountain of data, this alone is not always sufficient to give real insight into consumer behaviour. The story has frequently been told of an exercise undertaken by the company using data mining techniques, which apparently discovered a correlation between sales of beer and sales of babies' nappies. The two products were not in any way complementary to each other, so why should their sales appear to be associated? Was this just another spurious correlation, to be binned along with other gems of information such as a previously reported correlation between an individual's shoe size and their propensity to use a gym?

The company didn't give up, and refined its analysis to study the correlation for different categories of store and by different times of day. Where it also had details of customers' demographic characteristics (gathered through its Clubcard programme) it was able to probe for further insights. The company was edging towards a better understanding of why the sales of these two products should be closely correlated. However, the data alone could not provide a complete answer, and to achieve this, the company had to resort to more traditional qualitative research techniques. Having identified individuals where this correlation was evident, the company is reported to have undertaken qualitative research to probe why these consumers were buying the two products in combination. From this, it appeared that men were offering to run a household errand to the shops in order to buy babies' nappies. This was an excuse to leave the family home in order to buy more beer for their own consumption. The company is claimed to have learnt from this exercise and subsequently positioned the two products closer together in selected stores.

The story of Tesco's analysis of beer and nappy sales may have become distorted with telling, and may even come close to being an urban myth. But should it take a huge database and data mining techniques to reveal these insights to buyers' behaviour? The landlord of the traditional Irish bar spotted a very similar pattern of buyer motivation long ago, with bars doubling up as the local post office, bookseller, or grocer, giving the Irish drinker plenty of good excuses for visiting the pub. The Irish bar owner would have had none of the technology available to today's businesses, just a good set of ears and eyes.

It is sometimes said that today's marketers are drowning in data, but often short of common sense. Do we sometimes look for complex technological solutions to understand customers, when the answer might be much easier to find using more traditional judgements?

Based on: Clive Humby, Terry Hunt, and Tim Phillips (2003) *Scoring Points: How Tesco is Winning Customer Loyalty*. London: Kogan Page; Tesco corporate website (**www.tesco.com**)

. . . .

Case study review questions

1. Critically evaluate the relative merits of quantitative and qualitative approaches to data collection for a large retailer.

2. Discuss the limitations of statistically based consumer databases of the type discussed here. Do qualitative approaches based on small groups offer any advantages?

3. What effects do you expect the development of interactive electronic media to have on retailers' collection of marketing research information from consumers?

CHAPTER REVIEW QUESTIONS

1. In what ways does information contribute to a firm's competitive advantage? Can a company ever have too much information?

2. What factors should influence the amount of time and money that a firm commits to the collection, analysis, and dissemination of marketing information?

3. The view is often expressed that quantitative survey techniques fail to tell the whole truth about customers' perceptions of a company's products. To what extent is this true, and how can companies address this issue?

ACTIVITIES

1. If you are studying at a university or college, identify a list of likely key marketing research objectives for the university.

2. Gather a selection of printed customer surveys from restaurants, hotels, etc. Critically discuss the insights that you think the surveys' sponsors will be able to gain from the survey form.

3. If you were considering opening a new sushi bar in your local town, how would you go about researching likely demand? How would you try to identify the best location for your restaurant?

REFERENCES

Ashworth, L. and Free, C. (2006) 'Marketing Dataveillance and Digital Privacy: Using Theories of Justice to Understand Consumers' Online Privacy Concerns'. *Journal of Business Ethics*, 67 (2), 107–23.

Brown, S. (1998) *Postmodern Marketing 2: Telling Tales*. London: International Thomson Business Press.

Carson, D., Gilmore, A., Perry, C., and Gronhaug, K. (2001) *Qualitative Marketing Research*. London: Sage.

Carù, A. and Cova, B. (2008) 'Small Versus Big Stories in Framing Consumption Experiences'. *Qualitative Market Research: An International Journal*, 11 (2), 166–76.

Constantinides, E. and Fountain, S.J. (2008) 'Web 2.0: Conceptual Foundations and Marketing Issues'. *Journal of Direct, Data and Digital Marketing Practice*, 9 (3), 231–44.

Drucker, P. (1999) *The Frontier of Management: Where Tomorrow's Decisions are Being Shaped Today*. New York: Truman Talley.

Ericsson, K.A. and Simon, H.A. (1993) *Protocol Analysis: Verbal Reports as Data*. Cambridge, MA: MIT Press.

Flore, A.M. and Kim, J. (2007) 'An Integrative Framework Capturing Experiential and Utilitarian Shopping Experience'. *International Journal of Retail & Distribution Management*, 35 (6), 421–42.

Fugate, D.L. (2008) 'Marketing Services More Effectively with Neuromarketing Research: a Look into the Future'. *Journal of Services Marketing*, 22 (3), 70–3.

Holbrook, M.B. and Hirschman, E.C. (1982) 'The Experiential Aspects of Consumption: Consumer Fantasies, Feelings, and Fun'. *Journal of Consumer Research*, 9 (2), 132–40.

Humby, C., Hunt, T., and Phillips, T. (2003) *Scoring Points: How Tesco is Winning Customer Loyalty*. London: Kogan Page.

Jansen, B.J., Spink, A., and Saracevic, T. (2000) 'Real Life, Real Users, and Real Needs: A Study and Analysis of User Queries On The Web'. *Information Processing & Management*, 36 (2), 207–27.

Kozinets, R.V. (2006) Netnography 2.0. In R.W. Belk (ed.), *Handbook of Qualitative Research Methods in Marketing*, pp. 129–42. Cheltenham, UK: Edward Elgar.

Miller, K.D., Fabian, F., and Lin, S.J. (2009) Strategies For Online Communities'. *Strategic Management Journal*, 30 (3), 305–22.

Morton, H. (2001) 'Computer-mediated Communication in Australian Anthropology and Sociology'. *Social Analysis Journal of Cultural and Social Practices*, 45 (1), 3–11.

Nahl, D. and Tenopir, C. (1996) 'Affective and Cognitive Searching Behavior of Novice End-Users of a Full-text Database'. *Journal of the American Society for Information Science*, 47 (4), 276–86.

Nonaka, I. (1991) 'The Knowledge Creating Company'. *Harvard Business Review*, 69 (6), 96–104.

Pugh, K. and Dixon N.M. (2008) 'Don't Just Capture Knowledge—Put It to Work'. *Harvard Business Review*, 86 (5), May 2008.

Puri, A. (2007) 'The Web of Insights: The Art and Practice of Webnography'. *International Journal of Market Research*, 49 (3), 387–408.

Savage, M. (2001) 'A View from the Board Room'. *Research*, August, 16–18.

Schmitt, P. and Michahelles, F. (2008) *Economic Impact of RFID Report*. Zurich: ETH.

Smith, D. and Dexter, A. (2001) 'Whenever I Hear the Word Paradigm I Reach for my Gun: How to Stop Talking and Start Walking'. *International Journal of Market Research*, 43 (3), 321–40.

Tuckel, P. and O'Neill, H. (2002) 'The Vanishing Respondent in Telephone Surveys'. *Journal of Advertising Research*, 42 (5), 26–48.

🔍 SUGGESTED FURTHER READING

The market research process in general is described in more detail in a number of books. The following texts provide useful coverage of the principles introduced in this chapter:

Bradley, N. (2010) *Marketing Research, Tools and Techniques*. Oxford: Oxford University Press.

Wilson, A. (2006) *Marketing Research: An Integrated Approach*, 2nd edn. London: FT Prentice Hall.

Zikmund, W.G and Babin, B.J. (2010) *Essentials of Marketing Research*, 4th edition. Mason, Ohio: Thomson.

The important role played by information in business planning is discussed in the following texts.

Byrne, D. (2008) *Web of Knowledge: Essential Knowledge Management for Those Working with Information*. London: Facet Publishing.

Hislop, D. (2009) *Knowledge Management in Organizations: A Critical Introduction*. Oxford: Oxford University Press.

The following regularly updated UK government statistics are frequently used as a basis for marketing research:

Basic Statistics of the European Community

Economic Trends: a monthly compendium of economic data which gives convenient access from one source to a range of economic indicators

Family Expenditure Survey: a sample survey of consumer spending habits, providing a snapshot of household spending; published annually

Population Trends: statistics on population, including population change, births and deaths, life expectancy, and migration

Regional Trends: a comprehensive source of statistics about the regions of the UK allowing regional comparisons

Social Trends: statistics combined with text, tables, and charts which present a narrative of life and lifestyles in the UK; published annually

UK National Accounts (the Blue Book): the principal annual publication for National Account statistics, covering value added by industry, the personal sector, companies, public corporations, central and local government; published annually

ONLINE RESOURCE CENTRE

Visit the Online Resource Centre for resources that are relevant to this chapter, including a flashcard glossary, web links, multiple choice questions, and additional case studies:

www.oxfordtextbooks.co.uk/orc/palmer3e/

KEY TERMS

- Cluster analysis
- Conjoint analysis
- Desk research
- Environmental scanning
- Explicit knowledge
- Field research
- Focus group
- Knowledge
- Management by walking about
- Market research
- Marketing intelligence

- Marketing research
- Models
- Mystery shoppers
- Primary research
- Qualitative research
- Quantitative research
- Regression analysis
- Sampling
- Secondary research
- SERVQUAL
- Tacit knowledge

SEGMENTATION, POSITIONING, AND TARGETING

6

CHAPTER OBJECTIVES

Customers are becoming increasingly diverse in their needs and aspirations, and less inclined to accept an 'average' product. The purpose of segmentation is to identify groups of buyers who respond in a similar way to any given marketing stimuli. This chapter explores the bases for market segmentation and how these are used by companies to target selected groups. Some of the bases for identifying different types of customer are familiar and readily observable, such as age, gender, and geographical location. Others, such as attitudes and lifestyle, may be more difficult to identify, but can be crucial for understanding consumers' buying processes. To be effective, a company's products must be positioned relative to competitors' products in such a way that targeted segments find them the most attractive for satisfying their needs.

● Introduction

From Chapter 1 you will recall that a focus on meeting customers' needs is a defining characteristic of marketing. Organizations that make presumptions about customers' needs, or produce goods and services that are chosen for their convenience in production, are probably not truly marketing orientated. A true marketing orientation requires companies to focus on meeting the needs of individual customers. In a simple world where consumers all have broadly similar needs and expectations, a company could probably justify developing a marketing programme that meets the needs of the 'average' customer. In the early days of motoring, Henry Ford successfully sold as many standard, black Model T Fords as he was able to produce. In the modern world of marketing, few companies can have the luxury of producing just one product to satisfy a very large market. Some still can—for example water supply utility companies generally produce a single standard of water for all of their customers—but this is the exception rather than the rule. Most companies face markets that are becoming increasingly fragmented in terms of the needs customers seek to satisfy. So, while Henry Ford's customers may have been quite happy to have a plain black car, today's car buyers seek out differentiated products in order to satisfy a much wider range of needs. The 'average' customer that Henry Ford appealed to is increasingly becoming a myth.

Segmentation, then, is essentially about identifying groups of buyers within a marketplace who have needs that are distinctive in the way they deviate from the 'average' consumer (Figure 6.1). Some consumers may treat satisfaction of one particular need as a high priority, whereas others may regard this need as quite trivial. We saw in Chapter 4 how an understanding of needs is crucial to the study of buyer behaviour. We will pick up the question of needs again by considering the buying behaviour for cars. Buyers no longer select a car solely on the basis of a car's ability to satisfy a need to get them from A to B: in addition, they may seek to satisfy any of the following needs from a car purchase:

⦿ To give them status in the eyes of their peer group.

⦿ To provide safety and security for themselves and their families.

⦿ To project a particular image of themselves.

⦿ To provide a cost-effective means of transport.

⦿ To be seen making a gesture towards the environment by buying a 'green' car.

⦿ If it is a company car, to save company car tax.

There are many more possible factors that might influence an individual's choice of car. The important point here is that the market is composed of buyers who approach their decisions to buy a car in very different ways. Therefore, the features that each looks for in the product

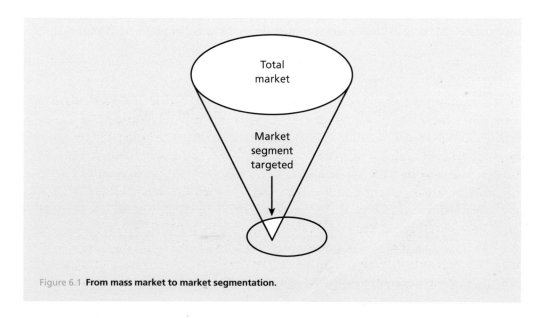

Figure 6.1 **From mass market to market segmentation.**

offer may differ quite markedly from the market 'average'. It follows that, with a wide dispersion of market needs, a marketing plan based on satisfying the needs of the average buyer will be unlikely to succeed in a competitive marketplace. If another company can better satisfy the needs of small specialist groups, then the company that seeks to serve them with just an 'average' product offer will lose the custom of this group.

We will define the process of market segmentation as the identification of sub-sets of buyers within a market who share similar needs and who have similar buying processes. In an ideal world, firms would tailor their product offering to the needs of each individual customer. In the case of some expensive items of capital equipment bought by firms, this indeed does happen. (For example, there are very few buyers of large power stations in the UK, so firms can justifiably treat each customer as a segment of one.) In the case of products that are relatively low in value and high in sales volume, it would be practically impossible for firms to cater to each individual's needs, although developments in technology are allowing for a much greater degree of customization than has previously been the case.

Segmentation should not be regarded as a technique that is unique to marketing. In fact, wise marketers are simply following a critical approach to decision making which is shared by many other professions and disciplines. The critical approach revolves around breaking a large problem down into a number of smaller problems and resolving those smaller problems in the most appropriate way. In this case, the 'problem' for the marketer is how to get the market to buy its products. The problem can be broken down into the sub-problems of how to get particular sub-groups within those markets to buy its products. The solution to each of these problems might be quite different. Analogies can be drawn with many other problems of decision making. An engineer designing a bridge breaks the bridge down into component parts when specifying materials to be used. The needs of the different parts of the structure would probably call for quite different strengths of material. Just as the marketer would not use one product to satisfy the needs of the entire market, the engineer would not use just one gauge of metal to build the entire bridge structure. Both the marketer and the engineer have used critical thinking to break a large problem down into smaller problems (Figure 6.2).

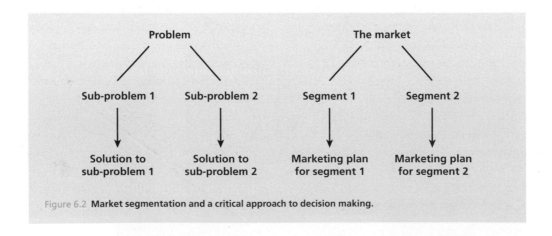

Figure 6.2 **Market segmentation and a critical approach to decision making.**

◉ Criteria for effective segmentation

Market segmentation should be regarded as the product of critical thinking rather than as some pre-determined set of procedures. There is no underlying theory to the process of market segmentation. It follows that what is an appropriate basis for segmenting one market may not be appropriate to all markets.

Before we begin to look at the bases on which marketers can segment any given market, we need to be aware of the criteria by which the effectiveness of any segmentation basis can be assessed. We will consider here four important criteria: usefulness to a company's marketing planning; size of the resulting segments; their measurability; and their accessibility.

Is the basis of market segmentation useful to the company?

It is easy to develop bases for market segmentation while losing sight of the purpose of the exercise. Essentially, the exercise is worthwhile only if it allows a company profitably to penetrate a greater proportion of its market than would have been the case if the exercise had not been undertaken. Groups identified as homogeneous market segments must be just that: similar in terms of the needs and buying behaviour of the individuals they contain. Many companies fail in their segmentation exercises because their assumptions about homogeneity within a segment overlook some critical differences within the segment which leads to varied responses to a product offer that has been specifically targeted at the segment. For example, a segment for overseas package holidays defined as 'affluent, married working women' may overlook the fact that women within this segment have very divergent views on the features they seek from a holiday, depending on the age and structure of their families. The buying behaviour of those affluent, married, working women who seek to take their children away with them is quite likely to be significantly different from those who seek to travel by themselves or just with their partners. To be more effective, market segmentation must recognize the diversity of needs within this group.

Are the segments of an economic size?

Any basis for segmentation should yield segments that are of a size that a company can profitably exploit. Companies face a dilemma here, because as segments get smaller they get closer to achieving the marketing philosophy of satisfying each customer's needs as though each one were the centre of all the company's attention. The problem for the company is that smaller segments may be uneconomic to provide for. What is a reasonable size of segment varies from one market to another, and is constantly changing over time. In the financial services industry, it is possible to develop quite specific products to target very small segments of a market. For example, it would involve relatively little effort by an insurance company to develop motor insurance policies that specifically meet the needs of people driving 'classic' vintage cars, further sub-divided into those who live in the north of England, and further sub-divided into those aged over 50 years. In principle, there are few operational reasons why an insurance broker should not focus on a segment that small. At the other extreme, a company manufacturing paint for the private household market might find it difficult to offer a range as customer-focused as this. For example, a paint manufacturer might wish to produce variants of paints for the following identified segments:

- users who are averse to painting (for this group, the manufacturer might develop a product that is non-spill and delicately perfumed);

- the 'professional' home decorator segment who seeks perfection through multi-coat application;

- the time-constrained perfectionist who seeks a one-coat paint with durable finish;

- the adventurous, who seek special-effect patterns from their paint (e.g. mottled effects).

To produce each new variant of paint, the manufacturer would probably have to interrupt its production lines to prepare for the next specialized product. Worse still, it would have to persuade its wholesalers and retailers to stock each such variant. When each colour variant is multiplied by the number of segment-specific formulations, it is clear that the stockholding problems for retailers and wholesalers could be immense.

Manufacturers are becoming increasingly able to offer specialized goods to meet the needs of small market segments (Figure 6.3). Service industries have had this flexibility for some time, and are now exploiting it to the full with the use of information technology. Within the manufacturing sector, flexible manufacturing systems are allowing smaller production runs to be achieved economically. For Henry Ford, producing even a slight variant of his original car would have meant stopping the production line and re-tooling for a new model. Today, car assembly lines employ computerized design and manufacturing systems, which, combined with interchangeability of components, allow many different models to come off the same production line.

Can the market segments be measured?

Ideally, companies should be able to know the precise size of all identified market segments. This is important in order that segments can be compared and their profit potentials assessed. Unfortunately, data are often not available to quantify market segments. Marketers therefore face a further dilemma in defining market segments. Should they go for segments that they believe exist but cannot measure, or should they define segments only on the basis of what can accurately be measured, but which may have little bearing on the homogeneity of consumers' needs and buying processes? As an example, the UK population census gives a lot of valuable information which is frequently used as a basis for identifying market segments (e.g. the age profile of an area, number of people per household, etc.). However, marketers are often interested in a more subjective assessment of individuals, such as their attitudes and lifestyles. Unfortunately, there is very little published information available

Figure 6.3 **The marketing environment has tended to allow firms to target increasingly small market segments.** Flexible manufacturing systems, interactive communication via the Internet and more flexible stock handling methods have contributed to this. In the consumer market for paint, which is dominated in the UK by two large manufacturers and a handful of major retail outlets, a market exists for specialist organic paints. Ecos Organic Paints offers a range of environmentally friendly paints targeted at niche markets of paint buyers who may be concerned about allergies or environmental damage. Using flexible manufacturing and stock handling systems, the company is able to offer next day delivery of a wide range of paints.
(Reproduced with kind permission of Ecos Organic Paints.)

on these more subjective aspects of market segments. While we can know quite accurately the size of the segment of people aged over 60 and living alone in a particular area, there is very little readily available information about how many people living in that area can be described as 'environmentally aware' or 'liberal in attitudes' or any other measure of attitudes or lifestyles. Inevitably, marketing managers must make a trade-off between the need for information that is objective and reliable on the one hand and subjective and creative on the other.

Fortunately for marketers, the sources of information available that can be used to segment markets are constantly increasing. In addition to traditional government statistical sources, many private-sector organizations (e.g. Mintel, Keynote, and nVision) frequently commission and publish research that is based on surveys of samples of the population.

Are the segments accessible to the company?

There is little point in going to a lot of effort in defining segments of a market when those segments are not accessible to the company, or ever likely to be. Inaccessibility can come about for a number of reasons.

- The company may be prohibited by law from entering certain markets. (For example, many overseas governments restrict the rights of foreign companies to serve their domestic market.)

- Some buyers in a market may be tied to suppliers by long-term supply contracts. In the case of subsidiaries of large corporations, the holding company may require its subsidiaries to obtain its purchases from within the group.

- Although it may be possible, the cost of gaining access to a market segment may be prohibitive. A manufacturer of building materials in the UK may in theory be able to supply a segment of small building contractors in southern Italy, but the cost of transporting its bulky goods over the distances involved may make the segment effectively inaccessible.

Although a segment may be inaccessible to a company now, this may not always continue to be the case. Changes in legislation may make possible something that was previously illegal for a company. Policies of large companies towards the contracting out of supplies may present new opportunities. Even segments that seemed inaccessible because of high transport costs may become accessible through the development of a joint venture company.

◉ Bases for market segmentation

A basis for segmenting a market should satisfy the criteria described above. It was noted that companies often need to make trade-offs in arriving at a basis for market segmentation that meets these criteria. It follows, therefore, that firms seldom use one basis for market segmentation alone. In Figure 6.4 a number of segmentation bases are plotted in terms of their measurability and usefulness to a typical manufacturer of ready-prepared meals. (Segmentation here is defined in terms of final consumers, although, as Chapter 10 will discuss, segmentation can also be applied to different types of intermediary who will handle the product.)

Markets can be segmented using a variety of approaches. In terms of operationalizing these approaches, demographic approaches, socio-economic approaches, and psychographic approaches are commonly used. Overlap often occurs between these approaches to segmentation.

Demographic bases for segmentation

Most methods of segmenting consumer markets make some use of demographic characteristics. In this section we will consider a number of demographic-related bases for segmenting markets: age, the stage in the family life-cycle, gender, and household composition.

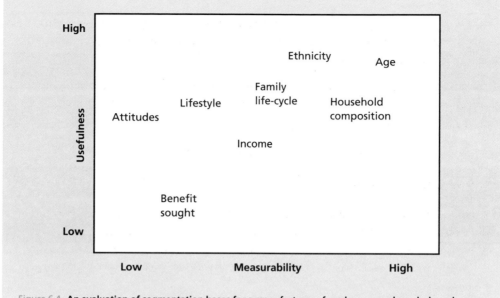

Figure 6.4 **An evaluation of segmentation bases for a manufacturer of ready-prepared meals, based on their usefulness and measurability.**

Age

Age is probably one of the most widely used bases for market segmentation. It satisfies many of the criteria for effective segmentation discussed above. It is useful to companies because demand for many products appears to be age related. There are many obvious examples; for example music buying peaks among the 18–25-year age group, and the purchase of cruise holidays increases after the age of 50. There are also more subtle age-related patterns of demand within particular categories of product. Within the UK retail sector, for example, many chains are associated with particular age groups. So, while the Arcadia clothing chain's Top Shop brand targets a mainly young 18–30 year age segment, its Principles brand is more attractive to the 21–40 year segment, and the Evans brand to 30+ shoppers. The usefulness of age can be partly explained by the observation that people's tastes change as they grow older. Some of this may be related to their stage in the family life-cycle, which is age related, as well as to changes in disposable income (see below).

Age segmentation meets another important criterion in that it is generally easy to measure the size of segments. Population censuses record respondents' ages, while many privately collected sources of information (such as company sponsored questionnaires) frequently ask for such information. A company can therefore be reasonably confident about how many people belong to a particular age segment within a specific area. This information might be vital to a retail chain seeking the best areas in which to locate new branches, given that demand for its format of stores is very age specific.

Of course, age alone is not usually a good basis for market segmentation. Within any age segment, individuals can be observed who exhibit quite different buying behaviour.

Stage in family life-cycle	Possible main emphasis of food buying
Dependent child	Main food purchased is for snacks. Attracted by the novelty and packaging of food.
Young independent adult	Eating out, possibly at fast food outlets. Minimum effort put into preparing food at home—home-consumed food is often from simple ready-made meals.
Adult, married, no children	Quite likely to eat out at restaurants. Willing to experiment in home cooking, although may still buy ready-made meals for home consumption.
Adult, married, dependent children	Eating out is reduced and cooking at home concentrates on meeting the needs of the whole family. Budgeting becomes tighter and economy replaces variety as a driving force behind food purchases.
Adult, married, independent children	Greater time and money now available for eating out and being adventurous with home-prepared food. Can afford ready-made meals, but prefers to prepare own food.
Sole survivor	Average size of food purchase declines. Emphasis on food items that are easy to prepare.

Figure 6.5 **Effects of stage in family life-course on an individual's food buying behaviour.**

However, differences often relate to the preference for specific brands rather than the consumption of a particular product. For example, while consumption of whisky is related to age, considerable diversity exists within age segments in brand preferences.

A further reservation on the use of age as a segmentation variable is that there may be differences between an individual's actual biological age and his perceived age. This can be seen at one extreme in 'wannabe' teenagers who seek to act out the lifestyle of their older peers, and at the other extreme by the elderly 'young at heart' who identify themselves with an age ten or twenty years younger than their actual age. There has been interesting research into the increasing desire of older people to perpetuate their youth and the effects on marketing of differences between actual age and self-ascribed age. It could be argued that the most important determinant of a person's buying behaviour is the age that he thinks he is, rather than his actual age. Many companies have exploited this opportunity; for example tour operators offer activity holidays targeted at retired people. However, while information on biological age is often readily available, data relating to perceived age can generally be established only by sample survey approaches.

Family life-cycle

Individuals typically go through a number of family roles, beginning with that of a dependent child and proceeding through a young single adult, a married adult with dependent children, a married adult with independent children, and finally a sole survivor. At each stage of development, an individual's buying preferences are likely to change—and, just as importantly, their ability to pay for those purchases will change too. There are many obvious marketing opportunities associated with specific stages in the life-course. For example, a young adult with no financial responsibilities is a prime target for many leisure related items such as music, while an individual with a young dependent family is an important target for firms selling childcare products. Figure 6.5 illustrates some of the changes in food buying habits which may arise as an individual progresses through the family life-course.

Marketers are often particularly interested in 'trigger' points in people's lives. These are events that suddenly change a person's behaviour, and they are frequently family related. Setting up home together, the birth of a first child, and the death of a partner are examples of events that can profoundly affect what an individual buys and how she buys it.

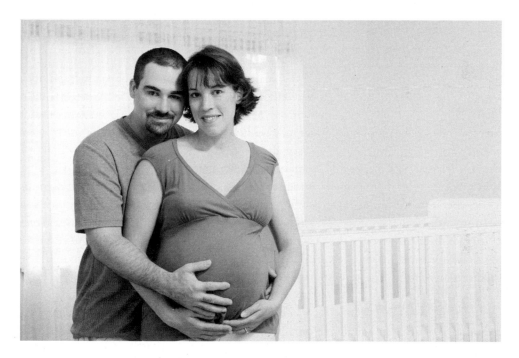

Figure 6.6 **Market segments are often defined in terms of individuals who are at transition points in their lives.** The birth of a child, marriage, divorce, and death of a family member are all events that can trigger a change in an individual's buying behaviour. Companies are therefore often keen to know more about these trigger points in individuals' lives. One example is Life-cycle Marketing Limited which publishes the pregnancy guide *Emma's Diary* and an interactive website (http://www.emmasdiary.co.uk) which guide parents-to-be through the various stages of pregnancy and childbirth. By registering with the company, individuals receive further information and offers appropriate to their needs at the different stages of their pregnancy. The company has built up a valuable database of customers who have come to trust the advice given by *Emma's Diary*. Advertisers in its book and website realize that the birth of a child, especially the first one, is a significant trigger to new patterns of expenditure. Targeted individuals are likely to be highly receptive to the firms' messages.

Of course, the family life-course shown in Figure 6.6 is an ideal type, and most western countries are seeing increasing deviation from it. Later marriage, adult children living with parents because they cannot afford to buy their own home, a rising divorce rate, and more single-parent families have created family units that do not fit into this ideal. Marketers have responded to such change, for example by offering domestic support services aimed at busy, affluent single-parent families.

Gender

It is quite evident that gender differences account for many variations in consumer buying behaviour. At first sight it might seem obvious that companies providing a wide range of goods and services will have developed product offers that are particularly targeted at males or females. So there are men's clothes and women's clothes; magazines aimed at women and those aimed at men; and cosmetics emphasizing their appeal to one gender or the other. Gender is a very commonly used basis for segmenting markets. Not only does it often correspond to crucial differences in buying behaviour, but it is also an easy one to measure. Firms can have a reasonably good idea of the gender-specific market in any given area.

We do, however, need to be careful how we use gender as a basis for market segmentation. In the first place, it has to be remembered that one of the criteria for effective segmentation is that it should identify homogeneity in *buying* behaviour. There is a lot of evidence that for many products a person of one gender may buy a product that is intended for use by someone of the other gender. It has been estimated, for example, that in the UK over half of all men's underwear is purchased by women, with men having a relatively minor part in the buying process. A segment of men's underwear buyers that should be of interest to manufacturers is therefore women. The way women buy underwear, the retailers that they buy from, and the features that they look for are likely to be quite different from these processes in men.

A further reservation to the use of gender as a segmentation basis is its frequent confusion with a classification based on sex. Sex is essentially a biological description, which in itself explains many of the observed differences in products sought by men and women (e.g. the use of bras and tampons). Gender is essentially a social construct and is influenced by social conditioning. Western societies have seen a convergence in many male and female values, although there remains argument about just how far this has gone. Concepts such as aggressiveness, competitiveness, and sensation seeking, which have traditionally been associated with male values, are increasingly being seen in females (e.g. heavy drinking 'ladettes'). Similarly, some observers have suggested that 'new men' are taking on traditional female traits of caring, nurturing, and reconciling. Many marketers have therefore moved on from segmentation based on a dichotomous male/female sex classification to a segmentation basis which recognizes a wide range of gender orientations. For example, the lifestyle and buying behaviour of career women is likely to be quite different from that of housewives, and may be more similar to career oriented men.

A further issue in gender-based segmentation is the emergence of segments of gay or lesbian people, whose buying behaviour may not fit neatly within dichotomous segments of male/female. Many companies have developed marketing programmes that are aimed at these groups, often seeking through promotional messages to promote accommodating and positive images of them. Manipulating gender images to accommodate different groups can create its own problems if not done carefully. If a company seeks to associate a product targeted at men with the values held by gay groups, it may alienate men with more traditional male values.

Ethnic group

The United Kingdom, like many other western countries, has become much more diverse in the ethnic backgrounds of its population. Despite years of integration, there is evidence that many ethnic groups retain distinctive preferences in their purchases which distinguishes them from the native community. A report published in 2010 by the Institute of Practitioners in Advertising identified a number of challenges in addressing the needs of segments of ethnic minorities. It has been noted that consumers from these groups are typically younger, more likely to own a business than others, tend to live in large urban centres—creating opportunities for cost-effective marketing—and are close-knit, making word-of-mouth recommendation a powerful force. However, they tend to be very fragmented, with intergenerational differences, requiring that businesses commission professional research to gain in-depth understanding of their target markets (IPA 2010). Ethnic groups remain important segments for travel related services—for visiting friends and relatives, and for pilgrimages.

As in the case of gender, segmentation purely on the basis of biological origins may not be as useful as an individual's self-ascribed ethnic background. While some members of an ethnic group may wish to associate themselves primarily with the values and lifestyle of their host community, others may be proud of their background and make purchases that reinforce their ethnicity. This may lead, among other things, to such groups being accessible to a consumer goods manufacturer only if that firm distributes through the ethnically owned businesses to which this group may be loyal.

Household composition

A wide range of goods and services are bought by households as an economic unit. The weekly household shopping, the annual holiday, and the family car are typically purchased to meet the needs of the economic unit as a whole rather than of individuals within it. Households differ in their size and composition, and these differences are associated with diverse buying behaviour. Segmenting markets on the basis of the size of the household buying unit therefore makes a lot of sense for many products. Furthermore, there is a lot of readily available information about household structure from the national census and other sources.

One indicator of household structure is the number of people that the household comprises. In the UK, as in most western countries, the average size of household units has declined as extended families have given way to nuclear families. More recently, there has been growth in the number of single-person households, which now account for over 10 percent of all households. The buying needs of a single-person household can differ quite markedly from those of a family unit; for example it is more likely to seek smaller pack sizes and products which satisfy the needs of the individual buyer rather than the whole household.

MARKETING in ACTION

Segmentation or discrimination?

Segmentation and targeting are central to the marketers' task of meeting consumers' needs at a profit to their organization. But to other social commentators, the practices of segmentation and targeting may appear to be more like discrimination, with all the connotations of social divisiveness that have been associated with various forms of social discrimination. Admittedly, marketers seldom find themselves practising the kind of discrimination that typified South Africa during its years of apartheid, but there can be a thin line between the desirable aims of segmentation and the undesirable consequences of discrimination.

Legislation in most western countries is gradually squeezing out the opportunities for marketers blatantly to sell their goods and services to one group but not to another. The days when the owner of a bar could admit customers on the basis of their colour are now long gone. Nightclubs in the UK that once advertised different prices for men and women would now most likely find themselves breaking the Sex Discrimination Act. However, marketers have found more subtle ways of pursuing their segmentation and targeting strategies. A bar may subtly make its atmosphere more conducive to one ethnic group and less attractive to others; nightclubs have learnt that discriminating on the basis of gender may be illegal, but a differential pricing policy based on whether a customer is wearing trousers or a skirt may come close to achieving the nightclub's objectives legally.

Despite a growing volume of legislation in developed countries to protect clearly identifiable groups based on sex, race, disability, and increasingly on age, concerns have been expressed by the UK Equality and Human Rights Commission that the processes of segmentation and targeting are leaving pockets of individuals who are denied access to many basic services (EHRC 2010). This is seen in the way that mainstream banks in most western countries have targeted relatively affluent individuals with a steady source of income. In the UK, a sizeable group of people find it difficult to borrow money from these banks, or even to open a basic bank account. Without a bank account, many life opportunities are closed to individuals, for example without a credit or debit card, it can be difficult to buy goods and services online. In the United States, banks have been suspected of 'redlining' certain areas of towns, from which the banks will not take new customers. Many states have responded with legislation making illegal such geographically generalized basis for selection. In the UK, geodemographics remains an important basis for banks' segmentation and targeting, but although there is no legislation to prevent geodemographic targeting, the government has shown its impatience with banks' reluctance to target poorer groups, even with basic bank accounts. One initiative in response to this apparent problem was the creation of a 'Basic Bank Account' based on collaboration between the main banks and local post offices, making banking facilities available to poorer people with a bad credit history. In many service sectors providing essential public services, such as electricity, water, and telephones, regulatory agencies ensure that private sector companies do not unduly disadvantage poorer groups in their pursuit of profits.

When does segmentation become discrimination? To what extent should commercial organizations be expected to do business with individuals who, on a narrow commercial basis, are unlikely to be profitable? How far will companies' shrewd analysis of their social and political environment—and a visible response to problems of emerging discrimination—allow these issues to be resolved? Or will it take further government legislation to protect the interests of disadvantaged groups who may be further marginalized in society by commercial firms' segmentation and targeting policies?

As with all bases of segmentation, it is important to avoid over-generalization, as the single-person household comprising a retired state pensioner is likely to behave very differently from that of a young, professional, single person.

A second indicator of household structure is the composition of individuals' roles within it. This is much more difficult to measure than size alone, but can be very useful because it is associated with quite distinctive buying patterns. In recent years, most western countries have seen a growth in the numbers of households that are composed of something other than the ideal type family of husband, wife, and two children. A rising divorce rate has meant that there is a growing segment of consumers who live in single-parent households, and who are often (but not always) poorer than a two-parent family in terms of money and time. Some travel companies have specifically targeted this segment to fill capacity at quiet times of the year.

Other types of household that may present opportunities to particular companies include those comprising groups of friends sharing, an elderly parent living with grown-up children, and people living in institutionalized homes.

Socio-economic bases for segmentation

It has been traditional to talk about class differences as a factor that affects the way goods and services are purchased. We saw in Chapter 4 that an individual's perception of her class may be an important influence on her buying behaviour. However, marketers find the concept of social class too value-laden and imprecise to be of much practical use. Instead, more measurable indicators of social class are generally used, in particular occupation and income.

Occupation

Since 1921, government statisticians in the UK have divided the population into six classes, based simply on occupation. This has resulted in the following familiar classification system:

Class category	Occupation
A	Higher managerial, administrative, or professional
B	Intermediate managerial, administrative, or professional
C1	Supervisory or clerical, and junior managerial, administrative, or professional
C2	Skilled manual
D	Semi-skilled and unskilled manual
E	State pensioners or widows (no other earners), casual or lower grade workers, or long-term unemployed

These segment labels have been widely used. For example, some newspapers have traditionally stressed the number of A/B readers they have. However, it became increasingly clear that six classifications could not fully explain the impact of class on buying behaviour. The government recognized that the uncertainty of work and the demise of a job for life had undermined the old classification system. From 2001 it implemented a new system, intended to take account of such things as the size of individuals' employing firms and their pension rights, effectively reflecting an individual's status in the purchasing marketplace.

Despite the improvements noted above, segmentation based on occupation remains fairly crude compared with the advances achieved using geodemographic methods (discussed below). Perhaps surprisingly, many marketers still refer to the old A/B/C1/C2/D/E basis of classification, perhaps because of its simplicity and a shared general understanding about the type of person contained in each of these groups.

Income

Many studies have shown that, as individuals' incomes increase, their expenditure on certain categories of product increases. For example, Mintel, in a study of the leisure industry, found a strong correlation between income and expenditure on a range of leisure activities.

There are three commonly used approaches to measuring income:

1. Total income before taxation: this is gross income, which is widely quoted and understood by most people.

2. Disposable income: this refers to the income that individuals have available to spend after taxation. It follows that, as taxes rise, disposable income falls.

3. Discretionary income: this is a measure of disposable income less expenditure on the necessities of life, such as mortgage payments. Discretionary income can be significantly affected by sudden changes in the cost of mortgages and other essential items of expenditure, such as heating and travel-to-work costs, which form a large component of household budgets.

All of these can be measured at the unit of the individual, or of the whole household.

Marketers are most often interested in consumers' discretionary incomes. A casual analysis of advertisements on television will show that most are aiming to gain an increased share of discretionary income—on an overseas holiday, a new mobile phone, or a takeaway meal, for example.

Despite its apparent correlation with buying behaviour, the use of income as a segmentation variable has some limitations. Obtaining data on individuals' incomes can be much more difficult than for occupation, and people are often reluctant to give this information when asked. Surveys that attempt to gather this information can be subject to mis-reporting by individuals. Even within segments of similar discretionary income, differences in actual spending levels arise, accounted for by differences in spending/saving ratios.

Psychographic bases for segmentation

So far, most of the bases for segmentation have been reasonably measurable. However, they are often criticized for missing the unique personality factors that distinguish one person from another, and many studies have suggested that psychographic segmentation has better predictive power than demographic bases (e.g. Lin 2002). Under the heading of psychographic factors, we will consider the effects of lifestyle, attitudes, values, benefits sought, and loyalty.

Lifestyles

People of a similar age and socio-economic status can nevertheless lead quite different life-styles, and firms have been quick to adapt their products to meet the needs of these lifestyles. Many companies in the tourism sector, for example, have been observed to base their segmentation and targeting on lifestyle factors (e.g. Gross et al. 2008) It is very difficult to describe a lifestyle accurately and even more difficult to have any realistic measure of the size of segments of different lifestyle groups. Nevertheless, as societies fragment into ever smaller groups of shared interests and activities, companies have recognized the need to develop ideal types of lifestyle segments. The depth of research that underlies these approaches to segmentation can be questionable, with many segments being held up as ideal-type segments on only a weak empirically derived basis. Thus, segments described by terms such as 'Yuppies' and 'Dinkies' have come to acquire a meaning among marketers, if only as unquantified ideal-types of the segment being targeted. Many lifestyle segmentation methods have been developed for specific sectors. For example, Sony's Consumer Segment Marketing Division has a mission to 'develop an intimate understanding of Sony's end consumers ... from cradle to grave', and divided its consumers into the following segments: Affluent; CE Alphas (early adopters); Zoomers (55+); SoHo (small office/home office); Young Professionals/DINKs (double income no kids, aged 25–34); Families (35–54); and Gen Y (under 25) (Elkin 2002). While such approaches may be very useful for defining possible target markets, they are difficult to measure because of the absence of data beyond small sample surveys.

Attitudes

Lifestyles are observable, even if it can be difficult to do so, and it is possible to estimate how many of each lifestyle group exist in a particular population. Attitudes are much more difficult to identify and to measure, and may be revealed only in subtle ways. More importantly for marketers, what is a hidden attitude for an individual today may tomorrow become a behaviour that is manifested in purchase decisions to support a chosen lifestyle. Many people may possess an attitude towards an item but are afraid of being an early adopter of behaviour associated with that attitude. Among males, there may be a significant segment of the population that possesses an attitude that it should be acceptable for men to use cosmetics traditionally associated with women. They may, however, be reluctant to buy and use male cosmetics until they consider that it has become socially acceptable to do so. For this segment, the marketing programme should emphasize the need to gain gradual acceptability of the product among this group, for example by appealing to wives/girlfriends as key influencers on the decision to purchase.

Values

Sociologists have distinguished a deeper level of individual distinctiveness in the form of values. Values are standards, rules, norms, goals, ideals, or underlying evaluative criteria which we use when making judgements. They are deep-seated and tend to be fairly enduring within an individual. Attitudes and lifestyles are built on this sub-structure of values. Individuals have been attributed with having a number of underlying values; for example values of self-centredness or of communality and sharing. Values can be even more difficult

MARKETING in ACTION

What your sandwich says about you

What does an individual's choice of sandwich say about him? The retailer Tesco has undertaken research that has revealed how complex the market for ready-made sandwiches has become, with clear segments emerging of people who look for quite different types of sandwich. In an attempt to define and target its lunch customers more precisely, the company found that well-paid executives invariably insisted on 'designer' sandwiches made from ciabatta and focaccia with sun-dried tomatoes and costing about £2.50. Salespeople and middle ranking executives were more inclined to opt for meaty triple-deckers. Upwardly mobile women aged 25–40 chose low-calorie sandwiches costing around £1.49. Busy manual workers tended to grab a sandwich that looked affordable, simple, and quick to eat, such as the ploughman's sandwich that Tesco sold for £1.15 Tesco's research claimed that sandwiches have become an important statement made by individuals and need to be targeted appropriately. What do your snack meals say about you?

to measure than attitudes, and apparent inconsistencies may question the existence of a deep-seated value system. An individual may appear to have a value system based on caution when driving a car, but may nevertheless be quite reckless when investing in financial services.

Benefits sought

The same product may provide a variety of benefits to different people. A watch, for example, can be purchased by one segment primarily as an accurate timepiece, by another as a fashion item above all else, and by still others as items of ostentatious consumption. There will also be segments who buy a watch as a gift for someone. Each segment is likely to respond in different ways to variations in product design, packaging, pricing, and promotion. Inevitably, overlap between benefit categories exists and it is really possible to determine the size of each segment only on the basis of sample surveys.

Loyalty

In many markets, a segment can be found that shows considerable loyalty to one brand, while other segments will be prepared to switch between brands in response to products offering more benefits and/or lower prices. This may reflect differences in individuals' willingness to take on the risk of switching to a new supplier. For some people, loyalty may occur through inertia and a reluctance to take the perceived risk of changing supplier.

Geodemographic bases for segmentation

Marketers have traditionally used geographical areas as a basis for market segmentation. Very often, there have been very good geographical reasons why product preferences should vary between regions. The long, dark, cold winter nights of northern England and Scotland have led the inhabitants of these regions to take proportionately more winter sun holidays than their counterparts in the south of England, despite their having lower average levels of disposable income. Many companies have managed to adapt their product offer to meet the needs of different regional segments. National newspapers, for example, produce regional editions to satisfy readers' needs for local news coverage and advertisers' needs for a regional advertising facility.

More recently, geographical segmentation has been undertaken at a much more localized level, and linked to other differences in social, economic, and demographic characteristics. The resulting basis for segmentation is often referred to as *geodemographic*. The premise of geodemographic analysis is that where a person lives is closely associated with a number of indicators of his socio-economic status and lifestyle. This association has been derived from detailed investigations of multiple sources of information about people living in a particular neighbourhood. An example of a widely used UK geodemographic segmentation system is MOSAIC, provided by Experian Ltd. By analysing a lot of sales data from people in each post-code area, it is possible to build up a good picture of the lifestyle and spending patterns associated with each classification (and also of individuals living at each address). It is also possible to see how the distribution of the population between different classifications changes over time (see Figure 6.7). Descriptions of each category can be seen by visiting the website www.upmystreet.com and entering any UK postcode.

Situational bases for segmentation

A further group of segmentation variables can be described as situational, because an individual may find herself grouped differently from one occasion to the next.

Stage in buying process

For some high-value goods, it may take a considerable time for an individual to arrive at a purchase decision. It has been estimated that the average time private buyers take in deciding on a replacement for their current car is about one year. At each stage of the process, their needs will be quite different. A price incentive aimed at a buyer in the early stages of the search process may achieve no success, while for a buyer who has gone through the search and evaluation processes and is now ready to commit himself to a particular product, it may prove successful.

Occasion of use

We often buy a product at different times for quite different reasons. A meal in a restaurant taken during the lunch hour will probably have to satisfy quite different needs compared with a meal taken during the evening. At lunchtime the most important selection criteria may be speed and value for money, whereas in the evening they may be good service and a relaxing atmosphere.

Frequency of purchase

Infrequent buyers of a product may approach their purchase decision with caution and seek reassurance throughout the process. Their knowledge of prices and competing facilities available in the market may be low. At the other end of this segmentation spectrum, frequent buyers may have become much more price-sensitive, or more demanding in the features they expect from a category of product. A promotional programme that guides buyers through the stages of purchase will be less appropriate for this group.

Group	Group Description	% Households	Type	Type Description	% Households
A	Symbols of Success	9.62	A01	Global Connections	0.72
			A02	Cultural Leadership	0.92
			A03	Corporate Chieftains	1.12
			A04	Golden Empty Nesters	1.33
			A05	Provincial Privilege	1.66
			A06	High Technologists	1.82
			A07	Semi-Rural Seclusion	2.04
B	Happy Families	10.76	B08	Just Moving In	0.91
			B09	Fledgling Nurseries	1.18
			B10	Upscale New Owners	1.35
			B11	Families Making Good	2.32
			B12	Middle Rung Families	2.86
			B13	Burdened Optimists	1.96
			B14	In Military Quarters	0.17
C	Suburban Comfort	15.10	C15	Close to Retirement	2.81
			C16	Conservative Values	2.84
			C17	Small Time Business	2.93
			C18	Sprawling Subtopia	3.08
			C19	Original Suburbs	2.41
			C20	Asian Enterprise	1.02
D	Ties of Community	16.04	D21	Respectable Rows	2.65
			D22	Affluent Blue Collar	3.12
			D23	Industrial Grit	3.82
			D24	Coronation Street	2.81
			D25	Town Centre Refuge	1.13
			D26	South Asian Industry	0.88
			D27	Settled Minorities	1.62
E	Urban Intelligence	7.19	E28	Counter Cultural Mix	1.36
			E29	City Adventurers	1.27
			E30	New Urban Colonists	1.36
			E31	Caring Professionals	1.08
			E32	Dinky Developments	1.10
			E33	Town Gown Transition	0.76
			E34	University Challenge	0.26
F	Welfare Borderline	6.43	F35	Bedsit Beneficiaries	0.71
			F36	Metro Multiculture	1.67
			F37	Upper Floor Families	1.72
			F38	Tower Block Living	0.49
			F39	Dignified Dependency	1.34
			F40	Sharing a Staircase	0.50
G	Municipal Dependency	6.71	G41	Families on Benefits	1.21
			G42	Low Horizons	2.64
			G43	Ex-industrial Legacy	2.86
H	Blue Collar Enterprise	11.01	H44	Rustbelt Resilience	3.00
			H45	Older Right to Buy	2.67
			H46	White Van Culture	3.17
			H47	New Town Materialism	2.17
I	Twilight Subsistence	3.88	I48	Old People in Flats	0.83
			I49	Low Income Elderly	1.63
			I50	Cared for Pensioners	1.43
J	Grey Perspectives	7.88	J51	Sepia Memories	0.75
			J52	Childfree Serenity	1.34
			J53	High Spending Elders	1.53
			J54	Bungalow Retirement	1.26
			J55	Small Town Seniors	2.71
			J56	Tourist Attendants	0.30
K	Rural Isolation	5.39	K57	Summer Playgrounds	0.29
			K58	Greenbelt Guardians	1.74
			K59	Parochial Villagers	1.64
			K60	Pastoral Symphony	1.31
			K61	Upland Hill Farmers	0.41

Figure 6.7 **MOSAIC is a widely used method of geodemographic segmentation.**

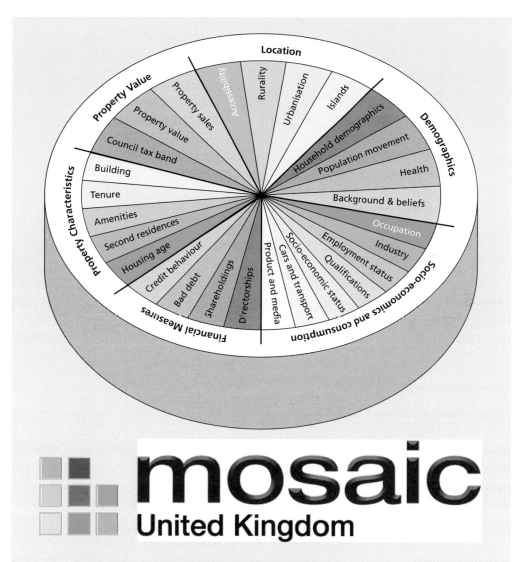

Figure 6.7 **Continued**

Many companies are in the business of providing customer analysis services to help firms' segmentation, targeting, and positioning strategies. One of the most widely used is Experian's MOSAIC consumer classification system. This gathers information about individuals from multiple sources under a number of headings shown in the diagram, and uses this to build up a picture of every household in the UK. From this information, each person has been assigned to one of 155 MOSAIC person types, aggregated into 67 household types (further aggregated into 15 broad groups). Each type has been given a distinctive and sometimes glib title, such as B05 'Mid-career climbers', D16 'Side street singles', and I41 'Stressed borrowers' For a company planning a mailshot, or deciding on the best location for new service outlets, such information about consumer behaviour at the individual and household level can avoid waste by targeting the company's efforts at those groups who are most likely to respond to a proposition. (*Source:* © Experian Limited. Reproduced with kind permission.)

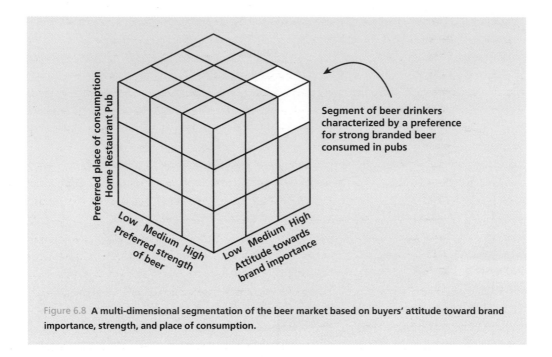

Figure 6.8 A multi-dimensional segmentation of the beer market based on buyers' attitude toward brand importance, strength, and place of consumption.

Comprehensive approaches to segmentation

The preceding discussion has presented a seemingly bewildering array of segmentation variables, each of which has its strengths and weaknesses. In practice, a company uses a number of key variables which are most relevant to its product/market, and companies commonly segment consumers on the basis of multiple-category purchase data. Geodemographic segmentation has become particularly popular because of the close correlation between where an individual lives and other indicators of income, occupation, and lifestyle (Figure 6.8).

E-Marketing

New gadgets targeted at consumers in poorer countries

Sometimes, the most promising market segments may appear in what might at first seem surprising places. During the past couple of decades, there has been a lot of talk about developing new, simple cashless payment devices, and in recent years there has been particular excitement about the prospect of using mobile phones as some form of 'electronic wallet'. Many people might have expected the most promising target markets to be sophisticated urban professionals living in London, Tokyo, or Singapore. In fact, adoption of mobile banking generally has been moving quite slowly in western countries and the west lags behind some developing countries such as Kenya and South Africa where many segments have adopted it.

In Kenya, about seven million people use the M-Pesa service, which was launched by Safaricom in partnership with Vodafone in 2007 and allows customers to use their mobile phone to pay bills, deposit cash, and send cash to other mobile phone users. The adoption of the M-Pesa service was speedy, with 11,000 new registrations per day during 2009. Even though the average transaction per person is very small, $1.9 billion has been moved in person-to-person transactions in the two years since the launch of the service (Mwangi 2009).

This rapid adoption of the M-Pesa service in Kenya can be largely explained by the lack of a land-line telephone network and a poorly developed banking infrastructure. The Financial Access Survey 2009 shows that only 23 per cent of the Kenyan adult population have a bank account but 48 per cent own a mobile phone, with the rate of ownership rising to 72.8 per cent in urban areas and 80.4 per cent in Nairobi (FSD Kenya and Central Bank of Kenya 2009). Furthermore, Africans with bank accounts have to pay high charges for moving cash around. M-Pesa provides a service which allows transferring cash safely without facing high costs. Setting up an account is straightforward. Similar successful m-banking examples exist in other non-western countries, for example Globe Telecom's GCash service is available in the Philippines, which transform the mobile phone into a virtual wallet for secure, quick, and convenient money transactions.

In a globalized business environment marketers often need to challenge their assumptions about market segments, and often the most promising target may be found in a surprising place.

Bases for segmenting business markets

The process of defining market segments for business buyers is similar in principle to that applied to consumer markets. Many of the bases described above, such as frequency of purchase and benefits sought, apply equally to private consumer purchases and business purchases. However, others, such as demographic and lifestyle bases, have little role to play, especially in segmenting very large corporate buyers. The following are additional bases for segmentation which are commonly used in business markets.

Size of firm

Within any industry sector, variations in corporate size are likely to be reflected in individual order sizes and the manner in which those orders are placed. In the printing industry, for example, very large printers obtain their inks direct from manufacturers, while smaller printers tend to rely on wholesale merchants. For a small intermediary, small printers may represent an important and accessible segment, whereas large printing companies may be considered inaccessible.

Formality of buying processes

As organizations grow, they have a tendency to formalize their buying processes. Nevertheless, within any size category of firm, variation can be observed in the formality of the buying process, in terms of the number of people involved in making a decision and the level of the management hierarchy at which approval is required. Large state-owned organizations have sometimes been noted for having slow and complicated ordering procedures. It was noted in Chapter 4 that, in general, the more complex a firm's buying process, the greater the complexity of a seller's marketing that is called for. Instead of having to appeal to one individual with one set of needs, it must appeal to multiple influencers, who may each seek different benefits from a purchase.

Industry sector

An industry sector may be a large user of certain types of product but have little use for others. Within particular product categories, niche segments may appear in industries with quite specific needs. Many suppliers of industrial goods and services therefore target particular industry sectors or sub-sectors. In the case of information technology (IT) equipment, Fujitsu ICL successfully targeted the special computing needs of the retail segment, while NCR targeted the special needs of the banking segment.

⊙ Evaluating market segments

Defining market segments is a relatively passive task of analysis. While sound analysis is always important, the next stages involve critically evaluating the identified market segments and selecting one or more for targeting. In this section we consider the questions that a company should ask in deciding whether a segment is worth going after. In fact, a company is likely to avoid a dichotomous classification of 'develop/ignore' and prefer instead a ranking of segments ranging from 'very attractive opportunity' to 'let's ignore this one'.

Size of segment

In our criteria for effective segmentation, it was stated that to be useful a segment must be of a sufficient size that the company can serve it economically. What is an economic size varies between companies. A package holiday company selling low cost holidays to popular destinations may be able to operate economically only with segments of several hundreds of thousands of customers. On the other hand, a small specialist holiday company with lower overhead costs may be able to justify serving much smaller segments of, say, a few thousand people who have distinctive needs. It was noted earlier that the size of market segments that can be economically served has tended to come down with the development of flexible production systems.

Growth prospects

Our definition of marketing (Chapter 1) spoke not only about identifying current customer demands, but also of anticipating what these will be in the future. Markets are seldom static, and what is an attractive segment today may not be so in the future. Many banks competed with each other in the buoyant 'buy-to-let' mortgage segment in the early 2000s, but from 2008, a 'credit crunch' among banks and falling property prices made the buy-to-let segment relatively unattractive. On the other hand, some segments that were once small have gone on to be very large before fragmenting into smaller sub-segments. In the UK the segment of adult ice cream consumers who sought sensual pleasures from consuming ice cream was small in the early 1980s, but grew significantly during the following decades. Suppliers of 'luxury' ice cream that had targeted this group saw their sales grow significantly faster than the ice cream industry average.

Profitability

The fact that a market segment is large does not necessarily mean that the segment can be served profitably. Many markets are characterized by a large segment which seeks low prices, and in which companies can make good profits only by stringent control of their costs, while a smaller segment is prepared to pay a premium for a product for which the additional cost of differentiation is less than the price premium charged.

Competition for the segment

Of course, the profitability of a segment is significantly affected by the level of competition for it. When a company is identifying potentially profitable segments to develop, the chances are that its competitors are doing exactly the same thing. The result is that an attractive segment soon becomes unattractive when large numbers of new entrants, all following the same logic, create intense competitive pressure. In evaluating a market segment, a company should consider not only how well *it* could develop the segment, but also how well its competitors could develop it. If its competitors in fact have more strengths with regard to this segment, the segment is likely to be less attractive to the company. Too many marketing plans fail because they make assumptions about a static market, when in fact markets are dynamic, with a changing composition of segments and of firms seeking to supply those segments.

Fit with company objectives

Many segments may appear large and profitable, but are then rejected because they would not sit easily within a company's broader marketing objectives and strategies (Figure 6.9). The following are some examples of market segments that might not 'fit' a company well.

- A manufacturer of high-value cars might be reluctant to serve a market segment that seeks more basic, low-value vehicles. What would happen to the image of BMW if it decided to develop the market segment for low-priced family hatchbacks using the BMW brand name?

- Will the image of a company be harmed by appearing to be too closely associated with a segment that is perceived by the public to be 'bad'? Many companies give priority to the preservation of their reputation, and being seen to supply products to a repressive government, for example, could cause unquantifiable damage to its long-term reputation.

⊙ Has the company a core competence in serving this segment? Would its funds and management effort be better applied to a project that better fits its competencies, leaving this segment to a competitor that may have a stronger base for developing it?

MARKETING in ACTION

Targeting or spamming?

In the early days of the Internet, the ability of firms to target millions of customers cheaply and quickly through email appeared to open up new opportunities. Schedules of press and TV advertising, optimized to minimize the cost per target audience, would be a thing of the past when the whole world could be targeted with a cheap email message. In reality, email may be an efficient way of targeting a lot of potential buyers, but is it effective?

Many online sites grew rapidly by building databases through sometimes dubious means. Some websites, such as 4anything.com, used the lure of a free sweepstake to build up a database of names which was subsequently used for sending promotional messages on behalf of other companies. Of course, to be effective, targeting requires a much more thorough understanding of potential customers than is possible using crude database building techniques. As with junk mail, 'spam', quickly finds its way to the bin. Many computer owners have installed anti-spam software to try and reduce the extent of the nuisance caused by junk email. In response, some companies have developed ingenious methods of getting round such anti-spam filters. They might just be lucky in achieving a sale that would not have been possible had their email been blocked, but their approach still appears very crude, and similar to targeting in the early days of modern marketing.

How can the Internet help segmentation and targeting for a company in a long-term and sustainable way? There are no surprises about the answer that traditional techniques work best. Targets are more likely to be responsive to a message where the message addresses a real need. Companies should amass information from multiple sources in order to build a profile of each potential target. The use of 'cookies' allows Internet-based companies to understand quite a lot about a target from the websites the target has visited, but this seldom gives much insight into an individual's attitudes and lifestyle. Integrating online information with traditional data sources can greatly improve the effectiveness of targeting.

In an age of mass information, consumers' concerns over their privacy have become increasingly important. This is reflected in the ideas of permission marketing. In his book of that title, Seth Godin, asserted that much of today's marketing is ineffective, as an overload of promotional messages is robbing people of one of their most precious assets—time. A target is more likely to be responsive to an email message if it has previously given a sender permission to target him. Data protection legislation is also increasingly requiring permission to be given before an individual can be targeted with messages.

For the future, mobile Internet is offering new opportunities for targeting, offering the possibility of targeting individuals just at the time and in the place when they will be most receptive to a message (a special offer from a nearby restaurant in the early evening). The possibility of walking down the high street and being bombarded with SMS messages from nearby shops may fill many people with horror. How can companies avoid the mistakes of spam email? If permission marketing is the way forward, how can that permission be obtained?

Figure 6.9 **The retailer Marks and Spencer is well known in the UK for adopting a fairly 'middle of the road' market position.** Its ranges of clothes and home furnishings are stylish but not too radical to alienate the values of its core market segments who tend to be quite traditional in their outlook towards style and value. In the past, the company has encountered problems when it tried to target younger segments of buyers, because this had the effect of alienating many people within its segments of older, traditional buyers. More recently, the company has taken a more detailed segmented approach in launching new products, for example its Per Una range which is positioned as slightly more adventurous than its core brand and likely to appeal to a younger segment, without alienating older segments. The company also has challenges in its efforts to expand internationally. In its UK market, Marks and Spencer may be regarded by most people as a fairly ordinary everyday store selling good value items at reasonable prices. However, when the company has entered a number of Asian markets it has been difficult to repeat this market position in the face of extensive local competition. Therefore the Marks and Spencer brand has been positioned as an aspirational one targeting, among others, segments of affluent local buyers who seek products that are exclusive and different to similar products that are more widely available in the local area.

◉ Selection of target markets

The time has now come for a company to select one or more market segments for further development. At this point, marketing becomes a blend of scientific analysis and creative thinking. The segmental analysis that we have just discussed cannot in itself produce answers: it can only guide decision making, which is influenced by a range of company and environment-specific factors, many of which cannot be easily quantified.

True entrepreneurs are able to understand their marketing environment and to use their knowledge of a market to identify target markets which will grow and give them a period of profitable sales before the market becomes saturated with competitors.

The following are some examples of successful targeting by entrepreneurs:

- Alan Sugar, founder of Amstrad, who had experience of launching low-cost versions of household electrical items and who correctly forecast the demand for a low-cost desktop computer for use by private households and small businesses.

- Stelios Haji-Ioannou, founder of easyJet, who understood the American airline market and sought to bring the benefits of low-cost domestic and European flights to the UK, where he had reasoned that there was a high level of suppressed demand from segments who were highly price-sensitive.

- Charles Dunstone, founder of the Carphone Warehouse, who foresaw the growth of privately owned mobile phones in the UK and of a segment that sought an impartial and independent retailer to guide them through the maze of competing networks and tariffs.

In each of these cases, success was a combination of good luck, good judgement, and good timing. Had there been a sudden rise in oil prices, or had its competitors responded more rapidly and vigorously, easyJet might have been sunk at an early stage. If mobile phones had failed to become popular consumer items (perhaps because of high taxes, network charges, or concerns over health), the ambitious plans of Carphone Warehouse might have come to nothing. The history books are littered with entrepreneurs (and large corporations) who have failed to understand and predict the dynamics of market segments, resulting in a failure to sell a product to a selected target market. The small C5 electric car is often cited as an example of an innovative product that just might have become a runaway success as a handy runabout or even a cult vehicle. It failed miserably, possibly because the entrepreneur behind the venture—Clive Sinclair—didn't have sufficient understanding of the market segment he was targeting. (Possibly its failure could also be put down to bad luck, as initial press coverage portrayed the car as ridiculous and dangerous rather than as a smart cult icon.)

A fundamental issue for a company is how many segments to exploit and how to enter those segments. A number of targeting strategies can be identified—for example undifferentiated mass marketing, single segment specialization, and multiple segment specialization (Figure 6.10). While these are three ideal-type targeting strategies, companies frequently combine elements of all these approaches. The characteristics of each approach are described below.

Undifferentiated mass marketing

This doesn't really involve segmentation and targeting at all, as here a company seeks to satisfy the entire market with a single formulation of its product. It worked well for Henry Ford, and cases can still be seen where companies serve the entire market with one product (for example electricity and water supply companies, which have traditionally

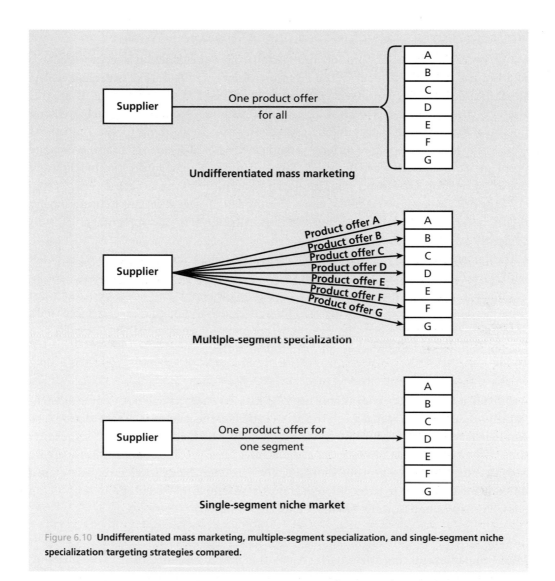

Figure 6.10 **Undifferentiated mass marketing, multiple-segment specialization, and single-segment niche specialization targeting strategies compared.**

offered one standard of service delivery to all of their domestic customers). Over time, however, consumers' needs tend to fragment into segments of different needs. Where markets are competitive, a company may no longer be able to ignore the special needs of small groups of its customers, because if it does its competitors may exploit the opportunities available. Very often, these groups with special needs represent the most profitable segments to serve. In the UK even the market for electricity has fragmented, spurred on by increasing competition which raises the expectations of consumers that their distinctive needs are capable of being met. Customers now have the choice of different pricing plans, bundling of electricity with other energy supplies, and a range of electrical appliance maintenance services to supplement the basic electricity supply.

Single-segment specialization ('niche' marketing)

Many companies succeed by producing a specialized product aimed at a very focused segment of the market (or 'niche'). The Freeminer Brewery in Gloucestershire targets the small proportion of beer drinkers who can be described as real ale enthusiasts. By this strategy, the company gets to know the needs of its target segment extremely well and puts all of its efforts into satisfying their needs. This can give it strength over competitors whose efforts are spread more diffusely among a number of segments. It also avoids the problem of tarnishing a brand by association with 'inferior' segments (Freeminer Brewery doesn't carry any of the bland, mass produced associations of the larger brewers). By specializing on one particular segment and achieving a high level of success in it, a company might be able to achieve economies of scale that give it cost advantages over its competitors.

The danger of targeting a single market segment is that a company's fortunes rise or fall with those of its chosen target. Upmarket UK hotels that had targeted premium-rate corporate and private clients had expanded steadily during the boom years of the mid-2000s, but some faced difficulty from 2008 when they were affected by a combination of reduced credit availability from banks and declining numbers of premium customers. The upmarket Van Essen hotel chain, for example became bankrupt in 2011.

Multiple-segment specialization

A third ideal-type strategy is for a company to seek to serve multiple markets, but to differentiate its products in a way that meets the needs of each of the segments it seeks to serve. The aim here is to develop slightly differentiated products which add to customer value faster than they add to production costs. Car manufacturers have become quite skilful at adapting a basic car to meet the needs of different groups (see vignette). Many retailers have developed different brand formats to target different groups (for example the Arcadia group with its Top Shop, Principles, and Dorothy Perkins chains, among others).

Segment development plans

Most companies entering a new market realize that it would be unrealistic to use their limited financial and management resources to satisfy all possible segments from the outset. They therefore develop a strategy to 'roll out' their marketing plan from an initial segment through further segments. The roll-out plan can be defined geographically. (McDonald's restaurants did this in the UK, working out from the London-based market to provincial markets.) Very often, companies initially target high-value segments. Such segments may be prepared to pay a premium for the benefits of novelty, but soon the premium attached to this novelty wears off. The company meanwhile has established an 'upmarket' image for itself from which to appeal to aspiring segments of potential buyers. In the UK, mobile telephone companies have moved from segments of business users who are prepared to pay a premium for a mobile phone that will give them a competitive advantage, to more price-sensitive segments for whom a mobile telephone is a useful but not essential accessory.

> **MARKETING in ACTION**
>
> **Cars in any colour except black**
>
> Henry Ford would have been amazed at the lengths to which the car company he founded now goes in order to satisfy the needs of specific market segments. Car manufacturers have for some time recognized the differing needs of differing groups of buyers, for example:
>
> - 'Boy racers' typically want plenty of features and external manifestations of the power and status of their car (e.g. 'GTI' badges and spoilers).
> - Affluent elderly males put the emphasis on refinement of the interior, comfort, and reliability, but seek no vulgar manifestation of status.
> - The family buying a 'runabout' car seeks low initial cost and subsequent low running costs; they are not too worried about comforts, but the car needs to be hard-wearing to stand up to rough treatment by dogs, children, etc.
> - The professional career woman, although a difficult market to typify, often seeks a light and airy colour, reliability, and easy maintenance.
> - Company car buyers look for an economical and reliable car which will have a high residual value after three years and will satisfy the status needs of employees.
>
> A look through the brochure for a Ford model such as the 'Focus' indicates how far the company has been able to adapt its cars to meet the needs of each of these segments: the 'ST' has been aimed at the 'boy racers', the 'Titanium' at the affluent young professional; The 'Studio' is a basic version aimed for use as a low-cost family runabout. In the past, Ford has produced a co-branded 'Elle' version of the car specifically targeted at professional career women. With an eye to the growing segment of car buyers that seeks to manifest its ecological responsibility through its car use, it has developed the 'Econetic' with many visible and invisible 'green' features.
>
> The logistical problems of satisfying so many segments have been significant, with one basic car available in three basic body forms, with five different engines, 12 colour options, and the choice of automatic or manual transmission. After allowing for permutations that are not available, Ford promotes 72 versions of the Focus. Making these available on demand at each of its dealers has called for flexible manufacturing systems and a centralized stock management system. Can the company be accused of offering too much choice? Can too much choice actually confuse customers, leading to them making no purchase decision at all? Or is the key to good market segmentation giving each targeted segment a small choice of, say four or five options which buyers in the segment think have been selected specially for them?

Market attractiveness analysis

Of all the market segments that a company has identified, which ones should it target? A conceptually useful analytic tool is a grid comprising two dimensions: market attractiveness and competitive position (Figure 6.11). Market attractiveness includes such factors as the size of a market, its projected growth rate, and its earnings performance. Competitive position refers to a company's brand strength, its experience in a market, and the availability of financial, technical, and human resources to serve that market. In developing an index, weights must be attached to each of these components and a sometimes subjective assessment made of each component. Ownership of a strong brand may be an essential element of competitive advantage for a soft drinks firm and would therefore be given a relatively high weighting, although the task of assessing how strong a brand is remains very subjective.

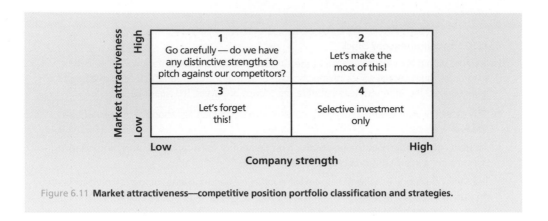

Figure 6.11 **Market attractiveness—competitive position portfolio classification and strategies.**

For the purpose of analysis, each of the scales in Figure 6.11 is divided into two classifications, resulting in a matrix of four cells.

- Box 1: a market may appear attractive, but if a company has only a weak competitive position, it should think carefully before investing large amounts of cash. The market will appear attractive also to other companies, which may have a stronger competitive position.

- Box 2: a highly attractive market in which a company has a strong competitive position is the best position in the matrix, and in such a market the company should invest and build for future growth.

- Box 3: unattractive markets for which a company does not have a strong competitive position should be avoided. However, a company may find that it has products in this box that were previously high performers, but whose market characteristics have changed. The best thing a company can do with the remaining products in this box is to refrain from new investment and to manage the products for the cash they generate.

- Box 4: market attractiveness is low, but the company's competitive position is strong. The company should exploit its strengths by selectively investing in this market and building for future market growth.

As a basis for targeting, the grid focuses attention on finding strategies that match an organization's internal strengths and weaknesses with the opportunities and threats presented by its operating environment. The key to making this model useful in formulating marketing strategy is to measure the two dimensions of the grid not only as they are at the present time, but as they are likely to become in the future.

◉ Developing a position within the target market

Having chosen a segment to target, a company must decide how to position itself in relation to the competitors for that segment. Positioning could be on the basis of the product's

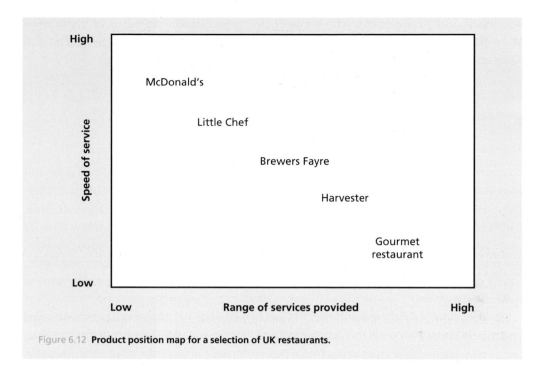

Figure 6.12 **Product position map for a selection of UK restaurants.**

unique selling proposition, its price, design characteristics, method of distribution, or any other combination of factors that allow for differentiation. Within any market, position maps can be drawn to show the relative positions adopted by the principal competing products in respect of key customer evaluation criteria. In Figure 6.12, a position map has been drawn relating two important criteria used by customers in selecting a restaurant: speed of service and the range of services provided by staff (e.g. whether the restaurant is self-service or waiter service). Position maps can use any criteria that are of relevance in influencing consumers' choices, and in reality they may be multi-dimensional rather than just two-dimensional, as in this example. Here, a number of UK restaurants have been plotted on this map in terms of two out of many possible relevant criteria.

The fact that a position on a map is unoccupied does not necessarily mean that it is an unexplored opportunity waiting to be targeted. There is always the possibility that a product offering in that position will not satisfy the needs of a sufficiently large market segment. However, many gaps on product position maps have been identified and exploited successfully. In the UK there was for a long time a gap between low-price fast-food restaurants offering little choice and higher priced gourmet restaurants offering a wide range of menu options. Restaurant chains such as Brewers Fayre and Harvester subsequently exploited this mid-market position.

It must be emphasized that a product position map is essentially product-focused rather than customer-focused. By itself, it does not address the underlying needs of customers that a company seeks to satisfy. The process of adopting a product position is essentially about selecting specific target markets. In a market-oriented company, product features are developed only in response to the needs of clearly identifiable segments of consumers. We will return to the subject of competitive positioning and discuss it in more depth in Chapter 7.

....

China—a lot of people, but a lot of differences

To many ill informed westerners, China is just one mass of people who all look alike and presumably all buy the same sorts of things. Such ignorance of the diversity of market segments in China can be dangerous for the many western companies who have targeted China. China is the world's most populous country and one that can bewilder westerners. With 22 provinces (23 if Taiwan is included), three municipalities, and five autonomous regions, there is tremendous diversity in consumer characteristics. Exporters seeking success in China must analyse the country carefully and choose the most promising target areas as their point of entry.

There is a significant income difference between urban and rural areas and between coastal and inland areas, with cities (especially the coastal cities) generally being much richer than rural areas. Examples of cities at the top of this purchasing power list are Shenzhen, Guangzhou, Shanghai, Beijing, Tianjin, Hangzhou, and Dalian.

Exporters are particularly interested in the distribution of 'trigger' levels of income, above which an individual's needs for necessities are satisfied and they can become purchasers of imported western luxury goods. It has been suggested that a per capita purchasing power of US$1000 per annum is the critical figure above which Chinese people can typically start buying colour TVs, washing machines, and imported clothing.

Rapid economic growth is bringing a wide variety of goods within reach of a growing number of consumers. China's per capita GDP was $3,744 in 2009, having risen sharply from just under $1,000 in 2000. By 2010, it was expected that 40 million households would earn more than 48,000 renminbi ($6000) per year, enough to qualify a household as middle-class by US standards. Income varies widely, with the GDP per capita average in Shanghai more than five times higher than in Chongqing, in the interior of the country.

However, care needs to be taken in interpreting official figures about wealth in China. The actual purchasing power of a dollar in China compared to the West is higher because many Chinese do not report all their income. There are also distortions caused by hidden savings and allowances received from family members living abroad. Furthermore, the Chinese typically pay very low or no rent, spend little on healthcare and education due to subsidies, and are allowed to have only one or two children. There is also a booming black market in labour, goods, services, and foreign exchange, which further distorts official statistics of wealth.

For exporters to China, getting their product to the market, at the right time and at the right place, can be very difficult, given the limitations of the communications infrastructure. This is especially true of the inland provinces and emphasizes the need for exporters to focus their marketing and distribution efforts on just a few of the richest areas. It has been observed that not even the largest multinational companies have attempted to take on the whole Chinese market at once.

◉ Chapter summary and linkages to other chapters

This chapter has emphasized the need for market-oriented companies to break markets down into segments comprising groups of people with similar needs and buying processes. Numerous bases for segmenting markets have been identified, but there is no unique 'right' way of segmenting a market. The best way is the one that allows a company most profitably to exploit the greatest possible share of a market. Segmentation alone does not produce a marketing plan. To this end, a company must evaluate the segment opportunities open to it and assess how well it will be able to exploit each of them. There are a number of approaches for entering a market, and companies often seek to exploit one segment at a time with products that are uniquely adapted to that segment.

The crucial importance of segmentation to the philosophy of marketing is reflected in the extensive linkages between this chapter and others. In Chapter 4 we saw how buying behaviour differs among individuals, and these differences form an important basis for segmentation. In Chapter 5 we explored methods by which companies can research the differences between individuals and thereby identify and evaluate segments. In the next chapter, we will pick up issues of competitive positioning which were introduced towards the end of this chapter. We will see how the development of brands facilitates the task of targeting and positioning. Subsequent chapters deal with the elements of the marketing mix that allow a company to develop products that are particularly suited to the needs of targeted segments.

✎ KEY PRINCIPLES OF MARKETING

- Segmentation is fundamental to marketing because of its emphasis on meeting the needs of identified groups of consumers.

- A trade-off must be made between the desire of individuals to be treated as a unique segment of one, and companies' desire to achieve segments that are large enough to achieve economic efficiencies.

- Segmentation exercises by themselves do not make decisions for management. Management must use creative thinking and a scientific analysis of segmentation data to decide which segments to target.

- Segments are rarely static in nature, and in deciding which segments to target, a company should focus on what each segment is likely to look like in the future.

CASE STUDY

A bar for all tastes

A few decades ago, the centre of most British towns would have had many small bars, all looking fairly similar to each other, with relatively few points of differentiation. The market for drinking in pubs was fairly homogenous, comprising mostly males, who went to the pub mainly to drink, and only very rarely to eat. Today, the bar scene in any British town centre is much more complex, and the key to understanding this complexity is the pub chain's increasingly sophisticated segmentation techniques which seek to address a market which is much more heterogeneous than a few decades ago.

Despite the closure of many pubs in recent years, going to pubs, clubs, and bars continues to be a popular leisure activity in the UK and pubs have benefited from a growth in eating out, which has increased faster than growth in GDP. This has been achieved despite numerous challenges facing pub operators, including higher taxes on alcohol, growing competition from supermarkets for 'off sales', a smoking ban introduced in most parts of the UK from 2007, and generally rising operating costs.

To achieve the greatest return from their investment, pub operators have had to focus the design of bars on meeting the needs of smaller and smaller market segments. No longer is the pub market dominated by males going out to drink—professional women and families are among many segments who may never have thought about going into the traditional bar, but may be tempted with a format which appeals to them. No loud music or big screen television? Good quality coffee served as well as beer? Bright, airy decor? Drinks served to the table, rather than queuing at the bar? These may have been design features that were unsought or unwanted by the traditional male heavy drinker, but may strongly appeal to other market segments.

Punch Taverns owns one of the largest pub portfolios in the UK and its portfolio is constantly developing through acquisition, investment, and the changing trends of the pub sector. It has identified 11 types of pubs which meet the needs of clearly defined market segments:

Basic local	These are community pubs, mostly located in high density residential areas. Trade is focused on regular drinkers and tends to be wet led with little food. Beer, cider, and spirits are the big sellers. Most show televised sport. Customers are predominantly male with the proportion of female customers relatively low.
Mid-market local	The 'traditional British pub' as depicted in television soaps. Again they are situated in residential areas and most offer some sort of food. There may also be themed evenings, quizzes, darts, or pool. Customers tend to use the pub to meet friends and relax.
Upmarket local	While still community pubs, upmarket locals are generally found in low density housing areas. It is likely to offer high quality food, representing a significant part of the trade. For this reason the proportion of women using these pubs is higher than most of the locals.

Young local	Younger customers aged 18–30 are the focus here. Pubs draw custom from the surrounding area—they are still 'locals' rather than on the drinking circuit. The pubs tend to have a modern, trendy feel. Amusements including pool tables and machines will feature and chart music, and video screens will be prevalent. Draught lagers are the most popular drink.
City local	As the name suggests, these are found in city or town centres but away from the young people's circuit. Trading is highly competitive and the offer will include basic pub food and snacks. Local workers and shoppers provide passing trade in the daytime—residents will normally use the pub in the evening.
City dry led	Centrally located but offering high levels of food, city dry led pubs target the same customers as city locals. These pubs tend to be larger and they may have function rooms and restaurant areas.
Chameleon	Also centrally located but the pub's character changes from day to night to attract different types of customers. The venue may be a subdued coffee bar in the day serving office workers and shoppers, but a vibrant young people's bar with loud music by night.
Circuit	These pubs will be on or near the young people's circuit. Expect loud music, possibly a dress code and door staff. Food is less important, while lager and spirits generate strong sales.
Premium dining	These are destination food-led pubs in more upmarket areas. Restaurant quality food served with flair will account for more than 50 per cent of sales. These pubs are a refuge for adults away from children.
Value dining	Again focusing on food these pubs offer good value for money, so often attract families. They are welcoming to families particularly during the weekend and early evening.
Venue	Distinctive, wet-led pubs, that draw clientele from a wide catchment area because they offer something special. This may be live music or entertainers. The pub could also be a meeting point for a specific customer group, for example bikers.

The company, like most of its competitors, has developed a computerized mapping programme that helps it to identify the best location for any given format of pub. Postcode data using ACORN analysis gives an indication of how many typical consumers for each pub format would live within range of any location. However, segmentation cannot be based simply on where people live, and must recognize their mobility and movement patterns. Therefore, for some sites located in town centres or on busy roads, an understanding of people's work patterns and commuting habits can be crucial. Being near a main train station may be crucial for attracting a target market of urban professionals who want somewhere to stop off to meet friends before catching a train home. Pub operators such as Punch make extensive use of consultants and geodemographic mapping systems to show the cultural, social, and economic make-up of an area. But data analysis on its own will not always provide a complete answer when choosing between locations or formats. Simply being on the wrong side of the road may be the difference between success and failure—will people be prepared to cross a busy road in order to get from a housing area to a pub? Data may drive the segmentation process, but simply getting out and having a feel for an area can provide a lot of detail not present in computerized systems.

What does the future hold for the pub industry in Britain? Operators face increasingly challenging times, and the British Beer & Pub Association—an industry association—estimated that at the beginning of 2010 there were 53,466 pubs operating in the UK, having fallen by a massive 2,377 in the previous year, the sharpest rate of decline on record. A lot of this decline could be attributed to higher taxes on beer, and the recently introduced ban on smoking in public places. In addition, many younger drinkers who might have previously gone to the pub now sought out coffee bars, which had been equally active in identifying different market segments and providing formats and drinks which appealed to different groups. In an increasingly competitive environment, in which pubs compete with other leisure outlets, identifying and comprehensively satisfying the needs of distinct market segments will become increasingly crucial for success.

Based on: Office for National Statistics, Social Trends; Mintel Oxygen Report—Lager, August 2007: Punch Taverns website (www.PunchTaverns.com); Campaign for Real Ale website (http://www.camra.org.uk;) British Beer & Pub Association website (http://www.beerandpub.com).

Case study review questions

1. Critically evaluate the bases that bars may use to segment their markets.

2. In the context of bars, discuss the relative merits of quantitative and qualitative approaches to market segmentation.

3. Examine the bars in your area and try to identify the segments—using those described above—to which the bars are appealing.

CHAPTER REVIEW QUESTIONS

1. 'Too much segmentation can be costly and can result in a paralysis by analysis.' Discuss the view that for many markets Henry Ford's approach of producing a limited range of products for the 'average' customer may be the most profitable option for a company.

2. Critically evaluate the likely future trend in segmentation techniques. Illustrate your answer with reference to a specific market sector.

3. Given the increasing fragmentation of society, and an apparent desire for greater individuality among consumers, are current scientific methods of analysis and segmentation a short-sighted over-simplification?

ACTIVITIES

1. If you are familiar with the UK, visit the website www.upmystreet.com and enter postcodes of yourself and your friends and family. You will see an 'ACORN' description of each postcode and associated spending patterns. How well do you think this classification system describes the spending pattern of individuals living in these areas? What are the limitations of such geodemographc methods of market segmentation?

2. Gather together a sample of national newspapers. Discuss the typical readership of these papers, and the extent to which this is reflected in who advertisers in the papers are targeting.

3. For a market sector of your choice, analyse the positions adopted by companies in the market. Use the framework in Figure 6.12 as a basis for your analysis.

REFERENCES

Elkin, T. (2002) 'Sony Marketing Aims at Lifestyle Segments'. *Advertising Age,*73, (11), 3–4.

Equality and Human Rights Commission *(EHRC) (2010) How Fair is Britain?* London: Equality and Human Rights Commission.

FSD Kenya and Central Bank of Kenya (2009) 'Results of the Finances National Survey: Dynamics of Kenya's Changing Financial Landscape', available at http://www.fsdkenya. org/finaccess/documents/09-06-10%20FinAccess%20FA09%20Brochure.pdf (accessed 29 March 2010).

Gross, M.J., Brien, C., and Brown, G. (2008) 'Examining the Dimensions of a Lifestyle Tourism Destination'. *International Journal of Culture, Tourism and Hospitality Research,* 2 (1), 44–66.

Institute of Practitioners in Advertising (IPA) (2010) *The Marketing Opportunities for Advertisers and Agencies in Multi-cultural Britain.* London: Institute of Practitioners in Advertising.

Lin, C.-F. (2002) 'Segmenting Customer Brand Preference: Demographic or Psychographic'. *Journal of Product & Brand Management*, 11 (4), 249–68.

Mwangi, B. (2009) 'M-PESA—Transforming the lives of Kenyans', available at http://www. safaricom.co.ke/fileadmin/template/main/downloads/m-pesa_resource_centre/M-PESA_ Presentations/09-09.16%20-%20AFI%20Conference.pdf (accessed 29 March 2010).

SUGGESTED FURTHER READING

Segmentation, and targeting are discussed in more detail in the following:

Cahill, D.J. (2006) *Lifestyle Market Segmentation.* New York: Haworth Press.

Dibb, S. and Simkin, L. (2007) *Market Segmentation Success: Making it Happen!* New York: Haworth Press.

McDonald, M. and Dunbar, I. (2010) *Market Segmentation: How to Do it, How to Profit from it.* Oxford: Butterworth-Heinemann.

Yankelovich, D. and Meer, D. (2006) 'Rediscovering Market Segmentation'. *Harvard Business Review*, February, 1–10.

Positioning is discussed in the following:

D'Aveni, R.A. (2007), 'Mapping Your Competitive Position'. *Harvard Business Review*, November.

Ries, A. and Trout, J. (2001) *Positioning: the Battle for Your Mind: How to be Seen and Heard in the Overcrowded Marketplace.* New York: McGraw-Hill.

 ONLINE RESOURCE CENTRE

Visit the Online Resource Centre for resources that are relevant to this chapter, including a flashcard glossary, web links, multiple choice questions, and additional case studies:

> www.oxfordtextbooks.co.uk/orc/palmer3e/

KEY TERMS

- Attitudes
- Differentiation
- Discretionary income
- Disposable income
- Family life-cycle
- Geodemographics
- Household structure
- Lifestyle
- Mass market
- Niche markets

- Permission marketing
- Positioning
- Position map
- Psychographic segmentation
- Segmentation
- Social class
- Targeting
- Trigger points
- Values

DEVELOPING THE MARKETING MIX

Part 3

7 COMPETITOR ANALYSIS AND BRAND DEVELOPMENT

CHAPTER OBJECTIVES

This chapter marks a transition point in the book. In previous chapters we have been focusing on how companies can gain a better understanding of the external environment from which they earn their sales revenue. In the following chapters we will consider how companies try to develop the right products, and sell them through the right channels at the right price and with the right promotional messages. In this chapter we introduce concepts associated with competitive markets. We will explore what is meant by a competitor and how a company can develop a sustainable competitive advantage over its competitors. A large part of this chapter is given to the development of brands. These form the focal point of a firm's product, pricing, promotion, and distribution plans, and aim to create a distinctive position for a product. Branding lies at the heart of marketing strategy and seeks to remove a company from the harsh competition of commodity-type markets. By differentiating its product and giving it unique values, a company simplifies consumers' choices in markets that are crowded with otherwise similar products.

◉ Introduction

Marketing is a dynamic process of ensuring a close fit between the capabilities of an organization and the demands placed upon it by its external environment. It follows that what a company offers to a market will need to evolve continually over time in order to meet changes in the company's internal objectives and in its external business environment. It is not good enough for a company to develop a marketing plan that works for a short period, but then fails to make good long-term profits for the company because the plan is not sufficiently responsive to changes in its marketing environment.

History is full of marketing plans that looked too good to be true. A company may have found a very high level of sales in the short term, but failed to earn sufficient profits over the longer term. It may be that such a company has underpriced its products, leaving it with an insufficient margin to cover its fixed costs. Or it may have invested heavily in product design and promotion but failed to generate a sufficient level of sales to pay for such investment. It is not difficult to develop short-term marketing strategies that at first appear highly successful when judged by sales levels. It is much more difficult to develop a marketing strategy that is sustainable over the longer term by producing adequate levels of continuing profits. Central to this long-term strategy is the development of strong **brands** which can allow a company to charge premium prices for products that consistently deliver a high level of customer-defined value.

Many companies that have been hailed as successful market-led businesses have not managed to achieve a sustainable long-term success. In the UK, companies such as Next, Amstrad, and Laura Ashley have risen rapidly and gained many 'Business of the Year' type of awards on the way. But each of these ended up in serious financial difficulties just a short while later. It has been noted that very few of the so-called 'excellent' companies identified by Peters and Waterman (1992) in their book *In Search of Excellence* were considered to be excellent 15 years later. The marketing strategy that had led to short-term success was not sustained.

⦿ Who are a company's competitors?

Any plan to develop a competitive advantage must be based on a sound analysis of just who a company's competitors are. At first sight, it may seem obvious who the competitors are, but, as Theodore Levitt pointed out (1960), a myopic view may focus on the immediate and direct competitors while overlooking the more serious threat posed by indirect and less obvious sources of competition. When railway companies in the 1930s saw their main competitors as other railway companies, they overlooked the fact that the most serious competition would come from road-based transport. More recently, banks have been made to realize that their competitors are not just other banks, or even other financial services organizations, but any organization that has a strong brand reputation and customer base. Through these, supermarkets, airlines, and car companies have all developed various forms of banking services which now compete with mainstream banks.

It is usually possible to identify direct and indirect competitors. **Direct competitors** are generally similar in form and satisfy customers' needs in a similar way. **Indirect competitors** may appear different in form, but satisfy a fundamentally similar need. Consider the examples of products and underlying needs shown in Figure 7.1. The table shows, for each product, possible direct and indirect competitors.

A sound analysis of the direct and indirect competitors of a firm is crucial in defining the business mission of an organization (Figure 7.2). (This is discussed further in Chapter 12.)

Product	Typical underlying need	Direct competitors	Examples of indirect competitors
Overseas holiday	Relaxation	Rival tour operators	Garden conservatories
Restaurant meal	Social gathering	Other restaurants	Ready-prepared gourmet meals for home consumption
Television programme	Entertainment	Other television programmes	Internet service providers
Rolex watch	Social status	Other watches	Armani suit; Gucci handbag

Figure 7.1 **Underlying needs, direct and indirect competitors for selected products.**

Figure 7.2 **What business is the Parker Pen company in?** At first sight, the company may appear to be in the pen business, or possibly the 'writing implement' or maybe even the 'communication' business. In fact, the company understands that the majority of its sales are made for gift giving. Gifts can be personal (e.g. to mark a relative's personal achievement or anniversary) or corporate (as when companies give away free pens as a sales incentive to reward a new order). The company is essentially in the 'gift' business, so its competitors are not just other pens, but any gift. Within this broad definition, MP3 players, alarm clocks, and overnight bags could all be regarded as competitors.

A useful framework for analysing the competition facing a company in a market has been provided by Michael Porter (1980). His model illustrates the relationship between existing competitors and potential competitors in a market and identifies five forces requiring evaluation:

1. The threat of new entrants

2. The threat of substitute products

3. The intensity of rivalry between competing firms

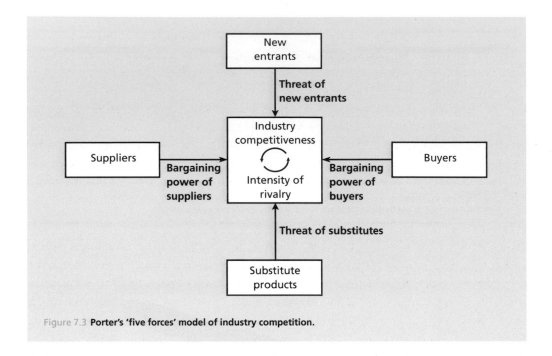

Figure 7.3 **Porter's 'five forces' model of industry competition.**

4. The power of suppliers

5. The power of buyers

Understanding the structure of competition within a market is a vital prerequisite for developing a strategy to develop a sustainable competitive advantage. The model is shown in Figure 7.3 and the nature of these five forces are discussed below.

The threat of new entrants

The threat of new entrants is greatest where there are low barriers to entry. New entrants may already be active in a similar market sector, but in another geographic market. The threat becomes reality when a company that is strong in one geographical market decides to exploit other geographical markets. As an example, the full service airlines have been challenged on many routes by newer low-cost 'budget' airlines. Having established a base, these airlines have often gone on to further challenge the established airlines by creating new operating bases. (For example, the budget airline Ryanair posed a new threat to Belgian and German carriers after expanding to those countries from its UK and Irish bases.)

Alternatively, new entrants may arrive from outside the industry. Bic, whose technology base was plastic moulding, was well established in the disposable ballpoint pen market. They were able to diversify successfully into the wet shave razor market with plastic disposable razors, thereby challenging established market leaders such as Gillette and Wilkinson in their core business.

The threat of substitute products

Substitute products are likely to emerge from alternative technologies, particularly as the economics of production change. Initially the new technology may have high costs associated with it and serve only small niche markets. As the technology and experience develop, the level of investment rises and production volumes increase, resulting in economies of scale that are associated with falling production costs. Many products have been consigned to obscurity by the development of new technologies; for example the market for typewriters has been almost eliminated by the development of personal computers, and the market for sugar has been reduced by the development of artificial sweeteners. These substitutes may change the whole economics of an industry and threaten the survival of manufacturers of the traditional product.

Intensity of rivalry between competing firms

The intensity of rivalry may be high if two or more firms are fighting for dominance in a fast-growing market. For example, this occurred in the UK's personal phone market during the mid-1990s. There may also be a fight to establish the dominant technology in a sector, something that occurred in the mid-2000s in the fight to establish a common standard for high definition DVD players. The Sony supported Blu ray system was pitched against Toshiba's rival HD-DVD system. By 2008, Blu-ray seemed to be winning the battle, with sales outnumbering those of HD-DVD, and more importantly, it had the support of Walt Disney, 20th Century Fox, and Metro Goldwyn Mayer who had chosen Blu-ray for their new releases. The need was for a format to become established as the dominant technology or brand before the industry matured. Companies are likely to engage heavily in promotional activity involving advertising and promotional incentives to buy. In a mature industry, particularly if it is characterized by high fixed costs and excess capacity, the intensity of competitive rivalry may be very high. This is because manufacturers or service providers need to operate at near maximum capacity to cover overhead costs. As the industry matures or at times of cyclical downturn, or when a number of companies have invested in new capacity, firms fight to maintain their maximum level of sales.

The power of suppliers

The power of suppliers is likely to be high if the number of suppliers is small and/or the materials, components, and services they offer are in short supply. The suppliers of silicone chips and patented medicines have at times held a powerful market position as a result of their dominance of technology and the high demand for their products.

The power of buyers

Buyers' power is likely to be high if there are relatively few buyers, if there are many alternative sources of supply, and if buyers incur only low costs in switching between suppliers. During the past couple of decades, Britain's grocery retailing sector has become increasingly dominated by a small number of very large organizations. According to a Competition Commission report Asda, Co-operative Stores, Iceland, Morrisons, Sainsbury's, Somerfield, and Tesco held over three-quarters of UK grocery market share by turnover in 2007 (Competition

Commission 2008). Power in the marketplace has shifted away from the manufacturers of grocery products to the retailers, seven of whom may buy around three-quarters of many manufacturers' total output.

Branding

Fierce competition may at first sight appear very attractive for the welfare of society as a whole, but it can pose problems for sellers. In a fiercely competitive market, an individual firm is subject to considerable direct competition from other firms and must take its selling price from the market. An implication of fierce competition is that firms will be unable to make a level of profits that is above the norm for their market. If they did achieve higher-than-normal profits, this would act as an invitation to new market entrants, whose presence would eventually increase the level of competition in the market and drive down profits to the minimum level that makes it attractive for firms to continue in the market.

To try to avoid head-on competition with large numbers of other suppliers in a market, companies seek to differentiate their product in some way. In doing so, they create an element of monopoly power for themselves, in that no other company in the market is selling a product identical to theirs. To some people, the point of difference may be of great importance in influencing their purchase decision, and they may be prepared to pay a price premium for the differentiated product. Nevertheless, such buyers remain aware of close substitutes that are available, and may be prepared to switch to these substitutes if the price premium is considered to be too high in relation to the additional benefits received. The co-existence of a limited monopoly power with the presence of many near substitutes is often referred to as *imperfect competition* (Figure 7.4). (We will come back to this again in Chapter 8.)

Figure 7.4 **Perfect competition, imperfect competition, and the role of brands.**

For a marketing manager, product differentiation becomes a key to gaining a degree of monopoly power in a market. It must be remembered, however, that product differentiation alone will not prove to be commercially successful unless the differentiation is based on satisfying clearly identified consumers' needs. A differentiated product may have significant monopoly power in that it is unique, but if it fails to satisfy consumers' needs, its uniqueness has no commercial value.

Out of the need for product differentiation comes the concept of branding. A company must ensure that customers can immediately recognize its distinctive products in the marketplace. Instead of asking for a generic version of the product, customers should be able to ask for the distinctive product that they have come to prefer. A brand is essentially a way of giving a product a unique identity which differentiates it from its near competitors. The means by which this unique identity is created are discussed in this chapter.

Through adding values that will attract customers, a company can provide a firm base for expansion and product development and protect itself against the strength of intermediaries and competitors. There has been much evidence linking high levels of advertising expenditure to support strong brands with high returns on capital and high market share (see de Chernatony 2006).

Branding through product differentiation may not be possible in all markets. Where products involve consumers in low levels of risk and there are few opportunities for developing a distinctive product, competitive advantage may be based on cost leadership rather than brand development. Examples of commodity strategies are evident in many low-value consumer and industrial markets where a significant segment of customers seek a product with a basic and substitutable set of characteristics. Milk and cheese are everyday items of consumer purchase where manufacturers' brands have had relatively little impact and most consumers are happy to buy the generic milk or cheese offered by a retailer.

⊙ The history of branding

The term 'branding' pre-dates modern marketing and is generally believed to have originated in agricultural practices of the Middle Ages. Farmers who allowed their cattle to graze on open common land needed some means of distinguishing their cattle from those that were owned by other farmers sharing common grazing rights. They therefore 'branded' their animals with a branding iron, leaving an indelible mark which would clearly identify the owner of a particular animal. The role of a brand in identifying products with a particular source is shared by the medieval farmer and the modern corporation.

Economies in an early stage of development are characterized by small-scale production processes and relatively local markets. Where there are few opportunities for economies of scale in production, brands had only a limited role to play. With poor transport facilities and few opportunities to expand business profitably beyond the immediate area of production, consumers could readily identify the source of goods. In early nineteenth-century Britain, most communities had their own baker, brewer, and carpenter. None had developed the

Figure 7.5 **In early nineteenth-century England, consumers of beer may have had little knowledge about the quality of beer from the expanding industrialized breweries.** Many brewers were reputed to add salt to their beer, in order to make the drinker thirstier, so that he would buy more beer—by which time he probably wouldn't notice any impurities. One of the growing brewers of the time, Bass, developed what is acknowledged to be one of the earliest brand logos in order to provide reassurance of quality to a segment of the market that was more discerning. By drinking Bass beer, the buyer could, over time, come to be reassured that it was worth specifically selecting that brand of beer, because it could be confident that no salt had been added. The logo was simply a plain triangle, and essentially the same logo is still in use today.

ability to achieve competitive advantage through economies of scale, while poor road and rail transport would have prevented their goods being exported to neighbouring communities. People in local communities knew where their goods had come from and were not confused by competing products from distant towns. Buyers were able to learn through personal experience of the abilities, consistency, and reliability of a supplier, while suppliers were able to adapt simple production methods to the needs of individual customers who were known personally. Through personal knowledge and trust, a supplier was likely to be able to judge the creditworthiness of each customer.

In the UK, the industrialization that occurred in the nineteenth century meant that many goods could now be produced efficiently in centralized factories rather than in small cottage industries. An efficient centralized factory could produce more output than could be consumed by the local community. Furthermore, improvements in transport infrastructure allowed the surplus production to be shipped to markets around the country. What one company could do efficiently in one factory, another company could probably do equally as well in another factory elsewhere. Therefore, firms became involved in competition in distant markets. This, however, led to a problem for buyers, whose buying process was now made more complicated. Instead of having just the local brewer's products available, they now had a range of beers to choose from. Buyers probably had little knowledge of the distant firms who were now supplying their market, or of the quality and consistency of their products. Branding emerged essentially to simplify the purchase processes of buyers who faced competing sources of supply (Figure 7.5).

◉ Key characteristics of a brand

A brand, then, is essentially a way of distinguishing the products of one company from those of its competitors. To have value, a brand must have consistency, reduce buyers' level of perceived risk, and offer a range of functional and emotional attributes that are of value to buyers.

Consistency

Consistency is at the heart of branding strategy. To have value in simplifying buyers' purchasing processes, consumers must come to learn that a brand stands for the same set of attributes on one purchase occasion as on all subsequent and previous occasions. Consider a brewery offering draft bitter to the market. The distinctive characteristics of the beer that contribute towards its brand values may be described as:

◉ Taste: light hop flavour

◉ Strength: above-average gravity

◉ Appearance: clear light colour

Consumers come to prefer the particular taste/strength/appearance of beer that is described in shorthand by a brand name. If the taste of a brand varies between one pint and the next, the ability of the brand name to act as a shorthand description of a whole bundle of attributes is significantly weakened. Next time the buyer may not bother sticking with the brand, which it does not now trust, if it has just as much chance of achieving the desired bundle of attributes from another product.

The ability of a company to secure consistency of product delivery is crucial to the development of branding. This helps to explain why branding was fastest to develop for those products that were produced using factory techniques in which quality control procedures could be used to ensure consistent standards every time. Soap powders, cigarettes, and soft drinks were all examples of products for which manufacturers developed an ability to control production standards and were early adopters of brands (Figure 7.6).

Brands have been relatively slow to develop in the services sector, partly because of the difficulty of maintaining consistent standards. Some service sectors have successfully taken on board the 'industrialization' of their production processes to ensure that a service delivered on one occasion is very similar to that delivered on all previous and subsequent occasions. Fast-food restaurants have been notable in this field, and have been associated with the

Figure 7.6 **Many of our most familiar fast-moving consumer goods brands have a long history.**
Typhoo tea, which can trace its origins back to 1820, is typical of a brand that has been associated with consistency in its appeal. Despite numerous changes in ownership of the brand and many new product formulations (such as different shapes of tea bags), many consumers remain loyal to the Typhoo brand, and this loyalty is often passed down through generations of families.

development of many strong international brands. On the other hand, many one-to-one services such as those provided by hairdressers, solicitors, and dentists have difficulty in 'industrializing' their service offer, and consequently corporate brands have had much more limited impact; the brand identity is essentially limited to the individual performing the service.

The term 'consistency' was noted above as an important attribute of a brand. As well as referring to specific product attributes (as in the case of the beer described earlier), consistency can refer to more general values about a producer or its range of products. As an example, the Co-operative brand name has been associated with ethical values, and these values have been applied consistently across the UK organization's activities, including retailing, banking, and travel services.

Risk reduction

In simple economies where buyers personally knew the producers of the goods and services they bought, the personal relationship helped to manage the buyer's exposure to risk. In the absence of that relationship, a brand acts as a substitute in managing buyers' exposure to risk. Branding simplifies the decision-making process by providing a sense of security and consistency for buyers which may be absent outside of a relationship with a supplier.

A brand addresses a number of dimensions of purchase risk, which have been identified as:

⊙ Physical (will the product cause me harm?)

⊙ Psychological (will this product satisfy my need for peace of mind?)

⊙ Performance (does the product work in accordance with my requirements?)

⊙ Financial (will this product provide adequate performance within my budget?)

Risk levels are perceived as being higher for products that fulfil important needs and for which there is a high level of involvement by the consumer.

Functional and emotional attributes

There have been many conceptualizations of the unique qualities of brands (see de Chernatony and McDonald 2003). These usually distinguish between dimensions that can be objectively measured (such as taste, shape, reliability) and the subjective values that can be defined only in the minds of consumers (such as the perceived personality of a brand). In an early study, Gardner and Levy (1955) distinguished between the 'functional' dimensions of a brand and its 'personality'. Similar attempts to distinguish the dimensions of brands have been made by others—for example utilitarianism versus value expressive (Munson and Spivey 1981), and functional versus representational (de Chernatony and McWilliam 1990). It has been suggested that brands need to be positioned somewhere in a 'brand space', defined by the degree of abstraction (whether the brand has become independent from its associated product) and the degree of enactment (whether the brand focuses more on the meaning of a product or its functionality) (Berthon et al. 2003). With increasing affluence, the emotional or non-functional expectations of brands have become more important.

A number of dimensions of a brand's emotional appeal have been identified, including trust, liking, and sophistication, and it has been shown that products with a high level of subjective emotional appeal are associated with a greater level of customer involvement than a product that provides essentially objective benefits. This has been demonstrated in the preference shown for branded beer as opposed to a functionally identical generic beer (Allison and Uhl 1964), and in the way that the emotional appeal of brands of analgesics

MARKETING in ACTION

Can a university be branded?

Are universities unique places of learning, or brands to be marketed just like any other product? The language of brand management has been entering the vocabulary of university vice-chancellors throughout the UK. 'Good' universities have known for some time that they have their reputation to preserve, but more recently many universities have begun talking about 'managing brand values'. Research among applicants to UK universities has consistently shown that prospective students have very poor knowledge about the actual facilities on offer, such as the standards of teaching, accommodation, and library facilities. However, some universities have come to be rated more highly than others, often on the basis of non-academic information, such as the triumphs of the university's sports teams or the nightlife in town.

Many of the UK's 'new' (post-1992) universities have made a priority of developing a strong brand image with which to challenge the established universities. Even students feel it is important to have a degree from a university that has a 'good' name, in the same way as people have always wanted to belong to 'good' clubs. The view has spread that a university's 'good' name needs to be nurtured and maintained in just the same way as any fast-moving consumer product. Simply having technical excellence is not good enough.

De Montfort University has been one of the pioneers in university brand building, supporting its efforts with television advertising. It undertook research among current students which showed, perhaps surprisingly, that many preferred limited university funds to be spent on a brand building advertising campaign than on improvements in academic facilities, such as additional books for the library. Graduating from a known rather than an unknown university was seen as being important to many students.

Cynics have been quick to criticize efforts to market universities as brands. How can any brand be sustained over the long term if the infrastructure and facilities of a university are under pressure from ever diminishing resources?

contributed significantly in relieving headaches (Branthwaite and Cooper 1981). As consumers buy products, they learn to appreciate their added value and begin to form a relationship with them. For example, there are many coffee shops competing for customers, but individual chains such as Starbucks and Costa Coffee have each tried to develop their own personality, expressed through the ambience of their stores, the personality of their staff, and their linking to good social causes.

There is an extensive literature on the emotional relationship consumers develop between a brand and their own perceived or sought personality. Brands are chosen when the image they create matches the needs, values, and lifestyles of customers. Through socialization processes, individuals form perceptions of their self, which they attempt to reinforce or alter by relating with specific groups, products, and brands. There is evidence that branding plays a particularly important role in purchase decisions where the product is conspicuous in its use and in situations where group social acceptance is a strong motivator.

◉ Creating a distinctive brand

Branding creates a product with unique physical, functional, and psychological values and can help to transform commodities into unique products. To be successful, a brand must have a competitive advantage in at least one aspect of marketing, such that it meets the complex needs of consumers better than competitors. This section discusses the strategic issues involved in creating a strong and distinctive brand.

Choice of name

A brand is much more just than a name. Nevertheless, a name is usually vital to the identity of a brand and can be the most difficult to change. Many products have been redesigned and relaunched as they have gone through their life-cycle, yet their brand name has remained unchanged. In the car market, Volkswagen introduced its first Golf model in 1974. Since then, the car has gone through four completely new body designs, three new series of engines, and countless minor modifications to styling, features, engine ranges, and colours. The Golf of 2008 is larger and much better equipped than its predecessor of a quarter of a century ago. Yet the brand name remains the same. Instead of symbolizing a set of narrowly defined product characteristics, the name 'Golf' has come to stand for reliable, mid-size, safe, value-for-money motoring. These values have been essentially unchanged for over 30 years. The public has come to learn what is associated with the name 'Golf', and therefore new model launches do not have to start from scratch in explaining what the car stands for.

Companies frequently engage specialist firms to develop brand names for their new products. This is often a wise investment, in view of the possible downside costs of getting a name wrong and the difficulties of subsequently changing it. A brand naming team may be made up of linguists, psychologists, sociologists, and media analysts, among others. The following are some of the factors that previous experience shows should lead to a brand name being successful.

- ◉ The name should have positive associations with the benefits and features of the product (e.g. 'Bostik' suggests adhesive qualities; 'Flash' sounds like it will clean thoroughly and quickly).

- ◉ There should be no negative associations with words that sound similar. (For example, Volkswagen had to think long and hard about the wisdom of using the name 'Sharan' in the UK for a new model. Although the name worked well in other countries, it sounded too similar to Sharon, a girl's name which at the time had been much maligned in the media.)

- ◉ The name should be memorable and easy to pronounce. (There is research evidence to suggest that names including the letter 'x' are particularly memorable, such as Andrex, Durex, Radox, etc.)

- ◉ The name must be in a tone of language that is understood and appreciated by the product's target market.

241

MARKETING in ACTION

A Bum name or a Sic brand?

Getting a brand name wrong can cost a company dearly. For a major brand, re-tooling to change product formulations can be a relatively minor matter compared with the costs of changing a brand name. Sometimes brands fail because the underlying product has failed to meet customers' expectations. At other times a brand fails because its name was chosen with insufficient care. Occasionally, the world outside a brand name changes in a way that destroys the appeal of a once well liked name; for example the slimmers' biscuits called Aids had to be renamed in the light of HIV scares.

With increasing globalization of markets, firms have to be careful that a brand name is capable of translation into overseas languages without causing offence or ridicule. The following brand names may have been well thought out in their own home market, but they failed to take account of local interpretations in potential overseas markets:

- General Motors may have wondered why its Nova car wasn't selling well in Spain, then realized that in the local language the brand name suggests that the car 'doesn't work'.

- British visitors to Spain are often amused to find 'Bum' crisps on sale—they probably wouldn't go down too well in an English speaking market.

- Similarly, the French drink 'Sic' wouldn't be easy to export to Britain.

Care must also be taken in choosing a corporate brand name. Corporate mergers and restructuring during the 1990s spawned numerous abstract names, many of which promptly had to be changed following public ridicule. Royal Mail should have had one of the most sought-after corporate brand names in the world, but nevertheless it decided to change the company's name to 'Consignia'. Public ridicule led it to abandon this name in 2002 and revert to its original name. There was incredulity in 2002 when the accounting firm Pricewaterhouse-Coopers proposed changing its name to 'Monday'. One financial analyst calculated that, during the period 1997–2000, just under half of all FTSE 100 companies that had taken on a new abstract corporate name were ejected from the FTSE 100 list within two years.

⊚ The name must be checked by legal experts to ensure that it does not infringe on another company's brand name.

⊚ A company must ensure that the product's name is available as an Internet domain name. Ideally, it should also be able to register all similar sounding domain names in order to prevent unauthorized sites appearing.

Despite these guidelines, brand names exist which appear to break all the rules and would almost certainly not have been chosen today. In a world that is sceptical of offal from animals, who would have named a range of meat products 'Brains'?

Distinctive product features

Sometimes the distinctive features of a product don't really require a brand name to prompt immediate recognition. Distinctiveness can be based on the physical design of a product (e.g. the distinctive shape of Toblerone chocolate); distinctive packaging (e.g. the lemon-shaped

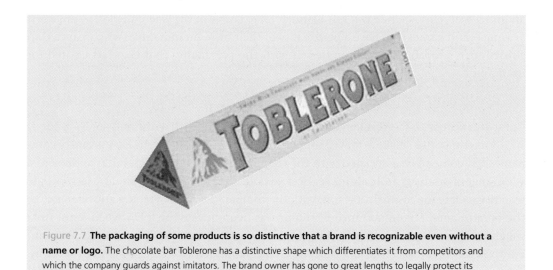

Figure 7.7 **The packaging of some products is so distinctive that a brand is recognizable even without a name or logo.** The chocolate bar Toblerone has a distinctive shape which differentiates it from competitors and which the company guards against imitators. The brand owner has gone to great lengths to legally protect its distinctive design from competitors who have imitated the triangular shape.

container used to package Jif lemon juice), or distinctive service processes (e.g. the manner in which waiting staff in a TGI Fridays restaurant serve customers). Companies make great efforts through the use of patents to protect the distinctive characteristics of their products from competition, although this can be much more difficult in the case of intangible service processes (Figure 7.7).

Creation of a distinctive brand personality

It will be recalled that a brand possesses functional and emotional attributes. The emotional attributes are of particular importance in contributing to a brand's personality. This can best be described as the psychological disposition that buyers have towards a particular brand. Brands have been variously described as having personalities that are 'fun', 'reliable', 'traditional', and 'adventurous'. The Virgin group has evolved a personality for its brand which can be described as reliable, slightly offbeat, and value for money. This personality has been developed consistently across the group's product ranges, from air travel to banking and investment services.

There has been some debate about whether the emotional aspects of a brand are becoming more or less important in consumers' overall evaluation of a product. One argument is that consumers are becoming more 'marketing literate' and increasingly sceptical of firms' attempts to create abstract images that are not underpinned by reality. On the other hand, there is no doubt that, as consumers become more affluent, they buy products to satisfy a much wider and more complex range of needs, which they seek to satisfy with distinctive brands. (Refer back to the discussion of needs in Chapter 4.) A brand personality can help an individual reinforce her own self-identity, for example in the way that clothes are worn bearing brand names that have a personality of their own. An individual who wears a Gap sweatshirt is probably identifying herself with the personality that Gap has created for its brand.

Distinctive visual identity

Companies often go to great lengths to invest their brands with a distinctive visual identity. Sometimes this can be achieved simply on the basis of a colour. The Easy group of companies has come to be associated with the colour bright orange, which it has applied to a wide range of products, from airline services, to hotels, car rental, and cinemas. Many people would associate the distinctive colour with the company, without needing any reference to the brand name. The importance of colour was demonstrated in 1996 when Pepsi Cola sought to adopt the colour blue in the UK cola market to distinguish itself from its predominantly red competitors. The fact that the change appeared to result in no short-term increase in sales provides a reminder that buyers may not be influenced simply by a superficial change which does not increase the product's perceived value. This may be especially true for low-involvement products such as soft drinks. One of Pepsi's arch rivals, Virgin, exploited the opportunity by stating in advertisements that it pays more attention to the *contents* of the can than to its colour.

The extent to which a company can legitimately 'own' an identifying colour is questionable. Many suppliers of generic products have copied the colours used by their branded competitors; for example many supermarkets' own brands of coffee have shared a very similar colour scheme to that of the market leader, Nescafé. This has frequently led to allegations that they are 'passing off' their goods as if they were the manufacturer's branded product, especially where the packaging and typography are also used to imitate the brand leader. The owner of easyJet successfully challenged the owner of easyRealestate.co.uk which had used easyJet's colour, orange. A court held that, by using a similar name and colour, the company had sought to wrongly imply an association with easyJet.

Colours have often come to be associated with certain product features. Bright reds and yellows are often used to signify speed (e.g. fast food, one-hour film developing), and white is often associated with purity (low fat, additive-free foods). However, the meaning of colours has to be seen in their cultural context—although white may be associated with purity in most western countries, in some other countries it is associated with bereavement.

To achieve maximum effect, corporate visual identity should be applied consistently. For a typical service-based company, this would mean applying a design and colour scheme to the company's advertising, buildings, staff uniforms, and vehicles. Logos are an important part of corporate visual identity. The aim of a logo is to encapsulate the values of a brand and to provide an immediate reminder of the brand each time it is seen by customers and potential customers. A good logo should:

◉ Give some indication of the business which a company is in, or the product category to which its output belongs (e.g. the logos for many water utility companies include stylized waves of water).

- Stress particular advantages of a product or organization (e.g. the most advanced, the fastest, most caring, longest established).

- Not be over-complicated. The simplest logos tend to stand the test of time best.

- Be updated to keep it in tune with styles and fashions of the time (e.g. the shell oil company's logo has gone through numerous minor styling changes during its 70-year history, which have retained the central theme of a shell, but adapted the shape and the emphasis on particular details.

....

E-Marketing

Branding in cyberspace

Companies would generally love their brand to be at the heart of a community, and many companies have developed their own blogs and online forums for this purpose. The power of social media for brand development is indicated by the research organization Virtue's social media index which measures the volume of conversations for brands on a variety of social media. In January 2009 it reported that the brands of iPhone, CNN, Starbucks, Apple, and iPod dominated the social space (Miller 2009). It has been suggested that 43 per cent of social networkers in Europe have visited a personal space of a brand and 16 per cent have already had a dialogue or sent a message to a brand (Microsoft Digital Advertising Solutions 2007). Another study noted that 36 per cent of active Internet users thought more positively about companies that have blogs and 32 per cent trusted bloggers' opinion on products and services (Universal Maccann International 2008).

However, there is a dilemma faced by companies planning to use online social media to develop their brands. On the one hand, they may seek to control the communication environment within the network, in an effort to make sure that their brand message comes through clearly. They may also be attracted by the availability of demographic and lifestyle information available to improve their targeting to individual members of the network. But on the other hand, a true social network implies members feeling a sense of ownership of the community, and there is evidence that individuals may be resentful of corporate intrusion into what is perceived to be their own community space (Croft 2008; Hitwise 2008). If online brand communities are perceived by users as not being trustworthy, open, interesting, relevant, and engaging with the target audience, they can rapidly harm a company's reputation. There have been reported cases of companies disguising their involvement in a community by falsely posting messages that purported to come from a member of the public, praising the company. While the company might have thought that it could influence opinion by manipulating the community, the subsequent uncovering of its covert actions generated bad publicity that undermined trust in the company.

Many companies are still trying to understand the impact of the Internet on their brands. Will the copious amounts of information available online reduce products to price led commodities? In this environment, how do companies build distinctive brand values?

How can a company work with a brand community and reduce the impacts when online communities turn against it?

Brand vision

It has often been suggested that a key factor in the development of a sustainable competitive advantage for a brand is for management and everybody in an organization to have a clear vision for the brand. There have been many definitions of what this term 'brand vision' means, but essentially it describes the company's perception of the values and qualities that its brand represents. A brand vision gives a clear statement about the 'soul' of the brand and provides a sense of direction to customers, and all of those employees and intermediaries who have responsibilities for delivering it. If a brand is to thrive, there must be a vision about what the brand will look like way into the future, in an environment that may be very challenging. A brand vision statement should be complementary to the company's corporate vision statement and sometimes can be combined with it. In fact, what is important is not what the statement is called, or the formalized procedures for developing it, but whether there is a shared sense of brand vision within an organization.

A brand vision should encapsulate the core values of the brand. There has been some discussion about how many values should be associated with a brand, and in what level of detail they should be described. There seems to be a consensus that the number of core values should be limited, ideally to four or five. As the number of brand values increases, confusion can set in about what are the most important values, and the opportunities for conflicts between core values can increase. In the case of people-intensive service businesses, staff become an important part of the brand promise, and therefore it is particularly important that they understand the values of the brand. If the values of a brand which are promoted to customers are not shared by staff, dissonance may result when customers do not receive the brand promise. Many labour intensive service organizations base their staff recruitment on matching the values of the brand with the values of potential employees. Some employers have taken the view that technical skills are relatively unimportant in the recruitment process, and instead it is more important that new recruits share core values. For example, it has been suggested that banks recruit to their call centre individuals who have values of honesty and integrity, rather than technical knowledge about banking skills.

There have been some notable entrepreneurs and CEOs who have had a passionate belief in their brand vision to the point of being evangelical. It is easy for bureaucratic, procedures-driven organizations to assemble a committee to write down brand vision statements, but this can easily fall into a trap of saying more and doing less. An example of a visionary brand evangelist is Sir Richard Branson who has had a consistent and passionate belief in the Virgin brand, which has been applied to a wide range of services, including air travel, music retailing, mobile phones, personal finance, and train services. The brand vision is based on a number of key values:

- Fun—enjoyment and humour, not offensive and incompetent.

- Value for money—simple, not cheap.

⦿ Quality—attention to detail, not expensive for the sake of it.

⦿ Innovation—challenging convention, not different for the sake of being different.

⦿ Competitive challenge—responding to consumer needs, not being irrelevant.

⦿ Brilliant customer service—empowered, not unprofessional people.

⦿ Branding strategy

Once a firm has decided on a distinctive brand identity for a product, the next issue is to have a strategy for developing the brand. In this section, a number of alternative strategic routes are explored which each lead to a company differentiating its products from those of its competitors. One strategy is to develop a single strong brand. As an alternative, differentiated brands or brand families may be developed (Figure 7.8). Finally, once a strong brand has been developed, companies are often keen to extend its use.

Development of a single strong brand

One approach to branding is to apply the same brand name to everything that a company produces. The big advantage of this approach is the economies of scale in promotion that this can bring about. Instead of promoting many minor brands through small campaigns, a company can concentrate all of its resources on one campaign for one brand. This approach has been used successfully by many large multinational companies, such as IBM, Kodak, and Cadbury, who, with a few exceptions, put their single brand name on everything they sell.

The main disadvantage of this approach is that it can pose significant risks of confusing the values of a brand. If a company positioned its product range as premium priced, top quality, confusion may arise in consumers' minds if it applied the same brand name to a budget version of its product—does the brand still stand for top quality?

Worse still for a company, a poorly performing product carrying its brand can tarnish all products carrying that name. This is a particular problem for new product launches which are of unproven reliability. (For example, the Virgin group's reputation for dependable, no-nonsense service undoubtedly suffered when it applied its brand name to train services with a very poor reliability record.)

A final problem of the strong single corporate brand is that it can make it more difficult for a company to dispose of the manufacture and marketing of products that no longer fit in its corporate plan. Very often, the main value of the products to a corporate buyer is their brand name, so the company may be forced into a monitoring agreement to protect its brand name from abuse by a company that has acquired the right to use it. Because of changes in corporate strategy, many of the products carrying the Cadbury and Virgin brand names are not in fact made or sold by these companies, yet they still need to preserve the values that the names stand for.

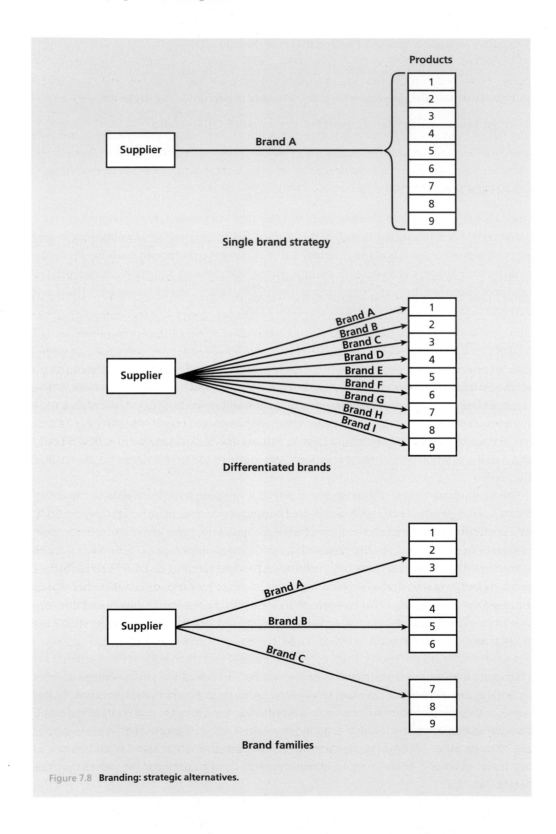

Figure 7.8 **Branding: strategic alternatives.**

Differentiated brands

To overcome the problem of confused brand values, firms often develop different brand names to serve different market segments. In this way, the clothing retailer Arcadia uses a number of different brand names to target different segments of the clothes buying market in terms of buyers' age, disposable income, and lifestyle. So Top Shop serves a price conscious young female segment, while Top Man serves a similar, but male, segment; the company's Dorothy Perkins and Burtons brands target older segments, female and male respectively. The company also operates a number of other store brands which target segments that are different in terms of their age/income/fashion consciousness/price sensitivity.

Brand families

A brand family occurs where a company uses a number of brand names, but identifies each product range or market segment served with a different brand name. The range is then developed to include a line of products. In this way, the Colgate Palmolive company has developed a number of product ranges, including soap, shampoos, and toothpaste, each with its own brand name. Within each range are a number of variants; for example Colgate toothpaste comes in original, baking soda, and total protection formats, among others.

Very often, companies promote brand names at a number of levels. As well as the corporate brand name, the name of the product category might be promoted. In addition, a special package offer within the basic product category may be developed with its own brand name. British Airways has developed a corporate brand (British Airways), brands for Club Class and its Executive Club, and brands for special offer tickets (e.g. World Savers). The danger of brand proliferation is confusion in the minds of consumers about what each brand stands for.

Brand extension

Where a company has invested heavily in a brand so that it has many positive attributes in the minds of buyers, it may feel tempted to get as much as possible out of its valuable asset. Given the increasing costs of developing strong brands, many companies have attempted to extend their brand to new product ranges. The attraction is quite clear. Rather than having to start from scratch with a new product and a new name, the company can at least start with a name whose values buyers are familiar with. So if a manufacturer of chocolate has developed a brand that stands for good taste and consistency, those values will be immediately transferred to a new range of ice cream products that the company may consider adding to its range.

Of course, extending a brand to new products poses dangers as well as opportunities. If the extension goes too far into unrelated product areas, the core values of the brand may be undermined. Consider the case of BP, which introduced a line of dishwashing detergent to the private consumer market. How could consumers avoid the feeling that the detergent was oily? The line was subsequently withdrawn. Considerable research has been undertaken to assess the effects of brand extensions on consumers' perceptions of a brand (e.g. Grime et al. 2002).

Co-branding

Opportunities often arise for the owners of two quite different brands to work together jointly to develop a new product that carries the brand name of both partners, resulting in an otherwise unattainable gain to both. Co-branding is increasingly common in the food sector, where, for example, a branded manufacturer of meat products may develop a 'beef and ale pie' in which it co-brands the product with its own brand name and that of the beer brand that makes up one of the ingredients. The owner of the beer brand gets exposure and distribution through a new channel, while the pie brand owner adds to the distinctiveness and perceived value of its pies. As with any brand extension (see above), co-branding presents dangers where expectations of each brand are not met. A previously loyal customer of the beer brand used in the pie may have his faith in the brand reduced if the process of incorporating it into the pie leaves a nasty taste.

Protecting a brand

Once they have been created, brands can become very valuable assets to the companies that own them. Attempts to value brands usually try to estimate the price premium they command in their market, multiplied by estimated sales. A discounted cash flow calculation takes into account the value of earnings in future years. The enormous value of brands such as Coca Cola is a reflection of the significant price premium they can command and their enormous annual sales worldwide.

Like any asset of value, criminals will be tempted to appropriate the asset for themselves. If somebody else has developed a strong brand name, why not 'borrow' it to promote your own goods? The result is counterfeit goods, which carry all the superficial manifestations of brand identity, but may fail to deliver the performance that has come to be expected with the brand. Counterfeiting of goods with false brand names has been found in products as diverse as beverages, perfumes, watches, computer chips, and aircraft engine components. Sometimes consumers may be quite happy buying a low priced branded product knowing that it is a counterfeit copy—this is especially true of goods bought for conspicuous consumption, such as the fake Rolex watches that many tourists bring back from the Far East for just a few pounds. Research undertaken by CDR International, a brand protection consultant, suggested that the most desirable consumer demands for counterfeiting were Nike, Calvin Klein, Rolex, Adidas, and Levi Strauss. At other times buyers may be defrauded into thinking that they have bought the genuine brand, often with dangerous consequences where the integrity of the product has safety implications. There have been many cases of counterfeit drugs being sold cheaply, but having harmful effects on the consumer.

For the owner of a brand, counterfeit copies hit it in two ways. First, it loses sales to counterfeiters which it would probably have made itself. Second, and more importantly, buyers may come to mistrust the brand. How can they be sure that they are buying the genuine article? Firms often go to great lengths to stay one step ahead of counterfeiters, for example by regularly introducing new designs which are hard to copy.

Brand owners resort to the law to protect their assets. In the UK, the common law provides a general remedy against companies seeking to 'pass off' counterfeit products as though they were the real thing. 'Passing off' can include attempts to copy any of the distinctive brand characteristics discussed above. As an example, a bus operator was accused of passing off by painting its buses a similar colour to those of its main competitor and running on a similar route. It had been relying on public confusion to pass off its service as the one people had been expecting. Further protection is provided by legislation. The Trade Marks Act 1994, which implements the EU Trade Marks Harmonization Directive no. 89/104/EEC), provides protection for trademarks, which are defined as any sign that can be represented graphically which is capable of distinguishing goods or services of one undertaking from those of other undertakings (Trade Marks Act 1994, s. 1(1)). Where a company has a patent for a product, the Patents Act 1977 provides protection against unauthorized copying of the product specification during the currency of the patent.

The organization as a brand

The traditional role of a brand has been to differentiate a product from competing products and to create a liking of it by target customers. The process of branding has been increasingly applied to organizational image, too. This has been particularly important for services, where the intangibility of the product causes the credentials of the provider to be an important component of consumers' choices. The notion of an emotional relationship to a product has been extended to develop an emotional relationship between an organization and its customers.

Many service organizations have found the development of brands to be attractive where their service offer is highly complex and consumers find the offer mentally as well as physically intangible. In the UK the pensions industry has found it difficult to explain its products to an audience that is not receptive to technical details of a product, but nevertheless may consider a pension to be a vital provision for old age. Furthermore, the Financial Services Act 1986 limits the ability of companies to promote their pensions in creative ways. (For example, companies may quote only standard industry-wide expected rates of return.) This has led many companies to embark on comprehensive brand building programmes which say very little about the details of the products on offer, but a lot about the nature of the company offering them. The Prudential Assurance Company has built its brand image on the superior lifestyle that can result from dealing with the company, while Legal and General used the brand image of an umbrella as the symbol of a protective company.

Many companies have used their corporate image successfully to extend the range of products that they offer. Retailers such as Tesco and Sainsbury's have developed strong, trusted brands, associated with reliable products sold at good value prices, with a high standard of customer services. They have used this trusted brand reputation to extend their activities to banking services, insurance, and telephone services, among others. Customers may not be knowledgeable on these additional services, but by inference, if they trust Sainsbury's with weekly shopping, they will trust it with its banking services.

The development of global brands

With the volume of international trade growing at around four times the rate of world gross domestic product, companies are increasingly having to include exports as part of their marketing plan. It follows therefore that the process of branding should be considered in global terms. The world's top 20 global brands are shown in Figure 7.9. Economies of scale can be achieved by developing a global brand; for example visitors from overseas can automatically recognize a McDonald's restaurant, giving it an advantage over a local branded restaurant which starts with no overseas name recognition. There are many challenges for the development of brands that work in overseas markets as well as the domestic one. There is an argument that individuals' need for cultural identity is making it more difficult to justify the cost of developing a global brand (Williams 2002). This chapter has highlighted some of the problems that occur with an inappropriate choice of name.

◉ The changing role of branding

The philosophy and practices of branding have seen a number of developments in recent years. There is debate about whether these represent shifts in the underlying principles of branding, or merely a change in application.

Rank 2009	Brand	2009 Brand value ($ m)	Country of ownership
1	Coca-Cola	68,734	US
2	IBM	60,211	US
3	Microsoft	56,647	US
4	GE	47,777	US
5	Nokia	34,864	Finland
6	McDonald's	32,275	US
7	Google	31,980	US
8	Toyota	31,330	Japan
9	Intel	30,636	US
10	Disney	28,447	US
11	Hewlett-Packard	24,096	US
12	Mercedes-Benz	23,867	Germany
13	Gillette	22,841	US
14	Cisco	22,030	US
15	BMW	21,671	Germany
16	Louis Vuitton	21,120	France
17	Marlboro	19,010	US
18	Honda	17,803	Japan
19	Samsung	17,518	S. Korea
20	Apple	15,443	US

Figure 7.9 **The world's top 20 global brands. Note: the table was based on the asset value of global brands, defined as those that derived 20 per cent or more of sales from outside their home country.** The brand valuations draw upon publicly available information, assessed by Interbrand.
(*Source*: Business Week/Interbrand Top 100 Global Brands Scoreboard, 2009.)

As societies become more affluent, the emotional aspects of branding have tended to become more important than the functional elements. Characteristics such as purity, reliability, and durability may have traditionally added value to a brand, but these are increasingly enshrined in legislation and therefore are less capable of being used to differentiate one product from another. An example of the effects of legislation on brand loyalty can be observed in the taxi market by contrasting buyer behaviour in areas with strict licensing (e.g. London) with areas where a relatively unregulated market exists. In London, legislation has reduced the product to a commodity meeting strictly specified standards, whereas in the other towns customers are more likely to seek the reassurance of a branded operator. In western countries, consumers choice of beer brand is no longer dominated by questions about its purity (this is ensured by lots of food safety legislation, and government inspectors to enforce it), but by the emotional messages that the brand develops, and with which the buyer associates. A casual observation of nearly all advertising for beer will show very little mention of the beer itself, but a lot which is related to abstract lifestyle associations with its consumption.

Another issue affecting branding is the claim that consumers are becoming increasingly critical of the abstract messages for brands developed by big, faceless corporate organizations. In her book *No Logo*, Naomi Klein (2001) painted a bleak picture of a 'brandscape' in which public space is dominated by such unaccountable multinational organizations. To her, brands such as Nike, Shell, Walmart, Microsoft, and McDonald's had become metaphors for a global economic system gone awry and she made a call to arms to fight the dominance and abuses of multinationals. It has also been noted that individuals who are disillusioned with a brand are increasingly likely to use web-based social networking sites to challenge the authority of the brand (Hollenbeck and Zinkhan 2006).

Against this, proponents of branding have argued that the idea of a confident, educated consumer who despises big brands does not reflect reality. Some, such as Cova (1997) have argued that in an increasingly fragmented society, individuals need to belong to groups through which they acquire identity. Where once church and family provided an individual with their identity, today this role is more likely to be fulfilled by their attachments to brands. Some have spoken of tribal marketing, by which brands only acquire value if they have collective meaning to groups of people who adopt them and of a brandscape as an increasingly important type of community. In such communities, consumers feel emotionally linked to one another, either formally or informally through the brands that they consume (Ouwersloot and Odekerken-Schröder 2008). Members of a gym or up-market fashion retailer may feel this sense of linking, and increasingly the Internet has been used to develop online branded communities, such as YouTube and Bebo.com.

A significant development in most countries in recent years has been the emergence of strong retailers' brands, which have come to challenge manufacturers' brands. When Tesco sells large volumes of its own branded lager, some would say that this represents declining importance of brands—the customer is simply buying the cheapest alternative that is available in the supermarket. This essentially treats the product as a commodity which is evaluated solely on the basis of price and availability. An alternative view is that retailers have been very active in developing their own brands, which consumers have come to trust. The consumer may select the Tesco lager rather than the Carlsberg branded lager because they have come to trust Tesco for all the other products that they buy. The buyer may also come to have a favourable emotional attitude towards Tesco, which may be greater than the emotional attitude towards Carlsberg. Many retailers, such as Tesco, have also gone on to create distinctive sub-brands with their own product positioning (Tesco has developed a 'value' brand for the price conscious, and a 'Tesco finest' brand for more quality orientated buyers).

Finally, brands are not only aimed at customers, but also increasingly at employees. The brand values that appeal to customers should be the same as those which employees identify with, and there has been a lot of talk among labour intensive service organizations about delivering their 'brand promise' through employees (Knox and Freeman 2006). If employees don't believe in their employer's brand, why should customers?

Marketing and social responsibility

Can brands be socially divisive?

Some of the healthiest food products we could consume are inexpensive but are shunned because they are not supported by brand building activities, in contrast to possibly more harmful and expensive alternatives which have the power of branding behind them. Consider the following examples:

- The market for bottled water in the UK has increased markedly during the past couple of decades, helped by the development of strong brands including Perrier, Highland Spring, and Volvic. This is despite repeated analyses suggesting that filtered domestic tap water is purer and more beneficial than most bottled water, yet is a fraction of the cost. The water supply utility companies have not marketed the benefits of their water, partly held back by a regulatory system that prevents them raising prices for the water they supply. Meanwhile, bottled water suppliers have promoted their product, increasingly relying on 'lifestyle' associations to command ever-higher prices.

- Children are exposed to a vast amount of advertising for snack foods, and peer group pressure leads them to demand 'cool' brands of drinks and snacks. Meanwhile, fresh fruit—which is considered by nutritionists to be much more beneficial to children—is overlooked as it lacks strong brand building support. A fragmented industry made up of countless growers and importers and a generic range of products that cannot generally be protected by patent have resulted in very little investment being made available for brand building. Support is generally limited to national growers' associations promoting a national product, with little effort to develop lifestyle brands. Would children eat more apples and fewer crisps if apples were supported by a multi-million advertising campaign to portray them as a 'cool' brand?

- A comparison by *Which?* magazine suggested that retailers' own brand training shoes costing around £10 are just as hard wearing and beneficial to children's' feet as top brand shoes advertised using sports heroes, but costing over £60. Critics have accused branded sports shoes companies of exploiting the children's susceptibility to peer group pressure and their consequent desire to be seen in only the coolest brand of sports shoes.

Are brands a form of exploitation which creates social divisiveness? Critics of branding in particular, and the capitalist system in general, have argued that brands contribute towards a division in society between the 'haves' and 'have-nots', with ostentatious displays of brands creating a feeling of grievance among those who aspire for brands but cannot afford them. Brands may particularly appeal to less secure individuals as a means of establishing an identity for themselves, yet these are often the people who can least afford to pay for premium brands.

Would life be better without brands? Buying would certainly be a lot more difficult without the shorthand code of a brand which comes to stand for a whole bundle of functional and emotional benefits, and simplifying our choice processes. As far as the emotional aspects of lifestyle brands are concerned, haven't all societies had some means of differentiating individuals within the society? Maybe we don't have the tribal dresses that have been used in the past by individuals to give them identity, so are modern day marketers spot on when they talk about 'tribal marketing' by appealing to individuals' inherent desire to identify with a group?

⦿ Positioning the brand

Positioning strategy for a brand is a crucial part of developing a sustainable competitive advantage for the brand. Positioning puts a firm in a sub-segment of its chosen market, and so a firm that adopts a product positioning based on 'high reliability/high cost' will appeal to a sub-segment that has a desire for reliability and a willingness to pay for it.

For some marketers, positioning has been seen as essentially a communications issue, where the nature of the product is given and the objective is to manipulate consumers'

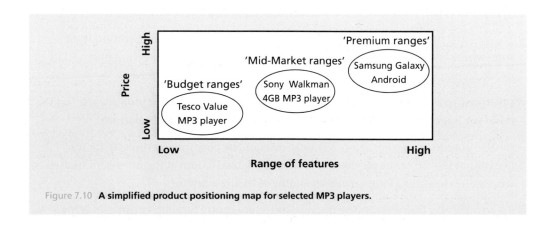

Figure 7.10 **A simplified product positioning map for selected MP3 players.**

perceptions of it. However, others have pointed out that positioning is more than merely advertising and promotion, involving the management of the whole marketing mix. Essentially, the mix must be managed in a way that is internally coherent and sustainable over the long term. A marketing mix positioning of high quality and low price may attract business from competitors in the short term, but the low prices may be insufficient to cover costs of delivering high quality, and therefore profits may be unsustainable over the long term.

A company must examine the strengths and weaknesses of its brands within their marketplace and the opportunities and threats that they face. From this, its brands take a position within their marketplace. A position can be defined by reference to a number of scales, such a price, quality, availability, durability, etc. Product features and price are two dimensions of positioning that are relevant to MP3 players. It is possible to draw a *position map* in which the positions of key players in a market are plotted in relation to these criteria. A position map plotting the positions of selected MP3 players in respect of their price and features is shown in Figure 7.10. Both scales run from high to low, with price being a general indication of price levels charged relative to competitors and features being a subjective evaluation of the functional and emotional benefits that users typically obtain from each MP3 player. The position map shows that most MP3 players lie on a diagonal line between the high features/high price (£250) position adopted by the iPod Touch and the low price/low features position adopted by the Tesco Value MP3 player which in 2011 was selling for just £18. Points along this diagonal represent feasible positioning strategies for car manufacturers. A strategy in the upper left quadrant (high price/low quality) can be described as a 'cowboy' strategy and generally is not sustainable. A position in the lower right area of the map (high quality/low price) may indicate that an organization is 'over delivering' by failing to achieve a sufficiently high price to match the level of quality that it is providing. Of course, this two-dimensional analysis of the MP3 player market is very simplistic, and buyers make judgements based on a variety of criteria. Low levels of features may be tolerated at a high price, for example if a player carries a strong, aspirational brand name.

The example of MP3 players used two very simplistic positioning criteria. Wind (1982, 79–81) has suggested six generic scales along which all products can be positioned. These are examined below by reference to the positioning opportunities of a leisure centre.

◉ Positioning by benefits or needs satisfied: The leisure centre could position itself somewhere between meeting pure physical recreation needs and meeting pure social needs. In practice, positioning may accommodate the two sets of needs.

◉ Positioning by specific product features: The leisure centre could promote the fact that it has the largest swimming pool in the area, or the most advanced solarium.

◉ Positioning by usage occasions: The centre could be positioned primarily for the occasional visitor, or the service offer could be adapted to aim at the more serious user who wishes to enter a long-term programme of leisure activities.

◉ Positioning by user categories: Should the leisure centre be aimed primarily at individual users, or institutional users such as sports clubs and schools?

⊙ **Positioning against another product:** The leisure centre could promote the fact that it has more facilities than its neighbouring competition.

⊙ **Positioning by product class:** Management could position the centre as an educational facility rather than a centre of leisure, thereby positioning it in a different product class.

Of all the position possibilities open to a company, which position should it adopt? Selecting a product position involves three basic steps (illustrated in Figure 7.11).

1. **Undertake a marketing audit to analyse the position opportunities relative to the company's strengths:** A SWOT analysis should be undertaken to assess the opportunities and threats in a marketplace and the strengths and weaknesses of the company in meeting opportunities as they arise. An important consideration is often the position that customers currently perceive a company as occupying. If a company is perceived as being 'down-market', this may pose a major weakness in exploiting opportunities arising for more 'up-market' products. An organization that is already established in a particular product position will normally have the advantage of customer familiarity to support any new product launch. A car manufacturer such as Mercedes Benz, which has positioned itself as a high quality/high price producer, can use this as a strength to persuade customers to pay relatively high prices for a new product range, in this case a premium small compact car. Sometimes a weakness can be turned into a strength for positioning purposes; for example the Avis car rental chain has stressed that, by being the number two operator, it has to try harder.

   It often happens that opportunities are greatest in budget range, low-quality, low-price positions. If a company has established a position as a premium position supplier, should it seek to exploit a lower market position when the opportunity arises? It must avoid tarnishing its established brand values by association with a lower quality product. One solution is to adopt a separate identity for a new product which assumes a different position. In this way, the Volkswagen car group offers different price/quality positions with its Volkswagen, Audi, and Skoda brands.

2. **Evaluate the position possibilities and select the most appropriate:** In undertaking a SWOT analysis, a number of potential positions may have been identified, but many may have to be discarded if they result in uneconomically small market segments, or are too costly to develop. Other positions may be rejected as being inconsistent with an organization's image. Selection from the remaining possibilities should be on the basis of the organization's greatest differential advantage in areas that are most valued by target customers. When it entered the Indonesian market, the UK retailer Marks & Spencer realized that its UK brand positioning of everyday clothes at good value prices would be unsustainable against low-cost local competition. It therefore adopted a much more exclusive position, with smaller shops, limited product ranges, and relatively high prices.

3. **Use the marketing mix to develop and communicate a position:** Organizations must develop programmes to implement and promote the position they have adopted. If a

257

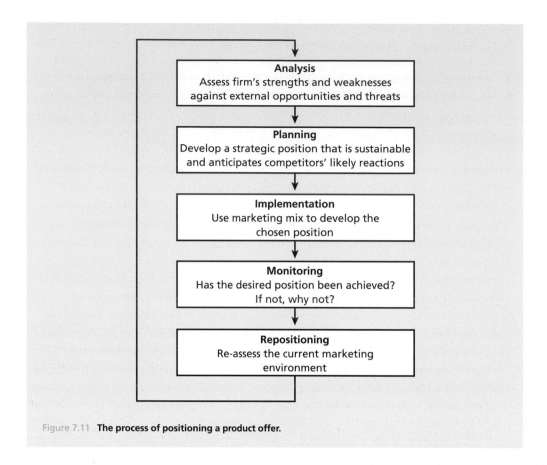

Figure 7.11 **The process of positioning a product offer.**

car manufacturer seeks to adopt a position as a supplier of premium quality cars at premium prices, it must have in hand production facilities for ensuring consistently high quality. It must also effectively communicate this quality to potential customers in order to justify their paying premium prices.

Repositioning

Markets are dynamic, and what was once an appropriate position for a brand may eventually cease to be so. Repositioning could become necessary for a number of reasons.

⦿ The original positioning may have been based on an overestimation of a brand's competitive advantage or of the size of the sub-segment to which the positioning was intended to appeal.

⦿ The nature of customer demand may have changed, for example in respect of preferences for high quality rather than low price. It has, for example, been suggested that UK customers' attitudes towards package holidays have changed in recent years, away from an emphasis on low price towards greater emphasis on high quality standards. Many tour operators accordingly repositioned their offering to provide higher standards at higher prices.

⦿ Companies often try to build upon their growing strengths to reposition their brands towards meeting the needs of more profitable high-value sub-segments. In many sectors, brands have started life as simple, no-frills, low-price operations, subsequently gaining a favourable image which they use to 'trade up' to relatively high quality/high price positions. This phenomenon is well established in the field of retailing and has become known as the 'wheel of retailing'. This contends that retail businesses start life as cut-price, low-cost, narrow-margin operations which subsequently 'trade up' with improvements in display, more prestigious premises, increased advertising, delivery, and the provision of many other customer services which serve to drive up expenses, prices, and margins. Eventually retailers mature as high-cost, conservative, and 'top-heavy' institutions with a sales policy based on quality goods and services rather than price appeal. This in turn opens the way for the next generation of low-cost innovatory retailers to find a position vacated by maturing firms.

⦿ The marketing mix

The marketing mix has already been mentioned a number of times in this book. In the following chapters we will look in detail at how companies go about using the marketing mix in order to build brands that satisfy consumers' needs and at the same time allow the company to make a sustainable level of profits.

So what exactly is the marketing mix? You may recall from Chapter 1 that the marketing mix is not a scientific theory, but merely a conceptual framework that identifies the principal decisions marketing managers make in configuring their offerings to suit customers' needs. The tools play a pivotal role in developing the sustainable competitive advantage which has been discussed in this chapter. The tools of the marketing mix can be used both to develop long-term strategies and short-term tactical programmes.

There has been a lot of debate in identifying the list of marketing mix elements. The traditional marketing mix has comprised the four elements of product, price, promotion, and place. A number of people have additionally suggested adding people, process, and physical evidence decisions, which are very important for services businesses. There is overlap between each of these headings, and their precise definition is not particularly important. What matters is that marketing managers can identify the actions they can take that will produce a favourable response from customers. The marketing mix has merely become a convenient framework for analysing these decisions. Some would go further and argue that the concept of a marketing mix is harmful because it encourages managers to take a narrow and compartmentalized approach to each of the mix elements. By this argument, customers buy the whole product offer and are not concerned about how decisions relating to individual components are arrived at—just so long as the total product offer is coherent and creates value in their eyes. Many critics of the marketing mix see the move towards relationship marketing (Chapter 4) as a move towards a focus on customers' holistic values and away from a narrower obsession with management of a producer-defined marketing mix.

The following chapters have been arranged in accordance with traditional definitions of the marketing mix elements, but it must never be forgotten that each element is closely related to all other elements.

◉ Chapter summary and key linkages to other chapters

Developing a sustainable competitive advantage involves a sound understanding of a firm's strengths and weaknesses relative to the opportunities and threats in its marketing environment. Research into buyer behaviour and appropriate targeting, issues discussed in Chapters 4, 5, and 6, provides input to the development of a distinctive marketing mix, discussed in the following chapters. A crucial link between the needs of customers and the capabilities of a firm is the development of a brand. The process of branding allows a company to develop a distinctive identity and position for itself and its products, so as to differentiate its products from those of competitors. By doing this, a company can avoid the worse excesses of price competition. We will look in more detail at how a company uses the marketing mix to develop a distinctive brand in the following chapters.

✎ KEY PRINCIPLES OF MARKETING

- An overriding aim of marketing is to develop a sustainable competitive advantage for an organization.

- Competitors for a firm's products can be direct or indirect. Indirect forms of competition are more difficult to identify.

- A brand is a means of identifying one company and its products from otherwise similar products supplied by other companies.

- The functional role of a brand should be distinguished from its emotional role.

- Brands are created through the management of the marketing mix. The marketing mix is merely a convenient listing of interrelated decisions to be taken by managers.

CASE STUDY

Fairy's brand bubble never seems to burst

It is often said that somebody who has been trained in marketing at Procter & Gamble can go on to successfully market anything. The markets in which Procter & Gamble operates—mainly low value consumer goods, such as household detergents—are among the most fiercely competitive, and building successful brands is key to long-term profitability. Differentiating one product from another in the minds of consumers can be extremely difficult, with one packet of detergent looking very much like another, and in many cases also performing similarly. An analysis of one of the company's flagship brands—Fairy Liquid—illustrates how the company has carefully nurtured the brand, adapting it to changes in consumers' preferences, and maintaining consistent standards while exploiting new market opportunities.

Fairy was rated as Britain's number one cleaning brand by *Marketing* magazine and in 2010 accounted for 3 per cent market share of the UK washing-up liquid category by value (Bainbridge 2011). The brand has been a regular household feature since the name first appeared in 1898 on a bar of soap. Procter & Gamble first launched Fairy Liquid in the UK market in 1960. At that time, the market for washing-up products was still in its infancy, with most consumers using solid soaps, and only 17 per cent of households using liquid soap. As market leader, Procter & Gamble stood to gain most from a change in consumers' habits. Its first task was therefore to educate the public of the benefits of using washing-up liquid. The launch of Fairy involved distributing 15 million trial bottles to about 85 per cent of households in the UK.

Creating early awareness and trial of the product led to Fairy gaining a market share of 27 per cent by 1969. Strong promotional support was, and remains, a key to the brand's success. Since its launch, promotional messages have focused consistently on the mildness of the product, its long-lasting suds, and a proud positioning as a slightly more expensive product which is better value and worth paying the extra for. Mother and child images have been used extensively in advertising. This helps to create brand values of a soft, caring, homely image. A discussion thread on the Bebo website featured many reminiscences from adults who associated the brand with happy days of their childhood. Fairy has a trusted heritage which has been passed down from generation to generation. However, messages have been adapted around the core theme in response to changing attitudes; for example a commercial in 1994 for the first time used a father instead of a mother at the kitchen sink. Various celebrities have been used to endorse the brand's values, including a lengthy spell of endorsement by the actress Nanette Newman. The consistency of the brand's message has been reinforced with a promotional jingle that has been modified only slightly since it was first introduced in 1960.

During the first twenty years of the brand's life, product innovation had been relatively modest. However, since then an increasingly competitive market and more discerning customers have forced the company to innovate in order to maintain and strengthen its market share. With the emergence of many 'me-too' competitors from supermarkets, Fairy needed to offer additional unique advantages to supplement its long-lasting suds.

In 1984/5 the company introduced a lemon variant of Fairy and its total market share increased to 32 per cent. By 1987 the market share had increased to 34 per cent, with the newly introduced lemon variant accounting for one-third of sales. In 1988 a new formulation was launched, offering '15 per cent extra mileage', as well as more effective grease eradication.

In 1992 the original Fairy Liquid was replaced with Fairy Excel, which claimed to be '50 per cent better at dealing with grease'. This helped to increase the market share to 50 per cent. In the following year a concentrated version of Fairy Excel Plus was launched, with the slogan 'The power of four for the price of one'. The company launched this low-bulk, high-concentration product with one eye to retailers, who were tiring of filling their valuable shelf space with more and more variants of basically low-value products. Excel Plus offered supermarkets more cost-effective and profitable use of their shelf space.

Increased ownership of domestic dish washing machines posed a threat and also an opportunity to Fairy. The threat came from a relative decline in sales of liquids used for hand washing of dishes. The opportunity arose from increased demand for dishwasher cleaning fluid and the Fairy brand was extended to dishwashing detergents. In 2006 Procter & Gamble introduced Fairy Active Bursts for dishwashers.

During the lifetime of Fairy, the market for detergents in different European countries has gradually converged. As a result, Excel Plus was launched simultaneously in the UK, Belgium, Denmark, Finland, Germany, Holland, Ireland, and Sweden.

Innovation and reliability have been at the heart of Fairy's branding strategy, in a market which has been fiercely contested by other manufacturers' brands, and increasingly by supermarkets' own label brands. In what other ways could Fairy evolve to retain its brand leadership? Preferences for new scents of detergent are continually emerging and provide an opportunity for innovation. Following a series of food safety scares, some observers of the market have pointed to a potential market for anti-bacterial food washes which would satisfy consumers' increasing concern over residues on the surface of fruit and vegetables.

Based on Procter & Gamble website (www.pg.com), accessed 25/4/08; British Brands Group, case study—Fairy Liquid (http://www.britishbrandsgroup.org.uk/brands/case-studies/brands); Talking Retail, 'Fairy adds two new dishwashing products' (http://www.talkingretail.com/products/9181/Fairy-adds-two-new-dishwash-pr.ehtml). Accessed 25 April 2008

Case study review questions

1. How would you explain the success of the Fairy brand?

2. How do you think Procter & Gamble has been able to increase its market share at a time when competition from supermarkets' own-label brands has intensified?

3. To what extent can the principles and practices of brand management used for Fairy Liquid be applied to other goods and services, such as televisions and package holidays?

CHAPTER REVIEW QUESTIONS

1. In the context of a sustainable competitive advantage, what is meant by customer value? How can a company ensure that it continues to deliver value?

2. With increasing levels of consumer protection legislation designed to protect buyers from faulty products and misleading advertising claims, do we still need brands? How can brands adapt to increasing levels of legislation?

3. Using examples, discuss the problems that are likely to result from a firm seeking to reposition its product offer.

ACTIVITIES

1. Consider the case of a restaurant in your local town. Identify the restaurant's direct and indirect competitors. Think far and wide about what may constitute an indirect competitor and justify your reasoning.

2. Look through a Sunday newspaper magazine supplement and examine a selection of adverts. What brand message is communicated by these adverts? Identify the functional and emotional elements of the firms' branding strategy.

3. Examine the branding strategy used by banks or financial services organizations with which you are familiar. Critically examine the message that is communicated by the brand. Which market segment is a brand particularly addressing? Are there any important segments that may be alienated by the brand message? To what extent has the service provider used brands and sub-brands to segment its market?

REFERENCES

Allison, R. and Uhl, K. (1964) 'Influence of Beer Brand Identification on Taste Perception'. *Journal of Marketing Research*, 1 (3), 36–9.

Bainbridge, J. (2011) 'Sector Insight, Dishwashing Detergents'. *Marketing*, 1 April 2011.

Berthon, P., Holbrook, M.B., and Hulbert, J.M. (2003) 'Understanding and Managing the Brand Space'. *MIT Sloan Management Review*, 44 (2), 49–55.

Branthwaite, A. and Cooper, P. (1981), 'Analgesic Effects of Branding in Treatment of Headaches'. *British Medical Journal*, 282 (16 May), 1576–8.

Competition Commission (2008) *The Supply of Groceries in the UK Market Investigation*, 30 April 2008 (online). Available at: http://www.competition-commission.org.uk/rep_pub/reports/2008/538grocery.htm

Cova, B. (1997) 'Community and Consumption—Towards a Definition of the "linking value" of product or services'. *European Journal of Marketing*, 31 (3/4), 297–316.

Croft, M. (2008) 'Consumers in control'. *Marketing Week*, 31 (14), 29–30.

De Chernatony, L. (2006) *From Brand Vision to Brand Evaluation*. Oxford: Butterworth-Heinemann.

De Chernatony, L. and McDonald, M. (2003) *Creating Powerful Brands*, 3rd edition. Oxford: Butterworth-Heinemann.

De Chernatony, L. and McWilliam, G. (1990) 'Appreciating Brands as Assets through Using a Two-Dimensional Model'. *International Journal of Advertising*, 9 (2), 111–19.

Gardner, B. and Levy, S. (1955) 'The Product and the Brand'. *Harvard Business Review*, 33 (Mar/Apr.), 33–9.

Grime, I., Diamantopoulos, A., and Smith, G. (2002) 'Consumer Evaluations of Extensions and their Effects on the Core Brand: Key Issues and Research Propositions'. *European Journal of Marketing*, 36, 1415–28.

Hitwise (2008) 'The impact of social networking in the UK', available at: www.
bergenmediaby.no/admin/ressurser/QCetFnO$_11_Social_Networking_Report_2008.pdf
(accessed 2 April 2009).

Hollenbeck, C.R. and Zinkhan, G.M. (2006) 'Consumer Activism on the Internet: the Role of
Anti-brand Communities'. *Advances in Consumer Research*, 33 (1), 479–85.

Jacques, E. (2002) 'The Traps and Pitfalls of Rip-Off Marketing'. *Daily Telegraph*, 9 May, 66.

Klein, N. (2001) *No Logo*. London: Flamingo.

Knox, S. and Freeman, C. (2006) 'Measuring and Managing Employer Brand Image in the
Service Industry'. *Journal of Marketing Management*, 22 (7), 695–716.

Levitt, T. (1960) 'Marketing Myopia'. *Harvard Business Review*, Sept–Oct, 41–52.

Microsoft Digital Advertising Solutions (2007) 'Word of the Web Guidelines for Advertisers:
Understanding Trends and Monetising Social Networks', available at: http://advertising.
microsoft.com/uk/WWDocs/User/en-uk/Advertise/Partner per cent20Properties/Piczo/
Word per cent20of per cent20the per cent20Web per cent20Social per cent20Networking
per cent20Report per cent20Ad5.pdf (accessed 10 February 2009).

Miller, G. (2009) 'Biggest Brand Movers on the Vitrue Social Media Index for January 2009',
Vitrue, available at: http://vitrue.com/blog/2009/02/10/biggest-brand-movers-on-the-
vitrue-social-media-index-for-january-2009/ (accessed 20 May 2009).

Munson, J.M. and Spivey, W.A. (1981) 'Products and Brand Users: Stereotypes among Social
Classes'. In K. Munroe (ed.) *Advances in Consumer Research*. Mich., CAR: Ann Arbor.

Ouwersloot, H. and Odekerken-Schröder, G. (2008) 'Who's Who in Brand Communities—
and why?' *European Journal of Marketing*, 42 (5/6), 571–85.

Peters, T.J. and Waterman, R.H. (1982) *In Search of Excellence: Lessons from America's Best
Run Companies*. New York: Harper & Row.

Porter, M.E. (1980) *Competitive Strategy: Techniques for Analysing Industries and
Competitors*. New York: Free Press.

Sherry, J.F. (1998) 'The Soul of the Company Store: Nike Town Chicago and the Emplaced
Brandscape'. In Sherry, J.F. Jr (ed.), *Servicescapes: The Concept of Place in Contemporary
Markets*, Lincolnwood, IL: NTC Business Books.

Universal Maccann International (2008) 'Power to the People—Social Media Tracker Wave
3', available at: www.slideshare.net/mickstravellin/universal-mccann-international-
social-media-research-wave-3 (accessed 20 May 2009), 33, 470–85.

Williams, L. (2002) 'Pursuit of Holy Grail Comes with Global Warning: the Jury is Out on
Whether the Cost of Creating a World Brand is Worth it'. *Daily Telegraph* (London), 14
November, 6.

Wind, Y.J. (1982) *Product Policy: Concepts, Methods and Strategy*. Reading: Addison-Wesley.

✎ SUGGESTED FURTHER READING

The following provide insights into competitor analysis:

Aaker, D. (2010) *Building Strong Brands*. New York: Simon & Schuster.

Brakus, J.J., Schmitt, B.H., and Zarantonello, L. (2009) 'Brand Experience: What is it? How is it Measured? Does it Affect Loyalty?' *Journal of Marketing*, 73, 52–68.

D'Aveni, R.A. (2007) 'Mapping Your Competitive Position'. *Harvard Business Review*, November.

de Chernatony, L. (2010) *From Brand Vision to Brand Evaluation*, 3rd edition. Oxford: Elsevier.

Hooley, G., Saunders, J., and Piercy, N.F. (2011) *Marketing Strategy and Competitive Positioning*, 5th edition. London: FT Prentice Hall.

Kapferer, J.-N. (2008) *The New Strategic Brand Management: Creating and Sustaining Brand Equity Long Term.* London: Kogan Page.

Porter, M.E. (2004) *Competitive Advantage*. New York: Free Press.

 ONLINE RESOURCE CENTRE

Visit the Online Resource Centre for resources that are relevant to this chapter, including a flashcard glossary, web links, multiple choice questions, and additional case studies:

 www.oxfordtextbooks.co.uk/orc/palmer3e/

KEY TERMS

- Brand extension
- Brand family
- Brand personality
- Brands
- Co-branding
- Commodity
- Counterfeiting
- Differentiation
- Direct competitors
- Five forces model

- Global brands
- Indirect competitors
- Patent
- Positioning
- Repositioning
- Trademark
- Tribal marketing
- Visual identity

DEVELOPING THE PRODUCT

CHAPTER OBJECTIVES

The product is at the heart of a company's marketing mix planning. Customers buy a firm's products in order to satisfy their needs as cost effectively as possible. This chapter begins by discussing the nature of the product offer. Products comprise complex bundles of attributes which must be translated into valuable benefits for customers. Companies typically offer a range of products, each of which can be expected to go through some form of life-cycle.

Product mix planning is discussed in the context of the product life-cycle. This chapter explores the methods used by companies to keep their product ranges up to date. Innovation is an important differentiating factor for many firms, and this chapter explores methods by which innovative products can be developed, tested, and brought to market. When products approach the end of their life-cycle, it is important that they are deleted in a rational and cost-effective manner.

● What do we mean by a product?

Products are the focal point through which companies seek to satisfy customers' needs. It must be remembered that people do not buy products as an end in themselves. Products are only bought for the benefits they provide. In other words, a product is of value to someone only as long as it is perceived as satisfying some need.

Most people, when they consider the marketing of products, tend to think of fast moving consumer goods such as soap powder or chocolate bars. In fact, the term 'product' can mean many things. In this chapter a 'product' is any tangible or intangible item that satisfies a need. A product can be any of the following:

- a material good

- an intangible service

- a combination of the above

- a location

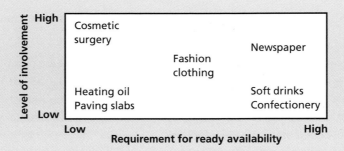

Figure 8.1 **A schematic classification of products based on buyers' levels of involvement and desired levels of access to the product, showing examples of product positions.**

◉ a person

◉ an idea

Most products that we buy are actually a combination of two or more of the above.

It is useful to begin this chapter by trying to classify products in a way which reflects differences in the way they are marketed. Within the different categories of products that are described below, some broad similarities in marketing requirements can be identified. Figure 8.1 attempts to classify products according to two important dimensions:

1. The level of involvement required on the part of the purchaser (e.g. the purchase of sugar calls for only very low levels of emotional involvement by the buyer, whereas in the case of fashion clothing involvement may be very high).

2. The level of accessibility to the product that is typically required by purchasers (e.g. a buyer will expect a can of soft drink to be available immediately and without having to travel to get it, whereas she would be prepared to travel further, and possibly wait, to purchase some specialist hi-fi equipment).

These are just two dimensions that contribute towards the design of an appropriate marketing mix. Others could include buyers' price sensitivity, brand loyalty, frequency of purchase, etc. The idea of placing products somewhere on a position map is introduced at this stage to emphasize an important reason for categorizing products in the first place: to explore whether marketers of one product can learn from the marketing of another product which may at first appear to be quite different, but is really quite similar in terms of the needs that it satisfies.

Tangible goods

Tangible goods can be classified under two major headings: consumer goods, and business-to-business goods. (The latter are also often referred to as industrial goods.)

Consumer goods

Consumer goods are purchased to satisfy individual or household needs. They can be classified as follows:

- **Convenience goods:** These items tend to be relatively cheap and are purchased on a regular basis—tea, coffee, toothpaste, etc. They are often referred to as fast moving consumer goods (FMCGs). The purchase of this type of product is likely to involve very little decision-making effort by the buyer, and in many cases an individual will tend to purchase a particular brand on a regular basis.

  Within the broad category of convenience goods, products as diverse as ice cream and toothpaste may at first appear to have very little in common; but in fact the marketing of them can be quite similar. Convenience goods are generally sold through many retail outlets so that buyers have easy access to the product. There is therefore a tendency to spend large amounts on advertising and on sales promotions. The packaging aspect of the marketing mix is also likely to be important, with the package acting as promotional tool in its own right. A company must invest in an extensive network of distributors, so that its product is easily available to large numbers of people. These items tend to be cheaply priced with the aim of selling high volumes at low margins.

- **Shopping goods:** Consumers generally put a lot more effort into choosing 'shopping' goods. Their bases for evaluation may be much wider than those used for FMCGs, and may typically include price, credit facilities, guarantees, after-sales service, etc. Examples of shopping goods: include dishwashers and freezers (which are examples of what are known as 'white goods'), mobile phones, and cameras.

  These products are distributed through fewer retail outlets and therefore there is likely to be a higher margin for the retailer. Customers are usually more willing to travel to an outlet to find a product, rather than expecting it to be available on their doorstep. Large amounts of money may be spent on advertising these goods and developing strong brands, and the amount of effort put into personal selling tends to be greater than for FMCGs.

- **Speciality goods:** For these products, consumers may spend a great deal of effort in the decision-making process. Speciality goods have one or more unique characteristics and are sold in relatively few outlets. A quality image is usually communicated as a result. Designer clothing would be an example of a speciality good. Such goods are bought infrequently, and tend to be expensive. Buyers may go to considerable effort to find the product of their choice.

- **Unsought goods:** Some goods initially may be considered by an individual not to be necessary, but they are nevertheless sold aggressively on the market. Many home owners may not be aware of, or concerned about, limescale damage to their dishwasher, and may therefore not seek out products which may reduce such damage. Consumers may only purchase these products if they are sold aggressively.

Business-to-business goods

These are purchased for use in a firm's production processes or to make other goods. They are often bought by a large decision-making unit in which organizational as well as individuals' needs have to be satisfied (see Chapter 4).

Business-to-business goods can be divided into the following types:

- **Raw materials:** These are basic materials that are needed as inputs to the early stages of production of a product or its components, for example iron ore, chemicals, etc. They are often purchased in bulk and sold as a commodity, with little attempt at product differentiation which would justify a price premium.

- **Major equipment:** This category includes large machines and tools used in production processes. They tend to be expensive and are expected to last a number of years. The decision to purchase this type of equipment tends to be made at a high level in an organization, and the purchase process can take a long time and involve a number of people. There is a need to build important relationships between buyers and sellers in this process, as it is likely to involve not only the agreement to purchase the equipment but also agreement on financing, maintenance contracts, guarantees, future purchases, etc.

- **Support equipment:** This includes goods that are used in the production process or allied activities but are separate from the final 'product' itself. Examples of support equipment include computer software, tools, etc. These goods are generally cheaper than major equipment and the purchase process is less involved.

- **Component parts:** When put together, component parts produce a finished good. Buyers purchase such items according to their own requirements for quality and delivery time so that they can ensure that their own end product can be produced effectively and efficiently. Just-in-time delivery of component parts has become an important element of the total product offer.

- **Consumable supplies:** These goods help in the production process and do not become part of the product; for example lubricating oil is vital to many production processes but does not become incorporated into the product. These items are typically purchased routinely by organizations with very little search effort.

Intangible services

Services can be described as 'products', although some people still find it amusing that bank accounts, package holidays, and even pop stars can be described as products. Although the term 'product' is traditionally associated with tangible goods, it can be more correctly defined as anything of value that a company offers to its customers. This value can take tangible or intangible forms.

There has been a big increase in recent years in service industries, which do not offer physical goods for sale but instead offer intangible benefits to buyers. A car mechanic offers expertise in maintaining vehicles; a decorator or plumber sells his service. It is essentially their skills in performing a service process that are being offered for sale, rather than any physical good. At other times, the service is essentially about paying for use of an asset, such as a rental car or car parking space. In many western economies, services now account for around three-quarters of gross domestic product.

The marketing of services can be quite different from the marketing of goods, although in practice most products are a combination of a good and a service. (For example, a meal in a restaurant combines the tangible elements of the food with the intangible service that is provided.) The distinguishing characteristics of services are described below:

⊙ Intangibility: Services cannot be seen, tasted, or touched. This means that it is very difficult for a customer to examine a service in advance. In fact, most material goods have some intangible service aspects to them, and likewise most services have at least some physical elements. Indeed, it is likely to be a question of degree of intangibility that will help in the identification of whether a product is a service.

⊙ Inseparability: The provision of a service normally requires the involvement of both customer and service provider simultaneously. Production and consumption cannot be separated in the way that manufacturing companies are able to mass-produce their goods in a central factory and transport them to customers for consumption.

⊙ Variability: As a result of inseparability, each service tends to be unique, and the standard of service delivery can vary from one occasion to the next. A consequence of this is that service quality is difficult to standardize and to guarantee. The best that can be achieved are minimum standards (e.g. answering the telephone after a stated number of rings) or standards relating to the physical aspects of the service (such as the percentage of time that a bank ATM machine is available for use).

⊙ Perishability: Services cannot be inventoried like material goods. If a service is not sold at the time it is produced, for example an empty airline seat after a plane has departed, then the service offer disappears for ever. This has important implications for service providers as they cannot store up services when demand is low in order to satisfy demand when it increases.

In much the same way as for goods, services can be further broken down into categories, although there tend to be fewer commonly used shorthand classification titles, such as FMCGs and 'white goods'. However, some important bases for classifying services are:

⊙ Consumer services—these are used up by the final consumer and no further economic benefit arises (e.g. a meal in a restaurant, a visit to the cinema).

⊙ Business-to-business services—these are bought by businesses in order to add value to their own production processes (e.g. the services of a commercial bank or courier delivery service).

⊙ People-based v. equipment-based services—the nature of interaction between a company and its customers tends to be different depending on whether the service is primarily provided by machines (e.g. a telephone service) or people (e.g. many personal health services).

- Knowledge-based services—some services essentially comprise the exchange of specialized knowledge, rather than the exchange of goods or undertaking of a service process (e.g. consultants may be engaged primarily for their knowledge).

The debate about the factors that distinguish or unite goods and services was crystallized recently in an article by Vargo and Lusch that talked about a new 'service dominant logic' of marketing (Vargo and Lusch 2008). They argued that marketing was originally built on a goods-centred, manufacturing-based model of economic exchange developed during the Industrial Revolution. Services were then added to these frameworks, but in seeking to broaden its scope to include services, marketing was constrained by the language and models of manufactured goods. Vargo and Lusch have turned this logic around, by arguing that everything we buy is essentially service-based, and goods play a secondary, facilitating role in any product offer. Services provide *value in use* for a tangible product which might otherwise be of little value to the consumer. Think of a bottle of beverage that you have bought and all of the services that were essential to create value in use at a time and place where you need it. Without the services of intermediaries and transport companies, the beverage would still be in the manufacturer's factory and of no value to you.

Ideas

Ideas can also be considered as 'products'. Political parties have developed marketing strategies to promote their own particular policies to the electorate, as have groups that are

---

MARKETING in ACTION

Service dominant logic?

To some people, the services sector may be seen as economically quite inferior to the manufacturing sector, conjuring up images of fast food, restaurants, and hairdressers. But services have in recent years been seen by many as the driving force of the economy rather than simply an 'add on' to traditional manufacturing sectors. The emerging theory of 'service dominant logic' holds that raw materials and manufactured goods have no value without services which create 'value in use' (Vargo and Lusch 2008). Think about trees which have just been felled in the forest to provide timber. Without transport services to move them to customers; intermediaries to handle and process them; and possibly banks to finance stock, the timber would have no value. In many markets, suppliers begin with designing the service level, then developing the physical product offer comes second. Within the manufacturing sector, many companies now compete on service, for example office equipment is often sold with the benefit of financing schemes, delivery, installation, maintenance contracts, and warranties. These may be an important point of differentiation in markets where product design features are fairly standard. Inevitably, when a new idea such as 'service dominant logic' comes along, there are critics who argue about the validity of the new idea. Services can certainly be seen to be driving many sales of manufactured goods, but if the product itself is not well designed, would the service offer make up for this? The photocopying machine may come with a very good maintenance and breakdown repair service, but wouldn't it be better to design a machine that didn't break down in the first place?

attempting to market particular issues, such as the environment, equal opportunities, etc. The key feature of these types of product is that they are intangible and have many similar characteristics to services. However, where an idea is the focus of marketing, it can be unclear just who the 'customer' is, and it can be difficult to conceptualize the exchange that takes place between the 'buyer' and the 'seller' of the idea.

Locations and people

The term 'product' can also be used to denote places (e.g. holiday resorts) and people (e.g. footballers, rock stars). These involve both tangible and intangible elements, and therefore the marketing mix should be configured accordingly.

◉ Analysis of the product offer

Products can be complex entities, and it is useful to identify a number of levels of the product offer. Three levels will be identified here (see Figure 8.2):

1. **The core level:** The best way to think of this is to consider an item and identify the key benefit from its ownership. For example, the core benefit of buying food is to overcome hunger, and the core benefit of undertaking a marketing course is personal development. Every product has a core element, and it is the secondary and augmented elements that put 'flesh on the bones' and give a product an individual identity.

2. **The secondary level:** The secondary level of a product includes those physical features that the product actually possesses. Such elements include colour, design, shape, packaging, size, etc. A television, for example, may have entertainment as a core benefit but the secondary elements would include such features as the shape of the box, the type of screen, the size of screen, the quality of sound, the colour of the unit, whether there is a stand, etc.

3. **The augmented level:** It is this that differentiates a particular product from its competitors. The augmented level of a product tends to include intangible features such as pre-sales and after-sales service, guarantees, credit facilities, brand name, etc.

This is a fairly traditional three-level analysis, which may be appropriate to tangible goods, but it has less value in the analysis of intangible services. For services, the augmented level may be the key distinguishing feature of the service. It is more appropriate, therefore, to talk about two levels of the product offer, with a core level representing the primary benefit and a secondary level representing the distinguishing characteristics of the service. Remember also the argument of Vargo and Lusch who see services as the focal point of all marketing activity. By their argument, it is goods which become the differentiator to a service, rather than services being one of the elements of the secondary offer which differentiates one good from another.

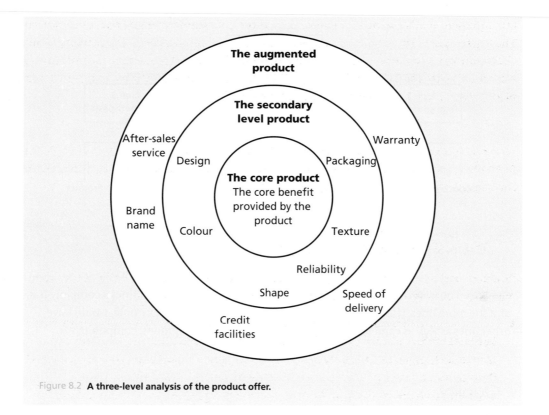

Figure 8.2 **A three-level analysis of the product offer.**

⊙ The product mix

The product mix comprises the complete range of products that a company offers to the market. A number of elements of a typical product portfolio can be identified and the following terms are commonly used (see Figure 8.3).

⊙ Product item: This is the individual product, with its core, secondary, and augmented elements (e.g. a Fuji A340 camera).

⊙ Product line: This is a collection of product items that are related by the type of raw materials used, similar technology used, or merely as a common-sense grouping (e.g. a line in digital cameras). A truly effective product line should be customer focused and therefore should link to the range of needs of the particular segment/s targeted by the firm (e.g. the need for recording memories).

⊙ Product mix: This is the total range of products that the company has on offer to customers and within this product mix there is what is known as the depth and the width of the product. The *depth* of the product mix refers to the number of products offered within a product line. The more products within a line, the greater the depth of the product mix. For example, the electrical retailer Currys has many different types of camera within its line of

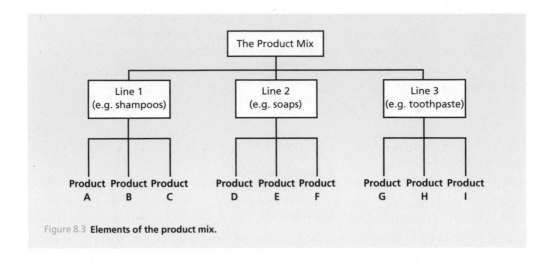

Figure 8.3 **Elements of the product mix.**

cameras. The *width* of the product mix refers to the number of product lines a company has, and the more lines, the greater the product mix width. Currys, for example, would have other lines as well as cameras, including televisions, audio equipment, computers, etc.

◉ Quality

Quality is an important feature of a product, and buyers make choices among competing products on the basis of the ratio of quality to price. Most people would accept that a Sony DVD recorder is of higher quality than one marketed by Alba and would be prepared to pay a higher price for it. Many will nevertheless be quite happy with the quality of the Alba machine, preferring its lower price.

But what do we mean by product quality? Quality is an extremely difficult concept to define in a few words. At its most basic, quality has been defined as 'conforming to requirements' (Crosby 1984). This implies that organizations must establish customers' requirements and specifications. Once established, the quality goal of the various functions of an organization is to comply strictly with these specifications. However, the questions remain: whose requirements, and whose specifications? A second series of definitions therefore state that quality is all about fitness for use (Juran 1982), a definition based primarily on satisfying customers' needs. These two definitions can be brought together in the concept of customer-perceived quality. Quality can be defined only by customers, and exists when an organization supplies goods or services to a specification that satisfies their needs and expectations.

The problem remains of identifying precisely what consumers' needs and expectations are. A company may think that it has the best-quality product based on its own criteria, but customers may have completely different criteria for judging quality. Sometimes there are benchmarks for measuring quality which can be readily agreed upon, for example that an 18 carat gold ring is better quality than one that is only nine carats. At other times, the quality of a tangible good can only be defined in the mind of the buyer, for example some people might rate fast food as being higher quality than a gourmet meal in a fine restaurant. In the case of intangible services, it can be much more difficult to agree the criteria for assessing quality, because few tangible manifestations exist. This has led many people to draw a distinction between the technical and functional dimensions of quality.

Technical quality and functional quality

Technical quality refers to the relatively quantifiable aspects of a product, which can easily be measured by both customer and supplier. Examples of technical quality include the waiting time at a supermarket checkout and the reliability of a new car. However, consumers are also influenced by *how* the technical quality is delivered to them. This is what Gronroos (1984) has described as *functional quality*, and it cannot be measured as objectively as the elements of technical quality. In the case of the queue at a supermarket checkout, functional quality is influenced by such factors as the environment in which queuing takes place and consumers' perceptions of the manner in which queues are handled by the supermarket's staff.

A lot of research has gone into trying to understand the processes by which buyers form expectations about the quality of a product. It is widely accepted that a product could be deemed to be of poor quality simply because it did not meet the buyer's expectations. A company's promotional material may have built up unsustainable expectations, resulting in perceptions of poor quality, even though an objective outside observer may have considered the technical quality to be high.

To try to provide reassurance to buyers, many companies incorporate some sort of guarantee of quality into their product offer. These can take a number of forms, including:

- The manufacturer may specify the standards in the product descriptions (e.g. bread made without preservatives; light bulbs tested for a life of 10,000 hours; clothing manufactured to be water-resistant).

- Often, product quality statements are backed up by specific guarantees of performance (e.g. the paintwork on a new car may be guaranteed to remain intact for six years).

- 'Customer charters' are often used to state the standards of service that a customer can expect. (Train operating companies have customer charters which, among other things, can provide compensation for late-running trains.)

◉ Distinctive design

It has been noted many times in this book that the development of a distinctive product is the basis for strong brand development. However, distinctiveness in itself is irrelevant if buyers do not value the distinction. Marmite-flavoured ice cream may be distinctive, but would you buy it (Ofek and Srinivasan 2002)?

A product's distinctiveness can be protected by a patent. This is a right given to an inventor which allows her exclusively to reap the benefits from the invention over a specified period. To qualify for a patent, a product must satisfy certain criteria: it must be novel and it must include an inventive step. In the case of services, for which patent protection is difficult to obtain, the registration of a trademark can protect a company's distinctive identity. If a patent or trademark is infringed, the patent holder will be entitled to an injunction and to damages. A company can also challenge a 'copycat' product under the common law doctrine of 'passing off'. It can be difficult to define the point where a competitors' copycat product infringes on the original company's legal protection. There have been many examples of alleged infringement. The crisp maker Walkers challenged Tesco over what it believed to be a similarity in packaging between its premium Sensations range and Tesco's Temptations crisps. Coincidentally, one of Walkers' more unusual flavours, Sea Salt and Cracked Black Pepper, also appeared in the Tesco range.

Ownership of patents can make enormous differences to the profitability of a product range, especially within the pharmaceutical sector. The shares of the pharmaceutical company Merck fell sharply in April 2008 after regulatory authorities refused a licence for its new anti-cholesterol pill, wiping out most of the value of its patent on the drug (*Financial Times* 2008a). However, the ownership of patents alone may not be sufficient for market success. It has been noted that the cosmetics company L'Oréal owns over 28,000 patents for components of its cosmetics, but the main reason behind its market success is the image that it has successfully created for its products (Mills 2003).

⦿ Packaging

The packaging of goods performs four major functions: handling, transport, storage, and the communication of product information.

Packaging is needed to ensure that goods are delivered to customers in a sound condition. The packaging should enable distributors and end users to handle and transport the product from one place to another. In addition, packaging should allow the product to be stored, and therefore the shape should be conducive to its being stocked on shelves and, where appropriate, in the home, office, or business. Packaging should protect the product from deterioration and from breakage.

Where goods are sold to customers using self-service methods, packaging can perform an important information and promotional role. The package can inform the customer of what is inside and can communicate the brand name, both directly through name association and indirectly by associating the brand with a distinctive type of packaging. (For example, most people would recognize a bar of Toblerone chocolate by the shape of its packaging alone.)

The results of redesigning packaging without changing the contents can sometimes be quite dramatic—see the Marketing in action vignette on how long-life milk sales were boosted by changing its packaging.

A pint of powder pulls a punch

The British have a long tradition of buying fresh bottles of milk delivered daily to the front door. Although today most milk is bought in plastic or cardboard containers, buying milk in a bottle still seems appealing to most people. Powdered milk had been around for a long time and, despite being nutritious, has been looked down upon by most people as an inferior product. Yet a market existed for dried milk as a 'reserve supply' of milk for those times when fresh milk was temporarily not available. But the product still had an image problem, not helped by many people's wartime memories of rations of dried milk being provided in tins and boxes. One solution identified by St Ivel was to put its dried milk in familiar shaped milk bottles. It could then sit in the fridge next to the fresh milk. The image of the product improved and sales soared.

'Greening' the product range

We saw in Chapter 3 that many consumers and governments are showing increasing concern for the ecological impacts of the products that they consume. The idea of individuals reducing their 'carbon footprint' has become a topical subject for discussion, even if, as we saw in Chapter 3, most consumers probably do not have a thorough understanding of the complexities of ecological impacts.

Ecologically concerned consumers can present marketers with product development opportunities, as well as problems. Pro-active companies have capitalized on ecological issues by reducing their costs and/or improving their organizational image. Many companies have seen recent ecological concerns as an opportunity to develop new products. Recyclable packaging, wind turbines, lightweight vehicle batteries, and technologies for carbon capture and storage are recent examples. By 2010 it appeared that the UK had lost in the design and construction of wind turbines, but the government pursued a policy of giving incentives to companies to support the development of innovative carbon capture and storage technologies in the hope that a strong home market would provide the basis for global competitive advantage.

Go back to Chapter 3 to review some examples of firms' responses to the need to make their product ranges more ecologically responsible.

The product life-cycle

There is a general acceptance that most products go through a number of stages in their existence, just as humans and most living organisms go through a number of life-cycle stages. When a new product comes on to the market, there is likely to be a lot of promotional effort by a company to secure sales. It is likely that the company will have incurred high costs in the development of such a product, costs that in the early stages may not be covered by revenue. Potential customers for a new product may be few and far between and therefore sales in the early stages may be quite slow. This stage is known as the *introduction stage*.

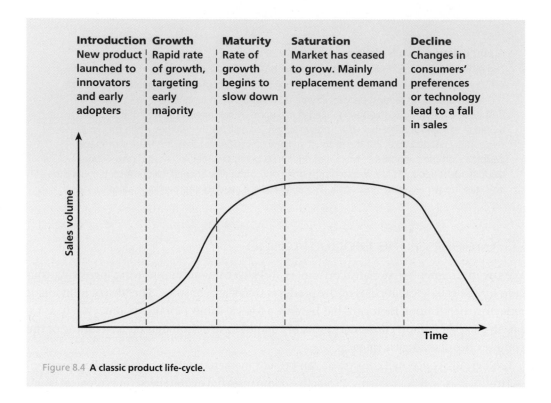

Introduction	Growth	Maturity	Saturation	Decline
New product launched to innovators and early adopters	Rapid rate of growth, targeting early majority	Rate of growth begins to slow down	Market has ceased to grow. Mainly replacement demand	Changes in consumers' preferences or technology lead to a fall in sales

Figure 8.4 **A classic product life-cycle.**

If the new product proves popular, more people will show an interest and start purchasing it. As more people buy, the firm will discover a number of cost savings in producing larger quantities. Raw materials can be purchased in bulk and therefore at a cheaper cost per unit. Machinery and employees will become more efficient at producing larger quantities, resulting in economies of scale. Any initial teething problems with the product will start to be ironed out and more people will purchase the product on the basis of word of mouth rather than merely the firm's formal promotion campaign. Falling costs and rising revenues will improve profitability in what is usually referred to as the *growth stage*.

As sales of the product increase, other competitors are likely to be attracted to the market, and as a result there will be increasingly fierce competition and a tendency for downward pressure on prices. Promotion on the part of all competitors will tend to increase, and yet the number of customers for the product will have ceased to grow. Over a period of time, the increase in sales starts to slow down and this is known as the *maturity stage*.

As time goes by, sales start to stabilize, marking the *saturation stage*. At this point most demand is replacement demand rather than new demand, and total sales start to fall. The mobile phone market in the UK reached this point in 2002 when total sales fell for the first time (*The Times* 2002). Falling sales eventually lead to the *decline stage*. Figure 8.4 displays this classical product life-cycle.

The product life-cycle fits well with the explanation put forward of how new products are adopted (Rogers 2003). Different types of customer are identified according to the speed at which a new product is adopted, and we will turn to this now.

The product life-cycle and consumer adoption processes

When an innovative product is introduced on to the market, only a small number of people will be interested in purchasing it as it is an untested item and usually quite expensive. Such people are categorized as *innovators*, and they tend to buy new products because they like to be seen owning something that is new and generally untried. People in this category are likely to have been among the first to buy mobile phones, digital cameras, and wide-screen televisions when they were launched. Despite the existence of innovators, new product launches may nevertheless be unsuccessful, as witnessed by the launch of WAP mobile phone services and the Sinclair C5 vehicle.

As the successful product begins to move to the growth stage, more people show an interest in it. The price of the product by this time has started to fall and, as innovators inform other people of the benefits of the product, more people begin to purchase it. The next wave of people to buy the product are known as *early adopters*. A key characteristic of early adopters is that they can be very influential in the groups with whom they interact, so they can be considered as opinion leaders. These individuals are generally looked on as experts in a particular field among the group, and therefore if they feel generally happy with the purchase of this relatively new product, they are likely to influence others to purchase it as well. This next group of customers are known as the *early majority*, and the product is now firmly in the growth stage of its life-cycle. As the competition starts to enter the market and prices begin to fall ever more quickly, the next group of people start to consider purchase. These are known as the *late majority*. It is after this point that the number of potential new customers for a product starts to decline, as the product starts to move through to its maturity and saturation stages. Products are sold at lower prices as companies try and sell excess stock. The market has by now almost ceased to grow, with most demand now being replacement demand rather than new demand. There is a relatively small group of people who tend to purchase products at the end of their life-cycles, and such people are known as *laggards*. The pattern of product adoption is illustrated in Figure 8.5.

The concept of the life-cycle is useful in that any marketing activity applied to a product can be closely related to the stage in the life-cycle that the product has reached. Promotional planning, for example, can be closely related to the life-cycle. In the introductory phase emphasis will typically be placed on creating awareness through public relations activity, building on this through the growth phase with advertising. Sales promotion activity will typically be used as the market reaches maturity and becomes more competitive. Finally, all promotional activity may be dropped in the decline stage as the product is allowed to die naturally.

All aspects of the marketing mix can be altered to fit the various life-cycle stages. For example, for an innovatory product, a high price may be achievable in the introductory stage,

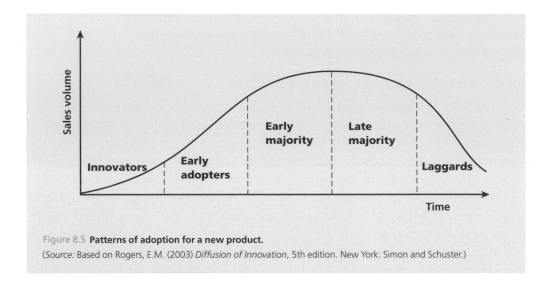

Figure 8.5 Patterns of adoption for a new product.
(*Source:* Based on Rogers, E.M. (2003) *Diffusion of Innovation*, 5th edition. New York: Simon and Schuster.)

eventually falling as the competition gets stronger and costs fall. Different distribution policies can be applied to the different stages.

Is there one particular pattern of product life-cycle that is applicable to all products? In
fact, different products move through the stages at different speeds, and not all products
follow the 'classic' shaped cycle. Some have an introduction stage but fail to go any further.
Others reach the growth stage and then for some reason sales fall very rapidly. Still other
products go through the introduction, growth, and maturity stages but then stay at the
maturity stage for a seemingly indefinite period. In reality, a number of different types of
life-cycle can exist, and some of these can be seen in Figure 8.6.

In the first example, the product has a high level of sales at an early stage but then there
seems to be no change in sales. In the second example, there is a constant increase in sales
volume in each subsequent time period. The third example displays the complete opposite:
here, each subsequent period of time brings with it a fall in sales volume after a period of
initially strong sales. This could be a result of the entry of strong and powerful competition.
The fourth type of life-cycle displays the situation where a firm actually influences the degree to which a product follows the life-cycle. In this situation the product has been saved
from decline, either through intense sales promotion activity or possibly through some
form of product modification; alternatively, external factors such as a change in customer
tastes, etc., may have led to the improvement in sales. Whatever the cause, the product here
displays further growth before moving once again through to a decline phase, although sales
are still higher now than they were at the original decline phase. The fifth example once
again shows that the product has been saved from decline, but in this case the new cycle is at
a lower stage than existed at first. The final example displays a typical life-cycle pattern for a
fashion item where there is a steep drop in sales once the product is considered unfashion-
able, but it may subsequently become popular again.

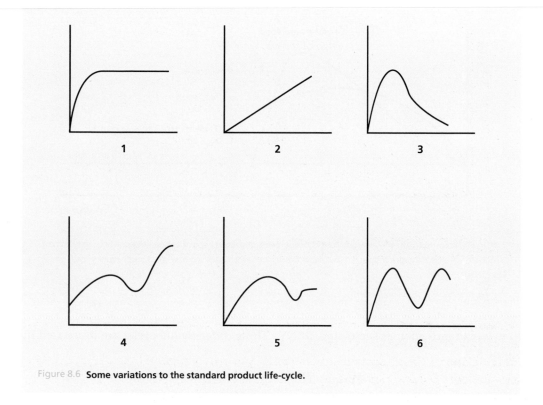

Figure 8.6 **Some variations to the standard product life-cycle.**

Limitations of product life-cycle theory

Life-cycle theory may look intuitively appealing when viewed with hindsight, but can be difficult to apply for short-term forecasting purposes. More fundamentally, it is difficult for marketers to identify where a product currently lies on its life-cycle. For example, if sales are stabilizing, it is difficult to ascertain whether the product has reached its peak in terms of growth and is about to decline, or whether there is just a temporary stabilization owing to external influences and that, if left alone, sales may start to increase once again in the near future. Indeed, the shape of the life-cycle can be influenced by the actions of the marketer, and as a result there could be a self-fulfilling prophecy. For example, if there is a belief that the product is about to reach the decline phase, marketers may consciously reduce the marketing effort in response to this belief; as a result of this action, sales may fall and the product may indeed move into the decline phase.

Another observation is that the shape and duration of a life-cycle is dependent upon whether it is the product class, the product form, or a specific brand that is being considered. For example, the life-cycle of mens' trousers is quite flat, taken over a long period of time, compared with specific types of trousers (e.g. jeans, chinos), which come and go out of fashion. Within each type of trouser, brand names will go through a life-cycle of popularity. (For example, Levis rose in the 1980s but lost ground by the end of the 1990s

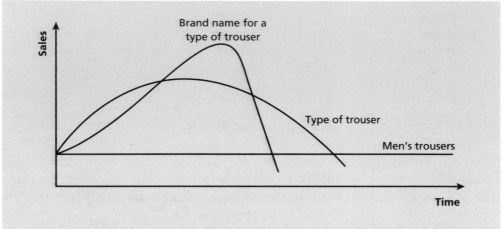

Figure 8.7 **A comparison of life-cycles for different levels of product specification.** When defined very broadly, a product life-cycle may appear quite flat, but individual variants and brands can have much more pronounced life-cycles.

to newer brands such as Diesel and DKNY.) These differing life-cycles are illustrated in Figure 8.7.

◉ Innovation and new product development

We have seen how products go through a life-cycle, and that therefore most products can expect eventually to go into decline. It is therefore important for a company to develop new products to replace those that have reached the end of their life. Marketing managers must recognize the need to develop new products in response to shortening life-cycles, which in turn result from rapidly changing technology and competitive pressures.

E-Marketing

Will 'virtual travel' take off?

You live in London and fancy going to New York to experience the sights and sounds of the city that never sleeps. But you can't really afford the fare for the plane ticket and the prospect of sitting in a plane for seven hours and the hassle of airport security doesn't appeal to you. So what about using virtual technologies to bring New York to you? Should companies be putting serious money into the development of virtual tourism?

A report 'Tomorrow's Tourist' published in 2010 by the Future Foundation claimed that young people are increasingly likely to play computer games and indulge in social net-working than enjoy leisure activities outside. As 3-D technology improves, will more people be tempted to sightsee from the comfort of their own home instead of actually visiting other places?

Dr Ian Yeoman, author of *Tomorrow's Tourist* and a consultant on the report pointed to what had happened in Japan. The Japanese, it seems, had over the last ten years spent more on in-home entertainment and technology than travelling the world. The technologies that the Japanese adopt today are likely to be those adopted by the rest of the world before too long.

The report, shows that spending on out-of-home leisure activities fell during the Japanese recession of the late twentieth century, but sales of in-home electronics had grown, and since 2000 had increased by 2.5 times in real terms. It also seemed that people had been gaining increasing enjoyment from in-home activities such as socializing via social network websites.

Some of the hype about virtual tourism may not be so far-fetched when it is remembered that 10 or 20 years ago many said that children would not give up kicking a football around in favour of computer games. Since then, the number of children taking part in sports has fallen, while many sit for hours behind their playstations playing virtual games. As virtual reality systems improve, and the cost, hassle, and security risks of travel increase, there may well be a scenario in which people decide that the virtual world of Paris is better than the reality. What else could trigger this transformation? Could the technology improve to the point where friends can have virtual meetings in Paris quite effortlessly? How can the experiential values of virtual reality systems be improved so that users get a greater sense of actually being there? Will virtual tourism become an aspirational first choice, or will it only ever become the second choice when real travel becomes too difficult and expensive? Will the availability of virtual tours whet people's appetite, so that in fact instead of being a substitute for travel, it will encourage even more travel to explore real destinations? If you were managing a museum or gallery in a tourist town, how could you adapt to the needs of virtual tourists?

What is innovation?

For many marketing managers, innovation means new or better products, and innovation has often been identified as a source of a company's long-term competitive advantage. Indeed, some nations as a whole can be described as more innovative than others, and there appears to be a link between a country's spending on research and development and its economic performance.

It should be remembered that innovation is not confined to a company's product offer, but applies to all marketing functions, including distribution and promotion. Innovation must be linked to a firm's objectives, and of course must relate to creating value in the eyes of customers.

What are new products?

It may not be that easy actually to define what is meant by a 'new product'. Companies' routine efforts at continuous quality improvement are often closely linked to innovation, and it can be difficult to distinguish between the two. New products could in fact comprise any of the following:

- improvements/revisions to existing products

- additions to existing lines

- 'new to the world' products

- repositioning (existing products in new segments/markets)

We will consider below the distinction between product modifications and innovative products.

Product modifications

Many so-called new products are in fact modifications of existing products. Changes tend to be incremental and may include the following:

1. Minor changes can be made to how the product actually performs: this could involve the addition of new features and/or changing the packaging.

2. The quality of the basic product can be improved.

3. The style of the product can be modified, without changing its basic function. (For example, cars tend to undergo styling changes to keep in line with current design preferences.) In style-conscious industries such as fashion clothing, regularly updating a product's style can be crucial to continuing success. A Mintel report noted that soft drinks manufacturers have responded to consumers' desire for novelty and variety with a raft of new flavours and bottle designs (Mintel 2002).

4. Non-product attributes can be altered to produce a change of image. A change in advertising message can be used to alter the image of a product. This occurred, for example, with the change in image of Guinness from a working man's stout to a trendy social drink, and the repositioning of After Eight mints as an all-time chocolate for all ages (Mills 2002).

Innovative products

Truly new products are comparatively rare compared with product modifications, but they can be very important in certain circumstances.

- If consumer tastes are changing radically, existing products may no longer satisfy their needs. (This is often the case in many parts of the fashion clothing industry.)

- Technological change may make existing products obsolete. (For example, dot matrix printers were made obsolete by the development of ink jet and laser printers.) However, it has been noted that new technologies need not necessarily have a better performance than those they replace (Adner 2002). For example, many professional photographers still prefer to use traditional 35 mm cameras than the newer digital cameras.

- New products may be required as a result of changes in internal processes such as accounting, office management, or labour relations. If a product becomes dangerous or illegal to produce (as has happened in the UK with many derivatives of beef products), a motivation is provided to develop a new replacement product.

- New products may be required to meet the need of intermediaries. (For example, concentrated forms of soap powder were introduced partly to satisfy retailers' demand that they take up less shelf space.)

- The social and economic environment may have changed, creating new needs in the market. For example, a growing number of Muslims in the UK population led many UK Banks to develop bank accounts based on the principles of Sharia law to target this group (*Financial Times* 2008b).

- If competitors are actively developing new products, a company must do likewise if it is not to lose market share.

- New products may be developed to fill under-utilized capacity. (For example, many business hotels have filled their empty rooms at the weekend by offering innovatory weekend leisure activity breaks, such as a course in aromatherapy.)

The focus for new product development can differ between countries (Figure 8.8). In some newly industrializing countries people may view the rush in western economies to automated self-service products as perplexing. In India and other Asian countries, where labour is relatively cheap and plentiful, the rising incomes of the middle classes would be used to employ more domestic help rather than buying a washing machine or vacuum cleaner, for example. Consumers in different parts of the world will have different priorities according to wealth and circumstances. In China, where the opportunity to buy your own home or car is more limited than in the UK, consumers with rising incomes are more likely to spend on TVs and mobile phones.

Critical to the development of many new products has been a 'product champion' within an organization. A champion can continually press the case for a new product to be developed and provide the impetus for development which may be lost if responsibility is dispersed too widely. Without such people, it is likely that many innovations that we take for granted today would not have been seen through to development and launch.

The new product development process

Having a formal new product development process in place is generally more likely to be effective than adopting a haphazard approach to developing a product. Indeed, where costs and risks are high (as they are in many major infrastructure developments), a system needs to be in place to help keep such risks to a minimum.

It is usual to talk about a new product development process comprising a number of stages which span from having an initial idea through to the launch of the new product. We will look at each of these stages in turn, although it must be recognized that the stages often overlap each other (Figure 8.9).

Figure 8.8 **Many people regard tea as an easily substitutable commodity product, so it can be a tough market for a company to gain a competitive advantage.** Innovation has been a key to successful marketing of this age-old product. Some niche players have innovated with herbal teas, but not all innovation has been successful (e.g. 'instant' powdered tea never became as popular as instant coffee). PG Tips has used innovation to gain a competitive advantage in the UK tea market. It has successfully launched new formats of tea bags which improve the taste of the tea and which are easier for consumers to use. More recently, it has capitalized on consumers' growing familiarity with cafetières by launching 'Plunger Tea' specifically for cafetières.
(Reproduced with kind permission of Unilever Bestfoods UK Ltd.)

Idea generation

New products come from a variety of sources rather than merely being initiated by the firm through the use of market research and the identification of untapped needs.

An important source of new product ideas is the customer. For products bought by businesses, new uses for an existing product or new ideas for a new one tend to be communicated

Here's the product, now where's the market?

Marketers might like the idea that they carefully study consumers' needs and then develop the products which satisfy their needs. You may recall from Chapter 1 this is essentially what distinguishes marketing orientation from production orientation. But the world is full of products which appeared almost by accident out of research laboratories, with no prior analysis of what customer needs were being targeted by new product development. Consider these examples:

- 'Post-it' notes were a by-product of 3M researchers looking for new forms of permanent adhesive. A partially sticky material was found, and a use subsequently found for it.

- The drugs manufacturer Pfizer was researching an anti-angina drug, when it noticed side effects in trials with patients. It capitalized on this and eventually launched Viagra.

- Even champagne, which we now take for granted, was developed by the accidental discoveries of a seventeenth century Benedictine monk Dom Pierre Perignon who had been trying to eradicate bubbles from white wine.

When researchers make a discovery, it can be difficult to tell whether it will satisfy a need. If consumers have no experience of the product, it may be difficult for them to articulate their thoughts, which may be dominated by familiarity with what is currently available. After all, it took Dom Perignon some time to convince the seventeenth century aristocracy that white wine with bubbles was not a sign of a dud vintage, but a refreshing drink in its own right. But he persevered, and the rest, as they say, is history.

Idea Generation
↓
Idea Screening
↓
Concept Development and Testing
↓
Business Analysis
↓
Product Development and Testing
↓
Market Testing
↓
Product Launch

Figure 8.9 **The new-product development process.**

to the sales force. For services, the important characteristic of inseparability means that there are plenty of opportunities for customers to inform service providers of new ideas or possible improvements to service processes.

Another source of new product ideas is a firm's competitors. Creative imitation does not carry the same risks as developing something totally new. A consideration of the flaws that exist in a competitor's product can also produce useful ideas for new products.

Some organizations see the importance of developing new products as part of their long-term competitive strategy and try to instil an internal organizational culture that positively thrives on new ideas. For example, Sony, the electronics company, encourages employees to move around and get involved in other departments. New perspectives and new ideas therefore come from every level of the organization, resulting in hundreds of new products every year. Similarly, 3M expects to receive new product ideas regularly from all members of staff, rather than just the research and development department. Its corporate ethos has for some time included two rules: the '15 per cent rule' and the '25 per cent rule'. The '15 per cent rule' states that employees should commit 15 per cent of their time to thinking of new ideas, and the 25 per cent rule states that every manager must ensure that at least 25 per cent of his portfolio of products is less than five years old. A number of products that are now accepted in the marketplace have originated from this approach, for example Post-it notes.

Many new products emerge from 'blue skies' research laboratories, or more applied research exercises in which the aim is not to develop a particular customer focused product, but to develop a particular area of technology. Sometimes, new products can emerge quite by accident without any planning or prior analysis of buyers' needs (see Marketing in action 'Here's the product, now where's the market?')

Idea screening

Whether a firm responds positively to ideas for new products very much depends on its internal resources. As well as considering whether there are the financial resources to develop a new product (in particular, the availability of cash flow in the short term), a firm needs to consider other internal issues. For example, is there enough production capacity to cope with likely demand? Are there suitably trained personnel? Will new staff have to be recruited or present staff retrained? In addition, the firm needs to consider the availability of the raw materials or components required to produce the new product (Figure 8.10).

Another consideration is time. New product development can take a long time from inception to final production and launch. Some developments can take as little as a few months whereas others can take years to come to fruition, especially where safety testing is protracted, as in the case of new drugs. The pressures of competition today mean that speed is becoming increasingly important.

Another important aspect that needs to be considered is the possibility that a new product could take sales from a product that is already in the firm's portfolio, through a process of 'cannibalization', resulting in only a small increase in total company sales. Alternatively, adding a new product may help to improve the sales of existing products as the product line becomes more comprehensive. This may be particularly important to companies that seek to expand their relationships with key customers and obtain a greater share of their total expenditure.

Screening should ensure that the new product fits within the firm's overall image. With current concern among many consumers about ecological issues, how well does a new product contribute to a company's image as an ecologically responsible organization.

Figure 8.10 **Would you ever want to travel into outer space? Would you invest millions in developing space tourism?** In 2001, the world's first space tourist, Dennis Tito, paid a reported $20 million for a visit to the International Space Station. Already a number of companies are looking at the possibilities for mass-market space tourism. Although the price of travelling into space may still appear prohibitive, analogies have been drawn with the early days of transatlantic air travel. In 1939, it cost the equivalent of £79,000 in today's inflation-adjusted money to make a return flight from Britain to the USA, something which can be routinely done today for around £400. Sir Richard Branson's Virgin Galactic plans to begin commercial passenger flights into space, departing from RAF Lossiemouth, by 2011. The flights will allow the public to experience the thrill of weightlessness outside the Earth's atmosphere at a cost of £120,000 per ticket. Would space tourism go the same way as transatlantic air travel by eventually becoming mass-market? What would be the price at which space tourism really begins to grow? Who would be the innovators, and just how many people in the later adopter groups would really want to experience weightlessness? A greater uncertainty in planning for the future is the effect of aircraft emissions on global warming, which could lead to prohibitively high taxes on operations, or a feeling of guilt by potential passengers about the effects of their travel into space on climate change.

(*Source:* www.virgingalactic.com.)

At this stage, many new product ideas will be dropped because they do not fit with the overall marketing strategy. If the proposal passes this filter, the company can proceed to the next stage. Although the filtering stage has been portrayed here as a rational process, there is evidence that the final selection of ideas for further development is typically affected by intuitive and political factors (Bolton 2003; Forlani et al. 2002).

Concept development and testing

It has often been claimed that around three-quarters of all new products fail. One way of reducing the failure rate is to ensure more rigorous screening so that 'no hope' ideas do not get through to the next stage. But even this can be easier said than done, because by this approach Sony would have rejected its Walkman concept and IBM the idea of developing a photocopier. At the time, both were dismissed as concepts with no potential.

A new product concept can be tested using a number of methods, and such testing should take place before any significant amount of further investment in product development takes place. Initial market research should aim to discover potential customer attitudes to the concept and, more particularly, whether they would be interested in purchasing the product if it came on to the market. This may be quite a difficult task if the new product is a major innovation and customers have no experience of such an idea (E-Marketing 'The unimaginable may be indescribable')

E-Marketing

The unimaginable may be indescribable

When it comes to forecasting take-up for completely new products, simply asking potential buyers whether they would buy it can be fraught with difficulties. In the case of intangible services, it can be difficult to present potential customers with a mock-up of the product in a way that manufacturing companies often do to test likely reaction to a new product. Around the year 2000, for example, there was a lot of discussion about just what features and benefits customers would use when high speed mobile Internet services became widely available and affordable.

Simply asking somebody what they would use such a service for is likely to be limited to the scope of respondents' imagination. In the context of developing a low cost car, Henry Ford is famously reported as saying that if he had asked people what they wanted, they would have simply replied 'faster horses', rather than being able to imagine ever owning a car. For intangible services, the problem of consumers' limited vision can be even greater, requiring more sophisticated research methods that seek to understand deep-seated needs and motivators.

Where possible, companies have sought to experiment with new goods and services targeted at trial groups, before committing themselves to large-scale provision. This may be a valid approach where capital commitments are high and the market is relatively stable, but in fast-moving markets, too much time spent understanding consumer behaviour may lead competitors to gain a lead in an emerging new service sector.

In the early days of the Internet, many new online services were developed with very little research. Indeed in those days, the problem of Henry Ford's horses was even more present, with most consumers having little idea of how they might use the Internet. So, in order to be first to market and have a 'first mover' advantage, the process of concept testing was often based more on intuition and judgement than rigorous analysis.

A financial analysis needs to take place in order to assess whether the product concept can be made into a profitable proposition. An income and expenditure statement, together with the associated balance sheet and cash flow analysis, therefore need to be prepared. The key to this financial analysis is that the product should at least break even over a period of time. However, any financial forecasts may be based on very crude assumptions about the likely volume of sales, the selling price, distribution costs, and the cost of producing the item. Cost and revenue estimates can be closely linked with each other, so that high-volume sales result in lower unit production costs, which in turn improves profitability. This can be a very difficult and speculative part of the process. According to one estimate, 30,000 new products annually vie for the 25,000 total spots in the average supermarket. Will a new consumer product even get supermarket shelf space? Of all new package-goods products, 52 per cent fail before their second year (Dipasquale 2002).

Because there are many unknowns in the financial analysis, a sensitivity analysis is often carried out to assess the impact on overall profitability of changes in the underlying assumptions. Would the concept still be profitable if selling prices were only half those that had been predicted?

This is the translation of the idea into an actual product that can be delivered to customers. It is at this point that the decision is made to physically develop the product, and large amounts of money can be poured in at this stage. The various elements of the product have to be designed and tested. However, this testing should be more rigorous than at the concept testing stage. In the case of tangible goods, customers can now see the product as it might actually look, and the company can identify possible problems that need to be resolved.

There is a need to consider the requirements for repeat purchase in addition to the single one-off purchase decision, and therefore the factors that influence trial, first purchase, adoption, and purchase frequency need to be identified. In addition, customer response to promotional material needs to be assessed.

Even given the increased rigour in this testing process, there are still difficulties. Testing consumers' responses to intangible elements of a new product can be more difficult.

A market test aims to replicate everything that is likely to exist in the entire market but on a smaller scale. A company is testing not only the product itself, but the way in which it is promoted, priced, and distributed. Test marketing can take place in a television viewing area, a test city, particular geographical regions, or, in the business-to-business context, on a sample of key customers.

Designing a market testing exercise involves making a number of decisions: Where should the test market be? What is to be tested? How long should the test last? What criteria should be used to determine success or otherwise?

Although market testing should reduce the potential risks before launch, it is important to realize that there are still potential problems. Market testing is not cheap, and in some cases can be nearly as expensive as a full-scale launch. Even a large test market is unlikely to be totally representative of the market, because in reality small test markets may lead to distortions that wouldn't be present in a national launch. Market testing is also likely to warn competitors of what is to come, and as a result the competition may act more quickly in response or may interfere with the test itself. Competitors may study the test very carefully through retail audits and their own qualitative research and may learn a lot which will allow them to launch a competitive product, but without having incurred much of the development and testing costs so far.

Product launch

Actually launching the product (assuming that it has survived this far) involves a number of issues. Replacing an existing product with a new one tends to be a popular approach. There is likely to be an existing customer base for the new product and therefore the risks are lower, although even here mistakes can be made. When Coca Cola sought to replace its existing cola with a new formulation, it became apparent that it had misinterpreted its market research and had to reinstate the old product as 'Classic' Coke. A company may choose to sell both the old and new products simultaneously for a period of time, although this might meet with reluctance from retailers who will be required to commit twice as much shelf space to the products.

Time is a key issue. The longer a new product goes through the various developmental stages, the greater the chance that competitors will enter the market before launch. The firm can be a pioneer and enter the market first or be a follower and reduce its risks considerably. In the UK there was a race in 2003 to launch the first 'third-generation' mobile phone network. The new operator Three created some publicity as the first to launch a network (on 03/03/2003), despite the fact that no handsets were available until sometime afterwards (Fagan 2003). There is also the issue of stock levels—a company would normally avoid launching a new product when it had large unsold stocks of an older model that would become more difficult to dispose of after the launch of the new one.

For companies operating globally, timing of the launch in different national markets can be critical, as markets are likely to be at different stages of development and a global rollout may be inefficient for a company to manage (Wong 2002). A staggered rollout allows a company to exploit profits from one market before moving on to progressively less attractive markets, thereby maintaining a portfolio of products at different stages of market development. However, in the case of some easily transported products such as computer software, it may not be realistic to have a staged rollout, as sales would soon occur through a 'grey' market. Most launches of new products by Microsoft have involved almost simultaneous launch, demanding a high level of global commitment by the company.

Integrating the new product development process

So far, the stages of new product development have been presented as if they are steps that necessarily have to be tackled in a sequential order. In fact, the time taken to go through this process can be considerable, allowing competitors to gain a lead. There have therefore been many attempts to carry out some of the steps simultaneously. Virtual reality systems, for example, are allowing customers to get a feel of the final product at a very early stage, allowing this to take place at the same time as concept testing and avoiding the need to wait until all steps of the process are progressed (Dahan and Hauser 2002).

The new product development process can be extremely complex, with many examples of cost overruns and delayed results (Kim and Wilemon 2003). A key to more effective new product development activity is close working relationships between marketing and manufacturing functions (Rodríguez et al. 2007). In one study of 467 completed product innovation projects, increased marketing–manufacturing joint involvement was associated with better project performance (Song and Swink 2002). Even simple administrative matters such as rapid communication following the results of one stage can help to speed up the new product development process.

As can be seen, the new product development process can be time consuming and complex. This has led many companies to outsource the whole process to specialist companies who have developed an expertise in product development and market testing (Howley 2002).

Our discussion of new product development processes has focused on how large companies might typically go about the process in a logical and structured manner. There is a lot of research evidence that in smaller companies the process is much more intuitive (e.g. Enright 2001). In one study of SMEs it was found that marketing-related activities were undertaken less frequently and were less well executed than technical activities in developing new products, and the existence of a new product strategy seemed to have a significant positive impact on marketing activities (Huang et al. 2002).

◉ Strategic issues in expanding the product range

Earlier in this chapter we introduced the idea of a product mix, which comprises the range of products offered by a company. Product life-cycle theory reminds us that a product mix cannot remain static, as some products will eventually cease to be profitable elements of that mix. But which direction should the new product mix take?

Product management involves ensuring that there is a succession of products available that are at different stages of their life-cycles. The planning process should involve the firm's business being managed in the same way as an investment portfolio, with attention paid to developing, maintaining, phasing out, and deleting specific elements. This process can lead management to identify where there may be market potential and therefore where investment can be most profitably made.

For a company to put all of its efforts into supplying a very limited range of products to a narrow market segment is potentially dangerous. Risk spreading is therefore often an important element of portfolio planning which goes beyond marketing planning. Some companies deliberately provide a range of products that—quite apart from their potential for cross selling—act in contrasting manners during the business cycle. There is a long tradition to this practice; for example, the ice cream manufacturer Walls became more sustainable as a business unit by adding sausages to its product portfolio. Sausages tended to have their highest demand in winter, counterbalancing the sharp peak in summer for ice cream. Similarly, accountancy firms have become potentially more stable units as they have amalgamated, by allowing pro-cyclical activities such as management buy-out expertise and venture capital investment to be counterbalanced by contra-cyclical activities such as insolvency work. Sometimes statutory requirements may require a balanced portfolio of products. The Bank of England's regulation of the UK banking system, for example, imposes constraints on banks' freedom to be market-led in the pattern of their lending decisions. Also, with the development of relationship marketing strategies, firms are increasingly keen to develop opportunities for offering customers a broad range of products which attract a higher share of their total expenditure. For all of these reasons, organizations seek to manage their growth in a manner that maintains a desired portfolio of products.

⊙ Planning for growth

Most private-sector organizations pursue growth in one form or another, whether this is an explicit aim or merely an implicit aim of its managers. Growth is often associated with

MARKETING in ACTION

From dairymen to hypermarket operator

Should a company 'stick to its knitting' and do what it is good at, or should it search continually for new products and new markets? Countless companies have reported disastrous results after going into areas they knew very little about. The rapid growth of Next from its core of fashion retailing into newsagents, travel, and home furnishings contributed to its near collapse in the late 1980s. WHSmith went through bad years in the mid-1990s when the newsagent's diversification into DIY retailing and television failed to work. Abbey National expanded in the late 1990s from its core of domestic mortgage lending into merchant banking and train and aircraft leasing, only to have to write off millions of pounds of losses and withdraw from these sectors in 2003.

But isn't change essential for companies, especially those facing static or declining markets for its core products? One of the UK's leading grocery retailers, Asda (now a subsidiary of Walmart), would not be where it is today had not the Associated Dairy Company taken a risk and set up a retailing operation. Milk was a facing a mature market, but new opportunities for product development were available further down its distribution chain as more people sought the benefits of shopping in large supermarkets. The company therefore created its Asda superstores. The security services company Securicor knew that it was taking a risk when it invested in a joint venture with British Telecom to create the Cellnet (now O$_2$) mobile phone network. And a small company manufacturing shopping baskets called WPP (standing for Wire Plastic Products) took huge risks in diversifying its product range on its way to becoming owners of some of the world's leading advertising agencies.

It is fine, with hindsight, to criticize a firm's decisions about which direction its product portfolio should take. But in an uncertain world risks have to be taken. A sound analysis of a company's strengths and weaknesses and of its external environment certainly helps, but success also depends upon an element of luck.

increasing returns to shareholders and greater career opportunities for managers. Growth may be vital in order to reach a critical size at which economies of scale in production, distribution, and promotion can be achieved, thereby contributing to a company's sustainable competitive advantage. But where should the growth be focused?

The development of new products or new markets are more risky options than simply selling more of its existing product to existing customers. More risky still is diversification into new markets and new products. The dimensions of product development and market development form the basis of the product/market expansion grid proposed by Ansoff (1957). Products and markets are each analysed in terms of their degree of novelty to an organization, and growth strategies are identified in terms of these two dimensions. In this way, four possible growth strategies can be identified. An illustration of the framework, with reference to the specific options open to a company that is currently marketing a range of organic fruit and vegetables, is shown in Figure 8.11.

The four growth options are associated with differing sets of problems and opportunities for a company. These relate to the resources required for implementation, and the level of risk associated with each. It follows, therefore, that what might be a feasible growth strategy for one organization may not be for another. The characteristics of the four strategies are described below.

1. Market penetration strategies: This type of strategy focuses growth on the existing product range by encouraging higher levels of sales to current target customers. In this way, a food manufacturer serving the growing market for organic produce could grow—all other things being equal—simply by maintaining its

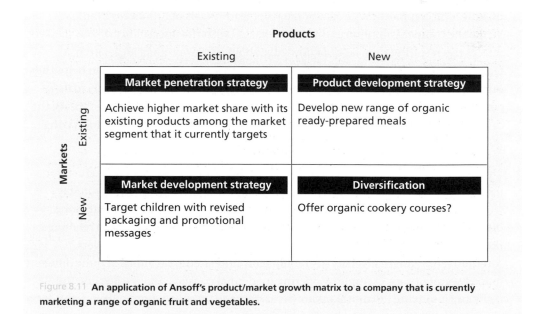

Figure 8.11 **An application of Ansoff's product/market growth matrix to a company that is currently marketing a range of organic fruit and vegetables.**

current marketing strategy. If it wanted to accelerate this growth, it could do this first by seeking to sell more products to its existing customers and second by attracting customers from its competitors. If the market was in fact in decline, the company could grow only by attracting customers from its competitors through more aggressive marketing policies and/or cost reduction programmes. This strategy offers the least level of risk to an organization—it is familiar with both its products and its customers.

2. Market development strategies: This type of strategy builds upon the existing product range that an organization has established, but seeks to find new groups of customers for them. In this way the organic foods manufacturer that had saturated its current market might seek to expand its sales to new geographical regions or overseas markets. It could also aim its marketing effort at attracting custom from groups beyond its current age/income groups—for example by targeting children with organically produced snacks. While the company may be familiar with the production side of its growth plans, it faces risks because it may have poor knowledge of different buyer behaviour patterns in the markets it is attempting to enter. For an organic food company that has built its business in the UK, it may have little knowledge about consumer buying behaviour in continental European countries, for example. It may face even greater risk in developing a marketing strategy aimed at children, whose needs it has little previous experience of satisfying.

3. Product development strategy: As an alternative to selling existing products in new markets, a company may choose to develop new products for its existing markets. The organic food company may add new ranges of ready meals or drinks, for example. While the company minimizes the risk associated with the uncertainty of new markets, it faces risk resulting from lack of knowledge about its new product area. Often, a feature of this growth strategy is collaboration with a product specialist who helps the organization produce the new product, leaving it free to market it effectively to its customers. Rather than setting up its own facility to produce ready prepared meals, the organic foods company may leave the specialized task of doing this and undertaking quality controls to a more experienced food manufacturer.

4. Diversification strategy: Here, a company expands by developing new products for new markets. Diversification can take a number of forms. The company could stay within the same general product/market area, but diversify into a new point in the distribution chain. For example, the organic food producer may move into retailing its products, rather than just selling them exclusively to wholesalers and retailers. Alternatively, it might diversify into completely unrelated areas aimed at quite different market segments, for example by offering residential cookery courses. Because the company is moving into both unknown markets and unknown product areas, this form of growth carries the greatest level of risk from a marketing management perspective.

Diversification may, however, help to manage the long-term risk of the organization by reducing dependency on a narrow product/market area.

In practice, most growth that occurs is a combination of product development and market development. In very competitive markets, a company would most likely have to adapt its product slightly in order to become attractive to a new market segment (Figure 8.12).

Deleting products

Good product management demands not only that new products are developed, but also that failing ones are deleted. Deciding when a product has reached the decline stage of its life-cycle can be quite difficult, because a downturn could simply be a temporary blip. If a downturn seems to have set in, it can sometimes be difficult to decide whether it is worth trying to revive the product, or to just let it die. Even the manner of a product's deletion requires careful thought—should it be allowed to die gradually, or suddenly killed off?

In general, there is a tendency to 'add on' rather than subtract, and therefore many products do not die but merely fade away, consuming resources of an organization which could be better used elsewhere. 'Old' products may not even cover overheads. In addition, there are a number of hidden costs of supporting dying products that need to be taken into consideration, for example:

- A disproportionate amount of management time can be spent on them: this can delay the search for new products.

- Short and relatively uneconomic production runs may be required where the demand for a product is small and irregular.

- They often require frequent price and stock adjustments.

Firms should have a logical planning system for deciding which products to delete. It would be naive, however, to assume that deletion is a simple process. In reality, there are a number of reasons why logical deletion procedures are not readily followed:

- Often firms do not have the information they need to identify whether a product needs to be considered for elimination. Even if an organization is aware of a potential deletion candidate, the reasons for its failure may not be known and therefore management may just leave things as they are and hope that the problem will go away by itself.

- Managers often become sentimental about products, hoping that sales will pick up when the market improves. Sometimes marketing strategy will be blamed for the lack of success, and there may be a belief that a change in advertising or pricing, for example, will improve the situation.

YOUNG FRUIT PICKERS WANTED.

This year the fruit picking season starts early with the introduction of the McDonald's Happy Meal Fruit Bag. The slices of fresh apple and seedless red grapes provide one of the Department of Health's recommended five daily portions of fruit and vegetables. It's available for 59p because we appreciate money doesn't grow on trees.

Figure 8.12 **Fast food was a great marketing success story of the 1980s and 1990s.** Chains developed in response to changes in the pattern of family meal eating, growing levels of disposable income (especially among younger adults), a growing desire for variety seeking and increasing concern with value for money. McDonald's has a long record of innovation with the development of new menus and new formats in new countries. However, by the end of the 1990s, there was growing concern in many western countries about problems of obesity caused by eating too much high fat food. McDonald's has continued its pattern of innovation with products which address the changed needs of the early 21st century, including McCafés and, shown here, a fruit bag which is aimed at making fresh fruit more appealing to children (and their parents).

(Reproduced with kind permission of McDonald's Corporation.)

- Political issues within organizations may create barriers to deletion. Some individuals will have vested interests in a product and may fight elimination efforts. In fact, some individuals may hide the true facts of a product's performance to ensure that deletion is not considered at all.

- Finally, a company may fear that the sale of other products in the product range will fall if a product is deleted. With the growing importance of relationship marketing, many firms are keen to ensure that they are able to satisfy all of their target customers' needs for a particular category of product. If a product is deleted, the whole relationship may be lost.

Where weak products are identified, a number of possibilities may be open for trying to revive a product, including:

- modifying the product so that it meets changed market requirements;

- decreasing promotional expenditure, in order to minimize costs: this may be a sensible idea if there is a small loyal market;

- increasing promotional expenditure, assuming that sales are sufficiently responsive to this increased promotion;

- decreasing the price, if demand is elastic and an increase in sales revenue is likely to result;

- increasing the price, if there remains a core market that is strongly loyal to the product: by doing this, total revenue may be increased, even if sales volumes decline;

- changing the distribution system, in order to cut costs, and/or open up sales opportunities in new market segments.

If none of these options is considered feasible, the company must decide how best to delete the product. This is not always a simple task, and a number of options can be identified:

1. Ruthlessly eliminate 'overnight'. This may seem the simplest solution, but will customers take their business to competitors? Will they take their business for other products in the company's mix with them? There may also be the problem of what to do with existing stocks of finished goods and work in progress. Sometimes a company may be contractually obliged to continue supplying a product for many years into the future, especially in the financial services sector, where products such as mortgages and pensions cannot be completely deleted until all customers' policies have reached the end of their contracted term. A sudden withdrawal of a product without notice may create bad publicity for a company, especially if customers have come to depend upon it.

2. Increase the price and let demand fade away. This may sound to many loyal customers like exploitation, but it could mean that the firm makes good profits on the product while demand lasts.

3. Reduce promotion or even stop it altogether. Again, this could increase profitability while demand lasts.

◉ Chapter summary and linkages to other chapters

Products are the means by which a company satisfies its customers' needs. However, it must be remembered that customers seek the benefits of the product rather than the product itself. Products can be grouped according to the similarity of their marketing requirements, and a number of bases for classifying products have been suggested. Services can be described as products, but the characteristics of 'pure' services can be quite distinct from those of 'pure' goods. For all products, quality is an important defining characteristic. Change in the marketing environment (Chapter 2) causes most products to go through some form of life-cycle which affects the way they are marketed.

Because most products eventually go into decline, it is important that a portfolio of established and new products is maintained in order to develop a sustainable competitive advantage (Chapter 7). This chapter has emphasized new product development as a process. The length of this process will depend upon product and market characteristics. Shortening the new product development process can give a firm a competitive advantage, but can also increase the risk of a failed launch.

The opposite of new product development is deletion, and a rational approach to deletion can prevent a firm becoming weighed down with a large number of minor products which consume a lot of management time but return very little, if any, profit.

Product decisions are just one element of the marketing mix, and the following chapters will discuss how price, distribution, and promotion are used to develop a distinctive and profitable market position for a product.

⬩ KEY PRINCIPLES OF MARKETING

- A customer's definition of a product focuses on the benefits provided and how the product will satisfy a need.

- A product can comprise anything that can be offered to a market. Marketers classify types of product according to the similarity of their marketing needs.

- In a dynamic marketing environment, products can expect to go through a life-cycle of development, launch, growth, saturation, and decline.

- Product life-cycle theory implies that new products will be required to replace products that go into decline and are eventually deleted from a product portfolio.

CASE STUDY

Small new phones, big investment risk?

The mobile phone industry is no stranger to product innovation. In fact, it is hard to believe that the sector barely existed just 20 years ago, now most people in western developed countries own a mobile phone. In fact, according to the telecoms regulator Ofcom, there are now more mobile phones in use in Britain than there are people. Although we are all now familiar with mobile phones, we probably wouldn't recognize a mobile phone of 20 years ago—much heavier and without the cameras, MP3 players, and web-browsing gizmos that we associate with today's mobile phones.

The life-cycle of mobile phones as a broad product category is now at the mature stage—some would say saturated. But when individual product formats are examined, a pattern of continual development, launch, growth, and eventual decline is evident. First-generation phones based on analogue technology were soon replaced by digital technology. From 2003, it seemed that the 'new' digital technology would be replaced by a third generation of mobile phones (3G). By 2008, work was well underway with the development of the next generation of fourth-generation mobile phones.

The pace of growth has posed enormous risks for the companies involved, especially where new technologies displace the technology which went before them, calling for ever increasing capital investment, and no chance of a return from customers until long after the initial investment has been made in new capacity. Each time, the stakes involved in new product development seemed to get bigger, with uncertainty about just what take-up there would be for the new technology. Companies had in the past been wrong in their predictions of mobile phone usage. WAP (wireless access protocol) phones capable of surfing the Internet turned out to be a flop. On the other hand, SMS text messaging, which was originally considered not worth including in the specification for GSM phones, went on to be a runaway hit.

Many commentators saw '3G' technology as the key to a whole new world of mobile telephony in which the mobile phone would be positioned not just as a device for voice communication, but a vital business, leisure, and information tool. In 2000 the UK government held an auction for five new 3G mobile phone licences, and the mobile phone companies paid a total of £22 billion for licences. Would they get back their huge investment, not only in licence fees paid, but also the infrastructure that was needed to support the new 3G networks?

During 2003, the Hong Kong-based Hutchison Whampoa became the first company to launch a 3G service in the UK, with its '3' network. The launch was accompanied by endless hype about the wireless Internet and video capabilities. The world was going to be transformed by streaming of video and football matches live to customers' mobile phones, and a whole new world of mobile advertising media would open up. Location-Based Services (LBS) had been a small but growing sector of the mobile phone industry. A report by Concise Insight (2004) noted that Vodafone UK's mobile content reached 1.9 per cent of total revenue for March 2004, almost double the 1.0 per cent a year before. It seemed that location technology was underpinning value-added data services. Even the emergency services stood to benefit from 3G's ability to precisely pinpoint a caller's location. By 2004, 60 per cent of calls to the UK emergency services were made from mobiles, but in many instances callers didn't know exactly where they were, and ambulances and fire brigades only had very approximate locations.

But after long delays in rolling out the new phones and networks, followed by sluggish uptake of the early services, 3 found itself in 2004 focusing on more mundane marketing issues, such as the cost of old-fashioned voice calls. The costs of recruiting new customers were high, with Mark James, telecoms analyst at Japanese investment bank Nomura, estimating that 3's customer acquisition costs in its first year were £600 per customer—around four times the European average. Analysts estimated that Hutchison, which had placed a $US22 billion bet on the fledgling technology, was seeing a worldwide 3G cash-burn of about HK$100 million ($12.8 million) per day. Rival operators that were preparing their own 3G launches would aim to start by pricing the technology at a premium. But their problem was that 3 was already pricing its phones and services—which offered ITN news and premiership football clips among other features—at cutthroat prices. Their best hope was that 3's model would prove unsustainable. After all, anyone can get customers if they effectively give their product away.

Hutchison is not new to taking big risks in the mobile phone market. It was behind the 'Rabbit' network of semi-mobile Telepoint phones launched in the UK in the 1980s. These allowed callers to use a compact handset to make outgoing calls only, when they were within 150 metres of a base station, these being located in public places such as railway stations, shops, petrol stations, etc. As in the case of many new markets that suddenly emerge, operators saw advantages of having an early market share lead. Customers who perceived that one network was more readily available than any other would—all other things being equal—be more likely to subscribe to that network. Operators saw that a bandwagon effect could be set up—to gain entry to the market at a later stage could become a much more expensive market challenger exercise.

Such was the speed of development that the Telepoint concept was not rigorously test marketed. To many, the development was too much product led, with insufficient understanding of buyer behaviour and competitive pressures. Each of the four companies forced through their own technologies, with little inclination or time available to discuss industry standard handsets which could eventually have caused the market to grow at a faster rate and allowed the operators to cut their costs. The final straw for the Rabbit network came with the announcement by the UK government of its proposal to issue licences for a new generation of Personal Communications Networks; these would have the additional benefit of allowing both incoming and outgoing calls, and would not be tied to a limited base station range. While this in itself might not have put people off buying new Rabbit handsets, it did have the effect of bringing new investment in the network to a halt, leaving the existing networks in a state of limbo.

Could the point about leapfrogging technology—which had wiped out Hutchison's Rabbit network—happen again with 3G technology? By 2006 the next generation of mobile phone services were under development, with Japanese trials of '4G'—faster than 3G. 3G phones were also challenged by the development of alternative wireless access services, notably WiFi. Many companies, such as T-Mobile had begun offering mobile WiFi services, which allow users to log on to local access points and gain access to their email and browse the Internet. Subscribers to

'VOIP' telephony services could also effectively make free phone calls from a WiFi access point. For many business travellers, using their laptop, WiFi access seemed a more attractive and less expensive option than using a 3G phone connection to check for email. It was likely to become even more attractive, with development of longer range WiMax services that extended beyond the very limited 50 metre or so range of WiFi. The pressure on 3G services was intensified when the UK government announced in 2006 that it would license the development of a national WiFi network.

Could 3G become old hat before it had even reached a profit table stage in its life-cycle? Would the history of the short-lived Rabbit network be repeated? Had the owners of the '3' network, Hutchison, failed to learn from the Rabbit failure? In 2010 it seemed that 3G technology would become obsolete as the UK government announced plans to sell lexemes for a '4G' network, capable of speeds up to ten times those of 3G.

Based on: *Financial Times*, '3UK seeks to project a new image', London, *Financial Times*, 18 October 2005, 25; *Financial Times*, 'Hutchison 3G unit hits profitability target', London, *Financial Times*, 27 May 2008, 31; Concise Insight Europe, 'European Location-Based Services 2004'. London: Concise Insight.

Case study review questions

1. Critically evaluate methods that mobile phone companies could use to assess buyer's likely response to new features, such as video on demand.

2. In terms of a new product development process, how could the development and launch of Telepoint services have been improved in order to avoid the problems that were experienced? What lessons can be learnt for the development of 3G (or 4G services?

3. Consider how the launch of 3G services in a less developed country with a less sophisticated telecommunications infrastructure may differ from a launch in a western developed country??

CHAPTER REVIEW QUESTIONS

1. Critically discuss the usefulness of the product life-cycle concept to marketing managers

2. To what extent can the various stages in the new product development process be distinguished? How could they be integrated more fully?

3. With reference to specific examples, examine the practical problems of deleting products from a company's product range.

ACTIVITIES

1. Take a look inside your local post office. Post offices have been undergoing a transformation in many countries, as governments deregulate mail services, and many of the functions traditionally undertaken by post offices are migrated online. Identify ideas for possible new product development by the post office, and critically evaluate their likelihood of success.

2. Consider a poorly performing service that you are familiar with, such as a bus service which seems to run empty, or a university course that has a falling number of students. Consider the merit of deleting the selected service. If you consider that the service justifies deletion, identify the most cost-effective strategy for deleting it, so that the reputation of the service provider is maintained and as many customers as possible are maintained.

3. If you are following a course of study at a college or university, list your ideas for new services, or service improvements offered by the college or university. Explore how your ideas could be most effectively communicated to senior decision makers, and identify possible barriers to actually implementing your ideas.

REFERENCES

ABA Banking Journal (2002) 'What's Egg?'. *ABA Banking Journal*, 94 (9), 60–61.

Adner, R. (2002) 'When Are Technologies Disruptive? A demand-based view of the emergence of competition'. *Strategic Management Journal*, 23 (8), 667–88.

Ansoff, I.H. (1957) 'Strategies for Diversification'. *Harvard Business Review*, 35 (5), 113–24.

Bolton, L.E. (2003) 'Stickier Priors: the Effects of Nonanalytic Versus Analytic Thinking in New Product Forecasting'. *Journal of Marketing Research*, 40 (1), 65–80.

Concise Insight (2004) *European Location-Based Services 2004: Market Opinions*. London: Concise Insight.

Crosby, P.B. (1984) *Quality Without Tears*. New York: New American Library.

Dahan, E. and Hauser, J.R. (2002) 'The Virtual Customer'. *Journal of Product Innovation Management*,19 (5), 332–51.

Dipasquale, C.B. (2002) 'Catalina Service to Track New Products'. *Advertising Age*, 73 (38), 59.

Enright, M. (2001) 'Approaches to Market Orientation and New Product Development in Smaller Enterprises: a Proposal for a Context-rich Interpretative Framework'. *Journal of Strategic Marketing*, 9 (4), 301–13.

Fagan, M. (2003) 'Three Launches 3G Services—But Without Handsets'. *Sunday Telegraph*, 2 March.

Financial Times (2008a) 'Commodities Sell-off Drags Materials Lower'. *Financial Times*, 30 April, 36.

Financial Times (2008b) 'UK Leads in Sowing Seeds for a Sector'. *Financial Times*, 17 June.

Forlani, D., Mullins, J.W., and Walker, O.C. Jr (2002) 'New Product Decision Making: How Chance and Size of Loss Influence What Marketing Managers See and Do'. *Psychology & Marketing*, 19 (11), 957–81.

Gronroos, C. (1984),'A Service Quality Model and its Marketing Implications'. *European Journal of Marketing*, 18 (4), 36–43.

Howley, M. (2002) 'The Role of Consultancies in New Product Development'. *Journal of Product & Brand Management*, 11 (7), 447–58.

Huang, X., Soutar, G.N., and Brown, A. (2002) 'New Product Development Processes in Small and Medium-Sized Enterprises: some Australian evidence'. *Journal of Small Business Management*, 40 (1), 27–42.

Juran, J.M. (1982) *Upper Management and Quality*. New York: Juran Institute.

Kim, J. and Wilemon, D. (2003) 'Sources and Assessment of Complexity in NPD Projects'. *R & D Management*, 33 (1), 16–30.

Mills, D. (2002) 'Ad of the Week'. *Daily Telegraph*, 5 November.

Mills, D. (2003) 'L'Oréal Patents: Are They Worth It?' *Daily Telegraph*, 18 February.

Mintel (2002) *The Sports Drinks Market*. London: Mintel.

Ofek, E. and Srinivasan, V. (2002) 'How Much Does the Market Value an Improvement in a Product Attribute?' *Marketing Science*, 21 (4), 398.

Rodríguez, N.G.M., Sanzo Pérez, J., and Trespalacios Gutiérrez, J.A. (2007) 'Interfunctional Trust as a Determining Factor of a New Product Performance'. *European Journal of Marketing*, 41 (5/6), 678–702.

Rogers, E.M. (2003) *Diffusion of Innovation,* 5th edition. New York: Simon and Schuster.

Song, M. and Swink, M. (2002) 'Marketing–Manufacturing Joint Involvement across Stages of New Product Development: Effects on the Success of Radical *v.* Incremental Innovations'. *Academy of Management Proceedings*, B1–B6.

The Times (2002) 'Mobile Phone Sales Fall'. *The Times*, 12 March, 25.

Vargo, S.L. and Lusch, R.F. (2008) 'Service-dominant Logic: Continuing the Evolution'. *Journal of the Academy of Marketing Science*, 36, 1–12.

Wong, V. (2002) 'Antecedents of International New Product Rollout Timeliness'. *International Marketing Review*, 19 (2/3), 120–32.

SUGGESTED FURTHER READING

The following provide contemporary insights into the role of innovation in organizations and the relationship between marketing and R&D:

Dodgson, M., Gann, D., and Salter, A. (2008) *Management of Technological Innovation: Strategy and Practice*. Oxford: Oxford University Press.

Trott, P. (2008) *Innovation Management and New Product Development*, 4th edition. London: FT Prentice Hall.

The methods used by organizations to search for new product ideas are discussed in the following:

Blazevic, V. and Lievens, A. (2008) 'Managing Innovation Through Customer Coproduced Knowledge in Electronic Services: an Exploratory Study'. *Journal of the Academy of Marketing Science*, 36, 138–51.

Füller, J., Matzler, K., and Hoppe, M. (2008) 'Brand Community Members as a Source of Innovation'. *The Journal of Product Innovation Management*, 25, 608–19.

Toivonen, M. and Tuominen, T. (2009) 'Emergence of Innovations in Services'. *The Service Industries Journal*, Volume 29, (7), 887–902.

The management of the new product development process is explored in the context of services in the following articles:

Seegy, U., Gleich, R., Wald, A., Mudde, P., and Motwani, J. (2008) 'The Management of Service Innovation: an Empirical Investigation'. *International Journal of Services and Operations Management*, 4 (6), 672–86.

Smith, A.M. and Fischbacher, M. (2005) 'New Service Development: a Stakeholder Perspective' *European Journal of Marketing*, 39 (9/10), 1025–48.

Stevens, E. and Dimitriadis, S. (2005) 'Managing the New Service Development Process: Toward a Systematic Model'. *European Journal of Marketing*, 39 (1/2), 175–98.

Consumer adoption processes for innovative products are discussed in the following:

Hossain, L. and de Silva, A. (2009) 'Exploring User Acceptance of Technology Using Social Networks'. *Journal of High Technology Management Research*, 20, 1–18.

Vlachos, P.A. and Vrechopoulos, A.P. (2008) 'Determinants of Behavioural Intentions in the Mobile Internet Services Market'. *Journal of Services Marketing*, 22 (4), 280–91.

Walker, R.H. and Johnson, L.W. (2006) 'Why Consumers Use and Do Not Use Technology Enabled Services'. *Journal of Services Marketing*, 20 (2), 126–35.

ONLINE RESOURCE CENTRE

Visit the Online Resource Centre for resources that are relevant to this chapter, including a flashcard glossary, web links, multiple choice questions, and additional case studies:

www.oxfordtextbooks.co.uk/orc/palmer3e/

KEYWORDS

- Consumer goods
- Convenience goods
- Diversification
- Fast moving consumer goods (FMCGs)
- Innovation
- New product development
- Packaging
- Patent

- Product life-cycle
- Product line
- Product mix
- Quality
- Research and development
- Shopping goods
- Speciality goods
- Trademark

PRICING

CHAPTER OBJECTIVES

Pricing can be a very difficult part of the marketing mix to get right, but getting it right can have a big impact on sales volumes and profitability. In the first part of this chapter we will look at the economic theory underlying price decisions. Perfectly competitive markets are introduced as one extreme in which the marketer must take prices as given from the market. From this, various other market structures are discussed and their impact on pricing decisions assessed. The second part of the chapter focuses on situations where a firm has developed some degree of uniqueness for its product, such as a brand, which sets it aside from perfectly competitive markets. Here firms have more discretion over pricing, and this chapter explores firms' objectives, strategies, and tactics in setting their prices.

Introduction

Most of the decisions made by marketing managers involve spending their company's money—on advertising, paying sales personnel, setting up distributor networks, new product development, and so on. Price is the one element of the marketing mix that directly affects the income that a company receives. In businesses with high turnover and low profit margins, a miscalculation of selling prices can have a big effect on a firm's annual profits. If the company charges too little for its products, it may find that, although it has achieved a very respectable level of sales, the low price charged is insufficient to give it any profit. Too high a price, and it may be unable to sell sufficient output to cover its fixed overhead costs. It may also end up with unsold stocks of obsolete products.

For most firms, setting prices is a difficult task which involves both scientific analysis and intuitive trial and error. This is especially true of new product launches, where a company has no historical precedent on which to base its expectations of how much customers will be prepared to pay.

In the first part of this chapter, we will look at some of the basic theory underlying firms' pricing decisions. Taking a broad perspective, firms cannot ignore market forces, so it is important to understand the relationship between market structure and the way in which prices are determined. The approach to pricing of a firm operating in a fiercely competitive market will differ quite markedly from the approach of a firm in a market where there are very few competitors.

The second part of this chapter considers more applied issues of pricing, which are applicable to companies that have some discretion in the prices they charge. (That is, they are not operating in a perfectly competitive market where prices are determined solely by the market.) Firms develop strategies in order to respond to the competitive nature of their environment; for example they may aim to be a price leader across their range of products. For individual new product launches, a company may pursue a strategy of starting with a high price, and gradually lowering it over time. In terms of setting prices for individual products, firms pursue a variety of approaches, including basing their selling price on their production costs, on the prices that competitors are currently charging, and on customers' ability and willingness to pay.

Governments often seek to regulate the prices of key goods and services, such as electricity and telephones, so it is important to understand how firms can reconcile the sometimes conflicting approaches of market forces and regulation.

Of course, pricing should never be seen as an isolated element of a firm's marketing decision making. What the company is able to charge is closely related to, among other things, the quality of its products, the advertising images that it has created, and the effectiveness of its distribution strategy.

Effects of market structure on pricing

The market conditions facing suppliers of goods and services vary considerably. Customers of water supply companies may feel they are being exploited by high prices and poor service levels provided by companies that know that their customers have little choice of supplier. On the other hand, customers are constantly being wooed by seemingly countless credit card companies, all trying to offer deals that buyers will consider to be better than those offered by competitors. The differences in the pricing behaviour of these two groups of organizations can be related to the structure of the markets in which they operate. The term 'market structure' is used to describe:

- the number of buyers and sellers operating in a market;

- the barriers that exist to prevent new firms from entering the market (or prevent existing companies from leaving it);

- the extent to which the supply of goods and services is concentrated in the hands of a small number of buyers (or, less frequently, the extent to which purchases are concentrated in the hands of a few buyers);

- the degree of collusion that occurs between buyers and/or sellers in the market.

An understanding of market structure underpins all pricing decisions made by marketers. Market structure influences not only the pricing decisions made by marketers within a firm, but also the nature of the response from other firms operating in the market.

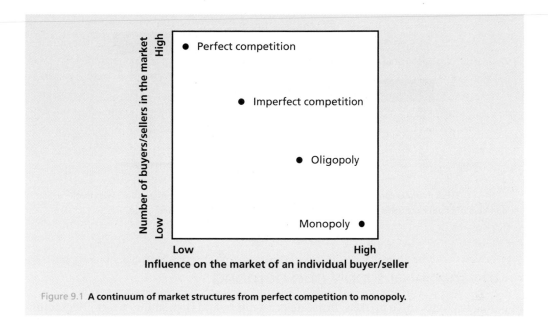

Figure 9.1 **A continuum of market structures from perfect competition to monopoly.**

Economists have developed a number of labels to describe different types of market structure. At one theoretical extreme is the model of perfect competition and at the other is pure monopoly. In practice, examples of the extremes are very rare, and most markets are referred to as being in a state of *imperfect competition* (Figure 9.1).

We are first going to spend some time looking at perfectly competitive markets. These are characterized by the following conditions:

- There are many producers supplying the market, each with similar cost structures and each producing an identical product. No single supplier on its own can influence the market price.

- There are also many buyers in the market, none of which can, on their own, influence the market price.

- Both buyers and sellers are free to enter or leave the market; that is, there are no barriers to entry or exit.

- There is a ready supply of information for buyers and sellers, for example about competing alternatives.

These may seem quite unrealistic conditions for many markets, although a few markets do come close to meeting them (e.g. the 'spot' market for oil products, and stock markets where shares are bought and sold). However, the real value of studying competitive markets is that it teaches us the basic rules of supply, demand, and price determination (Figure 9.2).

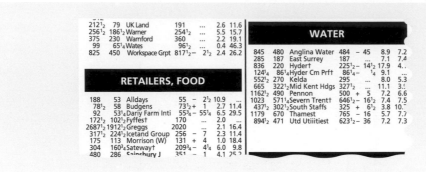

212¹₂	79	UK Land	191	...	2.6	11.6
256¹₂	186¹₂	Warner	254¹₂	...	5.5	15.7
375	230	Warnford	360	...	2.2	19.1
99	65¹₄	Wates	96¹₂	...	0.4	46.3
825	450	Workspace Grpt	817¹₂–	2¹₂	2.4	26.2

RETAILERS, FOOD

188	53	Alldays	55	– 2¹₂	10.9	...
78¹₂	58	Budgens	73¹₂+ 1	2.7	11.4	
92	53¹₄	Dariy Farm Inti	55³₄ – 55¹₄	6.5	29.5	
172¹₂	102¹₂	Fyffest	170	...	2.0	...
2687¹₂	1912¹₂	Greggs	2020	...	2.1	16.4
317¹₂	224¹₂	Iceland Group	256	– 7	2.3	11.4
175	113	Morrison (W)	131	+ 4	1.0	18.4
304	160³₄	Satewayt	209³₄ – 4¹₄	6.0	9.8	
480	286	Sainsbury J	351	– 1	4.1	25.2

WATER

845	480	Anglina Water	484	– 45	8.9	7.2
285	187	East Surrey	187	...	7.1	7.4
836	220	Hydert	225¹₂– 14¹₂	17.9	4..	
124¹₄	86¹₄	Hyder Cm Prft	86¹₄– ¹₄	9.1	...	
552¹₂	270	Kelda	295	...	8.0	5.3
665	322¹₂	Mid Kent Hdgs	327¹₂	...	11.1	3.!
1162¹₂	490	Pennon	500	+ 5	7.2	6.6
1023	571¹₄	Severn Trentt	646¹₂– 16¹₂	7.4	7.5	
437¹₂	302¹₂	South Staffs	325	+ 6¹₂	3.8	10.˜
1179	670	Thamest	765	– 16	5.7	7.7
894¹₂	471	Utd Utiiitiest	623¹₂– 36	7.2	7.3	

Figure 9.2 Stock markets come close to meeting the requirements of perfect competition, with large numbers of buyers and sellers resulting in daily fluctuations in a company's share price.

The theory of supply and demand

In perfectly competitive markets, firms are price-*takers*, and their ability to set prices is limited by the level of demand and supply within the market they serve. If total demand goes up, all other things being equal, the going rate of prices in the market for their product will rise. Likewise, if there is a drop in total supply for whatever reason (e.g. because of bad weather), there will be further pressure for prices in the market to rise. The final price paid in the market will reflect the balance between supply-side and demand-side factors.

A market as defined here need not be a physical location where exchange takes place (as happens in retail and wholesale grocery markets). A market in the economist's sense refers to all individuals and firms who wish either to buy or to sell a specified product. A market is defined in terms of product and geographic descriptions, so the UK soft drinks market refers to all individuals in the UK who seek to buy soft drinks and the suppliers to that market.

Demand

Demand refers to how many people in a market are actually willing and able to buy a product at a given price and given a set of assumptions about the product and the environment in which it is being offered. Demand is also expressed in terms of a specified time period, for example thousands of litres of soft drinks per week. It is important to add the caveat that demand is about the quantity of a product that consumers are *willing* and *able* to buy at a specific price over a given period of time. It is important to distinguish these conditions from what people would merely *like* to buy—after all, most people would probably *like* to buy more expensive holidays and cars.

For most products, as their price falls, so the demand for them (as defined above) can be expected to rise. Likewise, as the price rises, demand could be expected to fall. This relationship can be plotted on a simple graph. In Figure 9.3, a *demand curve* for dessert strawberries is shown by the line D1. This relates—for any given price shown on the vertical axis—the price to the volume of demand, which is shown on the horizontal axis. So at a price of £8 per kg

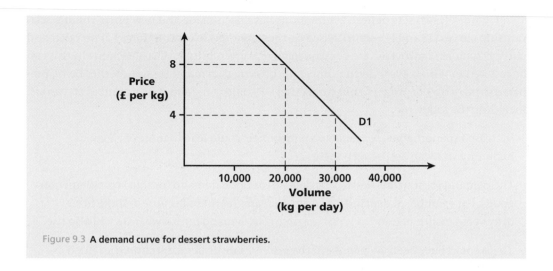

Figure 9.3 **A demand curve for dessert strawberries.**

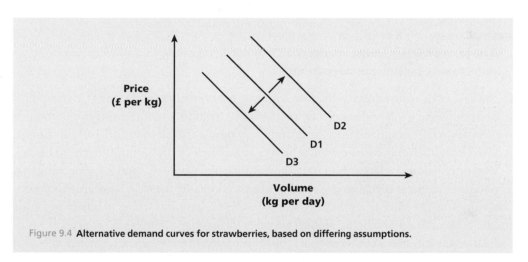

Figure 9.4 **Alternative demand curves for strawberries, based on differing assumptions.**

demand is 20,000 units per period within a given area, while at a price of £4 the demand rises to 30,000 units.

The demand curve shown in Figure 9.3 refers to *total* market demand from all consumers, and is not simply measuring demand for one strawberry grower's output. The importance of this distinction will become clear later, because in imperfect markets each producer seeks to develop a unique demand function for its own differentiated product.

In drawing the price–volume relationship D1, a number of assumptions were made. These include, for example, assumptions that the price of substitutes for strawberries will not change, and that consumers will not suddenly take a dislike to strawberries.

Demand curve D1 measures the relationship between price and market demand for *one given set of assumptions*. When these assumptions change, a new demand curve is needed to explain the new relationship between price asked and quantity demanded.

In Figure 9.4, two sets of fresh assumptions have been made and new price–volume relationship curves D2 and D3 drawn, based on these new sets of assumptions. For new demand curve D2, more strawberries are demanded for any given price level. (Alternatively, this can be restated in terms of any given number of consumers demanding strawberries being prepared to pay a higher price.) A shift from D1 to D2 could come about for a number of reasons, including the following:

- Increased spending power available to consumers could lead to more of all goods, including strawberries, being bought.

- The demand for strawberries may be dependent upon demand for some complementary goods. For example, if demand for cream increases (perhaps because of some newly discovered health benefit), it is just possible that demand for strawberries will also rise.

- There could have been an increase in the price of substitutes for strawberries (such as peaches or raspberries), thereby increasing demand for strawberries.

- Heavy advertising of strawberries may increase demand for strawberries.

- Consumer preferences may change. This may occur, for example, if strawberries are found to have positive effects on health.

In the case of the movement in the price–volume relationship from D1 to D3, corresponding but opposite explanations can be put forward, including reduced spending power of consumers; a fall in demand for a complementary product; a fall in the price of substitutes; reduced advertising; and new evidence linking strawberries with harmful effects on health.

Most price–volume relationships slope downwards, as in Figures 9.3 and 9.4, indicating that as price rises demand falls, and vice versa. While this is usually the case, there are exceptions. Sometimes, as the price of a product goes up, buyers are able and wiling to buy more of the product. This can occur where a product becomes increasingly desirable as more people consume it. Many Internet websites were of little value to advertisers when only small numbers of people used the site, but as more customers used it the price of advertising on the site increased.

Although the price–volume relationships shown in Figures 9.3 and 9.4 are straight, this is a simplification of reality. Demand curves are usually curved, indicating that the relationship between price and volume is not constant for all price points. There may, additionally, be discontinuities at certain price points where buyers in a market have psychological price barriers, for example an MP3 player costing £100 may be perceived as unaffordable, whereas one costing £99.99 may be perceived as affordable (Figure 9.5) (see Bray and Harris 2006).

Drawing a conceptual diagram relating price to volume of demand is relatively easy compared with the problems of collecting data and actually measuring the relationship. The problems are both theoretical and practical.

Data can be obtained by one of two principal methods:

1. They could be collected at one point in time by comparing sales volumes in one area, at a given price, with sales volumes in another area, where a different price is charged.

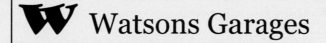

SPECIAL OFFER!

FULL SERVICE FOR YOUR CAR

ONLY

£99.99

AVAILABLE UNTIL AUGUST 31 2011.
BOOK YOUR APPOINTMENT NOW

Terms and conditions apply

W Watsons Garages

Figure 9.5 **£99.99 represents an important price point in many people's minds.** Through a process of rationalization, customers of this shop may be able to justify to themselves spending £99.99 on a luxury, whereas £100.00 may be considered unacceptable. Where the market allows it, companies use various forms of psychological pricing to induce a response that would probably not be expected on the basis of assumptions about a linear demand curve.

Retailers often experiment by charging different prices at different stores to build up some kind of picture about the relationship between price and volume. This is referred to as *cross-sectional data*. To be sure that this is accurately measuring the price–volume relationships, there must be no extraneous differences between the points of observation (such as differences in household incomes) which could partly explain differences in price–volume relationships.

2. Alternatively, a firm can change the price of a product over time and see what happens to sales volumes. This is referred to as *longitudinal data*. Again, it can be difficult to keep assumptions constant throughout the duration of the data collection, so that rising incomes or changing consumer preferences could explain sales variations just as much as changes in a product's selling price.

Supply

Firms' willingness to supply products to a market will be influenced by the prevailing price in the market. If the price they receive for selling their goods is low, they will be less willing to supply to the market than if the selling price is high. As in the case of demand, a price-volume line can be drawn, relating the market price of strawberries to volumes supplied by all farmers to the market (Figure 9.6).

The supply curve in Figure 9.6 slopes upwards from left to right, indicating that, as the market price rises, more suppliers will be attracted to supply strawberries to the market. Conversely, as prices fall, marginal producers (such as those who operate relatively inefficiently) will drop out of the market, reducing the daily supply available.

Supply curve S1 is based on various assumptions about the relationship between price and volume supplied. If these no longer hold true, a new supply price–volume relationship needs to be drawn, based on the new set of assumptions. In Figure 9.7, two new supply price–volume relationships, S2 and S3, are shown. The curve S2 indicates a situation where, for any given price level, total supply to the market is increased. This could come about for a number of reasons, including the following:

- In the short term, extraneous factors (such as favourable weather conditions) could result in a glut of perishable strawberries which must be sold, and the market would therefore be flooded with additional supply.

- Improvements in production methods could result in suppliers being prepared to supply more strawberries at any given price (or, looked at another way, for any given volume supplied, suppliers are prepared to accept a lower price).

- Governments may give subsidies to strawberry growers, thereby increasing their willingness to supply to the market at any given price level.

New supply curve S3 indicates a situation where, for any given price level, total supply to the market is reduced. This could come about for a number of reasons, including adverse extraneous factors (e.g. bad weather for growers), increased production costs (e.g. rising wage costs), and reduction of government subsidies and/or imposition of taxes.

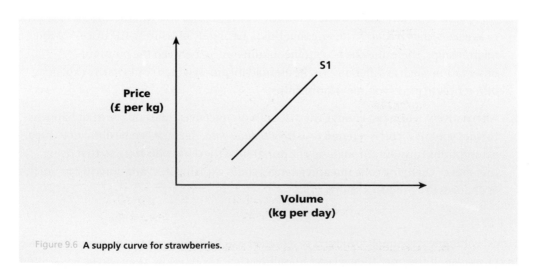

Figure 9.6 **A supply curve for strawberries.**

It should be noted that some changes in the actual volume of supply might take time to occur. So if strawberry prices went up today, this might not result in increased planting of strawberry plants and hence a larger supply of strawberries to the market, until the next growing season. Refer back to the discussion in Chapter 1 of the organic vegetable market and the time that it took firms to satisfy customers' demand for more organic produce.

Price determination

In competitive markets, selling prices are determined by the interaction of demand and supply. This can be illustrated by superimposing the supply curve on the demand curve (Figure 9.8).

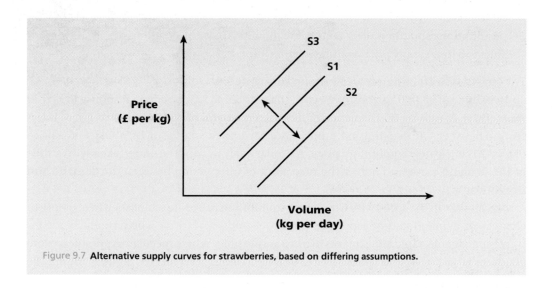

Figure 9.7 **Alternative supply curves for strawberries, based on differing assumptions.**

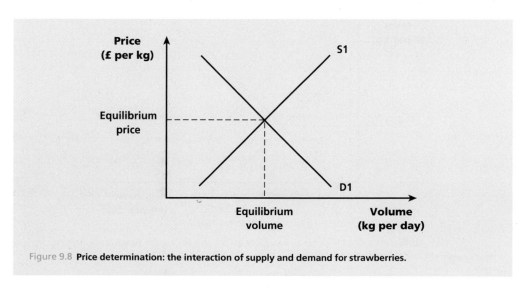

Figure 9.8 **Price determination: the interaction of supply and demand for strawberries.**

The supply curve indicates that at lower prices fewer strawberries will be supplied to the market. But at these lower prices, customers are willing and able to buy large volumes of strawberries—more than the suppliers collectively are willing or able to supply. The demand and supply curves intersect at precisely the point where the price–volume relationship is similar for both buyers and sellers. This is the point of equilibrium where demand and supply are precisely in balance. At any lower price, there will be more demand than suppliers are willing to cater for. At any higher price, excessive supply could result in the build up of unsold stocks.

Changes in the equilibrium market price can come about for two principal reasons.

1. Assumptions about buyers' ability or willingness to buy may change, resulting in a shift to a new demand price–volume relationship.

2. Assumptions about suppliers' ability or willingness to supply may change, resulting in a shift to a new supply price–volume relationship.

The effects of shifts in supply are illustrated in Figure 9.9. From an equilibrium price of £7 and a volume of 15,000 kg, the supply curve has shifted to S2 (perhaps in response to higher wage costs). Assuming that demand conditions remain unchanged, the new point of intersection between the demand and supply lines occurs at a volume of 12,000 kg and a price of £6. This is the new equilibrium price. A similar analysis could be undertaken with a shift in the demand curve and noting the new point of intersection between the demand and supply lines.

Markets vary in the speed with which new equilibrium prices are established in response to changes in demand and/or supply. In pure commodity markets where products are instantly perishable, rapid adjustments in price are possible. Where speculators are able to store goods, or large buyers and sellers are able unduly to influence a market, adjustment may be

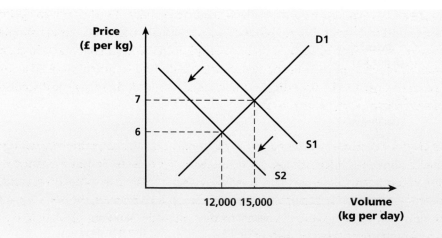

Figure 9.9 **New equilibrium market price for strawberries, based on a shift in the supply price–volume relationship.**

slower (see Bell et al. 2002). The extent of changes in price and volume traded is also dependent on the elasticity of demand and supply, which are considered later in this chapter.

Imperfections to competition

The model of perfect competition presented above is rarely seen in practice. The forces of competition may be ideal for consumers because of the tendency of market forces to minimize prices and/or maximize firms' outputs. But in such markets, suppliers are forced to be price-*takers* rather than price-*makers*. In a perfectly competitive market, firms are unable to use marketing strategies to affect the price at which they sell. At a higher price, buyers will immediately substitute identical products from other suppliers. Lower prices would be unsustainable in an industry where all firms had similar cost structures.

It is not surprising, therefore, that firms try to overcome the full effects of perfectly competitive markets. There are two principal methods by which a firm can seek to deviate from the workings of perfectly competitive markets to its own advantage: operating at lower costs than other firms in the market and differentiating its products.

Operating at a lower cost

If a company operates at a lower cost than other firms, and is able to remain at a lower cost than other firms, it will be able to sustain lower prices than its competitors. In many industries economies of scale are available to firms, so that as they grow bigger their unit costs fall. This allows them to charge lower prices and still make an adequate profit. Lower prices result in a greater demand for a firm's products, which in turn can allow it to achieve even more economies of scale. This virtuous circle of lower costs leading to competitive advantage can result in a small number of firms gaining a dominant position in the marketplace, thereby violating an important assumption of perfect competition. This can lead to a situation of oligopoly or monopoly (see below), in which the dominant firms have significant power to dictate prices.

Of course, gaining a competitive advantage through economies of scale is not an option open to firms in all industries. Where production and distribution methods are simple, there may be no economies of scale available to exploit. As an example, many firms in service industries such as plumbing and decorating would find it difficult to gain a cost advantage over competitors by operating at a larger scale. Indeed, there may be diseconomies of scale associated with being too large.

Differentiating the product

We saw in Chapter 7 that an entrepreneur can try to avoid head-on competition by selling a product that is somehow differentiated from competitors' products. So in the market for strawberries, a strawberry grower may try to get away from the fiercely competitive conditions that occur in wholesale fruit and vegetable markets. In such markets, the price of products is determined by the market forces alone. Instead, the strawberry supplier could try a number of differentiating strategies, including:

- concentrating on selling specially selected strawberries, for example ones that are of a particular size or ripeness;

- offering strawberries in distinctive protective packaging;

- offering a delivery service to local customers;

- offering a money-back guarantee of quality;

- offering strawberries in combination with other complementary elements of a fruit salad;

- processing the strawberries by tinning or freezing them;

- as a result of any of the above actions, it could develop a distinctive brand identity for its strawberries, so that buyers don't ask just for strawberries, but for 'brand x' strawberries by name.

In this example, the supplier has taken steps to turn a basic commodity product into something that is quite distinctive, so it has immediately cut down the number of direct competitors it faces. In fact, if its product really was unique, it would have no direct competition. (In other words, it would be a monopoly supplier of a unique product.) For some differentiated products, this may seem very true in many customers' minds; for example some people would see a Rolex watch as being quite different to any other watch. Part of the differentiation may be only in buyers' minds, resulting from brand images and lifestyle associations that have been built up over time.

It must not, however, be forgotten that, although the way a supplier has presented its product may be unique, the product is still broadly similar to many competing products in terms of the ability to met buyers' basic needs. The strawberry trader therefore will still face indirect competition from suppliers of other types of fruit.

If a supplier has successfully differentiated its product, it is no longer strictly a price-taker from the market. So the strawberry supplier that has specially selected or packaged its strawberries may be able to charge a few pence per kilogram more than the going rate for basic commodity strawberries. However, it will achieve this higher price only if customers consider that the higher price is worth paying for a better product. It will be able to experiment to assess how customers value a product, and to see just how much more buyers are prepared to pay for its differentiated product.

Elasticity of demand

Price elasticity of demand refers to the extent to which demand changes in relation to a change in price. It is a useful indicator for business organizations because it allows them to predict what will happen to volume sales in response to a change in price.

Price elasticity of demand can be expressed as a simple formula:

$$\text{Price elasticity of demand} = \frac{(\%)\,\text{change in demand}}{(\%)\,\text{change in price}}.$$

Where demand is relatively unresponsive to price changes, it is said to be *inelastic* with respect to price. Where demand is highly responsive to even a small price change, it is described as being *elastic* with respect to price.

We have seen that firms face a downward-sloping demand curve for their products, indicating that as prices fall demand increases, and vice versa. By lowering its price, a firm may be able to increase its sales, but what is important to firms is that they increase their total revenue (and profits). Whether this happens depends upon the elasticity of demand for the product in question.

- If it is possible to substitute a product with another that is very similar, price elasticity is said to be high. What constitutes a similar and substitutable product can be defined only in the minds of customers. Two pairs of training shoes may seem technically similar, but their images may be so different that for many buyers they are not at all substitutable.

- The absolute value of a product and its importance to a buyer can influence its elasticity. As an example, most people would not bother shopping around for the best price on infrequently purchased boxes of matches. However, the same percentage difference in price between competing brands of television sets makes a sufficiently large difference to encourage buyers to shop around.

- It is important to understand how price cuts will be perceived by people who are the target of the cuts. A large price cut may lead some people to ask 'Why do they have to make such a cut—surely the product cannot be very good?'

A number of demand curves describing a firm's market can be drawn, ranging from the general product form to the specific brand, each with differing elasticity. For example, in the market for beverages the demand curve for beverages in general may be fairly inelastic, on the basis that people will always want to buy drinks of some description (Figure 9.10). Demand for one particular type of beverage, such as cola, will be slightly more elastic, as people may be attracted to cola from other drinks such as carbonated fruit juices and soda water on the basis of their relative price. Price becomes more elastic still when a particular brand of cola is considered. To many people, Coca Cola can be easily substituted with other brands of cola, so if a price differential between brands developed, switching might occur.

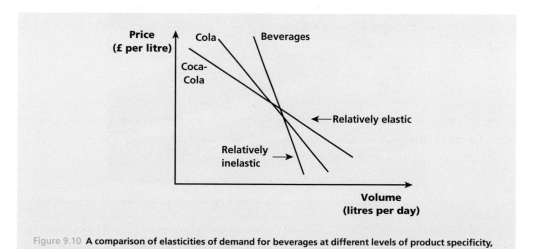

Figure 9.10 **A comparison of elasticities of demand for beverages at different levels of product specificity, from a general product form to a specific brand.**

In general, firms will find that their products are much more inelastic to changes in price over the short term, when possibilities for substitution may be few. But over the longer term, new possibilities for substitution may appear. (For example, petrol is very inelastic over the short term but much more elastic over the long term, when motorists have a chance to adapt to less fuel-intensive cars and alternative methods of transport.) In addition to *price* elasticity of demand, economists measure a number of other types of elasticity that are of relevance to marketers in determining selling prices (Figure 9.11). Probably the most important of these

Figure 9.11 **Budget airlines discovered a highly elastic demand for air services and have grown rapidly as a result.** The price of a return fare from London to Glasgow can now cost less than the price of a pair of jeans and low prices have tempted more people into the airline market. For some, low prices by air meant that they switched from competing rail and road services. For others, new possibilities for taking short holidays or visiting friends were opened up which had previously not been affordable.

A small penny—a big price difference?

Many business sectors have been accused of deliberately confusing customers in the way prices are presented, and the 'No frills' airline sector has attracted particular criticism from government agencies and consumer groups. Many of the 'tricks of the trade' used by the sector go back a long way, for example the use of '99' ending prices rather than whole pound pricing to make a buyer feel that the price is below a psychologically important price barrier (Bray and Harris 2006). Airlines have been fined for advertising low 'lead in' prices in bold print, but when customers have tried to find such prices, they have not been available. Airlines may have had an excuse for non-availability when printed price lists became out of date, but how could they excuse misleading lead-in prices for web-based adverts which can be automatically updated in real-time from a database?

The practice of some airlines of showing a low basic price in large figures, while hiding compulsory additional costs in small print has been widely criticized. For many budget airline tickets, taxes and security charges may amount to more than the basic price of the ticket, but the total cost of the ticket might only be found at the point where a potential buyer is about to complete their purchase. One critic has likened airlines' practice of making separate charges for taxes and security charges as being similar to car manufacturers making an additional charge for the steering wheel.

There is some evidence that consumers may make irrational choices, based on apparently misleading price information. This may be evidenced by paying a higher price for a ticket with a low basic price, compared with a similar ticket for which total price is expressed upfront (Palmer and Boissy 2009). Should governments intervene to stop such practices? Or should the old maxim apply that a buyer should beware, and study the small print before committing to a purchase? Do most buyers have the time or inclination to go through every company's small print with a fine toothcomb? One sign of governments' impatience with airlines' pricing practices was a statement in 2006 by the EU Transport Commissioner Mr Barrot, that the EU would press ahead with proposals to make fares easily comparable between airlines. In 2011, UK airlines finally gave in and showed most of their additional charges within the total amount, but many still sought to create new 'optional' charges, including fees for paying by credit card which many would argue were not really optional at all.

is *income* elasticity of demand, which measures the responsiveness of demand to changes in buyers' incomes and can be expressed in the following way:

$$\text{Income elasticity of demand} = \frac{(\%)\,\text{change in demand}}{(\%)\,\text{change in income}}.$$

In general, as an individual's income rises, her demand for most products rises, giving rise to a positive income elasticity of demand. Where there is a particularly strong increase in demand in response to an increase in incomes, a product is said to have a high income elasticity of demand. This is true of luxuries such as long-haul package holidays and fitted kitchens, whose sales have increased during times of general economic prosperity but declined during recessionary periods. On the other hand, there are some goods and services for which demand goes down as income increases. These are referred to as inferior goods, and examples in most western countries include rural bus services and household coal.

Oligopoly

Imperfect competition can develop to a point where market structure can be described as oligopolistic. Oligopoly lies somewhere between the two extremes of perfect competition and pure monopoly. An oligopoly market is dominated by a small number of sellers that provide a large share of the total market output. The crucial point about oligopoly markets is that all suppliers in the market are interdependent. One company cannot take price or output decisions without considering the specific possible responses of the other companies.

Markets are most likely to be oligopolistic where economies of scale are significant; for example oligopoly is typical of oil refining and distribution, pharmaceuticals, car manufacturing, and detergents. Customers of oligopoly organizations may not immediately appreciate that the products they are buying come from an oligopolist, as such firms frequently use a variety of brand names. (The detergent manufactures Unilever and Proctor & Gamble between them have over 50 apparently competing detergent products on sale in the UK.)

Oligopolists pay particular attention to the activities of their fellow oligopolists, and there is often a reluctance to upset the established order. One firm is often acknowledged as the price leader, and the other firms await its actions before adjusting their prices. In the UK household mortgage market, for example, Halifax has often been the initiator of price changes which other banks and building societies then follow. It has been suggested that firms may not match upward price movements, in the hope of gaining extra sales, but would match downward price changes for fear of losing market share. Oligopolists have often been accused of collusion and of creating barriers to entry for newcomers (such as signing exclusive distribution rights with key retailers).

Price wars between oligopolists can be very expensive to participants, so there is a tendency to find alternative ways to compete for customers, such as free gifts, coupons, added value offers, and sponsorship activities. This occurred in the UK in 2010 as the main cable television suppliers—Sky and Virgin—challenged each other with price cuts and special bundles of additional services which were included free of charge.

Monopolistic markets

In its purest extreme, monopoly occurs where there is only one supplier to the market, perhaps because of regulatory, technical, or economic barriers to entry which potential competing suppliers would face. A pure monopoly means that one person or organization has complete control over supply to that market. A monopolist can determine the market price for its product and can be described as a 'price-maker' rather than a 'price-taker'. Where there are few substitutes for a product, and where demand is inelastic, a monopolist may be able to get away with continually increasing prices in order to increase its profits.

Sometimes monopoly control over supply comes about through a group of suppliers acting in collusion in a cartel. As with the pure monopoly, companies would join a cartel in order to try and protect themselves from the harmful consequences of competition. Cartels have been suspected in many industry sectors, for example rings of cement suppliers in a region, who covertly agree to share markets between themselves and not to undercut each other's prices.

A pure monopoly rarely occurs in practice. Even in the former centrally planned economies of Eastern Europe, there were often active 'shadow' markets that existed alongside official monopoly suppliers. Most products have some form of substitute which reduces the monopolist's ability to set prices. Also, a firm that has significant monopoly pricing power at home may nevertheless face severe price competition in its overseas markets.

A company may have monopoly power over some of its users, but it may face competition if it wishes to attract new segments of users. It may therefore resort to differential pricing when targeting the two groups. As an example, many rail operators in the London area have considerable monopoly power over commuters, who need to use their train services to arrive at work by 9 am on weekdays. For such commuters, the alternatives of travelling to work by bus or car are very unattractive. However, leisure travellers wishing to go shopping in London during off-peak periods may be much more price sensitive. For them, the car or bus provide realistic alternatives, and so train companies offer a range of price incentives aimed at the off-peak leisure market, while charging full fare for their peak period commuters.

In theory, a company with significant monopoly power could continually raise its prices in order to exploit its monopoly. However, marketing managers who think strategically may be reluctant to exploit their monopoly powerfully. By charging high prices in the short term, a monopolist could give signals to companies in related product fields to develop substitutes that would eventually provide effective competition. Blatant abuse of monopoly power could also result in a referral to the regulatory authorities (see below).

Regulatory influences on pricing

Because of the presumed superiority of competitive markets, prevailing laws in most developed countries have been used to try to remove market imperfections where these are deemed to be against the public interest. Private-sector companies must take account of various regulations in setting their prices. These can be classified as:

- direct government controls to regulate monopoly power;

- government controls on price representations.

Direct government controls to regulate monopoly power

Governments have a range of measures which can be used to prevent exploitative pricing by monopolists. At a European level, Articles 85 and 86 of the Treaty of Rome limit the ability of firms to collude with their fellow producers or distributors in fixing prices. In the UK, the Enterprise Act 2002 strengthened the previous Competition Act 1998 by making provision for criminal sanctions with fines and a maximum penalty of five years in prison for individuals that operate agreements to fix prices, share markets, limit production, and rig bids. The Director-General of the Office of Fair Trading (OFT) has the power to order an investigation by the Competition Commission of alleged anti-competitive practices that may have the effect of restricting choice or causing prices to be higher than they need be. In 2010 an OFT investigation found that individuals in Royal Bank of Scotland's Professional Practices Coverage Team had disclosed confidential future pricing information to their counterparts at Barclays Bank. The OFT found evidence that the information was taken into account by

Barclays in determining its own pricing. RBS agreed to pay a fine of £28.6 million after admitting breaches of competition law between October 2007 and February 2008. The Competition Commission does not just involve itself with national organizations—it also investigates local abuse of monopoly power. In the Lancashire town of Preston, for example, the bus operator Stagecoach acquired Preston Bus in 2009, prompting an investigation by the Competition Commission which found evidence of a monopoly situation which was against the public interest, and therefore ordered the Scottish-based Stagecoach to sell its recent acquisition.

Utility companies with a monopoly position usually have their prices limited by the regulator for that industry. In the UK, Ofgem, Ofwat, and Ofcom regulate certain prices of gas/electricity, water, and broadcasting/telephone service providers, respectively. Governments have deregulated some utility markets, in the hope that this will result in lower prices through competitive pressures (e.g. numerous companies have been licensed to compete with British Telecom in the UK.) However, in many cases measures to increase competition have had only limited effect, as in the very limited competition faced by the privatized water supply companies; hence the continuing need for direct price controls. Even within the apparently more competitive telecommunications sector, the regulator has frequently intervened with instructions to operators to reduce specific categories of prices. In 2006, Ofcom—with the European Regulators Group (ERG), a body of EU telecoms regulators—investigated mobile phone roaming charges throughout Europe and was instrumental in the development of an EU directive to regulate these charges throughout Europe.

Government controls on price representations

In any marketplace, buyers and sellers need rules to govern their conduct and prevent abuses of their respective positions. So, as well as controlling or influencing the actual level of prices, government regulation can have the effect of specifying the manner in which price information is communicated to potential customers. At a general level, the Consumer Protection Act 1987 requires that all prices shown should conform to the Code of Practice on pricing—misleading price representations which relegate details of supplementary charges to the small print or give attractive low lead-in prices for services that are not in fact available are made illegal by this Act. Other regulations affect specific industries. The Consumer Credit Act 1974 requires that the charge made for credit must include a statement of the annual percentage rate (APR) of interest. Also within the financial services sector, the Financial Services Act 1986 has resulted in quite specific requirements regarding the manner in which charges for certain insurance-related services are presented to potential customers.

In the UK, the OFT has the power to investigate cases of misleading price representations. In 2009, it received complaints from local trading standards offices about alleged misleading price representations made on the website of the UK-based airline Jet2.com. The OFT investigated whether the airline was complying with the 2008 Consumer Protection from Unfair Trading Regulations. The OFT found evidence of misleading price information and the airline subsequently agreed to amend its pricing, in particular by ensuring that consumers are made aware of any fixed non-optional costs early in the booking process and by clearly displaying in the website's running total price the inclusion of costs which are not taxes (e.g. airport charges).

⊙ Pricing objectives of companies

We are now going to look at the decisions taken by firms that are able to act as price-*makers* rather than price-*takers*; in other words, those that have established some degree of differentiation from the rest of the market. Marketers must consider pricing not just at one point in time, but over the life of a product. So a price based on differential advantage over competitors may need to change over time as competitors gradually erode a company's differential advantage. Simplistic economic analyses of pricing tend to overlook the complex interdependencies that can exist between different products within a firm's product range, and we will explore the subject of product mix pricing.

First, we need to consider the objectives of an organization as an important influence on its pricing decisions. Simple models of perfect competition assume that firms are motivated primarily by the desire to maximize their short-term profits. In a commodity market, where prices are taken from the market, a company cannot be expected to have any other objectives, or it would soon go out of business. However, where a company has differentiated its products to give it a degree of monopoly power, it is able to pursue a more diverse range of possible objectives. Below we consider the effects of diverse objectives on an organization's pricing policies.

Profit maximization

Economists' models of perfect competition assume that firms in a market act rationally in order to maximize their profits. In less competitive markets, the notion of profit maximization becomes much more complex to understand. The first complicating issue is the possible divergence between short-term and long-term profit objectives. A company that aims to maximize its profits over the short run may unwittingly reduce its ability to achieve long-term profit objectives. By charging high prices in a new market, it may make that market seem very attractive to new entrants. This could provide a major incentive for new competitors to appear, thereby increasing the level of competition in subsequent years, and therefore reducing long-term profitability. Drugs companies selling medicines that have just come out of their period of patent protection must decide whether to continue charging the high prices buyers have been accustomed to, or to lower the price to a point where it deters new market entrants who can no longer be sure of making a quick short-term profit.

Organizations differ in the urgency with which they need to make profits from a new product. It is frequently suggested that the open shareholding structure of UK firms makes shareholders restless for short-term profits. Managers are therefore likely to set prices to achieve these short-term objectives, even if this is at the expense of longer-term profitability. By contrast, the relatively closed capital structure of many Japanese companies has allowed them to take a longer-term view on profitability, relatively free of short-term stock market pressures. A longer-term profit objective may allow an organization to tap relatively small but high-value segments of its markets in the first year and save the exploitation of lower-value segments until subsequent years.

Finally, while it is easy to talk about firms calculating the effects of their pricing on their profits, in reality many marketing managers have little understanding about the relationship between costs, sales volumes, and profitability. This can be especially true of new and emerging markets where there are few historical data on which to predict the outcome of price changes.

Sales growth

Management often does not directly receive any reward for increasing its organization's profits, so its main concern may be to achieve a *satisfactory* level of profits rather than the *maximum* possible. Managers often benefit personally where their company pursues a sales growth strategy, a point that has been made by many behaviourial studies of how managers act (e.g. Cyert and March 1963).

There are also some very good reasons why a company may benefit over the longer term by seeking to boost its short-term sales growth, even if this does mean charging very low prices and sacrificing short-term profits in order to do so. In many industries it is essential to achieve a critical size in order to achieve economies of scale in buying, production, promotion, and distribution. On the basis of these economies of scale, a firm may be able to achieve a competitive advantage. Companies in sectors as diverse as grocery retailing, civil aviation, and publishing have used low prices to achieve short-term sales growth in the hope that this will lead to long-term profit growth.

Finally, sales growth may be an important objective, influencing pricing, because managers may have practical difficulties in establishing relationships between marketing strategy decisions and the resulting change in profitability. Going for growth may be perceived by managers to be their safest option.

Survival

For many struggling companies, the objective of maximizing profits or sales volume is quite unrealistic when they are fighting desperately to avoid bankruptcy. In these circumstances, prices may be set at very low levels, simply to get enough cash into the organization to tide it over. Many retailers have found themselves in this situation when there has been a sudden downturn in consumer demand and they are left with too much stock and expensive overheads to pay. Cash is now tied up unnecessarily in stock. In a bid to stay afloat, many desperate retailers have held stock liquidation sales, in which stocks have been sold at almost any price, just to keep cash flowing in (*Daily Telegraph* 2007). Even if the prices charged did not cover the original cost of goods, such pricing could satisfy managers' short-term objective of survival (Figure 9.12).

Social considerations

Talk about maximizing sales or profits may have little meaning within the public and not-for-profit sectors, where there is more emphasis on maximizing social benefits (e.g. the

Figure 9.12 **Sometimes the use of advertising statements such as 'Closing Down Sale', 'Everything Must Go', and 'Stock Liquidation Sale' may be just advertising spin.** Often, however, these sales reflect the fact that the company is desperately short of cash and will sell its stock at very low prices, just so that it can raise enough cash quickly enough to satisfy its creditors. Low prices may be vital just for survival, but such prices will not sustain the business indefinitely.

number of operations performed by a hospital). The price of many public services represents a tax levied by government based not on market forces, but on an individual's ability to pay, with many services being provided at no charge. In the UK, many basic health services are provided without charge to patients, and where charges are made these often reflect the ability of individuals to pay, rather than the need for the health authority to maximize its revenue (e.g. lower dental and prescription charges for disadvantaged groups).

Although social objectives are normally associated with public-sector services, they are sometimes adopted by private-sector organizations also. Many companies provide goods and services for their staff (such as canteens and sports facilities) at below their market price, with the aim of adding to staff motivation and sense of loyalty to their organization.

Pricing strategy

Strategy is the means by which an organization seeks to achieve its objectives. Strategic decisions about pricing cannot be made in isolation from other strategic marketing decisions; so, for example, a strategy that seeks a premium price position must be matched by a product development strategy that creates a superior product and a promotional strategy that establishes in buyers' minds the value that the product offers.

The concept of positioning was discussed in Chapter 7, where it was noted that combinations anywhere along a line from high price/high quality to low price/low quality are sustainable strategic positions to adopt. A strategy that combines high price with low quality may be regarded by customers as poor value and they are likely to desert such companies where they have a choice of suppliers. For most companies such a strategy is not sustainable. A high quality/low price strategic position may appear very attractive to buyers, but it too may not be sustainable. Many companies in their public pronouncements claim this to be their strategic position, but it can pose problems for them, in the following ways.

- Are they selling themselves short and failing to recover their full costs in their bid to please customers? Unless they are operating more efficiently than other companies in their sector, there is the possibility that they will fail to make sufficient profits. In the mass market restaurant sector, for example, portion control can be quite critical to financial success. Customers may love the value offered by bigger servings, but many restaurants have gone out of business because they offered their customers too much value.

- If a company is genuinely able to offer lower prices for any given level of quality on the basis of greater efficiency, it must realize that its competitors may soon learn and copy its own levels of efficiency. Its prices will therefore no longer be the only sustainable low prices in the sector. In the European scheduled airline industry, many low-cost operators such as easyJet and Ryanair have undercut the established airlines' prices. However, their competitive advantage has often been eroded when the established operators have then implemented many of the cost-cutting measures pioneered by their new competitors.

Pricing and the product life-cycle

In Chapter 8 the concept of the product life-cycle was introduced, and you will recall that many aspects of a product's marketing strategy are closely related to the position that it has reached in its life-cycle. Pricing strategy is no exception. An effective marketing strategy must identify how the role of price is to function as a product goes through different stages in its life from the launch stage through growth to maturity.

Where a company is supplying a market in which product differentiation is possible, it is able to take a long-term view on its price position. However, pressure on the product's price, and hence on its profitability, will vary during the life of the product. Figure 9.13 illustrates the typical pressures on a product's price as it progresses through its life-cycle.

Price-skimming strategy

One approach to product life-cycle pricing is for a firm to start by charging a high price for a newly launched product, on the basis of its uniqueness. As its uniqueness is copied by other firms, the price will then have to be reduced to match those of the competitors.

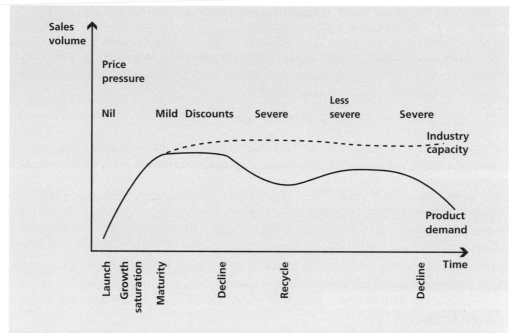

Figure 9.13 **As a product passes through its life-cycle, the pressures on pricing will change.** This graph shows the likely pricing response for a typical innovatory high-tech product.

This strategy is suitable for products that are genuinely innovative—the first microwave cookers in the 1970s; the first portable phones in the 1980s; the first digital cameras in the 1990s, and the first video mobile phones in the 2000s, for example. Such products are aimed initially at the segment of users who can be described as 'innovators' (discussed in Chapter 8). These are typically consumers who have the resources and inclination to be the trend-setters in purchasing new goods and services. Following these will be a group of 'early adopters', followed by a larger group often described as the 'early majority'. The subsequent 'late majority' group may take up the new product only when the product market itself has reached maturity. 'Laggards' are the last group to adopt a new product and would do so only when it has become commonplace and/or its price has fallen sufficiently.

The basic principle of a price-skimming strategy is to gain the highest possible price from each market segment, beginning with the highest-value segments and moving on to the next lower-value one when the purchasing ability of the first segment appears to be approaching saturation level. At this point the price level is lowered in order to appeal to the 'early adopter' segment, which has a lower price threshold at which it is prepared to purchase the product. This process is repeated for the following adoption segments.

As with so much of product life-cycle theory, identifying the points during the life-cycle at which action is needed can be very difficult, and it can also be very difficult to map out a price strategy with any degree of confidence. Consider the following problems, all of which make a price-skimming strategy difficult to formulate.

⊙ What is the saturation level of individual market segments? At what point should the company decide to lower its prices to appeal to lower value segments?

⊙ How long will the firm's product remain genuinely innovative in the eyes of consumers? To what extent will the appearance of competitors diminish its uniqueness and therefore the firm's ability to charge premium prices?

⊙ How quickly are new competitors likely to appear?

⊙ Should the firm avoid charging very high initial prices, as this may be a signal to competitors to enter the market? How strong are the barriers to entry for new competitors?

Price-skimming strategies work for consumer markets as well as business-to-business markets. Diffusion patterns for products sold mainly to business buyers can be different from those for consumer products. Business buyers generally have less of a desire to be a trend-setter for its own sake, and a different kind of rationality in purchase decisions. This limits the opportunities for price-skimming to situations where commercial buyers can use innovative products to give them a productivity advantage, which in turn will give them a competitive advantage in selling their own products to their customers at a lower price and/or a higher standard.

For many innovative products, falling prices may be further stimulated by falling production costs. Lower costs can occur because of economies of scale in production, promotion, and distribution. (For example, the cost of microwave cookers and mobile phones came down partly as a result of improved production efficiency, which itself was partly a reflection of economies of scale.) Costs may also fall as a result of the *experience effect*. This refers to the process by which costs fall as experience in production is gained. By pursuing a strategy to gain experience faster than its competitors, an organization lowers its cost base and has a greater scope for adopting an aggressive pricing strategy (Figure 9.14).

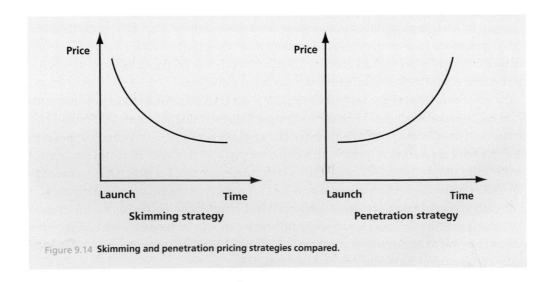

Figure 9.14 **Skimming and penetration pricing strategies compared.**

⦿ Penetration pricing strategy

Genuinely innovative new product launches are few and far between. The vast majority of product launches are simply copies of products that consumers can already buy in substantially the same form. Consider the following product launches:

- a new television listings magazine;

- a new type of chocolate biscuit;

- a new coffee shop.

The principle of initially appealing to high-value segments and then dropping the price will be unlikely to work with any of these, as buyers in all segments have access to competitors' products which are essentially similar. Buyers must have a good reason for choosing to try the new product instead of sticking with the product they are currently purchasing. There are many ways in which a company can encourage trial of its product, including a product design that offers real benefits to buyers, heavy advertising, sales promotion, and sponsorship activity. One method used by many companies to encourage trial is to offer prices that are sufficiently low that a large number of buyers will switch from their existing suppliers. Sometimes the new product will even be given away, in order to get potential buyers to try it. (For example, cosmetics companies often give away free samples with magazines.)

Naturally, companies will not want to go on charging low prices for very long. Their hope is that, once buyers have tried and enjoyed their product, they will come back again. At this stage, the price can be raised to something that approaches competitors' price levels. The buyers no longer have to be tempted with a low price. Over time, they may even come to prefer the product over competitors, so the company may be able to charge a price premium.

- -

Marketing and social responsibility

One nibble and customers are nobbled

Companies use many pricing techniques to get people to try out a product and then seek to lock in the customer at ever-increasing price levels. Is this exploitation, or just good marketing? Knowing that customers who were attracted by a low price may just as easily be lost to a competitor who tries to tempt them back with low prices, companies try to lock customers in once they have tried a new product. Many new magazines launch with low prices and include series or articles which it is hoped readers will get attached to and so will carry on buying the magazine, even after the publisher has put the price up midway during the series. Many fast moving consumer goods manufacturers include competitions or gift offers with their launch sales, for which tokens need to be collected. Where the collectible items include children's toys, 'pester power' may add to the motivation to carry on buying the product. Meanwhile, the company may have taken a strategic decision to increase the price of the product while customers are part way through collecting the required number of tokens. Is this ethical?

In some cases a company can exploit the fact that customers have become physically hooked on their product. Tobacco companies have recognized the power of addiction for some time, even though they may have not publicly accepted that it happens. The effects can be seen in other products too. So with the biscuit 'Hob Nobs', a suspicion arose that individuals could become addicted to the biscuit after their initial trial, regardless of its price. Is this brilliant marketing, in that the manufacturer has perfected its product to such an extent that buyers are prepared to pay a premium price for it? Or is this an example of cynical manipulation of buyers to put them in a position of dependency?

Of course, penetration pricing strategies have their dangers. Companies often find it difficult to develop sufficient loyalty from customers that will allow them to raise prices. Customers who were attracted by low penetration prices may be just as easily lost when a competitor or another new market entrant tries offering low prices in its turn. This pricing strategy also presupposes that buyers have a high awareness of prices. Research has shown that in many markets buyers have a very poor knowledge of prices, so competing for market share on the basis of low price alone may not work (Shugan 2006).

Customer lifetime pricing

As well as the product life-cycle, we can also consider the customer life-cycle. You will recall from Chapter 4 that the development of ongoing buyer–seller relationships is becoming a much more important part of business strategy. Rather than bargaining over each transaction, companies are trying to view each transaction with a customer in the context of those that have gone before, and those that they hope will follow. The price offered to a prospective new client may start off relatively low and build up progressively as both buyer and seller come to recognize the value of their relationship. Think back to our example in Chapter 4 of a new customer going into a restaurant. Should the profit of that individual be measured just in terms of that one meal, or in terms of the lifetime of meals it is hoped that he may buy? Viewed in the latter context, there may be scope for offering a low price incentive to encourage newcomers to give the restaurant a try.

◉ Pricing methods

Strategies need to be translated into methodologies for actually setting prices. Faced with a new product, the task of determining a selling price can sometimes appear to be quite daunting. If it is a completely new product, there may be very little historical guidance for setting prices. Companies may resort to a hunch or guesswork. However, even guesswork can be reduced to a series of rule-based decisions. Essentially, there are three questions that need to be asked when setting the price for any product:

1. How much does it cost us to make the product?

2. How much are competitors charging for a similar product?

3. What price are customers prepared to pay?

An additional factor affects marketing managers in many public utility sectors:

4.   How much will a government regulator allow us to charge customers?

The relationship between these bases for pricing is shown in Figure 9.15. Each will be considered in turn.

Cost-based pricing

The cost of producing a product sets the minimum price that a company would be prepared to charge its customers. If a commercial company is not covering its costs with its prices, it cannot continue in business indefinitely (unless, perhaps, the business has a wealthy owner and the business is kept going for reasons of prestige, as in the case of many national newspapers). The principle of a direct linkage between costs and prices may be central to basic price theory, but marketing managers rarely find conditions to be so simple. Consider some of the problems in relating costs to prices:

- The cost of a particular product is often very difficult to calculate. This is especially true where production costs involve high levels of shared overhead costs which cannot easily be allocated to specific products.

- While it may be relatively easy to calculate historic costs, it is *future* costs that may be crucial in determining profitability. An office furniture manufacturer, for example, may find it difficult to set fixed prices for customers today for furniture that will be built and delivered at some time in the future. It may be difficult to predict inflation rates for labour and materials used.

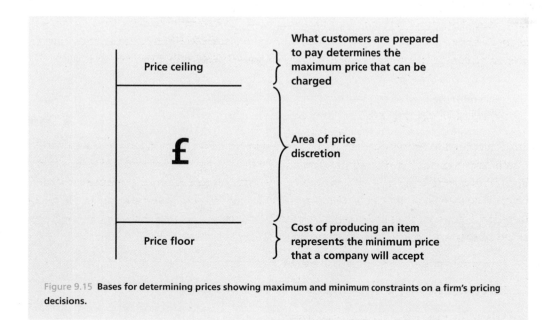

Figure 9.15 **Bases for determining prices showing maximum and minimum constraints on a firm's pricing decisions.**

⊙ Cost-based pricing in itself does not take account of the competition that a particular product faces at any particular time, nor of the fact that some customers may value the same service more highly than others.

Despite these shortcomings, cost-based pricing is widely used in many sectors. In its most straightforward form, 'cost-plus' pricing works like this: a company calculates it total costs and divides these by the total volume of resources used, in order to determine the average cost of each unit of resource used; it then calculates a selling price by estimating the number of units of resources to be used, multiplying this by the unit cost and adding a profit margin. Cost-based pricing is widely used by solicitors, plumbers, and other labour-intensive service industries where the cost of labour is a major component of total costs. So a plumber may price a job on the basis of the total number of hours estimated to complete a job, multiplied by the historical cost per hour (including overheads) of its employees, plus materials used, plus a profit margin. The principles are illustrated in Figure 9.16.

Marginal cost pricing

Another form of cost-based pricing that is widely used is referred to as marginal cost pricing. Here, a company calculates the *marginal* cost of producing one additional unit of a product (that is, the addition to the company's total costs of selling one extra item). In some industries with high levels of fixed costs, the marginal cost of producing one extra unit of output can be surprisingly small. The cost of carrying one extra passenger on an aeroplane that is about to depart with some empty seats can be little more than the cost of the airport handling charges, possibly a meal, and marginally additional fuel. This explains why many airlines and holiday companies are keen to offer last-minute standby airfares, as some

Cost information for most recent trading year:	
Total employees' wage cost	£1,000,000
Total hours worked	70,000
Cost per employee-hour	14.28
Total other overhead costs	£600,000
Overhead cost per employee hour worked	8.57
Total chargeable amount per hour	22.85
Required profit mark-up	40%
Price calculation for a job requiring 100 hours of labour and £500 materials:	
100 hours @ £22.85 per hour	£2,285
Materials	500
Sub-total	2,785
Add 40% mark-up	1,114
Price	3,899

Figure 9.16 **An example of a cost-based approach to pricing for a building contractor.**

revenue is better than having an unsold seat, just so long as the price charged more than covers the marginal costs.

Pricing based on marginal costs may work up to a point, but companies must realize that a sufficient number of customers must be willing to pay full costs in order for others to be charged a much lower price reflecting only marginal costs. Many airlines and holiday companies have gone bankrupt because too high a proportion of their customers have been sold tickets at the marginal cost, leaving the fixed overhead costs uncovered.

Calculating marginal costs can sometimes be quite difficult. In the long term, all of a company's costs are marginal in that there is always the option to close down entire business units or even the whole company. While the marginal cost of one seat on an aeroplane may be low, if the unit of analysis is the whole journey or even the whole route, the level of marginal costs becomes much higher (see Figures 9.17 and 9.18).

Product	Fixed costs	Marginal costs
Meal in a restaurant	Building maintenance Rent and rates Head chef	Food
Bank mortgage	Head office staff time Building maintenance Corporate advertising	Sales commission Paper and postage
Hairdresser	Building maintenance Rent and rates	Shampoos used

Figure 9.17 **A classification of typical fixed and marginal costs for three service industries.** Note that even fixed costs could in the long term become marginal costs if the whole business unit is being evaluated.

Figure 9.18 **Travel companies have for a long time used marginal cost pricing, mindful that some revenue is better than an empty plane seat or hotel room.** They have realized that some people could be tempted by low price offers to fill its spare capacity at very short notice. The online travel intermediary lastminute.com makes full use of marginal cost pricing by bringing together companies that have spare capacity with buyers who are looking for a bargain.
(Reproduced with kind permission of lastminute.com.)

Competitors and pricing

Very often, a marketing manager may go about setting prices by examining what competitors are charging. But what is the competition against which prices are to be compared? From Chapter 7, you will recall that competitors can be defined at different levels:

⦿ similar in terms of product characteristics, or, more broadly,

⦿ similar just in terms of the needs that a product satisfies.

As an example, a DVD film rental company can see its competition purely in terms of other film rental services, or it could widen it to include cinemas and satellite television services, or widen it still further to include any form of entertainment.

Once it has established what market it is in and who its competitors are, a company can go about setting comparative prices. First, it must establish what price position it seeks to adopt relative to its competitors. This position will reflect the wider marketing mix of the product, so if the product is perceived by buyers as being superior in quality to the competitors' products, it may justify a relatively higher price. Similarly, heavy investment in promotion or distribution channels may give it a competitive advantage which is reflected in buyers' willingness to pay relatively high prices.

In markets that show some signs of interdependency among suppliers, firms can often be described as price-makers, or price-followers. Price-makers tend to be those who, as a result of their size and power within a market, are able to determine the levels and patterns of prices, which other suppliers then follow. Smaller estate agents in a local area may find it convenient simply to respond to pricing policies adopted by the dominant firms— for them to take a proactive role themselves might bring about a reaction from the dominant firms which they would be unable to defend, because of their size and standing in the market.

Where it is difficult for a company to calculate its production costs (perhaps because of the high level of fixed costs), charging a 'going rate' can simplify the pricing process. As an example, it may be very difficult to calculate the cost of renting out a video film, as the figure will be very dependent upon assumptions made about the number of uses over which the initial purchase cost can be spread. It is much easier to take price decisions on the basis of the going rate charged by close competitors.

Many business-to-business goods and services are provided by means of a sealed bid tendering process where interested parties are invited to submit a bid for supplying goods or services in accordance with specifications. In the case of many government contracts, the organization inviting tenders is often legally obliged to accept the lowest priced tender, unless exceptional circumstances can be proved. The first task of a bidding company is to establish a minimum bid price based on its costs and the required rate of return, below which it would not be prepared to bid. The more difficult task is to try and put a maximum figure on what it can bid. This will be based on expectations of what its competitors will bid, based on an analysis of their strengths and weaknesses.

Demand-based pricing

What customers are prepared to pay represents the upper limit to a company's pricing possibilities. In fact, different customers often put different ceilings on the price they are prepared to pay for a product. Successful demand-oriented pricing is therefore based on effective segmentation of markets and price discrimination which achieves the maximum price from each segment.

The bases for segmenting markets were discussed in Chapter 6 and are of direct relevance in determining discriminatory prices. It was noted that, in addition to socio-economic factors, geographical location of buyers, their reason for purchase, and the time of purchase are all important bases for segmentation. Their impact on price determination is considered below (Figure 9.19).

Price discrimination between different groups of buyers

Sometimes price discrimination can be achieved by simply offering the same product to each segment, but charging a different price. This is possible with some services which are not transferrable from one individual to another. So a hairdresser can offer students a haircut that is identical to the service offered to all other customer groups in all respects except price. The justification could be that this segment is more price-sensitive than other segments, and therefore additional profitable business can be gained only by sacrificing some element of margin. By supplying more haircuts, even at a lower price, a hairdresser may end up deriving increased total revenue from this segment, while still preserving the higher prices charged to other segments.

On other occasions, however, where one segment was paying more than other segments for an identical product, price discrimination would not be sustainable. It would always be open for members of the segment being charged a higher price to try to buy the goods in lower-price markets. Sometimes they will do this directly themselves, as seen by the number of British buyers who have taken advantage of lower cigarette and alcohol prices in continental Europe. Sometimes entrepreneurs will seek out goods in low-priced market segments and offer them for resale in the higher-price market (a practice that retailers such as Superdrug and Tesco have carried out in respect of branded perfumes, which are sold in many overseas markets at lower prices than in the UK).

To be sustainable, price discrimination is often associated with slight changes to the product offer. This can be seen in the market for air passenger services. Airlines offer a variety of fare and service combinations to suit the needs of a number of segments. One segment has to travel at short notice and is typically travelling on business. For the employer, the cost of not being able to travel at short notice may be high, so this group is prepared to pay a relatively high price in return for ready availability. A sub-segment of this market may seek extra comfort and space and is prepared to pay more for the differentiated business class accommodation. For non-business travellers, another segment may be happy to accept a lower price in return for committing themselves to a particular flight just two weeks before departure. Another segment with even less income to spend on travel may be

MARKETING in ACTION

Entrepreneurial senior citizens seize price discounts

Many service-sector companies have offered reduced prices for segments of senior citizens, calculating that these segments are more price sensitive than others and could usefully fill spare capacity at a profit, even at the lower prices charged. But can this apply to the sale of goods? With services, a supplier can insist that only senior citizens receive the benefit of the service they have paid for (e.g. by insisting on seeing proof of age during a train journey). But goods can be bought by members of a low-price segment and sold on to those of a relatively high-price one. The pitfalls of this approach to market segmentation were learnt by a German grocery retailer which offered 20 per cent off the price of all purchases made by senior citizens. Entrepreneurial senior citizens were then seen lining up outside the supermarket offering to do other customers' shopping for them. The 20 per cent price saving was split between the senior citizen and the person needing the goods, saving effort for the latter, providing additional income for the former—but making a mockery of the retailer's attempts at price discrimination.

prepared to take the risk of obtaining a last-minute standby flight in return for a still lower priced ticket.

Charging different prices to different groups can raise ethical issues where a group associates price discrimination with discrimination on the basis of clearly identified social or demographic characteristics. As an example, gas and electricity companies have been accused of offering better prices to affluent consumers who can afford to shop around, while poorer households are given less favourable tariffs. Discriminatory pricing may also be perceived as unfair by customers where it is carried out covertly and they perceive that they are disadvantaged as a result (see vignette 'Cookies allow price discrimination at Amazon').

Price discrimination by point of sale

Some companies charge different prices in different places. Hotels frequently charge much higher prices in some prime locations, despite there being little difference in facilities offered between locations. The reason for this discrimination can be a combination of cost factors (e.g. land and staff costs for a hotel are higher in central London than in northern England) and demand factors. (To large segments of potential buyers, a hotel room in central London will be considered more valuable than one located in northern England.)

Price discrimination by location is much more effective for services than for goods. Services cannot generally be transferred from the point where they are produced to another area where a buyer most wants to consume them. (For example, a Sheffield hotel room can be consumed only in Sheffield and cannot be brought to London where it would be more valuable.) Airlines often charge more at one end of a route than the other, depending on strength of demand in different national markets. By contrast, differences between areas in the price of goods will soon be exploited by entrepreneurs who are able to buy in the lower-price market and sell on in the higher-price one (as has happened with cosmetics sourced from low-price Far Eastern markets and resold in the UK).

MONICA'S SALON

tel: 375336

PRICE LIST

Cut	Ladies	£25
	Gentlemen	£17
Cut & blow dry	Ladies	£32
	Gentlemen	£25
Permanent waving	*from*	£42
Colouring		by quotation
Highlights		by quotation

SPECIAL RATES

Senior citizens	10% off all prices Monday-Thursday only
Students	20% off on Wednesday afternoon
Children	25% off all prices

Figure 9.19 **It is not just large companies that practise price discrimination.** Many smaller businesses, such as this hairdressing salon, charge different prices for different groups, typically offering discounts for students and senior citizens. Price discrimination would work for a haircut (unlike most goods), because one person cannot buy a cheap haircut and sell it on to another person who is not eligible for the lower price. However, even small businesses must ensure that discriminatory pricing does not create feelings of resentment from those who pay a higher price for an essentially similar service.

Price discrimination by channels of access

Price discrimination is frequently based on the channel of access, so, for example, an intermediary may be offered a preferential price to stimulate recommendation by the intermediary to its clients. Services are increasingly distributed through Internet-based intermediaries, and the issue of differential pricing by channel is becoming increasingly complex. An airline, for example, may sell a ticket on its own website at one price, but may have negotiated special rates with intermediaries who can often sell the same ticket on their own website for a lower price. It is not uncommon to find the same air ticket being simultaneously offered by many intermediaries at different prices.

For the service provider, charging different prices for different points of access may make sense because of the different competitive environment of each point of access. A loyal customer of an airline may be less inclined to search for a lower price, especially if they are travelling on business and they feel tied to the airline because of a frequent flyer programme that they belong to. A bargain hunting leisure traveller visiting the site of an intermediary such as Expedia or Opodo will be in a competitive environment where prices are compared with other airlines, and to have any hope of gaining a sale, the airline must offer prices which are competitive with comparable airline offers. For the customer, different prices between intermediaries may be sustainable where different levels of service are offered, for example good after sales service without the need to use a premium rate telephone number.

Discriminatory pricing online is becoming more complex as channels of distribution for many services multiply. The airline's intermediaries, for example, are increasingly likely to work through intermediaries of their own, and these can take many forms, such as price comparison sites. Some intermediaries described generically as 'cashback' sites (e.g. www. topcashback.co.uk) offer part of the payment that they receive for a 'click through' back to the customer, effectively lowering the final price.

Price discrimination by type of use

A similar product can be bought by different people to satisfy quite different needs. A train journey may be perceived as an optional leisure purchase by one person, but as a means of getting work done on the way to an important business meeting by another. Train operating companies have therefore developed different fares aimed at groups with different journey purposes (e.g. off-peak fares for price-sensitive leisure travellers and first class facilities for business executives).

Even the same person may buy a product repeatedly but seek to satisfy different needs on each occasion. There are many examples of this. Most people when eating out are more likely to be price sensitive for a regular midday meal during their lunch hour than to a social meal with friends in the evening. Many restaurants have responded to this by offering special lunchtime menus which are very similar to meals offered in the evening, except that the price is lower.

Price discrimination by time of purchase

It is quite common for suppliers of services to charge different prices at different times of supply. Services often face an uneven demand which follows a daily, weekly, annual, seasonal, cyclical, or random pattern. At the height of each peak, pricing is usually a reflection of:

- The greater willingness of customers to pay higher prices when demand is strong, and

- The greater cost that often results from service operators trying to cater for short peaks in demand.

The greater strength of demand that occurs at some points in a daily cycle can be for a number of reasons. In the case of rail services into the major conurbations, workers generally must arrive at work at a specified time and may have few realistic alternative means of getting to work. A train operator can therefore sustain a higher level of fares during the daily commuter peak period. Similarly, the higher rate charged for telephone calls during the daytime is a reflection of the greater strength of demand from the business sector during the day. Price variation can also occur between different periods of the week (e.g. higher fares for using many train services on a Friday evening), or between different seasons of the year (e.g. holiday flights at busy holiday periods).

Price discrimination by time can be effective in inducing new business at what would otherwise be a quiet period. Hotels in holiday resorts frequently lower their prices in the off-peak season to try to tempt additional custom. Many utility companies lower their charges during off-peak periods in a bid to stimulate demand—for example lower telephone charges at weekends.

Bartering and auctions

Price discrimination between groups of buyers may sound fine in theory, but there can be problems in actually implementing it. First, it can be very difficult to identify homogeneous segments in terms of individuals' responsiveness to price changes. Second, it can be very difficult to predict just what level of price will be acceptable to that group and much trial and error may be necessary to establish the most appropriate price. One alternative adopted by some companies is to leave price determination to a process of individual negotiation between buyer and seller. For high-value commercial goods and services, individual negotiation of prices has always been quite commonplace, especially in the case of products such as houses or second-hand industrial equipment, which are difficult to value.

In less developed economies, instances of bartering in consumer markets can still be found. It is still normal practice in many Middle Eastern and Asian bazaars, where buyer and seller go through a process of determining each other's price limits before eventually converging on an agreed price. The seller will try to establish the maximum price that an individual is prepared to pay. To western tourists visiting these markets this may seem quite daunting, but the seller has doubtless worked out in his mind principles for negotiating. From previous experience, the seller may have come to recognize that such factors as the buyers' nationality, the size of their group, the length of time that they have been in the country, and their general appearance all give clues about the sales price that could be achieved.

In developed economies, it has been quite rare for relatively low-value consumer sales to be individually negotiated. However, auctions provide an opportunity for a seller to get the highest price possible for an individual consumer product. Internet-based auction sites have offered new opportunities for sellers to set their prices on the basis of what the highest bidder is prepared to pay.

Auction sites such as ebay.com essentially put the onus of pricing on the buyer by allowing customers to disclose the price at which they would be prepared to purchase. Faced with surplus aircraft seats or hotel rooms, sellers can make them available on a website and sell

341

them to bidders who bid the highest amount, as long as this is above a minimum reserve price. If the system is working effectively, the seller can be reasonably sure that it has secured the maximum achievable price for its products.

While auctioning of products to the highest bidder has numerous attractions, there are also problems. An auction may be good in the short term for clearing products, but in itself does nothing to develop strong brand values. In fact, auctions may treat a service like a commodity in which the only distinguishing feature is price. Auctions can be administratively challenging, even with the use of the Internet. Price lists were developed in order to simplify the purchasing process, especially where high-volume, low-value goods are concerned. Going round Sainsbury's supermarket haggling over the price of every item of groceries would take up a lot of time and effort for buyer and seller alike. Anybody who has used an Internet auction site will appreciate the uncertainty created by the buying process, in which you may not know for some time whether you have got yourself a bargain or will have to start the purchase process all over again. Many consumers would prefer the certainty of fixed prices rather than taking a chance with an auction where neither the availability of a specific service nor its price can be guaranteed.

As well as consumer sales, Internet auctions have found a valuable role for business-to-business procurement. A company can put out a tender and invite suppliers to bid, following which it would choose the lowest-price bidder.

◉ Pricing a product range

Most organizations sell a range of products, and the price of each individual item should recognize the pricing strategy adopted for other products in the range. Some companies may have many thousands of individual items, for each of which a price must be set.

For any given product, a company can allocate the other items in its product range to one of three categories for the purposes of pricing.

1. Optional additional items are those that a buyer may or may not choose to add to the main product purchased, often at the time the main product is purchased. As a matter of strategy, an organization could seek to charge a low lead-in price for the core product, but to recoup a higher margin from the additional optional items. Simply breaking a product into core and optional components may allow for the presentation of lower price indicators, which through a process of rationalization may be more acceptable to many customers. Research may show that the price of the core product is in fact the only factor that potential customers take into account when choosing between alternatives. In this way, mobile phone companies may cut the basic monthly charges for their calling plans, but make this up with higher prices for optional extras such as multimedia message bundles, or insurance.

2. Captive items occur where the core product has been purchased and the provision of additional services can be provided only by the original provider of the core product.

Where these are not specified at the outset of purchasing the core product, or are left up to the discretion of the supplier, the latter is in a strong position to charge a high price. Against this, the company must consider the effect that the perception of high exploitative prices charged for these captive items will have on customer loyalty when buyers are next considering the purchase of the core product. An example of captive product pricing is provided by car manufacturers, which compete on price for the sale of new cars, but many specialized replacement parts may be charged at very high prices, reflecting the lack of competition and captivity of the customer whose car will not function without a specific part.

3. Competing items within the product range occur where a new product targets a segment of the population that overlaps the segments served by other products within the organization's mix. By a process of cannibalization, a company could find that it is competing with itself. In this way, a confectionary company with a large market share that launches a new organic chocolate bar may find that its new launch is taking sales away from its existing range of chocolate bars.

Price bundling

Price bundling is the practice of marketing two or more products in a single package for a single price. Bundling is particularly important for goods and services that have a high ratio of fixed to variable costs. Furthermore, where there is a high level of interdependency between different types of output from an organization, it may be difficult and meaningless to price each individual item. In this way, the provision of an ATM card and Internet banking become an interdependent part of the current bank account offering, which most UK banks do not charge for separately.

Price bundling of diverse products from an organization's product mix is frequently used as a means of building relationships with customers. In this way a health insurance policy could be bundled with a travel insurance policy or a legal protection policy. Where the bundle of service represents ease of administration to the consumer, the service organization may be able to achieve a price for the bundle that is greater than the combined price of the bundle's components.

Different groups of consumers have differing expectations about what they would expect to see in a price bundle. Car buyers in the UK, for example, expect a high level of equipment (radio, wheel trims, etc.) to be bundled in with the main price of a car, while many buyers in continental Europe would expect to pay for each item separately.

Pricing models

A pricing model reflects the fact that companies can generate revenue through a variety of combinations of the basic price and prices charged for optional additional items. Some price models may be sustainable by giving away a product at very low price initially, but then charge higher prices for essential items that are needed to make the product function (razor manufacturers may make only a small charge for the initial razor unit, but make more money out of selling the replacement blades, which are specific to that brand). Sometimes, the dominant pricing model in a market is challenged by a new entrant, with the result that consumers' expectations are changed. This was seen in the pricing models adopted for broadband services in the UK. Until 2006, the dominant model was for firms to charge a fixed monthly fee for broadband services, in addition to basic telephone line rental charges. But in that year, Carphone Warehouse introduced a new model with its 'Talk Talk' plan, in which broadband was given away for (almost) free, and the company made up for this with its pricing of line rental.

The pricing of public services

Many of the pricing principles discussed above, such as price discrimination and competitor-based pricing, may be quite alien to some public services. It may be difficult or undesirable to implement a straightforward price–value relationship with individual users of public services for a number of reasons (Figures 9.20 and 9.21):

- Pricing can be actively used as a means of social policy. Subsidized prices are often used to favour particular groups; for example prescription charges favour the very ill and unemployed, among others. Sometimes the interests of marketing orientation and social policy can overlap. Charging lower prices for unemployed people to enter

Figure 9.20 **Companies often bundle a number of products together and charge one inclusive price.**
Like many sellers of lunchtime snacks, the Co-op offers a discounted 'Meal Deal' to customers who buy a sandwich, a drink and selected crisps/snack bars together. For many buyers, the 'Deal' price becomes the reference price which they use to compare prices between retailers. For the retailer, a bundled price offer encourages additional spending by the customer and the discounted price of the bundle is likely to be made up from the additional margin from selling three, rather than just one item.
(Reproduced with kind permission of Oxford, Swindon, and Gloucester Co-op.)

museums may provide social benefits for this group, while gaining additional revenue from a segment that might not otherwise have been able to afford a visit to the museum.

⊙ Benefits to society at large may be as significant as the benefits received by the individual, so there may be a case for the government subsidizing low prices. Education and training courses may be provided at an uneconomic charge in order to add to the level of skills available within an economy generally.

Figure 9.21 **Road users within the UK have not generally been charged directly for the benefits they receive from the road system, largely because of the impracticality of road pricing and issues of equity between users.** Instead, users have paid for the use of roads through direct and indirect taxation. However, with improved technology and growing realization of the social and economic costs of traffic congestion, there has been a move towards pricing the use of roads. The London Congestion Charge, introduced in 2003, provides evidence that pricing a public service can change consumers' behaviour, with traffic volumes falling by about 10 per cent since the introduction of the charge.

Problems can occur in public services that have been given a largely financial, market-oriented brief, but in which social policy objectives are superimposed, possibly in conflict. Museums, leisure centres, and car park charges have frequently been at the centre of debate about the relative importance to be attached to economic and social objectives. Museums have sometimes overcome this dilemma by retaining free or nominally priced admission charges for the serious, scholarly elements of their exhibits, while offering special exhibitions which match the private sector in the standard of production and the prices charged.

◉ Chapter summary and linkages to other chapters

This chapter began by discussing the underlying theory of price determination. Perfect competition is an idealized market structure which rarely occurs in its pure extreme, but the principles of such competition provide a relevant background to many of the pricing decisions made by marketers. Firms seek to create a distinctive product, which reduces the impact on them of intense price competition. Because imperfect markets are generally held to be against the public interest, various regulatory measures exist to improve the competitiveness of markets.

Where a company has developed a distinctive product, it becomes a price-maker rather than a price-taker. Its pricing behaviour will be influenced by its organizational objectives. Prices can be set in relation to production costs, the strength of demand, competitors' prices, or a combination of all three. Market segmentation (Chapter 6) is used to identify groups that may be able and willing to pay higher prices than average. Pricing strategy contributes towards a company's sustainable competitive advantage (Chapter 7). However, pricing must be closely related to a firm's product policy (Chapter 8), its distribution (Chapter 10), and its promotional strategies (Chapters 11) in order to create a coherent positioning for its products.

✎ KEY PRINCIPLES OF MARKETING

- In competitive markets, prices are influenced by the interaction of supply and demand.

- Marketing seeks to develop a unique product which is subject to less direct competitive pressure and therefore allows marketers more discretion in setting prices.

- The maximum price that a company can charge is what customers are able and willing to pay (or what a government regulator will allow it to charge).

- Price should be distinguished from costs. Costs determine the minimum price that a company will charge.

A fair price for 'free' hospital treatment?

Organizations with a broad range of products often price different products within their portfolio in quite different ways. They may have developed a price 'model', which describes the way that it uses pricing of its product portfolio to maximize its overall revenue. So, one product may be charged at a very low price, on the assumption that this will bring in business which is then prepared to pay relatively high prices for related products. There are many examples of this practice in action, ranging from humble household goods, through to complex industrial equipment. A simple refillable air freshener unit may initially be sold at a very low price, but the refills sold at a much higher-price. With a patent on the refills—preventing copycats undercutting its price—a manufacturer may benefit from several years of revenue from high price refills, more than offsetting the low-priced base units which were sold as a 'loss leader'. In some sectors, a number of different pricing models co-exist. For example, in the emerging multi-channel television broadcasting market, some channels are provided free of charge to users, but make revenue from selling advertising space, while others charge a subscription to users, either on a monthly/annual basis, or a 'pay to view' basis. In the UK, the BBC provides a further model, where most services are provided without charge to users or advertising revenue. Instead, government provides funding.

The idea of a pricing model is familiar to private sector organizations, but do they have a role to play in the public sector? In the UK, pricing models are increasingly being discussed and developed for services which have previously been considered a vital service and available freely to all. The National Health Service (NHS) has a long and proud tradition of providing health services to all, according to an individual's need, paid for out of general taxation, according to individuals' means. Pricing has historically had very little role to play in the NHS. Both socialist and right wing Conservative governments have encountered opposition when they suggested an American-style market-based approach to charging for health services. But the need to increase revenue became a priority for cash strapped NHS trusts from the 1990s, at a time when increasing demand for services was not fully matched by increased government funding. Could NHS trusts copy some of the ideas of pricing models from the private sector?

Although the principle of a health service free at the point of use has been firmly enshrined in the minds of politicians and users, a number of charges have been introduced over the years, for example for prescriptions. However, these tended to be centrally determined with exemptions for those in greatest need. But from the mid-1990s, individual NHS trusts began exploiting charges for ancillary services as a means of boosting their revenue. One of the first targets for charging was users of hospitals' car parks. Trusts argued that providing car parks was not central to the mission of NHS trusts, and conveniently, government was encouraging more people to use public transport and leave their cars at home. Critics argued that patients were essentially captive and public transport was not a realistic alternative for most people. What began for most hospitals as a small charge soon became a cash cow for hospital finance directors, mindful of the lack of alternatives available to patients. A House Commons Health Select Committee investigation in

2006 found evidence that some patients did not go to hospital for treatment because of the cost of parking. It showed that at one hospital in London, a patient who attended A&E on the advice of her GP, was charged £3.75 for the first two hours' use of the hospital car park and £7.50 thereafter.

She was ten minutes over the two hour period and therefore had to pay the higher charge. She also questioned the fact that charges were reduced to £1 per hour after 6 pm, when many hospital departments were closed. For private sector services, a lower evening price, when there is not much demand from customers, and plenty of spare capacity, is quite common. But is it right that a hospital should only charge lower prices at the very time when much of the hospital itself is closed? If lower prices are designed to stimulate additional demand, is this a realistic prospect when many hospital departments are only available between 9 am and 5 pm?

Another source of revenue exploited by many hospital trusts comes from the use of bedside telephones by patients. Many trusts entered agreements with private telephone service providers which allowed incoming and outgoing patient calls only through the officially appointed system, which used a premium rate number. A proportion of the revenue was retained by the hospital. Conveniently, hospital trusts pointed to evidence that mobile phones could harm sensitive medical equipment, and therefore used this to eliminate competitive pressure from patients' mobile phones, forcing them to use the hospital's own telephone system. The ethics of hospital telephone pricing was challenged by the House of Commons Health Select Committee, which accused some trusts of using excessively long recorded messages at the beginning of each incoming and outgoing call, adding to patients' costs, and boosting hospital revenues. It cited a hospital in Essex where people wishing to telephone patients were being charged 49p per minute at peak time and 39p off-peak. By comparison, a typical household rate for a long distance phone call was around 7p in the peak and 2p in the off-peak. One relative of a patient in a Gloucester hospital claimed to have run up a bill of nearly £1200 for phoning a disabled patient in hospital. The select committee also expressed doubts about whether a ban on mobile phones in hospitals was actually a result of possible interference with medical equipment and recommended visitors should be able to use mobile phones within certain areas of hospitals. By banning mobile phones, had hospitals been more concerned about creating a monopoly environment for pricing their telephone service, than any possible risk to their equipment? Summing up, the Select Committee on Health described the system of NHS pricing as a mess, with Lord Lipsey of the Social Market Foundation describing it as 'a dog's dinner'. Successive governments had shied away from an overt market-based framework for pricing services provided by the NHS. However, it appeared that pricing was coming in through the backdoor, raising issues about the ethics of charging apparently exploitative prices that reflect patients' captivity. Or were managers of NHS trusts simply being realistic and pragmatic, charging as much as they could for ancillary services so that they could invest more in what a hospital is essentially all about—providing better health treatments?

Based on:
The Times, 'Hospitals making £78 m a year from car park charges', July 18, 2006; House of Commons Health Select Committee, NHS Charges, 2006; NHS, 'Our NHS, our future', http://www.ournhs.nhs.uk/, accessed 20 June 2008

Case study review questions

1. What do you understand by the concept of a 'pricing model'? Critically discuss their relevance to a public sector service such as the NHS.

2. What factors should influence the level of charges at an NHS car park?

3. If you are studying at a university or college, critically reflect on the pricing strategy that it has adopted for ancillary services.

CHAPTER REVIEW QUESTIONS

1. Critically assess methods used by companies to reduce the effects on them of intense price competition.

2. 'Elasticity of demand is a fine theoretical concept of economists, but difficult for marketers to use in practice.' Critically assess this statement.

3. What are the main challenges facing an oligopolist when determining prices? Is the task of an oligopolistic marketer more or less difficult than that of a marketing manager in a sector dominated by small businesses?

ACTIVITIES

1. Gather together price lists from a selection of any of the following service organizations in your area: sports centres; cinemas/theatres; restaurants. Analyse their pricing and the extent to which cost-based; customer-based; and competitor-based pricing is being applied.

2. Examine prices charged by a selection of public sector organizations with which you are familiar, for example swimming pools, museums, and universities. Assess the extent to which prices are influenced by market forces rather than government social policy considerations.

3. Study the price list shown in Figure 9.19. What if any changes in pricing practice would you suggest, based on a similar service provider with which you are familiar?

REFERENCES

Bell, D.R., Iyer, G., and Padmanabhan, V. (2002) 'Price Competition under Stockpiling and Flexible Consumption'. *Journal of Marketing Research*, 39, 292–303.

Bicknell, C. (2000), 'The Amazon Story', *Wired News*, 21 July.

Bray, J. and Harris, C. (2006) 'The Effect of 9-ending Prices on Retail Sales: A Quantitative UK Based Field Study'. *Journal of Marketing Management*, 22 (5/6), 601–7.

Cyert, R.M. and March, J.G. (1963) *A Behavioural Theory of the Firm*. Englewood Cliffs, NJ: Prentice-Hall.

Daily Telegraph (2002) 'High-Price Airlines Fail to Get Message'. *Daily Telegraph*, 4 November, 36.

Daily Telegraph (2007) 'Wet Weather Compounds High Street Turmoil'. *Daily Telegraph*, 8 July.

Daily Telegraph (2008) 'Ten Simple Tips to Save Money on Your Mobile': *Daily Telegraph*, 16 June.

Fletcher, R. (2003) 'Urgent Email to Sugar; Nobody Believes your Electronic Message'. *Sunday Telegraph*, 5 January.

Gourville, J. and Soman, D. (2002) 'Pricing and the Psychology of Consumption'. *Harvard Business Review*, 80 (9), 90–6.

Palmer, A. and Boissy, S. (2009) 'The Effects of Airline Price Presentations on Buyers' Choice'. *Journal of Vacation Marketing*, 15 (1), 39–52.

Shugan, S.M. (2006) 'Are Consumers Rational? Experimental Evidence'. *Marketing Science*, 25 (1), January–February, 1–7.

Streitfeld, D. (2000) 'Ads on Web Don't Click'. *Washington Post*, 29 October, PA1.

Sunday Times (2003) '*Mirror* Prepares to End Price War'. *Sunday Times* (Business), 9 February, 3.

Sunday Times (2003) 'Price Fixers Face Jail, Fines and Disqualification in Crackdown'. *Sunday Times* (Business), 23 February, 15.

Timmins, N. (2003) 'A Bid to Save Money for the Government: online auctions'. *Financial Times*, 29 January, 12.

White, D. (2003) 'Mobile Pricing Riles Operators'. *Daily Telegraph*, 18 January.

✎ SUGGESTED FURTHER READING

This chapter has provided only a very brief overview of the principles of economics as they affect pricing. For a fuller discussion, one of the following texts would be useful.

Begg, D. (2009) *Foundations of Economics*, 2nd edition. Maidenhead: McGraw-Hill.

Begg, D. and Ward, D. (2009) *Economics for Business*. Maidenhead: McGraw-Hill.

Lipsey, R.G. and Chrystal, K.A. (2011) *Economics*, 12th edition. Oxford: Oxford University Press.

For an overview of pricing strategy as practised by marketers, the following provide useful insights:

Avlonitis, G.J. and Indounas, K.A. (2005) 'Pricing Objectives and Pricing Methods in the Services Sector'. *Journal of Services Marketing,* 19 (1), 47–57.

Bray, J. and Harris, C. (2006) 'The effect of 9-ending prices on retail sales: a quantitative UK based field study'. *Journal of Marketing Management*, 22 (5/6), 601–7.

Naylor, G. and Frank, K.E. (2001) 'The Effect of Price Bundling on Consumer Perceptions of Value'. *Journal of Services Marketing,* 15 (4), 270–81.

Indounas, K. (2009) 'Successful Industrial Service Pricing'. *Journal of Business & Industrial Marketing*, 24 (2), 86–97.

ONLINE RESOURCE CENTRE

Visit the Online Resource Centre for resources that are relevant to this chapter, including a flashcard glossary, web links, multiple choice questions, and additional case studies:

www.oxfordtextbooks.co.uk/orc/palmer3e/

KEY TERMS

- Auctions
- Bartering
- Cannibalization
- Cartel
- Commodity market
- Cost-based pricing
- Demand
- Economies of scale
- Elasticity of demand
- Equilibrium price

- Marginal cost pricing
- Market structure
- Monopoly
- Oligopoly
- Perfect competition
- Price bundling
- Price determination
- Price discrimination
- Price-skimming strategy
- Profit maximization

CHANNEL INTERMEDIARIES

CHAPTER OBJECTIVES

Most companies selling consumer goods and services would encounter administrative and logistical problems if they tried to deliver their products directly to each of their end consumers. Instead, companies will most likely use intermediaries to distribute their products. The first aim of this chapter is to develop an understanding of the 'place' element of the marketing mix and the role of intermediaries in making goods and services available to buyers, at a time and place that is convenient to them. Approaches to designing a channel of distribution and issues in the management and control of intermediaries are discussed.

The second part of the chapter considers *how* goods are physically moved between the producer and the end consumer. It seeks to develop an understanding of how efficient and effective distribution can add to a firm's competitive advantage. The chapter reviews the objectives of physical distribution management, strategic approaches to supply chain management, and the key elements of a physical distribution system. The influence of information technology (IT) on channels of distribution will become apparent as we proceed through the chapter.

⊙ Introduction

This chapter discusses issues concerning what is often called the 'place' (P) of the traditional marketing mix. Decisions about channel intermediaries (or 'middlemen', to use an outdated, yet user-friendly, term) and the management of physical distribution fall under this heading. 'Placing' products involves managing the processes supporting the flow of goods or services from producers to consumers. The process has sometimes been described as developing the best 'routes to market' for a firm's products.

We shall examine the distribution of services later in this chapter, but most of our initial attention will focus on making goods available to buyers. Goods must be made available in the right quantity, in the right location, and at the times when customers wish to purchase them—all at an acceptable price (and cost to the producer and/or inter-mediary). Achieving these concurrent aims is not easy, but is essential for an organization wishing to gain a sustainable competitive advantage. There is evidence that the design of distribution channels can explain differences in marketing and sales performance (Löning and Besson 2002).

Sometimes a manufacturer will decide to dispense with intermediaries altogether. The computer manufacturer Dell has pursued a distribution strategy which makes very little use of intermediaries, but instead relies on the company communicating directly with customers through advertising and direct mailshots (among others), and delivering computers directly from the company's factories to the buyer's home or office. But many companies have realized that not all buyers want to deal with the manufacturer, so they must develop multiple 'routes to market' involving intermediaries. Even Dell—which for a long time emphasized the benefits of dealing directly with the company—now sells its computers through a number of intermediaries. In the following pages we will explore the complex set of issues involved in managing distribution channels in today's fast-shifting economic environment.

◉ What is a marketing channel?

A marketing channel has been defined by the American Marketing Association as:

> A set of practices or activities necessary to transfer the ownership of goods, and to move goods, from the point of production to the point of consumption and, as such, which consists of all the institutions and all the marketing activities in the marketing process.

Channel *intermediaries* are those organizations that facilitate the distribution of products to the ultimate customer. The roles of intermediaries, which are explored in the following section, may include taking physical ownership of products, collecting payment, and offering after-sales service. Since these activities can involve considerable risk and responsibility, it is clear that, in attempting to ensure the availability of their goods, producers must consider the needs of channel intermediaries as well as those of the end consumers. Marketing channel management refers to the choice and control of these intermediaries, although, as we shall see, the ability of manufacturers to exert influence over intermediaries such as retailers varies considerably, especially in channels for fast moving consumer goods (FMCGs).

In addition to deciding who should be involved in a channel of distribution, it is important for marketing managers to understand the *overall* movement, storage, and availability of goods. Later in this chapter we will look at the physical distribution processes that allow goods to flow from materials suppliers to manufacturers and on to the end customer. In taking a wider perspective that extends beyond marketing channel considerations, it is common to visualize this entire supply chain as a *pipeline*.

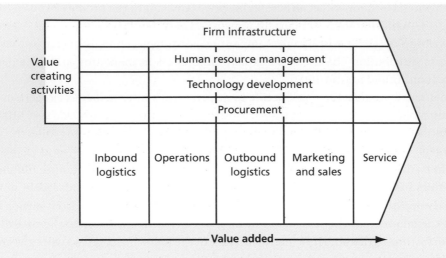

Figure 10.1 **A value chain showing how value is progressively added to a product as different processes are preformed.** Some of these processes may be performed more efficiently by intermediaries than by the manufacturing firm itself.

◉ The role of intermediaries in a value chain

The value chain was introduced in Chapter 2; it describes the activities involved in the manufacture, marketing, and delivery of goods or services by a firm (see Figure 10.1). You will recall that value can be added at all points in a value chain, from transformation of basic raw materials into components, and then into finished goods, and later through making those goods and services available at a time and place that is most highly valued by the buyer. Another way of looking at a value chain is as a supply chain. Although the two terms are not strictly synonymous, a value chain implies channels through which goods and services are supplied from the producer to the end consumer.

Marketing channels can perform an important role in the later stages of a value chain, in particular outbound logistics (e.g. order processing, storage, and transportation); marketing and sales (e.g. market research, personal selling, sales promotions), and after sales service (e.g. repair, training, spare parts). It is rare for a producer to undertake all of these activities itself, and therefore the management of channel intermediaries, in terms of both minimizing costs and maximizing competitive advantage, plays a vital part in boosting the value added by any marketing channel. The concept of a value chain applies to services as well as goods, in fact many sources of added value are essentially service-based. Value chains can also exist in an Internet environment, even though no physical goods may be directly involved, as a service offer is jointly created by a number of different companies, for example an Internet travel agent can add value by providing choice to consumers (Porter 2001).

In order to decide whether a firm should undertake its own distribution direct to consumers or whether it would be more efficient and effective to use intermediaries, it is necessary to understand the functions of intermediaries.

● Functions of intermediaries

Perhaps the most significant role of channel intermediaries is to reconcile the differing needs of manufacturers and consumers. Essentially, producers like to produce their product in bulk in order to achieve economies of scale, whereas consumers typically just want to buy one or two units. Furthermore, the producer would typically prefer to make the product in one central location where production economies can be maximized, whereas the buyer wants the product to be available close to them, where their own costs of obtaining the product are minimized. A manufacturer may prefer to operate its factory during the working day, but the buyer may prefer to buy its products in the evening.

Intermediaries play a valuable role by reducing this *discrepancy of assortment* between what the producer wants to produce and what the buyer wants to buy. They do this by dramatically reducing the number of contacts required between suppliers and the end customers. If a manufacturer had to deal with each consumer individually, it would have to maintain thousands, possibly millions of individual distribution channels. Furthermore, if there were many manufacturers competing in the market, each would maintain large numbers of direct channels. For low value, high volume goods, it is not very efficient to have such a large number of lines of contact between producers and consumers. This pattern can be greatly simplified if the manufacturers only deal with a smaller number of intermediaries, rather than the thousands or millions of individual consumers. There is a further benefit to consumers, because they can now go to any of the intermediaries and obtain a selection of products from a number of producers. They don't have to go to each producer separately. Look at Figure 10.2, and it should become apparent that the use of intermediaries greatly simplifies communication between a company and its customers, In this case, the use of intermediaries has reduced the number of potential channels between producers and consumers from 30 to 13.

Intermediaries can add value by breaking bulk. This might involve purchasing in large quantities from a manufacturer and then selling smaller, more manageable, volumes of stock on to retailers. *Discrepancies of quantity* are reduced by intermediaries who provide consumers with individual items that suit their needs.

In many cases, intermediaries can offer superior knowledge of a target market compared with manufacturers. Retailers can therefore add value to the producer's goods by tailoring their offerings more closely to the specific requirements of consumers, for example by ensuring that goods are stocked that match the economic and lifestyle needs of shoppers who live in the area.

Intermediaries might also offer after-sales services in the form of guarantees and customer advice hotlines. If these services can be provided with a high level of expertise, then manufacturers may feel able to relinquish control of these parts of the value chain. Ahmad and

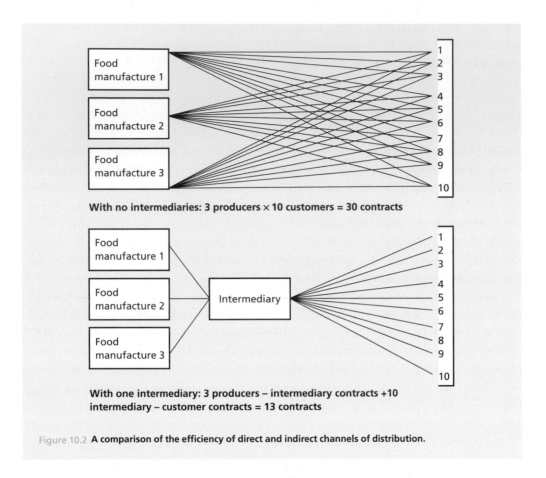

Figure 10.2 **A comparison of the efficiency of direct and indirect channels of distribution.**

Buttle (1998) described the relationship between a foreign-based manufacturer of office equipment (fax machines, photocopiers, printers, etc.) and its UK dealers. The manufacturer provided basic service training for the dealers' technical staff and allowed the dealers to sell consumables such as toners. More complex repair queries, however, were handled by a head office telephone helpline for both dealers and end users.

Probably the most important gaps between consumers and producers in channel management are those of location and time. A *location gap* occurs owing to the geographic separation of producers and the consumers of their goods and services. Goods manufacturers (and many service providers) generally want to produce their goods and services in one central location, but consumers typically want to buy them locally. A *time gap* arises when consumers want to purchase products at a time when a manufacturer may consider it inconvenient to make them available. Manufacturers may like producing goods and services from 9 am to 5 pm on weekdays, but consumers may want to buy in the evenings or at weekends. Intermediaries can facilitate the task of making goods and services available at these times.

⊙ Types of intermediary

Many types of intermediary can participate in a value chain. For most FMCG manufacturers, the two most commonly used intermediaries are wholesalers and retailers. These organizations are normally described as distributors (or 'merchants'), since they take title to products (that is, they take ownership), typically building up stocks and thereby assuming risk, and then resell them. Wholesalers sell to other wholesalers and retailers; retailers sell to the ultimate consumers. Other intermediaries, such as agents and brokers, do not take title to goods. Instead, they arrange exchanges between buyers and sellers and in return receive commissions or fees. The use of agents often involves less of a financial and contractual commitment by the manufacturer and is therefore less of a risk, but their lack of commitment to the manufacturer can sometimes be problematic.

Wholesalers are typically less obvious to us as individual consumers than retailers, but they play an important role in servicing retailers (in consumer markets) and organizational clients (in industrial or business-to-business markets). It can prove prohibitively expensive for a manufacturer of industrial goods, such as a simple bolt fastening, to maintain a large sales force. In this case, access to a wide range of industrial customers may be facilitated more efficiently via a few specialist wholesalers. Smaller retailers are often serviced by wholesalers specializing in sourcing and selecting stock for a particular product line. These wholesalers can offer detailed product knowledge and in-store merchandising services to retailers.

⊙ Classification of retailers

We now turn our attention to retailing, which represents a highly visible form of intermediary. A *retailer* is simply an organization that buys products for the purpose of reselling them to end consumers. Having said this, a number of different types of retailer may be identified.

⊙ Department stores for example Debenhams. Here, we find product lines laid out into separate departments, such as ladies' and men's clothing, home furnishings, cosmetics, etc. Companies may operate as 'shops-within-shops' and pay rent as a percentage of takings to the host store.

⊙ Supermarkets for example Sainsbury's and Carrefour. These are large, self-service stores carrying a very wide range of FMCGs. The supermarket chains are often the first with new customer initiatives such as loyalty cards and in-store bakeries. Low prices based on large-scale efficiency are hard for smaller independent stores to match.

⊙ Discount sheds or 'category killers' for example Toys 'R' Us. These stores often stock bulky items such as furniture and electrical goods. The 'category killer' terminology results from the tendency of some very large specialist stores to put competing independent retailers out of business.

- **Speciality** shops, for example clothing (Next), music (HMV), mobile phones (Carphone Warehouse). These are typically found in central business districts of towns where prime sites are vitally important. As it is frequently only the large national chains that can afford the high rents of such sites, it might be said that many central shopping areas in the UK are now very similar in the choice they offer to the shopper.

- **Convenience stores** for example Spar, 7-Eleven. Geographically, and also in terms of the range of products on offer, these stores fill the gap between edge-of-town supermarkets and the 'traditional' corner shops situated close to housing and work areas. While independently owned convenience stores have declined in number in recent years, the major UK supermarket operators have expanded into this area.

- **Cash and carry warehouses** for example Costco. These usually offer cheaper groceries and durable goods to consumers or catering trades and small retailers.

- **Catalogue showrooms** for example Argos. These stores lower their costs by maintaining only a limited display of goods, with consumers making their selection via a catalogue and collecting their purchase from a stockroom attached to the store.

- **Market traders** These remain significant outlets for many low-value products. Although they have generally declined in importance in recent years, some types of market, for example farmers' markets, have expanded.

- **Online retailers** Some online retailers, for example Amazon.com, have no physical shops that interface with the public. However, most online retailing is in fact accounted for by 'bricks and mortar' retailers. According to the annual IMRG-Experian Hitwise Hot Shops List, the largest UK online retailer in 2010 measured by number of hits on its website was Amazon, followed by Argos and Play.com.

Within these differing types of store, we can find some interesting trends. One of the most significant changes in retailing structure has been the increased proportion of trade taken by large multiple store retail chains. In the grocery sector, multiples are usually defined as retailers with over ten outlets. This change has taken place largely at the expense of independent retailers, but has also eroded the market share of the cooperatives. It is notable that, collectively, the cooperative societies represent one of the largest retailers in the country. The problem for the Co-op is that it comprises a large number of mostly autonomous societies and does not pool its buying resources into a fully integrated retailing organization. Independent retail stores are typically run by a sole trader or as a family business. Changing social trends conspire against the independent convenience store, which is constantly having to look for ways to differentiate itself, usually through flexible opening hours and specialist inventory (Figure 10.3). One response of independent retailers has been to form voluntary or 'symbol' groups where buying and marketing is provided centrally in return for the retailers buying a proportion of their goods from particular wholesalers. Examples include Spar for groceries, and Euronics for electrical goods.

Figure 10.3 **New forms of retailing are continually emerging.** Common for some time in the United States, one recent innovation in the UK is the outlet mall, which sells a range of brand name products at clearance prices. For shoppers, outlet malls, such as this one in Bicester, Oxfordshire, have been developed into day out attractions in their own right, attracting visitors from a wide area. For retailers and manufacturers, they provide an opportunity to sell old-season stock which would otherwise clutter their high street outlets.

◉ Designing a channel of distribution

Manufacturers need to take a holistic view of distribution, and to adopt a 'channel vision' to maximize their opportunities to reach customers. The starting point for designing a channel of distribution should be a producer's distribution objectives. These should be derived from the organization's positioning strategy and must be consistent with the remaining marketing mix tools used by the marketing manager to gain a sustainable competitive advantage (see Chapter 7). For example, a strategy to sell large volumes of a low priced FMCGs in a fiercely competitive market may be inconsistent with a distribution strategy which concentrates on just a small number of retailers.

We can identify three approaches to designating a channel of distribution:

1. Intensive distribution: This is generally used for FMCGs and other relatively low priced or impulse purchases. Put simply, the more outlets that are stocking your product, the greater the likelihood of it being bought. Convenience and availability is

often very important for these goods. An interesting development here is the increasing range of products available from petrol stations—everything from groceries to flowers and gifts. In terms of the discrepancies of assortment and location discussed earlier, a highly intensive distribution network with wide geographical cover can prove extremely efficient. Although not a conventional 'product', consider the huge number and variety of outlets where National Lottery tickets may be bought.

2. Exclusive distribution: Here, distribution may be limited to a small number of intermediaries that manage to gain better margins and exclusivity. In return, the manufacturer seeks more control over how the product is marketed, and there is likely to be dedicated merchandising and sales support from the retailer. The intermediary may also agree not to stock competing lines. This is often done for expensive products with an upmarket brand image, such as designer label clothing and sunglasses. Manufacturers can become upset when retailers who they see as not having the appropriate brand image attempt to stock their products or, worse, offer them at discounted prices. This can be seen in the reaction of the perfume industry to Superdrug's stocking of fine fragrances, or Calvin Klein's protests at Tesco selling its underwear range.

3. Selective distribution: This represents a compromise between intensive and exclusive distribution. The manufacturer is looking for adequate market coverage, but still hopes to select supportive dealers. This usually occurs for 'shopping' products such as audio and video hardware.

◉ Influences on channel selection

So, which type of intermediaries should a company use on its routes to market? There are a number of key influences on channel selection strategies.

1. First, the expectations of *end customers* must be addressed. Do they expect to buy locally, or are they prepared to travel to a retailer that stocks a product? This might mean taking into consideration factors such as a geographical preference to buy locally, or a tendency to feel more comfortable visiting a particular type of store. Do they expect the retailer to be capable of undertaking warranty repairs? Decisions must be made based on sound marketing research into buyer behaviour patterns (see Chapters 4 and 5). This is also true for business-to-business markets. For example, suppliers of electronic components need to determine whether business customers prefer to deal with the company's direct sales force (often the case for larger organizational clients with expert purchasing departments) or with a specialist distributor (typically used by smaller clients without this in-house expertise). In international markets, it may be essential to use an agent with an intimate knowledge of the cultural nuances of doing business in target countries (see Chapter 12).

2. *Producer-related factors* include a number of issues in addition to the distribution levels sought. An important constraint is the resources that are available to the manufacturer

to bring the product to market. Some companies lack the finances to recruit and reward a sales force and so will use a wholesaler or agent instead. This is often the case for companies making a very narrow range of products. Also critical is what the manufacturer believes to be its core competence. If, for instance, this is the design and production of innovative goods, then the distribution of these goods may well be better left to a specialist channel intermediary. Another consideration is the desired level of channel control sought by the manufacturer.

3. *Product attributes* can be important. Fresh produce that is highly perishable requires fairly short channels. Northern Foods, a manufacturer of chilled meals for Marks & Spencer, claims that it takes just 24 hours from the time a fresh egg arrives at the factory to its appearance in a custard tart on the shelves of an M&S store anywhere in the country. Heavy or large goods are frequently not suited to inner-city retail locations where consumers cannot easily drive to pick up their purchases: instead, they may be more suitable to out-of-town retailers or sold to order via direct distribution. Some products may be so complex that personal contact between producer and buyer is essential. This can be the case for the installation of highly technical machinery.

4. Finally, the activities of the *competition* must be considered. If competitors have exclusive deals with intermediaries, the choices open to a new market entrant seeking to place its products may be limited. Beverage manufacturers seeking to build distribution have often encountered refrigerator exclusivity deals between small retailers and the major suppliers such as Coca Cola, preventing them getting immediate access to such stores. In fact, such agreements are increasingly being scrutinized by competition regulators, and outlawed where they are held to be an anti-competitive practice. Sometimes, a manufacturer's most significant competitor is the 'own label' product of the supermarket itself. When this happens, it can be very difficult to gain retailer support, as shown by the battles of Coca Cola to gain what it saw as adequate display space in Sainsbury's. A solution may be for the manufacturer to target convenience stores instead, or to set up alternative distribution channels such as company-owned chilled vending machines.

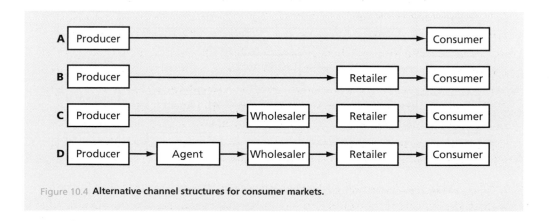

Figure 10.4 **Alternative channel structures for consumer markets.**

◉ Channel alternatives

Figure 10.4 shows some alternative *consumer* channels. Channel A represents a direct producer-to-consumer channel, using direct marketing techniques (e.g. Dell, Avon Cosmetics). Channel B represents the producer–retailer–consumer route. This is typically used by large retailers such as Sainsbury's, who have the buying power to order large quantities of goods direct from manufacturers with no need of a further middleman. The addition of the wholesaler in Channel C is more commonly used by smaller retailers with relatively small order quantities and, from the producer's perspective, by manufacturers of convenience goods, such as cigarettes, which need intensive distribution. The even longer structure of Channel D, with the inclusion of agents, is often used by producers entering foreign markets, where a local agent's expertise may be essential to overcome trade barriers (see Chapter 12).

Figure 10.5 shows alternative channels used in order to reach business customers. In general, these channels are shorter than those for consumer goods. The shortest structure, that of Channel E, represents the direct manufacturer-to-customer course. This is a viable alternative for many high-value industrial products, as customer numbers here are fewer and often less geographically widespread than for consumer markets. Channels for large, expensive, and highly technical products such as railway engines, may require considerable negotiation between the buyer and seller, therefore channel design frequently follows this pattern.

Channel F represents the manufacturer–industrial distributor–customer route. It is used for more frequently purchased, less expensive products that are required by a wider range of industrial customers, for example tools used by garage repair workshops. The use of an agent, as in Channel G, can occur when a manufacturer chooses not to set up its own dedicated sales force, and has therefore to 'outsource' the agent's marketing and selling services. This can be a relatively quick option, but, as we noted previously, the support offered by agents may be less than that provided by a title-taking distributor. Finally, the lengthier structure of

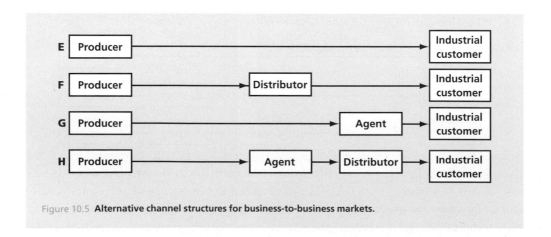

Figure 10.5 **Alternative channel structures for business-to-business markets.**

Channel H may arise where organizational buyers in a particular market prefer to use nearby distributors. This can happen when customers need to be resupplied frequently, for instance with paper used by office photocopiers.

◉ Multiple channels

In reality, many producers use a combination of channels to distribute their products. Think of the many different places you can purchase a can of Coca Cola, for instance. Also, some manufacturers, such as those in the personal computer sector, sell to both consumers and organizations. There is rarely one simple solution to the decision concerning which channel type should be selected by a company. Indeed, bearing in mind the power of some retailers, the problem for producers often comes down to: which channel intermediary will select *us*? This complexity is explored further in the following section.

◉ Selecting specific intermediaries

Once a decision has been made regarding the type of channel or channels to use, it is necessary to choose individual organizations with which to work. The selection of intermediaries can have a major impact on what happens afterwards, for example the success or failure of a product launch. A number of *criteria* can be used to assess the relative merits of potential channel participants, including:

◉ The firm's financial position

◉ Depth and width of product lines carried

◉ Whether competitive lines are carried

◉ Evidence of marketing, sales, and promotional ability

◉ Approach to order processing and order fulfillment

◉ Evidence of investment in new technologies

◉ Reputation within industry

◉ Willingness to share data

◉ Local market knowledge

Some of these selection criteria may be particularly important to the company, for example if it is entering a completely new market, an intermediary's local knowledge may be critical.

The issue can arise of *reverse selection* in a channel of distribution, in which the intermediary effectively selects the producer, rather than the other way round. This is becoming increasingly common among large supermarket chains, who may design a new food product in their research laboratories, then approach different specialist meal manufacturers for their ability to mass-produce the products to the supermarket's specification. The flexibility of such manufacturers as S&A Foods in providing Asian-style chilled meals to order, as well as in developing their own recipes, has resulted in the growth of a number of large food manufacturers whose products are sold under supermarkets' own labels, with customers completely unfamiliar with the identity of the manufacturer (e.g. Northern Foods and Samworth Brothers).

Power and conflict within distribution channels

From the previous discussion, it is clear that some members of a distribution channel may have dominant power over the others. Sometimes, it may be a manufacturer who has a strong brand which retailers feel they must stock in order to satisfy the expectations of their customers. Increasingly though, it is the retailers themselves who are exercising power within the channel. If power is used in a manner believed to be unfair by one or more channel members, then conflict may arise. Conflict need not necessarily be destructive, since it can encourage managers to question the *status quo* and find ways of improving their distribution systems. Sometimes, however, strategies employed by firms can create unstable, adversarial relationships between producers and intermediaries. The following are examples of conflict which may arise in channels:

- **Bypassing channels:** A producer may seek to cut out intermediaries by dealing directly with the public. Retailers may feel aggrieved that they have opened up a market for the producer, but are now cut out of any resulting benefit.

- **Over-saturation:** A manufacturer may be accused of using too many distributors within a given geographical area, making it difficult for any individual distributor to achieve a satisfactory level of sales.

- **Too many links:** In the supply chain: an intermediary may be required to buy stocks from a larger dealer, who may be perceived as a competitor, rather than a cooperative channel member.

- **New channels:** These can have a similar effect to bypassing an intermediary, for example many manufacturers have opened up Internet sales channels, thereby taking sales away from established intermediaries.

- **Cost-cutting:** In order to increase volume sales, a manufacturer may seek to distribute through higher volume, low cost intermediaries, which may make it more difficult for a smaller, full service intermediary to sell that product.

- **Inconsistency:** Appearing arbitrarily to treat some intermediaries more favourably than others, for example through incentives and rewards.

In recent years, power in UK distribution channels has tended to pass to a small number of dominant retailers and away from manufacturers. The growing strength of grocery retailers has put them at the focal point of a value chain. By building up their own strong brands, large retailers are increasingly able to exert pressure on manufacturers in terms of product specification, price, and the level of promotional support to be given to the retailer. According to market research group Kentar Worldpanel, the UK's 'big four' grocery retailers—Tesco, Asda, Sainsbury's, and Morrisons—accounted for more than three-quarters (76.1 per cent) of the grocery market value in 2010. However, while many manufacturers may be dependent on the big four retailers, this dependency is not reciprocated, with retailers generally not relying on one single supplier for more than 1 per cent of their supplies. Most countries have legislation which prevents one company having dominant power in a market, unless there are public interest benefits.

Some evidence of the power of grocery retailers was provided in a 2008 report by the UK Competition Commission on supermarkets (Competition Commission 2008). It found evidence of the large supermarkets using their dominant position to retrospectively demand discounts from suppliers, who felt obliged to pay, for fear of losing a large contract. It also highlighted how supermarkets had used their power to charge the cost of shoplifting to manufacturers, when the manufacturers' products were stolen while in the supermarket. The competition commission argued that the retailers were transferring excessive risk to suppliers, and proposed a new ombudsman, dubbed 'Offshop', to investigate grievances by suppliers at the hands of supermarkets. The new regulator would be able to hear and investigate complaints from farmers and any other traders in the grocery supply chain, including abattoirs, dairies, processors, the food service industry, wholesalers, and manufacturers.

◉ Integrated distribution channels

It follows from the previous discussion of conflict, that channel participants may be keen to integrate their functions, in order to reduce conflict and improve efficiency and effectiveness. An integrated channel is seen as having a number of advantages over a channel where the individual components operate quite independently:

◉ They reduce channel costs by eliminating duplication of functions.

◉ They minimize conflict among channel members.

◉ They maximize the experience and expertise of members.

There are three general types of integrated marketing channel:

1. The first of these, the *corporate* system, involves one company owning many stages in the distribution channel, for example a coffee producer may own farms, wholesalers, or retailers to provide it with raw materials, or outlets for its manufactured product. This form of channel integration is becoming less common, as companies outsource peripheral activities—which typically may involve raw material supplies or distribution—and concentrate on their 'core competencies'.

2. In *contractual* systems channel members' rights and obligations are defined by legal agreements. These can include collaborative agreements such as the voluntary chains discussed earlier in this chapter, where separate firms share resources and agree to joint purchasing initiatives and franchise arrangements. The level of detail specified in a contract can vary, with some ongoing relationships relying on goodwill between the parties as much as precise specification of all terms of business.

3. *Administered* systems arise when participants are financially independent but are effectively controlled by the most powerful channel member. Franchising is an important variant of this type of integration and is explored in more detail below.

Franchising systems

Franchising refers to trading relationships between companies in which a franchisor grants the right to a franchisee to operate a business using the franchisor's business format (see Figures 10.6 and 10.7). Franchising has been a rapidly growing type of business relationship. According to the annual NatWest/British Franchise Association survey, the total number of franchise systems in the UK in 2009 was 842. These were linked to a total of 34,800 franchisees, with an annual turnover of £11.8 billion and employed an estimated 465,000 people (British Franchise Association 2010). Franchising offers a ready-made business opportunity for entrepreneurs who have capital but do not want the risk associated with setting up a completely new business afresh. A good franchise operation will have a proven business format and would already be well established in its market. The franchisee would be required to pay an initial capital sum for the right to use the name of the franchisor. The NatWest/British Franchise Association survey found that in 2009 the average initial cost of starting a franchise was £46,700 (including franchise fee, working capital, equipment and fittings, stock, and materials) (British Franchise Association 2010). Franchisees typically pay between 5 per cent and 10 per cent of their sales in recurring fees to their franchisors.

Having said this, problems in controlling standards among individual franchisees can occur. This, for example, is claimed to have contributed to the failure of some of the Body Shop's franchised outlets in France. With poor control of franchisees, the image of the franchisor can be seriously dented. From a different perspective, Benetton's franchisees in Germany were outraged at the company's controversial advertising campaigns, which they blamed for poor sales. Bitter disputes can develop where franchisor and franchisee differ in their assessment of the costs and benefits associated with their involvement in a franchise.

◉ Global channels of distribution

Increasingly, channels of distribution are designed to cross national borders. There are a number of reasons for this. Retailers, who we have seen now have increasing power in a value chain, have sourced their goods from overseas countries where costs can be considerably lower than production at home. In recent years, retailers such as Tesco and Primark have been able to compete with extremely low prices, such as a pair of jeans for £5.00, or an

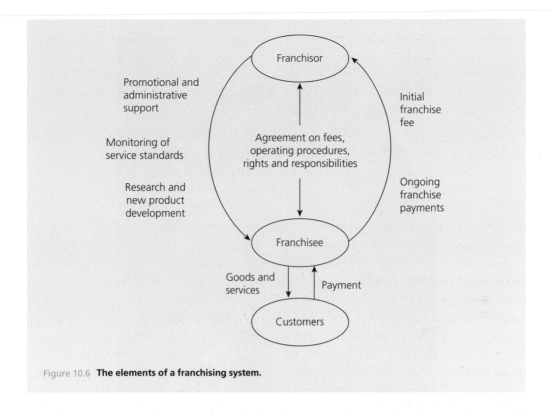

Figure 10.6 **The elements of a franchising system.**

espresso coffee machine for just £6.00, because they have sourced these from the cheapest manufacturers in the world. If the lowest price of a delivered pair of jeans involves manufacture in the Philippines, then the retailer's supply chain must be extended back to incorporate overseas manufacturers. We will consider logistics later in this chapter, when it will become evident that part of the retailer's competitive advantage lies not just in obtaining a cheaper pair of jeans at the factory gate, but also shipping it quickly and cheaply to its shelves.

The second reason for channels of distribution becoming increasingly international derives from retailers' desire to serve international, rather than purely national or regional markets. By operating internationally, retailers can achieve significant economies of scale through buying in bulk more cheaply; spreading the cost of product design over a greater range of output; and extending their management skills across a large network of outlets. Many west European retailers have moved into less developed markets, where their skills of inventory control, merchandising, and information technology can shake up the local market.

There are many examples of retailers who have sought to become truly global, including America's Walmart, Britain's Tesco, and France's Carrefour. However, many retailers have encountered problems in overseas markets, where the business environment may be quite different to what they have been used to. Even Tesco, which has successfully developed stores in Eastern Europe and the Far East, is reported to have faced problems when it sought to develop its 'Fresh and Easy' convenience stores in the United States (*Financial Times* 2008a).

We will return to the subject of global marketing in Chapter 12.

Figure 10.7 **Domino's Pizza is now recognized as the world's leading pizza delivery company.** Founded in 1960, Domino's makes and delivers nearly six million pizzas a week in more than 60 countries around the world. In 2010, it operated 665 stores in the UK with a total sales turnover of £485 million and a profit before tax of £18.7 million. Franchising has been a key element of the company's mission to bring pizza to the world, and by 2010, 85 per cent of its outlets were owned by franchisees. The UK was an early target for Domino's expansion, and it established a subsidiary company, Domino's Pizza Group Limited which holds the exclusive master franchise to own, operate, and franchise Domino's Pizza stores in the UK and Ireland. For Domino's, franchising allowed the company to expand quickly, by using the capital and entrepreneurial skills of independent franchisees. And in 2004, Domino's reported that 10 of its 100 plus UK and Ireland franchisees owned businesses which were worth more than £1,000,000 each. Domino's franchisees earned around £120,000 a year on average (although some considerably more), which was more than three times the average income of a typical business manager (£38,107). Although franchising is the dominant form of distribution for Domino's, the company retains a proportion of directly managed outlets. As well as providing an internal benchmark against which franchisees can be judged, these outlets are useful for developing new service ideas which may be too risky for individual franchisees to undertake on their own. One outcome of this process has been the development of a bluetooth and GPS enabled system which can pinpoint a pizza delivery person's exact location via satellite. The company has also developed an iPhone ordering app, which accounted for over £1 million sales in the three months after its UK launch in September 2010. The company has also become active in the social media arena. Would such developments be possible without the support of a strong, centrally managed franchise?

⊙ The Internet and channel design

The Internet has added to the complexity of channels of distribution (Figure 10.8). In the early days of the Internet, it was widely predicted that many companies would be able to dispense with intermediaries and distribute their goods and services directly to each customer. The growth of direct-selling intermediaries such as Direct Line Insurance appeared to confirm the ability to cut out intermediaries, who were often portrayed as parasitic and delaying middlemen. The inelegant term 'disintermediation' has been used to describe the process of removing intermediaries from a distribution channel and developing direct communications. However, the reality has in many cases been quite different, with the proliferation of new types of Internet-based intermediaries. Companies providing search engine optimization, affiliate marketing sites, and price comparison sites, among others, have made the task of getting through to final customers more complex.

Attracting the attention of web surfers can be a big challenge for Internet-based companies such as motor insurance and electricity suppliers who are selling a fairly generic service. Many have therefore chosen to pay a range of affiliate sites, price comparison sites, and 'cashback' sites to help in the task of bringing potential customers to their site.

The traditional manufacturer-to-customer distribution channel has also been challenged by the growth of peer-to-peer social network websites. In many cases, a buyer's choice is strongly influenced by what their peers are saying through blogs and review sites. In this way, the peer group can create value by providing advice to buyers and information to the seller about how it could improve its product offer, replacing one of the traditional functions of intermediaries.

Although online ordering may be administratively efficient, the problem of buyers being at home to accept goods ordered online has been slow to resolve. Retailers have experimented with 24-hour collection points at local convenience stores and delivery companies have experimented with evening and weekend deliveries. In the UK, the Royal Mail announced in October 2010 that it was to experiment with evening deliveries of mail to cater for busy professionals who are out at work all day and unable to receive deliveries at the time when retailers and delivery companies have traditionally made their deliveries.

The cost of delivering tangible goods has tended to increase in real terms. Many goods can only be evaluated by experiencing them through touch or smell, something that is difficult to achieve online. The failed Internet clothes retailer boo.com found that many people would probably find it much easier and reassuring to try on clothes in a shop than rely on a computer image, thereby ensuring a continuing role for traditional high street retailers (although 'bricks and clicks' retailers such as Next have quietly developed a substantial level of clothes sales via their website). There have been hopes that three-dimensional virtual reality systems may help to tangibilize services, for example by allowing potential buyers to have a virtual tour of a hotel, or have the semblance of a face-to-face meeting with an employee of a bank. Many companies now use 'Virtual assistants' in their websites to put a face to answers provided for the most frequently asked questions or to allow customers

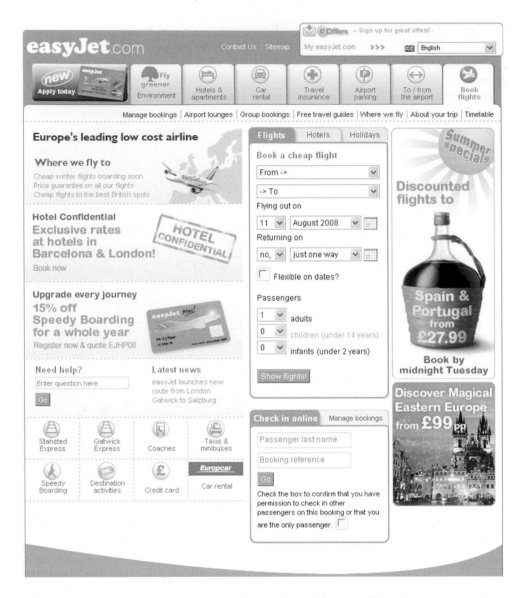

Figure 10.8 **The Internet has opened up a powerful distribution channel by which a company can communicate directly with each of its customers, providing rapid, low-cost distribution which need not involve intermediaries.** The budget airline easyJet has embraced the Internet and claims to be the 'Web's favourite airline', with over 90% of the airline's customers using the company's website for booking their tickets. The company boasts that it does not pay commission to intermediaries, and can pass on these savings in the form of lower ticket prices.

(*Source*: reproduced with kind permission of easyJet Airline Company Ltd.)

some limited experience of a product (e.g. the use of personalized avatars to try on clothes). However, expectations that large-scale virtual environments, such as 'Second life' (www. secondlife.com) do not yet appear to have gained the widespread popularity many had expected.

The end of shops?

There are many high-involvement goods where buyers feel more comfortable being able to see and feel the goods before they commit to a purchase. When buying clothes, many buyers would prefer to try the items on and to feel the texture of the clothes. Some online retailers have introduced 'virtual reality' systems to help simulate the shop buying experience, and some companies allow customers to develop a personal avatar which they can use to judge how an item of clothing would look on them. Despite a lot of hype about the potential of virtual reality systems, and hope that these could be used in a peer-to-peer environment, progress appears to have been slow. Uptake of the virtual reality social network websites 'Second Life' is reported to be lower than the original expectations.

Retailing often fulfils a social function, for example a group of friends may 'have a day out shopping' which might include stopping for coffee and having a meal and sharing experiences of new purchases. Many have doubted the ability of the Internet to replace this social function, even with further development of virtual reality social media networks.

As e-retailing has developed, customers' expectations have risen. When ordering online, customers expect to have prices and stock confirmed as well as a delivery date and preferably the time. Customers are also expecting to be told of any delays, particularly when they are waiting in for the delivery.

Although many companies have set up Internet retail sites in an attempt to cut out intermediaries, routes to the market for the retailers have become increasingly complex. E-retailing can be extremely competitive, with customers being just a click away from a competitor—they don't even have to make the effort of walking into the competitor's shop. Getting a customer into your site increasingly involves the use of online intermediaries, including search engines, affiliates, and price comparison sites. These would usually seek a percentage of the sales revenue, or a payment per 'click through' in return for providing a link to the retailer's site.

◉ Physical distribution management

A channel of distribution must support the task of moving goods from the producer to the consumer so that the right goods are available to the right people in the right place at the right time. This must be done as cheaply as possible. In other words, the distribution must be both *efficient* and *effective*. Physical distribution also concerns most services organizations that have to move supporting goods (e.g. supplies of brochures for travel agents; supplies of burgers for a fast-food chain). In western countries we have often come to take for granted that our favourite products will be on the shelves in a shop when we visit. Business buyers have come to depend on the prompt delivery of inputs to their production process. But when physical distribution goes wrong, customers will soon notice, and the financial effects on a company whose distribution has failed can be harsh, even threatening the survival of the company. When the UK children's retailer Mothercare opened a new UK distribution centre at Daventry, it hoped to achieve increases in efficiency and effectiveness of deliveries to the company's nationwide store network. In reality, poor IT systems caused stock to be lost within its system instead of getting 'hot' products to the shelves where customers were eager to buy them. By the time they had arrived, market preferences had changed and goods had to be sold at discounted 'clearance' prices. As a direct result of its distribution problems, the company was forced to issue a series of profit warnings and its share price slumped, threatening the continued independent existence of the company (Keers 2002).

In the next few pages, as well as examining the movement of goods between producers and these downstream channel participants, we shall also be considering the flow of raw materials and components from suppliers that are *upstream* from the manufacturer. Furthermore, we shall explore the vital role played by the flow of information between supply chain members, as shown in Figure 10.9. In this figure, second-tier suppliers usually provide the raw materials (e.g. plastic resin) for first-tier suppliers to convert to component parts (e.g. steering wheels), which are then manufactured into the end product (e.g. cars) by the producer. Note that not all supply chains will contain both tiers of suppliers; we shall discuss more examples of supply chains later.

Let us begin with some definitions, and attempt to show how the terms 'physical distribution' and 'logistics' differ. *Physical distribution* refers to the movement of finished goods outward from the end of the manufacturer's assembly line to the customer, frequently via intermediaries. Functions under this heading can include warehousing, transport (often undertaken by third-party specialists), customer service, and administration. *Logistics* describes the entire process of materials and products moving into, through, and out of a firm. The US Council of Logistics Management (CLM) has defined logistics as 'the process of planning, implementing, and controlling the efficient, effective flow and storage of goods, services, and related information from the point of origin to the point of consumption for the purposes of conforming to customer requirements'. Physical distribution may therefore be seen as 'outbound logistics', while 'inbound logistics' covers the movement of materials from suppliers and is closely linked to the manufacturer's purchasing or procurement function. 'Materials and inventory management' describes the movement and stockholding of goods within a firm.

It should also be remembered that distribution is often a two-way process. Most companies have to deal with customers' returns, and a facility to move these backwards through the distribution chain should be incorporated. Increasingly, legislation is requiring companies to recycle used products, requiring collection and return services.

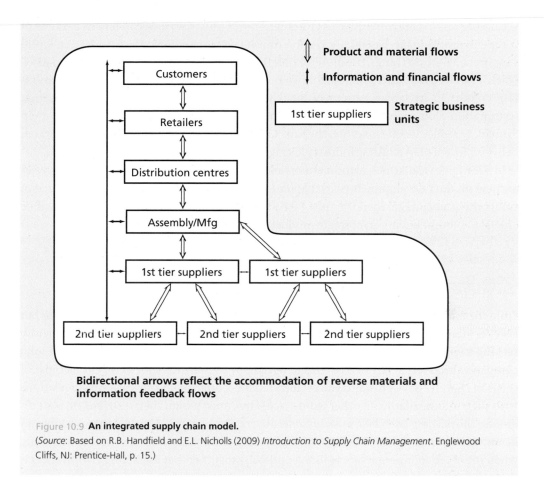

Figure 10.9 **An integrated supply chain model.**
(*Source*: Based on R.B. Handfield and E.L. Nicholls (2009) *Introduction to Supply Chain Management*. Englewood Cliffs, NJ: Prentice-Hall, p. 15.)

● Physical distribution objectives

As with all elements of the marketing mix, the ultimate objective of a firm's physical distribution management is to develop a sustainable competitive advantage. However, this is becoming increasingly difficult as customers, instead of just seeking a better designed product, seek value in a much wider sense. A critical component of such customer value is *service*, and a key part of service value is *availability*. In other words, there is no value in a product until it is in the hands of the customer. Recall in Chapter 8 it was noted that 'service dominant logic' holds that goods only have *value in use*, in other words they are of no value until they are actually made available to the end user (Vargo and Lusch 2008).

Customers often only have a *preference* for a particular brand, rather than strong brand loyalty; so when their preferred brand is not available, many customers will quite readily choose an acceptable substitute. This is equally true in both business-to-business and consumer markets. The choice of suppliers by a just-in-time (JIT—see later) manufacturer will be greatly influenced by delivery reliability, and not just product quality.

Companies that are responsive to customers' needs must also focus on *time* as a source of competitive advantage. Essentially, the less time it takes for a company—or indeed an entire supply chain—to do things, the more flexible it can be in response to changes in the market-place. The clothes retailer Primark, for instance, is able to respond to the popularity of certain colours in its ranges extremely quickly, thanks to efficient and effective logistics. Information from points of sale, flexible manufacturing, and global distribution help Primark to reduce its *lead times* (i.e. the time taken from receipt of a customer's order to final delivery) to less than clothing industry averages.

In addition to lead times, manufacturers should consider the impact of shorter life-cycles on new product development (see Chapter 8). If innovation is a company's key source of competitive advantage, then the time taken to get a new product onto the shelves will be crucial to prevent having an obsolete product range on display.

Customer service objectives in logistics

From the manufacturer's perspective, customer service impacts not only on the end user but also on intermediate customers. Marketing has traditionally focused on the consumer by seeking to promote brand values and to generate a demand 'pull' within the market for a company's products. It is now recognized that this by itself is often not sufficient. Because of shifts in channel power towards the retailer, it has become vital to develop strong relations with such intermediaries. In other words, marketers must design their distribution systems around the needs of both *trade* and *consumer* buyers. The benefits of both of these groups can be enhanced or diminished by the efficiency of the supplier's logistics system. It is only when the three components are working optimally together that marketing effectiveness is maximized.

The primary objective of any logistics customer service strategy must be to reduce the customer's cost of ownership. Ownership in this context can include the cost of ordering, holding stocks, and the consequences of running out of stock. As an example, a delivery twice a week instead of once reduces the customer's average inventory by half and therefore cuts the cost of carrying that inventory. Similarly, reliable on-time delivery means that a retailer can reduce the need to carry safety stock, again resulting in lower stockholding costs.

In a physical distribution context, customer service objectives can be described based on three sets of questions:

1. Pre-transaction elements: how quickly should we respond to requests for information from new potential customers? What level of flexibility should we offer individual customers?

2. Transaction elements: what should be the time taken from order to delivery? What is the target reliability of this lead time? What percentage of demand should be met from stock? What proportion of orders should be completely filled? How long should it take us to provide order status information?

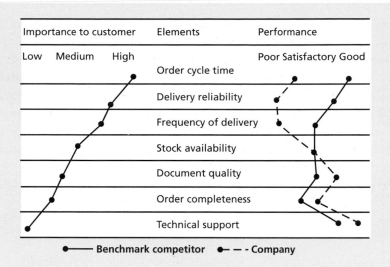

Figure 10.10 **Customer service benchmarking—a comparison of one company's performance against a benchmark competitor.**

3. Post-transaction elements: what level of availability of spare parts should we provide? What should be the target call-out time for our engineers? How quickly should we aim to deal with customers' complaints?

Precise questions will inevitably vary from one company to another. However, a key issue for marketers to grasp is that it is essential first to understand the differing requirements of different market segments, and then to tailor the company's service offering accordingly. For some customers, frequent deliveries of small quantities may be more important than occasional deliveries of large volumes at lower price. It has become fashionable to talk about 'marketing logistics', which starts by asking how customers want to receive the product (see Chapter 4 on buyer behaviour) and then works backwards to the retailing, warehousing, transport, inventory, and design of the goods in order to meet customers' expectations. The amount of information needed by managers to make appropriate marketing logistics decisions is clearly vast. Fortunately, it is becoming increasingly available, due to advances in technology, and we shall discuss some of these advances in more detail at the end of this chapter.

◉ Identification of segments by service requirements

The marketing logistics manager first needs to determine the elements of service that customers most value, for example speed, reliability, or availability. Some form of marketing research is likely to be needed here. It is probable that the market will not be homogeneous: some market segments may be willing to pay high prices to obtain premium service, while others

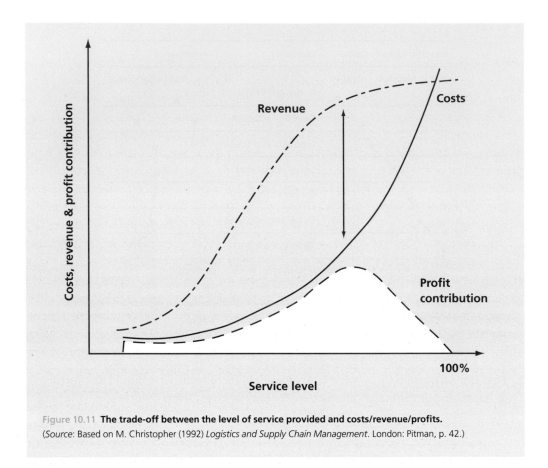

Figure 10.11 **The trade-off between the level of service provided and costs/revenue/profits.**
(*Source*: Based on M. Christopher (1992) *Logistics and Supply Chain Management*. London: Pitman, p. 42.)

may attach greatest importance to low prices and be willing to accept minimum service levels. In attempting to meet buyers' requirements, managers must, of course, also consider cost/ service trade-offs and the logistics standards set by the competition. Looking at the company's performance in relation to its main competitors is known as *benchmarking*, and allows it to identify areas for improvement. An example of a benchmarking study is shown in Figure 10.10. Which service elements do you think should be addressed by the company concerned?

Once target service levels have been identified (e.g. to deliver 95 per cent of orders within two days; to ensure 98 per cent availability in selected stockists of product X), the company must design a physical distribution system which can deliver them at minimum cost. The key issues for marketing logistics managers to consider include:

⦿ How can we speed up communications and order processing?

⦿ Where should we produce goods and store them?

⦿ How much stock should be held?

⦿ How can we best handle transport?

Cost/service trade-offs

We need to recognize that there are costs as well as benefits in providing high levels of customer service, and therefore the appropriate level of service will need to vary from customer to customer. While companies want to attract and retain customers by offering superior service to that provided by competitors, there comes a point when diminishing returns set in. For example, a chemicals supplier might continually have to keep very large stocks of a particular product because of the demands of a key customer. Eventually the cost of holding that inventory (perhaps in terms of storage space, or insurance bills) may force the supplier to reconsider the service levels it offers to the customer, or the price that it charges for the level of service provided. Figure 10.11 shows the typical nature of the cost–benefit trade-offs in service-level decisions.

Figure 10.11 indicates that the shape of the revenue curve is dictated by customers' response to the service level offered. The slope is initially fairly flat, since in many markets there will be a minimum threshold of acceptable service which most competitors will be providing, for example delivery within seven days. Once the threshold is passed, increasing returns to service improvements (say, getting delivery times down to five, then three, days and so on) should be achieved as customers place more orders with the company. At the top, the curve flattens out again when additional returns can only be achieved with greatly increased amounts of expenditure. At this point, there may be a case of 'service overkill'. The cost curve is usually a steeply rising curve, as shown, because of the need to keep high levels of inventory. By investing in IT to improve the flow of information about customer requirements, a company might, however, be able to push this curve to the right, thereby boosting overall profitability at all levels of service.

In setting physical distribution objectives, it is important for managers to understand the *total cost* of attempting to meet a specified service level. When assessing alternative approaches, the costs of some functions will increase, others will decrease, and still others may remain unchanged: the objective is to find the approach with the lowest overall cost. The concept of cost trade-offs recognizes these changing patterns, for example the 'trading' of additional information, via IT-based control systems, as an alternative to higher inventory levels; or perhaps the 'trading' of an extra regional warehouse as an alternative to a larger fleet of national delivery trucks.

Commercial organizations seek to maximize their ROI (return on investment) with a 'reduced asset base'. The need for marketing managers to work closely with other functional areas, such as finance, is vital. An understanding of accounting should tell you that, since ROI is a ratio of returns to investment, a company might attempt to improve this ratio by increasing sales revenue through improved service levels/volumes, and/or it might reduce the asset base on which the ratio is calculated. This can be achieved by a better management of inventory, thereby tying up less money in stocks. The use of 'just in time' (JIT) techniques to address this issue is discussed later in the chapter.

Inventory management

You should by now be aware of the strategic importance of inventory management. Ultimately, stockholding represents costs such as storage space, obsolescence, deterioration, and interest payments. Yet, ideally, a company should carry enough stock to meet customers' orders immediately. If the desired goods are not available, then a sale may be lost, and a customer may be lost to a competitor. If too much stock is held, the company may find itself with large quantities of goods which it is later forced to mark down. This is often the case in fashion retailing, as we saw with Mothercare. The objective of inventory management is therefore to find a balance between customer service and the cost of carrying stock.

A number of methods are used to achieve the desired balance in stockholding. Perhaps the most basic method is that of the *reorder point*. This approach recognizes that waiting to reorder stock until an extremely low level has been reached is risky, because it takes time to replenish stock. The reorder point system triggers reordering at a stock level a little higher than this 'danger' level, so that by the time new stock is received the danger level of the old stock has only just been reached. Stock levels may be counted manually in smaller organizations selling low volumes, but today extensive use is made of 'electronic point of sale' (EPOS) systems to calculate stock levels and to trigger reordering (see below). Safety stock levels are usually based on historical sales data, often seasonally adjusted. Another approach is to use the economic order quantity (EOQ) formula:

$$\text{EOQ} = \sqrt{2do/ic,}$$

where d = annual demand in units; o = cost of placing an order; i = carrying costs as a percentage of cost of one unit; and c = the cost of each unit. The principle of the EOQ model is shown in Figure 10.12. This shows an idealized theoretical relationship between order processing costs and inventory carrying costs to give the order quantity size that minimizes total costs.

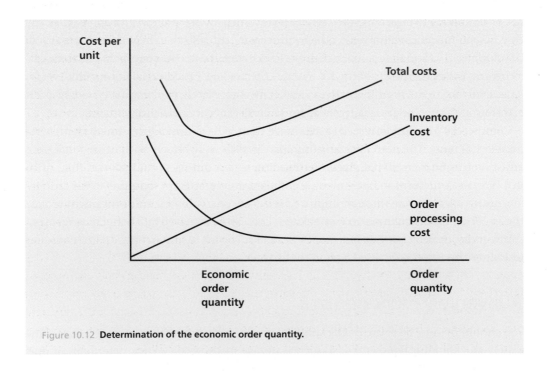

Figure 10.12 **Determination of the economic order quantity.**

Unfortunately, as with many economic models, the EOQ model does not take into sufficient account variations in customer and supplier behaviour. Where demand is unpredictable, or when stocks cannot be replenished relatively quickly, the model may be inadequate. Also, the reorder quantity means that a company will be carrying more inventory than is actually required over practically the complete order cycle (the time between placing separate orders with the supplier); for example if the EOQ is 100 units and daily usage is 10, then on the first day of the cycle the buyer would be overstocked by 90 units, on the second day by 80, and so on.

Just-in-time systems

The just-in-time (JIT) philosophy is based on the view, commonly attributed to the Japanese, that inventory is waste and that large inventories merely hide problems such as inaccurate forecasts, unreliable suppliers, quality issues, and production bottlenecks. The JIT concept aims to eliminate any need for safety stock, with parts for manufacture (or goods for reselling) arriving just as they are needed. As a result, small shipments must be made more frequently. Order requirements can specify the exact unloading point and time of day, with suppliers having to respond accordingly. For example, Toyota schedules its car production to minimize sharp fluctuations in daily volume, and to turn out a predicted number of each model every day. Suppliers are automatically notified of orders and given a stable production schedule so they will not deliver the wrong components on the date of final assembly. This level of planning also occurs, for instance, with retailers like Marks & Spencer stipulating delivery 'windows' for its carriers. In the fast changing world of personal computers, many companies have taken the lead of Dell, which builds computers to customers' specific requirements. This reduces the risk of obsolescence, but requires carefully planned logistics if promised delivery dates are to be met.

The increasing popularity of JIT delivery among business customers clearly means that, for suppliers, the logistics service elements of availability and reliability, plus, of course, uniformly excellent product quality become paramount. Successful implementation of JIT systems relies on high levels of cooperation between supplying and buying organizations, and on the development of long-term partnerships. These closer relations can exist both upstream and downstream from the producer/manufacturer. This can affect the whole culture of an organization and the way that it goes about business. Figure 10.13 summarizes the changes within an organization as it moves from a 'just-in-case' mentality to one of 'just-in-time'.

The JIT concept is not without its problems. The *Financial Times* (1994) reported that suppliers in the Japanese plastics industry have been in 'revolt' against JIT, claiming that it was too expensive. During the 1980s, suppliers tolerated the system because it strengthened the relationship between supplying firms and customers. Once manufacturers had become used to a steady flow of materials from one company, they were unlikely to go elsewhere. The cost to the suppliers of additional freight and stockholding was bearable because the Japanese plastics sector was highly profitable. However, when the demand for plastics fell, many suppliers felt that the costs of frequent small deliveries (up to three per day) had become

	Traditional 'just-in-case' logistics	With the development of a 'just-in-time' approach to logistics
Inventory levels	Large inventories resulting from manufacturing economies of scale and safety stock provision	Low inventories resulting from reliable, 'continuous flow' delivery
Flexibility	Minimal flexibility with long lead times	Short lead times and customer service drive flexibility
Relationships between logistics channel members	Tough, adversarial negotiations	Joint venture partnerships
Number of logistics channel members	Many, to avoid sole dependency	Fewer, but in long-term relationships
Communications	Minimal and with many secrets	Open communication and sharing of information to enable joint problem-solving

Figure 10.13 **The effects on organizational behaviour of the transition to a 'just-in-time' logistics system.**

insupportable. Eventually, *en masse*, the Japanese petrochemicals industry association decided to tell its customers that deliveries would be limited to once a day, with additional calls available, only if paid for by the customer.

Information processing

It should be clear from the previous sections that an effective and efficient supply of information is crucial to logistics management. Information technology is facilitating the creation of *integrated logistics systems* that link the operations of a company, such as production and distribution, with suppliers' operations on the one hand and customers on the other. A model of information within the logistics function is shown in Figure 10.14. This shows how information about customers should drive strategic issues, such as the design of channels of distribution, through to implementation issues such as order processing and delivery. Information technology is providing more information to improve management decision making. The support activities of the value chain have also benefited from developments such as computerized accounting and costing procedures, electronic mail, and online ordering procedures. We will now look at some of the impacts of IT on logistics activity.

Order processing

The physical distribution process starts when the company *receives an order*. This may be direct from the end consumer, as in the case of Dell's sales of personal computers; it may

Channel member	Focus for information collection
Final customer	Preferences with respect to product configuration and delivery. Payment/order processing
Intermediaries	Availability of stocks Availability of warehouse capacity Order/delivery preferences Availability and location of transport
Manufacturer	Manufacturing schedule Raw material supplies Availability of stocks Availability of warehouse capacity Availability and location of transport

Figure 10.14 **Levels of information within a logistics system.**
(*Source*: Based on M. Christopher (1992) *Logistics and Supply Chain Management*, London: Pitman, p. 215.)

involve a head office 'order-taker' noting a replenishment order from a major retailer; or it may be generated by an account manager visiting a client and entering its order onto a laptop. Copies of this order are then usually directed to relevant company departments, which may include those responsible for purchasing, credit control, manufacturing, dispatch, warehousing, and invoicing. As far as possible, the company should ensure that this communication takes place *concurrently*, rather than consecutively. This avoids an order being slowed down because it gets 'stuck' in one particular department before being passed to the next. Increasingly, integrated computer systems can automatically pick goods from warehouse shelves, produce shipping documentation, bill customers, update stock records, and confirm delivery arrangements to the customer. An integrated system can inform the production department of the potential need to make new stock, and the purchasing department of the need to order new supplies, as well as warning suppliers of the producing company's imminent requirements. A good IT system allows account managers to provide instant status reports on the progress of their customers' orders, to check inventory levels, and to make alternative recommendations for out-of-stock items.

Delivery planning

You will recall the earlier discussion of value in use—a product is of no value to a customer until it is delivered to them. Information technology can increase this value by improving the speed and reliability of the delivery process, and doing so at reduced cost. A good example of the impact of IT on physical distribution can be seen in the scheduling and

Figure 10.15 **Some express parcel companies have extended their parcel tracking facility to allow customers to log on to the Internet to find out for themselves where an expected delivery is.** DHL, a leading express parcel and logistics company with worldwide operations, whose operations add value to supply chains by speeding up deliveries and improving the confidence of channel members that goods will actually arrive in the place where they are needed, and at the time that they are needed. DHL allows customers to track the status of their parcels at any time of the day, anywhere in the world. With increasing importance of just-in-time production methods, this valuable facility allows customers to manage their production and inventory levels more effectively (Reproduced with kind permission of DHL International (UK) Ltd).

routing of delivery vehicles. Manual methods for this process are slow and relatively inefficient, and have been superseded by *computerized vehicle routing and scheduling* systems (CVRS). These allocate vehicles to sets of delivery locations and build routes linking these destinations. More recently, CVRS systems have been linked to global positioning systems (GPS), allowing a company to track delivery vehicles and to alert drivers to any need to re-route during their journey (Figure 10.15).

◉ Production and warehouse location

In traditional models of distribution, the production facility was taken as given, then it was the task of the manufacturer's marketing department to find customers for its output. We saw earlier that the more modern idea of marketing logistics works backwards from the customer, so using this logic, the location of factories also becomes a marketing decision, and not just a production decision.

Regarding the logistic chain as a whole, it is important to ask how many manufacturing plants there should be, and where they should be located. Larger factories generally achieve lower levels of cost per unit of output, but this has to be set against the cost and time involved in getting finished goods to customers. The trend in most industries has been for small manufacturing plants to be replaced by larger factories, operating at a national, European, or even world level.

Companies in fiercely competitive markets often calculate that it is cheaper to manufacture a product in a low-cost country such as China and to ship the finished product to the country where there is demand for it. Most British clothes companies now manufacture the bulk of their clothing in less developed countries where wages paid to staff can be a fraction of what would be paid to UK staff. This can more than offset higher transport costs and allow the company to compete on price, especially where there are significant price points above which buyers will not buy an item. However, locating manufacturing facilities a long way from customers extends the time between identification of a market need and the delivery of goods to meet that need. While fashion for basic underwear and socks may not change much over time, outerwear tends to be much more volatile, with preferred styles and colours changing frequently. If it takes several weeks to get the latest 'hot' fashion from China to Chichester, it might arrive in the shops just as customers have moved on to a new 'hot' fashion. For this reason, manufacturers supplying goods to highly volatile markets are more likely to favour manufacturing facilities—or at least finishing and final assembly facilities—closer to home. There is also an issue of maintaining quality control in low cost countries.

Locational advantages can change over time, and what was once a cost-effective production location may cease to be so if local production costs or transport costs change. It has been noted, for example, that many German car component manufacturers who relocated production to low cost Eastern European countries in the early 2000s found their cost advantage undermined by local increases in wage costs, and some subsequently relocated again to cheaper Far Eastern countries (Maskell et al. 2007). The rapid increase in fuel costs which occurred from 2008, led many supply chains to reconsider the merits of manufacturing goods a long way from their markets. In 2008, the FMCG manufacturer Procter and Gamble claimed that it was spending more on transport and storage than on running its factories, causing a major rethink of its extensive supply network (*Financial Times* 2008b).

Warehouse location decisions also have to be made to balance the often conflicting needs for low handling costs per unit, against the need for rapid delivery to customers. We may view decisions here in terms of the familiar 'trade-offs' concept: the greater the number of warehouses used, the greater the potential for rapid delivery. But more warehouses will increase costs and capital employed, thus reducing ROI. Warehouses may not necessarily be owned by manufacturers: many manufacturers and retailers use the warehouse facilities of specialist companies in order to achieve economies of scale, and to improve their operational flexibility.

◉ Transport

The appropriate choice of transport mode is a key part of physical distribution management. This is especially important in markets where JIT delivery is the norm. A number of criteria should be used to select transport, including costs, transit time, reliability, capability (important if goods require special handling, such as chilled temperatures), security, and traceability.

For most goods, road transport continues to be the dominant mode, although increasing road congestion in many countries has had serious consequences for the reliability and efficiency of distribution channels. For companies seeking to operate with 'lean' production methods, paying a truck driver to sit in a traffic jam, and being unsure when the truck will arrive can greatly increase the cost of a distribution channel, because of the need to keep spare stocks 'just in case'. In 2003 the DIY chain B&Q claimed that congestion on southern England's roads had become so severe that it moved its main import centres from Felixstowe and Tilbury to Humberside. Congestion (or 'southern discomfort', as the company called it), was contributing to a reported 5 per cent or 10 per cent failure rate in getting goods delivered on time. The company even estimated that the cost of UK road haulage was accounting for about half the total cost of getting a product from a Far East factory into a B&Q store (*The Times* 2003).

◉ Trends in logistics management

In a landmark article in 1962, the management guru Peter Drucker claimed that physical distribution was the US economy's 'dark continent'. He said: 'We know little more about distribution today than Napoleon's contemporaries knew about the interior of Africa. We know it is there, and we know it is big; and that's about all' (Drucker 1962). In the fifty years since Drucker made this claim, there have been massive advances in the efficiency and effectiveness of distribution systems. The impact of improved logistics on national economies should not be underestimated. The UK's Chartered Institute of Purchasing and Supply has claimed that a 1 per cent improvement in the cost of managing the supply chain can boost the bottom line of a company by as much as 15 per cent.

So far in this chapter we have identified a number of trends that have influenced the shape of logistic systems as they are today. Now we will summarize some of the key trends for the future.

Rising expectations of end consumers

Logistics for the most part is an invisible part of marketing—it is unseen by the final consumer, and we tend to appreciate its significance only when things go wrong, such as a supermarket running out of potatoes, or an expected home delivery not arriving. Logistics managers deliver what other people in the marketing function promise. Consumers' expectations of availability and reliability of delivery have tended to increase over time. Whereas consumers might previously have readily accepted that an item they had ordered was not available when they expected it, today they may complain and take their business elsewhere. The rising expectations of consumers have sharpened minds throughout the channel of distribution. In recognition of consumers' rising expectations, some companies have offered guarantees about delivery and/or availability, with compensation paid where they fail (Posselt et al. 2008).

From functions to processes

Effective and efficient logistics focus on processes rather than functional responsibility. It is a challenge to overcome the problem of functional isolation where senior managers come to regard functional area as their 'territory' and who often jealously guard their own departmental budgets. A typical problem is a production manager wanting to minimize costs by running large batch quantities, even though this may mean creating an inventory greater than what is needed.

The solution to these problems lies in recognizing that a customer order and its associated information flows should be at the heart of any business. This means moving from an *input-focused and budget-driven* organization to an *output-focused, market-driven* one, managing processes rather than functions; and ensuring the rapid sharing of accurate information. These are not solutions that are quick to implement and, furthermore, shared responsibility may sound fine in theory, but somebody should be accountable and responsible for achieving objectives.

Competition between supply networks

It is becoming too simplistic to see competition as existing between companies at just one level of the supply chain; rather, it takes place between integrated supply chains. A retailer may be the public face of competition to most consumers, but their source of competitive advantage increasingly lies in the networks of suppliers and distribution companies that provide the right goods at the right time for their stores, as cheaply as possible. Many commentators have pointed to weaknesses in its supply chain as a contributor to the difficulties that Marks & Spencer faced in the late 1990s, in contrast to the well-developed, flexible, responsive, and low-cost distribution network developed by upcoming competitors such as Primark and Zara.

Closer working relationships

We have seen how the need to share information has led to close working relationships becoming crucial to a successful distribution chain. In most channel relationships issues of power are never far from the surface, and they can destabilize the whole channel where one party seeks to exert power in the chain that others regard as unreasonable. Power in distribution channels has tended to move towards retailers and away from producers of goods.

Fewer channel members

There has been a tendency for channels to be simplified by reducing the number of members involved at each level. A good example of this is provided by the major car manufacturers, which have progressively reduced their number of component suppliers while from their remaining suppliers demanding a commitment to quality, innovation, and cost reduction.

Virtual organizations

With the growth of outsourcing as a business philosophy, some commentators have suggested that formal company structures are giving way to informal networks, giving rise to a *virtual organization* (Holcomb and Hitt 2007). In the case of logistics, key teams might be linked electronically to perform critical activities in an integrated fashion. Work teams could share common information regarding customer requirements and performance measures while retaining local control to achieve a high level of logistical core competency. This is essentially a form of 'electronic keiretsu'. ('Keiretsu' is a Japanese term for a loosely affiliated group of firms that share common practices and are committed to cooperation.)

Increasingly complex consumer needs

Society is fragmenting into smaller and smaller groups with specialized interests, needs, and expectations. We saw in Chapter 8 how marketers have responded by trying to develop products that closely meet the needs of each group. This can itself create a logistical challenge, as the proliferation of variants of a basic product means higher stockholdings if buffer stocks of each product variant are to be kept. For a simple product such as Coca Cola, the product range has proliferated from one flavour, three packaging types, and three sizes in the 1970s to today's five flavours/formulations (e.g. Diet/Caffeine-free), five basic packaging types, and five sizes, plus special promotional packages. In order to satisfy the needs of each group that has been targeted with these differentiated products, stocks of all must be continually available.

With the development of a 24-hour society and increasingly busy lifestyles, logistics management has to face the challenge of delivering goods to individual consumers' front doors not just between 9 am and 5 pm, but at other times that are convenient to consumers.

The Internet

We have seen that information technology has drastically changed the nature of logistics management. It is increasingly changing the way that consumers buy goods, with Internet sales set to grow further. The Internet has enabled many retailers to service customers without having to maintain expensive high street shops, but just a warehouse on a relatively low cost industrial estate. However, the delivery of goods to the final consumer has not shown the productivity gains that Internet-based ordering has achieved. This is probably not surprising when it is remembered that home delivery remains a labour-intensive activity in which two of the main costs—labour and transport—are likely to continue to increase in real terms. We should not forget that in the UK the milkman has almost disappeared because efficiency of delivery cannot be improved relative to the cost of consumers' collecting milk from large, efficient supermarkets. The logistics function must also face the challenge of being able to deliver goods when somebody is at home, or of providing alternative secure storage arrangements.

Increasing public concern over the environment

Ecological concerns have impacts on logistics in a number of ways. To a large extent, public concerns over ecologically harmful practices in logistics have not attracted the same level of attention as the goods themselves, possibly reflecting the point noted earlier that logistics tends to be a relatively invisible process, which is only noticed when things go wrong. It is much easier to focus attention on a visibly harmful product such as 'gas guzzling' 4x4 vehicles, rather than the resources used up in transporting manufactured goods between warehouses. However, this situation is changing, for example the subject of 'food miles' is gaining more public attention. The case study (below) discusses impacts of distribution systems which some critics have argued causes goods to be transported unnecessarily long distances, with impacts on greenhouse gas emissions.

Governments seem increasingly likely to impose environmental constraints which directly impact on distribution systems. The transport of goods, for example, is affected by measures to restrict trucks from town centres. Proposals to impose taxes on air freight may change the rationale for very long distance supply chains (e.g. will it continue to be cost effective to use air freight to move exotic fresh fruits from low cost Far East countries to western markets?) Recycling will become an increasingly important environmental issue, and an EU Directive has placed on certain manufacturers a responsibility to recycle discarded products after their use (e.g. car components that have reached the end of their life). This calls for reverse logistics. Many distribution channels already collect waste materials for recycling (e.g. cardboard packaging) and use empty vehicles to return such material to the distribution centre where it is consolidated and forwarded to a recycling plant. With higher recycling targets being set, getting waste products from consumers will need to be considered more carefully as part of the logistics plan.

◉ Chapter summary and key linkages to other chapters

The management of channel intermediaries plays a key part in a company's attempts to ensure that its goods or services are made available to the desired market segments. Making goods available where and when buyers need them is an important value adding activity which contributes towards a company's competitive advantage over rival producers (Chapter 7). Availability of a company's products must be consistent with its promotional messages (Chapter 11) and its price position (Chapter 9). The design of a marketing channel requires careful analysis and planning. For this to be done effectively, firms must be aware of the roles that intermediaries can perform and of their relative power bases.

Logistics is concerned with coordinating the flow of goods from suppliers to the manufacturer, through the production process, and on to the customer. The overall aim of marketing logistics management is to provide customer value through service, which for many customers (both consumers and commercial) comprises the key elements of availability and timeliness. There have been numerous developments in physical distribution and logistics in the past few decades, most of which has been facilitated by advances in IT.

KEY PRINCIPLES OF MARKETING

- Value chains are at the heart of marketing. Value is added to a product as it passes through a channel of distribution.

- There is not one channel design that is appropriate in all situations; the design of an optimal channel is influenced by a range of customer, product, supplier, and competitor characteristics.

- Physical distribution may be a largely unseen activity, but it is crucial for delivering promises communicated in a company's promotional messages.

- Distribution efficiency and effectiveness must be consistent with a company's product/ price/promotional positioning.

- Logistics involves a series of trade-offs in order to optimize a cost/service/profit level.

CASE STUDY

Tesco tries to cut food miles from its supply chain

For previous generations, the availability of fresh fruit and vegetables was governed by the time of year, and where you lived. If you lived in the heart of the countryside, you would probably be spoiled for choice of fruit and vegetables during summer and autumn. But the middle of the great conurbations in winter might have seen choice reduced to basic items such as potatoes, cabbage, and apples, supplemented by canned fruit and veg. Look in a Tesco supermarket today, and you may find it difficult to tell the season of the year or the distance from the countryside, simply based on the fruit and vegetables which are on display. With so many exotic fruits available, you might even wonder which part of the world you are in.

The UK supermarket sector is intensely competitive, and has seen continuous innovation in the way it seeks to satisfy customers' needs. As consumers have become wealthier, the supermarkets realized that buyers would no longer be content with the staple foods such as cabbage and potatoes in the depths of winter—significant numbers of them now wanted excitement on a plate, and all year round. Furthermore, if they were planning a menu, they wanted to be sure that when they went to their local supermarket, the Jerusalem artichoke or mangetout which their recipe demanded would be on the shelves, and not sold out.

By and large, supermarkets have been key drivers of the value chain for the groceries that they sell. They have been close to their customers and identified their changing needs. They have built confidence with their customers, who can trust the freshness and provenance of the food they sell, and the reliability of supply. It is therefore the supermarkets who have gone seeking sources of supply, rather than the growers aggressively seeking to sell the produce that they have available. Before the development of very large supermarket chains, retailers were more fragmented. They did not have the power or resources to innovate with new product lines which they could then commission a grower to produce. Today, supermarkets such as Tesco invest heavily in their food technology laboratories, and can then go to suppliers and place large orders with exacting standards with regard to price, quality, and delivery. Above all else, supermarkets have put themselves at the centre of a slick distribution system which connects an international network of growers through transport networks of trucks, ships, and planes to put fresh produce in their network of stores, every day, all year round. The efficiency of the logistics, and the bargaining power of the supermarkets has often led to the price being charged at a British supermarket being lower than the price charged in supermarkets thousands of miles away where fruit and vegetables were grown. Tomatoes grown in Bulgaria and sold in Britain can be cheaper in Britain than in local Bulgarian shops.

The bizarre situation has occurred where the supermarkets import apples from France to be sold in Kent, the traditional home of British apple growing; plums from Poland to be sold in the traditional plum growing area of Worcestershire, and cauliflowers from Spain to replace the locally grown product in Lincolnshire. Supermarkets argue that sourcing from overseas is not just an issue of cost-saving: more importantly, the supermarkets seek a continuity of supplies from large growers who can guarantee to deliver a specified quantity at a specified time and place. The supermarkets have claimed that the fragmented nature of agricultural growers and distributors in Britain is not capable of achieving this. British supermarkets are among the most efficient in the world, and their desire to ensure that customers can always get what they want may explain the mass transport of food. Local farmers' markets may sound environmentally friendly, but they rarely guarantee a continuity of supplies.

As part of their drive for efficiency, supermarkets have a tendency to move food between large warehouses and processing centres. Friends of the Earth have noted the paradox of potatoes being transported several hundred miles between distribution centres before they end up on a supermarket shelf just a few miles from where they were grown. The environmental campaigning group Sustain has estimated that the average chicken travels 2,000 km between the farm where it was grown and the supermarket shelf and furthermore the distance products travel from farm to end consumer increased by an estimated 25 per cent between 1980 and 2007 (Priesnitz 2007).

By the mid-2000s, the supermarkets' slick supply chains appeared to be coming under greater challenge. Global warming had become an important issue with many consumers, and there was growing concern that supermarkets' practice of transporting fresh produce long distances around the world was irresponsibly adding to greenhouse gas emissions. Conscientious consumers who did not want to be seen harming the ecological environment were apparently seeking out local produce, and often telling their friends about their moral stand. A survey for the Institute of Grocery Distribution in 2008 found that one in six (16 per cent) of respondents claimed that distance travelled was one of their top five concerns about food production, up from 9 per cent in 2003. The most contentious food miles are clocked up by fresh fruit and vegetables flown in by plane from overseas. Although air-freighted produce accounted for less than 1 per cent of total UK food miles, it was the fastest-growing way of moving food around, according to figures published in 2007 by the Department for Environment, Food and Rural Affairs (Defra). Furthermore, air transport is responsible for around 11 per cent of the total CO_2 emissions from UK food transport, because transport by plane generates 177 times more greenhouse gases than shipping per unit of food.

One response by Tesco was to introduce a greater proportion of local produce. To achieve this, it placed buyers and marketing teams in the regions in order to get a clearer picture of local markets and to develop closer relationships with suppliers. By 2007, Tesco claimed to have 7,000 regional lines from throughout the UK, which were promoted as local produce, supporting local growers and reducing greenhouse gas emissions. Later that year, the company announced that contracts for the supply of organic fruit and vegetables worth £12 million had been reallocated from overseas suppliers to UK growers.

Throughout its history, Tesco has demonstrated its ability to listen to what customers want, and this has been true in respect of its distribution system. At a time when the media enjoyed bashing the big supermarkets, being seen to source products locally and being good to the environment helped to restore the standing of the company. However, critics were quick to point out some of the weaknesses and occasional hypocrisy in Tesco's approach. One observer from Friends of the Earth noted that 'local produce' sold at a branch of Tesco in Essex had in fact travelled several hundred miles as it was moved from the grower to a regional processing centre, then to a regional distribution centre, and finally back to the supermarket where it was sold. There has also been debate about whether sourcing fruit and vegetables locally actually reduces greenhouse gas emissions.

There is an argument that it would be better for the environment to grow them in countries where they need less heating and artificial fertilizers than if they were grown in Britain. The greenhouse gas emissions resulting from growing them locally in Britain may be more than the emissions associated with transporting them from warmer countries.

Another distribution quandary facing Tesco and its customers occurred with respect to its home delivery service. With the launch of its Tesco online service, the company effectively extended the supply chain right through to customers' own homes, adding value to its product offer by avoiding the need for customers to even visit a supermarket. Was it good for the environment to have fleets of delivery vans scurrying around town and countryside? Simple evaluations were difficult to make, but again, Tesco was keen to be seen as a good citizen in this final leg of its value chain, for example by launching electric delivery vehicles which the company claimed had a low carbon footprint.

Based on: Institute of Grocery Distribution, Shopper Trends—Five Years On, 2008; *The Times*, Buy British food? No thanks, we're from the Government, 13 November 2007, p. 13; Tesco PLC website (www.tesco.com)

Case study review questions

1. Identify the elements of the value chain involved in the supply of fresh fruit and vegetables to Tesco stores.

2. Critically discuss the factors influencing Tesco's sourcing of fresh fruit and vegetables.

3. Assess the level of power that Tesco exercises in the supply chain for fruit and vegetables.

CHAPTER REVIEW QUESTIONS

1. Why does conflict so often occur between manufacturers and intermediaries? How might this conflict be resolved?

2. Contrast JIT inventory management with conventional reorder methods. Do you think the adoption of JIT techniques is viable for every sector? Where might it not be so relevant?

3. Giving examples from both the manufacturing and retailing sectors, discuss the effects of the Internet on logistics and physical distribution management.

ACTIVITIES

1. Compare the prices of a bottle of soft drink/jar of coffee/chocolate bar in different retail outlets in your area. What do the different prices for an identical product say about the nature of its value chain? Is there a consistent trend of retailers charging a price premium for providing availability of the item in prime locations and/or at anti-social hours?

2. Construct a diagram showing the channel alternatives for a manufacturer of coffee to get its products to the final consumer.

3. Undertake an audit of local fast-food restaurants in your area. Can you tell whether there are differences in the style and standard of service provided between franchised and company owned outlets? If you were a franchisor, how would you go about monitoring and maintaining the standards of service provided by the franchised outlets that you have observed?

REFERENCES

Ahmad, R. and Buttle, F. (1998) 'Bridging the Gaps between Theory and Practice: a Case of the Retention of Dealers of Office Equipment Products'. In *Proceedings of Academy of Marketing Conference* (Sheffield Hallam University, 8–10 July), Sheffield Hallam University, Sheffield, pp. 16–21.

British Franchise Association (2010) *The NatWest/British Franchising Association Annual Survey of Franchising*. Henley-on-Thames: BFA.

Christopher, M. (1992) *Logistics and Supply Chain Management*. London: Pitman.

Competition Commission (2008) *Grocery Markets Investigation*. London: Competition Commission.

Deloitte (2006) 'The Global Powers of Retailing 2006', London: Deloitte.

Drucker, P. (1962) 'The Economy's Dark Continent'. *Fortune*, April, 103.

Financial Times (1994), 'Just-in-time Now Just Too Much'. *Financial Times*, 14 Jan, 20.

Financial Times (2008a) 'Tesco's Trolley May Have Started to Wobble'. *Financial Times,* 4 April.

Financial Times (2008b) 'Oil Costs Force P&G to Rethink its Supply Network'. *Financial Times*, 27 June, 22.

Handfield, R.B. and Nicholls, E.L. (2009) *Introduction to Supply Chain Management*. Englewood Cliffs, NJ: Prentice-Hall. p. 15.

Holcomb, T.R. and Hitt, M.A. (2007) 'Toward a Model of Strategic Outsourcing'. *Journal of Operations Management*, 25 (2), 464–81.

Keers, H. (2002) 'Mothercare Slips into Red as Warehouse Woes Grow'. *Daily Telegraph*, 22 November.

Löning, H. and Besson, M. (2002) 'Can Distribution Channels Explain Differences in Marketing and Sales Performance Measurement Systems?' *European Management Journal*, 20 (6), 54–62.

Maskell, P., Pedersen, T., Petersen, B., and Dick-Nielsen, J. (2007) 'Learning Paths to Offshore Outsourcing: From Cost Reduction to Knowledge Seeking'. *Industry & Innovation,* 14 (3), 239–57.

Nairn, G. (2003) 'Not Many Happy Returns: Reverse Logistics Causes Headaches and Eats into Already Thin Margins'. *Financial Times*, 5 February, 5.

O'Cass, A. and Fenech, T. (2003) 'Web Retailing Adoption: Exploring the Nature of Internet Users Web Retailing Behaviour'. *Journal of Retailing & Consumer Services*, 10 (2), 81–94.

Porter, M.E. (2001) 'Strategy and the Internet'. *Harvard Business Review,* March–April, 63–78.

Posselt, T., Gerstner, E., and Radic, D. (2008) 'Rating E-Tailers' Money-Back Guarantees'. *Journal of Service Research*, 10 (3), 207–19.

Priesnitz, W. (2007) 'Counting our Food Miles'. *Natural Life*, 1 July.

The Times (2003) 'B&Q Plans Freight Escape from Southern Route'. *The Times*, 20 January, Business, 4.

Timmins, N. (2003) 'Online Auctions: E-commerce has Arrived in the Public Sector as a Way to Reduce the Civil Procurement Bill'. *Financial Times*, 29 January, 12.

Vargo, S.L. and Lusch, R.F. (2008) 'Service-dominant Logic: Continuing the Evolution'. *Journal of the Academy of Marketing Science*, 36, 1–12.

Yrjölä, H. (2001) 'Physical Distribution Considerations for Electronic Grocery Shopping'. *International Journal of Physical Distribution & Logistics Management*, 31 (10), 746–61.

SUGGESTED FURTHER READING

For a general review of the channels of distribution literature, the following develop many of the issues raised in this chapter:

Arikan, A. (2009) *Multichannel Marketing*. New York: John Wiley.

Coughlan, A., Anderson, E., Stern, L.W., and El-Ansary, A. (2007) *Marketing Channels*, 7th edition. London: FT Prentice Hall.

Fung, P.K.O., Chen, I.S.N., and Yip, L.S.C. (2007) 'Relationships and Performance of Trade Intermediaries: an Exploratory Study'. *European Journal of Marketing*, 41 (1/2), 159–80.

For discussion of issues relating to the use of intermediaries by services organizations, the following provide useful insights:

Cassab, H. and MacLachlan, D.L. (2009) 'A Consumer-based View of Multi-channel Service'. *Journal of Service Management*, 20 (1), 52–75.

Hughes, T. (2006) 'New Channels/Old Channels: Customer Management and Multichannels'. *European Journal of Marketing*, 40 (1/2), 113–29.

The effects of the Internet on service distribution channels are discussed in the following:

Dall'Olmo, R.F., Scarpi, D., and Manaresi, A. (2009) 'Purchasing Services Online: a Two-country Generalization of Possible Influences'. *Journal of Services Marketing*, 23 (2), 92–102.

Kim, J.-H., Kim, M., and Kandampully, J. (2009) 'Buying Environment Characteristics in the Context of E-service'. *European Journal of Marketing*, 43 (9/10), 1188–204.

Franchising of services is discussed in the following:

British Franchise Association (2010) *The NatWest/British Franchising Association Annual Survey of Franchising*. Henley-on-Thames: British Franchise Association.

Combs, J.G., Michael, S.C., and Castrogiovanni, G.J. (2009) 'Institutional Influences on the Choice of Organizational Form: The Case of Franchising'. *Journal of Management*, 35 (5), 1268–90.

Doherty, A.M. and Alexander, N. (2006) 'Power and Control in International Retail Franchising'. *European Journal of Marketing*, 40 (11/12), 1292–316.

For further discussion of logistics and supply chain management, consult the following:

Rushton, A., Croucher, P., and Baker, P. (2010) *The Handbook of Logistics and Distribution Management*, 4th edition. London: Kogan Page.

Christopher, M. (2010) *Logistics and Supply Chain Management*, 3rd edition. London: FT Prentice Hall.

 ONLINE RESOURCE CENTRE

Visit the Online Resource Centre for resources that are relevant to this chapter, including a flashcard glossary, web links, multiple choice questions, and additional case studies:

www.oxfordtextbooks.co.uk/orc/palmer3e/

🔍 KEY TERMS

- Direct marketing
- Distributors
- Economic order quantity
- Franchising
- Intermediary
- Inventory
- Just-in-time

- Logistics
- Marketing channel
- Physical distribution management
- Retailers
- Supply chain
- Value chain
- Wholesalers

MARKETING COMMUNICATIONS

CHAPTER OBJECTIVES

It is sometimes said that a well-designed product, appropriately priced and distributed, should require little or no promotion. Instead, customers should be queuing to buy it. Some new products do find themselves in a seller's market, and their producers can sell all they can make without a need for promotion. But the reality of most markets is fierce competition between suppliers in which each supplier has to communicate to potential buyers the unique benefits of buying its products rather than the competitor's. This chapter aims to develop an understanding of promotion planning as an integral part of the marketing and business planning process. It then discusses the key stages of the promotion planning process, the range and variety of promotional techniques, basic models of communication, and how promotional activity can be monitored. The characteristics of the different media that make up the promotion mix will be explored.

◉ Introduction

As consumers, we are surrounded and constantly bombarded by marketing communications stimuli. These stimuli derive from a range of promotional activity, such as television advertising, mailshots, email messages and face-to-face selling, delivered through a variety of different channels and media. Alongside such overt messages, the broader marketing mix is also communicating messages to us, more covertly (e.g. the packaging of a product and its price send out messages about the nature of the product).

This chapter focuses on firms' efforts to communicate the features and benefits of their products in particular, and their corporate image in general. Communication in its broadest sense can incorporate firms' communication with key stakeholder groups, including shareholders, employees, and government agencies. This chapter will concentrate on communications which take the form of promotional activity aimed at customers. Although the words 'communications' and 'promotion' are sometimes used interchangeably, this chapter will focus on this narrower understanding of promotion.

A key theme of this chapter is the need for companies to integrate their communications, and this integration can take a number of forms. The message that is sent out by the firms' promotional material must be consistent with the product that it is selling, or the distribution channels that it is using. The promotional media themselves must be integrated, so that, for example, the message seen on a television advert is reinforced by Internet banner ads. 'Integrated marketing communications' has become an important concept, and although this chapter looks in detail at individual aspects of promotion, you should never forget the need to develop an integrated approach, which is what customers will see.

Managing an organization's communications involves a lot of detail. As an example of recent developments, many people are employed to optimize a company's search engine rankings, which can involve complex knowledge of algorithms. This introductory chapter cannot hope to go into great detail on operational issues, which are covered in more specialist books. This chapter will adopt a more strategic approach to managing communications. It may not give you the answers to the detailed questions that communications managers ask every day, but at least it will help you to identify the important questions that need to be asked within a strategic marketing management framework.

Communication between a company and its customers has become increasingly interactive. With very simple technology, a company could communicate with its customers but it was difficult for them to reply immediately through the limited media available (e.g. the dominant media of newspaper and television advertising may have required the customer to send away a coupon or make a telephone call). Improvements in technology allowed customers to respond immediately and directly (e.g. through interactive TV or the Internet). Further developments in communications technology have allowed real time interaction not only between the company and its customers, but between customers themselves. This peer-to-peer

MARKETING IN ACTION

Airport's high-tech dream turns into communications disaster

For British Airways, the opening of its new Heathrow Terminal 5 involved carefully planned communications in the build-up to the launch. The public had been kept informed of development of this exciting new £4.3 billion state-of-the-art terminal through carefully planned press releases, behind the scenes television documentaries, and the promise that the misery of travelling through the aged and cramped Heathrow would be transformed with the new terminal. Then when the terminal finally opened in March 2008 calamity struck and the years of carefully planned communications seemed to be undone in just a couple of days. The baggage system failed in a big way, resulting in piles of baggage going missing. Flights had to be cancelled and British Airways, which the British still had an affection for, was humiliated and became the laughing stock of the world. News reports carried endless stories about missing bags and ruined holidays. Bloggers were actively warning travellers to avoid Terminal 5 and YouTube carried videos of mountains of misplaced baggage and angry customers. British Airways had seemingly lost control of its carefully thought out communication plan. The Terminal 5 fiasco reminds us that communication planning can be very difficult in practice, and the development of social network media is making it increasingly easy for customers to set the communication agenda rather than the company itself.

communication has potential to spread good and bad news stories about the company very rapidly, and organizations are still learning how to manage this communication.

● Marketing and promotional objectives

To some people, marketing is the same thing as advertising. This is quite wrong. Advertising is just one element of the marketing mix which helps to sell a product. If a product is well designed, and it has earned a good reputation among customers it may not need to do any advertising. This is unusual, and most organizations will need to put some effort into communicating the benefits of their service compared to the competition.

We will begin by exploring the link between promotional activity and other aspects of marketing activity. To understand fully the role of promotion planning, it is necessary to see it within the context of an organization's overall business and marketing plan, and in particular its objectives and strategy. Promotion activity should not be seen as a stand-alone series of activities which bear little relation to the organization's goals, purpose, and markets.

At its most basic, promotion planning can be visualized as a top-down process which is just one element of business and marketing planning (Figure 11.1), with the aim of ensuring that:

- The messages being communicated are consistent with an organization's corporate and marketing activity.

- Promotion activity supports the overall business and marketing strategy.

- Consumers hear 'one voice' and not a range of disparate messages and behaviour.

The starting point of a company's promotional planning is a clear understanding and articulation of the promotional objectives, in order that appropriate messages are accurately targeted through the most appropriate channels in the most cost-effective manner possible. Typical communication objectives might be:

- to develop an awareness of an organization and its products;

- to communicate the benefits of purchasing a product;

- to build a positive image of the organization and its products;

- to influence eventual purchase of the product;

- to differentiate the company and its products from its competitors;

- to remind people of the existence of the organization and its products.

Ideally, promotional objectives should be quantified as far as possible. From the general objectives specified above, the following specific objectives are typical of those that might be set by a newly established budget airline.

- Thirty per cent of all A/B/C1 adults within the south-east region of England should be aware of the airline's brand name by the end of year 1, rising to 50 per cent after year 2 and 70 per cent after year 3.

- Awareness levels among A/B/C1 adults who regularly fly from London area airports should be 60 per cent, 80 per cent, and 90 per cent over the same time periods.

- The airline should receive five million hits on its website during year 1, rising to ten million in year 3.

- By the end of year 3, the airline should be the first low-cost airline to be recalled by regular air travellers in the south-east region of England in an unprompted survey of brand recognition.

- Ultimately, promotion effort should contribute to the sale of one million seats in year 1, rising to three million in year 3.

Promotional objectives are likely to change throughout the life-cycle of a product, as the above example would suggest. We will see later in this chapter how firms' promotion planning responds to changing objectives.

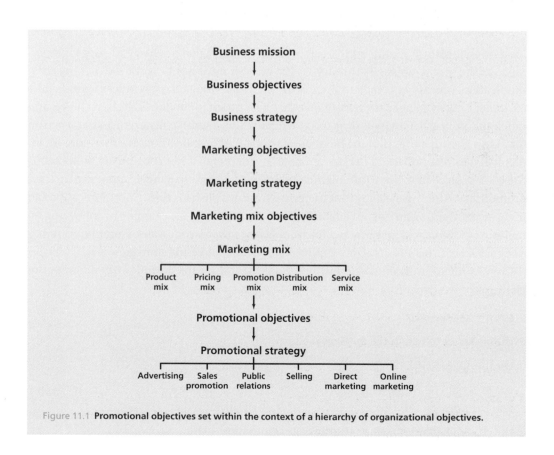

Figure 11.1 **Promotional objectives set within the context of a hierarchy of organizational objectives.**

◉ The communication process

To understand the principles of promotion, we first need to understand what is happening when a company sends messages to potential customers telling them about the benefits of buying its product. Some people see promotion as essentially a proactive means of persuading people to do something that they would not otherwise have done. (For example, they would not have gone to a new nightclub if they hadn't known about it.) An alternative view is that promotion is essentially a communication process which aims to remove the barriers that prevent an individual doing something. Think further about why you might not have visited a new nightclub in town:

◉ You may not have been aware of its existence.

◉ If you had known about it, you might not have had sufficient information to allow you to take action. (Where is it? What times does it open?)

◉ You might have wondered what benefits it would offer over the nightclub that you regularly patronize—what motivation would there be for you to break away from your present club, with which you are perfectly happy?

◉ You may have regarded a visit to the new nightclub as risky. (Will there be a rough clientele? Will they rip me off for drinks prices?)

Promotional planning must address all of these issues, which are likely to vary in importance as the nightclub passes through its life-cycle. It must not be assumed that the communication process is complete once a targeted individual has become a customer. A customer is likely to need the reassurance that her chosen nightclub is the best choice, and much promotional activity is directed at reducing the cognitive dissonance that a person may have if she believes that she has made a wrong purchase decision. Furthermore, an individual may fear ridicule of her peer group if the nightclub is not continually promoted as the coolest place in town. Other nightclubs, including new challengers, may step up their promotional efforts in a bid to attract defectors from established clubs. Communication can involve maintaining an ongoing dialogue with the customer, for example by informing established customers of new product offers, or giving rewards for loyalty. Communication is a key aspect of firms' efforts at developing relationship marketing strategies.

Communication, then, is a continual process, and we need to identify a number of elements of this process:

◉ the message source;

◉ the audience to which the message is addressed;

◉ the message itself;

◉ the processes by which a message is encoded by the sender and decoded by the receiver, and the noise factors that may cause distortion of the message;

◉ the channels through which the message is communicated;

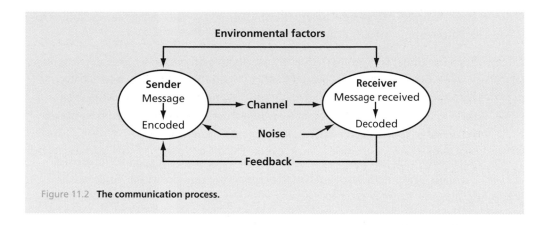

Figure 11.2 **The communication process.**

⊚ the desired and actual response of the audience;

⊚ a feedback loop by which future communication with the target audience may be reconfigured following evaluation of the current communication.

The development of electronic channels of communication is making this process increasingly interactive, so now, instead of waiting a long time for feedback following a communication, this can often come back instantly. The elements of the process are illustrated in Figure 11.2 and are described in more detail below.

⊙ The message source

The company seeking to promote a product is the ultimate source of a message. Sometimes the identity of the source may be quite clear, but very often a company will use distinctive individuals as the apparent source of its messages. The identity of the message source can be important, because the source of a message—as distinct from the message itself—can influence the effectiveness of any communication. The following factors affect the credibility of a message source:

1. If a source is perceived as having power, then the audience response is likely to be compliance.

2. If a source is liked, then identification by the audience is a likely response. Important factors here include past experience and the reputation of the organization, in addition to the personality of the actual source of the communication. A salesperson, any contact personnel, a TV/radio personality, etc., are all very important in creating *liking*.

3. If a source is perceived as credible, then the message is more likely to be internalized by the audience. Credibility can be developed by establishing a source as important, high in status, power, and prestige, or by emphasizing reliability and openness. Consider the

following examples of messages in which companies have selected a message source to add to the credibility of its products:

(a) Pharmaceutical companies frequently use doctors dressed in white coats to explain the benefits of an over-the-counter medication in their television adverts. Even if the role of doctor is played by an actor, the presence of the doctor's white coat is likely to increase the chances that we would trust the message. (Would we believe the message as much if it were communicated by a comedian?)

(b) Many companies seeking to stress the robust design of their product have used Germans—popularly associated with engineering superiority—to endorse the product.

(c) For many low-involvement products, endorsement by an individual's peer group can be important. 'If people who are like me are happy with the product, then I will be happy with it as well' is a typical rationalization.

Celebrities are often used to endorse a product or an organization. We have a tendency to impute to the endorsed product the qualities that we have come to like about our favourite celebrity characters. There have been numerous studies of the effects of celebrity endorsement (e.g. Chung-kue and McDonald 2002; Cummings 2007). To be effective, the celebrity must be carefully chosen to match the aspirations of a product's target market. Consider the following examples of celebrity endorsement.

1. Children develop a liking for television and film characters, whether they are real or inanimate. The popularity of Harry Potter books and films with children (and their parents) has led to manufacturers of products as diverse as breakfast cereals, confectionery, stationery, and computer hardware being endorsed with the character of Harry Potter (Lynch 2001).

2. The TV chef Jamie Oliver has developed a loyal following among aspirational cooks which has been exploited by the grocery retailer Sainsbury's, which employed the chef to front its advertising campaign demonstrating meals made with Sainsbury's groceries.

3. Companies often pay to have their products 'placed' in films. When the James Bond movie Casino Royale was released in 2006, several companies, including Sony, Ford, Dell, and Federal Express helped to pay for the film, in return for having their products used by the stars of the film.

Of course, a celebrity endorsement loses a lot of its value if the celebrity subsequently acquires a negative reputation. Naomi Campbell, for example, was notoriously dropped from her involvement in a charity campaign against wearing animal skins when she was photographed draped in fur on the catwalk. And in 2010 the golfer Tiger Woods was dropped by several companies who sponsored him, including ATandT, Accenture, Tag Heuer, and PepsiCo, because the image of him in the public's mind was no longer consistent with the companies desired brand image.

◉ The message

Central to an organization's communication effort is the message that it wants to communicate. The message must be derived from a sound analysis of an organization's product offer and the positioning of its brand. To be effective, a message must identify the target audience and communicate in a manner that addresses its needs and expectations. A message may be communicated for a number of reasons. Usually, the focus for a message is communication of specific product features and benefits. Often, however, a message will say very little about specific product details, but will instead focus on communicating core brand values that encourage customers and other stakeholders to trust the organization and its brands. Sometimes, messages have to be communicated following a crisis, for example in the aftermath of a food poisoning incident.

A message must be able to move an individual along a path from awareness through to eventual purchase. In order for a message to be received and understood, it must gain attention, use a common language, arouse needs, and suggest how these needs might be met. All of this should take place within the acceptable standards of the target audience. However, the product itself, the channel, and the source of the communication also convey a message, and therefore it is important that these do not conflict.

Three aspects of a communication message can be identified: content, structure, and format. It is the content that is likely to attract attention, and change attitude and intention. The appeal or theme of the message is therefore important. The formulation of the message must include some kind of benefit, motivator, identification, or reason why the audience should think or do something. Appeals can be rational, emotional, or moral.

Messages can be classified into a number of types, according to the dominant theme of the message. The following are common focal points for messages:

1. The nature and characteristics of the organization and the product on offer: For example, television advertisements for Volkswagen have traditionally stressed their robust build quality.

2. Advantages over the competition: Promotion by the airline Ryanair has emphasized the low cost of its fares compared with its competitors.

3. Adaptability to buyers' needs: Many insurance companies stress the extent to which their policies have been designed with the needs of particular age segments of the population in mind.

4. Experience of others: Testimonials of previous satisfied customers are used to demonstrate the benefits resulting from use and the dependability of a company. (For example, Weight Watchers has used real customers to say how they successfully managed to lose weight using the company's products.)

Recipients of a message must see it as applying specifically to themselves, and they must see some reason for being interested in it. The message must be structured according to the job it has to do. The points to be included in the message should be ordered (strongest arguments first or last) and consideration given to whether one-sided or two-sided messages should be used. Some messages use criticism of competitors' products, although there is some research evidence that negative advertising may be counterproductive (Richardson 2001).

Encoding, decoding, and noise

The message that a company seeks to put across to its audience may be lengthy and involve a lot of technical description. However, the audience may have an attention span of only a few seconds; moreover, it is likely to be expensive to buy sufficient access to channels of communication to allow the company to put across its message in full. Furthermore, a company may define its products in terms of their features, but it is important to remember that the audience must be *rapidly* made aware of its *benefits* to them. The creator of a message must therefore encode it into some acceptable form for an audience, which will then decode it (Figure 11.3).

Unfortunately, there is likely to be interference between the stages of encoding and decoding, so the message that a company sends out may not be the one the audience picks up. Noise occurs between the encoding and decoding of a message. Although it is difficult to eliminate such interference in the communication process totally, an understanding of the various elements of this 'noise' should help to minimize its effects.

Noise factors can be divided into two major types:

1. **Psychological factors:** No two individuals are the same in terms of their psychological makeup. Each person undergoes different experiences influencing their personality, perceptions of the world, motives for action, and attitudes towards people, situations, and objects. Therefore, it is not surprising to find that different people will interpret an advertisement differently.

    An individual's past experience of a product or supplier is an important influence on how messages about that company's products are interpreted. Both positive and negative experiences predispose an individual to decode messages in a particular way. For example, a person may have a negative attitude towards an insurance company as a result of having previously had an insurance claim turned down by that company. This negative attitude is likely to distort their interpretation of any marketing communication from the company. Also, an individual's current motives can influence how a message is decoded (an advert for food may be viewed differently when you are hungry, compared to when you have just eaten).

2. **Sociological factors:** In addition to the essentially personal characteristics that influence their behaviour, people are influenced by the presence of others around them. Individuals develop attitudes as a result of a conditioning process which is brought about by the culture they live in and the specific actions of family, friends, and work associates. People develop attitudes from a number of sources (Figure 11.4). In addition to the family, there are many other social groupings that influence how consumers see the world and how they decide what to purchase. These include

Figure 11.3 **Advertisers must fight to gain the attention of an audience; simply stating the benefits of a product may be inadequate to gain attention or to create a distinctive identity.** This advertisement does not say much about the product on offer and is not likely to achieve any sales in the short term, but it does raise awareness of the KitKat brand and it helps to give it a distinctive and humorous position in the competitive market for confectionary products.

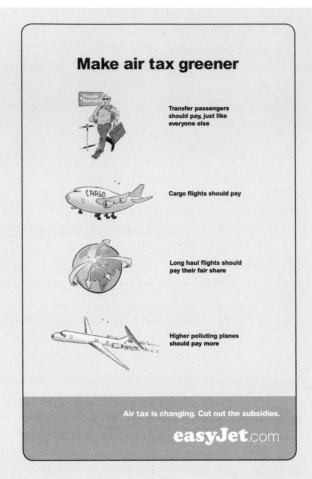

Figure 11.4 **Addressing customers' concerns for the ecological environment has become an increasingly important basis for films' messages.** During its first ten years of operation, the low-cost airline easyJet stressed low fares above all else. In early adverts, the company likened the price of an air ticket to a low-cost item of clothing. Over time, the airline placed a little more emphasis on the extensiveness of its route network, and for passengers travelling on business, it promoted ease of booking, and flexible tickets which would allow business people the possibility of changing their travel arrangements at short notice. But from 2007, a potentially serious threat faced easyJet, and other low cost airlines, in the form of EU proposals to tax airlines more heavily. The public had become increasingly concerned about the harmful ecological effects of aviation. Some passengers may have even felt guilty about flying, and many more people thought that 'something must be done' to tackle the problem of greenhouse gas emissions caused by aircraft. But a new tax on airlines could have hit easyJet hard. Had the company ignored pressure for greater controls on civil aviation, and simply carried on advertising cheap flights, it might have alienated the public it sought to serve, and more importantly, the legislators who would decide its fate. An important message of easyJet therefore turned towards addressing the needs of these wider groups of stakeholders. In this advert, the company is accepting the need for some form of increased taxation on aviation. In doing so, it comes over as a more responsible airline, and may overcome some passengers' feelings of guilt about flying. Just as importantly, the company was keen to preserve its business model and sought to engage in debate about how new taxes should be implemented, so that low-cost airlines did not lose competitive advantage to airlines with different business models. The target of this advert was legislators, as much as passengers themselves.
(Reproduced with kind permission of EasyJet Airline Co Ltd.)

reference groups with which an individual closely identifies. Reference groups can be divided into those of which an individual is a member ('membership groups') and those to which membership is aspired ('aspirational groups'). Both types of reference group can affect how an individual makes decisions on goods and services purchases. (Think of how many people copy their best friend's or their favourite pop star's hairstyle or clothing.)

Perception and retention of the message

We are unlikely to remember, let alone notice, all of the messages that we come across. In a typical day, the average person in the UK may be exposed to hundreds of commercial messages, including television and newspaper adverts, messages on cereal packets at breakfast time, posters seen on the roadside on the way to work and banner ads encountered while surfing the Internet. Past experience, personality, motivation, attitudes, and the influence of reference groups can all affect what we perceive and retain, leading to 'noise', which can distort an audience's perception and interpretation of a promotional message.

Individuals are likely to select only the stimuli perceived as being important to them:

1. Selective perception occurs where communication is perceived in such a way that it merely reinforces existing attitudes and beliefs.

2. Selective reception occurs where individuals make active decisions as to which stimuli they wish to expose themselves to. For example, a committed Conservative Party supporter may consciously avoid advertising by the Labour Party.

3. Selective retention occurs when an individual remembers only those aspects of the message perceived as being necessary to him.

Even if an individual decides to give attention to a message, understands it, and remembers it, comprehension may still be different from what the communicator of the message expected. This perceptual distortion could be caused by those noise factors previously noted, poor encoding on the part of the communicator, or poor understanding by the audience itself. It is therefore important to pre-test all advertising before a full campaign is launched.

⊙ The target audience

A fundamental principle that underlies most promotional activity is that communication should be designed and placed to reach a specific type of audience. This audience represents a *market segment*. A market segment is any group of people who exhibit similar needs or demographic, social, psychological, or behavioural characteristics that will enable them to be targeted with a distinct marketing mix. Go back to Chapter 6 if you wish to review different bases for defining market segments. The importance of rigorous market segmentation and targeting varies between products and some promotion succeeds with only very broad definitions of their target market. One example is the UK national lottery, which has gained wide market appeal with a message aimed at a very wide target market. For the majority of products, however, such a homogeneous market and message is unlikely to be cost effective.

Once potential market segments have been identified and target audiences selected, a company will need to determine the positioning of its product in the marketplace and in the minds of consumers. It is not feasible to develop promotional plans until a clear understanding of the product positioning has been determined. Positioning was discussed in Chapter 7.

The matching of media to target markets is increasingly being done using state-of-the art technology to manipulate quantitative and qualitative data (Figure 11.5). The accuracy of such market information is critical for effective promotion management. The media industry has traditionally been provided with a wealth of market research data such as the Target Group Index, which mixes product usage data with demographic, socio-economic, and attitudinal data. The Broadcasters Audience Research Board (BARB) uses a panel of households to monitor television viewing data, and national readership surveys (NRS) provide data on newspaper and magazine readership. Internet-based advertisers have available to them a wealth of information measuring visitors' behaviour, for example the source of hits to a website, the length of time spent on specific pages, and the progression of visitors from one page to another. Embedded cookies can allow a company to analyse the websites that an individual had visited before coming to its own website. Alongside these data, advertising agencies and market research organizations conduct their own detailed research to help match target markets with the media audiences.

Buyer readiness state

It is often important to define an audience in terms of the level of involvement of potential recipients of the communication. For example, a distinction can be made between those people who are merely aware of the existence of a product, those who are interested in possibly purchasing it, and those who definitely wish to purchase it. This is crucial, because it was noted above that the aim of communication is to move target customers through the stages from mere awareness, through liking, to eventual purchase. Segmentation of audiences does not end there, however: many communication messages are aimed at people who have already bought a product, with the aim of reducing any *cognitive dissonance* they may have, and encouraging them to recommend the product to their friends. A communication can sometimes succeed in targeting buyers at all stages of the buying process, but generally it is more likely to be focused on buyers at just one or two stages of the process.

Figure 11.5 **Matching the target market with media audiences is key to successful communication.**
A message sent to the wrong audience is a message wasted. For this purpose, target markets have traditionally been defined in terms of economic, social, and demographic factors, and the stage that a consumer has reached in the buying process. Timing has always been crucial, and a message that is too late or too early for the target audience may be wasted. Increasingly the place that a message is received is becoming a basis for defining a target audience. Newspapers, television, and radio stations have for a long time segmented their audience by time and place (e.g. leisure attractions advertising in the local press just before the weekend). With the advent of smartphones, the ability to target messages to very specific geographic audiences is greatly increased. This is particularly important for inseparable and perishable services, so, for example, a restaurant with spare capacity can send special offer messages to people on its database who are in the area at the time. Smartphones also offer the chance of two-way feedback communication, for example the recipient of a message may use their Smartphone to book a table at the restaurant immediately.

It is also important to note that people differ markedly in their readiness to try new products, and a number of attempts have been made to classify the population in terms of their level of risk aversity or risk-seeking inclination. For purchases that are perceived as being highly risky, customers are likely to use more credible sources of information (e.g. word-of-mouth recommendation) and to engage in a prolonged search through information sources. Rogers (2003) defined a person's 'innovativeness' as the 'degree to which an individual is relatively earlier in adopting new ideas than the other members of his social system'. In each product area, there are likely to be 'consumption pioneers' and early adopters, while other individuals adopt new products only much later.

> **MARKETING IN ACTION**
>
> ### Magazines for men
>
> Until a few years ago, the shelves of most newsagents would have been loaded with many general interest women's magazines (e.g. *Woman's Own, Women's Weekly, Cosmopolitan*), but very few general interest magazines aimed at men. Why? Some cynics might have argued that women were more likely to have spare time at home and could sit around reading, while 'busy' men were out at work, in the pub, or watching sport, and did not have time to read magazines. There may just have been a bit of truth in this, but the main reason has been that women's magazines have been popular with advertisers, who generally provide a high proportion of total income for a magazine publisher. In the traditional household, it has been women who have made decisions on a wide range of consumer goods purchases. Advertising the benefits of toothpaste, yogurt, or jam would have been lost on most men, who had little interest in which brand was put in front of them, and played little part in the buying process.
>
> Take a look at the news-stand now and you will find that it carries a wide range of men's general interest magazines, such as *FHM, Loaded, Maxim,* and *Esquire*. Why have they suddenly mushroomed in number and in readership? Again, the answer lies in their attractiveness to advertisers. Talk of a male identity crisis may have spurred some sales, and it is evident that men are now involved in a much wider range of purchasing decisions than ever before. While some 'new men' may be taking a more active interest in the household shopping, many more are marrying later and indulging themselves in personal luxuries, an option that is less readily available to their married counterparts.
>
> With support from advertisers, the leading men's magazine in the UK, *FHM,* had a circulation of 192,596 copies per issue in 2010 (Audit Bureau of Circulation, 2011). Sales of all magazines—men's and women's—have suffered in recent years as more people seek out content online, but in the late 1990s, *FHM* magazine had even overtaken the leading women's monthly magazine, *Cosmopolitan*.

A typical adoption pattern, applied to the market for mobile video-phones, is illustrated in Figure 11.6. 'Innovators' are willing to try new ideas at some risk. Some people will always want to have the latest gadgets, and the promotion of new video mobile phones to this group should stress not only the technical features of the product, but also the status benefits that an early adopter of the new technology will receive. 'Early adopters' are opinion leaders in their community, adopting new products early but carefully. The 'early majority' adopt new ideas before the average person, taking their lead from opinion leaders; for this group communication should be moving towards an emphasis on the practical benefits of video mobile phones, rather than concentrating on their status benefits. The 'late majority' are sceptical, tending to adopt an innovation only after the majority of people have tried it. Finally, 'laggards' are tradition-bound, being suspicious of changes. This group adopts a new product only when it has become sufficiently widespread that it has taken on a measure of tradition in itself. Communication aimed at them would probably emphasize low price and easy availability.

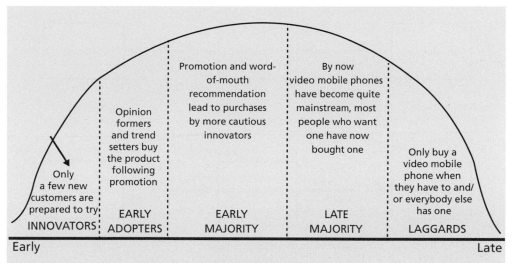

Figure 11.6 **A message has to reflect the position of a service in its life-cycle and differences between buyers in their motivations to try new services.** Rogers described a diffusion model in which a small group of 'innovators' are first to respond to a new service offer, and a message to them may emphasize the novelty of the purchase and the social benefits that may derive from being a consumption pioneer of an exclusive product. Over time, ownership will become diffused to progressively wider audiences, helped by falling costs and increasing competitive pressure. Instead of stressing exclusivity, the advertising message is likely to increasingly emphasize easy availability and an affordable price. A final group of 'laggards' may only become receptive to a message if it implies that what was once an exclusive product has now become a necessary item which even they can afford. Mobile phone services as a category have gone through this diffusion process, with previous 'snob appeal' messages about mobile phone messages giving way to more general price-based promotion. Nevertheless, mobile phone operators are continually developing new services, such as live sports events delivered to customers' phones, which has the effect of starting the process again with a new group of innovators, before this new product development itself becomes adopted by a mainstream audience.

Push v. pull messages

Should a company aim its message at the final consumer who will actually use its product? You should recall from Chapter 4 the existence of decision-making units (DMU) and note that the person who actually consumes a product may not be the best person to target a message at. (For example, a high proportion of men have very little influence in the purchase process for the socks that they wear.) Just as importantly, we need to consider whether messages should be aimed at the end buyer/user, or at intermediaries who will influence the purchase decisions of the end buyer/user.

This distinction forms the basis for 'push' and 'pull' models of communication (Figure 11.7). In a traditional push model, a manufacturer promotes its products heavily to wholesalers, which in turn promote to retailers, which in turn use their sales skills to sell to the

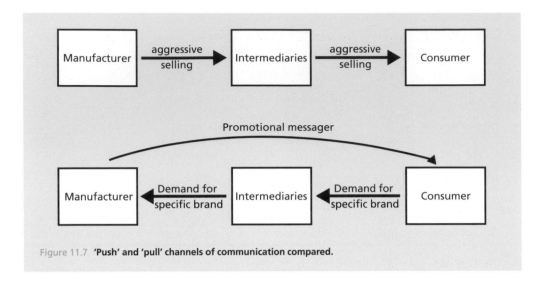

Figure 11.7 **'Push' and 'pull' channels of communication compared.**

final buyer/user. In many markets, the end consumer may have little awareness of brands and may rely totally on what is offered to them by an intermediary. How many patients visiting their dentist would specify a type of filling material by brand name that they would like the dentist to use in their filling? How many people visiting an independent financial adviser (IFA) for advice on pensions would have a preference for one pension company rather than another? In these circumstances, a company is most likely to achieve higher levels of sales by targeting its promotional efforts at intermediaries rather than the end consumer.

The problems to a manufacturer of a 'push' approach should be apparent. In order for its message to reach the end buyer/user, it must be transmitted efficiently and effectively by each of the intermediaries who handle the message. There is a great danger that 'noise' factors could drastically change the message from what is sent out by the manufacturer to what is received by the end buyer/user. Because the manufacturer has very little control over a message as it passes through a push channel, it may seek to go over the heads of intermediaries by developing a 'pull' channel. Here, the message is aimed at the end buyer/user. If it has an effect in changing their behaviour, buyers will go into a retail outlet and demand the brand by name. The retailer will then demand a particular brand from the wholesaler, which in turn will demand the product from the manufacturer. In the field of financial services, the efforts of savings and pensions companies to develop strong brands have been designed to bring buyers to an intermediary with a prior preference for one brand over others. In computing, Intel broke with tradition by going over the heads of dealers and computer assemblers with the message to end users that they would benefit by choosing a computer with an Intel processor.

Other important audiences for communication

It should be remembered that promotion is not always aimed solely at buyers or their immediate decision-making units. Other key audiences, or 'stakeholders' can include the following:

1. Suppliers

2. Distributors/agents

3. Competitors

4. Employees and trades unions

5. Political bodies and regulatory agencies

6. Financial institutions

7. Pressure groups and local community groups

8. The media and opinion leaders

Each of these stakeholder groups at varying times can have a significant influence upon the organization in terms of its overall effectiveness, efficiency, and image. Many privatized utility companies realize that the most important target for their communication is often not the consumers who buy or use their services, but the regulators who control the prices that can be charged, or politicians who can change the legislative framework within which the utilities do business. It is often necessary to strike a balance between the short-term goals of the organization and the longer-term interests of these key groups. Communication is a vital link between the organization and its key stakeholders and public relations (see below) is often the primary tool used for communicating with such stakeholders.

◉ The channel

A message must be communicated to the target audience by some means. In a very few cases, a company may be able to do the bulk of its communication face to face with its current and potential customers. A trader at a fruit and vegetable market probably has no advertising or paid promotional activity, but relies on attracting passing trade through a display of his products and face-to-face communication with each customer. Larger and more complex companies cannot rely on such simple methods. They must develop impersonal means of communication in place of face-to-face contact. We talk about communication being conducted through a *channel*, such as television, newspapers, or posters. Some of these channels may nevertheless still retain a high degree of personal contact, for example personal selling, where a company communicates its message through its sales personnel.

    Channels have a tendency to distort the message that was sent. We saw earlier how messages are encoded by the sender and also by the receiver, and part of the noise that occurs between the two can be explained by the nature of the channel. Some channels are able to accommodate a lengthy message without distortion. Contrast this to a typical 30-second radio advert, where a complex message must be conveyed in a short time using only one of the senses—sound. While some channels have a facility for immediate feedback from the person receiving a message (online channels are good at this), immediate response is lacking from many channels; for example a newspaper advert in itself doesn't allow a customer to speak back to a company that has transmitted a message through the pages of the newspaper.

Companies put a lot of effort into optimizing their use of channels so that they get the maximum number of messages through to the most number of people in their target market, at minimum cost. We will consider general approaches to evaluation later in this chapter.

The term promotion mix is often used to describe the range of channels, such as advertising, email, and face-to-face selling, which are available to companies as methods by which they can get their messages to target customers. We will look in more detail at the elements of the promotion mix, and their relationship to each other, later in this chapter.

◉ Response: marketing communications models

Having identified the target audience and its characteristics, the communicator must consider the type of response required from it. The required response will have an influence on the source, message, and channel of communication.

It was noted above that in most cases customers are seen as going through a series of stages before finally deciding to purchase a product. It is therefore critical to recognize these buyer-readiness states and to assess where the target audience is at any given time. The communicator will be seeking any one or more of three audience responses to the communication:

1. Cognitive responses: The message should be considered and understood.

2. Affective responses: The message should lead to some change in attitude.

3. Behavioural responses: Finally, the message should achieve some change in behaviour (e.g. a purchase decision).

Many models have been developed to show how marketing communication has the effect of 'pushing' recipients of messages through a number of sequential stages, finally resulting in a purchase decision. These models portray a simple and steady movement through the stages, and the probabilities of success in each stage cumulatively decline because of noise, and therefore the probability of the final stage eventually achieving an actual purchase can be very low.

We will now look briefly at some widely used marketing communication models which seek to understand buyers' responses to communication stimuli.

'Hierarchy of effects' models

These models propose a sequence of responses that occurs as a result of a message being received by a target audience. The two most common such models are referred to as AIDA and DAGMAR (Figure 11.8).

The principle that underlies these models is that communication acts as a stimulus which gives rise to a 'conditioned' response. Communication can therefore be developed to achieve the objective of moving people through a sequence of responses:

For example:

1. To gain initial awareness of a product, advertising may be the most effective method.

2. To gain liking, comprehension, and desire, brochures may provide more detail which will be needed to make a subsequent purchase decision.

3. To achieve an actual sale, personal selling and sales promotion activity may be best.

'Hierarchy of effects' models suggest how communications affect the mind and behaviour of the audience. The major benefit of such models is that they enable the purpose of a particular promotion to be defined and pre-and post-campaign surveys can be carried out to assess the communication effect.

The models have many weaknesses, the most significant being their simplification of complex psychological and behavioural processes. The audience is seen as a passive recipient of messages as opposed to active seekers and participants in the communication process. Consumer research has shown that many consumers set predetermined parameters within which a purchase decision might be made, such as price range and style of a product. The buyer therefore selects those messages that support her in her purchase decision as opposed to being passively pulled through the sequence. These models also ignore individual psychological factors, such as the influence of attitudes/beliefs, motivation, and perception on behaviour. Furthermore, they assume that the sequence of response is universal, when in fact instances occur where awareness of, and commitment to, a product can occur at the

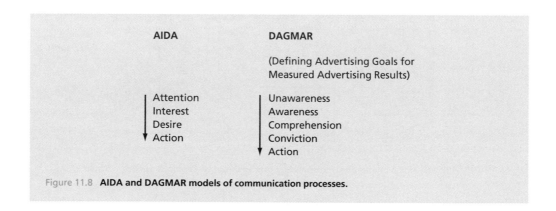

Figure 11.8 **AIDA and DAGMAR models of communication processes.**

same time as the point of purchase but with limited understanding, as happens with impulse purchases. Finally, the assumption that specific promotional effects can be measured in isolation is a simplification of a complex communication environment. In reality, it is difficult to isolate one single element.

Integrated models

A model that identifies and integrates psychological and behavioural elements was developed by Timothy Joyce and is shown in Figure 11.9. This model recognizes that to understand how promotions work we need to understand the nature of the promotion, people's purchase behaviour, their individual psychology, and the interrelationships between these factors. The effect of communication is seen not as a passive relationship but more as a continuing relationship, with habit and consistency forming an integral part of an individual's behaviour. The inclusion of perception and the selective attention to communication stimuli recognize that the consumer will not take in all of a communication message and that individuals make associations in their own minds as to the nature of the communication they have received. The model also recognizes that attitudes can be influenced by both pre- and post-purchase experience and that consumers may actively seek promotional material to reduce feelings of cognitive dissonance, which can occur where they believe that they may not have made the best purchase choice. Promotion can therefore help to overcome dissonance.

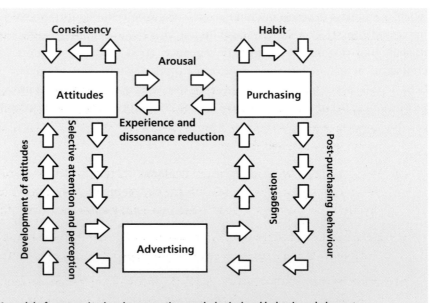

Figure 11.9 **A model of communication, incorporating psychological and behavioural elements.**
(*Source:* adapted from Joyce, T. (1967) 'What do we know about how advertising works?' ESOMAR.)

⊙ Stages of the promotion planning process

Promotional activity is unlikely to be effective unless it forms part of a cohesive and integrated promotional plan. A useful framework within which to consider promotional planning is the SOST '4Ms' proposed by Smith and Taylor (2004), which sees the process beginning with a general review of a company's situation, and proceeds through objectives, strategy, and tactics.

1. Situation:

    (a) Company—sales and market share trends, summary strengths, and weaknesses

    (b) Product service range—features, benefits, and unique selling proposition; product positioning

    (c) Market structure—growth, opportunities and hazards, target markets and competition

2. Objectives: short, medium, and long term:

    (a) Markcting objectives

    (b) Communication objectives

3. Strategy: how the objectives will be achieved; this can be a summary of the promotional mix and can include the marketing mix (no tactical details here)

4. Tactics: the detailed activities to implement strategy; the detailed planning of how, when, and where various promotional activities (communication tools) occur

5. 4Ms:

    (a) *Men*: men (and women!)—who is responsible for what? Are there enough suitably experienced men and women in-house to handle various projects? Have they got spare capacity to take on extra tasks? Are outside agencies needed, or should extra permanent staff be recruited?

    (b) *Money*: budget—what will it cost? Is it affordable? Is it good value for money? Should the money be spent elsewhere? Does the budget include research to measure the effectiveness of various other activities? Is there an allowance for contingencies?

    (c) *Minutes*: timescale and deadlines for each stage of each activity—proposals, concept development, concept testing, regional testing, national roll-out, international launch.

    (d) *Measurement*: monitoring the results of all activities helps the marketing manager to understand what works well and what is not worth repeating in the next campaign. Clearly defined and specific objectives provide yardsticks for measurement. The monitored results also help the manager to make realistic forecasts and ultimately to build better marketing communication plans in the future.

The situation analysis should ideally be part of a comprehensive audit of an organization's competitive position. It should highlight market trends, market position, competitor activity, consumer perceptions, etc. From this analysis a clearer understanding of the situation can be obtained and appropriate objectives and strategies agreed. It is also important to conduct an internal audit of the organization to determine resource requirements and availability.

After analysing the situation, objectives are set. A mnemonic that provides a useful framework by which to formulate objectives is SMARTT. Objectives should be **S**pecific, **M**easurable, **A**chievable, **R**elevant, **T**imed, and **T**argeted.

The choice of promotional strategy will be determined by the objectives. A range of promotional options are likely to be available, for example whether to have a low-key launch of a new product, or to go for an aggressive promotional build-up prior to launch. Strategy is not about doing things, but about setting the direction, scope, and breadth by which things will be done, and allocating resources. The strategy should provide guidance on the future implementation of promotional activity and its evaluation.

The promotion campaign

A campaign brings together a wide range of media-related activities so that, instead of being a series of unrelated activities, they can act in a planned and coordinated way to achieve promotional objectives. The term 'integrated marketing communications' is often used to describe the way in which one promotional medium works in conjunction with others, in order to convey a consistent message cost effectively. The first stage of campaign planning is to have a clear understanding of promotional objectives (see above). Once these have been clarified, a message can be developed that is most likely to achieve the objectives. The next step is the production of the media plan. Having defined the target audience in terms of its size, location, and media characteristics, media must be selected that achieve the desired levels of exposure/repetition with the target audience. This should specify the timing of media activities (Figure 11.10) A media plan must be formulated which specifies:

1. The allocation of expenditure between the different media.

2. The selection of specific media components—for example, in the case of print media, decisions need to be made regarding the type (tabloid *v.* broadsheet; national *v.* local), size of advertisement, and whether there is to be national or local coverage.

3. The frequency and timing of insertions.

4. The cost of reaching a particular target group for each of the media vehicles specified in the plan.

5. The interrelationship between different media (e.g. how an Internet banner ad may reinforce a newspaper advert).

The role of promotion agencies

Should a company undertake its own campaign management, or give the task to a specialist agency? There are many benefits in giving the task to an outside agency. The culture of

Product: Zarinda shampoo	Schedule of Promotional Activity									
	J	F	M	A	M	J	J	A	S	O
TV adverts	X	X				X	X			
Magazine adverts		X	X	X			X	X	X	
Press releases	X	X			X	X			X	X
Sales promotions			X	X	X				X	X
Trade promotions	X	X			X	X			X	X
Field sales	X	X			X	X			X	X
Telephone sales	X	X	X			X	X	X		
Sponsorship				X				X		
Exhibition				X						
Community event							X			

Figure 11.10 **A schedule such as the one shown above is typically used to plan media related activities over the coming 12-month period.** While a plan such as this helps to control budgets and provides more certainty in interfunctional planning, the media schedule may need to be revised at short notice, for example if consumer spending falls unexpectedly, or a new competitor appears with a large media budget.

a company, especially large ones operating in stable or regulated environments, may not be conducive to the creativity that promotion demands and therefore it may be better to leave promotional activity to an outside organization which has a more creative culture. It may be easier for an outsider to be more customer-focused and to see opportunities for promotion that are not immediately apparent to insiders who are too close to the product. A further major benefit of using an outside agency is its ability to use its expertise in developing and executing campaigns. Such agencies can usually purchase media on more favourable terms than a single company acting alone. External agencies have tended to become much broader in their abilities. While many still specialize in one type of promotion (e.g. advertising or direct mail), there has been a tendency for agencies to offer their clients a broad range of promotion management services. Clients' requirements for integrated marketing communications planning (sometimes referred to as 'media neutral planning') in an increasingly complex and fragmented media world has been one reason for the development of large multi-media promotion agencies. An integrated approach implies consistency in the structure of communications and the attitudes they develop (Fill 2009).

Against these benefits, external agencies are sometimes accused of losing sight of the true nature of a product and its target customers. While an agency may be free to take risky innovations, these can sometimes prove disastrous and need to be disowned by the client company. The relationship between an advertising agency and its client company is critical. There are many examples of very long-lasting relationships which have been mutually beneficial and have given the agency considerable experience in understanding the client's needs. Dissatisfaction with the relationship may result in the client company's inviting rival agencies to 'pitch' for its account. Large organizations frequently use a number of agencies to cover different product and/or geographical areas. Where a company uses the specialized services of different media agencies, there is a danger that these could seek to use more of the client's money on the medium they specialize in, rather than on the medium that is best suited to the client. A specialist advertising agency may see a direct marketing agency as a threat, rather than part of an integrated solution which would benefit the client.

◉ Setting budgets for promotional activity

Promotional expenditure can become a drain on an organization's resources if no conscious attempt is made to determine an appropriate budget and to ensure that expenditure is kept within the budget. A number of methods are commonly used to determine the promotional budget.

1. **What can be afforded:** This is largely a subjective assessment and regards promotion as a luxury which can be afforded in good times and cut back during lean times. In fact, expenditure may need to be increased rather than reduced in bad times. This approach is used by many smaller companies to whom advertising spending is seen as the first and easy short-term target for reducing expenditure in bad times.

2. **Percentage of sales:** By this method, advertising expenditure rises or falls to reflect changes in sales. In fact, sales are likely to be influenced by advertising rather than vice versa, and this method is likely to accentuate any given situation. If sales are declining during a recession, *more* advertising may be required to induce sales, but this method of determining the budget implies imposing a cut in advertising expenditure.

3. **Competitive parity:** Advertising expenditure is determined by the amount spent by competitors. Many market sectors see periodic outbursts of promotional expenditure, often accompanying a change in some other element of firms' marketing mix. As an example, operators of satellite and cable television services in the UK became involved in an escalating campaign during 2010, as the two main contenders—Sky and Virgin—launched a series of new services, backed by levels of promotion expenditure which were designed to outbid the other. However, merely increasing advertising expenditure may hide the fact that other elements of the marketing mix need adjusting in order to gain a competitive market position in relation to competitors.

4. **Residual:** This is the least satisfactory approach, and merely assigns to the advertising budget what is left after all other costs have been covered. It may bear no relationship to promotional objectives, especially as a downturn in the business cycle may call for greater expenditure rather than less.

5. **Objective and task:** This approach starts by defining promotional objectives. Tasks are then set that relate to specific targets. In this way, advertising is seen as a necessary—even though risky—investment in a brand, ranking in importance with other more obvious costs such as production and salary costs. This is the most rational approach to setting a promotional budget.

It has been common to talk about 'above-the-line' and 'below-the-line' promotional budgets, referring respectively to advertising and other forms of promotion. In large organizations, having separately managed budgets for different elements of the promotion mix may have served the status needs of individual managers, but the result may have been a fragmented promotion plan. With increasing emphasis on integrated communications, this distinction has become increasingly irrelevant. Also, instead of the advertising manager engaging an advertising agency and the direct marketing manager recruiting a direct marketing agency, there has been a tendency for agencies to become multi-channel, operating 'through the line', thereby allowing a client company to hand its entire promotional planning activity over to one agency.

It was also noted above that many of a firm's activities that communicate messages about the firm and its products do not fit neatly under the heading of 'promotion', and therefore may not be included in the promotional budget. While there has been a tendency to bring under the budget heading some items that were previously considered outside it (e.g. direct marketing activities), others are difficult to include. Should a company's website be included within the promotional budget, or should it be seen as part of a company's wider budget for supporting its distribution system? More seriously, how should temporary price discounts be handled? Should these be included as a promotional item of expenditure, perhaps on the basis that they are a temporary means of stimulating sales by communicating a temporary price advantage? Or should they be regarded not as a cost, but as a reduction in revenue budgets? There are also issues about the extent to which promotion managers should have budgetary responsibility for the customer-facing messages that are given out by a company's buildings and staff. Some would argue that the promotion budget for a fashion retailer should include provision for a designer-look store frontage that conveys a message about the clothes within the store.

◉ Monitoring and evaluating the promotional effort

It is very important to monitor and evaluate the effectiveness of an organization's promotional activities, in order to better inform future campaign planning. However, it can be very difficult to assess effectiveness, and in respect of advertising, Lord Rothermere once famously said that half of all advertising was wasted, but the trouble was he couldn't tell which half. In one study of 135 campaigns by 40 advertising agencies, it was found that almost none of the agencies really knew, or ever could know, whether or not their campaigns were successful (Henderson 2000). While much evaluation relies on instinct and gut feeling, methods of evaluation are becoming increasingly sophisticated. Databases are making it possible for direct marketing companies to measure the response to a message, allowing them to refine their efforts in future targeting. The development of the Internet has allowed previously unimaginable levels of information about an audience's behaviour with respect to a message. Cookies embedded in an individual's computer can enable a company to learn how the viewer arrived at a company's site, the range of sites that she had previously visited, her movements around the site, how long she spent on different pages, where she went to subsequently, and whether she made a purchase/enquiry for further information.

It should not be forgotten that evaluation of communication must be made against the objectives set for that communication. A message that had the objective of creating awareness of a brand should not be criticized if it failed to achieve a short-term increase in sales. Instead, evaluation should be based on changes in the level of awareness of the brand among the target market.

In combination, a number of techniques can be used to try to assess the effectiveness of an individual advert or an advertising campaign:

1. Prior to launching a message, companies use focus groups to test its effectiveness. Researchers are particularly concerned to identify memorable parts of the message and how far an individual progressed before he skipped to the next subject. Prior evaluation of an advert can help companies to avoid running adverts that subsequently turn out to be offensive or misinterpreted.

2. Routine monitoring of a sample panel's television viewing is undertaken by BARB. Similar monitoring of the press is undertaken by the National Readership Survey. While such monitoring can estimate how many people see an advertisement, they provide little evidence of whether the advert was recalled or acted upon.

3. To overcome the above problem, a number of panels are retained by market research agencies and are consulted regularly to ascertain which recent advertisements or other promotional messages they can recall, either spontaneously or with prompting. One example is the NOP weekly telephone omnibus survey carried out among 1,000 adults on behalf of sponsoring companies.

◉ Introducing the promotion mix

Communication is received by audiences from two principal sources: those within an organization, and those external to it. The latter includes word-of-mouth/word of mouse recommendation from friends, editorials in the press, etc., which may have high credibility in the product evaluation process. Sources originating within an organization can be divided into those originating from the traditional marketing function (which can be divided into personal two-way channels such as personal selling and impersonal one-way channels such as advertising), and those originating from front-line production resources. In the case of services that involve consumers in the production process, the promotion mix has to be considered more broadly than is the case with manufactured goods. Front-line operations staff and service outlets become a valuable channel of communication.

The promotion mix comprises those activities and channels that a company uses to promote its products and its corporate image to customers, potential customers, and the key stake-holder groups described above. These activities are conventionally identified by a number of headings, although they overlap. As with the marketing mix itself, definitions of the promotion mix elements are not in themselves particularly important—what is more important is to recognize the interdependencies between them. The most commonly used headings for promotion mix elements are advertising, sales promotion, selling, public relations, direct marketing, and online marketing. Within each of these categories a further range of options can be identified. (For example, advertising involves mixing a variety of media, such as newspaper, television, and radio advertising.) Figure 11.11 outlines the key elements of the promotion mix.

The choice of a particular combination of communication channels will depend primarily on the characteristics of the target audience, especially its habits in terms of exposure to messages. Other important considerations include the present and potential market size for the product (advertising on television may not be appropriate for a product that has a local niche market, for example), the nature of the product itself (the more personal the product, the more effective the two-way communication channel), and of course the costs of the various channels.

An important trend affecting promotional planning is the increasing fragmentation of markets, resulting in smaller market segments, and hence smaller audiences for a highly specific message. Fortunately, this has occurred at a time of growing media availability and choice. Sophisticated database technology and the Internet have opened new possibilities for communicating messages to narrowly defined audiences, while the development of the mobile Internet through 3G mobile phones, WiFi, and global positioning systems allows targeting not only of individuals, but also according to where and when a company believes that the individual will be most responsive to a message. Such fragmentation of both markets and media availability confirms the need for increased sophistication of market segmentation and targeting techniques within the promotion planning process. Another key trend is the emergence of peer-to-peer communication through the Internet. Social networking sites such as Facebook and YouTube can provide user generated sources of messages which compete with the 'official' message from the company whose products are being talked about.

The elements of the promotion mix vary in the extent to which they can achieve the diverse communication objectives described earlier in this chapter. Advertising, for example, is generally fairly good at developing an image for a company, but is less capable of conveying complex factual information about a product. Direct marketing is much better

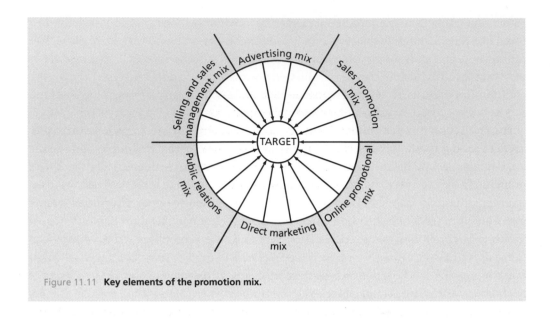

Figure 11.11 **Key elements of the promotion mix.**

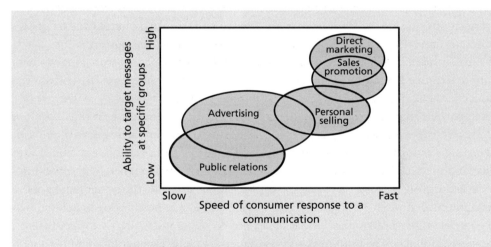

Figure 11.12 **A schematic map showing the capabilities of the main promotional mix elements in terms of their ability to target specific audiences and to achieve short-term rather than long-term results.**

at adapting a message to very small audiences, but is less useful for image building. Two important aspects of communication objectives are shown in Figure 11.12:

1. the extent to which a message can be adapted to the needs of a specific audience;

2. the extent to which a message can achieve a short-term or a long-term response from the audience.

Figure 11.12 shows a two-dimensional grid, in which the main elements of the promotional mix have been located. It shows that, while different mix elements may have distinctive functions, there is nevertheless some overlap. Some media, such as advertising, are capable of spanning a range of objectives.

Different elements of the promotion mix are brought together in a promotional campaign, and for any given product, the emphasis placed on different elements is likely to change as a product goes through its life-cycle. Advertising and public relations are more likely to form important channels of communication during the introductory stage of the life-cycle, where the major objective is often to increase overall audience awareness. Sales promotion can be used to stimulate trial, and sometimes personal selling can be used to acquire distribution coverage. During a product's growth stage the use of all communication channels can generally be reduced, as demand during this phase tends to produce its own momentum through word-of-mouth communications. However, as the product develops into its maturity stage, there may be a call for an increase in advertising and sales promotion activity. Finally, when the product is seen to be going into decline, advertising and public relations are often reduced, although sales promotion can still quite usefully be applied. Sometimes products in decline are allowed to die quietly with very little promotion. In the case of many long-life financial services, which a company would like to delete but cannot for contractual reasons, the service may be kept going with no promotional support at all.

An organization's image can be projected through channels other than the formal promotional process. There is a lot of evidence, for example, that, when comparing professional and personal services providers, customers prefer to be guided by information from friends and other personal contacts rather than a company's formal promotion mix (e.g. Susskind 2002; Walker 2001). Of course, positive word-of-mouth recommendation is generally dependent on customers having good experiences with an organization. An important communication objective for firms is often therefore to leverage 'free' positive promotion through word-of-mouth recommendation, and to limit the damage caused by negative word of mouth. Word-of-mouth recommendation has been further facilitated by the Internet. As well as telling their friends, messages left with social network sites can spread a message very rapidly.

The nature of promotion channel decisions has been changing rapidly in recent years. Although the following sections distinguish between apparently separate components such as advertising and sales promotion, these are becoming increasingly integrated and one media channel is likely to be used alongside other channels as reinforcements. But perhaps the most fundamental change that has occurred has resulted from Web 2.0 technologies which make it much easier for communication messages from ordinary customers to be heard by very large audiences. 'Word of mouth' has always been important to service companies, keen to grow their business through personal recommendation, but now social network media allow individuals to spread their messages much more widely and quickly. Many organizations are still grappling with the issue of how to exploit the opportunities of social network media, and to restrict the possible damage that they can cause to brand reputation. As the Heathrow Terminal 5 example earlier in this chapter demonstrated, a lot of planned communication effort by an organization can be cancelled out by videos appearing on You-Tube, for example, with links to the video being spread virally through social network sites. We will return to the subject of viral marketing later in this chapter.

Many companies have embraced the Internet to develop 'viral' marketing, in which a message can be spread rapidly from one person to a handful of friends, who each in turn inform a handful of their friends (Ferguson 2008). In one case, the online marketing firm NewGate distributed advance excerpts of a new children's book to online forum leaders. When the forum leaders read the pre-released chapters they quickly spread the excitement and anticipation for the book, which ended up being on the *New York Times* bestseller list. The company had used more than 400,000 discussion boards and message forums across the net, targeting about 11 million 'e-fluentials', who in turn reached 55 million consumers by spreading the word (Cardwell 2002). However, Internet-based communication can also pose a threat to companies as social networking sites can rapidly spread the views of dissatisfied customers. As an example, two disgruntled employees of Domino's pizza in North Carolina posted a video on YouTube showing disgusting food preparation at a branch of Dominos and attracted huge audiences, which Dominos couldn't control effectively (Vogt 2009).

We will now look in more detail at each of the main elements of the promotion mix. We can only cover broad strategic issues relating to each of these, and for more discussion of the practical problems and opportunities of implementation, refer to the suggestions for further reading at the end of this chapter. Remember also as you read through the list of promotion mix elements that the headings used can overlap, for example Internet promotion may be seen as a form of advertising.

◉ Advertising

The role of advertising in the promotion mix

Advertising is defined here as: 'Any paid form of non-personal communication of ideas, goods, or services delivered through selected media channels'. This definition incorporates a wide range of activities, from a 30-second slot on prime-time television through to a postcard in a newsagent's window. Advertising 'media' simply refers to where the advert is placed. In addition to television and newspapers, a hot air balloon with an advertising message and football hoardings seen at stadiums are all different forms of advertising media.

The selection of media is critical. In an ideal world, a specific advertisement would be seen and read by all of its intended target audience. In reality, such coverage is difficult to achieve. Different media are therefore selected to increase the probability of a member of the target audience seeing the advert at least once. The combination of types of media used for this purpose is often referred to as the *media mix*.

Advertising is defined as non-personal. Advertisements are targeted at a mass audience and not to a specific individual. One of the benefits of advertising is its ability to reach a large number of people at relatively low cost. That is not to say that advertising costs are low. If an advertiser wishes to reach a prime-time television audience or to place a full-page advert in a high-quality magazine or newspaper, then the costs will range from tens of thousands of pounds to hundreds of thousands of pounds just for one spot or insertion. When we consider the cost per 1,000 people, however, this can work out to be relatively low. With large audiences or readerships, the cost of an advertisement per 1,000 viewers or readers can often fall to just a few pence. Advertising, like the other mix elements, cannot be seen in isolation. Advertising is frequently used, for example, to support sales promotion and direct marketing activity.

How does advertising work?

Think back to the discussion earlier in this chapter about the objectives of communication. You will recall that a message may be required to do a number of things, from simply creating awareness of a product, through to achieving a final sale. Advertising can be used to achieve a wide range of objectives, but it is generally best suited to building a longer-term image for an organization and its products. Advertising is also best at targeting broadly defined target audiences where dialogue is not called for.

An advertising message must be able to move an individual along a path from awareness through to eventual purchase. In order for a message to be received and understood, it must gain attention, use a common language, arouse needs, and suggest how these needs may be met. The content, structure, and format of an advert must be developed in order to achieve promotional objectives. A complex message needs to be encoded before being transmitted, but the presence of 'noise' may result in the receiver decoding a message quite differently to what had been intended.

The role of advertising often does not end when a sale has been achieved. Advertising is often aimed at customers after they have made a purchase, to encourage them to feel that they made the correct choice (thereby reducing 'cognitive dissonance') and to foster further purchases from the company. It was noted in Chapter 4 that organizations increasingly seek to build relationships with their customers, so the behavioural change (the sale) should be seen as the starting-point for making customers aware of other goods and services available from the organization.

Advertising media

Effective advertising requires a good understanding of the media habits of the target audience. If a firm's target market is not in the habit of being exposed to a particular medium, much of the value of advertising through that medium will be wasted. Information about target audiences' media habits is obtained from a number of sources. Newspaper readership information is collated by the National Readership Survey. For each newspaper, this shows reading frequency and average readership per issue (as distinct from circulation) broken down into age, class, sex, ownership of consumer durables, etc. Television viewing information is collected by the Broadcasters Audience Research Board (BARB). This indicates the number of people watching particular channels at particular times by reference to two types of television rating (TVR): one for the number of *households* watching a programme/advertising slot, and one for the number of *people* watching.

Using such sources of information, the media characteristics of a particular target audience can be ascertained and a media plan produced which achieves maximum penetration of the target audience. The choice of advertising media is influenced by the characteristics of each medium and its ability to achieve the specified promotional objectives. The following are some of the most common types of media and their characteristics.

Newspapers Daily newspapers tend to have a high degree of reader loyalty, reflecting the fact that each national title is targeted at specific segments of the population. This loyalty means that the printed message can be perceived by readers as having a high level of credibility. Therefore, daily papers may be useful for prestige and reminder advertising. They can be used for creating general awareness of a product or a brand as well as providing detailed product information. In this way, banks use newspapers both for adverts designed to create a brand awareness and liking for the organization, and for adverts giving specific details of savings accounts. The latter may include an invitation to act in the form of a website address or freephone telephone number where a transaction can be completed.

Daily newspapers, however, are normally read hurriedly, and therefore lengthy copy is likely to be wasted. Sunday newspapers also appeal to highly segmented audiences but are generally read at a more leisurely pace than daily papers. They are also more likely to be read at home and shared by households, which may be important for appealing to family-based purchase decisions.

Local newspapers offer a much greater degree of geographical segmentation than is possible with national titles. Within their circulation areas, they can also achieve much higher levels of readership penetration. In the case of free newspapers, high levels of circulation may be achieved, although actual readership levels are more open to question. While national advertising through local newspapers is expensive and inefficient, it is useful for purely local suppliers, as well as national organizations wishing to target specific areas with local messages, or to pretest national advertising copy.

The distinction between national, regional, and local papers has become blurred as flexible printing systems allow local editions of national and international newspapers to be produced, appealing to advertisers seeking tightly specified audiences. Many commentators have forecast the demise of newspapers in the face of competition from electronic sources of news, but newspapers have fought back and adapted. There is, however, a trend towards lower newspaper readership by some groups, especially young people (Lauf 2001). Local newspapers have suffered as much of their traditional classified advertising—for jobs, cars, and houses, has transferred to the Internet, which provides a constantly updated and searchable source of information, accessible from anywhere.

Magazines/journals Within the UK, and most western countries, there is an extensive selection of magazine and journal titles. While some high-circulation magazines appeal to broad groups of people (e.g. *Radio Times*), most titles are specialized in terms of their content and targeting. In this way *What Car?* magazine may be a highly specific medium for car manufacturers, dealers, and loan companies to promote their goods and services to new car buyers. Specialist trade titles allow messages to be aimed at intermediaries; for example manufacturers of catering equipment will gain access to an audience of key buyers through *The Caterer* magazine. The

What does your newspaper say about you?

In most countries, advertisers are attracted to national newspapers by the highly segmented audience of each newspaper. Not only do we tend to be loyal to our preferred newspaper, but we may be inclined subconsciously to regard advertisements placed in it as being more believable. An individual's choice of national newspaper can say a lot about his or her values, attitudes, and lifestyle. Researchers have developed a number of detailed indicators of the profile of a newspaper's readership, but the following tongue-in-cheek analysis of UK newspaper readership may not be too far from the truth:

The *Times* is read by the people who run the country.

The *Financial Times* is read by the people who own the country.

The *Telegraph* is read by people who think that the country should be run the way that it was in the past.

The *Mail* is read by the wives of the people that run the country.

The *Independent's* readers keep an open mind about who should run the country.

Sun readers don't care who runs the country, so long as she looks good on page 3.

What does your preferred newspaper say about you?

amount of advertising placed in magazines has been falling recently, as advertisers, especially specialist trade and classified advertisers, have moved to searchable online media and some specialist titles, such as *Hospital Doctor* and *Independent Practitioner* have closed.

Although advertising in magazines may at first seem relatively expensive compared with newspapers, it represents good value to advertisers in terms of the high number of target readers per copy and the highly segmented nature of their audiences (Figure 11.13).

Television This is an expensive, but very powerful, medium. Although it tends to be used mainly for the long-term task of creating brand awareness, it can also be used to create a rapid sales response. The very fact that a message has been seen on television can give credibility to the message source, and many companies add the phrase 'as seen on TV' to give additional credibility to their other media communications. The power of the television medium is enhanced by its ability to appeal to the senses of both sight and sound, and to use movement and colour to develop a sales message.

A major limitation of television advertising is its cost. For most small businesses, television advertising rates start at too high a level to be considered. The high starting price for television advertising reflects not only high production costs, but also the difficulty in segmenting television audiences, either socio-economically or in terms of narrowly defined geographical areas. Also, the question must be asked as to how many people within the target audience are actually receptive to a television advert. Is the target viewer actually in the room when an advertisement is being broadcast? If the viewer is present, is he receptive to the message? The use of video recorders and remote controls has important implications for the effectiveness of television advertising. Television advertisers must use their creative talents to ensure that a short 30-second slot creates sufficient impact for a viewer to pay attention to the whole of the advertisement.

With the development of digital broadcasting and the proliferation of television channels, the ability of the medium to segment audiences is increasing. There are now numerous channels that have developed distinctive audiences, such as the Discovery Channel, MTV, and Sky Sports. With the development of interactive television, advertising can be used to elicit an immediate response. (For example, a pizza company can use an advert to create an awareness and liking of its brand, as well as offering immediate ordering and delivery of a pizza.) The distinction between television and Internet has become more blurred and pure television companies should be worried by the tendency of young people, in particular, to increase their use of the Internet, at the expense of television viewing. A report by Ofcom in 2010 indicated that consumers increasingly watch Internet-based content via their PC and noted that 31 per cent of adults with Internet access had watched catch-up TV on their computer, up from 23 per cent in 2009 (Ofcom, 2010).

Commercial radio Radio advertising in the UK has seen considerable growth in recent years, recovering from its traditional perception as the poor relation of television advertising. The threshold cost of radio advertising is much lower than for television, reflecting much more local segmentation of radio audiences and the lower production costs of radio adverts. With radio, the audience can be involved in other activities—particularly driving—while being exposed to an advertisement. Inevitably, a radio message is less powerful than a television message, relying solely on the sense of hearing. Although there are often doubts about the extent to which an audience receives and understands a radio message, it does form a useful reminder medium when used in conjunction with other media (Figure 11.14).

Cinema Because of the captive nature of cinema audiences, this medium has the potential to make a major impact. It is frequently used to promote local services such as food outlets, whose target market broadly corresponds to the audience of most cinemas. However, without repetition, cinema advertisements have little lasting effect, although they can be useful for supporting press and television advertising.

Outdoor advertising This is useful for reminder copy and can support other media activities. The effect of an advertisement on television or in the national press can be prolonged if recipients are exposed to a reminder poster on their way to work the following day. Some poster sites can appeal to segmented audiences; for example London Underground sites in the City of London are seen by large numbers of affluent business people. The sides of buses are often used to support new products available locally (e.g. new store openings) and have the ability to spread their message as the bus travels along local routes. Posters can generally be used only to convey a simple communication rather than complex details.

Online media The Internet has opened up new opportunities for companies to communicate with their target markets. Much of the development in this area allows companies to enter into a one-to-one dialogue with customers, which is not strictly a form of advertising as defined here. The use of the Internet for one-to-one communication and distribution is considered in more detail later in this chapter. In addition, most companies have their own websites which address mass audiences. Creating an awareness of these sites has become a

Figure 11.13 **Trade journals are particularly valuable for targeting highly specific groups of business buyers.** *Construction News* is the most widely circulated publication within the UK building and civil engineering sector, with a total ABC average circulation figure of 16,523 (July 2008–June 2009). This makes it an ideal medium for promoting a range of construction-related products, such as plant and equipment. A fuller understanding of the publication's readers is provided by an in-depth readership survey which is conducted every two years. Among other things, the survey has established that four people on average read each copy of *Construction News,* giving an industry-wide readership of over 65,000 per week. (Reproduced with kind permission of Construction News.)

Figure 11.14 **Radio is a useful advertising medium for communicating with audiences when they are captive and/or open to persuasion.** This advertisement demonstrates the power of radio in communicating a message about a fast-moving consumer good, just at the moment when the audience may be most receptive to a message about the product.
(Reproduced with kind permission of the Radio Advertising Bureau.)

major challenge for companies, with conventional media often being used to promote the website address. As a further method of attracting 'hits', companies frequently pay for hot-links out of other companies' websites. 'Search' marketing has become very important for identifying web-based audiences who are actively seeking a particular category of product, and will be considered later (Jones 2008).

Getting viewers to a company's website is a continuing challenge, especially for people who are not looking for a company specifically, but seeking a category of service through a search-engine enquiry. Search-engine optimization (SEO) has become a specialist skill to ensure that a company's website comes top of the list when the user of a search-engine enters specified keywords. Many models exist by which companies can pay to improve their search engine ranking, for example by paying per 'click through'. Many other approaches are used to get visitors to the company's website, such as sponsored links from affiliates. The essential point is that in a competitive environment, it is not sufficient to just have a website, it is important to have a strategy for getting visitors to the website.

Other innovative media Advertising media can become very cluttered by the sheer volume of advertising. Companies that spot new media may avoid some of this clutter by having the field to themselves, at least until it too becomes cluttered. Innovative media that have targeted specific groups in recent years include:

1. adverts on milk bottles promoting breakfast cereals;

2. adverts on petrol pumps promoting car insurance;

3. adverts on the sides of cows promoting ice-cream.

◉ Media selection and evaluation

Faced with the availability of such a great variety of media, advertising managers need some criteria to assess the most effective mix of media to meet their objectives. Increasingly sophisticated computer programmes are available which produce a schedule of advertising activities, based on their ability to get through to the target audience cost-effectively. Such programmes take into account:

- The *cover* or *reach* of an advert, defined as the percentage of a particular target audience reached by a medium or a whole campaign.

- The *frequency*, or number of times a particular target audience has an 'opportunity to see/hear' an advertising message.

- The impact an advertisement will have on the target audience—how many people can remember seeing an advert?

- The extent to which the effects of a particular advertising message 'wear out' over time and require reinforcement.

◉ The cost of advertising through a particular medium. The cost of using different media varies markedly, and a medium that at first sight appears to be expensive may in fact be good value in terms of achieving promotional objectives. A key measure is the cost of each message that is actually seen by, or acted upon, by the target audience.

Although it is commonplace to think that advertising can increase sales, it is extremely difficult to prove that advertising alone is responsible for a sales increase. Sales, after all, can be the result of many intervening variables, some of which are internal to the organization (e.g. public relations activity, pricing policy), while others are external (e.g. the state of the national economy).

Constraints on advertising

You will recall from Chapter 3 that firms are increasingly expected to act in a socially responsible manner, and this is particularly the case in respect of their advertising. Britain, like most developed countries, recognizes the possibly harmful effects that advertising can have on vulnerable buyers and the values of society. Advertisers therefore face a number of controls on the content and distribution of their adverts. The content of advertisements is influenced by both volun-tary codes and legislation, although the effect of EU legislation has been to move more towards legislation; for example from 2003 it has been illegal to advertise tobacco products. Refer back to Chapter 3 for more discussion of the voluntary and legislative constraints on advertisers.

Personal selling

Personal selling involves interpersonal dialogue between a prospective customer and a sales-person. Such dialogue may occur face to face or by other personal forms of communication. Personal selling is not simply about persuasion and persistence, although undoubtedly such skills and attributes do come in useful. Professional selling is also about gathering market and customer information; listening, interpreting, and understanding customer needs; managing the customer–supplier relationship interface; and communicating clearly to the customer the benefits of purchasing a particular product that meets their needs.

Selling as a profession is often devalued and misunderstood. Much of this misunderstanding comes from the activities of sectors of the profession itself, particularly the sleazy end represented by pressurized selling techniques, which traditionally were (and still commonly are) practised in several consumer service and goods industries such as double glazing, time-share property, and kitchens/bathrooms. In a business-to-business context, professional selling is more highly regarded.

The interrelationship between sales and marketing has been discussed at length. There is only limited evidence to support the view of Drucker (1973), who stated that if organizations got their marketing activity right they would not need a sales force, as customers would come beating a path to their door. Such a statement is naive and does not recognize the complex nature of many purchase decisions and the importance of human relationships and the sales function in business transactions. Steward (2002) suggested that to omit the importance of selling as an integral component of the marketing activities of an organization is akin to 'omitting a striker from a football team, a gun without a firing pin, and a chemical formula without a catalyst. . .'.

Types of selling

Selling includes activities that range from a shop assistant selling a bar of chocolate for a few pence to teams negotiating a multi-million pound contract to supply aircraft. A sales person's role can be described as any of the following, or a combination of them:

1. Deliverer: Although a person may have the title of 'salesperson', their job is mainly concerned with delivering the product, for example milk, beer, bread, and there are few selling responsibilities. Increases in sales are more likely to stem from a good service and a pleasant manner.

2. Order taker: The salesperson is predominantly an order taker but works in the field and is sometimes able to negotiate additional sales. Here, selling may be done at a central or regional office, and the salesperson simply records and processes the customers' orders. Sometimes, there is scope for making additional sales, for example a waiter in a restaurant may have a role to encourage customers to add additional items to their order. Good service and a pleasant personality may lead to more orders, but the salesperson has only limited opportunity for creative selling.

3. Missionary selling: The salesperson does not actually take orders but rather builds up goodwill, educates the actual or potential user, and undertakes various promotional activities, for example a salesperson for a pharmaceutical company who makes doctors and pharmacists aware of the benefits of prescribing a new drug.

4. Technical selling: Many companies in business-to-business markets use sales engineers or salespeople with technical knowledge where product and application knowledge is a central part of the selling function.

5. Managing key accounts: With the development of relationship marketing strategies, many companies have appointed people to manage the relationship that the company has with its most important customers. They are given responsibilities for selling the company's range of products, based on a thorough understanding of the client's specific and changing needs. They are also likely to have responsibility for ensuring the customer's satisfaction, although they may be given little authority over operational people who are responsible for delivering the company's promises.

Tasks of a salesperson

A number of tasks undertaken by salespeople can be identified. The importance of each of these tasks depends on the type of selling situation in which a salesperson is employed. The most common tasks are:

1. Prospecting: A key function of many selling roles is to help in identifying and generating sales leads. Unsophisticated prospecting involves door knocking; searching through telephone directories, trade directories, and other general listings of companies; etc. The probability is that only a small percentage of those contacted will

be interested in what the organization has to offer. The generation of sales leads from referrals by customers, suppliers, or other business/social contacts will usually provide better prospects. Similarly, leads generated by exhibitions, conferences, seminars, and responses to advertisements will prove to be 'warmer' leads.

2. Targeting: Deciding how to allocate time among prospects and customers. Having established a customer prospect list, the salesperson should conduct some form of evaluation of each potential buyer in terms of their business, markets, products, and probability of purchase. Those prospects that appear to offer the most potential can then be shortlisted for contact.

3. Selling: This is at the heart of many sales peoples' roles and involves clearly understanding the needs of a buyer; recognizing the barriers to them making a purchase (financial, psychological, administrative, etc.); communicating the benefits of the product as they affect the buyer; overcoming objections from the buyer; recognizing buying signals; and eventually closing the sale. A good sales person will have the flexibility to adapt their communication to the emerging requirements of the buyer. This is most likely to be important for complex, high value sales, and less important for selling situations where the sales person is essentially an order taker.

4. Servicing: sales people are often expected to check that an order has been successfully delivered. They may also have a role of routinely checking with the buyer about their future requirements. With the development of key account management, the servicing function has become an increasingly important task linked to selling.

5. Information gathering: Sales people need to gather information about a buyer so that they can adapt their sales pitch to their needs. In addition, sales personnel may be expected to conduct market research and intelligence work to inform a company's sales and marketing decisions.

6. Allocating: where goods or service capacity is in short supply relative to demand, sales personnel may become involved in deciding which customers will get priority for deliveries.

The range of these roles and responsibilities will vary between organizations and sectors, particularly in terms of the level of complexity. For a retail salesperson the primary role may be to meet customers who enter the shop and through dialogue to encourage purchase of a product. Such a salesperson may also be responsible for maintaining the appearance of the stock on the shelf and providing support and advice to customers. A telephone salesperson requires a different range of skills, often following a predetermined and well-tested script.

◉ Sales promotion

Sales promotion involves those activities—other than advertising, personal selling, and public relations—that stimulate customer purchase and the effectiveness of intermediaries.

The Institute of Sales Promotion defines sales promotions as 'a range of tactical marketing techniques designed within a strategic marketing framework, to add value to a product or service in order to achieve a specific sales and marketing objective'.

Although sales promotion activity can be used to create awareness, it is usually used for the later stages of the buying process, that is to create interest and desire, and—in particular—to bring about action. Sales promotion can quite successfully complement other tools within the promotion mix, for example by reinforcing a particular image or identity developed through advertising. Traditionally, sales promotion has been used tactically to encourage brand switching, as a response to competitors' activity, or to create a short-term increase in the level and frequency of sales. Whereas advertising tends to encourage brand loyalty, sales promotion tries to undermine loyalty to competitors' brands with a short-term incentive to switch brands. Increasingly, sales promotions are being used more strategically and are being integrated into an overall communications strategy. Sales promotions can be targeted at consumers with the aim of pulling sales through a channel of distribution, or at intermediaries with the aim of pushing products through the channel, or at a combination of both.

Over the last few years there has been a rapid increase in the use of sales promotion. This can be attributed to the increasingly competitive nature of many markets, and new technology in targeting, which has resulted in an increase in the efficiency and effectiveness of sales promotion.

Sales promotion tools

A wide and ever increasing range of sales promotion tools are available to marketers. Some of the more commonly used tools aimed at the final consumer include the following.

1. Free samples/visits/consultations: These encourage trial of a product and can be valuable where consumers are currently loyal to another supplier. They could, for example, be used by a breakfast cereal manufacturer to entice potential customers to try their brand. In the case of new products which are perceived as being expensive and of poor value to a consumer, they can encourage trial. Satellite television companies, for example, have often used this approach with free trial offers. However, for established products, excessive offering of free samples can demean the value of the product and buyers may become reluctant to pay for a product that they have seen being given away freely (Figure 11.15).

2. Money-off price incentives: Price incentives can be used tactically to try to counteract temporary increases in competitor activity. They can also be used to stimulate sales of a new product shortly after launch or to stimulate demand during slack periods where price is considered to be a key element in a customer's purchase decision. Price incentives tend to be an expensive form of sales promotion, as the incentive is given to customers regardless of its motivational effect on them. A restaurant reducing its prices for all customers is unable to extract the full price from those customers who may have been willing to pay the full price. There is also a danger that price incentives can become built into consumers' expectations so that their removal will result in a fall in business.

435

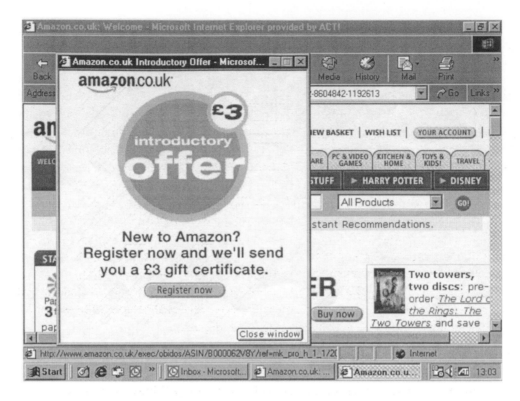

Figure 11.15 **Coupons have been used by marketers for a long time to promote sales.** Coupons allow groups of prospective or actual customers to be targeted with an incentive to encourage them to become a new customer, or to become a bigger spending customer. By restricting the distribution of coupons to those who it is most interested in, a company avoids giving a price reduction to everybody, including those who are loyal and probably find its prices good value. More recently, the Internet has allowed electronic coupons to be distributed efficiently and effectively. By studying site visitors' previous behaviour, unique coupons can be generated. These can either be used online or printed for use elsewhere. The online retailer Amazon.com has made extensive use of coupons to promote sales, such as this one, which is configured according to the information that the company has available about specific targets. Combined with a carefully planned Internet-based promotion programme and an active affiliates programme, Amazon has become the leading online book retailer in the UK.
(Reproduced with kind permission of Amazon.com.)

3. Coupons/vouchers: These allow holders to obtain a discount off a purchase and can be targeted at quite specific groups of users or potential users, often combined with the direct marketing techniques discussed later in this chapter. To encourage trial by potential new users, vouchers can be distributed to non-users who fit a specified profile. In this way, a manufacturer of cosmetics may provide a voucher with a women's magazine whose readership corresponds with the manufacturer's target market. To encourage repeat usage, vouchers can be given as a loyalty bonus. Voucher offers tend to be much more cost effective than straight price incentives because of their ability to segment markets. As an example, a tourist attraction can recognize that visitors from

overseas might see the full price as being only a small part of their total holiday cost and representing good value, while a local family might need an incentive to make more frequent visits to the attraction.

4. Gift offers: Companies often provide the incentive of a gift to encourage short-term sales. Gifts can take many forms, such as a Marks & Spencer gift token or a T-shirt, and can encourage immediate and/or repeated purchase. The gift can satisfy a number of objectives. In order to promote initial enquiry, many firms offer a gift for merely enquiring about their products. This provides an opportunity to submit, with the gift, samples and brochures of the firm's products. A gift can also be used to bring about immediate action—for example a free clock radio if a purchase is made within a specified period. For existing customers, gifts can be used to develop and reward loyalty. Sometimes, a company might charge a small amount for a 'gift'. If the gift is inscribed with the company's logo, the message will be seen by the user and others for some time to come. Some gifts are provided collaboratively between companies with quite different product ranges. For example, a grocery retailer may give rewards of money-off vouchers at a chain of restaurants, satisfying the promotional criteria of the retailer (rewarding loyalty) and the restaurant (encouraging trial).

5. Competitions: The offer of a competition adds value to the total offer. Instead of simply buying an insurance policy, a customer buys the policy plus a dream of winning a prize to which she attaches significance. Competitions can be used both to create trial among non-users and to encourage loyalty among existing customers (e.g. a competition for which a number of proofs of purchase are necessary to enter).

The sales promotion tools described above are predominantly aimed at the final consumer of a product. In addition, a company may use sales promotions aimed at the intermediaries who sell its products. The following are commonly used:

1. Short-term sales bonuses: These can be used to stimulate sales during slack periods or to develop loyalty from intermediaries in the face of competitor activity.

2. Competitions and gifts: These can be aimed at sales personnel working for intermediaries and can help increase awareness of a brand and, if entry to the competition is dependent upon sales, can encourage additional sales.

3. Point of purchase material: To stimulate additional sales, a supplier can provide a range of incentives to help intermediaries. Many consumer goods suppliers offer retailers and field sales staff a range of eye-catching displays to demonstrate the benefits of their product at the point of purchase.

4. Cooperative advertising: Suppliers can agree to subscribe to local advertising by an intermediary, for instance when a car manufacturer promotes the location of its dealers as well as the core benefits of its cars. Cooperative advertising is often undertaken in

conjunction with a significant event, such as the opening of a new outlet by the intermediary, or the launch of a new product.

Evaluation of sales promotion

The performance of the promotion needs to be assessed against the objectives set. If objectives are specific and quantifiable, measurement would seem to be easy. However, extraneous factors can account for the apparent success of many sales promotion activities; for example competitive actions or seasonal variations may influence customers' decision making. It can also be extremely difficult to separate out the effects of sales promotion activity from other promotional activity—or indeed from other marketing mix changes, such as a lower price. A further problem is that sales promotion activity may simply bring demand forward, resulting in buyers building up stockpiles which depresses demand for the product in future periods. This is especially true of products that are of low value and have a long shelf-life. This effect is illustrated in Figure 11.16.

While some firms would use sales promotion tactically to boost sales at specific times and/or locations (e.g. during a quiet time of year, or to support a new store opening), others have a tendency to use a continuous series of sales promotions in a strategic way. A retailer may, for example, have a strategy of always offering a small number of lines at exceptionally low prices in order to attract people into its store, and it is hoped they will buy other products as well as the promotional items. However, it should be remembered that sales promotion activities in themselves generally do not create long-term customer loyalty.

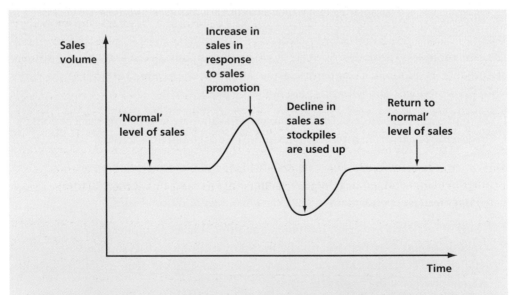

Figure 11.16 **Sales promotion activity, such as a short-term 'Buy one, get one free' offer, can simply bring demand forward, resulting in stockpiles which depress demand after the promotion has ended.** This graph illustrates the difficulties in trying to assess the effectiveness of sales promotion activities.

⊙ Public relations

Public relations (PR) is used to establish and enhance a positive image of an organization and its products among its various publics. It is defined by the Institute of Public Relations as 'the deliberate, planned and sustained effort to establish and maintain mutual understanding between an organization and its publics'.

The words 'deliberate', 'planned', and 'sustained' are crucial here, as companies cannot simply 'do a bit of PR' in isolated bursts and hope for the type of result that comes from a more concerted effort. Public relations as a professional activity is treated with suspicion by many people, but this probably reflects a perception of a short-term opportunistic activity, rather than the long-term commitment advocated by public relations professionals. A good long-term PR strategy will make it much easier for a company to use PR tools when it has a real emergency and needs to communicate with its audiences. As an example, a food manufacturer that has carefully used PR to develop a good mutual understanding between itself and its principal publics will be better placed to use PR to counter a food safety incident than a manufacturer that uses PR tools only as and when needed.

Because public relations is involved with more than just customer relationships, it is often handled at a corporate level rather than at the functional level of marketing management, and covers communication with investor and community groups, among others.

Public relations and corporate reputation

Public relations is very important for maintaining a firm's reputation, especially where it is facing a crisis, for example following a food poisoning scare. Public relations was called upon extensively by the chocolate manufacturer Cadbury following an outbreak of salmonella at one of its factories in 2007. The company had to carefully manage its reputation immediately following the outbreak by recalling all stocks swiftly, and also later on, when investigations suggested that poor working practices had led to contamination within its factory.

For highly variable goods and services (such as airline and train services), there is always the possibility that the media will pick up one bad incident and leave their audience thinking that this is the norm for a particular organization. Media editors have a tendency to write stories that they believe their audiences would like to hear, so if a bad news story about a train company can be assured of a sympathetic hearing it will most likely be run. It would take a lot of effort by train operators to prove to editors that they are out of touch with the reality facing their readers or viewers.

With the development of a 24/7 media environment and Web 2.0 social network sites, companies' reputations can be destroyed more quickly and easily than ever before. It took very little time for the accountancy firm Arthur Andersen to be brought down from having a multi-million-pound income with blue-chip clients and an international network, to being picked over by competitors and deserted by long-term clients. By all accounts, Andersen was still doing good work at its offices in Singapore and Auckland, but its involvement with just one client—Enron—had changed the public's perceptions of the company to the point where business leaders were going out of their way not to be associated with it. The pervasiveness of news media meant that what could have been a local difficulty had led to a multi-national organization being brought down.

The characteristics of public relations

Some of the more important characteristics of public relations are described below.

1. Relatively low cost: PR tends to be much cheaper, in terms of cost per person reached, than any other type of promotion. Apart from nominal production costs, much PR activity can be carried out at almost no cost, in marked contrast to the high cost of buying space or time in the main media. To make the most use of this apparently free resource, many companies pay outside PR consultants.

2. Can be targeted: Public relations activities can be targeted to a small specialized audience if the right media vehicle is used.

3. Credibility: The results of PR activity often have a high degree of credibility, compared with other promotional sources such as advertising. Where information is presented as news, readers or viewers may be less critical of it than if it is presented as an advertisement, which they may presume to be biased.

4. Relatively uncontrollable: A company can exercise little direct control over how its public relations activity is subsequently handled and interpreted. If successful, a press release may be printed in full, although there can be no control over where or when it is printed. At worst, a press release can be misinterpreted and the result can be unfavourable news coverage. This is in contrast to advertising, where an advertiser can exercise considerable control over the content, placing, and timing of an advert.

The tools of public relations

In general, the tools of public relations are best suited to creating awareness of an organization and its products, or a liking for them, and tend to be less effective in directly bringing about action in the form of purchase decisions (Figure 11.17). Some of the more important tools of public relations are described below.

1. Press releases: This seeks to secure *editorial* space in the media, as distinct from paid-for advertising space. Because of the competition from other organizations for press coverage, there can be no guarantee that any particular item will actually be used. Indeed, it is often suggested that over 90 per cent of press releases sent to media editors end up in the bin without being used.

2. Press conferences: These are used where a major event is to be announced and an opportunity for a two-way dialogue between the organization and the media is considered desirable.

3. Lobbying: Professional lobbyists are often employed by a company in an effort to inform and hence influence those key decision makers who may be critical to its

success. Lobbying can take place at a local level (e.g. a fast-food company seeking to convince members of a local authority about the benefits of allowing them to locate in a sensitive area); at a national level (e.g. lobbying by UK brewers to bring UK tax on beer down to the lower levels of many other European countries); and at a supranational level (e.g. the lobbying of the EU Commission by airlines campaigning against proposals to introduce additional taxes on airlines).

4. Education and training: In an effort to develop a better understanding—and hence liking—of an organization and its products, many firms aim education and training programmes at important target groups. In this way, food manufacturers frequently supply schools with educational material that will predispose recipients of the material to their brand. 'Open days' are another common method of educating the public by showing them the complex processes that occur 'behind the scenes' in order to ensure a high quality of output for customers.

5. Exhibitions and trade shows: Most companies attend exhibitions not with the intention of making an immediate sale, but to create an awareness of their organization which will result in a sale over the longer term. Exhibitions are used to target both consumer and commercial audiences. Many trade shows are important events in their respective business sectors, where a high proportion of key decision makers are likely to be present. The annual World Travel Market in London, for example, is an ideal opportunity for travel-related organizations to communicate with their key business customers.

6. In-house journals: The number of in-house magazines produced by companies is now huge, with examples spanning sectors from airlines to banks and supermarkets. By adopting a news-based magazine format, the message becomes more credible than if it were presented as a pure advertisement. Often, outside advertisers contribute revenue which can make such journals self-financing. Airlines often publish in-flight magazines that are read by a captive audience.

7. Sponsorship: There is argument about whether this strictly forms part of the public relations portfolio of tools. It is, however, being increasingly used as an element of the promotion mix and is described in more detail later in this chapter.

8. Internet: Companies now routinely use the Internet as one of their PR tools, often to support the activities described above. Press releases in practice are most likely to be circulated by email. Companies have also become active in creating blogs, and some, such as that associated with Innocent Smoothies, have developed a loyal following. At other times, PR professionals 'lurk' in social network sites, in order to understand better what the public is saying about a client company. Smart PR professionals also prepare to address issues raised through such networks, although there is debate about whether they should do this covertly, passing off as an ordinary member of the community, rather than declaring their attachment to the company being discussed.

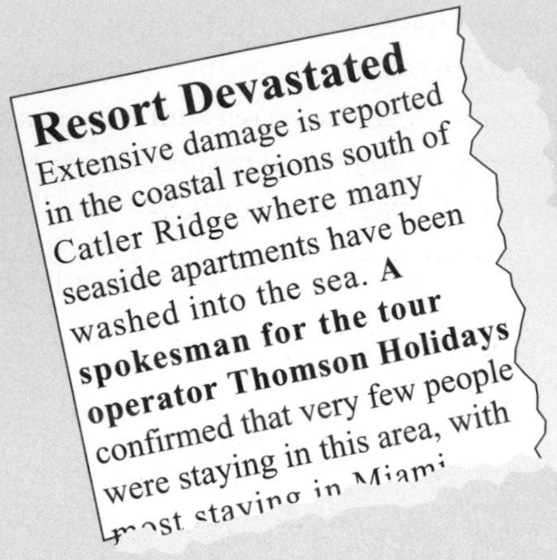

Figure 11.17 **Faced with a news story that the media wishes to cover, a newspaper or radio station may seek specialists within an industrial sector who are knowledgeable on the issues involved.** A local tour operator may be asked by a local newspaper to comment upon the consequences of a natural disaster in an overseas resort. This helps both the reporter and the tour operator in question, whose representative is fielded as an expert.

Evaluating public relations activity

The need for evaluation of PR activity was dismissed by many on the grounds that it was very difficult to do, and the low cost of PR activity didn't justify the effort. Today, there is greater awareness of the need for evaluation and an increasing range of tools to do so. Media content analysis and press cuttings are the most commonly used evaluation techniques, and companies typically measure, 'advertising value equivalents' and 'opportunities to see'. Innovations in computer software are providing new tools which can allow for rapid tracking of media coverage and a calculation of the likely audience.

Another important aspect of PR evaluation is the pre-testing of messages. Where time allows, this may identify any possibilities of misinterpretation that may subsequently arise.

Who should do the PR evaluation? Many PR consultancies provide an evaluation service to their clients, using agreed criteria. Meanwhile, many specialist evaluation companies have emerged that may be contracted directly by the client, or subcontracted by a consultant to provide detailed evaluation.

Sponsorship

Sponsorship does not fit neatly into a categorization of the main elements of the promotion mix. It uses a combination of advertising, public relations, sales promotion, and direct marketing to associate a company's product or corporate image that may be unknown or misunderstood with the image of something that is well understood. As the general clutter of media advertising has increased in recent years, sponsorship has come to play a more important role in the promotion mix. With consumers becoming increasingly critical of organizations' societal credentials, sponsorship has been seen by many organizations as a cost-effective means of enhancing their image.

Sponsorship involves a company's investment in events or causes in order to achieve objectives such as increased awareness levels, enhanced reputation, etc. Sponsorship activities include a brewer sponsoring tennis matches (e.g. the Stella Artois tournament) and an organization sponsoring specific television programmes (such as Cadbury's sponsorship of *Coronation Street*).

As with promotional planning in general, segmentation is crucial to successful sponsorship. A company must have a good definition of the audience to which it wishes to communicate its message, and must then seek sponsorship vehicles whose audiences match that target market. As an example, the tour operator Kuoni Travel's sponsorship of Classic FM programmes matches Kuoni's target market with Classic FM's audience. Sponsorship often takes place at a local level; for example an estate agency moving into an area may seek to increase awareness of it by sponsoring a school fete or a local theatrical group.

It is difficult to evaluate sponsorship activities because of the problem of isolating the effects of sponsorship from other elements of the promotion mix. Direct measurement is likely to be possible only if sponsorship is the predominant tool. Sponsorship should therefore be seen as a tool that complements other elements of the promotion mix (Figure 11.18).

⊙ Direct marketing

Direct marketing entails companies opening up a dialogue directly between themselves and the end consumers of their products, thereby avoiding the need to communicate through indirect media such as press and television advertising. It can also allow a firm to communicate directly with its customers without having to go through retail or wholesale intermediaries. However, direct marketing is also compatible with a company using intermediaries (e.g. the manufacturer may use direct marketing to direct potential customers to its intermediaries). Direct marketing activities described in this section are often used to support other elements of the promotion mix and should therefore not be seen in isolation.

There is no universally agreed definition of what constitutes direct marketing, but we will begin with the definition used by the UK Direct Marketing Association. It defines direct marketing as: 'communications where data are used systematically to achieve quantifiable marketing objectives and where direct contact is invited or made between a company and its customers'.

Direct marketing has been growing very rapidly. Direct marketing is a major element of many firms' communication activities. According to a 2010 report by the UK Direct Marketing Association, more than £102 billion in sales are attributed to direct marketing—36 per cent of the £285 billion in retail sales recorded by the British Retail Consortium in 2009.

Figure 11.18 **Sponsorship of sporting events allows a company's brand name to be seen by viewers of the event and to associate the brand with the values of the sport concerned.** Cheltenham & Gloucester is the third largest provider of household mortgages in the UK, and has to compete with dozens of other banks and building societies for buyers' attention. By sponsoring a public activity, the brand name is exposed to potential buyers, especially, in this case, cricket fans, for whom C&G may be high on the list of brands which are spontaneously recalled. The company's financial services products are also likely to be associated with some of the characteristics of cricket—traditional, very English, fair, reliable, etc.
(Reproduced with kind permission of Cheltenham & Gloucester.)

Direct marketing is also responsible for nearly £76 billion in revenue for the consumer financial services sector (DMA 2010). As a further indicator of its significance to the marketing community, the Institute of Direct Marketing has estimated that 10 per cent of all new graduates entering marketing careers begin in direct marketing.

An important advantage of direct marketing is that it can target segments as small as one. This is fine for companies that produce high-value goods and services that are tailored to the needs of specific customers. It helps to explain the popularity of direct marketing in such sectors as computer hardware and motor insurance. However, many goods and services are capable of appealing to large groups of customers in their 'standard' form without any attempt at differentiation. Where the value of the goods is low and volume sales are high, the cost of attempting to communicate directly with each individual customer may be prohibitive.

The development of customer databases

At the heart of companies' direct marketing efforts is a database identifying prospective customers, current customers, and lapsed customers. The effectiveness of direct marketing is critically dependent on the quality of customer details held on the database. To many people, direct marketing has become synonymous with 'junk mail'. But mail becomes junk in the hands of the recipient only if it has been poorly targeted so that it does not meet the needs of the person to whom it has been sent. Consider the following cases:

1. A company selling garden furniture for domestic gardeners sent its catalogues to people living in upstairs flats in an inner-city area of London.

2. A bank that had just refused a loan to an individual shortly afterwards sent out a mailing to that same customer enclosing details of its loans and an application form.

3. A company manufacturing baby nappies sent promotional material and a trial offer for its products to a resident of a retirement home.

In each of these cases, it is just possible that the companies concerned had carefully studied their target market and made a decision that successfully hit their target market, even though it seemed intuitively ridiculous. (For example, the firm supplying garden furniture may have identified a group of flat dwellers who went away to their country cottages at the weekend.) However, the above examples serve only to show that the individual dialogue that is a defining characteristic of direct marketing cannot exist where a company is speaking to people who have no motivation whatsoever to enter into a dialogue.

So how does a company develop a database that at least allows it to enter into an appropriate dialogue with the right people? The most commonly used sources are:

⊙ **Routine customer enquiries:** Increasingly, companies are taking an enquirer's postcode very seriously. By analysing postcodes using a geodemographic system such as MOSAIC, a lot can be learned about the background of an enquirer. At the very least, a careful analysis of postcodes tells the company something about the geographical spread of its enquiries, something that may be vital to planning future marketing communications. It should also be able subsequently to identify which postcode areas result in the highest 'conversion' rate (that is, in a sale). Companies often go beyond asking for an enquirer's name and address. Typical additional questions include: where did you see the advertisement? (helps monitor the effectiveness of the firm's advertising); when do you intend to buy? (helps the company follow up an enquiry at a later date if the purchase intention is not immediate); do you currently own a specified item? (can help to distinguish first-time purchasers from replacement purchasers who may approach the purchase decision in quite different ways); and basic demographic details, such as age group and marital status (helps to develop a profile of an enquirer's needs specifically, and a profile of enquirers generally). Of course, companies can go too far in the information they collect from a casual enquiry and risk alienating the enquirer. There is also a danger that a firm's intermediaries may be suspicious of its opening a dialogue directly with what they regard as their own customers.

◉ Customer orders: Once a prospect has become an actual customer, a company can track subsequent purchases, building up a more refined profile of the customer's needs. From this it should spot opportunities for opening a dialogue to sell related or replacement products. If a company has maintained its database effectively, it should instantly be able to build up a picture of each of its customers. So when a customer calls in with an enquiry, any individual within the company taking the call should have available full details of the enquirer's recent transactions, notes about his preferences, and any problems that he might have encountered in the past.

◉ Buying in mailing lists: Leasing mailing lists has become a major industry in its own right, with numerous specialist marketing services companies offering mailing lists tailored to the needs of individual client companies. These list brokers gather information from multiple sources, including the electoral register, credit rating reports, consumer survey data, and other geographic data accumulated by recording an individual's previous transactions with other companies. Lists can become out of date very rapidly, so some mailing lists may be of dubious reliability. People moving house, deaths, and companies going out of business are typical reasons for a name on a mailing list no longer being a prospect. The better suppliers of mailing lists use multiple sources of information to confirm the existence of an individual on the list and to delete any if they have not had a recent positive confirmation of their existence. Merging multiple lists can be a highly complex task, with electronically stored lists coming in a variety of formats.

The manner in which companies buy and sell information about individuals raises a number of ethical and legal issues. Should a customer of a company have a right to consider the dialogue she enters into with the company to be private between the two parties? Is it then unethical for the company to sell on information about its customers to third-party companies? In the UK, the Data Protection Act 1998 gives individuals a general right to prevent a company from passing on their details to organizations other than the one to which they initially gave the information. There are also voluntary codes of conduct which restrict the ability of firms to exchange customers' personal information, for example in the UK, the Mailing Preference Service allows individuals to opt out of receiving direct mail. The direct marketing industry has become concerned at the rising number of people who choose not to allow their details to be passed on to other organizations. While the volume of junk mail has been reduced by better targeting by companies, junk email ('spam') is a growing problem.

There has been much talk of 'permission marketing', in which dialogue is based on buyers' giving permission for a company to communicate with them (Godin 2007). This puts greater control of marketing communications in the hands of the buyer, and technology is increasingly facilitating buyers' ability to be selective in what communications they choose to receive (Figure 11.19).

Profiling and targeting

With direct marketing, a company can use its database to develop a profile of who its best customers are. Consider the case of a direct response company advertising in the national press to promote a satellite navigation system, a product it has no previous experience in selling. It would probably have a reasonable idea of its target market from previous related selling experience, and may choose to advertise in national newspapers and magazines whose audience closely matches its own target market. Prospective customers would be invited to return a coupon or telephone for further information about the offer. The company would learn about the geodemographic profile of customers who responded, and through which medium they originally saw the promotional message. From its initial response, a company can get a reasonable idea of what type of person is showing most interest in its product. A further analysis is made to establish which types of respondent are the most successful prospects in terms of conversion to paying customers. Very often a company may find that a high level of initial enquiry among one segment is matched by a below-average level of conversions. Where this is the case, the company needs to examine the appeal of the offer to this segment. Was the product appropriately specified? Was it overpriced? Were the benefits of ownership stressed sufficiently?

For the initial enquirers who were converted into customers, the company can seek to obtain further information at the time of ordering (e.g. do they already own a navigation system, whether the purchase was for their personal use, business use, or a gift for someone else). If the company is offering credit facilities, this gives a further legitimate reason to collect more information to build up a profile of customers wishing to buy on credit.

Having started out with only a general idea about who constitutes its target market, the company now has a fairly detailed profile of who its customers are. If it is offering a range of accessory products, it would be able to identify who the most profitable customers will be in terms of the total value of their orders. The company can go on to track the purchases of those customers it had attracted with its initial offer. It may find that some converts went on to become regular customers not only of its navigation systems, but of its related product offers. These represent particularly attractive customers for the company, and it would seek to establish whether frequent buying is associated with any particular combination of an individual's demographic characteristics (e.g. aged under 30, living in a better residential area, and reading *FHM* magazine). The company may offer attractive incentives to obtain an initial purchase from this group, in the knowledge that there is a high probability of such buyers' going on to become regular, profitable customers.

Finally, a profile analysis of an organization's customers may suggest that some are unprofitable and are unlikely to ever become profitable. Just as a company requires a means of adding new prospects to its database, it requires a means of 'exiting' those who have not responded profitably to its attempts to create a dialogue. Companies may adopt a graduated

GUARANTEE REGISTRATION CARD

Name   Mr/Miss/Mrs/Other _____   First Name _____   Surname _____

Address   _____

Postcode   _____

Model No. of product purchased   HN_____

Where did you buy this product? _____

Which of the following best describes your reason for purchase?

Gift _____
Replacement for existing equipment_____
Purchase of addition equipment_____
First time purchase of this type of product_____

What is your age group?   Under 18 ☐   18–25 ☐   25–35 ☐

                                 36–45 ☐   46–55 ☐   56–65 ☐

                                 65+ ☐

Male or female?   Male ☐   Female ☐

Your occupation_____

Please tell us whether you own, or are considering buying, the following:

	Already own	Considering buying
Smart phone	☐	☐
HD satellite receiver	☐	☐
Tablet computer	☐	☐

Tick this box if you would like to be informed from time to time of new products and special offers. ☐

THANK YOU

Now return this card to the address shown overleaf.
You will also be entered in our monthly prize draw.

Figure 11.19 **Guarantee registration cards can say a lot about an individual.** Cards such as this one offer consumers who complete it a number of benefits, such as priority attention in the event of a safety recall of the product and entry into a prize draw. But the main beneficiary is the manufacturer, who gets to learn a lot about the profile of the buyer and his reasons for buying its products.

process of removing individuals from their active database. They may invite individuals to confirm that they want to continue mailings or reduce the frequency of mailings.

Companies are amassing increasing volumes of data with which to profile their customers and prospective customers. However, it is felt by many that the ability of companies to use such data effectively is lagging behind the growth in volume of data. Techniques such as artificial intelligence, fuzzy logic, and neural networks have been used to find patterns in large databases, and in particular to identify those variables that are most closely associated with sales and profitability (Ratner 2001).

Direct marketing media

One of the problems in defining and quantifying direct marketing is that it uses a wide range of media. So advertising could be used as part of traditional mass marketing strategy, or it could be used to try and initiate a direct dialogue between a company and its prospective customers. Direct mail (sending printed materials to individual customers through the mail), and telemarketing (using the telephone inbound and outbound calls) are more likely to be used once a customer profile has been developed.

E-Marketing

Telecoms companies are particularly bad at communicating, says report

The phenomenal development of telecommunications over the past couple of decades should have opened up tremendous new opportunities for two-way communication between a company and its customers—actual and potential. But there is still evidence that service companies can be slow to embrace the interactive communication abilities of the telephone and Internet. Research undertaken in 2006 by the e-services provider Transversal showed that the UK telecoms sector, which should have been at the forefront of the telecommunications revolution, was actually performing badly at communication. The report found phone companies to be among the slowest at answering their phones, with some, such as Carphone Warehouse apparently being overwhelmed at their call centres. Answering a phone is generally more expensive than having customers communicating through a website, entering all data themselves and using their time rather than a call centre operator's time to search for results. But the phone companies didn't seem to do well here either. The report found that only a third provided an online customer search function, down from 70 per cent in 2005. Furthermore, the telephone companies' websites could answer an average of just 2 out of 11 most basic customer questions such as 'How do I upgrade my phone?' Online users who sent an email to the company to resolve a problem would typically wait 48 hours for a reply, and many email requests for information simply did not get answered.

It is easy to say that telecommunications improve the ability of companies to communicate with their customers, but technology alone will not improve communication. Telecommunications companies should be at the leading edge when it comes to the enabling technology, but did they have the management abilities to put the technology to good use? Or were they simply victims of their own success, and as they grew, their capacity to handle calls continually lagged behind customer demand? Had the communications revolution led to higher expectations by customers, who may have been happy to wait several days for an answer, but now want an instant response, 24/7? And with communication costing money, could facilitating easier communication simply result in more calls from customers, adding to a company's costs and putting it at a disadvantage in a price sensitive market?

◉ Online communication

We have already mentioned some of the advantages of online marketing in our previous discussion of the elements of the promotion mix and noted the overlap between promotion mix elements. Consider some of the overlaps with online promotion:

- ◉ The definition of advertising includes web pages which broadcast to large numbers of people but are not interactive.

- ◉ Personal selling is increasingly relying on online communication to support the efforts of sales personnel.

- ◉ Public relations professionals have understood the potential impacts of social networking websites on a company's reputation and have developed web-based tools of their own.

- ◉ Online media have become an integral element of direct marketing by opening up a channel through which a company can enter an interactive dialogue with its customers.

Communication using online media has gone through a number of stages of development. At the most basic level, a company's website can simply give additional information about its goods and services, for example many hotels have websites which give information about their location and the facilities available. At this stage of development, the Internet is being used simply as an online form of the traditional printed brochure. Although a static, one-to-all website may now seem quite unadventurous, we should nevertheless recognize the advantages that a web page has over traditional printed brochures:

- ◉ They are much less expensive to produce.

- ◉ They can be updated very rapidly (e.g. in response to a price change) without the need to destroy existing sticks of brochures.

- ◉ Information can be provided immediately to prospective customers anywhere in the world, without the need to wait for a postal delivery.

- ◉ Comprehensive information can be provided within the site—more than could realistically be provided within a printed brochure.

- ◉ Links can be provided to other related information (e.g. a hotel can include a link to local tourist attractions).

The second stage of online development allows some degree of interactive dialogue between a company and visitors to its website. At its simplest, this can allow a visitor to the site to send a message to the company, perhaps to request further information. Interactivity could be added by creating a script which allows the visitor to ask simple questions and for the site to generate answers which are of direct relevance to the customer (e.g. the bank's website may include a simple ready reckoner to allow the user to calculate the monthly repayments on a mortgage). More complex interactivity can be developed by linking the customer's request to a database of information. This is used by railway operators (e.g. www.nationalrail.co.uk) to provide precise information on possible rail journeys in response to a customer's request for information on train times between two specified points at a specified time. Many online service providers use targeted email services to encourage customers to visit their sites. The travel and leisure company Lastminute.com, for example, claims to send more than two million emails to customers every week. The content of the email is tailored to fit the recipient's age, lifestyle, and other factors (Kirchgaessner 2003).

The third stage of online development is to allow immediate fulfilment of a request, such as confirmation of a hotel booking or reservation of a plane ticket. By linking a customer's online request to a real-time database of availability, the company is able to immediately communicate a specific price/product offer. Many airline and hotel companies have used the principles of yield management to continually change their price and product offer to reflect the changing balance between supply and demand, so the message that it sends to a site visitor may be quite different to one that it sent even just half an hour previously.

Communication through social network media

More recently, Web 2.0 has allowed much more interactivity between customers themselves. More fundamentally, the question has been raised whether companies can ever again be in control of their communication in an environment of peer-to-peer social network media.

The development of social network media is having profound effects on patterns of communication. We have already seen how viral marketing can rapidly build or undermine the company's position in the markets it serves. Purchase decisions taken by customers are increasingly likely to be affected by peer group communication rather than 'official' communication from the company.

A distinguishing feature of social network sites is the apparent willingness and ability of individuals to communicate their thoughts to others, including people who they do not know. Many strong brands such as Skype have been built with very little paid for advertising and instead relied on referral through online communities.

Many companies have started to use Web 2.0 technologies, such as blogs and video clips, to increase the level of engagement with buyers. An example from the public sector was Transport for London's 2008 campaign to improve the safety of cyclists. In an effort to demonstrate the need to pay attention to cyclists, visitors to its website were shown a game of basketball and asked to count the number of basketball passes. Somebody in a bear suit danced through the team, but this was initially unseen by the majority of people until they were told about it afterwards. The film acquired a cult status and was reportedly viewed by over eight million people in the month after its launch, almost entirely through word of mouse referral (Readon 2009). Of course, although millions of people might have visited the site, it cannot be assumed that the attitude of visitors had been changed in the way that Transport for London had intended. A plethora of social networking sites, such as Facebook and Bebo, plus many specialized niche sites have emerged through which companies have sought engagement as part of a community.

Online communities present a number of opportunities for companies to get close to their markets, including observing and collecting information; hosting or sponsoring communities; providing content to communities (such as music, information or entertainment); and participating as members of online communities (Miller et al. 2009). A company's involvement in social network sites can result in a wide range of strategic and operational benefits. By inviting feedback, or simply observing conversations, a company can learn about customers' needs and inform its new product development policy (Constantinides and Fountain 2008).

Companies would generally love their product to be at the heart of a community, and there have been many examples of companies who have developed social network media to put them at the centre of a community. Starbucks, for example, has a Facebook site which claimed to have 1,727,314 'fans' in 2009; it is present on Twitter; has its own YouTube channel and its own online community web pages (MyStarbucksIdeas, Starbucks V2V, and StarbucksRed).

Online communities can pose a threat as well as an opportunity to companies as they can rapidly spread the views of dissatisfied, angry customers (Figure 11.20). As an example, the bank HSBC announced in 2007 that it intended to end interest-free overdrafts for students after they had graduated, but was subsequently forced to do a U-turn and restore the facility. Many commentators attributed this change of heart to the strength of feeling expressed through Facebook circles of friends.

E-Marketing

Firms face up to Facebook

The communication environment has changed rapidly in recent years and the development of Web 2.0 technologies has facilitated communication between customers themselves, as well as between companies and their customers. So-called 'social network' sites such as Facebook and YouTube have led to many widely-publicized problems for companies. For example, in 2005, the computer manufacturer Dell was hit by influential blogger Jeff Jarvis complaining about poor customer service provided by Dell.

Fellow consumers, no longer passive in their dissatisfaction, joined in with comments of their own, and stories of 'Dell Hell' rapidly became mainstream news. The company was rudely awoken to the power of social media and realized that simply trying to silence one individual or sue them for libel was never going to be effective. It subsequently put a lot of effort into engaging with social media, including the appointment of a 'coordinator of customer messages'.

Figure 11.20 **It should never be forgotten that the most powerful form of promotion is word-of-mouth recommendation. For many people, booking a hotel may involve a high level of perceived risk.**
Rather than relying on the hotel's own description, buyers are increasingly turning to customer review sites to find out whether other customers would recommend a hotel. Maybe the official hotel website didn't say anything about the factory opposite, whose workers noisily and abruptly woke people up at 6 am. Hiding this on the official hotel website wouldn't be a lie, but increasingly people are prepared to volunteer the whole story to other potential customers. However, even customer review sites can be ambiguous, with competitors trying to sabotage other hotels while covertly praising their own. Many companies have realized that they cannot ignore customer review sites, or hope to control them, so they need to find a way of engaging with them.

There is a lot of research indicating that for high involvement products, consumers turn initially to their friends for recommendations. But how can you trust friends in a global community comprising millions of users who contribute to peer-to-peer sites? Inevitably, when an Internet forum provides free access to all, it will include material posted by cranks, criminals, and smart companies who have learnt how to anonymously provide a good recommendation about their own organization, and to criticize their competitors. Peer review sites for restaurants and hotels have become difficult to manage, with many allegations that hotels have simply submitted a glowing recommendation for their establishment, passed off as the comments of a very satisfied customer. Inevitably, some sites have become more trusted than others, on account of their greater diligence in spotting false postings. It seems that there will always be a role for impartial communication by companies and intermediaries that can be trusted. Despite the availability of a plethora of free hotel review sites, paid for hotel guides such as Frommer's travel guides, continue to prosper, based on the trust that they have developed as a communication source.

Increasingly, companies have been mingling in social networks sites, and have sometimes created their own sites as community forums. Dell, for example, established the Dell2Dell blog, in an attempt to gain some control over communication about it. But on other occasions, companies have sponsored blogs without declaring their hand. The retailer Walmart covertly sponsored a blog which was supposedly operated by a couple camping in the store's car parks. It had hoped to manipulate content to show the company in a good light, but eventually the exercise turned into a PR disaster when news broke that the company had in fact been controlling the blog.

A significant challenge for companies is the sometimes blurred distinction between communication that is internal and external to company. Social networking sites allow employees to spread stories of dissent about their company among their circle of friends. Using simpler communication technologies, a slanderous comment about a bad employer might have gone no further than a small circle of friends and family. But with large numbers of friends linked through Facebook and Twitter, dissent can spread much more widely. For example, there have been many reported cases of disgruntled restaurant workers who have told the world about disgusting kitchens that they work in, but which customers do not ordinarily get to see. Some websites, such as www.wikkileaks.com make a point of publicizing business and government policy documents that they would rather keep secret. Previously a document marked 'Top Secret' would have had to have been physically stolen and copied to have an impact. Today the disgruntled employee can download the document and have it on the screens of millions of people within hours.

Choice of online channels

As use of the Internet as a communication medium has increased, it has become increasingly cluttered. This effect has been seen during the development of all media, and companies using the Internet have faced increasing challenges in drawing people to their website. Getting a high ranking in search engines has become a critical skill and specialist companies are often employed to raise a client's rankings. From being a very cheap source of messages, companies have to spend increasing amounts of money promoting their web presence, both online and offline.

According to data from the UK Online Measurement Company (UKOM) and Nielsen, by December 2010 the UK's active online user base had grown to 40.3 million and social networks accounted for 25 per cent of the time spent online in the UK. Internet advertising continues to grow rapidly. In its annual survey of the UK, the Internet Advertising Bureau estimated that total UK Internet advertising expenditure in 2010 was £4 billion, up by 12.8 per cent over the previous year and it claimed that as much as 25 per cent of all firms' advertising spend went on Internet media. In 2010 the biggest gain was display advertising, attributed to a nearly 200 per cent increase in display advertising in a social media environment and 91 per cent year-on-year increase in video formats. Paid search continued to perform strongly, with growth of 8 per cent year-on-year to £2,346 million, representing 57 per cent of total online spend (61 per cent in 2009) (IAB 2011).

There are several methods that online service providers use to charge for advertising. 'Pay per click' involves a company paying a fee every time their advert on another site is clicked on. Google, Yahoo, and other companies offer these facilities, but they are susceptible to abuse—companies can click on a competitor's banner adverts to drive up its costs, possibly getting them removed from the search results page if they reach their maximum ad budget. Other methods of buying advertising include paying per visitor to a website; paying per thousand people exposed to a message; and paying commission only if an actual transaction takes place.

Search marketing typically involves an advertiser paying to sponsor individual key words on Internet search engines such as Google or Yahoo. When a visitor to the search engine enters the keywords, the advertiser's entry is listed as a sponsored link. This puts the advertiser at the top of a long list—possibly thousands or even millions—of websites which match the search criteria. The visitor can then click on this link to arrive at the advertiser's website. Very often, the advertiser will have prepared slightly different pages, to reflect the keyword which was originally searched for. Search marketing is becoming increasingly sophisticated, and can involve intermediaries and affiliates all competing for the same keywords, providing alternate routes to potential customers. For example, somebody searching for a flight from Manchester to Paris might find at the top of their search list the site of an airline (e.g. Air France), or they may find the site of a travel agency offering flights (e.g. Opodo), or they may find a customer review or 'cashback' site (e.g. topcashback.co.uk) which earns a commission for referral of customers. Search is also becoming increasingly sophisticated in its geographic targeting. Until recently, geographical targeting was based on very crude national boundaries, for example a user based in the UK entering 'mobile phone deals' would see UK-based mobile phone companies, while the visitor based in the USA would see American-based companies. As the Internet becomes more widely available through mobile phones and PDAs linked to a global positioning system, search can be made geographically very specific.

While the level of sophistication in search marketing has been going up, the cost of entry has also been rising. It is no longer realistic to plan the launch of a major brand from a small home office with a budget of just a few hundred pounds—as many entrepreneurs in the early stages of Internet development managed to do. Pricing of keywords has risen steadily as more advertisers have been drawn into the market. Companies in highly competitive markets are likely to bid up the prices paid for key terms such as 'cheap car insurance' or 'mobile phone deals'.

Integrating online with other media

For most companies, online cannot really be considered in isolation from other elements of the promotion mix. Online adverts are increasingly used to support printed and broadcast media, and such ads now routinely include a website address where a reader or viewer can find more information. The Internet should be used to provide a form of communication which is not possible using other media, for example a bank's press advertising may give

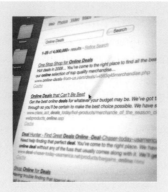

Figure 11.21 **For many generic type services which can be searched using easy to specify criteria, search engines have become an important battleground for capturing the attention of buyers.** If you are a hotel offering budget accommodation in London, you would want to be top of the list of results for people who enter the term 'London budget hotel' into a search engine such as Google, rather than being lost somewhere on page 24, which very few users would click through to. If you are a big hotel with lots of other websites providing links to your site, you may just come close to the top of the list without much effort. But in reality, you may need to bid for key words so that you come top of the page as a sponsored link. Generic and popular search terms can be expensive to purchase. Further complication arises because your agents may be bidding against you for the same keywords. Even if you include your hotel name as a paid for search term, competitors might have outbid you, in the hope that anybody looking for your site will instead find the competitor's site at the top of their search results. In the early days of the Internet, many people expected the Internet to make inexpensive advertising available to all. However, with the growing sophistication of online promotion, many companies have had to increase their budgets sharply for search engine optimization and employed specialists to undertake the task.

general information about personal loans, but its website can incorporate a personalized loan repayment calculator. A picture of a car in a glossy Sunday magazine can be supplemented on the manufacturer's website with video clips and information about how the car can be personalized to suit their preferences.

The Internet Advertising Bureau (www.iabuk.net) has made a number of recommendations for companies planning to engage in online marketing, and these emphasize integration with the offline environment. It has noted, for example, the importance of including words used in offline campaigns in their paid for search advertising.

Although some companies, such as Amazon, rely on online channels for almost all of their promotion, most companies recognize that the medium is not suitable for all products or all target customers. Although the majority of the population in most western countries now has access to the Internet, there are still large groups, especially of elderly people, who do not routinely have access and must be targeted through alternative media. Some products are more suitable than others for online promotion. In the case of high involvement purchases, which require a sense of touch, smell, or feel to fully evaluate the product, promotion through the medium of the Internet may be a limitation. Doubt has been expressed whether it is possible to build a strong brand using Internet media alone (Figure 11.21).

⦿ Chapter summary and linkages to other chapters

Very few products can be sold in competitive markets without some form of promotion. This chapter has shown how the features of a product need to be communicated to potential buyers as benefits that will satisfy a need. We saw in Chapter 4 that needs can be complex, and can change over time for an individual. Promotion can help to take people through a number of stages of the buying process, from merely being aware of a product through to committing themselves to a purchase. Messages are communicated through channels to reach a target audience. The existence of 'noise' means that the message that was encoded and sent is not the same as the one that is received and decoded. This chapter has reviewed the elements of the promotion mix. Although each element of the mix has a different role to play, they are very much interdependent. The headings this chapter has used to define the elements of the promotion mix are to some extent arbitrary, and we have seen, for example, how advertising is often an important part of sales promotion and direct marketing activity.

This chapter has stressed that promotion planning is an integral part of the marketing and business planning process. The promotional message must be consistent with the positioning of a product (Chapters 6 and 7), its price position (Chapter 9), and its availability (Chapter 10). Promotion becomes more complex where overseas markets are involved (Chapter 12).

🔍 KEY PRINCIPLES OF MARKETING

- Promotional messages should translate product features into benefits for buyers.

- Objectives set for individual elements of the promotion mix must be consistent with overall marketing objectives.

- The audience for a promotional message should correspond to the target market for the product being promoted.

- There can be multiple targets involved in promoting a product, including all members of a decision-making unit and the intermediaries that handle the product.

- Communication is a process that aims to take a target through stages from awareness to action.

- The promotional objectives for a product must be related to the stage of the product's life-cycle.

- Definitions of the elements of the promotion mix are not watertight and all elements overlap with each other.

- The effects of any promotional medium will be greater if its message is integrated with other media.

- All elements of the promotion mix involve a process of analysis, objective setting, development of strategies, implementation, and evaluation.

CASE STUDY

Online advertising goes mobile

In life generally, it is widely recognized that there can be a time and a place to communicate a message. Your friend may not appreciate an invitation to spend a night on the town just before their pay day when they are broke, but a couple of days later, the message may be more keenly taken up. In the world of advertising media, the past hundred years has seen a dramatic improvement in the ability of media to target messages on the basis of time and place. Ten years ago, the main medium for advertising was the printed press, which had only a very crude ability to segment by time, but nevertheless it did happen; for example Friday editions of newspapers have tended to carry more advertising than other days, ahead of weekend shopping trips. Segmentation by place was technically very difficult for national newspapers, and it has only been quite recently that regional editions of national newspapers have become widespread, supplementing local titles for a share of local advertising expenditure. Television improved segmentation by time, for example the typical audience profile for daytime television can be quite different to the audience for evening peak hour programmes.

The Internet has opened up tremendous new possibilities for segmentation by time and place. The time aspect has been well developed by many companies' Internet-based communication. The live nature of the Internet means that a company can change its message throughout the day or week to cater for visitors' fluctuating motivations. As an example, some insurance companies have been reported to charge different premiums depending upon the time of an inquiry. The rationale could be that an enquirer for car insurance at 9 am on a Monday morning might have been desperate to renew their insurance because it had just expired, therefore will be less likely to shop around for the best deal, and will more readily accept a higher premium. On the other hand, an enquirer at 5 pm may be casually surfing a few sites before they go home from work, and may be more price sensitive than the morning shopper.

A problem for Internet advertising so far has been its inability to fully exploit segmentation by place. An advertiser generally has little idea about the geographical location of the visitors to its site. Online advertisers would normally expect statistics showing the domain where a visitor came from, and the country with which that domain is associated. However, it has been technically very difficult to show even in which region, let alone which town or part of the town the visitor is based. There is also a problem that the buyer may be using an office computer with a different location to their home address.

Is mobile marketing about to exploit the opportunities for time- and place-specific advertising? As with any new technology-based advertising medium which comes along, there were initial doubts about the true potential of the medium. According to the UK's Internet Advertising Bureau, mobile advertising experienced a massive 116 per cent year-on-year growth from 2009 to 2010. Advertisers spent £83 million on mobile advertising in 2010, led by the entertainment and media sectors, with significant growth from finance, telecoms, and consumer goods advertisers.

For search-based advertising companies such as Yahoo and Google, which dominate Internet advertising, the mobile market offers a new, much larger market of more than three billion consumers worldwide, compared to about one billion on the fixed-line Internet. Media buyers have been enthusiastic about the mobile phone's ability to tailor advertising to specific audiences, particularly teenagers. Moreover, messages could be targeted precisely at the time and a place when the receiver is most likely to be receptive to a message. They were encouraged by early reports of high response rates for mobile campaigns. Vodafone claimed in 2007 that it was obtaining a two per cent click-through rate on banner ads on its mobile Internet pages, more than ten times the response rate to ads on the fixed-line Internet. Rival UK operator 3 UK claimed an 8–10 per cent click-through in ads on its mobile portal. However, sceptics urged caution over these apparently good early results, and pointed out that high response rates could be attributed to the novelty of the medium. A decade earlier, when the Internet was still a novelty, click-through rates were similarly high, but have since declined.

Key to the success of mobile marketing is the creation of a user friendly experience. Many critics have pointed out that navigating the Internet on a tiny screen can be extremely difficult, so mobile advertisers and network operators have been keen to simplify this process, and to link mobile advertising with offline advertising. To this end, mobile operators have been carrying out experiments to try and judge the likely take-up of mobile advertising. As on previous occasions when new mobile technologies have emerged, they have looked to the affluent, technologically savvy countries of the Far East to try and assess the likely take-up in western markets.

In Singapore, the operator M1 launched a location-based marketing service. Having opted-in, a user walking along Orchard Road, Singapore's main shopping street, would receive messages offering discounts in stores or restaurants as they approached them. Shopkeepers, who typically cut 10 per cent off their prices, were able to address customers who might otherwise have passed them by. Restaurants could offer discounts to attract early and late diners, filling capacity during their quieter hours. The operator also undertook a trial to link the world of mobile advertising with the real physical world. It had acknowledged that navigating the Internet on a mobile phone was slow and difficult, so sought to simplify the process by linking outdoor billboards to websites. A number of billboards appeared with bar codes, which could be read by mobile phone cameras. As soon as the bar code was read, the mobile phone would be linked to the advertiser's website, giving more information about the product.

Providing a link between the mobile world and the real physical world may be the key to overcoming the problem of navigating the Internet on a small screen. Many have seen hope in the idea of widespread use of barcodes printed on physical objects, such as magazines or product packaging, at which a mobile phone user could point their camera phone and find out more about the product directly from the advertiser's website. This vision led to the creation of the Mobile Codes Consortium, an initiative launched in 2008 by Hewlett-Packard, Publicis, and NeoMedia to push for greater technology standardization in the emerging field of '2D barcodes'.

There may be many more problems to overcome before mobile advertising becomes truly mainstream. Many people have bought mobile phones which are capable of accessing the Internet, but simply do not use this facility. In 2007, the mobile phone manufacturer Motorola claimed that typically only 10–20 per cent of owners of smart phones had used the browser on their mobile to connect to the Internet. Many may have been deterred by the mobile phone companies' practice of charging on the basis of cost per minute or per byte downloaded. This issue was addressed when operators such as Vodafone moved to a flat rate charging method, but this itself created problems as some users used their unlimited data allowance to download lengthy videos, causing capacity problems on the operators' networks.

A further challenge is data protection legislation, which requires customers to opt in before they receive unsolicited messages. Targeting hungry diners as they pass a restaurant with empty tables may seem attractive in principle, but the legislation of most countries requires permission from the receiver before they can be sent unsolicited messages. There was clearly a great need for the mobile sector to put its house in order if users were not to be deterred from giving permission by stories of relentless spam mail.

Measuring the effectiveness of mobile ads has been a big problem. Click-through rates on banners and messages can be counted, but there is little agreement on how to calculate the reach of a display or video ad, for example. A study by Jupiter Research in 2006 indicated that 47 per cent of executives responsible for mobile advertising said they had problems with measurement and reporting of mobile campaigns. To make matters worse, mobile phone operators have historically been secretive with their key customer data, and nearly half of advertising buyers polled in the Jupiter survey identified measurement difficulties as an important obstacle in mobile advertising. In 2008, the principal UK mobile phone operators agreed, under the auspices of the GSM Association—the global trade association for the handset industry—to pool information on customer numbers and usage patterns. The aim was to develop a common set of metrics for measuring the reach of mobile advertising.

A final problem that mobile advertisers had to face up to was a proliferation of mobile technologies. The 3G phone was just one medium through which to target buyers on the move. It had to compete for attention with WiFi networks, and the prospect of national rollouts of such networks and longer range WiMax networks, which did not directly involve 3G technology. Podcasts which could be downloaded onto a person's home computer and listened to on their MP3 player may have been a more attractive alternative for many people seeking content over which they have control.

Case study review questions

1. Critically assess the likely opportunities and problems of mobile advertising for a national chain of restaurants.

2. Discuss methods that could be used to assess the effectiveness of mobile advertising.

3. Discuss the relationship between mobile advertising and other elements of the promotion in campaign planning.

CHAPTER REVIEW QUESTIONS

1. What is the relationship between selling and marketing?

2. Critically evaluate the steps that companies can take to ensure that their direct mail does not become 'junk' mail.

3. What do you understand by the term 'promotional campaign', and how can a firm assess whether its campaign has been successful?

ACTIVITIES

1. Collect publicity material and media reports for a selection of major football clubs (e.g. Manchester United) or leading theatrical companies (e.g. Royal Shakespeare Company). Identify which commercial organizations sponsor them, either as primary or secondary sponsors. Evaluate how well you think the sponsorship works for all parties.

2. Undertake a critical assessment of the last time you purchased a reasonably high involvement product such as a holiday or university course. Identify the main sources of communication that influenced your eventual choice, noting the effects of messages derived from within and beyond the service provider. Now repeat the exercise on friends to see if a consistent pattern emerges.

3. Go through a glossy magazine and select a sample of adverts for durable consumer goods. Critically assess the messages contained in the adverts and in the context of a buyer response model, try and understand what the intended response of the message may be.

REFERENCES

Audit Bureau of Circulation (2011) Certificate Reports. www.abc.org.uk/Certificates-Reports/Our-Reports (accessed 12 August 2011).

Cardwell, A. (2002) 'Subliminal Advertising'. *Ziff Davis Smart Business*, 15 (3), 51–2.

Chung-kue, H. and McDonald, D. (2002) 'An Examination on Multiple Celebrity Endorsers in Advertising'. *Journal of Product & Brand Management*, 11 (1), 19–29.

Constantinides, E. and Fountain, S.J. (2008) 'Web 2.0: Conceptual Foundations and Marketing Issues'. *Journal of Direct, Data, and Digital Marketing Practice*, 9 (3), 231–44.

Cummings, P. (2007) 'The Power of Celebrity Endorsement: Do Celebrities Add Value to a Brand Campaign? How to Get the Best and What to Expect in Return'. *Journal of Sponsorship*, 1 (1), 67–71.

DMA (2010) *Value of Direet Marketing*. London: Direct Marketing Association.

Drucker, P. (1973) *Management: Tasks, Responsibilities and Practices.* New York: Harper & Row.

Ferguson, R. (2008) 'Word of Mouth and Viral Marketing: Taking the Temperature of the Hottest Trends in Marketing'. *Journal of Consumer Marketing*, 25 (3), 179–82.

Fill, C. (2009) *Marketing Communications: Interactivity, Communities and Content.* London: FT Prentice Hall.

Forrester Research (2006) *Information Fabric, Enterprise Data Virtualization.* Cambridge, MA: Forrester Research.

Godin, S. (2007) *Permission Marketing: Turning Strangers into Friends and Friends into Customers*. New York: Pocket Books.

Henderson B.S. (2000) 'Are So-called Successful Advertising Campaigns Really Successful?' *Journal of Advertising Research*, 40 (6), 25–31.

IAB (2011) Online Adspend 2010, London, Internet Advertising Bureau. Available at http://www.iabuk.net/en/1/adspendbreaks4billionmilestone280311.mxs; (accessed 5 May 2011).

Jones, K. (2008) *Search Engine Optimization: Your Visual Blueprint for Effective Internet Marketing*. Chichester: John Wiley.

Joyce, T. (1967) 'What do we know about how advertising works?' Brussels: ESOMAR seminar.

Kirchgaessner, S. (2003) 'Need Inflatable Sheep, Fast? Lastminute.com: Speed and Reliability are Essential Ingredients for Online Success'. *Financial Times*, 5 February, 4.

Kotler, P., Rackham, N., and Krishnaswamy, S. (2006) 'Ending the War Between Sales and Marketing'. *Harvard Business Review*, July.

Kwak, H., Fox, R.J., and Zinkhan, G.M. (2002) 'What Products Can Be Successfully Promoted and Sold via the Internet?' *Journal of Advertising Research*, 42 (1), 23–38.

Lauf, E. (2001) 'The Vanishing Young Reader'. *European Journal of Communication*, 16 (2), 233–44.

Lynch, D. (2001) 'The Magic of *Harry Potter*'. *Advertising Age*, 72 (50), 26.

Miller, K.D., Fabian, F., and Lin, S.J. (2009) 'Strategies for Online Communities'. *Strategic Management Journal*, 30 (3), 305–22.

OFCOM (2010) *Seventh Annual Communications Market Report*. London: OFCOM.

Ratner, B. (2001) 'Finding the Best Variables for Direct Marketing Models'. *Journal of Targeting, Measurement & Analysis for Marketing*, 9 (3), 270–96.

Readon, J. (2009) 'Viral marketing: Alternative reality' (electronic version), *Brand Strategy*, 44 (23 February), accessed 5 May 2010.

Richardson, G.W. (2001) 'Looking for Meaning in All the Wrong Places: Why Negative Advertising is a Suspect Category'. *Journal of Communication*, 51, 775–90.

Rogers, E.M. (2003) *Diffusion of Innovation*. New York: Free Press.

Smith, P. and Taylor, J. (2004) *Marketing Communications: An Integrated Approach*, London: Kogan Page.

Steward, K. (1993) *Marketing Led, Sales Driven: Professional Selling in a Marketing Environment*. Oxford: Butterworth-Heinemann.

Susskind, A.M. (2002) 'I Told You So! Restaurant Customers' Word-of-mouth Communication Patterns'. *Cornell Hotel & Restaurant Administration Quarterly*, 43 (2), 75–85.

The Times (2002), 'Media Age Poses Threat to Reputations'. London: *The Times* (Business), 1 May, 29.

Vogt, P. (2009) 'Brands Under Attack: Marketers Can Learn From Domino's Video Disaster'. *Forbes*, available at: www.forbes.com/2009/04/24/dominos-youtube-twitter-leadership-cmo-network-marketing.html (accessed 20 May 2009).

Walker, L. J.-H. (2001) 'The Measurement of Word-of-mouth Communication and an Investigation of Service Quality and Customer Commitment as Potential Antecedents'. *Journal of Service Research*, 4 (1), 60–75.

SUGGESTED FURTHER READING

For a fuller discussion of the general principles of promotion, the following texts cover the main elements of the promotion mix:

Egan, J. (2007) *Marketing Communications.* London: Cengage.

Fill, C. (2009) *Marketing Communications: Interactivity, Communities and Content.* London: FT Prentice Hall.

Advertising is explored in more detail in the following:

Burtenshaw, K., Mahon, N., and Barfoot C. (2006) *The Fundamentals of Creative Advertising.* Worthing: AVA Publishing.

Ogilvy, D. (2007) *Ogilvy on Advertising.*, London: Prion Books.

Pricken, M. (2008) *Creative Advertising: Ideas and Techniques from the World's Best Campaigns.* London: Thames and Hudson.

Public Relations is explored in more detail in the following:

L'Etang, J. (2007) *Public Relations: Concepts, Practice and Critique.* London: Sage.

Tench, R. and Yeomans, L. (2009) *Exploring Public Relations.* London: FT Prentice Hall.

For an overview of direct marketing and online media, the following are useful:

Chaffey, D., Ellis-Chadwick, F., Johnston, K., and Mayer, R. (2008) *Internet Marketing: Strategy, Implementation and Practice.* London: FT Prentice Hall.

Fox, V. (2010) *Marketing in the Age of Google.* New York: John Wiley.

Scoble, R. and Israel, S. (2006) *Naked Conversations: How Blogs are Changing the Way Businesses Talk with Customers.* Hoboken, NJ: John Wiley.

Tapp, A. (2008) *Principles of Direct and Database Marketing*, 4th edition. London: FT Prentice Hall.

The challenges of integrating media channels are discussed in the following:

Clow K.E. and Baack, D.E. (2008) *Integrated Advertising, Promotion, and Marketing Communications.* Harlow: Pearson.

Shimp, T. (2009) *Integrated Marketing Communications in Advertising and Promotion*, 8th international edition. Boston, MA: South Western.

ONLINE RESOURCE CENTRE

Visit the Online Resource Centre for resources that are relevant to this chapter, including a flashcard glossary, web links, multiple choice questions, and additional case studies:

   www.oxfordtextbooks.co.uk/orc/palmer3e/

KEY TERMS

- Advertising
- Buyer-readiness state
- Communication models
- Communication process
- Decoding
- Direct mail
- Direct marketing
- Encoding
- Key account management
- Lobbying
- Mailing lists
- Noise
- Online marketing
- Personal selling

- Press release
- Promotion mix
- Prospecting
- Public relations
- Sales promotion
- Search marketing
- Social network sites
- Sponsorship
- Target audience
- Telemarketing
- Viral marketing
- Voluntary codes
- Word-of-mouth

BRINGING IT TOGETHER

Part 4

MANAGING THE MARKETING EFFORT IN A GLOBAL ENVIRONMENT

12

CHAPTER OBJECTIVES

This chapter brings together the theory of the previous chapters in a framework that can be implemented by marketing managers. Too many marketing plans fail to be implemented effectively, and this chapter explores the bases for effective marketing management. Marketing management involves a never-ending process of analysis, planning, implementation, and control. Timely and relevant information, acted upon by appropriately structured and motivated management, is crucial to success. Marketing is becoming increasingly globalized, and this chapter brings together issues and challenges for marketing management as it goes global.

Introduction

A frequently heard comment about some aspects of marketing is that it is 'fine in theory, but doesn't work in practice'. This book has presented a lot of the theory that underlies marketing management decisions, but theory and good ideas alone will not create long-term profitability. Nor is it good enough just to have the right product at the right time. Good management is crucial to bringing about *sustainable* success.

Most people will have had experience of companies that do not appear to have the management capabilities necessary for success. At the operational level, inadequate investment in staff training and a distribution system that results in the wrong products being delivered late to the wrong place can be signs of bad management. At a strategic level, poor management can be seen by a preoccupation with declining products at the expense of new opportunities and a lack of information about current market conditions.

The challenges of putting marketing into practice become even greater in a globalized marketing environment. The number of companies who can regard their markets purely in terms of their home country is rapidly diminishing. Airlines, commercial banks, and consulting engineers have for a long time seen their markets in world terms. Companies operating in sectors such as electricity supply, office cleaning, and bus services would only a few years ago have most likely considered globalization to be something which only concerned other sectors, and not theirs. However, all of these sectors have seen companies expanding outside their domestic market. It may be fair to say that 'going global' is no longer an additional activity which companies may decide to become involved in. The reality for more and more companies is that they are already part of the globalized business environment. Even if they are not taking their products to overseas customers, they are quite likely to be facing competition from companies who are based abroad.

The purpose of this final chapter is to provide an overview of marketing implementation issues in an increasingly complex, globalized environment.

◉ What does a marketing manager do?

A good marketing manager has probably read something about the theories of marketing, but that alone is not enough. Being able to turn theory into practice demands a critical set of creative, analytical, and organizational skills.

There is an ongoing debate about whether marketing management is an art or a science. Those who advocate a scientific approach set great value in disciplined, structured procedures, for example in the way information is routinely collected and analysed. Rationality and reassurance underlie the scientific approach. Most of the top hundred UK companies have systematic procedures for management which make them a relatively safe bet for investors, even if they lack the occasional sparkle of smaller and more volatile companies.

Advocates of a more creative, artistic approach would argue that the business environment is changing rapidly and therefore a scientific framework, which works on the basis of previous models, may no longer be valid in the future. Furthermore, under the scientific approach it may take a long time to reach a decision, putting a firm at a competitive disadvantage in a fast-moving market. By taking a scientific approach, managers often end up breaking a large problem down into component sub-problems, and fail to take a holistic overview. If all other firms are following a similar scientific approach, using similar business models, they may all end up with 'me-too' strategies. A more creative approach is likely to encourage unique solutions which may either succeed spectacularly or fail miserably. Some would argue that large organizations stifle creativity in an individual, and point to entrepreneurs who have been creative in their thinking when they were setting up and growing a business, but who did not fit within the culture of a larger, structured organization which follows more rational, scientific processes.

Whether you accept marketing management as being essentially a structured, scientific process, or a creative one, knowledge is likely to be at the heart of the marketing manager's job. Many entrepreneurs have used a creative approach to obtaining, managing, and retaining knowledge about their marketing environment, but in larger organizations, a more structured approach is likely to be needed. We saw in Chapter 5 how, in large organizations, information is a medium for keeping in touch with customers, employees, suppliers, and intermediaries. Getting the right information to the right people at the right time is crucial if the management of a company is to be able to develop and implement a strategy. Without appropriate information, strategy formulation can become guesswork and the implementation of that strategy may be half-hearted. Inadequate monitoring may not warn of problems until it is too late to do anything about them.

◉ The marketing management process

Some companies are born, they grow quickly, and then rapidly go into decline and disappear. Sometimes, companies are set up to achieve a particular aim, and then when that is achieved, there is no need for the company to continue to exist. Most marketing managers, however, expect that their company will continue to operate into the future and it is therefore essential that the management continually reviews its achievements to date, and where it is going in the future. Marketing management can be seen as a continual process of analysis, goal setting, strategy, implementation, monitoring, and control. At the end of each period of marketing activity, managers should assess how well they have done, learn from their experience, and begin planning for the next period.

There are five key stages in the marketing management process (Figure 12.1):

1. **Where are we now? Analysis of the organization's current market position:** A vital starting-point for marketing planning is an analysis of a company's current marketing

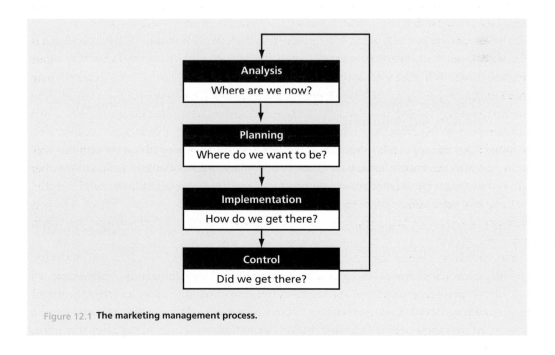

Figure 12.1 **The marketing management process.**

environment, often undertaken by means of a SWOT analysis or a marketing audit. A *marketing audit* has been defined as: 'a systematical, critical, and unbiased review and appraisal of the environment and of the company's operations. A marketing audit is part of the larger management audit and is concerned with the marketing environment and marketing operations' (McDonald 2002).

A marketing audit typically includes analysis of the organization's current market share, the size and nature of its customer base, customer perceptions of the organization's output, and the internal strengths and weaknesses of the organization in terms of production, personnel, and financial resources. A marketing audit addresses these issues using both quantitative and qualitative methods where appropriate. But what information should be collected? A company's mission statement can provide its employees with guidance about what is relevant and irrelevant in analysing its current position.

How much analysis of the current situation should a company undertake? While it is nearly always true that a sound analysis of the current situation is an essential prerequisite to developing a marketing plan for the future, excessive preoccupation with the current situation can have its costs. Analysis on its own will not provide the management decisions that are necessary for defining the future marketing plan. A 'paralysis by analysis' can occur in organizations that avoid making hard decisions about the future because they are continually seeking more information about the present. A plateau is usually reached at which little additional information is available that will improve the quality of marketing plan decisions. Worse still, in markets that are fast changing, excessive analysis of the current position can put a company at a competitive disadvantage to firms that are more willing to take a risk and exploit a market opportunity ahead of its competitors.

2. Where do we want to be? Setting marketing objectives: Without clearly specified objectives, marketing management can drift aimlessly. Objectives have a number of functions within an organization:

   (a) They add to the sense of purpose within the organization, without which there would be little focus for managers' efforts.

   (b) They help to achieve consistency between decisions made at different points within the organization; for example it would be inconsistent if a production manager used a production objective that was unrelated to the marketing manager's sales objective.

   (c) Objectives are used as motivational devices and can be used in a variety of formal and informal ways to stimulate increased performance by managers.

   (d) Objectives allow for more effective control within an organization. Unless clear objectives have been set at the outset, it is very difficult to know whether the firm has achieved what it set out to achieve, and what corrective action to take if its efforts seem to be going adrift during the plan period.

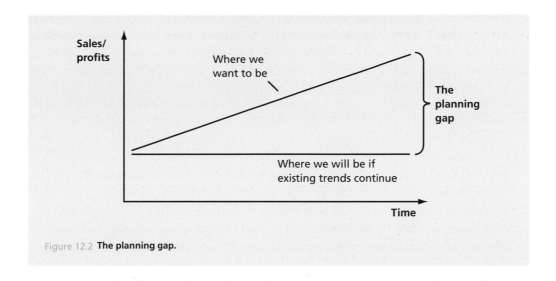

Figure 12.2 **The planning gap.**

To be effective, objectives must be capable of realistic achievement and must be accepted as such by the people responsible for acting on them. If objectives are set unattainably high, the whole process of planning can be brought into disrepute by the company's employees. Wherever possible, objectives should be quantified and should clearly specify the time period to which they relate. Inconsistency between objectives should be avoided. This sometimes occurs, for example, where sales objectives can be achieved only by reducing selling prices, thereby making it impossible to achieve a profitability objective.

3. How can we get there? Developing a marketing strategy: There are usually many ways in which marketing objectives can be achieved. For example, a financial return objective could be satisfied equally well by a high sales volume/low price strategy or a low volume/high price strategy. Identifying the strategic alternatives open to an organization relies on interpreting data and evaluating a number of possible future scenarios. Within this evaluation, factors such as the likelihood of success, the level of downside risk, and the amount of resources required to implement a strategy need to be taken into consideration. What may be an appropriate strategy for one company may be quite inappropriate for another, on account of differences in financial resources, past history, and personnel strengths, among other things.

It often happens that the objectives set for the planning period are greater than what could be achieved if growth occurred at the historic trend rate. Where such a 'planning gap' exists, the aim of the planning process is to develop a strategy that will close this gap. This can be done either by reducing the original objective downward to a level that is more realistic, given the historical pattern, or by accelerating the trend rate from its historical pattern to a higher level by means of marketing strategy. In practice, the planning gap is reduced by a combination of revising objectives and amending marketing strategies (Figure 12.2).

There have been many prescriptions for developing marketing strategies, some of which were discussed in Chapter 7 in the context of the development of a sustainable competitive advantage.

4. **How will we implement the strategy?** Having chosen a strategy, the next step is to implement it. This is usually done through a 12-month marketing plan, although the length of the plan period can depend on the amount of turbulence in a company's marketing environment. The marketing plan sets out programmes for, among other things, the timing and costing of promotional programmes, pricing plans, and the recruitment and payment of distributors. The plan should clearly show who is responsible for implementing each aspect of the plan. The detailed marketing plan should flow directly from the marketing strategy, which itself starts from marketing objectives. The plan may go through a series of iterative stages of consultation before it is finally accepted. Too many companies develop a strategy that sounds fine, but they fail to think through fully the detail of implementation.

5. **Did we get there? Monitoring and controlling the marketing programme:** Marketing plans are of little value if they are to be implemented only half-heartedly. An ongoing part of the marketing management process is therefore to monitor the implementation of the plan and to seek an explanation of any deviation from it.

Effective control systems demand timely, accurate, and relevant information about an organization's operations and environment. Control systems require three underlying components to be in place:

(a) setting of targets or standards of expected performance;

(b) measurement and evaluation of actual performance;

(c) corrective action to be taken where necessary;

Many control systems fail because employees within an organization have been given inappropriate or unrealistic targets. Even where targets are set and appropriate data are collected, control systems may fail because of a failure by management to act on the information available. Control information should identify variances from target and should be able to indicate whether the variance is within or beyond the control of the person responsible for meeting the target. If it is beyond that person's control, the issue should become one of revising the target so that it once more becomes achievable. If the variance is the result of factors that are subject to a manager's control, a number of measures can be taken to try to revise their behaviour, including incentive schemes, training, and disciplinary action.

After the monitoring and control stages of the marketing management process, managers should have learned from their analysis of past performance, and this provides the basis for reviewing objectives and strategies for the period ahead.

◉ Strategic, tactical, and contingency planning

From the above description, marketing *planning* is best viewed as a continuous *process*. However, it is necessary to produce periodic statements of a *plan* which all individuals in an organization can work towards. Three types of periodic plan can be identified.

1. The **strategic** element of a marketing plan focuses on the overriding direction that an organization's efforts will take in order to meet its objectives.

2. The **tactical** element is more concerned with plans for implementing the detail of the strategic plan.

The division between the strategic and tactical elements of a marketing plan can sometimes be difficult to define. Typically, a strategic marketing plan is concerned with mapping out direction over a five-year planning period, whereas a tactical marketing plan is concerned with implementation during the next 12 months. Many business sectors view their strategic planning periods very differently, and in the case of large-scale infrastructure projects such as airports or railways, the strategic planning period may be very long indeed. On the other hand, many small-scale, low-technology businesses may find little need for a strategic plan beyond the immediate operational period.

3. A contingency plan seeks to identify scenarios where the assumptions of the position analysis on which strategic decisions were based turn out to be false. For example, a food manufacturer might have assumed that there would be no significant change in consumers' attitudes towards a particular category of food. However, this assumption may be false if subsequently its food products become associated with harm to health. A contingency plan would allow a firm to react quickly to such a scenario, for example by increasing its promotional expenditure and cutting back on production capacity.

◉ The dynamic marketing environment

In developing a marketing plan, it can be very easy to assume a stable market. In Chapter 7 we saw that, in reality, most markets are dynamic and a marketing plan needs to take account of not just competitors' current strategies, but also their likely future strategies. If a market appears attractive to one organization, then it probably appears equally attractive to others as well. These other organizations may possess equal competitive advantage in addressing the market. If all such firms decide to enter the market, oversupply results, profit margins become squeezed, and the market becomes relatively unattractive. This could be observed in the semi-conductor market, which in the mid-1990s looked highly attractive, with a rapid growth in demand and a shortage of supply. This was the signal for many companies to enter the market, with the result that by 2000 oversupply had resulted, the price of semi-conductors had fallen from over £4 to less than 50p, and many manufacturing operations had become unprofitable.

Marketing planning and corporate planning

Marketing management is just one of the specialist management functions that can be identi-fied within most commercial organizations. What is the relationship between marketing man-agement and corporate management? At one extreme, the two can be seen as synonymous. If an organization stands or falls primarily on its ability to satisfy customer needs, then it can be argued that marketing planning is so central to the organization's activities that it becomes corporate planning. The alternative view is that marketing is just one of the functions of an organization that affects its performance. Marketing takes its goals from corporate plans just as the personnel or production functions of the organization do. In business sectors where customers have relatively little choice and production capacity is limited, the significance of the marketing plan to the corporate plan will be less than for a company facing fierce competi-tion. Many public sector service organizations operating in relatively uncompetitive markets claim to go through a marketing planning process, when in fact, although the term 'marketing planning' may be referred to by name, it is given much less significance than the development of production plans or personnel plans to serve a stable market.

The relationship between the processes of marketing and corporate planning can be two-way, again reflecting the importance of marketing to the total planning process. Marketing in-formation is fed into the corporate planning process for analysis and formulation of the corporate plan in a process sometimes referred to as 'bottom-up planning'. In a 'top-down' process, the corporate plan is developed and functional objectives are specified for marketing.

◉ Planning as an inter-functional integrator

The marketing planning process helps to integrate the efforts of a diverse range of people throughout an organization. The plan allows everybody to 'sing from the same hymn sheet'. Without the plan, individuals may end up doing things that are in direct conflict with their colleagues.

Corporate and marketing planning processes act as integrators in horizontal and vertical dimensions (see Figure 12.3).

1. *In the horizontal dimension*, the planning process brings together the plans of the specialized functions that are necessary to make the organization work. Marketing is just one function of an organization which generates its own planning process. Other functional plans found in most organizations are financial plans, personnel plans, and production plans. The components of these functional plans must recognize their interdependencies if they are to be effective. For example, a car manufacturer's marketing strategic plan which anticipates a 20 per cent growth in sales of its cars over a five-year planning period should be reflected in a strategic production plan that allows for output to increase by a similar amount, as well as a financial plan that identifies strategies for raising the required level of finance for new investment and work in progress and a personnel plan for recruiting additional staff. Within the marketing department, a plan helps to ensure that the activities of advertising personnel are mutually supportive of the activities of sales and market research staff, for example.

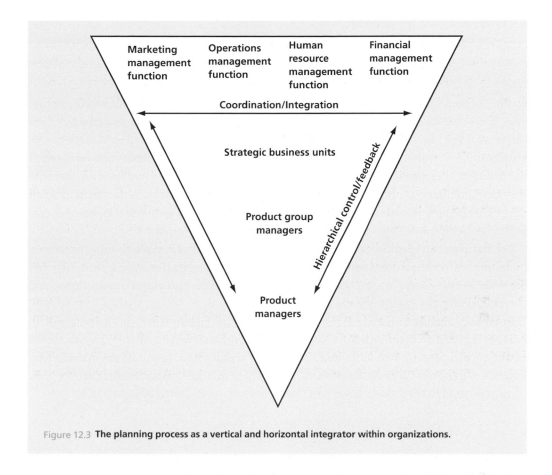

Figure 12.3 **The planning process as a vertical and horizontal integrator within organizations.**

2.   *In the vertical dimension*, the planning process provides a framework for decisions to be made at different levels of the corporate hierarchy. Objectives can be specified in progressively more detail, from the global objectives of the corporate plan, to the information required to operationalize these objectives at the level of individual operational units (or strategic business units) and, in turn, for individual products.

⊙ The mission statement

A corporate mission statement provides a focal point for the marketing planning process. It can be likened to a hidden hand which guides all employees in an organization in developing and implementing marketing plans. Drucker (1973) identified a number of basic questions that management needs to ask in drawing up a mission statement:

1.   What is our business?

2.   Who is the customer?

3. What is value to the customer?

4. What will our business be?

5. What should our business be?

By forcing management to focus on the essential nature of the business it is in and the nature of customer needs it seeks to satisfy, the problem of 'marketing myopia' identified by Levitt can be avoided. Levitt argued that, in order to avoid a narrow, shortsighted view of their business, managers should define their business in terms of the needs that they fulfil rather than the products they produce. In the classic example, railway operators lost their way because they defined their output in terms of the *technology* of tracked vehicles, rather than in terms of the core benefit of *movement* that they provided. They lost out to the development of cars and buses, which provided similar benefits using different technologies.

The nature of an organization's mission statement is a reflection of a number of factors, including the organization's ownership (e.g. public sector *v.* private sector statements); the previous history of the organization; the resources available; and major opportunities and threats faced by the organization.

In services organizations where the interface between consumers and production personnel is often critical, communication of the values contained within the mission statement can be very important. The statement is frequently repeated by organizations in staff newsletters and in notices at the place of work. An example of a mission statement that is widely communicated to the workforce—as well as to customers—is shown in Figure 12.4.

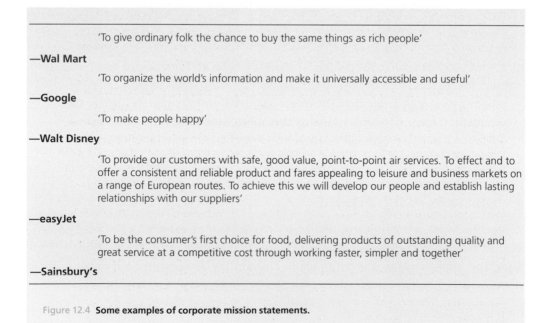

'To give ordinary folk the chance to buy the same things as rich people'

—Wal Mart

'To organize the world's information and make it universally accessible and useful'

—Google

'To make people happy'

—Walt Disney

'To provide our customers with safe, good value, point-to-point air services. To effect and to offer a consistent and reliable product and fares appealing to leisure and business markets on a range of European routes. To achieve this we will develop our people and establish lasting relationships with our suppliers'

—easyJet

'To be the consumer's first choice for food, delivering products of outstanding quality and great service at a competitive cost through working faster, simpler and together'

—Sainsbury's

Figure 12.4 **Some examples of corporate mission statements.**

MARKETING in ACTION

Marketing the unmanageable?

In any organization, the aspirations of marketing managers can be quite different from those of the employees who have to deliver the promises that marketers make. It can be naive to imagine that marketers simply concentrate on identifying customers' needs, then operations people develop products which will satisfy those needs. In reality, front-line employees may have cherished ways of working which they may feel are threatened by new ideas of the marketing department. This is especially true in services, and the problem can be acute where the front-line employees have considerable knowledge and power. An analysis of marketing management in the National Health Service (NHS) illustrates some of the challenges that marketing managers may face.

The NHS has seen an increase in the number of managers who have no clinical background. Increasingly, marketing managers are being appointed by health service trusts, mindful of the fact that in an increasingly market-driven health sector, understanding and responding to patients' needs becomes increasingly important. Indeed, the language of some hospital managers now talks about 'customers' rather than 'patients'.

Although the chief executive of a National Health Service trust in principle has ultimate authority over all employees, many people would recognize that it is the medical consultants who have the real power in a hospital. If they do not like a change that is proposed by the chief executive, they can point to their professional codes of conduct and years of training that have given them knowledge-based power. Consultants may argue that they have patients' long-term interests at heart, because they have invested heavily in their specialized training and will be around for many years to pick up the consequences of their actions. By contrast, a marketing manager may be perceived as having relatively simple training, and will soon move on to another job with no professional responsibility to see through the consequences of their actions. Marketing managers with a non-clinical background may become too focused on relatively superficial quality of service issues such as car parking and food, while consultants could argue that only they can judge the true quality of the core service of a hospital, namely the outcome of medical and surgical procedures. They point out that a typical patient is incapable of assessing clinical performance, owing to their limited knowledge, and the fact that the outcome of many clinical procedures will not fully present themselves for many months or even years into the future. In short, only consultants, with their professional training and codes of conduct can manage the nature of interaction between the hospital and its patients.

For a marketing manager, the professional, knowledge-based power of consultants may be seen as a source of frustration. As an example, it has been claimed that many NHS hospitals' operating theatres are under-utilized on Friday afternoons. For a marketing manager, one method of increasing the number of patient admissions would be to use these very expensive facilities on Friday afternoons, rather than to leave them idle. Consultants would argue that it is bad professional practice to commence operations just before the weekend, when there is only limited cover available in a hospital to rectify any clinical complications. Cynics may claim that consultants are using professional arguments as a smokescreen for giving themselves a long weekend, and a chance to get away early to play golf. Some have pointed out that consultants may nevertheless use Friday afternoons to undertake profitable private surgery elsewhere. How can a chief executive or marketing manager with a non-clinical background argue with the knowledge and professional responsibilities of a consultant? What does marketing management mean in the context of highly-skilled professionals? Many would argue that management is not about command and control, but more about facilitating others to achieve their goals. Which model of management is right? Who decides whether consultants are right in their goals of keeping Friday afternoons free for professional reasons, or whether they are doing it because they know a good personal opportunity when they see one?

⦿ Integrating marketing management with other management functions

Should an organization actually have a marketing department? The idea is becoming increasingly popular that the existence of a separate marketing department within an organization may in fact hinder the development of a true customer-centred marketing orientation. By placing all marketing activity in a marketing department, non-marketing staff may consider that responsibility for getting new or repeat business is nothing to do with them, but should be left to the marketing department. While it is becoming fashionable to talk about everybody becoming a 'part-time marketer' (see Gummesson 2008), a marketing department is usually required in order to coordinate and implement those functions that cannot sensibly be delegated to operational personnel. Advertising, sales management, and pricing decisions, for example, usually need some central coordination by a marketing department. The importance that a marketing department assumes within any organization is a reflection on the nature of its operating environment. An organization operating in a fiercely competitive environment would typically attach great importance to its marketing department as a means of producing a focused marketing mix strategy by which it could gain competitive advantage over its rivals. On the other hand, a company operating in a relatively stable environment would be more likely to allow strategic decisions to be taken by personnel who were not marketing strategists—for example pricing decisions may be taken by accountants with less need to understand the marketing implications of price decisions.

In a marketing-oriented organization, customers are at the centre of all of the organization's activities. Customers are the concern not simply of the marketing department, but of all the production and administrative personnel whose actions may directly or indirectly impinge upon the customers' service. In the words of Drucker (1973), marketing is so basic that it cannot be considered to be a separate function. It is the whole business seen from the point of view of its final result, that is, from the customer's point of view.

The activities of a number of functional departments can impinge on customers' perceptions of the value they get from a company.

1. Personnel plans can have a crucial bearing on marketing plans. The selection, training, motivation, and control of staff cannot be considered in isolation from marketing objectives and strategies. Possible conflict between personnel and marketing functions may arise where, for example, marketing demands highly trained and motivated staff, but the personnel function pursues a policy that emphasizes cost reduction and uniform pay structures.

2. Marketing managers may try to respond as closely as possible to customers' needs but encounter opposition from production managers, who argue that a product of the required standard cannot be achieved. A marketing manager may want large numbers of product variants in order to satisfy market niches, whereas a production manager may seek large production runs of standardized products.

3. Ultimately, finance managers assume responsibility for the allocation of the funds that are needed to implement a marketing plan. At a more operational level, finance managers' actions in respect of the level of credit offered to customers, or towards stockholdings, can also significantly affect the quality of service and the volume of customers that the organization is able to serve.

The problem of how to bring people together in an organization to act collectively, while also being able to place responsibility on an individual is one which continues to generate considerable discussion. Organizations which produce many different products for many different markets may experience difficulties if they adopt a purely product or market-based structure. If a product management structure is adopted, product managers would require detailed knowledge of very diverse markets. Likewise, in a market management structure, market managers would require detailed knowledge of possibly very diverse product ranges. To avoid the problem of functional managers acting and thinking with a 'silo' mentality, there has been a tendency for organizations to develop clusters of individuals who focus on creating value for targeted groups of consumers and profits for their company.

Within such a cluster, product managers can concentrate on excellence in production, while market managers focus on meeting consumer needs without any preference for a particular product. An example of a matrix structure as these are sometimes known can be found in many vehicle distributors where market managers can be appointed to identify and formulate a market strategy in respect of the distinct needs of private customers and contract hire customers etc., as well as being appointed to manage key customers (Figure 12.5). Market managers work alongside product managers who can develop specialized activities such as servicing, bodywork repairs, and vehicle hire which are made available to final customers through the market managers.

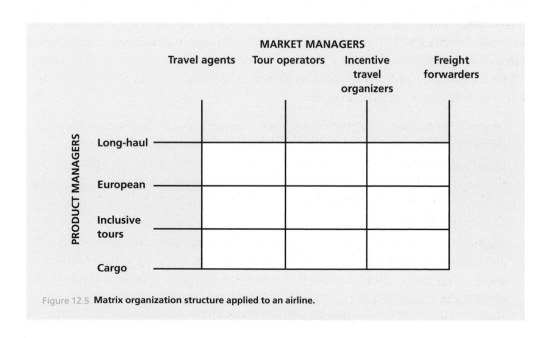

Figure 12.5 **Matrix organization structure applied to an airline.**

The most important advantages of such clusters are that they can, in principle, allow organizations to respond rapidly to environmental change. Short-term project teams can be assembled and disbanded at short notice to meet changed needs. Project teams can bring together a wide variety of disciplines and can be used to evaluate new services before full-scale development is undertaken. A bank exploring the possibility of developing a mobile phone-based payment system might establish a team drawn from staff involved in marketing to personal customers and staff responsible for technology-based research and development. The former may include market researchers and the latter software developers.

The flexibility of such structures can be increased by bringing temporary workers into the structure on a contract basis as and when needed. During the past two decades there has been a trend for many services organizations to lay off significant numbers of workers, including management, and to buy these back when needed. As well as cutting fixed costs, such organizations have the potential to respond very rapidly to environmental change.

Where inter-functional clusters exist, great motivation can be present in effectively managed teams. Against this, matrix type structures can have their problems. Most serious is the confused lines of authority which may result. Staff may not be clear about which superior he or she is responsible to for a particular aspect of their duties, resulting in possible stress and demotivation. Where a matrix-type structure is introduced into an organization with a history and culture of functional specialization, it can be very difficult to implement effectively. Staff may be reluctant to act outside a role which they have traditionally defined narrowly and guarded jealously. Finally, such structures invariably result in more managers being employed within an organization. At best this can result in a costly addition to the salary bill. At worst, the existence of additional managers can also slow down decision-making processes where the managers show a reluctance to act outside a narrow functional role.

Having multi-functional clusters of individuals may represent a desirable structure for an organization, but getting there can be a slow and painful process. Most management change within organizations occurs incrementally. The result of this is often a compromised organizational structure which is unduly influenced by historic factors which are of no continuing relevance. Vested interests within an organization frequently result in an organization which is production rather than customer focused.

◉ Marketing management and smaller businesses

Much of what has been written so far in this chapter about marketing management processes and structures might sound fine for larger organizations, but what about smaller businesses where the very idea of a 'management structure' and a formalized marketing planning system may seem quite alien?

The term 'small business' (or SME, standing for small and medium-sized enterprise) is difficult to define. In an industry such as car manufacture, a firm with one hundred employees would be considered very small, whereas among solicitors, a practice of that size would be considered large. The term 'small business' is therefore a relative one, based typically on some measure of numbers of employees or capital employed. A large category of 'micro' or 'size class zero' businesses exist which do not have any employees. In these companies, production, finance, and marketing are all vested in the same person.

In terms of marketing management, SMEs have a number of important characteristics.

1. They generally offer much greater adaptability than larger firms. With less bureaucracy and fewer channels of communications, decisions can be taken rapidly. A larger organization may be burdened with constraints which tend to slow the decision-making process, such as the need to negotiate new working practices with trade union representatives, or the need to obtain the board of directors' approval for major decisions. As organizations grow, there is an inherent tendency for them to become more risk-averse by building in systems of control that make them slower to adapt to changes in their business environment.

2. Small businesses tend to be good innovators. This comes about through their greater adaptability, especially where large amounts of capital are not required. Small firms can also be good innovators where they operate in markets dominated by a small number of larger companies and the only way in which a small business can gain entry to the market is to develop an innovatory product aimed at a small niche. The soap powder market in Britain is dominated by a small number of large producers, yet it was a relatively small company that identified a niche for environmentally friendly powders and introduced innovatory products to the market.

It is not only small entrepreneurs who have been creating new small businesses. Many larger organizations have also recognized their value and have tried to replicate them at a distance from their own structure. Many large manufacturing organizations operating in mature markets have created autonomous new small business units to serve rapidly developing or specialist niche markets, free of the bureaucratic culture of the parent organization. In the education sector, many universities have established small research companies at arm's length from the universities' organizational structures. However, while small businesses have certainly seen a resurgence in recent years, it should also be recognized that they have a very high failure rate compared to larger corporations.

⊙ Marketing leadership

Many of the most successful market-led companies, such as Virgin Group, J.D. Weatherspoon, and Dell Computers, attribute their success in part to the quality of leadership within their organizations. The results of poor leadership are evident in many failing service organizations. Many commentators attributed the temporary decline in fortunes of Marks & Spencer and Sainsbury's during the 1990s to leadership rifts within their senior managements.

What is good leadership for one organization need not necessarily be so for another. Organizations operating in relatively stable environments may be best suited with a leadership style that places a lot of power in a hierarchical chain of command. In the UK, many banks until recently had leadership styles that were drawn from models developed in the armed forces, as evidenced by some managers having titles such as 'superintendent' and 'inspector'. Such rigid,

481

MARKETING in ACTION

Are entrepreneurs born or bred?

Is there such a thing as an 'entrepreneurship gene'? Further developments in the science of genetics may one day add some evidence to the debate about whether entrepreneurs are born or bred. But what about students leaving university today? Evidence abounds of students who are attributed with an 'entrepreneurship' gene. As an example, a company called Innocent was set up in 1999 by three entrepreneurial Cambridge University graduates—Adam Balon, Richard Reed, and Jon Wright—to produce fresh fruit smoothies. By 2002 the company was already producing 200,000 smoothies a week with an annual sales turnover of £7 million. The budding entrepreneurs initially tested their dream by buying £500 of fresh fruit and selling their smoothies at a stall during a weekend jazz festival in London. In December 2007 Innocent Drinks appeared at number 40 in the Sunday Times Fast Track 100, a list of the fastest growing private companies in the UK. Such was their success that by 2010 the company was selling two million smoothies a week and had an annual turnover of £110 million, fighting competition from rivals such as Pepsico's Tropicana and Nestlé's Boost, which caused annual sales to fall temporarily for the first time. Even after this competitive skirmish, Innocent's share of the UK smoothie market remained at 85 per cent, according to the company. One potential competitor who decided that it would be better to work with Innocent rather than compete against them was Coca Cola, which bought an 18 per cent stake in Innocent in 2009, increasing it to a majority stake in 2010. Would the founding entrepreneurs, who continued with the company, be able to adapt to life as part of a big multinational corporation? Or could Coca Cola adapt to preserve the values and style of Innocent?

Of course, for every entrepreneurial success story there are scores of failures, and it is commonly estimated that a third of new entrants to self-employment leave within three years—even more in periods of economic recession. Very often, an entrepreneur can be good at creating a business, but much less good at handling the procedures that are necessary to keep a larger organization on track. Typical of this tendency is Michelle Mone, inventor of the cleavage enhancing Ultimo bra. She launched her business, MJM International, in 1996 and enjoyed an annual turnover of more than £1 million within just a few years. Her products went on to achieve global fame when Julia Roberts wore an Ultimo bra for her role in the Oscar-winning film *Erin Brockovich*. In 2001 turnover reached £3 million, and Mone announced plans to float her company. But when the planned float failed to take off, her fortunes seemed to unwind. The bank called in the company's overdraft, she began experiencing problems with designers, and a department store cancelled its order, leaving her business with 15,000 unsold bras. It seemed that designing stylish bras for the rich and famous was one thing, but handling relationships with large retail buyers was quite another. Mone pulled her products out of department stores in 2001 to sell direct to the public via an Internet site, but sales have remained static.

So what are the characteristics of an entrepreneur? Most commentators agree that a willingness to take risks is crucial—it really does seem to be necessary to speculate in order to accumulate. Of course, taking risk implies that, while some entrepreneurs will succeed beyond their wildest dreams, many will fail. Good entrepreneurs are able to pick themselves up quickly following a failure. Being optimistic and spotting opportunities is important, as is the ability to work long hours, and to have a belief in yourself and your ideas.

It would seem that many would-be entrepreneurs don't set out on the road to entrepreneurship because they have a fear of failure. Some cultures condemn individuals who have failed, but in other countries, such as the United States, there is an environment in which failure is recognized as a sign of a well-intentioned individual who hit a bit of bad luck, and success is about more than having a bit of undeserved good luck. Can this difference in cultural values explain why some countries seem to have a larger number of entrepreneurial companies?

hierarchical patterns of leadership may be less effective where the marketing environment is changing rapidly and a flexible response is called for (as has happened in the banking sector).

What makes a good leader of a marketing-oriented company? And are leaders born, or can individuals acquire the skills of leadership? On the latter point there is little doubt that development is possible, and successful companies have invested heavily in leadership development programmes. As for what makes a successful leader of people, there have been many suggestions of desirable traits, including:

1. setting clear expectations of staff;

2. recognizing excellence appropriately and facilitating staff in overcoming their weaknesses;

3. leading by example;

4. being able to empathize with employees;

5. showing adaptability to changing circumstances.

In too many companies, bad leadership is characterized by:

1. 'management by confusion', in which expectations of staff are ambiguously stated and management actions are guided by a secretive 'hidden agenda';

2. reward systems that are not based on performance and are perceived as being unfair;

3. the deliberate or inadvertent creation of an 'us-and-them' attitude;

4. failure to understand the aspirations of employees;

5. failure to take the initiative where environmental change calls for adaptation.

⦿ Managing information

We saw in Chapter 5 how information represents a bridge between an organization and its environment. It is the means by which a picture of the changing environment is built up within the organization. Marketing management is responsible for turning information into specific marketing plans. The marketing management function of any organization requires a constant flow of information for two principal purposes:

1. To provide information as an input to the planning of marketing activities.

2. To monitor the implementation of marketing programmes and allow corrective action to be taken if performance diverges from target.

A timely supply of appropriate information provides feedback on an organization's performance, allowing actual performance to be compared with target performance. On the basis of this information, control measures can be applied which seek—where necessary—to put

MARKETING in ACTION

Managing by example

Beginning with a small shop in Dundalk in 1960, the Irish grocery retailer SuperQuinn has grown to a successful chain, in 2010 owning 23 stores throughout Ireland and employing over 3,000 people. A large part of this success has been attributed to the leadership style of the company's founder, Feargal Quinn, and the emphasis on linking employees' activities to excellence in service. But what makes such leadership style distinctive?

An important principle is that managers should lead by example and should never lose contact with the most important person in the organization—the customer. It is the task of a leader to set the tone for customer-focused excellence. To prevent managers losing sight of customers' needs, Quinn uses every opportunity to move them closer to customers, including locating their offices not in a comfortable room upstairs, but in the middle of the sales floor. Managers regularly take part in customer panels where customers talk about their expectations and perceptions of SuperQuinn. Subcontracting this task entirely to a market research agency is seen as alien to the leadership culture of the company. The company requires its managers to spend periods doing routine front-line jobs (such as packing customers' bags), a practice that has become commonplace in many successful services organizations. This keeps managers close to the company and improves their ability to empathize with junior employees.

Does this leadership style work? Given the company's level of growth, profits, and rate of repeat business, it must be doing something right, contradicting much of the scientific management theories that management is a specialist task which can be separated from routine dealings with customers and employees.

the organization back on its original targets. Organizations also learn from the past in order to understand the future better. For making longer-term planning decisions, historical information is supplemented by a variety of continuous and *ad hoc* studies, all designed to allow better informed decisions to be made.

Marketing information cannot in itself produce decisions: it merely provides data which must be interpreted by marketing managers. As an inter-functional integrator, marketing information draws data from all functional areas of an organization, which in turn use data to focus on meeting customers' needs more effectively.

You will recall from Chapter 5 that, to be useful to management, information should be collected from a variety of sources in a systematic manner and turned into knowledge that can be shared throughout the organization and acted upon. An important task of marketing management is to plan the collection, analysis, and dissemination of information in a way that balances the costs of collecting the information against the costs of a poor decision based on inadequate information. A number of factors will determine the efficiency and effectiveness of these activities:

1. The accuracy with which the information requirements have been defined: It can be very difficult to identify what information should be of relevance in a company's information gathering activities and to separate relevance from irrelevance. This is a particular problem for large multi-output firms expanding into new markets/products.

The mission statement of an organization may give some indication of the boundaries for its information search.

2. **The extensiveness of the search for information:** A balance has to be struck between the need for information and the cost of collecting it. The most critical elements of the marketing environment must be identified and the cost of collecting relevant information weighed against the cost that would result from a poorly informed management decision.

3. **The appropriateness of the sources of information:** Information for decision making can usually be obtained from numerous sources; for example customers' attitudes towards a product can be measured using a variety of quantitative and qualitative techniques. Companies often rely on the former when more qualitative techniques are really called for. Successful companies use a variety of sources of information.

4. **The speed of communication:** A marketing manager must facilitate rapid communication of information to the people capable of acting on it. Deciding what information to withhold from an individual and the concise reporting of relevant information can be as important as deciding what information to include if information overload is to be avoided.

Of course, information itself will not produce decisions, and it was noted earlier that a preoccupation with data collection and analysis can lead to a 'paralysis by analysis'. A crucial skill of management is to interpret information, and a variety of quantitative and qualitative techniques are used to support management decisions. We have seen in previous chapters how rules-based systems have been used to help decisions in relation to such issues as retail location and the allocation of advertisements between different media. Rules-based techniques often need to be supplemented with the intuition and experience of the marketing manager. Rules-based systems for decision support may be fine in stable and predictable environments, where historically collected data may be a good guide to the future. They can be of much less value where the environment is changing and the old 'rules' are no longer appropriate. Many successful entrepreneurs have spotted such changes and, using a combination of intuition, experience, and analysis, have exploited new opportunities.

Using information for control

So far, we have looked at information primarily as a means of improving planning for the future. But it must not be forgotten that marketing managers have a control function as well as a planning function. Indeed, many people have criticized the marketing profession for being good on planning, sometimes lacking in implementation skills, but much worse at monitoring and evaluating their efforts. Control is an important and often overlooked function of marketing, and the key to effective control is to give the right information to the right people at the right time. Providing too much information can be costly in terms of the effort required to assemble and disseminate it and can also reduce effective control where the valuable information is hidden among information of secondary importance. A control system will show variances between budgeted performance and actual performance, and will highlight those differences that are beyond a specified zone of tolerance. An analysis of variance from target should also indicate whether the variance is within or beyond the control of the person responsible for meeting the target. If it is beyond her control, the issue should become one of revising the target so that it becomes once more achievable. If the variance is the result of factors that are subject to an individual's control, a number of measures can be taken to try to revise behaviour.

The following are some of the things that most organizations will need information on if they are to monitor adequately the implementation of their marketing plan:

1. Financial targets—sales turnover/contribution/profit margin, disaggregated by product/business unit.

2. Market analysis, for example market share.

3. Effectiveness of communication—productivity of sales personnel, effectiveness of advertising, effectiveness of sales promotion.

4. Pricing—level of discounts given, price position.

5. Personnel—level of skills achieved by employees, survey of customer comments on staff performance.

6. Quality levels achieved—for example reliability, complaint level.

Where performance is below target, the reasons may not be immediately obvious. A comprehensive marketing information system can allow an organization to analyse variance. A uniform fall in sales performance across the organization, combined with intelligence gained about the state of the market, would suggest that remedial action aimed at improving the performance of individual sales personnel may not be as effective as a reassessment of targets or strategies in the light of the changed sales environment.

Successful control mechanisms require three underlying components to be in place:

1. The setting of targets or standards of expected performance.

2. The measurement and evaluation of actual performance.

3. The means to take corrective action where necessary.

Marketing managers now have a lot more information available to them which they can use to spot trends and take corrective action where marketing activities are not meeting the specified objectives. In previous times, managers may have been able to rely on instinct to gauge their success, but today regular reporting and analysis of quantifiable data are frequently expected. In some sectors, for example online retailing, the challenge can be to identify the most relevant control statistics from the mass of data that is typically available.

Despite the greater availability of data, there is some evidence that many marketers are reluctant to measure their effectiveness. Nearly all firms compare actual sales with sales targets, and there is an increasing focus on shareholder value, but relatively few measure customer value. Ambler (2000) noted a number of reasons why managers may be reluctant to measure their marketing performance.

1. The board is not marketing or customer oriented, and has no senior marketing representation on it. Little board agenda time is made available to discuss marketing issues.

2. Determination and effort may be considered more important than objectivity. To use an analogy, the First World War would never have been won if the soldiers had known the score—it was won by sheer determination.

3. Some company boards believe that accountants should be solely responsible for accounting for all that matters. Internal measures may be interpreted as navel gazing, and are no substitute for measuring sales and market share.

4. Marketers may argue against having their effectiveness measured too closely by pointing out that marketing is the business of the whole company, and so they cannot be held specifically accountable.

5. Marketers are often too busy fighting the next battle and feel that this should take priority over worrying about the last one.

6. In reality, the status of a marketer is determined by the size of the department's marketing budget. Size of budget, which can be measured, looks more credible on a CV than subjective outcomes.

7. Marketing effectiveness may be perceived as something essentially unmeasurable, which should be assessed by more subjective 'feel good' or 'good news' aspects.

8. Marketers may argue that past experience has shown that marketing expenditure cannot be related to sales and profits; that is, profit and loss account measures do not work.

9. The environment changes too fast, so results need to be judged by the new realities, not those in place or forecast when the plan was drawn up.

10. Creating new measurement systems takes too long—the current marketing team will have moved on by the time the report comes out.

It is important to note that measuring overall marketing performance is not the same as measuring marketing expenditure effectiveness. Think back to Chapter 1 where the distinction was made between marketing as a philosophy and as a set of techniques. Techniques such as advertising may be performing well, but if the wrong products are being advertised to the wrong people, marketing effectiveness overall may be quite poor.

   Some have seen measurement of brand equity as a fundamentally important metric. You will recall from Chapter 7 that brand equity corresponds to the premium that buyers are prepared to pay for a specified brand rather than a generic product. There is plenty of evidence that organizations whose marketing is ineffective are often those who have seen their brand equity diminish. Banks who were once trusted institutions have caused anger among many of their customers through perceptions of overcharging, reckless lending, and excessive bonus payments to staff. One result has been that many customers have shifted their bank accounts and credit cards to supermarkets and other rivals to banks, which have achieved high levels of brand equity. Many of these misgivings about banks can be attributed to operational functions, but this only serves to emphasize the point that marketing should be a company-wide integrator. Customers may not care who in the bank is the source of their grievance, but the result is the same: the value they place on a bank's brand is lower than it was before.

◉ Improving organizational effectiveness for marketing

What makes some organizations more effective at marketing than others? And what practical steps can a company take to become one of the best at marketing? One widely used framework for analysis—the McKinsey 7S framework developed by Peters and Waterman (1982)—identified seven essential elements for a successful business, based on a study of the most successful American companies. The elements are broken down into the hardware (strategy, structure, and systems) and the software (skills, staff, styles, and shared values). Formalized strategies, structures, and systems on their own were not considered to be sufficient to bring about success—these could be operationalized only with appropriate intangible 'software'. In other words, the quality of management, in terms of leadership and working with people to achieve stated goals, is critical.

At a strategic level, companies have used a number of methods to try to develop a pervasive marketing orientation throughout their organization:

1. In-house educational programmes can aim to train non-marketing employees to empathize with customers' expectations. Some organizations have tried 'job swaps', in which backroom production people spend time at the sharp end of their business, in front of customers and learning about their needs.

2. By appointing senior managers who have experience of marketing, marketing values may permeate throughout an organization in a top-down manner.

3. The introduction of outside consultants is sometimes used as an external change agent. Consultants can impartially apply their previous experience of introducing a marketing culture to an organization.

4. Getting top management to empathize with customers, to understand what they value in a brand, is generally not a problem for small businesses, but formal or informal processes, such as 'management by walking about', can help managers in larger organizations to gain the necessary understanding.

5. A commonly used method of making management think in marketing terms is to introduce a formal market-oriented planning system. When proposing any initiative,

How do patients measure up?

The UK's National Health Service (NHS) has increasingly been driven to meet higher 'customer service' standards, in addition to the standards of clinical excellence that have traditionally been expected from health care professionals. Starting with the publication of a 'Patients' Charter' in the mid-1990s, governments have steadily increased the targets placed on health care administrators, often linking funding to the achievement of targets. But, like many performance targets, their value in the NHS has been questioned by many.

The idea of introducing targets that relate mainly to customer handling rather than to clinical issues has been dismissed by many as mere window dressing. But even the meaning of these non-clinical statistics is open to doubt, as hospitals find ways of making their performance look good on paper, if not in practice. For example, Accident and Emergency (A&E) departments use triage nurses to assess new patients upon arrival, thereby keeping within their Patients' Charter target for the time taken to see a new patient initially. However, A&E departments may be slower in providing actual treatment. In 2003, a number of ambulance services were reprimanded for trying to make their response times appear better than they actually were by measuring the response time from when an ambulance set out, rather than when a call for help was received.

Even the whole value of publishing performance indicators for hospitals has been questioned by many. What does it mean if a consultant or a department has a long waiting time for appointments? Rather than being an indicator of inefficiency, could it be that a long waiting list is an indicator of a consultant who is very popular with patients? And doesn't the very fact that performance indicators are published push up users' expectations of service delivery, so that in the end they may become more dissatisfied even though actual performance has improved?

managers must work through a list of market-related headings, such as an analysis of the competitive environment and an identification of market opportunities when developing their annual plans. This prevents a myopic focus on the product alone.

6. It was noted above that building brand equity is a primary function of marketing management and is likely to be developed by using brand equity as a basis for rewarding managers.

The overall result of these activities should be to develop a customer-focused marketing culture within an organization. Within many organizations, it has proved very difficult to change cultural attitudes when the nature of an organization's operating environment has changed significantly, rendering the established culture a liability in terms of strategic marketing management. As an example, the cultural values of UK clearing banks have for a long time continued to be dominated by prudence and caution, when in some product areas, for example insurance sales, a more aggressive approach to marketing management is called for.

As an organization develops, it is essential that the dominant culture adapts. While a small business may quite successfully embrace a centralized power culture, continued growth may cause this culture to become a liability. There are many cases of businesses, such as the electronics company Amstrad, that have reportedly failed to make the cultural transition from small entrepreneur to large corporate entity. Similarly, the privatization of many public utilities called for a transformation from a bureaucratic role culture to a task-oriented culture (see Handy 1994).

Managing marketing in a global business environment

At some point, many businesses recognize that their growth can only continue if they exploit overseas markets. However, entering overseas markets can be extremely risky, as evidenced by examples of recent failures where companies failed to foresee all the problems involved.

- The mobile phone company O2 invested over £1.5 billion in the Dutch mobile phone operator Telfort but failed to achieve higher than fifth ranking in the Dutch market. In April 2003 the company admitted defeat and sold the entire Dutch operation for just £16 million.

- The grocery retailer Sainsbury's pulled out of Egypt in 2001, only two years after investing in a chain of 100 supermarkets. Sainsbury's had gone out on a limb in Egypt, which had no tradition of supermarket shopping, and the company was not helped by persistent rumours of links with Jewish owners. Sainsbury's two years of involvement in the Egyptian market incurred a loss of over £100 million.

- Even the fast-food retailer McDonald's initially failed to make profits when it entered the UK market in the 1970s and had to rapidly adjust its service offer in order to achieve viability.

Nevertheless, a company that has successfully developed its business strategy should be well placed to extend this development into overseas markets. There are many examples of companies that have successfully developed overseas markets, including the following.

- The retailer Tesco successfully reduced its dependence on the saturated UK grocery market by developing outlets in the Far East and Eastern Europe.

- The mobile phone company Vodafone has expanded from its UK base and now provides service in 30 countries, reducing the company's unit costs through economies of scale, and offering seamless, added-value services to international travellers.

- The Irish airline Ryanair started life with a route network that focused on Dublin. With successful expansion of its route network, most of its services now do not call at its Irish base.

- Carphone Warehouse was the brainchild of entrepreneur Charles Dunstone and, after a small-scale start in London, it has successfully expanded to more than 1,100 stores throughout Europe, operating under the Carphone Warehouse banner in the UK, and the Phone House in France, Spain, Germany, Sweden, and the Netherlands.

Although the focus of this book is on the UK and European environment, it should never be forgotten that UK organizations increasingly have to co-exist with a global business environment. Frequent reference has therefore been made throughout this book to the global context of business.

For an individual company, development of foreign markets can be attractive for a number of reasons. These can be analysed in terms of 'pull' factors, which derive from the attractiveness of a potential foreign market, and 'push' factors, which make an organization's domestic market appear less attractive.

- For firms seeking growth, foreign markets represent new market segments, which they may be able to serve with their existing range of products. In this way, a company can stick to producing products that it is good at. Finding new foreign markets for existing or slightly modified products does not expose a company to the risks of expanding both its product range and its market coverage simultaneously.

- Saturation of its domestic market can force an organization to seek foreign markets. Saturation can come about where a product reaches the maturity stage of its life-cycle in the domestic market, while being at a much earlier stage of the cycle in less developed foreign markets. While the market for fast-food restaurants may be approaching saturation in a number of western markets, especially the USA, they represent a relatively new service opportunity in the early stages of development in some eastern European countries.

- As part of its portfolio management, an organization may wish to reduce its dependence upon one geographical market. The attractiveness of individual national markets can change in a manner that is unrelated to other national markets. For example, costly competition can develop in one national market but not others; world economic cycles show that lagged effects between different economies and government policies—through specific regulation or general economic management—can have counter-balancing effects on market prospects.

- The nature of a service may require an organization to become active in a foreign market. This particularly affects transport-related services such as scheduled airline services and courier services. A UK scheduled airline flying between London and Paris would most likely become involved in exploiting a foreign market at the Paris end of its route.

- Companies operating in a number of foreign countries may require their services suppliers to be able to cater for their needs across national boundaries. A company may wish to engage accountants who are able to provide auditing and management accounting services in its foreign subsidiaries. To achieve this, the firm of accountants would probably need to have created an operational base overseas. Similarly, firms selling in a number of foreign markets may wish to engage an advertising agency that can organize a global campaign in a number of foreign markets.

⦿ Some products are highly specialized and the domestic market is too small to allow economies of scale to be exploited. Foreign markets must be exploited in order to achieve a critical mass which allows a competitive price to be reached. Specialized aircraft engineering services and oil exploration services fall into this category.

⦿ Economies of scale also result from extending the use of brands in foreign markets. Expenditure by a fast-food company on promoting its brand image to UK residents is wasted when those citizens travel abroad and cannot find the brand that they have come to value. Newly created foreign outlets will enjoy the benefit of promotion to foreign visitors at little additional cost.

⦿ Analysing overseas market opportunities

Foreign markets can represent very different opportunities and threats compared to those that an organization has been used to in its domestic market. Before a detailed market analysis is undertaken, an organization should consider the overseas business environment in general terms to assess whether a market is likely to be attractive. By considering in general terms such matters as political stability or cultural attitudes, an organization may screen out potential markets for which it considers further analysis cannot be justified by the likelihood of success. Where an exploratory analysis of a foreign marketing environment appears to indicate some opportunities, a more thorough analysis might suggest important modifications to a product, which would need to be made before it could be successfully offered to the market.

Questions to be asked in analysing a foreign marketing environment can be examined under the same overlapping headings as would be used to analyse the domestic market—the political, economic, social, demographic, and technological environments. However, the combination of environmental factors that contributed to success within an organization's domestic market may be absent in a foreign market, resulting in the failure of attempts to export a product. Foreign market data needs to be carefully analysed, for example a country with a low level of GDP may nevertheless be attractive if it is growing rapidly and income is distributed between different groups in such a way that allows an affluent middle class to purchase the company's products (see Figure 12.6).

Overseas marketing environments are dynamic and what might have been a promising overseas markets a few years ago may no longer be so. On the other hand, many companies have achieved success by identifying overseas markets which have potential to expand rapidly, for example the 'BRICs' countries (Brazil, Russia, India, and China). So as well as undertaking a thorough analysis of what an overseas market is like today, it is very important to try and get a view of what the market will be like in a few years' time. Timing of market entry can be critical (Figure 12.7).

The measure of political freedom comprises a composite of two separate indicators, political rights and civil liberties. The combined score is between 1 and 7, 1 being the freest and 7

MARKETING in ACTION

Is the glass half full or half empty?

In a twist to an old tale, the story is told of a business development team from a tour operator that was sent abroad to investigate the possibilities for offering package holidays in the format that had worked well at home. The main finding was that very few people in that market bought package holidays. But what did this mean? One member of the team concluded that the current level of sales indicated a lack of interest in the product and the market should therefore be best avoided in favour of other possible markets. But, to another member of the team, this was the sign of huge potential—'Just wait until these people discover the advantages of buying package holidays!'. This simple example emphasizes that any analysis of overseas market potential can only be based on a combination of factual analysis and judgement.

being the least free. The organization Freedom House considers countries with scores of between 1.0 to 2.5 'free'; those scoring between 3.0 and 5.0 as 'partly free'; and those scoring between 5.5 and 7.0 as 'not free'. The ranking of Economic Freedom consists of one index, in which the freest economy (Hong Kong) is ranked 1 and the least free economy (North Korea) ranks 179. Ranking of corruption is based on data provided by Transparency International (2009), with the least corrupt country being ranked 1.

E-Marketing

How do you find a needle in an international haystack?

In the early days of the Internet, many people assumed, perhaps naively, that international markets could be opened up through the Internet at very little cost. An entrepreneur with a bright idea and a good product proposition would no longer need to distribute expensively printed brochures around the world or employ a network of agents. With direct communication through the Internet, a buyer seeking supplies of fasteners or needles could trawl the Internet for the best source of supplier. The supplier just had to have a website, and buyers would come. Of course, life is not so simple, and one of the biggest challenges is simply to get a potential customer to your site. In the case of many consumer goods and services, the only sensible solution may be to pay one of the many information intermediaries who act as a cyber exchange between often geographically separated buyers and sellers.

But what about the case of specialized business-to-business sales where intermediaries may be few and far between? Here, the importance of getting a high ranking in search engines becomes even more important. It is claimed that there are over 20,000 search engines available to Internet users, but the reality is that the top ten search engines account for over 90 per cent of all searches. Being close to the top of these search engines has become an important part of marketing strategy. Consider the case of a company that specializes in buying redundant manufacturing machinery from factories that have closed down, and reselling it

	GDP per capita 2008	Index of political freedom 2009	Ranking of economic freedom 2009	Ranking of corruption 2009
Burundi	144	4.5	160	168
Liberia	222	3.5	163	97
Tanzania	482	3.5	97	126
Haiti	729	4.5	141	168
Pakistan	991	4.5	117	139
India	1017	2.5	124	84
Zambia	1134	3.5	100	99
Nigeria	1370	4.5	106	130
Philippines	1847	3.5	109	139
China	3267	6.5	140	79
Hong Kong	30863	3.5	1	12
Canada	45070	1	7	8
UK	43541	1	11	17
Ireland	60460	1	5	14
Switzerland	64327	1	6	5
Norway	94759	1	37	11

Figure 12.6 **If you were planning to expand your restaurant chain to an overseas market, which of the countries listed would appeal to you most?** The table above reports data for a selection of countries linking annual GDP per capita with an index of political freedom within the country (e.g. the extent of universal voting rights). It also gives a ranking of economic freedom (e.g. the ease with which new entrants can enter a market) and ranking of corruption. A casual glance at this table will reveal that many of the poorest countries of the world are associated with lower levels of political freedom and a high level of corruption. However, should you instinctively go for a country such as Switzerland, which has a high level of GDP and a relatively open, incorrupt system of government? At first sight, Switzerland may appear much more attractive than Tanzania or Zambia, where it may be necessary to bribe your way into the country, only to find a very poor population. The problem with this simplistic analysis is that a country that is attractive to you will also be attractive to your competitors. So, the competitive pressure for a restaurant is likely to be much greater in Switzerland than Zambia. If you invest time and effort into Zambia, you may have the market to yourself, reasonably secure in the knowledge that a new overseas competitor would first have to go through the pain barrier that allowed you to enter the market. Also, the figures for GDP per person can be quite misleading, because what really matters is the number of people in the population who have disposable income above the level at which they start eating out in restaurants. In many less-developed countries, a low GDP may mask big differences in income distribution. A small but expanding middle class may be a very attractive proposition for a new entrant to the market. (*Source:* Based on United Nations 1998; World Bank 2008; Freedom House 2010; Transparency International 2009; and World Factbook 2009.)

to buyers looking for second-hand equipment. Addressing global markets is often key to success here. After all, if a shoe factory that has just closed down in Leicester is selling off its injection moulding equipment, it is unlikely that there will be many potential buyers for the equipment in Leicester, or indeed the UK—if one company in the UK couldn't profitably use the equipment, then it is likely that no UK companies will be able to. But the equipment may be just what an entrepreneur in Romania is looking for.

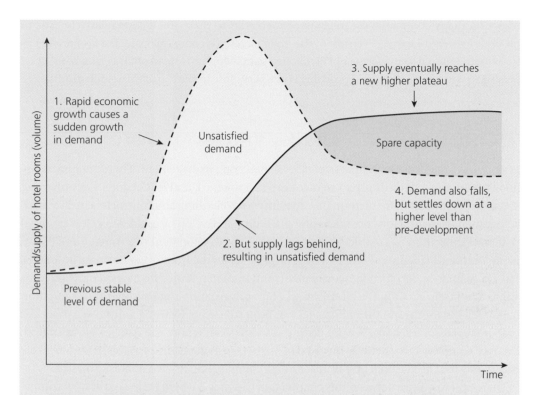

Figure 12.7 **In emerging markets, timing can be a crucial aspect of market entry strategy. In the past two decades, major opportunities for hotel operators have emerged as the economies of China, India, Eastern Europe, and Latin America have grown rapidly.** When these economies emerged as centres for economic growth, one of their first requirements has been for hotels to accommodate the army of architects, engineers, and business people who headed out to these countries to create new infrastructure and trading links. The result was that, in the early stages of rapid growth, hotels were very scarce and operators could charge premium prices. As an example, China and Eastern Europe are associated with low costs of labour and many manufacturers and service businesses have moved operations there to exploit these low costs. However, their capital cities often had some of the highest hotel costs in the world, reflecting their scarcity at a time of rapid economic growth. This has been a signal for more hotel chains to move into the market, but eventually the steam goes out of the economic boom, probably just at the time when the additional hotel capacity is becoming available. The result is greater pressure on prices, and a less attractive overseas investment opportunity for newly arrived companies compared with that achieved by earlier arrivals. Of course, it is easy with hindsight to spot the right time to invest, but much more difficult to predict which economies are going to grow, when and by how much.

How can a UK-based trader in second-hand equipment get its site top of the list that the Romanian is looking at? Relying on searches for 'machinery' or even 'second-hand machinery' is unlikely to be very fruitful—after all, there are likely to be thousands of sites in this category across the world. But including market-specific terms such as 'injection moulding' and 'shoes' in the web page text and meta-tags will help to put a company's site higher in a specialized search category. Having several pages with different titles, text, and meta-tags provides more opportunities to target specific international market segments. And there's another trick that many companies use to get overseas buyers to their site. It costs relatively little to produce a foreign-language version of the main pages of a company's site. If a Romanian entrepreneur entered 'preyyforma bprVlykh' in a search engine instead of 'injection moulding' or 'shoes', the seller's site would probably come very close to the top of the search results.

◉ Chapter summary and key linkages to other chapters

This chapter has provided a brief overview of marketing management. There are now many books about how marketing management can be improved, and this chapter has only been able to provide a summary of the main issues involved. Planning and control is central to marketing management. However, marketing plans do not develop by accident, so it is essential that an organization has a structure that facilitates the development of a strategy and its implementation. Marketing management cannot be separated from other business functions, especially finance, production management, and human resource management. Numerous approaches to improving the effectiveness of an organization's marketing implementation have been discussed, and the importance has been stressed of focusing around key processes that create customer value. Few marketing managers can ignore the issue of globalization. Even if a company is not actively involved in exporting its goods and services, it is quite likely that it may find itself competing against foreign companies in its own domestic market.

There are close links between this chapter and Chapter 7, where we looked at how companies can develop a sustainable advantage through the management of the marketing mix (Chapters 8–11). Information is crucial to management (Chapter 5) in order that it can build a better picture of its operating environment (Chapter 2). It is the task of a marketing manager to ensure sustainable competitive advantage through such means as new product development (Chapter 8) and the development of appropriate distribution channels (Chapter 10).

✎ KEY PRINCIPLES OF MARKETING

- Marketing management is a continual process of analysis, planning, implementation, and control.

- Good information and knowledge management can be crucial for success in a market.

- Marketing managers have to work closely with other managers within an organization.

- The basic principles of marketing apply whether a firm is dealing with its domestic market or a foreign market.

- The competing demands of global standardization and local adaptation must be reconciled.

- Understanding the effects of cultural differences on buyer behaviour is crucial to successful overseas marketing.

Viva España! Marketing Spain as a tourism destination

It used to be said that the toughest training ground for a budding marketer was to work at one of the fast moving consumer goods companies such as Procter & Gamble—in such a fiercely competitive market, you would need to use all of your skills and expertise to keep your brand in a strong market position. But more recently, it can be argued that an even more challenging environment for a marketer to cut their teeth is in the increasingly important field of destination marketing. Look through any Sunday newspaper supplement, and it is quite likely that you will see plenty of advertisements enticing you to take a holiday in exotic sounding places. Destination marketing is now a big and a competitive business. A visit to the annual World Travel Market in London will find hundreds of local regional and national destination marketers jostling with each other to persuade tour operators to include their destination in tourists' itineraries, rather than other destinations.

However, although the marketing of tourism destinations as brands has acquired a lot of attention in recent years, the very idea of an all embracing destination brand can be very difficult to achieve. The main problem is that the destination brand manager has very little control of the 'product' which the consumer receives. The experience of staying in one of the destination's hotels, drinking at its bars and coffee shops, or visiting its shops is dependent upon the activities of organizations over whom the destination brand manager has very little, if any direct control. There is also a problem that a destination brand manager has to address the interests of different stakeholders who would like the brand positioned in very different ways. Very often, those promoting tourism would like the brand image to emphasize quaint and old characteristics, while those seeking to promote inward investment want an image based on modernness and the latest technology. Ireland is just one of many countries that has faced this dilemma—should its brand image reflect the traditional image of a rural country with slightly quirky ways, or a high tech country with an increasingly ethnically diverse population? A further group of stakeholders are the inhabitants themselves—how do they want to be portrayed. Many attempts at creating brand identities for tourists have met with ridicule from local people who do not recognize the brand representations.

Many experts in destination marketing agree that Spain has overseen the most successful implementation of a destination marketing programme. Key to this success was a tourism marketing campaign launched in 1982 on the occasion of the football World Cup held in Spain. The campaign used Joan Miro's sun design to symbolize the modernization of Spain. This logo has since become Spain's tourism logo.

Overseeing the brand is the Instituto de Turismo de España (TURESPAÑA), an administrative unit of the Spanish central government. Its main responsibilities are the planning, development, and execution of activities aimed at promoting Spain as a tourism destination in international markets, and support of the marketing of Spanish tourism services abroad, in cooperation with regional and local authorities and the private sector. The organization operates with a staff of 505 working through a network of offices located in Spain and abroad. Nearly three-quarters of its 2009 budget of 165 million euros was used for direct investment in campaigns and activities for tourism promotion abroad. This included not just conventional media advertising (more than 3,100 communications activities in total), but also public relations activity, such as hosting 2200 visits by journalists to Spain, resulting in published articles and reports which the organization estimated to be worth over €126 million in advertising equivalent expenditure. TURESPAÑA recognized the importance of intermediaries in influencing the holiday choices of consumers, and for this reason, it organized familiarization trips for over 3500 tour operators and travel agents.

Key to TURESPAÑA's strategy has been the development of a brand communication strategy which highlights the unique and differentiating elements which a visit to Spain would provide, compared with other competing destinations. The brand values of Spain have particularly focused on: the way of living and the general lifestyle existing in Spain; the cultural traditions of Spain; and the size and diversity of the country.

TURESPAÑA is particularly keen to broaden the brand appeal beyond its association with sun and sea vacations. Like many tourist destinations, Spain experiences seasonality, and over-concentration of tourism in a few key areas. A key part of its marketing strategy has therefore been to encourage visitors to come out of the peak summer season, and to explore the diversity of tourism attractions beyond the coastal resorts.

With a country as big and diverse as Spain, TURESPAÑA recognizes that it must leverage as much as possible out of its budget by working with others. It has therefore worked with regional and local authorities on a variety of regional brand destination campaigns, including the Pyrenees, Green Spain, the Silver Route, the Jacobean Way to Santiago de Compostela, and the World Heritage Sites.

Many commentators agree that Spain has developed and executed one of the most successful examples of national tourism destination branding. The advertising guru Wally Olins noted how until just a few decades ago, Spain was seen as an isolated, backward, poor country on the fringes of Europe. The reality of Spain has changed, and today it is a modern, vibrant, and democratic economy. The branding campaign has reflected the reality of Spain's new position in Europe. But it can be difficult to tell which was cause and which was effect. Much of the change in perception of Spain has occurred beyond the domain of tourism management; for example the Barcelona Olympics of 1992 and the Seville International Exhibition put the country on the map in many people's minds. The growth, privatization, and globalization of Spanish companies such as Repsol, Telefonica, and Union Fenosa have made many people aware that Spain is now an economic powerhouse. The restoration of Spain's major cities, including Barcelona, Valencia, and Bilbao soon inspire confidence among visitors that this is not a backward country.

But brand management for Spain still faces problems. Within Europe, changing perceptions of Spain have matched the changing reality. However, in the United States, the brand image of Spain tends to be confused with that of Latin American countries, where Spain has a historical influence. In Asia and Africa, it is claimed that Spain is largely unknown, and indistinguishable from other European countries.

The marketing of Spain as a tourism destination has succeeded where many other countries have failed. Other countries have tried to promote an image which does not reflect reality, or identified particularly indistinctive aspects of a brand. Many new countries have emerged during the past two decades in central and Eastern Europe, but the brand development in many of these has made little impact because of the lack of truly distinctive positioning which has value in the minds of potential tourists. Many attempts at destination branding have failed because of the often conflicting demands of tourism marketers to position their brand on the basis of a country's history, while those responsible for inward investment want to drop these images as quickly as possible and portray their country as thoroughly modern. A great achievement of the Spanish tourism branding campaign has been to incorporate many modern icons, such as the Guggenheim museum in Bilbao, into the brand image, without having to rely exclusively on outdated images of flamenco dancing.

Based on: Instituto de Turismo de España (TURESPAÑA) website (http://www.tourspain.es/TourSpain/Home?Language=en); Wally Olins, Trading identities, why countries and companies are taking on each other's roles, 1999.

Case study review questions

1. Contrast the objectives of public and private sector organizations that are involved in tourism.

2. Summarize the benefits of collaboration between public and private sector organizations in the tourism sector.

3. Identify the main problems of collective marketing of a tourism destination, compared with the marketing of an individual hotel.

CHAPTER REVIEW QUESTIONS

1. What is the difference between marketing planning and corporate planning? Should they be considered synonymous?

2. Do you agree with the notion that a marketing department can actually be a barrier to the successful development of a marketing orientation? Give examples.

3. Discuss the macro- and micro-level reasons why a UK-based general insurance company might seek to expand into continental Europe

ACTIVITIES

1. 'Mission statements are the result of senior managers undertaking management development courses. They may have the language, but mission statements are invariably ignored by the very people who they are aimed at.' Visit the website of a selection of large and small organizations that you are familiar with and note their

mission statement, if they have one. Discuss whether these are useful in guiding the business, its employees, and customers.

2. Choose two or three international service providers from the following sectors: hotels, airlines, fast food, car rental, accountancy services. Go to their websites and click through to a selection of their national sites in countries with a different socio-economic profile to your own. Analyse what is common between the service offer and the promotional messages between the different countries in which the company operates. Then try and identify ways in which the service offer has been adapted to meet local conditions.

3. Refer to Figure 12.6 which gives information about GDP per person and the level of corruption and economic freedom in a selection of countries. If you were a European hotel operator seeking international expansion for its budget hotel format, how would this information influence your choice of target country to expand into? What specific additional information would you need to further guide your choice between those countries listed?

REFERENCES

Ambler, T. (2000) 'Marketing Metrics'. *Business Strategy Review*, 11 (2).

Bateson, J.E.G. (1989) *Managing Services Marketing: Text and Readings*, 2nd edition. Fort Worth, Texas: Dryden Press.

Denton, D.K. (1990) 'Customer Focused Management'. *HR Magazine* (Lexington, Mass.), August, 62–7.

Drucker, P. (1973) *Management: Tasks, Responsibilities and Practices*. New York: Harper & Row.

Freedom House (1997) Freedom in the World. Available at www.freedomhouse.org/ template.cfm?page=15 (accessed 12 August 2011).

Gummesson, E. (2008) *Total Relationship Marketing: Marketing Management, Relationship Strategy and CRM Approaches for the Network Economy*. Oxford: Butterworth-Heinemann.

Handy, C. (1994) *Understanding Organizations*, 4th edition. Harmondsworth: Penguin.

Levitt, T. (1960) 'Marketing Myopia'. *Harvard Business Review*, 38 (4), 45–56.

Lukas, B.A. and Maignan, I. (1996) 'Striving for Quality: the Key Role of Internal and External Customers'. *Journal of Market Focused Management*, 1, 175–97.

McDonald, M. (2002) *Marketing Plans: How to Prepare Them; How to Use Them*, 5th edition. Oxford: Butterworth-Heinemann.

O'Sullivan, D. and Abela, A.V. (2007) 'Marketing Performance Measurement Ability and Firm Performance'. *Journal of Marketing*, 71 (2), 79–93.

Peters, T.J. and Waterman, R.H. (1982) *In Search of Excellence: Lessons From America's Best Run Companies*. New York: Harper & Row.

Porter, M. (1980) *Competitive Strategy: Technique for Analyzing Industries and Competitors*. New York: Free Press.

Reynoso, J.F. and Moores, B. (1996) 'Internal Relationships'. In F. Buttle, (ed.), *Relationship Marketing: Theory and Practice*. London: Paul Chapman. pp. 55–73.

Seggie, S., Cavusgil, E., and Phelan, S.E. (2007) 'Measurement of Return on Marketing Investment: A Conceptual Framework and the Future of Marketing Metrics'. *Industrial Marketing Management*, 36, (6), 834–41.

Transparency International (1998) '1998 Corruption Perceptions Index: Transparency International Ranks 85 Countries in Largest Ever Corruption Perceptions Index'. Transparency International, Berlin, available at www.transparency.org/news_room/latest_news/press_releases/1998/1998_09_22_cpi (accessed 12 August 2011).

United Nations (1998) *Human Development Report*, available at http://hdr.undp.org/reports/global/1998/en/ (accessed 12 August 2011).

Varey, R.J. (1995) 'Internal Marketing: a Review and Some Interdisciplinary Research Challenges'. *International Journal of Service Industry Management*, 6 (1), 40–63.

World Bank (1999) *World Development Report, 1998/99*. Available at www.worldbank.org/wdr/wdr98/contents.htm (accessed 12 August 2011).

World Factbook (2005). Available at https://www.cia.gov/library/publications/the-worldfactbook/ (accessed 12 August 2011).

✎ SUGGESTED FURTHER READING

There are many texts on the subject of marketing management which focus on how an organization can implement measures to respond to a changing external environment. The following are useful:

Johnson, G., Whittington, R., and Scholes, K. (2010) *Exploring Corporate Strategy*, 9th edition. London: FT Prentice Hall.

Kotler, P. (2011) *Marketing Management*, 14th edition. Harlow: Pearson Education.

Piercy, N. (2008) *Market-led Strategic Change: Transforming the Process of Going to Market*, 4th edition. Oxford: Butterworth-Heinemann.

Sargeant, A. (2009) *Marketing Management for Not-for-Profit Organizations*, 3rd edition. Oxford: Oxford University Press.

The important role played by information in business planning is discussed in the following texts:

Byrne, D. (2008) *Web of Knowledge: Essential Knowledge Management for Those Working with Information*. London: Facet Publishing.

Hislop, D. (2009) *Knowledge Management in Organizations: a Critical Introduction*. Oxford: Oxford University Press.

The following references offer a general review of the factors that influence firms' foreign expansion decisions.

Doole, I. and Lowe, R. (2008) *International Marketing Strategy*, 5th edition. Dundee: Thomson.

Keegan, W.J. and Green, M.C. (2007) *Global Marketing*, 5th edition. Upper Saddle River, NJ: Prentice Hall.

Lee, K. and Carter, S. (2009) *Global Marketing Management: Changes, Challenges and New Strategies*, 2nd edition. Oxford: Oxford University Press.

ONLINE RESOURCE CENTRE

Visit the Online Resource Centre for resources that are relevant to this chapter, including a flashcard glossary, web links, multiple choice questions, and additional case studies:

www.oxfordtextbooks.co.uk/orc/palmer3e/

KEY TERMS

- Contingency plan
- Control systems
- Corporate planning
- Exporting
- Leadership

- Marketing planning
- Matrix structure
- Mission statement
- SMEs
- Strategic business units

GLOSSARY OF MARKETING TERMS

Above-the-line Expenditure on paid-for advertising

Accelerator effect The sales of some categories of products tend to disproportionately increase the level of activity elsewhere in a national economy

ACORN ('A Classification of Residential Neighbourhood') A widely used geodemographic database of residential locality types

Adoption process Rate at which individuals start buying a product

Advertising The process by which an advertiser communicates with target audiences through paid-for messages

Advertising agency An organization which specializes in communication on behalf of clients

Advertising campaign A coherent and planned approach to communication over a specified period of time

Advertising media Communication channels such as radio, television, and newspapers

Agent An individual or company acting in a capacity on behalf of a principal (e.g. a sales agent); an agent does not generally take ownership of goods

AIDA model ('Attention, Interest, Desire, Action') A mnemonic used to describe the process of communicating a series of messages

Anti-competitive practices Efforts made by firms or individuals to prevent the proper functioning of competitive markets

Attitudes A positive or negative predisposition a person has towards products, people, events, ideas, etc.

Auctions A process by which the price of an exchange is based on the price that the highest bidder is prepared to pay

Augmented product The core product offer with the addition of differentiating benefits, e.g. additional services

Awareness The proportion of a target audience who have heard of a particular product of service (either 'prompted' or 'unprompted')

Banner advertisements Paid-for advertisements on other companies' websites

Barriers to entry Obstacles facing a company when it wishes to enter a market

Bartering Goods or services are exchanged on the basis of bargaining between the parties

Below-the-line Expenditure on promotional activities that involves non-commission paying media

Benchmarking Setting performance goals for an organization based on those achieved by its competitors

Birth rate The number of people born in the population, commonly expressed as the number of births per 1,000 women

Black box model of buyer behaviour A simplified model of the buying process, which sees inputs as stimuli to the decision-making process and the output is a decision to buy/rebuy/not buy

Brand A combination of name, visual identity and distinctive design which distinguishes the products of one company from its competitors

Brand equity The capitalized value of price premiums that customers are prepared to pay for a brand, compared with a similar generic product

Brand extension A company with a strong brand seeks to extend the brand to new categories of products

Brand family A brand is applied to a range of loosely related products, for example a range of shampoos

Branding The process of creating a distinctive identity for a product that differentiates it from its competitors

Brand personality The essence of a brand, which evokes emotional responses from consumers

Budget The amount of money scheduled to be spent or received in future periods

Business cycle Fluctuations in the level of activity in an economy, commonly measured by employment levels and aggregate demand

Business-to-business marketing Targeting goods and services at businesses, who use the products to add value in their own production processes, as distinct from consumers who are the final consumers of the product

Business-to-business products Goods and services targeted at businesses who use the products to add value in their own production processes, as distinct from consumers who are the final consumers of the product

Buyer readiness state The recognition that buyers may be simply thinking about a purchase, actively looking, or about to make an actual purchase

Buying behaviour The way in which customers act, and the processes involved in making a purchase decision

Buying process All of the activities involved as the buyer goes through the stages of having an idea to make a purchase, to actually completing the purchase and reflecting on it afterwards

Cannibalization Occurs where one product within a company's range reduces sales of other products in its range

Cartel An association of suppliers that seeks to restrict costly competition between its members

Channel of communication A medium through which a company directs its messages to customers and other key influencers

Cluster analysis A statistical process of identifying similarity among individual pieces of data, commonly used for identifying market segments

Co-branding Two or more brands apply their brands to a single product

Codes of conduct A formal or informal statement of behaviours to be followed by those individuals or organizations who agree to follow the code of conduct

Cognitive dissonance Mental discomfort that occurs following a purchase decision which the buyer may subsequently believe to have been a poor decision

Commodity A product which is easily substituted with other similar products

Commodity market A market in which homogeneous products are traded, largely on the basis of price

Communication mix The various media and messages that are used to communicate with a target audience

Communication models A simplified representation of the processes of communication

Communication process The stages involved in communicating a message from the sender to the receiver, including methods of encoding and decoding of the message

Competitive advantage A firm has a marketing mix that the target market sees as meeting its needs better than the mix of competing firms

Competitor orientation A company orients its strategy and tactics based on what its competitors are doing

Competitors Companies and products that compete with the focal company, either directly by offering a similar product form, or indirectly by satisfying a similar underlying need

Conjoint analysis A statistical process for analysing how the individual components of a product offer influence buyers' choices

Consumer The final user of a good or a service

Consumer goods Goods or services which are targeted at private individuals, rather than at organizations

Consumer panel Research involving a group of consumers who report on their purchases over a period of time

Contingency plan An alternative plan which can be rapidly implemented if the assumptions underlying the original plan turn out to be false

Control systems Procedures aimed at ensuring that performance matches targets

Convenience goods Non-specialist goods which are selected because of their ease of purchase

Cookies A small program embedded in a computer which collects information that can be forwarded and interrogated by a remote computer

Core product The essential benefit provided by a good or service

Corporate governance Procedures and codes by which an organization manages itself

Corporate planning Planning which involves all functions within an organization

Correlation analysis Measuring the extent to which variation in values for two or more variables are related to each other

Cost-based pricing Calculating the selling price of a product on the basis of how much it costs to make the product

Cost per thousand Used in advertising as a measure of cost per thousand people viewing or reading an advertisement

Cost plus pricing A pricing method in which a percentage 'mark-up' is added to the costs of producing a product

Counterfeiting Passing off a copy of a product as though it was an original branded product

Coverage The percentage of a targeted audience that have an opportunity to see a particular advertisement

Cultural convergence The notion that differences in cultural values held by different groups are becoming less important

Culture The whole set of beliefs, attitudes, and ways of behaving shared by a group of people

Customer Person who buys a firm's products (although customers may not be the actual consumers of the product)

Customer lifetime pricing An approach to pricing that is based on developing a profitable long-term relationship with customers

Customer orientation A company develops its strategies and tactics by focusing on the needs of customers

Customer panels A sample (not necessarily representative) of customers who provide regular feedback to the company

Customer relationship management (CRM) A process of intergrating the multiple contacts which a customer may have with an organization to create a shared knowledge base about the customer's history, preferences, and likely future needs

DAGMAR model ('Defining Advertising Goals for Measured Advertising Results') An acronym for a model of the communication process

Database marketing (DBM) The use of a list of customers (potential and actual) which drives communication between an organization and its customers

Data protection Ensuring that a company's data is not allowed to get into the hands of individuals or organizations who have no right of access to it and who may misuse it

Decision-making unit (DMU) The group of individuals who are involved in making a purchase decision

Decision support system Models which are used to inform management decisions on the bases of available data

Decoding The interpretation that an individual puts on a message coming from an organization

Demand The willingness and ability of buyers to buy a particular product at a particular time at a given price

Demography The study of population characteristics, e.g. relating to broad population statistics, such as age, sex, household composition

Desk research Research which uses existing (secondary) sources of information

Differentiation Creating a product which is different in some way from its main competitors, in the eyes of the target market

Diffusion The rate at which new products are adopted by different customer adoption categories

Direct competitors Competing products which are essentially similar in form to those provided by a company

Direct mail A form of below-the-line promotion, which uses personalized communication, sent directly from the advertiser to potential and actual customers

Direct marketing Direct communication between a seller and individual customers using a promotion method other than face-to-face selling; direct mail is one communication channel used by direct marketing

Discretionary income Income which is available to individuals or households after essential purchases, such as housing, transport, and food have been paid

Discriminatory pricing Selling a product at two or more prices, where the difference in prices is not based on differences in costs

Disintermediation A term sometimes used to describe the processes by which companies seek to simplify their distribution channels by reducing or eliminating intermediaries

Disposable income Income which is available to individuals or households after committed expenditure has been incurred

Distributor A person or organization who assists in the task of making goods and services available to end users; distributors of goods generally take ownership of goods from suppliers and are responsible for collecting payments

Diversification Broadening the spread of markets served and/or products supplied by a business

Door-to-door A labour intensive form of communication involving visiting households to communicate a message

E-business The ability to integrate local and wide area networks through the use of Internet protocols to effectively remove the barriers between businesses, their customers, and their suppliers in global markets

Ecological environment The natural environment comprising natural resources and living plants and animals

Ecological responsibility Organizations act in a way that minimizes harmful impacts on the natural environment

E-commerce Transactions of goods or services for which payment occurs over the Internet or other wide area networks

Economic growth The value of activity in an economy is greater in one year than in the previous year

Economic order quantity The most efficient size of order for a company to place with its supplier, reflecting the economic efficiency of large orders and the cost of stockholding

Economies of scale Costs per unit fall as total output increases

Elasticity of demand Responsiveness of customer demand to changes in price or some other variable

Encoding Reducing a complex message or argument to a very short one for communication to a target audience

Entrepreneur An individual who takes risks with a view to profitably exploiting business opportunities

Environment Everything that exists outside the boundaries of a system

Environmental scanning Keeping a watchful eye on developments in an organization's business environment, broadly defined

Environmental set The elements within an organization's environment that are currently of major concern to it

Equilibrium price The price for the exchange of goods and services at which buyers' willingness to buy is matched by sellers' willingness to sell

Ethics Statements of what is right and wrong

Ethnographic research Interpretative research which seeks a greater understanding from the perspectives of the value systems of those being researched

Exchange Something is given by one party in return for something that is received, typically (though not necessarily) goods exchanged for money

Exchange rate The price of one currency expressed in terms of another currency

Experimental research A research approach which evaluates alternatives within a controlled framework

Explicit knowledge Knowledge which can be recorded relatively objectively

Exploratory research Initial marketing research used to review a problem in general before committing larger expenditure to a study

Exporting A company sells goods to customers who are located in another country

Family life-cycle A term used to describe different stages of family life, from single adults, to married without children, married with children etc., and finally lone remaining adults

Fast-moving consumer goods (FMCGs) Frequently purchased products, usually of low value

Field research Primary research, not using existing published sources

Five forces model A model developed by Michael Porter which analyses competitive position in terms of the threat of new entrants; the threat of substitute products; the intensity of rivalry between competing firms; the power of suppliers; and the power of buyers

Fixed costs Costs that do not increase as total output increases

Flexible organization An organization arranges its structures and processes so that it can respond rapidly to change in its external environment

Focus group A qualitative research technique in which groups of consumers are brought together to discuss their views and attitudes to a specific topic

Franchising An agreement where a franchisor develops a product format and marketing strategy and sells the right for other individuals or organizations ('franchisees') to use that format

Gatekeepers Members of a decision-making unit who control access to information about available choices

Geodemographic analysis The analysis of markets using a combination of geographic and demographic information

Global brands Goods and services which can have universal appeal and are marketed in numerous countries with little modification to product or image

Global marketing A company sees its markets as worldwide, rather than purely national or local

Green consumers There are many definitions of 'green consumers', but the term essentially describes consumers who consider ecological implications when making a purchase

Gross domestic product The value of wealth created in an economy

Guerrilla marketing The use of unconventional promotion tactics which are unexpected by the target audience

Hierarchy of effects model A model which portrays consumers' responses to cues as a linear process

Hierarchy of needs A model of consumer motivation proposed by Maslow

Horizontal integration Merging of firms' activities at a similar point in a value chain

Household structure The people who make up the occupants of a household

Image The perceptions of a product, brand, or company

Imperfect competition Market forces which are constrained in some way, for example by the existence of a dominant competitor or a barrier to entry

Imperfect market A market in which the assumptions of perfect competition are violated

Income elasticity of demand A measure of the responsiveness of demand for a product to changes in household incomes

Indirect competitors Goods or services provided by a competitor which are different in form, but satisfy the same underlying needs as the company's products

Industrial goods Goods which are bought by industrial organizations, often also referred to as business-to-business goods

Industrialization of services The process of standardizing and mass-producing services

Influencers Individuals or organizations who do not actually purchase a product, but may influence others in their product purchase decisions

Innovation Developing a significantly new product or process

Inseparability The inability to separate consumption of a service from its production

Intangibility The inability to assess a service using any tangible evidence

Interfunctional coordination An organization tries to ensure that the strategies and tactics of all departments are coordinated with each other

Intermediaries Individuals or organizations who are involved in transferring goods and services from the producer to the final consumer

Internal environment The people, processes, and structures within an organization which influence its ability to respond to external opportunities and threats

Internal marketing The application of the principles and practices of marketing to an organization's dealings with its employees

Internet An open access system of communication between computers

Internet marketing Use of the World Wide Web to communicate with customers and potential customers with a view to making a sale

Intranet A restricted access, local Internet communication channel

Inventory Stock held by a company

Involvement The extent to which an individual has a high level of emotional attachment to a purchase

Joint venture An agreement between two or more firms to exploit a business opportunity, in which capital funding, profits, risk, and core competencies are shared

Just-in-time production Reliably producing goods and getting them to customers just before customers need them

Key account management The recognition that some customers are more important than others and are allocated a specific manager to manage their relationship with the company

Key client A customer who is particularly important to an organization

Knowledge The accumulation of information about an object acquired through a formal or informal learning process; it can be implicit or explicit

Ladder of loyalty A representation of the stages through which a buyer goes in the process of becoming a committed and loyal customer of a supplier

Leadership Giving direction to individuals

Learning organization An organization-wide sharing of knowledge which leads to better decisions being made by the organization

Life-cycle A phenomenon that exhibits cyclical patterns (e.g. in respect of products, markets, and buyer–seller relationships)

Lifestyle The behavioural manifestations of an underlying attitude, influenced by an individual's economic and social background and their peer group

Lobbying Applying pressure at key points in policy forming processes, with a view to influencing the outcome of policy decisions

Logistics The processes involved in moving goods through a supply chain efficiently and effectively

Loyalty Non-random repeat purchasing from a seller, with behavioural and attitudinal dimensions

Macro-environment The general external business environment in which a firm operates

Mailing lists Lists of addresses of individuals who meet some predefined criteria set by the purchaser of the list, typically a company seeking to target a particular profile of buyer

Management by walking about Understanding how an organization creates value by having managers listening informally to employees and customers at all points in the organization

Marginal cost The addition to total cost resulting from the production of one additional unit of output

Marginal cost pricing The addition to total cost resulting from the production of one additional unit of output

Market A group of potential customers with similar needs who are willing to exchange something of value with sellers offering products that satisfy their needs; economists define a market more widely by including sellers who interact with buyers, either in a tangible market (e.g. Covent Garden vegetable market), or a conceptual market (e.g. the UK market for vegetables)

Market development A strategy used by an organization to increase sales by offering its existing products in new markets

Market leader The organization which has the greatest share of sales in a given market

Market penetration A strategy used by an organization to increase sales by trying to sell more of its current range of products to its current target customers

Market research Activity to acquire knowledge of external factors relating to an organization's marketplace

Market research agencies Organizations employed by client companies to collect information about the client company's marketplace (although market research agencies do not strictly act in an 'agency' capacity)

Market segmentation A process of identifying groups of customers within a broad product market who share similar needs and respond similarly to a given marketing mix formulation

Market share One company's sales value (or volume) as a proportion of the total sales (or volume) for that market

Market structure The nature of a market, reflected in the number of buyers and sellers and their relationships to each other

Marketing environment The political, economic, social, and technological factors impinging on an organization's decision making

Marketing The management process which identifies, anticipates, and supplies customer requirements efficiently and profitably (Chartered Institute of Marketing definition)

Marketing audit A systematic review of a company's marketing activities and of its marketing environment

Marketing channel The route by which the producer of a product gets their product to the final consumer, typically involving intermediate handling by wholesalers and retailers

Marketing environment The social, economical, legal, political, cultural, and technological factors, external to the marketing function of an organization, that affect its actions

Marketing information system A systematic way of collecting, analysing, and disseminating information which is relevant to a company's marketing

Marketing intelligence Relatively unstructured information about trends and events in a company's marketing environment

Marketing management Comprises processes by which marketing decisions are made, and the structures within which those decisions are made

Marketing mix A series of convenient headings for decisions to be made by marketing managers in eliciting a profitable consumer response

Marketing orientation An organization makes its strategic and tactical decisions on the basis of what the market needs

Marketing planning A systematic process of analysing a company's environment, then developing objectives, strategies, and action appropriate to the company's resources

Marketing research Distinguished from market research because marketing research is concerned with research into all of a company's marketing functions (e.g. research into pricing and distribution effectiveness)

Mass market A segment of the market which is large and fairly homogenous

Matrix structure An organization structure which relies on coordination of management through cross-functional group leaders

Media Channels of communication, e.g. television, radio, newspapers, etc.

Micro-environment The organization's customers, suppliers, and other institutions with whom it deals (or may potentially deal) and who may affect the actions of the organization

Mission statement A means of reminding everyone within an organization of the essential purpose of the organization

Model of buyer behaviour A simplified representation of the processes that buyers go through in making a purchase decision

Models A simplification of reality, expressed as a series of hypothesized relationships between variables

Monopoly A market in which there is only one supplier, rarely achieved in practice, as most products have some form of substitute

Multiplier effect A small item of expenditure in one part of the economy has a cumulatively much larger effect in other parts of the economy

Mystery shoppers An observational form of marketing research

Needs The underlying forces that drive an individual to make a purchase which will remove a feeling of deprivation

New product development The process of identifying, developing, and evaluating new product offers

Niche A small sub-segment of a market which can be targeted with a distinct marketing strategy

Noise Factors that distort the flow of communication between sender and receiver

Non-price competition Non-price benefits such as warranties or additional features, or merchandising which can give a company's product a competitive advantage

Not-for-profit organization An organization which exists primarily to maximize the public good, rather than the wealth of shareholders

Objective A target towards which to work

Observational research Research which studies customers' reactions and behaviour without any direct interaction

Oligopoly A market dominated by a few interdependent suppliers

Omnibus survey A regular questionnaire undertaken on behalf of multiple clients, usually involving very large samples

Online marketing Marketing which is undertaken through the medium of the Internet

Organic growth A 'natural' form of growth in which a company's growth rate is influenced by its previous success rate

Packaging Methods used to protect products and to communicate a message at the point of purchase; it can also be used describe the way in which diverse services are offered in combination with each other

Patent The legal right to prevent others copying a product or component

Peer group Friends and associates who have the capacity to influence an individual's attitudes and decisions

Penetration price strategy A company seeks to develop a new market as quickly as possible by charging very low prices

Perception Signals received by the brain, which result from physical stimulation of sensory preceptors (e.g. eyes, ears)

Perfect competition An ideal-type market in which there are no barriers to entry, no one firm can dominate the market, there is full information available to all buyers and sellers, and all sellers sell an undifferentiated product

Perishability Services perish instantly, as the service offer cannot be stored for sale at a future time

Permission marketing Communication by a company with customers and potential customers that is based on consent to receive communications

Personal selling A face-to-face communication between an organization and its customers, with a view to achieving a sale

PEST analysis (or 'STEP' analysis) Elements of the macro-marketing environment, comprising political/legal, economic, social/cultural, and technological environments

Pester power A term used to describe the processes by which children try to influence the purchasing decisions of adults

Physical distribution management The process of ensuring that the right goods get to the right place at the right time, cost effectively

Place The point where a product is to be made available to consumers

Point-of-sale (or point of purchase) In retail, the area where customers make their final decision to buy

Portfolio analysis An analysis of the range of products offered by a company, typically in terms of their growth rate and profitability

Portfolio planning Deliberately planning to bring about a preferred portfolio of products offered by the company, for example by balancing risky products with less risky ones

Positioning Decisions about how the marketing mix for a company's product should be developed in comparison to the marketing mix of competing products

Position map A graphical representation of a company's products in relation to competing products, typically expressed in terms of relative price and quality positions

Positivist approach A logical, rational approach to studying a problem which rejects intuition and personal judgement

Press conference A meeting organized by a company or agency appointed by the company with a view to disseminating a news story to members of the press

Press release News story written for, and distributed to, the news media with a view to inclusion in media editorial

Pressure group A group which is formed to promote a particular cause

Price bundling The practice of charging a combined price for a number of service elements, rather than setting prices for each individual element

Price determination The process by which prices are determined in a market, resulting from the interaction of supply and demand for a product

Price discrimination The practice of selling a product at two or more prices, where the difference in prices is not based on differences in costs

Price elasticity of demand A measure of the responsiveness of demand for a product to a change in the price of the product

Price-maker A company that is in a dominant position in its markets and can effectively set prices, which others follow

Price-skimming strategy Pricing strategy in which a marketer sets a relatively high price for a product or service at first, then lowers the price over time

Price-taker A company that has very little power in its market, and takes prices from those determined by others

Pricing The process of determining what money should be paid by customers in exchange for goods or services

Primary data New, original data obtained from field research

Primary research Collecting new information specifically for the task in hand

Privacy Ensuring that personal information is not disseminated improperly

Product life-cycle The different stages through which a product develops over time, reflecting different needs, sales levels, and profitability

Product line A number of related products offered by a supplier that often cover a broadly similar type of need

Product mix The total range of goods and services offered by an organization

Production orientation Where the focus of an organization is on production capability rather than consumers' needs

Productivity The efficiency with which inputs are turned into outputs

Products Anything that an organization offers for sale to meet a need—the term can include goods as well as services

Profiling A description of the characteristics of actual or target customers, based on data analysis

Profit The excess of revenue over costs (although it can be difficult to calculate costs for particular products, and therefore their profitability)

Profit maximization An organization develops its business strategy and tactics with the aim of maximizing its profits

Promotion Communicating messages to customers and potential customers in order to increase purchases of product

Promotion mix The combination of media and messages which a company uses to communicate with actual and potential customers

Prospecting Techniques to identify potential new customers

Psychographic segmentation Identifying distinct groups of customers on the basis of their lifestyle and personality, rather than simply on the basis of demographic factors

Psychographics A basis for segmentation derived from attitudinal and behavioural variables

Public relations A deliberate and planned effort to create mutual understanding between an organization and its various publics

Pull strategy A marketing strategy in which the manufacturer promotes directly to the final customers, who then demand products from intermediaries, who in turn 'pull' goods from the manufacturer

Push strategy A marketing strategy in which the manufacturer promotes primarily to intermediaries, relying on them to promote to their customers

Qualitative research Research which produces essentially attitudinal, non-numerical data

Quality The standard of delivery of goods or services, often expressed in terms of the extent to which they meet customers' expectations

Quantitative research Research based on large samples, but which may be lacking in interpretation, sometimes called 'hard data'

Questionnarie A set of questions used to obtain information from a respondent

Quota sample A sampling method where those questioned are numerically in proportion to pre-defined characteristics, e.g. sex, age, occupation

Random sample A sampling method where everyone in the population has an equal chance of being included in the sample

Reference groups Groups of people that an individual makes a comparison with when making purchase decisions—can be primary in the case of groups who are personally known, or secondary in the case of groups with whom there is no direct contact

Regression analysis A statistical technique for trying to find a relationship between a dependent variable and one or more independent variables, often with a view to developing a predictive model

Relationship marketing A means by which an organization seeks to maintain an ongoing relationship between itself and its customers, based on continuous patterns of service delivery, rather than isolated and discrete transactions

Repositioning The development of a new marketing mix relative to that of competitors, to replace the existing mix

Research and development A structured process for finding new products and processes and improving existing ones

Retailers Companies who buy in bulk and sell individual units of the products to the end user

Sales orientation The focus of an organization is on selling its products more aggressively, while probably not fully understanding the needs of customers and the types of product they would prefer to buy

Sales promotion Techniques and incentives used to increase short-term sales

Sampling A process of selecting a small part of a population for study, rather than studying the whole population

Scientific approach Using the rules of scientific procedure in order to develop objectivity and repeatability

Sealed bid pricing Submission of a price quotation for supplying goods or services, in which the identity or price of competing bids is not known

Search marketing A term used to describe strategies and tactics used by companies to have their messages seen by users of search engines

Secondary research Using previously conducted research data

Segment A grouping of customers who have similar needs and respond in a similar way to a given marketing stimulus

Segmentation The process of identifying groups of customers who have similar needs and respond in a similar way to a given marketing stimulus

Selling orientation An organization's strategy and tactics are influenced by a focus on selling, rather than necessarily understanding what the customer wants to buy

Services Products which are essentially intangible and cannot be owned

SERVQUAL A method of measuring service quality

Shareholders The individuals and organizations who own a business

Shopping goods Consumer purchases that are routine and for which comparisons are regularly made

SMEs Small and medium-sized enterprises

Social class A basis for classifying individuals, based on their background, attitudes, values, and status in society

Social network sites Internet-based methods by which individuals and organizations can communicate with each other

Social responsibility Accepting corporate responsibilities to customers and non-customers that go beyond legal or contractual requirements

Societal marketing Marketing which attempts to improve social benefits

Socio-economic groups A grouping of the population based on occupation

Spam Unsolicited e-mail

Speciality goods Consumer goods for which buyers are prepared to make an effort to acquire

Sponsorship Payment by a company to be associated with a particular event or activity

Stakeholder Any person with an interest in the activities of an organization (e.g. customers, employees, government agencies, and local communities)

Stimulus–response models Models which vary in complexity, but essentially show a causal relationship between a stimulus, which leads to a response

Strategic alliances Agreements between organizations that are based on a long-term recognition that they could each benefit by cooperating on some aspect of their marketing

Strategic business units Divisions, or clusters of divisions within a large organization which form a group for which strategy is developed

Strategy The overall, long-term direction or approach which a company aims to follow, in order to achieve its objectives

Supply chain All the organizations and processes involved in getting products from the manufacturer to the end consumer

Sustainability A system which is capable of continuing in a stable state without intervention from outside

SWOT analysis An acronym for strengths and weaknesses, opportunities, and threats and used to assess the internal strengths and weaknesses of an organization against its external threats and opportunities

System Interrelationships between individuals, companies, products, etc., which result in a response from one component when changes affect another component; in business, systems can be closed (all of the elements of the system are known) or open (it may be difficult or impossible to specify all of the elements of the system)

Tacit knowledge Knowledge which is difficult to record objectively, and is essentially subjective in the minds of individuals

Tactics Operational activities that put into effect a company's marketing strategy

Target audience Listeners, viewers, readers, etc., who are sought by a communication channel

Target market The segment of a market at which a marketing mix is aimed

Targeting The process of deciding which groups of customers a company should aim its products at

Telemarketing Sales activity which focuses on the use of the telephone to enter into a two-way dialogue with present and potential customers

Test marketing A trial launch of a product into a limited area to test its marketing mix prior to a full national launch

Trademark A name, symbol, or logo which has legal protection to prevent unauthorized copying

Tribal marketing The idea that people make purchases to identify with particular groups, or 'tribes' of people

Trigger points Something happens to stimulate consumer behaviour, for example becoming a student for the first time typically triggers the purchase of a range of products previously not purchased

Unique selling proposition (USP) A selling claim based on a differentiated product feature or unique element of the marketing mix

Value The ratio of benefits to costs

Value chain The sequence of activities and organizations involved in transforming a product from one which is of low value to one that is of high value

Vertical integration The extension of a firm's activities to previous or subsequent points in a value chain

Vertical Marketing Systems (VMSs) The integration of intermediaries at different levels of a distribution chain to improve efficiency and effectiveness of the chain as a whole

Viral marketing Encouraging recommendation of a company or its products through word of mouth

Visual identity A combination of visual cues (e.g. colour, typeface, packaging design), which are used to create a unique identity for an organization and its products

Voluntary codes An organization agrees that its behaviour should be governed by a code of conduct agreed with other organizations in its sector

Vulnerable customers Customers who may be incapable of making an informed purchase decision, and who therefore need some form of protection against companies who may exploit their vulnerability

Wants A manifestation of underlying needs, expressed in terms of a particular product form

Wholesaler An intermediary who buys products in bulk and resells them in smaller quantities to retailers

Word-of-mouth Passing on views to friends and colleagues

Word-of-mouth promotion The act of recommendation by existing customers to their friends

Yield management Using variable pricing to maximize the earnings from fixed resources, e.g. hotel rooms, airline seats

SUBJECT INDEX

AUTHOR INDEX

INDEX OF COMPANIES AND ORGANIZATIONS